PATTERNS IN
COMPARATIVE
RELIGION

Patterns in
Comparative Religion

by

MIRCEA ELIADE

Translated by Rosemary Sheed

A MERIDIAN BOOK

NEW AMERICAN LIBRARY

NEW YORK AND SCARBOROUGH, ONTARIO

MERIDIAN TRADEMARK REG. U.S. PAT. OFF. AND FOREIGN COUNTRIES
REGISTERED TRADEMARK—MARCA REGISTRADA
HECHO EN WESTFORD, MASS., U.S.A.

SIGNET, SIGNET CLASSIC, MENTOR, PLUME, MERIDIAN AND NAL BOOKS
are published by New American Library,
1633 Broadway, New York, New York 10019

First Printing/World Publishing Company, April, 1963
First Printing/New American Library, March, 1974

5 6 7 8 9 10 11 12 13

PRINTED IN THE UNITED STATES OF AMERICA

CONTENTS

ABBREVIATIONS

Acta Orientalia	AOA
American Anthropologist	AA
American Journal of the Semitic Languages and Literatures	AJSL
Annales Academiæ Scientiarum Fennicæ	AASF
Année sociologique	AS
Anthropos	APS
Das alte Orient	AOR
Archiv für Religionspsychologie	AFRP
Archiv für Religionswissenschaft	AFRW
Archiven für Völkerkunde	AFV
Archiv Orientální	AOI
Ars Islamica	AI
Art Bulletin	AB
Asiatica	ASA
Atharva Veda	AV
Bernice P. Bishop Museum Bulletin	BMB
Bulletin de la société française de philosophie	BSFP
Bulletin of the Museum of Far Eastern Antiquities, Stockholm	BMAS
Bulletin of the School of Oriental Studies	BSOAS
Corpus Inscriptionum Græcarum	CIG
Deutsche Forschungen	DF
Eranos Jahrbuch	EJ
Ethnos	ES
Etudes asiatiques	EA
Folklore	FRE
Folklore Fellowship Communications	FFC
Gazette des beaux-arts	GBA
Germanisch-Romanische Monatsschrift	GRM
Globus	GBS
Glotta	GLA
Harvard Journal of Asiatic Studies	HJAS
Hermes	HE
Indian Historical Quarterly	IHQ
Indogermanische Forschungen	IGF
Internationales Archiv für Ethnologie	IAFE
Jahrbuch des deutschen archäologischen Instituts	JDAI
Jahrbuch des kaiserlichen deutschen archäologischen Instituts	JKDAI
Journal asiatique	JA
Journal de la société des africanistes	JSA
Journal of American Folklore	JAF
Journal of the American Oriental Society	JAOS
Journal of the American Society for Semitic Languages	JASS

Journal of Egyptian Archæology	*JEA*
Journal of the Indian Society of Oriental Art . .	*JISOA*
Journal of the Polynesian Society	*JPS*
Journal of the Royal Anthropological Institute . .	*JRAI*
Journal of the Royal Asiatic Society . . .	*JRAS*
Man	*MN*
Mana	*MA*
Mannus-Bibliothek	*MB*
Mitteilungen der anthropologischen Gesellschaft in Wien	*MAGW*
Mitteilungen des Instituts für österreichische Geschichts-	
forschungen	*MIOG*
Mnemosyne	*ME*
Le Monde oriental	*MO*
Nova et Vetera	*NV*
Oceania	*OA*
Orientalia	*ORA*
Osterreichische Zeitschrift für Pflege religiöser Kunst .	*OZK*
Patrologia Latina	*PL*
Philologus	*PS*
Préhistoire	*PHE*
Revue anthropologique	*RAN*
Revue archéologique	*RAR*
Revue celtique	*RC*
Revue des études grecques	*REG*
Revue des études slaves	*RES*
Revue d'ethnographie et des traditions populaires	*RETP*
Revue de l'histoire ancienne	*RHA*
Rg Veda	*RV*
Revue d'histoire des religions	*RHR*
Revue des sciences religieuses	*RSR*
Revue hispanique	*RH*
Rivista del reale istituto d'archeologia e storia dell' arte	*RIASA*
Rivista di studi orientali	*RSO*
Studia Ægyptica	*SA*
Studia Orientalia	*SO*
Studi e materiali di storia delle religione . .	*SMSR*
Transactions of the American Association of Philosophy	*TAAP*
T'oung Pao	*TP*
Wiener Beiträge zur Kulturgeschichte und Linguistik .	*WBKL*
Wiener Zeitschrift für die Kunde des Morgenlandes .	*WZKM*
Wörter und Sachen	*WS*
Zalmoxis (Cahiers de Zalmoxis)	*ZCZ*
Zeitschrift der deutschen morgenländischen Gesellschaft	*ZDMG*
Zeitschrift für Ethnologie	*ZFE*
Zeitschrift für neutestamentlische Wissenschaft .	*ZNW*
Zeitschrift für Sozialwissenschaft . . .	*ZFS*
Zeitschrift für Völkerpsychologie und Sprachwissen-	
schaft	*ZVS*

AUTHOR'S FOREWORD

MODERN science has restored a principle which was seriously endangered by some of the confusions of the nineteenth century: " *It is the scale that makes the phenomenon.*" Henri Poincare queried with some irony whether " a naturalist who had studied elephants only under the microscope would think he knew enough about those animals ? " The microscope shows the structure and mechanism of the cells, a structure and mechanism which are the same in all multicellular organisms. But is that all there is to know ? At the microscopic level one cannot be certain. At the level of human eyesight, which does at least recognize the elephant as a phenomenon of zoology, all uncertainty departs. In the same way, a religious phenomenon will only be recognized as such if it is grasped at its own level, that is to say, if it is studied *as* something religious. To try to grasp the essence of such a phenomenon by means of physiology, psychology, sociology, economics, linguistics, art or any other study is false; it misses the one unique and irreducible element in it—the element of the sacred. Obviously there are no *purely* religious phenomena; no phenomenon can be solely and exclusively religious. Because religion is human it must for that very reason be something social, something linguistic, something economic—you cannot think of man apart from language and society. But it would be hopeless to try and explain religion in terms of any one of those basic functions which are really no more than another way of saying what man is. It would be as futile as thinking you could explain *Madame Bovary* by a list of social, economic and political facts; however true, they do not affect it as a work of literature.

I do not mean to deny the usefulness of approaching the religious phenomenon from various different angles; but it must be looked at first of all in itself, in that which belongs to it alone and can be explained in no other terms. It is no easy task. It is a matter, if not of giving an exact definition of the religious phenomenon, at least of seeing its limits and setting it in its true relation to the other things of the mind. And, as

Roger Caillois remarks at the beginning of his brilliant short book, *L'Homme et le sacré:* " At bottom, the only helpful thing one can say of the sacred in general is contained in the very definition of the term: that it is the opposite of profane. As soon as one attempts to give a clear statement of the nature, the *modality* of that opposition, one strikes difficulty. No formula, however elementary, will cover the labyrinthine complexity of the facts." Now, in my researches, what have primarily interested me are these facts, this labyrinthine complexity of elements which will yield to no formula or definition whatever. Taboo, ritual, symbol, myth, demon, god—these are some of them; but it would be an outrageous simplification to make such a list tell the whole story. What we have really got to deal with is a diverse and indeed chaotic mass of actions, beliefs and systems which go together to make up what one may call the religious phenomenon.

This book deals with a twofold problem: first, what *is* religion and, secondly, how far can one talk of the history of religion? As I doubt the value of beginning with a definition of the religious phenomenon, I am simply going to examine various " hierophanies "—taking that term in its widest sense as anything which manifests the sacred. We shall, therefore, only be able to consider the problem of the *history* of religious forms after having examined a certain number of them. A treatise on religious phenomena starting with the simplest and working up to the most complex does not seem to me to be called for, given the aims I have set myself in this book—I mean the sort of treatise that starts with the most elementary hierophanies (*mana*, the unusual, etc.), going on to totemism, fetishism, the worship of nature and spirits, thence to gods and demons, and coming finally to the monotheistic idea of God. Such an arrangement would be quite arbitrary; it presupposes an evolution in the religious phenomenon, from the simple to the complex, which is a mere hypothesis and cannot be proved; we have yet to meet anywhere a simple religion, consisting only of the most elementary hierophanies; and it would, besides, run counter to the aim I intend—that of seeing just what things *are* religious in nature and what those things reveal.

The path I have followed is, if not easier, at least surer. I have begun this study with an account of certain cosmic hierophanies, the sacred revealed at different cosmic levels—sky, waters, earth, stones. I have chosen these classes of hierophany not because I consider them the earliest (the historical problem does not yet arise), but because describing them explains on the one hand the dialectic of the sacred, and on the other what sort of forms the sacred will take. For instance, a study of the hierophanies of sky and water will provide us with data enabling us to understand both exactly what the manifestation of the sacred means at those particular cosmic levels, and how far those hierophanies constitute autonomous forms. I then go on to the biological hierophanies (the rhythm of the moon, the sun, vegetation and agriculture, sexuality, etc.), then local hierophanies (consecrated places, temples, etc.) and lastly myths and symbols. Having looked at a sufficient quantity of such material, we shall be ready to turn in a future book to the other problems of the history of religions: " divine forms ", man's relations with the sacred, and handling of it (rites, etc.), magic and religion, ideas on the soul and death, consecrated persons (priest, magician, king, initiate, etc.), the relationships of myth, symbol and ideogram, the possibility of laying the foundations for a history of religions, and so on.

This does not mean that I shall discuss each subject separately as in articles in an encyclopædia, carefully avoiding any mention of myth or symbol, for instance, in the chapter on aquatic or lunar hierophanies; nor do I promise that all discussion of divine figures will be restricted to a chapter on " gods ". In fact, the reader may be surprised to find quite a lot about gods of sky and air in the chapter on hierophanies of the sky, and to observe in that same chapter references to, and even discussions upon, symbols, rites, myths and ideograms. The nature of the subject necessitates constant overlaps between the subject matter of one chapter and another. It is not possible to talk of the sacredness attributed to the sky without mentioning the divine figures that reflect or share that sacredness, some of the sky myths, the rites connected with its worship, the symbols and ideograms in which it is personified. Each one in its own way shows some modality of the sky religion or its history. But since each myth, rite and " divine figure " is discussed in its proper place, I do not hesitate to use these terms in their precise meaning in the chapter about the sky. In the same way, when dealing with the hierophanies of earth, vegetation and farming, my concern is with the manifestations of the sacred at these bio-cosmic levels; all analysis of the forms of the gods of vegetation and agriculture will be left to the chapter on these forms. But that does not mean that I do not allude to the gods, rites, myths or symbols of vegetation and agriculture in the preliminary study. The object of these preliminary chapters is to examine as closely as possible the pattern to be found in the cosmic hierophanies, to see what we can discover from the sacred as expressed in the sky, in water, in vegetation, and so on.

If one is to weigh the advantages and disadvantages of this method of proceeding, I think the former are considerably greater, and that for more than one reason:

(1) We are dispensed from any *a priori* definition of the religious phenomenon; the reader can make his own reflections on the nature of the sacred as he goes.

(2) The analysis of each group of hierophanies, by making a natural division among the various modalities of the sacred, and showing how they fit together in a coherent system, will at the same time clear the ground for the final discussion on the essence of religion.

(3) By examining the " lower " and " higher " religious forms simultaneously, and seeing at once what elements they have in common, we shall not make the mistakes that result from an *evolutionist* or *occidentalist* perspective.

(4) Religious wholes are not seen in bits and pieces, for each class of hierophanies (aquatic, celestial, vegetal, etc.) forms in its own way, a whole, both morphologically (for we have to deal with gods and myths and symbols and every sort of thing) and historically (for often enough the study must spread over a great many cultures widely divergent in time and space).

(5) Each chapter will present one particular modality of the sacred, a series of relationships between man and the sacred, and, in these relationships, a series of " historical moments ".

This, and this only, is what I mean by calling this book " Patterns in Comparative Religion "; what I intend is to introduce my readers to the labyrinthine complexity of religious data, their basic patterns, and the variety of cultures they reflect. I have endeavoured to give each chapter a different plan and even a different style, to escape from the monotony which threatens every didactic work, and I have so arranged the paragraphing as to make reference as easy as possible. But the point of this book cannot be grasped except by reading it right through; it is in no sense a handbook for reference. The bibliographies are intended as a spur to elementary research; they are in no case exhaustive. I have, however, tried to include in them representatives of as many schools and methods as possible.

A great part of the morphological analyses and the methodological conclusions of this book was given as lectures in my courses on the history of religions at the University of Bucharest, and in two series of lectures at the Ecole des Hautes Études of the Sorbonne (*Recherches sur la morphologie du sacré*, 1946; *Recherches sur la structure des mythes*, 1948). For this English edition, corrections have been made in the text, and the bibliographies have been brought up to date.

M. E.

PATTERNS IN
COMPARATIVE
RELIGION

I

APPROXIMATIONS: THE STRUCTURE AND MORPHOLOGY OF THE SACRED

1. "SACRED" AND "PROFANE"

ALL the definitions given up till now of the religious phenomenon have one thing in common: each has its own way of
showing that the sacred and the religious life are the opposite
of the profane and the secular life. But as soon as you start to
fix limits to the notion of the sacred you come upon difficulties—
difficulties both theoretical and practical. For, before you
attempt any definition of the phenomenon of religion, you must
know where to look for the evidence, and, first and foremost,
for those expressions of religion that can be seen in the " pure
state "—that is, those which are " simple " and as close as
possible to their origins. Unfortunately, evidence of this sort
is nowhere to be found; neither in any society whose history
we know, nor among the " primitives ", the uncivilized peoples
of to-day. Almost everywhere the religious phenomena we
see are complex, suggesting a long historical evolution.

Then, too, assembling one's material presents certain
important practical difficulties. Even if one were satisfied
with studying only one religion, a lifetime would scarcely be
long enough to complete the research, while, if one proposed
to compare religions, several lifetimes would not suffice to
attain the end in view. Yet it is just such a comparative study
that we want, for only thus can we discover both the changing
morphology of the sacred, and its historical development.
In embarking, therefore, on this study, we must choose a few
among the many religions which have been discovered by
history, or ethnology, and then only some of their aspects or
phases.

This choice, even if confined to the major manifestations, is a
delicate matter. If we want to limit and define the sacred, we
shall have to have at our disposal a manageable number of
expressions of religion. If it starts by being difficult, the
diversity of those expressions becomes gradually paralysing.

1

We are faced with rites, myths, divine forms, sacred and venerated objects, symbols, cosmologies, theologoumena, consecrated men, animals and plants, sacred places, and more. And each category has its own morphology—of a branching and luxuriant richness. We have to deal with a vast and ill-assorted mass of material, with a Melanesian cosmogony myth or Brahman sacrifice having as much right to our consideration as the mystical writings of a St. Teresa or a Nichiren, an Australian totem, a primitive initiation rite, the symbolism of the Borobudur temple, the ceremonial costumes and dances of a Siberian shaman, the sacred stones to be found in so many places, agricultural ceremonies, the myths and rites of the Great Goddesses, the enthroning of an ancient king or the superstitions attaching to precious stones. Each must be considered as a hierophany in as much as it expresses in some way some modality of the sacred and some moment in its history; that is to say, some one of the many kinds of experience of the sacred man has had. Each is valuable for two things it tells us: because it is a hierophany, it reveals some modality of the sacred; because it is a historical incident, it reveals some attitude man has had towards the sacred. For instance, the following Vedic text addressing a dead man: " Crawl to your Mother, Earth ! May she save you from the void ! "[1] This text shows the nature of earth worship; the earth is looked upon as the Mother, *Tellus Mater*; but it also shows one given stage in the history of Indian religions, the moment when Mother Earth was valued—at least by one group—as a pro-tectress against the void, a valuation which was to be done away with by the reform of the Upanisads and the preaching of Buddha.

To return to where we began, each category of evidence (myths, rites, gods, superstitions, and so on) is really equally important to us if we are to understand the religious pheno-menon. And this understanding will always come about in relation to history. Every hierophany we look at is also an historical fact. Every manifestation of the sacred takes place in some historical situation. Even the most personal and transcendant mystical experiences are affected by the age in which they occur. The Jewish prophets owed a debt to the

[1] *RV*, x, 18, 10.

events of history, which justified them and confirmed their message; and also to the religious history of Israel, which made it possible for them to explain what they had experienced. As a historical phenomenon—though not as personal experience—the nihilism and ontologism of some of the Mahāyāna mystics would not have been possible without the Upaniṣad speculations, the evolution of Sanskrit and other things. I do not mean that every hierophany and every religious experience whatsoever is a unique and never-to-be-repeated incident in the working of the spirit. The greatest experiences are not only alike in content, but often also alike in their expression. Rudolf Otto discovered some astonishing similarities between the vocabulary and formulæ of Meister Eckhardt and those of Śaṅkara.

The fact that a hierophany is always a historical event (that is to say, always occurs in some definite situation) does not lessen its universal quality. Some hierophanies have a purely local purpose; others have, or attain, world-wide significance. The Indians, for instance, venerate a certain tree called *aśvattha*; the manifestation of the sacred in that particular plant species has meaning only for them, for only to them is the *aśvattha* anything more than just a tree. Consequently, that hierophany is not only of a certain time (as every hierophany must be), but also of a certain place. However, the Indians also have the symbol of a cosmic tree (*Axis Mundi*), and this mythico-symbolic hierophany is universal, for we find Cosmic Trees everywhere among ancient civilizations. But note that the *aśvattha* is venerated because it embodies the sacred significance of the universe in constant renewal of life; it is venerated, in fact, because it embodies, is part of, or symbolizes the universe as represented by all the Cosmic Trees in all mythologies. (Cf. § 99.) But although the *aśvattha* is explained by the same symbolism that we find in the Cosmic Tree, the hierophany which turns a particular plant-form into a sacred tree has a meaning only in the eyes of that particular Indian society.

To give a further example—in this case a hierophany which was left behind by the actual history of the people concerned: the Semites at one time in their history adored the divine couple made up of Ba'al, the god of hurricane and fecundity, and Belit, the goddess of fertility (particularly the fertility of the earth). The Jewish prophets held these cults to be sacrilegious. From their standpoint—from the standpoint, that is, of those Semites who had, as a result of the Mosaic reforms, reached a higher, purer and more complete conception of the Deity—such a criticism was perfectly justified. And yet the old Semitic cult of Ba'al and Belit *was* a hierophany: it showed (though in unhealthy and monstrous forms) the religious value of organic life, the elementary forces of blood, sexuality and fecundity. This revelation maintained its importance, if not for thousands, at least for hundreds of years. As a hierophany it held sway till the time when it was replaced by another, which—completed in the religious experience of an élite—proved itself more satisfying and of greater perfection. The " divine form " of Yahweh prevailed over the " divine form " of Ba'al; it manifested a more perfect holiness, it sanctified life without in any way allowing to run wild the elementary forces concentrated in the cult of Ba'al, it revealed a spiritual economy in which man's life and destiny gained a totally new value ; at the same time it made possible a richer religious experience, a communion with God at once purer and more complete. This hierophany of Yahweh had the final victory; because it represented a universal modality of the sacred, it was by its very nature open to other cultures; it became, by means of Christianity, of world-wide religious value. It can be seen, then that some hierophanies are, or can in this way become, of universal value and significance, whereas others may remain local or of one period—they are not open to other cultures, and fall eventually into oblivion even in the society which produced them.

2. DIFFICULTIES OF METHOD

But, to return to the great practical difficulty I mentioned earlier : the extreme diversity of the material we are faced with. To make matters worse, there seems no limit to the number of spheres whence we have drawn these hundreds of thousands of scraps of evidence. For one thing (as with all historical material), what we have to hand has survived more or less by chance (not merely in the case of written texts but also of monuments, inscriptions, oral traditions and customs). For another, what has chanced to survive comes to us from many different sources. If, for instance, we want to piece together the early history of the Greek religion, we must make do with the very few texts that have come down to us, a few inscriptions, a few mutilated monuments and some votive objects; in the case of the Germanic or Slavonic religions, we are obliged to make use of simple folklore, with the inevitable risks attaching to its handling and interpretation. A runic inscription, a myth recorded several centuries after it had ceased to be understood, a few symbolic pictures, a few protohistoric monuments, a mass of rites, and the popular legends of a century ago— nothing could be more ill-assorted than the material available to the historian of Germanic and Slavonic religion. Such a mixture of things would not be too bad if one were studying only one religion, but it is really serious when one attempts a comparative study of religions, or tries to grasp a great many different modalities of the sacred.

It is exactly as if a critic had to write a history of French literature with no other evidence than some fragments of Racine, a Spanish translation of La Bruyère, a few texts quoted by a foreign critic, the literary recollections of a few travellers and diplomats, the catalogue of a provincial library, the notes and exercise books of a schoolboy, and a few more hints of the same sort. That is really all the material available to a historian of religions: a few fragments from a vast oral priestly learning (the exclusive product of one social class), allusions found in travellers' notes, material gathered by foreign missionaries, reflections drawn from secular literature, a few monuments, a few inscriptions, and what memories remain in local traditions. All the historical sciences are, of course, tied to this sort of scrappy and accidental evidence. But the religious historian faces a bolder task than the historian, whose job is merely to piece together an event or a series of events with the aid of the few bits of evidence that are preserved to him; the religious historian must trace not only the *history* of a given hierophany, but must first of all understand and explain the modality of the sacred that that hierophany discloses. It would be difficult enough to interpret the meaning of a hierophany in any case, but the heterogeneous and chancy nature of the available evidence makes it far, far worse. Imagine a Buddhist trying to understand Christianity with only a few fragments of the Gospels, a Catholic breviary, various ornaments (Byzantine icons, Baroque statues of the saints, the vestments, perhaps, of an Orthodox priest), but able, on the other hand, to study the religious life of some European village. No doubt the first thing our Buddhist observer would note would be a distinct difference between the religious life of the peasants and the theological, moral and mystical ideas of the village priest. But, while he would be quite right to note the distinction, he would be wrong if he refused to judge Christianity according to the traditions preserved by the priest on the grounds that he was merely a single individual—if he only held to be genuine the experience represented by the village as a community. The modalities of the sacred revealed by Christianity are in fact more truly preserved in the tradition represented by the priest (however strongly coloured by history and theology) than in the beliefs of the villagers. What the observer is interested in is not the one moment in the history of Christianity, or one part of Christendom, but the Christian religion as such. The fact that only one man, in a whole village, may have a proper knowledge of Christian ritual, dogma and mysticism, while the rest of the community are ill-informed about them and practise an elemental cult tinctured with supersitition (with, that is, the remains of outworn hierophanies) does not, for his purpose at least, matter at all. What does matter is to realize that this single man has kept more completely, if not the original experience of Christianity, at least its basic elements and its mystical, theological and ritual values.

We find this mistake in method often enough in ethnology. Paul Radin felt he had the right to reject the conclusions reached by the missionary Gusinde in his researches because his enquiries were limited to one man. Such an attitude would be justified only if the object of the enquiry were a strictly sociological one: if it were the religious life of a Fuegian community at a given time; but when it is a question of discovering what capacity the Fuegians have of experiencing religion, then the position is quite different. And the capacity of primitives to know different modalities of the sacred is one of the most important problems of religious history. Indeed, if one can show (as has been done in recent decades) that the religious lives of the most primitive peoples are in fact complex, that they cannot be reduced to "animism", "totemism", or even ancestor-worship, that they include visions of Supreme Beings with all the powers of an omnipotent Creator-God, then these evolutionist hypotheses which deny the primitive any approach to "superior hierophanies" are nullified.

3. THE VARIETY AMONG HIEROPHANIES

The comparisons I have used to illustrate the tenuousness of the evidence the religious historian has at his disposal are, of course, imaginary examples and must be taken as such. My first object is to justify the method I have used in this book. How far—considering the diversity and tenuousness of our evidence—are we right to speak of different "modalities of the sacred"? That those modalities exist is proved by the fact that a given hierophany may be lived and interpreted quite differently by the religious élite and by the rest of the community. For the throng who come to the temple of Kalighat in Calcutta every autumn Durgā is simply a goddess of terror to whom goats are sacrificed; but for a few initiated *śāktas* Durgā is the manifestation of cosmic life in constant and violent regeneration. It is very likely that among those who adore the *lingam* of Śiva, a great many see it only as an archetype of the generative organ; but there are others who look to it as a sign, an "image" of the rhythmic creation and destruction of the universe which expresses itself in forms, and periodically returns to its primal, pre-formal unity, before being reborn. Which is the true meaning of Durgā and Śiva—what is deciphered by the initiates, or what is taken up by the mass of the faithful? In this book I am trying to show that both are equally valuable; that the meaning given by the masses stands for as authentic a modality of the sacred manifested in Durgā or Śiva as the interpretation of the initiates. And I can show that the two hierophanies fit together—that the modalities of the sacred which they reveal are in no sense contradictory, but are complementary, are parts of a whole. That is my warrant for giving equal weight to what records an experience of the masses, and what reflects only the experience of an élite. Both categories are necessary—to enable us not only to trace the history of a hierophany, but, even more important, to establish the modalities of the sacred which that hierophany manifests.

These observations—which are amply illustrated later on in this book—may be applied to the great variety of hierophanies I spoke of earlier. For—as I have said—this evidence is not only heterogeneous in origin (some coming from priests and initiates, some from the masses, some presenting the merest allusions, fragments and sayings, some whole texts), but also in form. For instance, plant hierophanies (or the sacred as expressed in vegetation) are to be found equally in symbols (like the Cosmic Tree) or " popular " rites (like " bringing home the May ", the burning of logs, or agricultural ceremonies), in beliefs bound up with the idea that mankind originated from plants, in the mystical relationships which have existed between certain trees and certain individuals or societies, in the superstitions relative to the fertilizing power of fruits or flowers, in the stories of dead heroes' being changed into plants, in the myths and rites of the gods of vegetation and agriculture, and so on. These things differ, not only in their history (compare, for instance, the symbol of the Cosmic Tree among the Indians and the Altai peoples with the belief of some primitive peoples that the human race is descended from a vegetable species)—but even in structure. Which should we take as our models in trying to understand plant hierophanies ? The symbols, the myths, the rites, or the " divine forms " ?

The safest method, clearly, is to make use of all these kinds of evidence, omitting no important type, and always asking ourselves what *meaning* is revealed by each of these hierophanies. In this way we shall get a coherent collection of common traits which, as we shall see later, will make it possible to formulate a *coherent* system of the various modalities of vegetation cult. We shall see in this way that every hierophany in fact supposes such a system; a popular custom bearing a certain relation to " bringing home the May " implies the same sacred meaning of plants expressed in the ideogram of the Cosmic Tree; some hierophanies are not at all clear, are indeed almost cryptic, in that they only reveal the sacred meaning embodied or symbolized in plant life in part, or, as it were, in code, while others (more truly *manifestations*) display the sacred in all its modalities as a whole. For instance, what I should describe as a cryptic, or insufficiently clear, *local* hierophany is the custom of carrying a green branch in solemn procession at the beginning of the spring; whereas what I should call a " clear " hierophany is the symbol of the Cosmic Tree. Yet both reveal the same modality of the sacred embodied in plant life: the rhythm of rebirth, the never-ending life that vegetation contains, reality manifested in recurring creation, and so on. (§ 124.) What must be emphasized at once is that *all* these hierophanies point to a system of coherent statements, to a theory of the sacred significance of vegetation, the more cryptic hierophanies as much as the others.

The theoretical consequences attendant on these remarks will be dealt with at the end of this book after we have examined enough of our material. For the moment it is enough to show that neither the variety of sources for the evidence (coming partly from the religious élite, partly from the uneducated masses, some being the product of cultured civilizations, some of primitive societies, etc.), nor the variety of forms it takes (myths, rites, divine forms, superstitions and so on), forms any obstacle to the understanding of any hierophany. Whatever the practical difficulties it causes, this very variety is what makes it possible for us to discover all the different modalities of the sacred—for symbol and myth will give a clear view of the modalities that a rite can never do more than suggest. A symbol and a rite (say) are on such different levels that the rite can never reveal what the symbol reveals. But let me say again, the hierophany present in one agricultural rite presupposes the entire system—the different modalities of the sacredness of vegetation revealed to us by all the other agricultural hierophanies all over the world.

Perhaps I can make these preliminary remarks clearer if I state the problem differently. When a sorceress burns a wax doll containing a lock of her victim's hair she does not have in mind the entire theory underlying that bit of magic—but this fact does not affect our understanding of sympathetic magic. What does matter to our understanding is to know that such an action could only have happened after people had satisfied themselves by experiment, or established theoretically, that nails, hair, or anything a person has worn preserve an intimate relation with their owner even when separated from him. This

belief is based on the notion of a " space connection " between
the most distant things whereby they are linked by means of a
kind of sympathy governed by its own specific laws—organic
coexistence, formal or symbolic analogy, and functional
symmetry. The sorceress can only believe what she does to
have any effect in so far as this " space-connection " exists.
Whether she knows what it is or not, whether or not she understands the " sympathy " that connects the lock of hair with
the person concerned does not matter at all. It is extremely
unlikely that most of those sorceresses to be found to-day
have a view of the world that corresponds with the magical
practices they perform. Yet, even if those who perform them
do not subscribe to the theories which underlie them, the
practices themselves can tell us much of the world from which
they come. We do not arrive at the mental universe of archaic
man by logical investigation, by means of men's explicit
beliefs; it is preserved to us in myths, symbols and customs
which still, in spite of every sort of corruption, show clearly
what they meant when they began. In a way they are a kind
of " living fossils "—and sometimes a single fossil is enough for
us to reassemble a whole organism.

4. THE MULTIPLICITY OF HIEROPHANIES

I shall return to the examples I have quoted here and support
them more fully later on in this book. For the moment let
them give a first approximation—not towards defining the
idea of the sacred, but towards familiarizing us with the evidence
we have to deal with. I have given each piece of evidence the
title *hierophany*, because each expresses some one modality of
the sacred. The modalities of that expression and the ontological value to be accorded to it are two questions which must
be left to the end of this study. For the moment we shall
consider each separate thing—rite, myth, cosmogony or god—
as a hierophany; in other words, we shall see each as a manifestation of the sacred in the mental world of those who believed
in it.

What I propose is by no means always easy. To the Western
mind, which almost automatically relates all ideas of the
sacred, of religion, and even of magic to certain historical
forms of Judaeo-Christian religious life, alien hierophanies

must appear largely as aberrations. Even for those disposed to consider certain aspects of exotic—and particularly of Oriental—religions quite sympathetically, it is hard to understand the sacred value attached to stones, say, or the mystique of eroticism. And even if he can see some justification for these queer hierophanies (labelling them " fetishism " or something of the sort), it is quite certain that there are others the modern man will never come to accept, which he cannot see as having the value of a hierophany at all, in which he can discern no modality of the sacred. Walter Otto noted in his *Die Götter Griechenlands*[1] how difficult it is for a modern to find any religious meaning in " perfect forms ", one of the categories of the divine current among the ancient Greeks. The difficulty is even greater when it comes to considering a symbol as a manifestation of the sacred, to thinking of the seasons, the rhythm or the fullness of forms (any and every form) as so many modes of the sacred. In the pages that follow I shall try to show that they were held to be such by primitive cultures. If only we can get away from the prejudices of the lecture-room, can consider such beliefs not simply as pantheism, fetishism, infantilism and so on, but as what they actually meant to those who held them, we shall be better able to understand the past and present meaning of the sacred in primitive cultures; and at the same time our chances of understanding the modes and the history of religion will increase too.

We must get used to the idea of recognizing hierophanies absolutely everywhere, in every area of psychological, economic, spiritual and social life. Indeed, we cannot be sure that there is *anything*—object, movement, psychological function, being or even game—that has not at some time in human history been somewhere transformed into a hierophany. It is a very different matter to find out *why* that particular thing should have become a hierophany, or should have stopped being one at any given moment. But it is quite certain that anything man has ever handled, felt, come in contact with or loved *can* become a hierophany. We know, for instance, that all the gestures, dances and games children have, and many of their toys, have a religious origin—they were once the gestures and objects of worship. In the same way musical and architectural instru-

[1] Bonn, 1929.

ments, means of transport (animals, chariots, boats and so on) started by being sacred objects, sacred activities. It is unlikely that there is any animal or any important species of plant in the world that has *never* had a place in religion. In the same way too, every trade, art, industry and technical skill either began as something holy, or has, over the years, been invested with religious value. This list could be carried on to include man's everyday movements (getting up, walking, running), his various employments (hunting, fishing, agriculture), all his physiological activities (nutrition, sexual life, etc.) ; perhaps too the essential words of the language, and so on. Obviously it would be wrong to imagine the whole of mankind's having gone through all these stages; to see every society in turn reaching the sacred in all these ways. Such an evolutionist hypothesis might have been conceivable a few generations ago, but is now completely impossible. But somewhere, at a given time, each human society chose for itself a certain number of things, animals, plants, gestures and so on, and turned them into hierophanies; and as this has been going on for tens of thousands of years of religious life, it seems improbable that there remains anything that has not at some time been so trans-figured.

5. THE DIALECTIC OF HIEROPHANIES

I mentioned at the beginning of this chapter that all the definitions that have ever been given of the religious phenomenon make the sacred the opposite of the profane. What I have just said—that anything whatever can become at any given moment a hierophany—may seem to contradict all these definitions. If anything whatever may embody separate values, can the sacred-profane dichotomy have any meaning ? The contradiction is, in fact, only a surface one, for while it is true that anything at all can become a hierophany, and that in all probability there is nothing that has not, somewhere, some time, been invested with a sacred value, it still remains that no one religion or race has ever been found to contain all these hierophanies in its history. In other words, in every religious framework there have always been profane beings and things beside the sacred. (The same cannot be said of physiological actions, trades, skills, gestures and so on, but I shall come to this distinction later). Further: while a certain class of things may be found fitting vehicles of the sacred, there always remain some things in the class which are not given this honour.

For instance, in the so-called "worship of stones" not all stones are held to be sacred. We shall always find that *some* stones are venerated because they are a certain shape, or because they are very large, or because they are bound up with some ritual. Note, too, that it is not a question of actually worshipping the stones; the stones are venerated precisely because they are not simply stones but hierophanies, something outside their normal status as things. The dialectic of a hierophany implies a more or less clear choice, a singling-out. A thing becomes sacred in so far as it embodies (that is, reveals) something other than itself. Here we need not be concerned with whether that something other comes from its unusual shape, its efficacy or simply its "power"—or whether it springs from the thing's fitting in with some symbolism or other, or has been given it by some rite of consecration, or acquired by its being placed in some position that is instinct with sacredness (a sacred zone, a sacred time, some "accident"—a thunderbolt, crime, sacrilege or such). What matters is that a hierophany implies a *choice,* a clear-cut separation of this thing which manifests the sacred from everything else around it. There is always something *else,* even when it is some whole sphere that becomes sacred—the sky, for instance, or a certain familiar landscape, or the "fatherland". The thing that becomes sacred is still separated in regard to itself, for it only becomes a hierophany at the moment of stopping to be a mere profane something, at the moment of acquiring a new "dimension" of sacredness.

This dialectic shows itself very clearly at the elementary level of those vivid hierophanies so often mentioned in ethnological writings. Everything unusual, unique, new, perfect or monstrous at once becomes imbued with magico-religious powers and an object of veneration or fear according to the circumstances (for the sacred usually produces this double reaction). "When a dog," writes A. C. Kruyt, "is always lucky in hunting, it is *measa* (ill-starred, a bringer of evil), for too much good luck in hunting makes the Toradja uneasy. The mystic virtue by means of which the animal is enabled to seize his prey must necessarily be fatal to his master; he will soon die, or his rice-crop will fail, or, more often still, there will be an epidemic among his cattle or his pigs. This belief is general throughout Central Celebes."[1] Perfection in any sphere is frightening, and this sacred or magic quality of perfection may provide an explanation for the fear that even the most civilized societies seem to feel when faced with a genius or a saint. Perfection is not of this world. It is something different, it comes from somewhere else.

This same fear, this same scrupulous reserve, applies to everything alien, strange, new—that such astonishing things should be present is the sign of a force that, however much it is to be venerated, may be dangerous. In the Celebes, " if the fruit of the banana appears, not at the end of the stalk but in the middle, it is *measa*. . . . People usually say that it entails the death of its owner. . . . When a certain variety of pumpkin bears two fruits upon a single stem (a similar case to a twin birth) it is *measa*. It will cause a death in the family of the man who owns the field in which it is growing. The pumpkin-plant must be pulled up, for nobody must eat it."[2] As Edwin W. Smith says, " it is especially strange, unusual things, uncommon sights, new-fangled habits, strange foods and ways of doing things that are regarded as manifestations of the hidden powers."[3] At Tana, in the New Hebrides, all disasters were attributed to the white missionaries who had just come.[4] This list could easily be made longer.[5]

6. THE TABOO AND THE AMBIVALENCE OF THE SACRED

I will come later to the question, how far such things can be considered hierophanies. They are in any case kratophanies, that is manifestations of power, and are therefore feared and venerated. This ambivalence of the sacred is not only in the psychological order (in that it attracts or repels), but also in

[1] Translated and quoted by Lévy-Bruhl in *Primitives and the Supernatural*, London, 1936, pp. 45–6.

[2] Kruyt, quoted by Lévy-Bruhl, p. 191.

[3] Quoted by Lévy-Bruhl, p. 192.

[4] Lévy-Bruhl, p. 164.

[5] Cf. for instance, Lévy-Bruhl, *Primitive Mentality*, London, 1923, pp. 36, 261–4, 352 sq; H. Webster, *Taboo, A Sociological Study*, Stanford, 1942, pp. 230 ff.

the order of values; the sacred is at once " sacred " and
" defiled ". Commenting on Virgil's phrase *auri sacra fames*,
Servius[1] remarks quite rightly that *sacer* can mean at the same
time accursed and holy. Eustathius[2] notes the same double
meaning with *hagios*, which can express at once the notion
" pure " and the notion " polluted ".[3] And we find this same
ambivalence of the sacred appearing in the early Semitic
world[4] and among the Egyptians.[5]

All the negative valuations of " defilement " (contact with
corpses, criminals and so on) result from this ambivalence of
hierophanies and kratophanies. It is dangerous to come near
any defiled or consecrated object in a profane state—without,
that is, the proper ritual preparation. What is called taboo—
from a Polynesian word that the ethnologists have taken over—
means just that: it is the fact of things', or places', or persons',
being cut off, or " forbidden ", because contact with them is
dangerous. Generally speaking, any object, action or person
which either has naturally, or acquires by some shift of ontological level, force of a nature more or less uncertain, is, or
becomes, taboo. The study of the nature of taboos and of
things, persons or actions that are taboo, is quite a rich one.
You can get some idea of this by glancing through Part II of
Frazer's *The Golden Bough, Taboo and the Perils of the Soul*,
or Webster's huge catalogue in his book *Taboo*. Here I will
simply quote a few examples from Van Gennep's monograph,
Tabou et totémisme à Madagascar.[6] The Malagasy word that
corresponds to *taboo* is *fady, faly*, which means what is " sacred,
forbidden, out of bounds, incestuous, ill-omened "[7]—really, in
other words, what is dangerous.[8] *Fady* were " the first horses
brought on to the island, rabbits brought by the missionaries,

---

[1] *Ad. Aen.*, iii, 75.

[2] *Ad Iliadem*, xxiii, 429.

[3] Cf. Harrison, *Prolegomena to the Study of Greek Religion*, 3rd ed., Cambridge, 1922, p. 59.

[4] Cf. Robertson Smith, *The Religion of the Semites*, 3rd ed., London, 1927, pp. 446–54.

[5] Cf. W. F. Albright, *From the Stone Age to Christianity*, 2nd ed., Baltimore, 1946, p. 321, n. 45.

[6] Paris, 1904.

[7] Van Gennep, p. 12.

[8] Van Gennep, p. 23.

all new merchandise, above all, European medicines " (salt, iodine, rum, pepper and so on).[1] Here again, you see, we find the unusual and the new transformed into kratophanies. They are generally mere lightning-flashes, for such taboos are not lasting in their nature; as soon as things are known and handled, fitted into the primitive cosmos, they lose all power to upset the order of things. Another Malagasy term is *loza*, which the dictionaries tell us means: " All that is outside, or runs counter to, the natural order; any public calamity, or unusual misfortune, sin against the natural law, or incest."[2]

Clearly death and sickness are phenomena that also come within the category of the unusual and frightening. Among the Malagasy and elsewhere the sick and the dead are sharply cut off from the rest of the community by " interdicts ". It is forbidden to touch a dead man, to look at him, or to mention his name. There is another series of taboos applying to women, to sex, to birth, and to certain special situations: for instance, a soldier may not eat a cock that has died in a battle, nor any animal whatever killed by a *sagaie*; one must not slay any male animal in the house of a man who is armed or at war.[3] In each case the interdict is a provisional one due to a temporary concentration of powers in some person or thing (a woman, a corpse, a sick man), or to someone's being in a dangerous situation (a soldier, huntsman, fisherman, and so on). But there are also permanent taboos: those attaching to a king or a holy man, to a name or to iron, or to certain cosmic regions (the mountain of Ambondrome which none dares approach,[4] lakes, rivers, or even whole islands).[5] In this case the taboos are based on the specific mode of being of the person or thing tabooed. A king is an absolute powerhouse of forces simply because he *is* a king, and one must take certain precautions before approaching him; he must not be directly looked at or touched; nor must he be directly spoken to, and so on. In some areas the ruler must not touch the ground, for he has enough power in him to destroy it completely; he has to be

[1] Van Gennep, p. 37.
[2] Van Gennep, p. 36.
[3] Van Gennep, pp. 20 ff.; cf. also R. Lehmann, *Die Polynesischen Tabusitten* Leipzig, 1930, pp. 101 ff.; Webster, pp. 261 ff.
[4] Van Gennep, p. 194.
[5] Van Gennep, pp. 195 ff.

carried, or to walk on carpets all the time. The precautions considered necessary when dealing with saints, priests and medicine men come from the same kind of fear. As for the " tabooing " of certain metals (iron, for instance), or certain places (islands and mountains), there may be various causes: the novelty of the metal, or the fact that it is used for secret work (by sorcerers and smelters, for instance); the majesty or the mystery of certain mountains, or the fact that they cannot be fitted, or have not as yet been fitted, into the local universe, and so on.

However, the elements of the taboo itself are always the same: certain things, or persons, or places belong in some way to a different order of being, and therefore any contact with them will produce an upheaval at the ontological level which might well prove fatal. You will find the fear of such an upheaval—ever present because of this difference in the order of being between what is profane and what is hierophany or kratophany—even in people's approach to consecrated food, or food thought to contain certain magico-religious powers. " Certain food is so holy that it must not be eaten at all, or be eaten in small portions only."[1] That is why in Morocco people visiting the sanctuaries or celebrating feasts eat only very little of the dishes they are offered. When the wheat is on the threshing-floor one tries to increase its " power " (*baraka*), yet if too much power accumulates it may become harmful.[2] For the same reason, if honey is too rich in *baraka* it is dangerous.[3]

This ambivalence, by which the sacred at once attracts and repels, will be more usefully discussed in the second volume of this study. What can be noted now is the self-contradictory attitude displayed by man in regard to all that is sacred (using the word in its widest sense). On the one hand he hopes to secure and strengthen his own reality by the most fruitful contact he can attain with hierophanies and kratophanies; on the other, he fears he may lose it completely if he is totally lifted to a plane of being higher than his natural profane

[1] Westermarck, *Pagan Survivals in Mahommedan Civilization*, London, 1933, p. 125.

[2] Westermarck, p. 126.

[3] Westermarck, p. 126.

state; he longs to go beyond it and yet cannot wholly leave it. This ambivalence of attitude towards the sacred is found not only where you have negative hierophanies and kratophanies (fear of corpses, of spirits, of anything defiled), but even in the most developed religious forms. Even such theophanies as are revealed by the great Christian mystics repel the vast majority of men as well as attracting them (the repulsion may appear under many forms—hatred, scorn, fear, wilful ignorance, or sarcasm).

As I have said, manifestations of the unaccustomed and the extraordinary generally provoke fear and withdrawal. Some particular examples of taboos, and of actions, things and persons tabooed have shown us the workings by which kratophanies of the unusual, the disastrous, the mysterious, and so on, are set apart from the round of ordinary experience. This setting-apart sometimes has positive effects; it does not merely isolate, it elevates. Thus ugliness and deformities, while marking out those who possess them, at the same time make them sacred. So, among the Ojibwa Indians, " many receive the name of witches without making any pretension to the art, merely because they are deformed or ill-looking ". All esteemed witches or wizards among these Indians are, as a rule, " remarkably wicked, of a ragged appearance and forbidding countenance ". Reade states that in the Congo all dwarfs and albinos are elevated to the priesthood. " There is little doubt that the awe with which this class of men is generally regarded, in consequence of their outward appearance, also accounts for the belief that they are endowed with secret powers."[1]

That shamans, sorcerers and medicine men are recruited for preference from among neuropaths and those who are nervously unbalanced is due to this same value set upon the unaccustomed and the extraordinary. Such stigmata indicate a choice; those who have them must simply submit to the divinity or the spirits who have thus singled them out, by becoming priests, shamans, or sorcerers. Obviously natural external qualities of this sort (ugliness, weakness, nervous disorder, etc.) are not the only means by which the choice is made; the

---

[1] G. Landtmann, quoted by N. Söderblom, *The Living God*, Oxford, 1933, p.15.

religious calling often comes as a result of certain ritual practices to which the candidate submits willingly or otherwise, or of a selection carried out by the fetish-priest.[1] But in every case a choice has been made.

7. *Mana*

The unknown and the extraordinary are disturbing epiphanies: they indicate the presence of something *other* than the natural; the presence, or at least the call of that something. A particularly cunning animal, anything novel, any monstrosity—all these are as clearly marked out as a man who is exceptionally ugly, neurotic, or shut off from the rest of the community by any sort of distinguishing mark (whether natural, or acquired by means of a ceremony whose object is to mark out the " elect "). Such examples may help us to understand the Melanesian idea of *mana* from which some authors have thought it possible to trace the origins of every religious phenomenon. *Mana* is, for the Melanesians, that mysterious but active power which belongs to certain people, and generally to the souls of the dead and all spirits.[2] The tremendous act of creating the cosmos could only be performed by the *mana* of the Divinity; the head of a family also possesses *mana*, the English conquered the Maoris because their *mana* was stronger, the worship of a Christian missionary has a higher *mana* than that of the old rites. Even latrines have a certain *mana* in that they are "receptacles of power "—for human bodies and their excretions have it.[3]

But men and things only possess *mana* because they have received it from higher beings, or, in other words, because and in so far as they have a mystical sharing of life with the sacred. " If a stone is found to have a supernatural power, it is because a spirit has associated itself with it; a dead man's bone has with it *mana*, because the ghost is with the bone; a man may have so close a connection with a spirit or ghost that he has *mana* in himself also, and can so direct it as to effect what he desires."[4] It is a force different in quality from physical

[1] Söderblom, pp. 13 ff.
[2] Codrington, *The Melanesians*, Oxford, 1891, p. 118.
[3] Cf. Van der Leeuw, *Religion in Essence and Manifestation*, London, 1938, p. 25.
[4] Codrington, pp. 119 ff.

forces, and it works arbitrarily. A man is a good fighter not because of his own strength or resources but because of the strength he gets from the *mana* of some dead fighter; this *mana* may lie in the little stone amulet hanging round his neck, in some leaves fastened to his belt, or in some spoken formula. The fact that a man's pigs multiply or his garden thrives is due to his possessing certain stones containing the particular *mana* of pigs and of trees. A boat is fast only if it has *mana*, and the same applies to a net catching fish, or an arrow delivering a mortal wound.[1] Everything that *is* supremely, possesses *mana*; everything, in fact, that seems to man effective, dynamic, creative or perfect.

The English anthropologist Marrett thought it possible to detect, in this belief in the existence of an impersonal force, a pre-animist phase of religion—in opposition to the theories of Tylor and his school, who held that the first phase of religion could only be animism. I do not want, at the moment, to discuss exactly how far one is right in speaking of any " first phase " of religion; nor do I want to see whether the identification of such a primal phase will prove to be the same thing as finding the " origins " of religion itself. I have only mentioned these few instances of *mana* to illuminate the kratophany–hierophany dialectic at its most elementary level. (And be it clearly understood that " most elementary " does not mean in any sense most primitive psychologically, nor oldest chronologically: the elementary level means a simple and undisguised modality of the sacred made manifest.) The instances I have quoted serve to illustrate the fact that a kratophany or hierophany singles out an object from its fellows in the same way as the unknown, the extraordinary and the new. However, note that in the first place the idea of *mana*, though it is to be found in religions outside the Melanesian area, is not a universal idea, and therefore can hardly be taken to represent the first phase of all religions, and, in the second, that it is not quite correct to see *mana* as an impersonal force.

There are certainly non-Melanesian peoples[2] who believe in

[1] Codrington, p. 120.

[2] And, besides, *mana* is not a concept of all Melanesians, for it is unknown at Ontong Java (North-East Solomons), at Wogeo (New Guinea) (Hogbin, " Mana ", *MN*, 1914, no. xiv, pp. 268 ff.), at Wagawaga, Tubetube, etc. (Capell, " The Word ' Mana '," *OA*, 1938, vol. ix, p. 92).

the same sort of force, a force that can make things powerful, *real* in the fullest sense. The Sioux call this force *wakan*; it exists everywhere in the universe, but only manifests itself in extraordinary phenomena (such as the sun, the moon, thunder, wind, etc.) and in strong personalities (sorcerers, Christian missionaries, figures of myth and legend, and so on). The Iroquois use the term *orenda* to mean the same idea: a storm possesses *orenda*, the *orenda* of a bird that is hard to bring down is very cunning, a man who is enraged is a prey to his *orenda*, etc. *Oki* to the Hurons, *zemi* to the West Indians, *megbe* to the African pygmies (Bambuti)—all these words mean the same sort of thing as *mana*. But, let me repeat, not everyone possesses *oki*, *zemi*, *megbe*, *orenda* and so on; only divinities, heroes, souls of the dead, or men and things in some way connected with the sacred, such as sorcerers, fetishes, idols and so on. To quote only one of the modern ethnologists who have described these magico-religious phenomena—and in this case our author is dealing with an ancient people whose belief in *mana* has been much controverted—Paul Schebesta writes: " *Megbe* is everywhere, but its power is not shown everywhere with the same intensity, nor in the same manner. Some animals are richly endowed with it; cne man may possess more *megbe*, another less. Capable men become eminent simply because of the amount of *megbe* they amass. Sorcerers too have a great deal. It seems to be power bound up with the soul-shadow, destined to disappear with it at death and either transfer itself to someone else, or become changed into the Totem."[1]

Although some scholars have added certain other terms to this list (the Masai's *ngai*, the Malagasy *andriamanitha*, the Dyaks' *petara*, and so on), and there are those who would place a similar interpretation upon the Indian *brahman*, the Iranian *xvarenah*, the Roman *imperium*, the Nordic *hamingja*— the idea of *mana* is not found everywhere. *Mana* does not appear in all religions, and even where it does appear it is neither the only nor the oldest religious form. " *Mana*, in other words, is by no means universal, and its use, therefore, as a foundation on which to build up a general theory of primitive religion is not only misleading but also fallacious."[2]

[1] *Les Pygmées* (French trans.), Paris, 1940, p. 64.
[2] Hogbin, p. 274.

Indeed, even among the varying formulæ (*mana, wakan, orenda,* etc.) there are, if not glaring differences, certainly nuances not sufficiently observed in the early studies. Paul Radin, for instance, when analysing the conclusions drawn by Jones, Fletcher and Hewitt from their researches on *wakanda* and *manito* among the Sioux and the Algonquins, remarks that these terms mean " sacred ", " strange ", " remarkable ", " wonderful ", " unusual ", " powerful "—without conveying the slightest notion of " inherent power ".[1]

Marrett—and others—thought that *mana* represented an " impersonal force ", although Codrington had already drawn attention to the fact that this power, though " itself impersonal, is always connected with some person who directs it. . . . No man has this force of himself; all he does he does with the help of personal beings, spirits of nature or the spirits of his ancestors."[2] Recent researches (Hocart, Hogbin, Capell) have specified more clearly the nature of these distinctions established by Codrington. " How can it be impersonal, if it is always bound up with personal beings ? " asks Hocart. In Guadalcanal and Malaita, for instance, *nanama* is exclusively possessed by the spirits of the dead, though they can use their power to benefit man. " A man may work very hard, but unless he wins the approval of the spirits, and they use their power for his benefit, he will never become wealthy."[3] " Every endeavour is made to secure the favour of the spirits so that *mana* will always be available. Sacrifices are the commonest method of winning approval, but certain other ceremonies are also supposed to be pleasing."[4]

Then, too, Radin notes that the Indian makes no opposition between personal and impersonal, or corporal and incorporeal. " What he seems to be interested in is the question of existence, of reality; and everything that is perceived by the senses, thought of, felt and dreamt of, exists. It follows, consequently, that most of the problems connected with the nature of spirit as personal or impersonal do not exist."[5] We must, it seems,

[1] " Religion of the North American Indians ", *JAF*, 1914, vol xxvii, p. 349.
[2] *The Melanesians*, pp. 119, 121.
[3] Hogbin, p. 297.
[4] Hogbin, p. 264.
[5] Hogbin, p. 352.

put the problem in ontological terms: what *exists* and what *is real*, what *does not exist*—rather than in the terms of personal or impersonal, and corporal or incorporeal—concepts to which the " primitives " did not attach the same significance as later cultures. Anything possessing *mana* exists on the ontological level and is for that reason efficacious, fecund, fertile. We cannot therefore really talk of *mana* as " impersonal ", for such a notion would have no meaning within the mental limits of the primitive. Nowhere do we find *mana* existing of itself, standing apart from things, cosmic events, beings or men. Further still, you will find, on a close analysis, that a thing, a cosmic phenomenon, in fact any being whatever, possesses *mana* thanks either to the intervention of some spirit, or to getting involved in an epiphany of some divine being.

There seems in fact to be no justification for seeing *mana* as an impersonal magic force. To go on from this to seeing a pre-religious phase—dominated solely by magic—must therefore be equally mistaken. Such a theory is invalidated in any case by the fact that not all peoples (particularly the most primitive) have any such belief as that in *mana*; and also by the fact that magic—although it is to be found more or less everywhere—never exists apart from religion. Indeed, magic does not dominate the spiritual life of " primitive " societies everywhere by any means; it is, on the contrary, in the more developed societies that it becomes so prevalent. (As instances I would quote the Kurnai of Australia and the Fuegians, among whom it is very little practised; and it is far less known among certain Eskimo and Koryak societies than among their Ainu and Samoyed neighbours, who are far above them in cultural and other ways.)

8. THE STRUCTURE OF HIEROPHANIES

Let us recall what the object was in mentioning the various startling and transient hierophanies, the kratophanies, *mana*, and so on. It was not to discuss them (which would imply that we already had clear notions of the sacred, the balance between religion and magic, and so on), but simply to illustrate the most elementary modalities of the sacred with a view to getting some sort of rough estimate. All these hierophanies and kratophanies indicate some sort of choice; what has been chosen is taken for granted as being *strong*, efficacious, dread or fertile, even if the " choice " is only a thing's being singled out by being unusual, new, or freakish; what is chosen and shown to be so by means of a hierophany or a kratophany, often becomes dangerous, forbidden or defiled. We have often found the notion of force or effectiveness connected with hierophanies, and I have called them kratophanies because their sacred character has yet to be proved. However, I have shown how unwise it is to make hasty generalizations; how wrong it is, for instance, to speak of *mana* as an impersonal force, since it is only by some sort of personification or embodiment that it becomes accessible to religious experience, or to the eyes of profane man; how it is wiser to set out the problem in ontological terms, saying that all that *exists fully* has *mana*; and lastly, how the distinction between personal and impersonal has no clear meaning in the mental universe of the primitive, and is therefore better left aside.

But what must be noted is that the elementary hierophanies and kratophanies I have mentioned above are far from being the whole of the religious theory and experience of " primitives ". No religion has ever been found consisting only of such elementary manifestations. The categories of the sacred invariably show themselves wider than merely manifestations of the unusual, of *mana*, of ancestor-worship, belief in spirits, nature cults and so on. In other words, no religion, however " primitive " (the religion, say, of an Australian tribe, of the Andaman Islanders, the Pygmies, etc.) is capable of being reduced to an elementary level of hierophanies (*mana*, totemism, or animism). Alongside these wholly simple religious theories and experiences we continually find more or less marked traces of other experiences and theories, traces, for instance, of worship of a Supreme Being. That these traces have little bearing on the daily religious life of the tribe does not concern us here. As I shall have occasion to show (§ 12 sq.), belief in a Supreme Being, creator, omnipotent, dwelling in the heavens and manifesting himself by epiphanies of the sky, appears to some extent among almost all primitives; but this Supreme Being has almost no place in the cult—his place is taken there by other religious forces (totemism, ancestor-worship, mythologies of sun and moon, epiphanies of fertility, and so on). Why such

Supreme Beings disappear from daily religious life is clearly a problem of *history*; it is due to forces which can in part be identified. But though they may not appear there as very important, Supreme Beings do belong to the religious patrimony of " primitives " and cannot therefore be left out of any world-wide study of early mankind's experience of the sacred. Elementary hierophanies and lightning-flash kratophanies are only elements of archaic religious experience, and though they sometimes dominate it, they are never the whole of it.

Besides, these elementary manifestations are not always " closed ", or monovalent. They can develop, if not in their religious content, at least in their formal function. A sacred stone will manifest one modality of the sacred at one moment of history: this stone shows that the sacred is something other than the cosmic surroundings, and like stone, the sacred *is* absolutely, invulnerable, steadfast, beyond change. This expression of *being* (interpreted on the religious plane) in the stone can change its " form " over the course of history; the same stone may be venerated later on not for what it reveals *directly* (not, that is, as an elementary hierophany) but because it has become a part of some sacred spot (temple, altar, or some such), or because it is held to be the manifestation of a god, or for some other reason (cf. § 74). It remains something other than its surroundings; it is still sacred in virtue of the primordial hierophany by which it was *chosen*, but the value attributed to it changes according to the religious theory in which that hierophany happens to fit at a given time.

We shall meet a great many such revaluations of primal hierophanies, for the history of religion is, from the scientific aspect, largely the history of the devaluations and the revaluations which make up the process of the expression of the sacred. Idolatry and its condemnation are thus attitudes that come quite naturally to a mind faced with the phenomenon of the hierophany; there is justification for both positions. To anyone who has received a new revelation (the Mosaic revelation in the Semitic world, for instance, or Christianity in the Graeco-Roman world), the earlier hierophanies have not only lost their original meaning—that of manifesting a given modality of the sacred—but they have now become obstacles to the development of religious experience. The assailants of idols,

of whatever sort and in whatever religion, are justified both by
their own religious experience and by the point in history
when their experience occurs. There is, in their lifetime, a
revelation more "complete", more consistent with their
spiritual and cultural powers, and they *cannot* believe, they
cannot see any religious value, in the hierophanies accepted in
previous stages of religious development.

On the other hand, the opposite attitude, called for the
purposes of this study "idolatry", is also fully justified both
by the religious experience itself and by history. This attitude,
which consists in preserving, in some sense, and constantly
revaluing the ancient hierophanies, is supported by the very
dialectic of the sacred, for the sacred is always manifested
through some thing; the fact that this something (which I have
termed "hierophany") may be some object close at hand, or
something as large as the world itself, a divine figure, a symbol,
a moral law or even an idea, does not matter. The dialectic
works in the same way: the sacred expresses itself through
something other than itself; it appears in things, myths or
symbols, but never wholly or directly. From this point of
view, therefore, a sacred stone, an avatar of Viṣṇu, a statue of
Jupiter, or an appearance of Yahweh will *all* be held by the
believer as at once real and inadequate simply because in every
case the sacred manifests itself limited and incarnate. This
paradox of incarnation which makes hierophanies possible at
all—whether the most elementary or the supreme Incarnation
of the Word in Christ—is to be found everywhere in religious
history; I shall be returning to this problem elsewhere. However, the attitude which I have labelled idolatrous is based
(whether consciously or not hardly matters) on this view of *all*
hierophanies as being part of a whole. It would preserve the
older hierophanies, by according them value on a different
religious level, and the performance of a function there. I will
give only two examples of this here, chosen from different
spheres and from different times in the past.

9. THE REVALUATION OF HIEROPHANIES

I have said (§ 5), that everything out of the ordinary, large-
scale, or novel could become a hierophany; could be looked
upon, in the spiritual perspective of the primitive, as a mani-

festation of the sacred. The Konde of Tanganyika believe in a Supreme Being, Kyala or Lesa, who, like all the Supreme Beings of the Africans, is endowed with all the majesty of a heavenly, creating, omnipotent and law-giving God. But Lesa does not only show himself by means of epiphanies of the sky: " Anything great of its kind, such as a great ox or even a great he-goat, or any other impressive object, is called Kyala, by which it may be meant that God takes up his abode temporarily in these things. When a great storm lashes the lake into fury, God is walking on the face of the waters: when the roar of the waterfall is louder than usual, it is the voice of God. The earthquake is caused by his mighty footstep, and the lightning is *lesa*, God coming down in anger. God sometimes comes also in the body of a lion or a snake, and it is in that form he walks about among men to behold their doings."[1] In the same way among the Shilluk, the name of the Supreme Being, Juok, is given to anything miraculous or monstrous, anything foreign, anything a Shilluk cannot understand.[2]

In this example we see elementary hierophanies and startling and transient kratophanies given their value by being seen as part of a manifestation of the Supreme Being: the unusual, the extraordinary, the novel, are all given their religious value as modalities of Lesa or Juok. I will not for the moment attempt to analyse this phenomenon layer by layer, or try to ascertain its history—to see whether belief in a Supreme Being came before the notion that the extraordinary was a sign of the sacred, or vice versa, or whether the two religious experiences happened at once. What concerns us is the religious act by which the elementary hierophanies are integrated into the epiphany of the Supreme Being—for it is not quite the same thing as idolatry, that generous view which sees idols, fetishes and physical signs all as a series of paradoxical embodiments of some divinity. This example is particularly instructive, as it concerns African peoples who, one supposes, have not experienced the severe systematization imposed by theologians or mystics. We may say that it is a spontaneous case of the integration of elementary hierophanies with the complex

---

[1] Frazer, *The Worship of Nature*, London, 1926, p. 189.

[2] Ibid., p. 312; cf. Radin (quoting the Seligmans) *Primitive Religion*, London, 1938, p. 260.

concept of the Supreme Being (who is a person, a creator, omnipotent, and so on).

My second example shows an attempt to justify the attitude of idolatry by a subtle interpretation of it. The Vaisnavite school of Indian mysticism gives the name *arka*, " homage ", to all the material things people have been venerating for centuries (the *tulasī* plant, *śālagrāma* stones, or the idols of Viṣṇu), and as a result considers them all as epiphanies of the great God. The mystics and theologians, however, interpret this paradoxical epiphany as a moment of its dialectic when the sacred, though eternal, absolute and unfettered, manifests itself in a precarious and contingent material thing. When Viṣṇu thus becomes incarnate in a *śālagrāma* or an idol it has, in Vaiṣṇavite teaching, a redemptive purpose (in his great love for men, the god *shows* himself to them by taking on their inferior mode of being). But it also has a theological meaning: by becoming thus embodied the god reveals his freedom to take on whatever form he wishes, just as the sacred can, paradoxically, coincide with the profane without nullifying its own mode of being. The paradox is admirably stressed by Lōcacārya: " Though he is omniscient Viṣṇu shows himself in the *arkas* as if he were without knowledge; though a spirit, he appears material; though truly God he appears to be at the disposal of man; though all-powerful he appears weak; though free of all care he appears to need looking after; though inaccessible [to sense], he appears as tangible."

One's first reaction is to see this as a mystical theologian giving a high-flown interpretation of an ancient and popular religious act; in itself the act reveals nowhere near all that the mystic and theologian see in it. But though this objection seems so reasonable, it is very hard to say whether or not it is justified. True, the idols of Viṣṇu existed long before we find the elevated theology and mysticism of a Lōcacārya; and, too, a devout Indian villager worships an *arka* for no other reason than because he thinks it embodies Viṣṇu. But the problem is to know whether this religious valuation of the idol—seen as sharing in some way or another in the essence of Viṣṇu—is not really saying the same thing as Lōcacārya—simply by giving a religious value to a material thing. In fact, the theologian is doing no more than translate into more explicit formulæ what

is implied in the paradox of the idol (and of all other hierophanies too): the *sacred* manifesting itself in something
profane.

In fact, this paradoxical coming-together of sacred and
profane, being and non-being, absolute and relative, the eternal
and the becoming, is what every hierophany, even the most
elementary, reveals. A mystic and a theologian like Lōcacārya
is merely explaining the paradox of hierophanies to his contemporaries. By thus rendering it explicit he is clearly making
a revaluation, that is, re-integrating the hierophany in a new
religious system. For, in fact, the difference between the
arka and Lōcacārya's intepretation is really a difference of
formula, of expression: the paradox of the coming-together
of the sacred and the profane was expressed in the concrete in
the case of the idol, and by analytical description in the case of
the verbal interpretation. This coming-together of sacred and
profane really produces a kind of breakthrough of the various
levels of existence. It is implied in every hierophany whatever,
for every hierophany shows, makes manifest, the coexistence
of contradictory essences: sacred and profane, spirit and
matter, eternal and non-eternal, and so on. That the dialectic
of hierophanies, of the manifestation of the sacred in material
things, should be an object for even such complex theology as
that of the Middle Ages serves to prove that it remains *the*
cardinal problem of any religion. One might even say that all
hierophanies are simply prefigurations of the miracle of the
Incarnation, that every hierophany is an abortive attempt to
reveal the mystery of the coming together of God and man.
Ockham, for instance, even went so far as to write: " Est
articulus fidei quod Deus assumpsit naturam humanam. Non
includit contradictionem, Deus assumere naturam assinam.
Pari ratione potest assumere lapidum aut lignum." It does
not, therefore, seem absurd in the least to study the nature of
primitive hierophanies in the light of Christian theology:
God is free to manifest himself under any form—even that of
stone or wood. Leaving out for a moment the word " God ",
this may be translated: the sacred may be seen under any sort
of form, even the most alien. In fact, what is paradoxical,
what is beyond our understanding, is not that the sacred can be

manifested in stones or in trees, but that it can be manifested at all, that it can thus become limited and relative.[1]

10. THE COMPLEXITY OF "PRIMITIVE" RELIGION

The examples I have so far quoted help, I think, to establish certain guiding principles:

(1) The sacred is qualitatively different from the profane, yet it may manifest itself no matter how or where in the profane world because of its power of turning any natural object into a paradox by means of a hierophany (it ceases to be itself, *as* a natural object, though in appearance it remains unchanged);

(2) This dialectic of the sacred belongs to all religions, not only to the supposedly "primitive" forms. It is expressed as much in the worship of stones and trees, as in the theology of Indian avatars, or the supreme mystery of the Incarnation;

(3) Nowhere do you find *only* elementary hierophanies (the kratophanies of the unusual, the extraordinary, the novel, *mana*, etc.), but also traces of religious forms which evolutionist thought would call superior (Supreme Beings, moral laws, mythologies, and so on);

(4) We find everywhere, even apart from these traces of higher religious forms, a system into which the elementary hierophanies fit. The "system" is always greater than they are: it is made up of all the religious *experiences* of the tribe (*mana*, kratophanies of the unusual, etc., totemism, ancestor worship, and much more), but also contains a corpus of traditional *theories* which cannot be reduced to elementary hierophanies: for instance, myths about the origin of the world and the human race, myths explaining present human conditions, the theories underlying various rites, moral notions, and so on. It is important to stress this last point.

One has only to glance through a few ethnological writings (Spencer and Gillen or Strehlow on the Australians, for instance, Schebesta or Trilles on the African Pygmies, Gusinde

---

[1] One could attempt to vindicate the hierophanies which preceded the miracle of the Incarnation in the light of Christian teaching, by showing their importance as a series of prefigurations of that Incarnation. Consequently, far from thinking of pagan religious ways (fetishes, idols and such) as false and degenerate stages in the religious feeling of mankind fallen in sin, one may see them as desperate attempts to prefigure the mystery of the Incarnation. The whole religious life of mankind—expressed in the dialectic of hierophanies—would, from this standpoint, be simply a waiting for Christ.

on the Fuegians) to note first, that the religious life of the " primitive " spreads beyond the sphere one normally allots to religious experience and theory, and second, that that religious life is always complex—the simple and one-dimensional presentation so often to be found in works of synthesis and popularization depends entirely on the author's more or less arbitrary selectiveness. Certainly some forms will be found to dominate the religious picture (totemism in Australia for example, *mana* in Melanesia, ancestor-worship in Africa, and so on), but they are never the whole of it. We find as well a mass of symbols, cosmic, biological or social occurrences, ideograms and ideas, which are of great importance on the religious plane, though their connection with actual religious experience may not always be clear to us moderns. We can understand, for instance, how the phases of the moon, the seasons, sexual or social initiation, or space symbolism, might have come to have religious value for early mankind, might have become hierophanies; but it is much harder to see how the same would apply to physiological actions such as nutrition or sexual intercourse, or ideograms like " the year ". We face in fact a double difficulty: first that of accepting that there is something sacred about all physiological life and, secondly, that of looking at certain patterns of thought (ideograms, mythograms, natural or moral laws and so forth) as hierophanies.

Indeed one of the major differences separating the people of the early cultures from people to-day is precisely the utter incapacity of the latter to live their organic life (particularly as regards sex and nutrition) as a sacrament. Psychoanalysis and historical materialism have taken as surest confirmation of their theses the important part played by sexuality and nutrition among peoples still at the ethnological stage. What they have missed, however, is how utterly different from their modern meaning are the value and even the function of eroticism and of nutrition among those peoples. For the modern they are simply physiological acts, whereas for primitive man they were sacraments, ceremonies by means of which he communicated with the *force* which stood for Life itself. As we shall see later, this force and this life are simply expressions of ultimate reality, and such elementary actions for the primitive become a rite which will assist man to approach reality, to, as it were, wedge himself into Being, by setting himself free from merely automatic actions (without sense or meaning), from change, from the profane, from nothingness.

We shall see that, as the rite always consists in the repetition of an archetypal action performed *in illo tempore* (before " history " began) by ancestors or by gods, man is trying, by means of the hierophany, to give " being " to even his most ordinary and insignificant acts. By its repetition, the act coincides with its archetype, and time is abolished. We are witnessing, so to speak, the same act that was performed *in illo tempore*, at the dawn of the universe. Thus, by transforming all his physiological acts into ceremonies, primitive man strove to " pass beyond ", to thrust himself out of time (and change) into eternity. I do not want to stress here the function fulfilled by ritual, but we must note at once that it is the normal tendency of the primitive to transform his physiological acts into rites, thus investing them with spiritual value. When he is eating or making love, he is putting himself on a plane which is not simply that of eating or sexuality. This is true both of initiatory experiences (first-fruits, first sexual act), and also of the whole of erotic or nutritional activity. One might say that here you have an indistinct religious experience, different in form from the distinct experiences represented by the hierophanies of the unusual, the extraordinary, *mana*, etc. But the part this experience plays in the life of primitive man is none the less for that, though it is, by its very nature, liable to escape the eye of the observer. This explains my earlier statement that the religious life of primitive peoples goes beyond the categories of *mana*, hierophanies and startling kratophanies. A real religious experience, indistinct in form, results from this effort man makes to enter the real, the sacred, by way of the most fundamental physiological acts transformed into ceremonies.

Then, too, the religious life of any human group at the ethnological stage will always include certain elements of theory (symbols, ideograms, nature- and genealogy-myths, and so on). As we shall see later, such " truths " are held to be hierophanies by primitive peoples—not only because they reveal modalities of the sacred, but because these " truths " help man to protect himself against the meaningless nothingness; to escape, in fact, from the profane sphere. Much has been said of the backwardness of primitives in regard to theory. Even if this were the case (and a great many observers think otherwise), it is too often forgotten that the workings of primitive thought were not expressed only in concepts or conceptual elements, but also, and primarily, in symbols. We shall see later on how the "handling" of symbols works according to its own symbolic logic. It follows from this that the apparent conceptual poverty of the primitive cultures does not imply an inability to construct theory, but implies rather that they belong to a style of thinking totally different from our modern style, with its roots in the speculation of the Greeks. Indeed we can identify, even among the groups least developed ethnologically, a collection of truths fitting coherently into a system or theory (among, for instance, the Australians, Pygmies and Fuegians). That collection of truths does not simply constitute a *Weltanschauung*, but a pragmatic ontology (I would even say soteriology) in the sense that with the help of these " truths " man is trying to gain salvation by uniting himself with reality.

To quote only one example, we shall see that the greater part of primitive man's actions were, so he thought, simply the repetition of a primeval action accomplished at the beginning of time by a divine being, or mythical figure. An act only had meaning in so far as it repeated a transcendent model, an archetype. The object of that repetition was also to ensure the *normality* of the act, to legalize it by giving it an ontological status ; it only became real in so far as it repeated an archetype. Now, every action performed by the primitive supposes a transcendent model—his actions are effective only in so far as they are real, as they follow the pattern. The action is both a ceremony (in that it makes man part of a sacred zone) and a thrusting into reality. All these observations imply shades of meaning which will become clearer when we are in a position to discuss the examples given in the following chapters. However, I felt it necessary to suggest these implications from the first so as to demonstrate the aspect of theory in " primitive " religion which is so often missed.

BIBLIOGRAPHICAL SUGGESTIONS

Puech, H. C., " Bibliographie générale ", *Mana, Introduction à l'histoire des religions*, 2nd ed., Paris, 1949, vol. i, pp. xvii-lxiii; Hastings, J., *Encylcopædia of Religion and Ethics*, Edinburgh, 1908–23, 13 vols; Schiele, F. M., Gunkel, H., Zscharnak, L., Bertholet, A., and others, *Die Religion in Geschichte und Gegenwart*. *Handwörterbuch für Theologie und Religionswissenschanft*, 2nd ed., Tübingen, 1926–32, 5 vols.

General Reading, Handbooks, and the History of Religion in General

Caillois, R., *L'homme et le sacré*, Paris, 1939; Dussaud, René, *Introduction à l'histoire des religions*, Paris, 1924; Toy, C. H., *Introduction to the History of Religions*, Oxford, 1926; Mensching, G., *Vergleichende Religionswissenschaft*, Leipzig, 1938; id., *Allgemeine Religionsgeschichte*, Leipzig, 1940; James, E. O., *Comparative Religion*, London, 1938; Bouquet, A. C., *Comparative Religion*, London, 1941.

La Saussaye, P. D. Chantepie de, *Lehrbuch der Religionsgeschichte*, Freiburg-im-Breisgau, 2 vols.; 4th ed., completely revised by A. Bertholet and E. Lehmann, Tübingen, 1924–5, 2 vols.; Moore, George Foot, *History of Religions*, New York, 1920, 2 vols.; Clemen, C. (in collaboration), *Die Religionen der Erde*, Munich, 1927 ; Michelitsch, A., *Allgemeine Religionsgeschichte*, Graz, 1930; Venturi, P. Tacchi (in collaboration), *Storia delle religioni*, 3rd ed., Turin, 1949, 2 vols.; *Histoire des religions*, Paris, 1939–47, 3 vols.; Gorce, M., and Mortier, R., *Histoire générale des religions*, Paris, 1944–9, vols. i–v; König, Franz, and others, *Christus und die Religionen der Erde*, Vienna, 1951, 3 vols.

Comparative Method and Historical Method

Jordan, L. H., *Comparative Religion, Its Genesis and Growth*, Edinburgh, 1905; De La Boulaye, H. Pinard, *L'Etude comparée des religions*, Paris, 1922, 2 vols., 3rd ed. revised and corrected, 1929; Pettazzoni, Rafaele, *Svolgimento e carattere della storia delle religioni*, Bari, 1924; Schmidt, W., *Handbuch der vergleichende Religionsgeschichte. Ursprung und Wesen der Religion*, Münster-in-Westfalen, 1930; Koppers, W., " Le Principe historique et la science comparée des religions ", *Mélanges F. Cumont*, Brussels, 1936, pp. 765–84; Martino, Ernesto de, *Naturalismo e storicismo nell'etnologia*, Bari, 1942; Widengren, George, " Evolutionism and the Problem of the Origin of Religion ", *ES*, Stockholm, 1945, vol. x, pp. 57–96; Kluckhohn, C., " Some Reflections on the Method and Theory of the *Kulturkreislehre* ", *AA*, 1936, no. xxxviii, pp. 157–96; Koppers, W., " Der historische Gedanke in Ethnologie und Religionswissenschaft ", *Christus und die Religionen der Erde*, vol. i, Vienna, 1951, pp. 75–109.

Palethnology, Ethnology and History of Religions

Mainage, T. ,*Les Religions de la préhistoire*, Paris, 1921 ; Luquet, G. H., *The Art and Religion of Fossil Man*, New Haven, 1930; Clemen, C., *Urgeschichtliche Religion. Die Religion der Stein-, Bronze- und Eisenzeit*, I–II, Bonn, 1932–3; Meuli, Karl, " Griechische Opferbräuche ", *Phyllobolia für Peter von der Mühl*, Basle, 1946, pp. 185–288, particularly 237 ff.; Laviosa-Zambotti, Pia, *Origini e diffusione della civiltà*, Milan, 1947; Blanc, Alberto Carlo, *Il sacro presso i primitivi*, Rome, 1945; Koppers, W., " Urmensch und Urreligion ", in F. Dessauer, *Wissen und Bekenntnis*,

2nd ed., Olten, 1946, pp. 25–149; " Der historische Gedanke in Ethnologie und Prähistorie ", *Kultur und Sprache* (*WBKL*, 1952, ix, pp. 11–65).*
LOWIE R. H., *Primitive Religion*, New York, 1924; RADIN, P., *Primitive Religion. Its Nature and Origin*, London, 1938; GOLDENWEISER, A., *Early Civilization*, New York, 1922; id., *Anthropology*, London, 1935; SCHMIDT, W., *The Culture Historical Method of Ethnology*, New York, 1929; id., " Untersuchungen zur Methode der Ethnologie: I ", *APS*, 1940–1, vols. xxxv–xxxvi, pp. 898–965; MARTINO, E. de, " Percezione extrasensoriale e magismo etnologico ", *SMSR*, 1942, vol. xviii, pp. 1–19; 1943–6, vols. xix–xx, pp. 31–84; id., *Il Mondo magico*, Turin, 1948; MAUSS, Marcel, *Manuel d'ethnographie*, Paris, 1947, particularly pp. 164 ff.

Religious Phenomenolgy and Sociology

OTTO, R., *The Idea of the Holy*, London, 1950; id., *Aufsätze das Numinose betreffend*, Gotha, 1923; VAN DER LEEUW, G., *Religion in Essence and Manifestation*, London, 1938; id., *L'Homme primitif et la Religion*, Paris, 1940; HIRSCHMANN, Eva, *Phänomenologie der Religion*, Wurzburg-Anmuhle, 1940.
LEVY-BRUHL, L., *How Natives Think*, London, 1926; id., *Primitive Mentality*, London, 1923; id., *Primitives and the Supernatural*, London, 1936; id., *La Mythologie primitive*, Paris, 1935; id., *L'Expérience mystique et les symboles chez les primitifs*, Paris, 1938; on Lévy-Bruhl's work, see VAN DER LEEUW, *La Structure de la mentalité primitive*, Paris, 1932; CAILLET, E., *Mysticisme et mentalité mystique*, Paris, 1938; LEROY, Oliver, *La Raison primitive. Essai de réfutation de la théorie du prélogisme*, Paris, 1926; MARTINO, E. de, *Naturalismo e storicismo nell' etnologia*, Bari, 1942, pp. 17–75.
DURKHEIM, Émile, *The Elementary Forms of the Religious Life*, London, 1915; HUBERT, H., and MAUSS, M., *Mélanges d'histoire des religions*, Paris, 1909; WEBER, Max, *Gesammelte Aufsätze zur Religionssoziologie*, 2nd ed., Tübingen, 1922–4, 3 vols.; HASENFUSS, J., *Die moderne Religionssoziologie und ihre Bedeutung für die religiöse Problematik*, Paderborn, 1937; GURVITCH, G., *Essais de Sociologie*, Paris, 1938, particularly pp. 176 ff. ; WACH, Joachim, *Sociology of Religion*, Chicago, 1944; MENSCHING, Gustave, *Soziologie der Religion*, Bonn, 1947; JAMES, E. O., *The Social Function of Religion*, London, 1940.
On the value of the individual in backward societies, see VIERKANDT, A., " Führende Individuen bei den Naturvölkern ", *ZFS*, 1908, vol. xi, pp. 1–28; BECK, *Das Individuum bei den Australiern*, Leipzig, 1925; KOPPERS, W., " Individualforschung unter d. Primitiven im besonderen unter d. Yamana auf Feuerland ", *Festschrift W. Schmidt*, Mödling, 1928, pp. 349–65; LOWIE, Robert H., " Individual Differences and Primitive Culture ", ibid., pp. 495–500; WACH, J., *Sociology of Religion*, pp. 31 ff.
LEENHARDT, Maurice, *Do Kamo. La personne et le mythe dans le monde mélanésien*, Paris, 1947.

Taboo, Mana, Magic and Religion

VAN GENNEP, A., *Tabou et totémisme à Madagascar*, Paris, 1904; FRAZER, Sir James George, *Taboo and the Perils of the Soul*, London, 1911; LEHMANN, R., *Die polynesischen Tabusitten*, Leipzig, 1930 (taboos

* A greatly expanded version of this study has appeared in translation as *Primitive Man and his World Picture*, London, 1952.

in economy and commerce, pp. 169 ff.; juridical symbols, pp. 192ff.; the spread of the word *tapu* in Oceania and Indonesia, pp. 301 ff.; comparative study, pp. 312, ff.); HANDY, E. S., " Polynesian Religion ", *BMB*, Honolulu, 1927, no. xxxiv, pp. 43 ff., 155 ff., and *passim*; WEBSTER, Hutton, *Taboo*. *A Sociological Study*, Stanford, California, 1942 (the nature of taboo, pp. 1–48; taboos of the dead, pp. 166–229; sacred persons, pp. 261–79; sacred things, pp. 280–310); RADCLIFFE-BROWN, A. R., *Tabu*, Cambridge, 1940; STEINER, Franz, *Taboo*, New York, 1956.

HOCART, A. M., " Mana ", *MN*, 1915, no. xiv, p. 99 ff.; LEHMANN, F. R., *Mana*. *Eine begriffsgeschichtliche Untersuchung auf ethnologische Grundlage*, Leipzig, 1915, 2nd ed., 1922; ROHR, J., " Das Wesen des Mana ", *APS*, 1919–24 vols. xiv–xv, pp. 97–124; THURNWALD, R., " Neue Forschungen zum Mana-Begriff "; *AFRW*, 1929, pp. 93–112; LEHMANN, F. R., " Die Gegenwärtige Lage der Mana-Forschung " (*Kultur und Rasse, Otto Reche zum 60. Geburtstag*, Munich, 1939, pp. 379 ff.

HOGBIN, H. Ian, " Mana ", *OA*, 1936, vol. vi, pp. 241–74; CAPELL, A., " The Word ' Mana '; a Linguistic Study ", *OA*, 1938, vol. ix, pp. 89–96; FIRTH, Raymond, " The Analysis of Mana: an Empirical Approach ", *JPS*, 1940, vol. xlix, pp. 483–510; Cf. WILLIAMSON, R. W., *Essays in Polynesian Ethnology*, Cambridge, 1939, pp. 264–5: " The beliefs, customs and usages connected with the Polynesian terms *mana* and *tapu* are so widely diverse that if we were to attempt to formulate definitions which would cover all of them, such formulations would be of such a general character that they might be attributed to any human culture."

HEWITT, J. N. B., " Orenda and a Definition of Religion ", *AA*, 1892, new series, pp. 33–46; RADIN, P., " Religion of the North American Indians ", *JAF*, 1914, vol. xxvii, pp. 335–73; MARRETT, " Preanimistic Religion ", *FRE*, 1900, vol. ix, pp. 162–82; id., *Threshold of Religion*, London, 1909, 2nd ed., 1914; ABBOTT, J., *The Keys of Power. A Study of Indian Ritual and Belief*, London, 1932.

On *brahman, hamingja, hosia, imperium*, etc.: ARBMAN, E., " Seele und Mana ", *AFRW*, 1931, vol. xxix; GRONBECH, V., *The Culture of the Teutons*, Copenhagen and London, 1931, vol. i, p. 127 ff., 248 ff.; WIDENGREN, G., " Evolutionism . . . ", *ES*, Stockholm, 1945, vol. x; BATKE, W., *Das Heilige im Germanischen*, Tübingen, 1942; WAGENWOORT, H., *Roman Dynamism*, Oxford, 1947; VAN DER VALK, H., " Zum Worte öolos ", *ME*, 1942, pp. 113–40; JEANMAIRE, H., " Le substantif Hosia et sa signification comme terme technique dans le vocabulaire religieux ", *REG*, 1945, vol. lviii, pp. 66–89.

FRAZER, Sir James George, *The Golden Bough. A Study in Comparative Religion*, 3rd ed., London, 1911 onwards, 12 vols., abridged ed., London, 1922; HUBERT, H., and MAUSS, M., " Esquisses d'une théorie générale de la magie ", *AS*, 1902–3, vol. vii, pp. 1–146; id., " Origine des pouvoirs magiques ", *Mélanges d'histoire des Religions*, Paris, 1909, pp. 131–87; VIERKANDT, A., " Die Anfänge der Religion und Zauberei ", *GBS*, 1907, vol. xxii, pp. 21–5, 40–5, 61–5; HARTLAND, E. S., *The Relations of Religion and Magic*, reprinted in *Ritual and Belief. Studies in the History of Religion*, London, 1914; CLEMEN, Carl, " Wesen und Ursprung der Magie ", *Nachrichten d. Gesell. d. Wissensch. zu Göttingen*, Berlin, 1926–7; MALINOWSKI, B., *Argonauts of the Western Pacific*, London, 1922 (pp. 392–463, magic and *kula*, the magic word, etc.); id., *Coral Gardens*,

London, 1935, vol. ii, pp. 214–50: " An Ethnographic Theory of the Magic Word "; ALLIER, R., *The Mind of the Savage*, London, 1929; id., *Magie et religion*, Paris, 1935; MARTINO, E. de, " Percezione extra-sensoriale e magismo etnologico ", *SMSR*, 1942, vol. xviii, pp. 1–19; RATSCHOW, C. H., *Magie und Religion*, 1946; EVANS-PRITCHARD, E. E., " The Morphology and Function of Magic: a Comparative Study of Trobriand and Zande Rituals and Spells ", *AA*, 1929, vol. xxxi, pp. 619–41; JAMES, E. O., *The Beginnings of Religion*, London, 1948.

II

THE SKY AND SKY GODS

11. THE SACREDNESS OF THE SKY

THE most popular prayer in the world is addressed to " Our Father who art in heaven ". It is possible that man's earliest prayers were addressed to the same heavenly father—it would explain the testimony of an African of the Ewe tribe: " There where the sky is, God is too ". The Vienna school of ethnology (particularly in the person of Fr. W. Schmidt, the author of the fullest monograph yet produced on the subject of the origins of the idea of divinity) even claims to have established the existence of a primitive monotheism, basing the proof chiefly on the belief in sky gods among the most primitive human societies. For the moment we will leave on one side this problem of primeval monotheism. What is quite beyond doubt is that there is an almost universal belief in a celestial divine being, who created the universe and guarantees the fecundity of the earth (by pouring rain down upon it). These beings are endowed with infinite foreknowledge and wisdom; moral laws and often tribal ritual as well were established by them during a brief visit to the earth; they watch to see that their laws are obeyed, and lightning strikes all who infringe them.

We shall look at a series of divine figures of the sky, but first it is necessary to grasp the religious significance of the sky as such. There is no need to look into the teachings of myth to see that the sky itself directly reveals a transcendence, a power and a holiness. Merely contemplating the vault of heaven produces a religious experience in the primitive mind. This does not necessarily imply a " nature-worship " of the sky. To the primitive, nature is never purely " natural ". The phrase " contemplating the vault of heaven " really means something when it is applied to primitive man, receptive to the miracles of every day to an extent we find it hard to imagine. Such contemplation is the same as a revelation. The sky shows itself as it really is: infinite, transcendent. The vault of heaven is, more than anything else, " something quite apart " from the tiny thing that is man and his span of life. The symbolism of its transcendence derives from the simple realization of its infinite height. " Most High " becomes quite naturally an attribute of the divinity. The regions above man's reach, the starry places, are invested with the divine majesty of the transcendent, of absolute reality, of everlastingness. Such places are the dwellings of the gods; certain privileged people go there as a result of rites effecting their ascension into heaven; there, according to some religions, go the souls of the dead. The " high " is something inaccessible to man as such; it belongs by right to superhuman powers and beings; when a man ceremonially ascends the steps of a sanctuary, or the ritual ladder leading to the sky he ceases to be a man; the souls of the privileged dead leave their human state behind when they rise into heaven.

All this derives from simply contemplating the sky; but it would be a great mistake to see it as a logical, rational process. The transcendental quality of " height ", or the supra-terrestrial, the infinite, is revealed to man all at once, to his intellect as to his soul as a whole. The symbolism is an immediate notion of the whole consciousness, of the man, that is, who realizes himself as a man, who recognizes his place in the universe; these primeval realizations are bound up so organically with his life that the same symbolism determines both the activity of his subconscious and the noblest expressions of his spiritual life. It really is important, therefore, this realization that though the symbolism and religious values of the sky are not deduced logically from a calm and objective observation of the heavens, neither are they exclusively the product of mythical activity and non-rational religious experience. Let me repeat: even before any religious values have been set upon the sky it reveals its transcendence. The sky " symbolizes " transcendence, power and changelessness simply by being there. It exists because it is high, infinite, immovable, powerful.

That the mere fact of being high, of being high up, means being powerful (in the religious sense), and being as such filled with the sacred, is shown by the very etymology of some of the gods' names. To the Iroquois, all that has *orenda* is called *oki*, but the meaning of the word *oki* seems to be " what is on high "; we even fin a Supreme Being of the sky called Oke.[1] The Sioux express magico-religious power by the word *wakan*, which is phonetically extremely close to *wakan, wankan*, which means, in the Dakota language, " on high, above "; the sun, the moon, lightning, the wind, possess *wakan*, and this force was personified though imperfectly in " Wakan ", which the missionaries translated as meaning " Lord ", but who was in fact a Supreme Being of the sky, manifesting himself above all in lightning.[2]

The supreme divinity of the Maoris is called Iho : *iho* means " raised up, on high ".[3] The Akposo negroes have a Supreme God Uwoluwu; the name means " what is on high, the upper regions ".[4] And one could multiply these examples.[5] We shall see soon that " the most high ", " the shining ", " the sky ", are notions which have existed more or less explicitly in the terms used by primitive civilizations to express the idea of Godhead. The transcendence of God is directly revealed in the inaccessibility, infinity, eternity and creative power (rain) of the sky. The whole nature of the sky is an inexhaustible hierophany. Consequently, anything that happens among the stars or in the upper areas of the atmosphere—the rhythmic revolution of the stars, chasing clouds, storms, thunderbolts, meteors, rainbows—is a moment in that hierophany.

When this hierophany became personified, when the divinities *of* the sky showed themselves, or took the place of the holiness of the sky as such, is difficult to say precisely. What is quite certain is that the sky divinities have always been supreme divinities; that their hierophanies, dramatized in various ways by myth, have remained for that reason sky hierophanies; and that what one may call the history of sky divinities is largely a history of notions of " force ", of " creation ", of " laws " and of " sovereignty ". We shall look briefly at several groups of sky divinities, which will help

[1] Pettazzoni, *Dio*, Rome, 1922, vol. i, p. 310. All references to Pettazzoni's work are to vol. i; vol. ii has not yet appeared. Schmidt, *Der Ursprung der Gottesidee*, Münster, 1926, vol. ii, p. 399.

[2] Pettazzoni, pp. 290 ff.; Schmidt, vol. ii, pp. 402, 648–52.

[3] Pettazzoni, p. 175.

[4] Pettazzoni, p. 244.

[5] Cf. Pettazzoni, p. 358, n. 2.

us to a better understanding both of the essence of these divinities and of the tenor of their " history ".

12. AUSTRALIAN SKY GODS

Baiame, the supreme divinity among the tribes of South-East Australia (Kamilaroi, Wiradjuri, Euahlayi), dwells in the sky, beside a great stream of water (the Milky Way), and receives the souls of the innocent. He sits on a crystal throne; the sun and moon are his " sons ", his messengers to the earth (more truly his eyes, as with the Fuegians' Halakwulup and among the Semang and the Samoyeds).[1] Thunder is his voice; he causes the rain to fall, making the whole earth green and fertile; in this sense too he is creator. For Baiame is self-created and has created everything from nothing. Like the other sky gods, Baiame sees and hears everything.[2] Other tribes on the East coast (Muring, etc.), believe in a similar divine being, Daramulum. This is an esoteric name (the name of Baiame is too) only made known to the initiate; the women and children know him only as " father " (papang) and " lord " (biambam). In the same way, the clumsy clay images they have of the god are shown only during the initiation ceremonies; they are afterwards destroyed and the pieces are carefully scattered. At one time Daramulum lived for a short time on earth, and inaugurated the rites of initiation; he was then raised once more into heaven whence his voice may be heard (in thunder) and whence he sends down the rain. The initiation consists, among other things, in a solemn demonstration of the " bull-roarer "; it is a piece of wood about six inches long and just under an inch and a half wide with a piece of string through a hole at one end; when it is swung round it makes a noise like thunder or like a bull roaring. The identity of the bull-roarer and of Daramulum are known only to the initiate. The strange groanings they hear from the jungle at night fill the uninitiated with holy fear, for they take them to mean that the god is coming.[3]

The Supreme Being of the Kulin tribes is called Bunjil; he

---

[1] Cf. Schmidt, vol. iii, p. 1087.

[2] Howitt, *The Native Tribes of South-East Australia*, London, 1904, pp. 362 ff., 466 ff.; Pettazzoni, pp. 2 ff.; Schmidt, vol. i, p. 416; vol. iii, pp. 846 ff.

[3] Howitt, pp. 494 ff., 528 ff.

dwells high in the heavens, beyond the " dark heaven " (it is to this dark heaven that medicine men ascend, as to a mountain top); there another divine figure, Gargomitch, welcomes them and intercedes for them with Bunjil;[1] cf. the mountain at whose summit there is a being inferior to Baiame, who carries men's prayers to him and brings back his answers to them.[2] It was Bunjil who created the earth, trees, animals, and man himself (whom he fashioned of clay, breathing a soul into him through the nose, the mouth and the navel). But Bunjil, having given his son Bimbeal power over the earth, and his daughter Karakarook power over the sky, has himself withdrawn from the world. He stays above the clouds, like a " lord ", with a great sword in his hand.[3] Sky characteristics attach to other supreme gods of the Australians too. Almost all manifest their will through thunder, thunderbolts (Pulyallana for instance), the wind (Baime), the *aurora borealis* (Mungangana) rainbows (Bunjil, Nurrendere) and so on. As I said, Baiame's sky home has the Milky Way running through it; the stars are the campfires of Altjira and Tukura (the supreme gods of the Aranda and Loritja tribes; see the Bibliography).

In general it is true to say that these divine beings of the Australians preserve a direct and concrete connection with the sky, with the world of stars and meteors.[4] Of all of them we know that they made the universe and created man (that is, man's mythical ancestor); in their short stay on earth they revealed mysteries (almost all of which could be reduced to a communication of the mythical genealogy of the tribe, and certain epiphanies of thunder like the bull-roarer, and so on), and instituted civil and moral laws. They are good (they are called " Our Father "), they reward the upright and defend morality. They play the major part in all initiation ceremonies (as for example with the Wiradjuri and Kamilaroi and the

---

[1] Howitt, p. 490.

[2] Schmidt, vol. iii, pp. 845, 868, 871.

[3] Schmidt, vol. iii, pp. 656–717.

[4] But one cannot sum them up, as Professor Pettazzoni does, as simply a personification of the vault of heaven. The primitive element is the anthropocosmic structure of their personality. The Wotjobluk, for instance, speak of Bunjil as a " great man " who used to be on earth and is now in heaven (Howitt, p. 489). Sky-nature characteristics are almost wholly absent from Mungangana (" our father ") who is none the less one of the earliest Supreme Beings of the Australians (cf. Howitt, pp. 616 ff.; Schmidt, vol. iii, pp. 591 ff.).

Yuin and Kuri) and prayers are even addressed directly to them (as with the Yuin and the Kuri in the South). But nowhere does the belief in such Supreme Beings dominate religious life. The characteristic element in Australian religion is not the belief in a heavenly being, a supreme creator, but totemism. We find the same situation elsewhere; the supreme divinities of the sky are constantly pushed to the periphery of religious life where they are almost ignored; other sacred forces, nearer to man, more accessible to his daily experience, more useful to him, fill the leading role.

13. SKY GODS AMONG THE ANDAMAN ISLANDERS, AFRICANS, ETC.

So, for example, Risley and Geden find traces of an almost forgotten belief in a Supreme Divinity among the aboriginal peoples of India—" a shadowy recollection rather than an active force ";[1] " fainéant unworshipped Supreme Beings ".[2] Yet, however nearly obliterated the traces of this Supreme Divinity of heaven, they still retain their connection with the world of the sky and weather. In the Andaman archipelago, among one of the most primitive peoples of Asia, Puluga is the Supreme Being; he is thought of very anthropomorphically,[3] but he dwells in the sky and his voice is the thunder, the wind his breath; hurricanes are the sign of his anger, for he sends thunderbolts to punish all who infringe his commandments. Puluga knows everything, but only knows men's thoughts during the day (a naturist quality—omniscient means all-seeing).[4] He has created himself a wife and they have children. He lives in the sky near the sun (feminine) and the moon (masculine), with their children, the stars. When Puluga sleeps there is a drought. When it is raining the god has come down to earth and is looking for food.[5] Puluga created the world, and the first man, Tomo. Mankind multiplied and had to disperse, and after the death of Tomo grew ever more forgetful of its creator. One day Puluga got angry and a flood

[1] Geden, in the *Encylopædia of Religion and Ethics*, vol. vi, p. 289.
[2] Risley, *The People of India*, London, 1915, pp. 226 ff.
[3] Schebesta, *Les Pygmées*, Paris, 1940, p. 161.
[4] Cf. Pettazzoni, vol. i, p. 96.
[5] The appearance of vegetation: Schmidt, *Ursprung*, vol. i, pp. 161 ff., vol. iii, pp. 122 ff.

covered the whole earth and destroyed mankind: only four people escaped. Puluga had mercy on them, but men still remained recalcitrant. Having once and for all reminded them of his commandments the god withdrew, and men have never seen him since. This myth of estrangement fits in with the total absence of any cult. One of the most recent explorers, Paul Schebesta, writes about it: " The Andaman Islanders have no worship of the god, no prayer, no sacrifice, no supplication, no thanksgiving. They are simply afraid of Puluga and therefore they obey his commandments, some of which are hard, such as that of avoiding certain fruits during the rainy season. By stretching a point one might explain some of their customs as a kind of cult."[1] Among those customs one might include the " sacred silence " of the huntsmen when they return to the village after successful hunting.

Among the Selk'nam nomad hunters of Tierra del Fuego, the god is called Temaukel, but from holy fear this name is never pronounced. He is ordinarily called *so'onh-haskan*, i.e., " Dweller in the Sky ", and *so'onh kas pémer*, " He Who is in the Sky ". He is eternal, omniscient, omnipotent, creator —but creation was accomplished through mythical ancestors who were also created by the Supreme God before he withdrew beyond the stars. For, in fact, this god is set apart from men, indifferent to the world's affairs. He has no images, no priests. He is the author of the moral law, he is the judge, and ultimately he is master of all destinies. But they pray to him only in case of illness: " Thou, on high, do not take my child; he is still too small ! " And they make special offerings to him in time of bad weather.[2]

All over Africa traces are to be found of a great sky god who has almost disappeared or is in course of disappearing from the cult (see the Bibliography). His place has been taken by other religious forces, particularly by the cult of ancestors. " The general bias of the negro mind," says Sir A. B. Ellis, " has been in favour of selecting the firmament for the chief Nature-god, instead of the Sun, Moon or Earth."[3] Mary

[1] *Les Pygmées*, p. 163.

[2] Cf. Martin Gusinde, " Das höchste Wesen bei den Selk'nam auf Feuerland ", *W. Schmidt-Festschrift*, Vienna, 1928, pp. 269–74.

[3] Frazer, *The Worship of Nature*, London, 1926, p. 99.

Kingsley writes: " The firmament is, I believe, always the great indifferent and neglected god, the Nyan Kupon of the Tschwis, and the Anzambe, the Naam, etc. of the Bantu races. The African thinks this god has great power if he would only exert it."[1]

I will return in a moment to the indifference of this great god. Note for the moment his celestial form. The Tschwis, for instance, use the word Nyankupon—the name of their Supreme Being—to designate sky and rain; they say *Nyankupon bom* (strikes) for " It is thundering "; *Nyankupon aba* (has come) for " It is raining ".[2] The Ba-Ilas, Bantu tribes in the Kafu valley, believe in an omnipotent Supreme Being and creator who dwells in the sky, and whom they call Leza. But in common speech the word " Leza " also describes meteorological phenomena; " Leza falls " means it is raining, " Leza is angry ", it thunders, and so on.[3] The Suks call their Supreme Being Tororut, that is, the Sky, and also Ilat, the Rain.[4] Among the negroes properly so-called, Nyame also means the firmament (from the root *nyam*, " to shine "; cf. *div*, § 20).

For most of the Ewe peoples, Mawu is the name of the Supreme Being (the name comes from *wu*, " to spread ", " to cover "); Mawu is also used to designate the firmament and the rain. The blue of the sky is the veil Mawu uses to cover his face; the clouds are his clothes and ornaments; blue and white are his favourite colours (his priest may wear no others). Light is the oil with which he anoints his body. Mawu sends the rain, and he is omniscient. But though he is still offered regular sacrifices, he is gradually disappearing from the cult.[5] Among the Masai, Ngai is a lofty divine figure. He still preserves sky characteristics; he is invisible, dwells in heaven, his sons are stars, etc. Other stars are his eyes; a falling star is one of his eyes coming towards the earth to see better. According to Hollis, Engai (Ngai) means literally, " rain ".[6]

---

[1] *Travels in West Africa*, London, 1897, p. 508.
[2] A. B. Ellis, quoted by Frazer, p. 99.
[3] Smith and Dale, *The Ila-Speaking Peoples of Northern Rhodesia*, London, 1920, vol. ii, pp. 198 ff.
[4] Frazer, p. 288.
[5] J. Spieth, *Die Religion der Eweer*, Göttingen and Leipzig, 1911, pp. 5 ff.
[6] *The Masai*, Oxford, 1905, pp. 264 ff.

The Pawnees believe in Tirawa Atius, "Tirawa Father of All Things", creator of all that exists and giver of life. He has created the stars to guide man's steps; lightning is his glance, and the wind his breath. His worship still has a definite and strongly-coloured sky symbolism. His home is to be found far above the clouds in the unchanging sky. Tirawa becomes a noble figure of myth and religion. "White men speak of a heavenly Father, we speak of Tirawa Atius the Father on High, but we do not think of Tirawa as a person. We think of him in everything. . . . What he looks like no one knows."[1]

14. "DEUS OTIOSUS"

The absence of cult—and above all the absence of any calendar of seasonal rites—is characteristic of most of the sky gods.[2] The Semang on the Malacca peninsula also have a Supreme Being, Kari, Karei or Ta Pedn, who is taller than a man, and invisible. When they speak of him, the Semang do not exactly say that he is immortal, yet they declare that he has always existed. He created everything except the earth and man who are the work of Ple, another and subordinate divinity.[3] The detail that the earth and man were not created by Kari is a significant one; it is a popular expression of the idea of the transcendence and passivity of the Supreme Being, too far removed from man to satisfy his innumerable religious, economic and vital needs. Like the other supreme sky gods, Kari lives in the sky and shows his anger by hurling lightning; in fact his very name means "thunderbolt" ("storm"). He is omniscient, for he can see everything that happens on earth. That is why he is "first of all the Lawgiver, ruling over the communal life of the men of the forest, and watching jealously to see that his commandments are kept".[4] But he is not

---

[1] Pettazzoni, p. 287.

[2] Pettazzoni (*Dio*, p. 365), gives a list of these primitive sky divinities with no cult or only a few elements of cult, a list which must, however, be corrected in the light of the material gathered and discussed by Schmidt in the first six volumes of his *Ursprung der Gottesidee* (Schebesta's researches among the Pygmies, those of Gusinde and Koppers among the Selk'nam, of Vanoverbergh among the Negritos of the Philippines, and so on). See the critical bibliography at the end of this chapter.

[3] Skeat and Blagden, *Pagan Races of the Malay Peninsula*, London, 1906, vol. ii, pp. 239, 297, 737 ff.

[4] Schebesta, p. 148.

worshipped in the true sense of the word; he is invoked, with expiatory blood-offerings, only when a tornado breaks out.[1]

The same is the case with most of the African peoples: the Great God of Heaven, the Supreme Being, Creator omnipotent, plays a quite insignificant part in the religious life of the tribe. He is too distant or too good to need worship properly so called, and they invoke him only in cases of extreme need. Thus, for instance, the Yorubas of West Africa believe in a sky god called Olorun (which means literally " Owner of the Sky "), who having started to create the world handed over the finishing and governing of it to a lower god, Obatalla. Olorun himself withdrew permanently from earthly and human affairs, and though he is a Supreme God, he has neither temples, statues, nor priests. He is, however, called on as a last resort in time of calamity.[2]

Among the Fang of the French Congo Nzame—or Nsambe —creator and lord of heaven and earth, once played a fairly important part in the religious life of the tribe, but he has now faded into the background.[3] Nzambi of the Bantus is also a great sky god now withdrawn from all worship. The natives look upon him as all-powerful, good and just; but for that very reason they do not adore him, they have no material representation of him as they have of the other gods and spirits.[4] Among the Basongos, the heavenly creator, Efile Mokulu, has no cult, and is invoked only by those swearing oaths.[5] The Hereros, a Bantu people from South-West Africa, call their supreme god Ndyambi. Withdrawn into the

---

[1] Schebesta was the first European to witness this ceremony. During the storm, the Semang cut their legs with a bamboo knife, pouring a few drops of blood on the ground as an offering to the goddess Manoid, and throwing the rest to the four points of the compass, and shouting, " Go! Go! Go! "; they invoke the god of thunder: " Ta Pedn! I am not obdurate, I am paying for my fault! Accept my debt, I am paying! " or else: " Oh! Oh ! listen, hear me, give me your ear, Ta Pedn. I am not deceiving you; I pay my debt. I fear thy thunder! " (Schebesta, p. 149; Schmidt, vol. iii, pp. 178 ff.; 190 ff.) This expiatory offering of blood—by which the Semang " pay for " their sins against the (sky) god of thunder—is their only act of worship; they have no other prayers at all.

[2] Frazer, pp. 119 ff.

[3] Frazer, p. 135.

[4] Frazer, pp. 142 ff.

[5] Frazer, p. 149.

sky, he has abandoned mankind to the lower divinities. For that reason he is not adored. " Why should we sacrifice to him ? " said a native. " We do not need to fear him, for he does not do us any harm, as do the spirits of our dead [ovakuru]." The Hereros, however, do offer prayers to him when they have some unexpected piece of good luck.[1] The Alundas, another Bantu tribe, believe that their Nzambi is very distant and inaccessible to men; their religious life is entirely given over to the fear and worship of spirits; even for rain they pray to the akishi, that is to their ancestors.[2]

We find the same situation among the Angonis, who have a Supreme Being, but adore their ancestors; with the Tumbukas, for whom the Creator is too unknown, too great " for the common affairs of man ";[3] with the Wembas, who know of Leza's existence but whose worship is demanded solely by their ancestors; with the Wahehes, who picture the Supreme Being, Nguruhi, as omnipotent creator, but who know also that it is the spirits of the dead (masoka) who really have control over the affairs of the world and so offer to them their regular worship; and so on. The Wachaggas, an important Bantu tribe of Kilimanjaro, adore Ruwa, the creator, the good God, guardian of the moral law. He is active in myth and legend, but plays only a moderate part in religion. He is so good and so kind that men have no need to fear him; all their anxiety centres on the spirits of the dead. And it is only when the prayer and sacrifice offered to the spirits remain unanswered that they sacrifice to Ruwa, particularly in the case of drought or serious illness.[4]

It is the same with the Tschwi-speaking negroes of West Africa and Nyankupon. Nyankupon is far from being adored; he has no cult, nor even any special priests, and they pay him honour only in rare circumstances—in time of famine or epidemic, or after a violent hurricane; at those times they ask him in what they have offended him.[5] Dzingbe (" The Universal Father ") leads the pantheon of gods of the Ewe

[1] Frazer, pp. 150 ff.

[2] Frazer, p. 168.

[3] Frazer, p. 185.

[4] Frazer, pp. 205 ff.; cf. the Bibliography.

[5] Pettazzoni, p. 239.

people. Unlike most of the other supreme sky beings, Dzingbe
has a special priest, called *dzisai*, "priest of heaven", who
invokes him when there is a drought: "O sky, to whom we owe
our thanks, great is the drought; make it to rain that the earth
may be refreshed and the fields thrive ! "[1] The remoteness and
impartiality of the Supreme Being of heaven are admirably
expressed in a saying of the Gyriamas of East Africa who
describe their God thus: "God [Mulungu] is on high, the
manes are below [literally, on earth]."[2]

The Bantus say: "God, after having made man, pays no
further attention to him." And the Negrilloes say again and
again: "God is far from us ! "[3] The Fang peoples of the
plains of Equatorial Africa express their philosophy of religion
in the following song:

> Nzame [God] is on high, man below.
> God is God, man is man
> Each is at home, each in his own house.

There is no cult of Nzame, and the Fang only address him
to ask for rain.[4] It is also for rain that the Hottentots invoke
Tsuni-Goam: "O Tsuni-Goam, thou, father of fathers, thou
our father, let Nanub [that is, the cloud] drop down rain in
torrents ! " As he is omniscient the god knows everyone's
sins, so he is also invoked thus: "O Tsuni-Goam, thou alone
knowest that I am not guilty."[5]

The prayers addressed to these gods by those in need sum
up perfectly their celestial nature. The Pygmies of Equatorial
Africa believe that God (Kmvum) shows his wish to enter into
contact with them by means of the rainbow. That is why,
whenever a rainbow appears, they pick up their bows and
direct them towards it and begin to chant: " . . . Thou, victor
in the fight, hast cast down beneath thee the thunder that
growled, that growled so loudly and so angrily. Was it angry
with us ? ", and so on. The litany closes with a prayer to the
rainbow to intervene with the supreme sky god so that he will

---

[1] Spieth, *Die Religion der Eweer*, Gottingen and Leipzig, 1911, pp. 46 ff.
[2] Le Roy, *The Religion of the Primitives*, London, 1923, p. 123.
[3] Trilles, *Les Pygmées de la forêt équatoriale*, Paris, 1932, p. 74.
[4] Trilles, p. 77.
[5] Pettazzoni, p. 198.

no longer be angry with them, no longer thunder and kill.[1]
Men only remember the sky and the supreme divinity when
they are directly threatened by a danger from the sky; at other
times, their piety is called upon by the needs of every day, and
their practices and devotion are directed towards the forces
that control those needs. But it is quite clear that all this in
no way lessens the autonomy, majesty and primacy of the
supreme sky beings; at most it shows that the "primitive"
man as well as the civilized quickly forgets them when he feels
no need of them; that the hardships of life drive him to look
more towards earth than towards heaven, and that he only
discovers heaven's importance when he is threatened with
death from that direction.

15. NEW "DIVINE FORMS" SUBSTITUTED FOR THE SKY GODS

In point of fact, nowhere in primitive religion do we find
Supreme Beings of the sky playing a leading role. The dominant
religious form among the Australians is totemism. In Polynesia, although there is belief in a Supreme Divinity of the sky
or a first divine pair (see *infra*), religious practice is marked by
a profuse polydemonism or polytheism. In the Yap islands of
the Western Carolines there is a quite clearly defined belief in
Yelafaz—a Supreme Being, creator, good, and so on—but in
fact the people venerate spirits (*taliukan*). The natives of the
Wetter islands in Indonesia, though they practise fetishism,
still believe in a Supreme Being, "the Old One", who lives in
the sun or in the sky. In Indonesia generally, the supreme
divinity of the sky has either been amalgamated with or replaced by the god of the Sun; for instance I-lai of the Celebes
has been assimilated into a sun god whom, however, the natives
see as continuing the work of creation begun by I-lai; it is the
same on Timor and innumerable other islands.[2]

In Melanesia what dominates religious life is the belief in
mana; but you also find animism there and traces of a belief
in the sky god. Fijian religious practice takes the form of
animism, despite certain survivals of a supreme sky divinity,
Ndengei, represented paradoxically as a great serpent who lives
hidden in a cave, or with a serpent's head and a stone body;

---

[1] Trilles, pp. 78, 79; *L'Ame du Pygmée d'Afrique*, Leipzig, 1933, p. 109.
[2] Cf. Pettazzoni, pp. 130 ff.

when he moves the earth quakes; they still believe he is the creator of the world, knows everything, punishes evil, and so on.[1] The peoples of Africa, as we have seen, though they may have kept more or less intact their belief in a Supreme Being of the sky, still have a religious life dominated by things other than monotheism or monolatry. In the religion of the Déné Indians shamanism and the worship of spirits are the main elements, but there is also a Supreme Being of the sky, Yuttoere (which means: " He who remains on high ").

In other places, a lunar divinity has been superimposed on the Supreme Being of the sky; such for instance is the case with the natives of the Banks islands,[2] and in the New Hebrides.[3] Very occasionally—and no doubt under the influence of a matriarchy—the Supreme Divinity of the sky is feminine; thus Hintubuhet of New Ireland, who has all the attributes of the Supreme Divinity of the sky (passivity and so on), but is female. Sometimes a Great Goddess has been substituted for the primitive Supreme Being of heaven, as with the Todas, the Kavis of Assam and so on. In Southern India the supreme divinity of the sky plays almost no part, religious life being entirely taken up with the worship of local female divinities, the grāma-devatā.

The motif of a primordial pair: Sky (male) and Earth (female), is fairly common. So, in the Indonesian island of Keisar, the masculine principle Makarom Manouwe, who lives in the sky and sometimes in the sun, and the feminine principle Makarom Mawakhu, present in the earth, form the central object of worship.[4] The first couple and the creation myth corresponding to them are characteristic of Polynesia and Micronesia—the Maori version of Rangi and Papa being the best known. Traces of the belief in a first divine couple are also to be found in Africa; among the Bantus of the south, and especially among the Bavili and Fjort peoples, the supreme sky god Nzambi has slipped into the background leaving in his place a divinity of earth who even bears the same name, and whose sacred secrets are revealed only to women.[5] The

---

[1] Pettazzoni, pp. 155 ff.
[2] Codrington, *The Melanesians*, pp. 155 ff.
[3] Pettazzoni, vol. i, p. 161.
[4] Pettazzoni, p. 134.
[5] Pettazzoni, pp. 210 ff.; Frazer, *Worship of Nature*, pp. 130 ff.

mythological motif of the Sky-Earth couple is found again in Southern California (they are brother and sister: from their union all things are born), among the Pima Indians, and in New Mexico among the Plains Indians, among the Sioux and the Pawnees, and in the West Indies.[1]

16. FUSION AND SUBSTITUTION

What is clear is that the supreme sky god everywhere gives place to other religious forms. The morphology of this substitution may vary; but its meaning is in each case partly the same: it is a movement away from the transcendence and passivity of sky beings towards more dynamic, active and easily accessible forms. One might say that we are observing a "progressive descent of the sacred into the concrete"; man's life and his immediate natural surroundings come more and more to have the value of sacred things. His belief in *mana*, *orenda*, *wakan*, etc., animism, totemism, devotion to the spirits of the dead and local divinities, and so on, place man in a quite different religious attitude from that which he held towards the Supreme Being of the sky. The very structure of the religious experience is changed; a Daramulum or a Tirawa, for instance, makes himself known very differently from the totems, the *grāma-devatā*, the spirits of the dead. Every substitution marks a victory for the dynamic, dramatic forms, so rich in mythological meaning, over the Supreme Being of the sky who is exalted, but passive and remote.

Thus, for the Maoris of New Zealand, Rangi, though present in their myths, is not the object of any worship; in his place we find Tangaroa, the supreme (sun?) god of the Maori pantheon. In Melanesia one constantly comes across the myth of the two brothers, one bright, the other dull (the two phases of the moon) created by the Supreme Being of the sky and eventually replacing him. Generally, the Supreme Being gives place to a demiurge whom he has himself created and who, in his name and following his instructions, sets the world in order; or to a sun god. So, for certain Bantu peoples the demiurge Unkulunkulu is the creator of the human race, but is subordinate to the supreme being of the sky Utikxo, although he

[1] Cf. Numazawa, *Die Weltanfänge in der japanischen Mythologie*, Lucerne, 1946, pp. 301 ff.

has since pushed the latter into the shade. Among the Tlingit Indians (North-West Pacific), the central divine figure is the Crow, primeval hero and demiurge, who made the world (or, more precisely, set it in order, and spread civilization and culture through it), created and liberated the sun, and so on.[1] But sometimes the Crow does all this under the command of a higher divine being (whose son he may be). Among the Tupi Indians, Tamosci is the mythical ancestor, the solarized demiurge who is substituted for the Supreme Being of the sky, and among the Guarani it is Tamoi.

In North America the Supreme Being of the sky generally tends to become amalgamated with the mythological personification of the thunder and the wind, represented as a large bird (the crow, etc.); he beats his wings and the wind rises, his tongue is the lightning.[2] Thunder was from the beginning, and still is, the essential attribute of the sky gods. Sometimes it is singled out and invested with individual autonomy. Thus, for instance, the Sioux Indians believe the stars and all meteorological phenomena, the sun, the moon, the thunder—the thunder particularly—are full of *wakan*. The Kansas Indians say they have never seen their god Wakan, but that they often hear his voice in the thunder. Indeed, among the Dakotas, Wakantanka is " a word meaning thunder " (Dorsey). The Omahas honour the thunder as Wakanda with a cult properly so called; in particular, at the beginning of spring the men go up to the hills to smoke in his honour, and to bring him offerings of tobacco.[3] The Algonquins make promises to Chebbeniathan, " The Man on High ", whenever a hurricane threatens or thunder seems to be coming near.

I said (§ 12) that in Australian initiation rituals the epiphany of thunder is shown by the noise of the bull-roarer. The same object and the same ceremonial were also preserved in the Orphic initiation rites. Thunder is a weapon of the sky god in all mythologies, and any spot he has struck with lightning becomes sacred (*enelysion* to the Greeks, *fulguritum* to the Romans)[4]; and any man he has struck with lightning is

---

[1] Schmidt, *Ursprung*, vol. ii, p. 390.

[2] Rendel Harris, *Boanerges*, Cambridge, 1913, pp. 13 ff.; Schmidt, vol. ii, pp. 44 ff.; 266 ff.; 299 ff.

[3] Pettazzoni, p. 290.

[4] Cf. Usener, *Kleine Schriften*, Leipzig-Berlin, 1912, vol. iv p. 478.

consecrate. The tree most often struck by lightning (the oak) is endowed with the majesty of the Supreme Divinity (I need only remind you of the oak of Zeus at Dodona, of Jupiter Capitolinus in Rome, the oak of Donar near Geismar, the sacred oak of Romowe in Prussia, the oak of Perun among the Slavs). A great many beliefs connected with the sanctity of thunder are to be found all over the world. People thought the so-called " thunder " stones—which are for the most part nothing more than prehistoric flints—were the very arrowpoints of the lightning, and they were venerated and piously preserved as such (§ 78). Everything that fell from above partook of the holiness of the sky; that is why meteorites, absolutely saturated with it, were venerated.[1]

17. THE ANTIQUITY OF SUPREME BEINGS OF THE SKY

We cannot say for certain that devotion to sky beings was the first and only belief that primitive man had, and that all other religious forms appeared later and represent corruptions. Though belief in a supreme sky being is generally to be found among the most archaic of primitive societies (Pygmies, Australians, Fuegians and so on), it is not found amongst them all (there is none, for instance, among the Tasmanians, the Veddas, the Kubu). And it seems to me, in any case, that such a belief would not necessarily exclude all other religious forms. Undoubtedly, from the earliest times man realized the transcendence and omnipotence of the sacred from what he experienced of the sky. The sky needs no aid from mythological imagination or conceptual elaboration to be seen as *the* divine sphere. But innumerable other hierophanies could coexist with this hierophany of the sky.

One thing we can say with certainty: generally speaking, the sky hierophany and the belief in Supreme Beings of the sky have been superseded by other religious conceptions. Generally speaking, again, it is clear that such beliefs in a Supreme Being of the sky formerly represented the very centre

[1] Eliade, " Metallurgy, Magic and Alchemy ", Paris, 1938, *CZ*, vol. i, pp. 3 ff. Among certain West African tribes, various stones are venerated as part of the cult of sky gods. So, for instance, the Kassunas and Buras call these stones We (from the name of their sky god); the Kassunas and Fras adore them and offer sacrifice to them; the Habés offer sacrifice to menhirs which they regard as incorporating the sky divinity Amma; elsewhere in Africa they adore thunderstones (cf. Frazer, pp. 91 ff.).

of religious life, not a mere sort of subsection on the periphery, as they are among primitives to-day. The present scant worship of these sky gods indicates purely and simply that the mass of religious practice is given over to other religious forms; in no case does it indicate that such sky gods are the abstract creations of primitive man (or simply of his " priests "), or that he has not had, or been able to have, any real religious relationship with them. Besides, as I have already said, the lack of worship indicates mainly the absence of any religious calendar; occasionally, sporadically, each of these supreme sky beings is honoured with prayers, sacrifices and so on. Occasionally they even have a real cult, as witness, for instance, the great ritual feasts of North America in honour of their supreme beings (Tirawa, Chebbeniathan, Awonawilona). Even in Africa, there are quite a number of examples: the night dances in honour of Cagn among the Bushmen, or the regular worship of Uwoluwu (who has priests, places of worship and sacrifices) among the Akposos; the Ibibios have periodic human sacrifices, in honour of Abassi Abumo, the Thunderer, and Abbassi still has a sanctuary in the courtyard of each house among the inhabitants of Calabar, who are the Ibibios' neighbours; there are prayers and sacrifices in honour of Leza; and so on. The Kondes adore their supreme god Mbamba with dances, songs, and prayers: " Mbamba, let our children thrive! May the cattle multiply! May our maize and sweet potatoes flourish! Take pestilence away! "[1] The Wachaggas address their prayers and sacrifices to Ruwa: " Thou Man of Heaven, O Chief, take this head of cattle. We pray thee that thou wouldst lead far past and away the sickness that comes on earth." Pious people offer prayers to Ruwa morning and evening without any sacrifice.[2] Goats are offered to Mulugu, and the Akikuyus offer numerous sacrifices to Engai of the first-fruits of their harvests and sheep.[3]

An analysis of the various stages of Australian religion shows clearly that the sky divinity held the central place in the most primitive religious life. Originally, Mungangana used to live on earth among men; only later did he withdraw to heaven

[1] Frazer, p. 190.
[2] Frazer, pp. 212 ff.
[3] Frazer, pp. 248 ff.

and leave them. All over Australia one can recognize to some extent the myth of the gradual withdrawal of divine beings. It would in any case be hard to trace the belief in these sky beings back to any earlier belief. It has been said, for instance, that it grew from the cult of the dead, but in South-Eastern Australia (where is one of the oldest of all) there is no cult of the dead.[1] And it is there, where the initiation ceremonies are most in force (that is, in South-East Australia) that we find the sky divinity connected with secret rites. Where, on the other hand, esoterism is gradually disappearing (as is the case with most of the Central Australian tribes—the Arunta and Loritja), the sky divinity (Altjira, Tukura) appears to have lost all religious force and to survive only in the mythological sphere; which means that belief in the sky divinity was undoubtedly once fuller and more intense. From initiation one learns the true theophany, the myth of the tribal genealogy, the corpus of laws, moral and social, in a word, man's place in the cosmos. Initiation is thus an occasion of learning and not merely a ritual of regeneration. Knowledge, the global understanding of the world, the interpretation of the unity of nature, the revelation of the final causes underlying existence, and so on—all these things are possible thanks to contemplation of the sky, the sky hierophany, and the Supreme Divinities of the sky.

However, we should be making a great mistake if we were to see these actions and reflections merely as things of the intellect (as, for instance, Schmidt does). They are, on the contrary, acts of the whole man, who, of course, has a certain preoccupation with causality, but has above all—in fact, finds himself in the midst of—the problem of existence. All these revelations of a metaphysical nature (the origin of the human race, sacred history of the god and of ancestors, metamorphoses, the meaning of symbols, secret names and so on), made within the framework of initiation ceremonies, are not simply aimed at satisfying the neophyte's thirst for knowledge, but primarily at consolidating his existence as a whole, promoting continuity of life and prosperity and assuring a happier fate after death.

To sum up, then: the most significant thing of all is the presence of sky divinities at the most primitive levels of Aus-

[1] Schmidt, vol. iii, p. 106.

tralian religion, in the framework of initiation ceremonies. This initiation, as I said, assures the regeneration of the initiate at the same time as revealing to him secrets of a metaphysical nature; it feeds at once life, strength and knowledge. It shows what a close bond there is between the theophany (for in the initiation ritual the true name and nature of the god are revealed), soteriology (for the ceremony of initiation, however elementary it may be, assures the salvation of the neophyte), and metaphysics (for revelation is given about the workings and origin of the universe, the origin of the human race and so on). But at the very heart of this secret ceremony you will find the sky god, the same divinity who originally created the universe and man, and came down to earth to establish culture and the rites of initiation.

That sky gods had, at first, this prerogative of being not only creators and omnipotent, but also all-knowing, supremely " wise ", explains why you find them changed in some religions into abstract divine figures, personified concepts used to explain the universe or express its absolute reality. Iho, the sky god of New Zealand and Tahiti, revealed only to those initiated into esoteric priestly learning, is more of a philosophical concept than a real divinity.[1] Other sky gods—Nzambi of the Bantu peoples, for instance, Sussistinako among the Sia Indians— are asexual: a phenomenon of abstraction which marks the changing of the divinity into a metaphysical principle. Indeed, Awonawilona, among the Zuñi Indians, is represented as without any personal characteristics, and may be considered equally well as feminine or as masculine (Lang called it " He-She ").[2]

These Supreme Gods of the sky could be transformed into philosophic concepts only because the sky hierophany itself could be transformed into a metaphysical revelation; because, that is, contemplation of the sky by its very nature enabled man to know not only his own precariousness and the trans- cendence of the divinity, but also the sacred value of knowledge, of spiritual " force ". Gazing into the clear blue sky by day or the multitude of stars by night, nowhere could one discern more

---

[1] Pettazzoni, p. 174.

[2] One must not, however, forget that bisexuality was a mark of divinity for the primitive; it represented a formula (approximative, like most mythological formulæ) of *totality*, of the *integration of opposites*, of the *coincidentia opposi- torum* (§159).

completely the divine origin and sacred value of knowledge, the omnipotence of him who *sees* and *understands*, of him who " knows " all because he is everywhere, sees everything, makes and governs all things. To the modern mind, of course, such gods, with their vague mythological outlines—Iho and Brahman and the rest—seem rather abstract, and we tend to look on them more as philosophical concepts than as divinities proper. But do not forget that to primitive man, whose invention they were, knowledge and understanding were—and still are— epiphanies of " power ", of " sacred force ". He who sees and knows all, *is* and *can do* all. Sometimes such a Supreme Being, celestial in origin, becomes the foundation of the universe, author and controller of the rhythms of nature, and tends to become amalgamated either with the principle or metaphysical substance of the universe, or with the Law, with what is eternal and universal among the phenomena of time and change—the Law which the gods themselves cannot do away with.

18. SKY GODS AMONG THE PEOPLES OF THE ARCTIC AND CENTRAL ASIA

When we turn from the religion of " primitive " peoples to so-called polytheistic religions, the main differences we encounter result from their own " history ". Naturally " history " has also modified primitive theophanies; none of the sky gods of primitive peoples is " pure ", none represent an original form. Their " forms " have been altered, either by outside influences, or simply because they have been part of a human tradition. But when it comes to the so-called polytheistic religions, history has had an effect of far greater violence. The religious conceptions, as well as the whole spiritual and mental life of these historically creative peoples, have undergone influences, symbioses, conversions and eclipses. Divine " forms ", like all the other " forms " produced by those civilizations, are made up of innumerable different elements. Fortunately, religious life, and all the creations that spring from it, are dominated by what one may call " the tendency towards an archetype ". However many and varied are the components that go to make up any religious creation (any divine form, rite, myth or cult) their expression tends constantly to revert to an archetype. We shall be able, for that reason, to glance at some of the sky gods of polytheistic religion, without having to know the "history" of each in order to understand his make-up and his career; for eacn one, whatever the history that has gone before, tends to work back to his original "form", to revert to his archetype. This does not mean, however, that the figures of these sky gods are simple, or that we can go very far in simplifying them.

The first new element these gods present by comparison with those we looked at in the preceding paragraphs is their sovereignty. The theophany can never be reduced simply to meteorological phenomena and what happens in the sky; their power is never shown merely by the creation of the cosmos. They become "masters", universal sovereigns. Consequently, in the so-called polytheistic religions, we cannot speak simply of sky gods without including this new element of sovereignty; it derives from the same celestial prerogatives, but it is in fact a new expression of the religious significance of "power", and it produces a definite change of outline in the concept of divinity.

We may begin our brief sketch with the supreme sky gods adored by the Arctic peoples, and the nomads of North and Central Asia. The Samoyeds worship Num, a divinity who dwells in the sky (or the seventh heaven) and whose name means "heaven".[1] But he cannot be physically identified with the sky, for, as Schmidt points out,[2] the Samoyeds also consider Num to be the sea and the earth, that is to say the whole universe. Among the Koryaks, the supreme divinity is called "the one on high", "the master of what is high", "the overseer", "he who exists", "force", "the world". The Ainu know him as "the divine master of the sky", "the heavenly god", "the divine Creator of the worlds", "the Protector", and so on; but also as Kamui, which means "sky".[3] The supreme divinity of the Koryaks dwells in "the village of heaven". The Central Eskimos believe that their Supreme God lives in the sky; they call him "heavenly being".[4] But I need hardly say these names and attributions

[1] Castren, *Reisen im Norden in den Jahren* 1838–1844, Leipzig, 1953, pp. 231 ff.
[2] *Ursprung*, vol. iii, p. 357.
[3] Batchelor, *The Ainu and their Folk-Lore*, London, 1901, pp. 248 ff., 258 ff.
[4] Cf. Schmidt, vol. iii, p. 345.

do not exhaust the personality of the Supreme God of the Arctic peoples. He is, above all, an omnipotent god, often the only one, and master of the universe. But the celestial nature of his theophanies is clear and ancient; and like the sky gods of the " primitives ", this Supreme God too shares the religious life of the Arctic peoples with lower gods and spirits. Sometimes, when prayer to the spirits has been fruitless, they pray to him alone. None the less, in sacrifice he is offered the head and long bones of the animal sacrificed, whereas the spirits and the chthonian divinities receive only the warm blood.[1]

The Mongol name for the Supreme Divinity is *tengri*, which means " sky " (cf. too *tengeri* of the Buriats, *tangere* of the Tatars of the Volga, *tingir* of the Beltirs, Tangar of the Yakuts, and probably *tura* of the Chuvashes.[2] Among the Cheremisses, the sky god is called Yume, originally " heaven ").[3] The most common name among the Ostyaks and the Voguls is Num-Turem, " Turem the high " or " Turem who dwells on high ".[4] Further south, among the Irtysh Ostyaks, the name of the sky god comes from *senke* whose original meaning was " luminous, shining, light ";[5] for instance Num-Senke (" Senke from on high "), Yem-Senke (" Senke the good "), etc.[5]

Other titles and epithets of the sky god complete our definition of his nature and functions. The Beltirs address their prayers to the " most merciful Khan " (Kaira-Kan) and to the " Master " (*cajan*).[6] The Tatars of Minusinsk call

---

[1] A. Gahs, " Kopf-, Schädel- und Langknochenopfer bei Rentiervölkern ", *W. Schmidt-Festschrift*, Vienna, 1928, pp. 231 ff.
Thus the Yurak-Samoyeds, for instance, to honour their sky god Num, sacrifice a white reindeer on a high mountain top (op. cit., p. 238), the Tunguses make their offering in the same way to Buga, the spirit of the sky (p. 243), and so on. Among the Koryaks, the Chukchi and the Eskimos, the ancient cult of the sky god has become involved with totemist, animist and matriarchal elements which Gahs holds to be secondary (p. 261).

[2] Holmberg-Harva, *Die religiösen Vorstellungen der altaischen Völker*, Helsinki, 1939, pp. 141 ff.

[3] Holmberg-Harva, " Die Religion der Tscheremissen ", Porvoo, 1926 (*FFC*, no. 61), p. 63.

[4] Karjalainen, " Die Religion der Jugra-Völker ", Porvoo-Helsinki, 1921, (*FFC*, no. 44), vol. ii, p. 250.

[5] Kai Donner tries to explain *Num* by the Sogdian *nom*, " law " (cf. the Greek *nomos*), a term which might have been carried to the far north by the peoples of Central Asia at the time of the Uighur supremacy. Even were this to be proved (which it is not; see the Bibliography), such a derivation could only be a borrowing of the actual word, for the notion of a supreme sky god is native to all Arctic and North Asiatic religions.

[6] Holmberg-Harva, *Rel. Vorst.*, p. 144.

their supreme god " Creator of the Earth " (*car cajany*);[1] the Yakuts " the wise master creator " (*urun ajy tojon*) or " the most high master " (*ar tojon*), the Tatars of the Altai " the great " (*ulgan, ulgen*) or " the very great " (*bai ulgen*) and in their invocations he is even " white light " (*ak ajas*; cf. the Ostyak *senke*, and " most luminous Khan " (*ajas kan*)).[2] The Ostyaks and the Voguls add to the name Turem the qualifications " great ", " luminous ", " golden ", " white ", " most high ", " Lord Master my father ", " good golden light from on high ", and so on.[3] In prayers and written texts the sky god is often called " Father ".[4]

Simply to list these names and titles shows the celestial, sovereign and creative character of the Uralo-Altaic supreme god. He dwells in the sky,[5] in the seventh heaven, or the ninth, or the sixteenth (Bai Ulgen, cf. § 33). His throne is to be found in the highest place in the sky, or on top of the cosmic mountain (cf. § 143). The Abakhan Tatars even speak of " the vault " of the sky god, the Buriats of " the house blazing with gold and silver ", and the Altai peoples of a " palace " (*orgo*) with a " golden door " and a " golden throne ".[6] The god has sons and daughters,[7] and is surrounded by servants and messengers whom the shaman meets on his ecstatic ascent into heaven. (One of these, Yajyk, lives on earth and plays the part of intermediary between Ulgen and men; another, Suila, watches the behaviour of men and informs the Master.)[8] But we do not find among the Uralo-Altaics any hierogamy myth, though the Buriats call the sky " Father " and the earth " Mother " in their invocations.[9]

The Supreme God of the sky is the creator of earth and of man. He is the " fashioner of all things " and " Father ". He created things visible and invisible, and it is still he who

[1] Ibid., p. 149.
[2] Ibid., p. 154.
[3] Karjalainen, vol. ii, pp. 250 ff.
[4] Holmberg-Harva, *Rel. Vorst.*, p. 284.
[5] Cf. Karjalainen, vol. ii, p. 257.
[6] Holmberg-Harva, *Rel. Vorst.*, p. 154.
[7] Ibid., pp. 156 ff.
[8] Ibid., pp. 155 ff.
[9] Ibid., p. 152.

makes the earth fruitful.[1]   Among the Voguls, Numi-Tarem
is not only the creator of mankind but also the civilizer who
taught men to fish and so on.[2]   The notion of creation is closely
bound up with the notion of a cosmic law.   The sky is the archetype of universal order.   The sky god guarantees the continuation and intangibility of cosmic rhythms as well as the
stability of human societies.   He is "Khan", "Leader",
"Master", that is to say, universal sovereign.   Consequently
his orders must be respected (in the titles of the god the notion
of "command", "commander", is clear).[3]   The Mongols
believe that the sky sees everything, and when they make a
vow they declare: "May heaven know it", or: "May
heaven witness it."[4]   In the signs of heaven (comets, droughts
and the rest) they read the revelations and orders of God.
As creator, knowing and seeing all, guardian of the law, the
sky god is ruler of the cosmos; he does not, however, rule
directly, but wherever there are political bodies, he rules by
his earthly representatives the Khans.

In the letter Mangu-Khan sent by William of Roubruck to
the King of France, we find the clearest possible profession of
the faith of the Mongol race: "Such is the order of the eternal
God: In heaven there is only one eternal God and there is to be
only one master on earth, Genghis-Khan, son of God!"
And Genghis-Khan's seal bore the following inscription:
"One God in heaven, and the Khan on earth.   The seal of
the Master of the World."   This notion of the universal
monarch, a son or representative of the sky god on earth, is
also found among the Chinese (as among certain Polynesian
peoples).   In ancient Chinese texts the sky god had two names:
T'ien ("Sky" and "God of the Sky") and Chang-Ti ("Lord
Highness", "Lord on High").   It is the sky that regulates
the order of the cosmos, that dwells as supreme sovereign
at the summit of the nine regions of heaven.   "The sky is a
dynastic providence, an all-seeing and law-giving power.   It
is the god of vows.   Men swear by the brightness of day and

[1] Ibid., p. 155; Karjalainen, vol. ii, p. 262.
[2] Karjalainen, vol. ii, p. 254.
[3] Cf. Holmberg-Harva, *Rel. Vorst.*, p. 144.
[4] Ibid., p. 150.

of dawn; they call to witness the blue vault, the blue sky, the sky on high that shines and shines."[1]

The Emperor is the " son of heaven ", T'ien Tsu, the sky god's representative on earth. The Chinese *T'ien Ming* corresponds to the Mongolian *dzajagan*—" the order of the sky ": The sovereign guarantees not only the proper organization of society but also the fertility of the earth, the normal succession of nature's rhythms. When there is an earthquake or some other calamity the Chinese sovereign confesses his sins and devotes himself to the practice of purification. In *Chi King*, the king moans during a dreadful drought: " Of what crime are we now accused, that the sky has unleashed death and torment ? . . . Would that this devastation and ruin of our country could fall on me alone ! " For the Emperor is the " unique man ", the representative of cosmic order and guardian of law.

The combination of Sky-Creator-Universal-Sovereign guaranteeing the cosmic order and the continuation of life on the earth, is completed by that specific trait of sky gods—passivity. In the great political organizations like China and the Mongol empires the sovereignty myth and the very existence of an empire reinforce the efficacy of the sky god. But when he gets no help from " history ", the supreme divinity of the Uralo-Altaics tends, in the minds of his worshippers, to become passive and remote. For some Siberian and Central Asiatic peoples, the sky god is so distant that he takes no interest in what men do. And for the Tunguses, Buga (" sky ", " world ") knows everything but does not meddle in the affairs of mankind, nor even punish evildoers. *Uran ajy tojon* or *aibyt aga* (Aga, " Father ") of the Yakuts dwells in the seventh heaven on a white marble throne, and governs all things, but does only good (in other words, does not punish). The Tunguses from round Turukhansk believe that the sky god sometimes brings them good luck and sometimes ill, but say that they do not understand by what criterion he decides which to do.[2]

Generally speaking, though, one may say that the sky gods of the Uralo-Altaic tribes have kept their primordial characteristics better than those of other races. They have no hiero-

[1] Granet, *La Religion des Chinois*, Paris, 1922, p. 57.
[2] Holmberg-Harva, *Rel. Vorst.*, p. 151.

gamies and are not transformed into gods of tempest or thunder.
(Like the North American mythologies, those of the Uralo-
Altaics picture thunder as a bird, but they never offer sacrifice
to it.)[1] They are venerated, people pray to them for food,[2]
they have a genuine cult, though they are not represented by
images,[3] and their sacrifices generally consist of white reindeer
and dogs.[4] But it cannot be said that the whole of religious
life is dominated by belief in the Supreme Being; there are a
whole series of rites, beliefs and superstitions with no reference
to him at all.

19. MESOPOTAMIA

The Sumerian term for divinity, *dingir*,[5] had as its earliest
meaning a sky epiphany: " bright, shining " (*dingir* was
translated into Akkadian as *ellu*, " bright, shining "). The
ideogram expressed in the word for " divinity " (which was
pronounced *dingir*) was the same as that expressed in the word
for " sky " (pronounced, in this case, *ana*, *anu*). To start
with, this written sign was a hieroglyph representing a star.
When it was pronounced *an(a)*, *an(u)*, the hieroglyph signified
the transcendence of space as such: " high, high being ".

The same sign *an* is also used to express " the rainy sky ",
and, by extension, rain. Thus, the intuition of divinity as
such (*dingir*) is based on hierophanies of the sky (high, bright,
shining, sky, rain). These hierophanies were fairly soon
detached from the notion of divinity as · such (*dingir*), and

---

[1] Ibid., pp. 205 ff.

[2] Cf. *Numi tarem*: Karjalainen, vol. ii, p. 255.

[3] Karjalainen, p. 280.

[4] Karjalainen, p. 273.

[5] Hommel connects the Sumerian *dingir*, " God ", " shining ", with the
Turco-Mongolian *tengri*, " Sky ", " God ". P. A. Barton thinks that the sky
god Anu was imported—before the end of prehistoric times—from Central
Asia into Mesopotamia (*Semitic and Hamitic Origins*, Philadelphia, 1934, pp.
245, 369). And one can indeed find, as early as the fourth millennium, certain
contacts between the paleo-Oriental cultures (Elam) and the " Caspian " and
Altaic cultures (i.e., the proto-Turks; see, in the Bibliography, the studies of
M. Ebert, G. Hermes, W. Amschler, W. Koppers, E. Erzfeld). But it remains
very unclear how much each of these civilizations contributed. On the other
hand, one can trace Oriental influences as far as the north of Russia as early
as the third millennium (cf. the works of Tallgren). And, in any case, it is
clear that the earliest proto-Turks had a sky god, that his likeness to the Indo-
European sky god is most striking, and that, generally speaking, the structure
of Indo-European religious life is closer to that of the proto-Turks than the
religion of any other near-eastern or Mediterranean people.

became centred upon one particular personalized divinity, Anu, whose name means " the sky ", and who had certainly appeared in history before the fourth millennium. Of Sumerian origin, Anu became the chief god of the Babylonians. But, like the other sky gods, he ceased in time to play a part of major importance. Anu is a somewhat abstract god, at least in historical times. His cult is not widespread;[1] in religious texts he is rarely invoked, and he does not figure among the lists of divine names.[2] He is not a creator god, like Marduk. No statues of Anu have been found[3]—which would seem to confirm that he has never actively affected Babylonian religious life or worship within historical times.

Anu dwells, of course, in the sky. His palace, standing at the high peak of the vault, was not touched by the waters of the flood.[4] There, as with Olympus in Greek mythology, the gods visit him.

His temple at Uruk is called *E-an-na*, " Sky House ". Anu sits on a throne in the sky, clothed with all the attributes of sovereignty: sceptre, diadem, headdress, staff.[5] He is the supreme ruler, and the symbols of his kingship are used by all kings as source and justification for their authority; symbolically, the king gets his power directly from Anu.[6] That is why only kings invoke him, never common men. He is " Father of the Gods " (*abu ilani*), and " King of the Gods ". He is called " Father "[7] rather in the sense of supreme authority than in the familiar sense.

In the Code of Hammurabi he is invoked as " King of the Anunnaki ", and his commonest titles are: *il shame*, " Sky God ", *ab shame*, " Sky Father ", *shar shame*, " Sky King ". Royalty itself comes from heaven.[8]

The stars are his army[9] for Anu, as universal sovereign, is a

---

[1] Jastrow, *Die Religion Babyloniens u. Assyriens*, Giessen, 1902, vol. i, p. 84.

[2] Furlani, *La Religione Babilonese-Assira*, Bologna, 1928, vol. i, p. 110.

[3] Furlani, p. 115.

[4] Epic of Gilgamesh, xii, 155.

[5] Dhorme, " Les Religions de Babylonie et d'Assyrie ", *MA*, Paris, 1945, p. 67.

[6] See Labat, *Le Caractère religieux de la royauté assyro-babylonienne*, Paris, 1939, particularly pp. 30 ff.

[7] Code of Hammurabi, 42, 46.

[8] Cf. Dhorme, pp. 46–7.

[9] Dhorme, p. 68.

warrior god (cf. the biblical " Lord of Hosts "). His principal feast occurs at the beginning of the New Year, when the creation of the world is also commemorated (§ 153). But as time went on, the feast of the New Year was consecrated to Marduk, a younger god (his rise dates from the time of Hammurabi, about 2150 B.C.), more dynamic (he battled with the sea-monster Tiamat and killed her), and more important still, a creator-god (Marduk created the world out of Tiamat's body). This change-over of Anu's principal feast to Marduk corresponds to the promotion of the storm-god Enlil-Bel to the rank of Supreme God of the Babylonians (§ 27). The consequences of substituting these dynamic, creating, and approaching divinities will become clearer as we go on.

20. DYAUS, VARUNA

There is no need to enter here into the discussion concerning Dieus, the hypothetical god of the light sky, common to all Aryan tribes. Certain it is that the Indian Dyaus, the Roman Jupiter, the Greek Zeus and the Germanic god Tyr-Zio, are forms evolved in the course of history from that primeval sky divinity, and that their very names reveal the original twofold meaning of " light (day) " and " sacred " (cf. the Sanskrit *div*, " shine ", " day ", *dyaus*, " sky ", " day "; *dios*, *dies*; *deivos*, *divus*). The names of these supreme Indo-Aryan divinities show their organic connection with the serene, shining sky. But this does not mean, as many scholars think,[1] that no meteorological phenomena—storms, lightning, thunder and such—are connected with the original notion of Dieus. The most primitive sky gods (such as Baiame and Daramulum, cf. § 12) governed those phenomena, and the lightning was their major attribute. The fact that the actual name of the Aryan sky god stresses his shining and serene quality, does not exclude the other sky theophanies (hurricanes and rain and so on) from Dieus' personality. It is true, as we shall see further on (§ 26), that a great number of these sky gods as it were " specialized ", and became gods of storm or of fertility. But these specializations must be seen as the result of various tendencies often to be found in the history of religion (the

---

[1] Like Nehring, for instance, " Studien zur indogermanischen Kultur- und Urheimat ", *WBKL*, vol. iv, pp. 195 ff.

tendency towards the concrete; the turning of the notion of "creation" into that of "fertility", and so on), and, in any case, they do not prevent meteorological functions from existing alongside the notion of a god of the bright sky.

It would be hard to reduce the *historical* forms of the Indo-Aryan sky divinities to any single theophany, or single series of sky theophanies. Their personality is richer, their functions more complex. The sacred forces they contain and govern appear to be spread over many spheres—spheres not always cosmic in form. A decisive element in the personality of all these divinities is their sovereignty, and sovereignty cannot be explained merely by the sacredness of the sky. Consider, for instance, the case of the Indo-Aryan sky god. Dyaus seldom appears in the Vedas or post-Vedic writings as a divinity proper;[1] normally his name is used to mean "sky" or "day" (*dyāvi dyāvi*: "from day to day"). There was certainly a time when Dyaus enjoyed the autonomy of a real divinity, and some traces of this remain to us in Vedic writings: the couple Dyāvapṛthivi, "Sky and Earth",[2] the invocation to the "Sky Father", to the "Sky who knows all".[3] Hierogamy, omniscience, and creativity are the specific attributes of a real sky divinity. But Dyaus has been the object of a process of "naturist" specialization; he has ceased, in other words, to be the revealer of the holiness of the sky and become an expression for the daily phenomena of the sky ("sky", "day"). Here, too, it is the result of his "passivity"; the sacred element is detached from the cosmic phenomena, and words once used to describe the sacred end by becoming profane; the divinity of the sky is replaced by a word meaning the "sky" and the "phenomenon of day". But such a "laicizing" of Dyaus in no way destroys or weakens the theophany of the sky; it simply means that Dyaus has given place to another divinity. By becoming "naturalized", by ceasing to express the *sacredness* of the sky, Dyaus has ceased to fulfil the function of a Supreme God of the sky.

This changeover took place early on, for ever since the beginning of Vedic times Dyaus' place has been filled by another

[1] Hillebrandt, *Vedische Mythologie*, Breslau, 1929, vol. iii, iii, 392.
[2] *RV*, i, 160.
[3] *AV*, i, 32, 4.

god, Varuna (*u-ru-va-na* in the Boghazkeui inscriptions of the
fourteenth century B.C.), who kept all the attributes of the sky,
but who cannot be called only a sky god. What we can be
certain of is that Varuna is *viśvadarśata*, " visible everywhere ",[1]
that he " separated the two worlds ",[2] that the wind is his
breath,[3] that he and Mitra are venerated as " the two powerful
and sublime masters of the sky ", and that " darkening the
clouds he shows himself at the first growl of thunder and makes
the sky rain by a divine miracle ", that it is he who " unfolds
their miraculous works in the sky ",[4] etc. At an early stage
Varuna acquired lunar qualities,[5] and was so closely connected
with rain that he became an ocean god.[6] Both changes can
be seen to spring from his original celestial form. The substitution of lunar divinities, or, more generally, the assimilation
of lunar elements by primordial divine figures is something
you will often meet in the history of religion. The rhythms of
the moon rule rain and sea; and the prerogative of rain passes
from sky god to moon god.

His original celestial structure explains still more of Varuna's
functions and glories; for instance, his omniscience. " His
spies come down from the sky, and with their thousands of
eyes they spy on the earth. Varuna the king sees all. . . . He
even counts how often men wink their eyes . . ."[7] Varuna is
omniscient and infallible, " he knows the trail of birds flying
in the air . . . he knows the direction of the wind . . . and he,
who knows all, spies out all secrets, all deeds and intentions . . ."[8]
With Mitra, he plants spies in plants and in houses, for these
gods never close their eyes.[9] Varuna is *sahasrākṣa*, " thousand-
eyed ",[10] the thousand eyes being a mythical formula for the
stars—a metaphor which at first, if not later on, indicated a

---

[1] *RV*, viii, 41, 3.
[2] *RV*, vii, 86, i.
[3] *RV*, vii, 87, 2.
[4] *RV*, v, 63, 2–5.
[5] Hillebrandt, vol. iii, p. 1 ff.
[6] Cf. abundant references in Meyer, *Trilogie altindische Mächte und Feste
der Vegetation*, Zürich-Leipzig, 1937, vol. iii, pp. 206 ff, 269 ff.
[7] *AV*, iv, 16, 2–7.
[8] *RV*, i, 25, 7 ff.
[9] *RV*, vii, 61, 3.
[10] *RV*, vii, 34, 10.

celestial divinity.[1] Varuna is not the only one with " a thousand eyes "; Indra and Vāyu have them also,[2] and Agni,[3] and Puruṣa.[4] We can establish some connection between the first two and the celestial regions (storms, winds, and such), but Agni is the god of fire, and as for Purusa, he was the mythical giant. Their having a thousand eyes was not due to any celestial prerogatives, but to the fact that in all the hymns to them they were regarded as omniscient and omnipotent gods or, in other words, as sovereigns.

21. VARUNA AND SOVEREIGNTY

To return to the question of whether Varuna can be considered as exclusively a sky divinity—in Vedic writings, the stress does not always fall on his sky characteristics, but often on his quality of sovereign: " Truly, Varuṇa is the supreme Kṣatra ";[5] and H. Güntert[6] and Dumézil[7] have found excellent formulæ to make clear this fundamental quality of Varuna. The faithful feel " like slaves " in his presence,[8] and the attitude of humility is to be found in the worship of no other god.[9] As universal sovereign, Varuna is guardian of the norms of cosmic order. That is why he " sees " all, and no sin escapes him, however hidden; it is to him that a man will pray when he feels thwarted, asking what sins he has committed, or how he has offended him.[10] He guarantees the contracts of men, " binding " them by their oaths. Anyone he wishes to ruin Varuna " binds ";[11] and Varuna's " nets " are to be feared[12] for they are bonds which paralyse and exhaust. Varuṇa is the divinity who " binds ", a privilege possessed by various other sovereign gods (§ 23), and one that reveals his magic powers,

---

[1] Cf. Pettazzoni, " Le Corps parsemé d'yeux ", *CZ*, i, pp. 1 ff.

[2] *RV*, i, 23, 3.

[3] *RV*, i, 79, 12.

[4] *RV*, x, 90, 1.

[5] *Śatapatha Brahmaṇa*, ii, 5, 2, 34; cf. *Maitri-Upaniṣad*, i, 6, 11.

[6] In *Der arische Weltkönig und Heiland*, Halle, 1923, pp. 97 ff.

[7] In *Oûranos-Varuna*, Paris, 1934, pp. 39 ff.

[8] *RV*, i, 25, 1.

[9] Cf. Geiger, *Die Amesa Spentas*, Vienna, 1916, pp. 154, 157.

[10] Cf. *RV*, vii, 86; *AV*, iv, 16, etc.

[11] *RV*, i, 24, 15.

[12] *RV*, i, 24, 15.

his possession of a power that is spiritual, of the supreme kingly power.

Even Varuṇa's name can be explained by his power of binding, for nowadays the etymology *var* (*vṛnoti*) " to cover ", " to close in " (which would point to his celestial qualities) has been abandoned in favour of the interpretation proposed by H. Petersson and accepted by Güntert[1] and Dumézil[2] whereby it comes from the Indo-European root *uer* " to bind " (Sanskrit *varatra* " strap, rope "; Lithuanian *weru, wert*, " to thread, to embroider "; Russian *verenica*, " broken thread "). Varuṇa is always pictured with a rope in his hand[3] and a great many ceremonies are performed with the object of loosing men from " the bonds of Varuṇa " (even knots are something special to him).[4]

This power of binding, though later chthonian and lunar influences Varuṇa has undergone may have increased it,[5] indicates that the sovereignty of the god is essentially magical. Dumézil, to complete Güntert's interpretation[6] of the magic value of the " bonds " and the " nets ", points out quite rightly their kingly function. " Varuṇa is supremely the master of the *maya*, of magic influence. The bonds of Varuṇa are magic as is his sovereignty itself; they are the symbol of those mystical powers held by the chief which are called: justice, administration, royal and public security, all powers. Sceptre and bonds, *daṇḍa* and *pāśāḥ*, in India and elsewhere, share the honour of representing all this."[7] Consequently, at the ceremony of a king's consecration in India, Varuṇa presides; *rājasūya*, in any case, does nothing more than reproduce the archetypal act with which the first sovereign, Varuṇa, was himself consecrated.[8]

[1] p. 144.
[2] p. 49.
[3] Cf. Bergaigne, *La Religion védique d'après les hymnes du Rig Veda*, Paris, 1878–83, vol. iii, p. 114; S. Lévi, *La Doctrine du sacrifice dans les Brahmanas*, Paris, 1898, pp. 153 ff.; Hopkins, *Epic Mythology*, Strasbourg, 1920, pp. 116 ff.
[4] See Dumézil, *Ouranos-Varuna*, Paris, 1934, p. 21, n. i; cf. Eliade, " Le ' Dieu lieur ' et le symbolisme des nœuds ", *RHR*, 1947–8, vol. cxxxiv, pp. 5–36.
[5] Cf. A. Closs, " Die Religion des Semnonenstammes ", *WBKL*, vol. iv, pp. 625 ff.
[6] *Der arische Weltkönig und Heiland*, Halle, 1923, pp. 120 ff.
[7] Dumézil, pp. 53 ff.
[8] Dumézil, pp. 42 ff.

It would therefore be a mistake to think of Varuṇa as simply a sky god, and to explain everything—personality, myth and rites—purely in the light of his celestial elements. Like others who are called sky gods, Varuṇa is a complex figure and cannot be reduced to "naturist" epiphanies nor limited to social functions. The prerogatives of sovereignty developed, and they augmented the sky prerogatives; Varuṇa sees and knows all because from his starry home he towers above the universe; but at the same time he can do everything because he rules over the cosmos, and he punishes all who break his laws by "binding" them (with illness or impotence) because he is the guardian of universal order. One common note is clear in all these attributions and functions: the serene, sacred, one may almost say passive, quality of his "power". He does not take to himself any rights, conquers nothing, does not struggle to win anything (as does Indra for instance); he *is* powerful, he *is* sovereign, while remaining a contemplative ("a priest who frequents assemblies").[1] Varuṇa is king, not by himself (*svarāj*, like Indra) but *saṁrāj*, universal king.[2] That is to say, power is his by right because of his very nature; this power enables him to act through magic, through "the power of the mind", through "knowledge".

In this way we can observe an extraordinary symmetry between what may be called Varuṇa's "celestial aspect" and his "kingly aspect" so that they fit together and complete each other; the sky is transcendent and unique in precisely the same way as the universal sovereign; the tendency to passivity is shown by all the supreme sky gods who live in the higher spheres, far from man and more or less indifferent to his daily needs. The passivity of primitive supreme figures of the sky is to be found in Varuṇa too; you can see it in his contemplative nature, and his ability to act, not by physical methods like Indra, but by magic, spiritual forces. You will find the same symmetry between the attributes of the sky god of the primitives and of the universal sovereign; both guarantee the order and the fertility of nature as long as the law is kept; rain ensures fertility, but any breaking of the law, any "sin", will endanger the normal functioning of the seasons, thus

[1] *RV*, vi, 68, 3.
[2] *RV*, vii, 82, 2; Bergaigne, vol. iii, p. 140; Dumézil, p. 40.

threatening the very life of society and nature. As we shall see, the sovereign stands as guarantor of the good ordering and fertility of the earth not only in myth, but also in actual worship. But let me point out at once that this notion of universal sovereignty, exercised purely by spiritual and magical means, owes its development and its definition of outline largely to the notion of the sky's transcendence. It was some such notion, developing at all sorts of different levels, that made the full picture of " magic sovereignty " possible. But, on the other hand, the theory of " magic sovereignty " has had a marked influence on the original figure of the sky god. So much so that Varuna, at least *historically* speaking (as he appears, that is, in Vedic and post-Vedic writings), cannot be called simply a sky god any more than he can be called a moon god or a sea god. He is, or tends to be, all these things at once, and at the same time, he is supremely the sovereign god.

22. IRANIAN SKY GODS

The Iranians also had a supreme sky god; for, according to Herodotus,[1] " they used to go up to the highest mountains and offer sacrifices to Zeus, whose name they gave to the circular expanse of heaven ". We do not know what name this primordial sky god was called in the Iranian languages. The divinity we find in the Avesta, the divinity Zarathustra attempted to transfigure, placing him at the heart of his religious reform, was called Ahura Mazda, " Lord Wisdom ", " omniscient ". One of his epithets was *vouru casani*, " the widely-seeing ".[2] which indicates a celestial structure. But in Zarathustra's reform Ahura Mazda was purified of his naturist elements, and it is rather in later writings—which reflect a return to the former polytheism of the Iranians—that we find the most clearly defined traces of the ancient sky god.

From the first, comparative studies in religion have indicated in Ahura Mazda a counterpart of Varuna. Though certain scholars have contested this theory,[3] I can see no serious reasons for abandoning it. The traits they have in common as shown fifty years ago by Oldenberg (in his study " Varuna

[1] i, 131.
[2] Nyberg, *Die Religionen des alten Iran*, Leipzig, 1928, p. 99.
[3] For instance H. Lommel, *Les Anciens Aryens*, pp. 99 ff.

und die Adityas ") are convincing; like Varuṇa, Ahura Mazda is the " sovereign god ".[1] An ancient formula fairly common in the Avesta is Mitra-Ahura;[2] here Mitra is associated with an Ahura who has not yet become the Ahura Mazda of historical times and is more reminiscent of the supreme Asura of Vedic writings, Varuṇa; the Mitra-Ahura of the Avesta thus corresponds to the Vedic twofold name, Mitra-Varuṇa. I cannot go as far as Hertel,[3] Nyberg[4] and Widengren,[5] and see Mithra as the night sky, and Ahura Mazda as the sky by day. But the sky structure in the epiphany of Ahura Mazda is beyond doubt. For he has " for his clothing the steadfast vault of heaven ";[6] he makes rain fall from all parts of it to nourish " men that are pious and animals that are useful ";[7] he is called " he who sees much, who sees best, who sees far, who sees best from afar, who spies, who knows, who knows best ";[8] " he who does not deceive ";[9] " he who knows ... he is infallible, he has an infallible, omniscient mind ".[10] " It is impossible to deceive Ahura, who sees all ", says the *Yasna*.[11] Like the other sky gods, Ahura Mazda is never sleepy and no narcotic has any effect on him.[12] That is why no secret escapes " his keen gaze ".[13] Ahura Mazda guarantees the inviolability of contracts, and the keeping of promises; when he revealed to Zarathustra why he had created Mithra, Ahura Mazda said that anyone who breaks a pact (*mithra*=" contract ") will bring bad luck on the entire land.[14] It is thus he who ensures good contractual relations among men, and also the steady balance of natural forces and general prosperity. That is also why Mithra is omniscient, why he has ten thousand eyes and

[1] Dumézil, *Naissance d'Archanges*, Paris, 1945, p. 82.
[2] Cf. Benveniste-Renou, *Vrtra et Vrthragna*, Paris, 1935, p. 46.
[3] *Die Sonne und Mithra im Awesta*, Leipzig, 1927, pp. 174 ff.
[4] *Religionen*, p. 99.
[5] *Hochgottglaube im alten Iran*, Uppsala, 1938, pp. 94 ff.
[6] *Yasna*, 30, 5; cf. *Yast*, 13, 2–3.
[7] *Videvdat*, 5, 20.
[8] *Yast*, i, 12–13.
[9] *Yast*, i, 14.
[10] *Yast*, 12, 1.
[11] 45, 4.
[12] *Videvdat*, 19, 20.
[13] *Yasna*, 31, 13–14.
[14] *Yast*, 10, 1–2.

a thousand ears[1] and, like Ahura Mazda, is infallible, powerful, never-sleeping, watchful;[2] he too is called " undeceivable " (*adaoyamna*) and " omniscient " (*vispo, vidva*).

But all these attributes and these functions imply not only a sky epiphany, but other prerogatives too—that, for instance, of sovereignty.[3] Ahura Mazda sees and knows all, not only because he is the god of the sky, but also because as sovereign, he is the keeper of the laws, and punisher of the wicked; because of his sovereignty, he must guarantee the good organization and prosperity both of nature and of society, for a single infringement would be enough to endanger the balance of order at every cosmic level. We have far too little in the way of Iranian religious writings—chiefly because of Zarathustra's reform—to be able to reconstruct the original figure of Ahura Mazda as a sky god. One might even wonder whether Ahura Mazda ever was a sky god pure and simple, whether being a supreme god did not at the same time make him the god of destiny,[4] the archetype of ruler and of priest,[5] the bisexual god,[6] whether in fact he did not show himself from the start of his " history " as a complex theophany in which elements of sky naturally played an important, but never an exclusive, part.

It is necessary, too, to point out the pre-Zarathustra notion of Ahura Mazda as *deus otiosus*[7] who does not create directly, but through the *spenta mainyu*,[8] that is, through the intermediary of a " good spirit ", rather like the demiurge that accompanies the Supreme Being of the sky in primitive religions. The phenomenon is so general that it seems as if it must correspond to some fundamental tendency in religious life; I shall come back to this tendency later. In the case of Ahura Mazda, this tendency was thwarted by Zarathustra's reform —just as so many religious reformers (Moses, the prophets, Mahomet for instance) brought back to life ancient supreme

---

[1] *Yast*, 17, 16; cf. Pettazzoni, " Le Corps parsemé d'yeux ", p. 9.
[2] *Yast*, 10, 7.
[3] See Widengren, pp. 260 ff.
[4] Widengren, p. 253.
[5] Widengren, p. 386.
[6] Widengren, p. 251.
[7] Cf. Nyberg, p. 105; Widengren, p. 374.
[8] *Yast*, 44, 7.

gods of heaven who had been turned into *dei otiosi* and whose place in the religious life of the masses had been taken by more concrete and dynamic divine figures (gods of fertility, Great Goddesses, and so forth). But religious reform implies an experience of the sacred quite different from the sort we are dealing with here, and can be discussed more usefully elsewhere.

23. OURANOS

In Greece, Ouranos preserved his naturist character more clearly; he *was* the sky. Hesiod shows him[1] drawing near, and spreading out in all directions as, " eager for love " and bringing night with him, he envelops the earth. This cosmic marriage is a clear statement of what the sky's function is. But apart from this myth, nothing of Ouranos remains to us; not even an image. His rather wavering cult was usurped by other gods, particularly Zeus. Ouranos too, in fact, bears witness to this fate of sky divinities to be gradually driven out of religious life and practice, to go through innumerable usurpations, substitutions and amalgamations, and at last to be forgotten. Completely forgotten as far as religion goes, Ouranos survives only in the myth handed down by Hesiod; a myth which, whatever rituals it may suggest, still does satisfy the desire to know how things began. It shows that there existed, at the beginning, if not the sky alone, at least the divine pair Sky-Earth.[2] From this ever-faithful sacred marriage were born the first gods (Oceanos, Hyperion, Theia, Themis, Phoebe, Kronos, etc.), and also the Cyclops and other monstrous creatures. Ouranos was supremely the male-who-makes-fruitful, as were all the sky gods; as was, for instance, Dyaus (he was known as *suretah*, " good seed ",[3] and from his embrace with his divine wife Pṛthivī were born men and gods).[4]

But, unlike other sky gods, Ouranos' fecundity was dangerous. His creatures were not like the inhabitants of the world we know, but monsters (with a hundred arms, fifty eyes, immensely tall and so on). As he " hated them from the very first day "

---

[1] *Theog.*, 126 ff.

[2] In Hesiod's myth, Earth (Gaia) gives birth to Ouranos; a remnant of the chthonian religion of prehellenic times.

[3] *RV*, iv, 17, 4.

[4] Cf. *RV*, i, 106, 3; 159, 1; 185, 4; iv, 56, 2, etc.

(Hesiod), Ouranos hid them in the body of the earth (Gaia), so that she suffered and groaned. Encouraged by Gaia, his youngest child, Kronos, waited for his father to come to the earth as he always did at nightfall, and cut off his genital organ and threw it in the sea. This mutilation put a stop to Ouranos' monstrous creations, and, by that very fact, to his sovereignty. As Dumézil has shown,[1] this myth has a counterpart in the myth of Varuṇa's impotence and the ritual for a sovereign's investiture in India. I shall be returning in a different context to the complex question of the " dangers of sovereignty ", but what must be noted for the moment is the essential meaning of the two myths and of their corresponding rituals (the control and assurance of fecundity). The symmetry between the two sovereignties of Varuṇa and Ouranos is also astonishing; despite the evolution of Ouranos towards naturism, he " was the first sovereign of the universe ";[2] his eldest daughter was called Basileia.[3] Just as Varuṇa is supremely the divinity who " binds ", so Ouranos too " binds " his children, hiding them one after another in the body of Gaia. Varuṇa " seizes the breath " of his son Bhṛgu and sends him to the subterranean world to study.[4] And the Cyclops Ouranos binds in chains and hurls down to " Tartarus ".[5] Kronos succeeds him as universal sovereign, and puts his adversaries in chains; the Orphics also invest Zeus with the same magic power.

What marks Ouranos out from the other sky gods is his monstrous fecundity and the hatred he nourishes for what he has himself created. All the sky gods are creators; they make the world, gods, living beings. Fecundity is only one element in their essential vocation as creators. " The holy Sky is drunk with penetrating the body of Earth ", says Aeschylus in one of his lost tragedies, the *Danaiads*.[6] That is why the sky gods of the Indo-Mediterranean religions are all in one way or another identified with bulls. The *Rg Veda* calls Dyaus " bull "[7] and as we shall see, most of the Aegean-Oriental

[1] In his *Ouranos-Varuna*.
[2] Apollodorus, *Bibliotheca*, i, 1.
[3] Diodorus Siculus, 3, 57.
[4] *Jaiminiya Br.*, I, 44; Lévi, *Doctrine*, pp. 100 ff.; Dumézil, p. 55.
[5] Apollodorus, i, 1, 2.
[6] Nauck, frag. 44.
[7] Cf. i, 160, 3; v, 6, 5; v, 58, 6, etc.

gods have this same quality. But with Ouranos, this fecundity is dangerous. As Mazon notes in his commentary on Hesiod's *Theogony*,[1] the mutilation of Ouranos puts an end to his hateful and unproductive fecundity, and introduces into the world through the appearance of Aphrodite (born out of the foam bloodied by Ouranos' genital organ) an order, a fixedness of species which was to prevent all disordered and dangerous procreation in the future.

This singularity of Ouranos, at least as Hesiod's myth presents it, has not been fully explained. Why should he, along among the sky gods, go on indefinitely procreating monstrous creatures while " hating " them, and going to the length of " chaining " them in Tartarus or in the belly of the earth ? Could it be some reminiscence, some negative caricature, of that mythical day, that *illud tempus*, when creation had as yet no fixed norms, when anything might be born of anything else, when the wolf lay down with the lamb, and the leopard with the kid ? A thing which characterized that " time " of dawn and of paradise was indeed utter liberty, which existed at every level of reality, and therefore among the various species. A good many traditions speak of the fluid and monstrous character of the beings created when the world first began. One wonders whether this strange monster-breeding of Ouranos might be a rationalization produced by the Greek mind to show the value of the régime brought about by Aphrodite and later governed by Zeus, in which the species are fixed, there is order, balance, and hierarchy. Or is the struggle of Ouranos' children to be seen simply as a process whereby the Hellenic gods were substituted for the divinities of pre-Hellenic times ?

24. ZEUS

Whatever the explanation of these aberrant creations, the fact remains that Ouranos had disappeared from the cult before histórical times. His place was taken by Zeus whose name shows that he was essentially celestial. Like Dyaus, Zeus preserves in his name the values of " brightness " and " day " (cf. the Sanskrit *div*, " shine ", " day "; the Cretans called the day *dia*),[2] and it is etymologically related equally to

[1] Coll. Budé, 1928, pp. 28 ff.

[2] Macrobius, *Saturnalia*, i, 15, 14; cf. Cook, *Zeus*, Cambridge, 1914–40, vol. i, pp. 1 ff.

dios and to the Latin *dies*. But obviously we must not limit his sphere to " the serene, light, shining sky ", looking upon his meteorological activities as later developments or outside influences. Zeus's weapon was the thunderbolt and places struck by lightning, *enelysia*, were consecrated to him. The meaning of all Zeus's titles is quite clear, and all more or less directly evidence his connection with storm, rain, and fertility. Thus, he is called Ombrios and Hyetios (rainy), Urios (he who sends favourable winds), Astrapios (who sends lightning), Bronton (who thunders), etc. He is called Georgos (farmer) and Chthonios (earth-dweller),[1] because he governs the rain, and assures the fertility of the fields. Even his animalesque aspect (Zeus Lykaios, as a wolf to whom human sacrifice was offered)[2] can be accounted for by the magic connected with farming (the sacrifices took place in time of drought, storm, and such).

It has long been observed that Zeus, though he is the supreme divinity of the Greek pantheon, has relatively few feasts and less of a cult than many other gods, and various explanations have been put forward for this anomaly.[3] I think that, in fact, like all sky divinities, he is not always to the fore in religious life; he does however dominate two important elements of it —agriculture and expiation. Everything that will ensure a good harvest (rain, everything to do with weather), and whatever purifies from sin, falls under the jurisdiction of the sky. " Purification " and " initiation "—by thunderbolt or something representing a thunderbolt (such as the bull-roarer or a thunder-stone)—are primitive rites (§ 12) which witness not only the antiquity of these sky gods, but also the antiquity of their dramatic, stormy elements. Many scholars are so fascinated with the etymology of Dieus that they forget the unity of structure of the primitive notion of sky divinities. Zeus is, of course, sovereign; but he has kept, more clearly than the other sky gods, his character of " Father ". He is Zeus Pater (cf. Dyaus Pitar, Jupiter), archetype of the patriarchal head of the family. The picture of him as *pater familias*

---

[1] Cf. Hesiod, *Works and Days*, v, 465.

[2] Cf. Nilsson, *Geschichte der griechischen Religion*, Münich, 1941, vol. i, pp. 371 ff.

[3] Cf. Nilsson, p. 369.

reflects the sociological conceptions of the Aryan races. It explains Zeus Ktesios, the *Hausvater* the Hellenes took with them in all their migrations, whom they represented as a veritable domestic genius under the form of a serpent. " Father " and " Sovereign ", Zeus quite naturally becomes the divinity of the city, Zeus Polienos, and it is from him that the kings get their authority. But this many-sidedness always comes back to the same basic form: supremacy belongs to the Father, that is to say, to the Creator, maker of all things. This " creative " element is very marked in Zeus, not on the cosmogonic level (for the universe was not created by him), but on the bio-cosmic level: he governs the sources of fertility, he is master of the rain. He is " creator " because it is he who " makes fruitful " (he too sometimes becomes a bull; cf. the myth of Europa). And his " creation " depends primarily on what the weather does, particularly the rain. His supremacy is at once fatherly and kingly; he guarantees the well-being of the family and of nature both by his creative powers, and by his authority as guardian of the order of things.

25. JUPITER, ODIN, TARANIS, ETC.

Like Zeus, Jupiter, in Italy, was adored on the heights. A manifold symbolism attaches to mountains (§ 31); they are " high ", they are nearer to heaven, they are the meeting-place of clouds and from them the thunder is loosed. Olympus was, of course, specially favoured; but Zeus, like Jupiter, was present on every hill. And Jupiter's titles are equally telling: Lucelius, Fulgur, Fulgurator. The oak was sacred to Jupiter (as to Zeus) because it was the tree most often struck by lightning. The oak tree on the Capitol belonged to Jupiter Feretrius, *qui ferit*, " he who strikes ", known also as Jupiter Lapis, and represented by a silex. Like all sky gods, Jupiter punished with thunderbolts, and he punished particularly all who failed to keep their word, all who violated treaties. Jupiter Lapis consecrated treaties between nations; a *fetialis* killed a pig with the sacred silex, declaring: " If the Roman people violate the treaty, may Jupiter strike them as I now strike this pig with the stone ! " Jupiter was the supreme divinity, the absolute sovereign; *Jupiter Omnipotens, Jupiter Optimus Maximus*. Even in literary writings these titles are to be found: *summe deum regnator;*[1] *meus pater, deorum regnator, architectus omnibus;*[2] *deum regnator, nocte caeca caelum e conspectu abstulit,*[3] and so on. As the true cosmic sovereign that he is, Jupiter intervenes in history not by physical, military force, like Mars, but by his magic powers. Dumézil[4] brings out this magic of Jupiter's by recalling an incident in Roman history; the Sabines, already in control of the Capitol, threaten to annihilate the whole Roman army through panic and Romulus begs of Jupiter: " Let the Romans stop being terrified, arrest their shameful flight ! " At that moment, as if by a miracle, their courage returns, and they counter-attack and conquer.[5] Jupiter had intervened by " magic ", by direct action on their spiritual forces.

Tacitus, speaking of the religion of the Semnones,[6] notes the belief of that Germanic tribe in a supreme god, *regnator omnium deus*, though he does not record his name.[7] The Germans (again according to Tacitus), worshipped above all Mercury and Mars; that is to say Wotan (Wotanaz; the Nordic Odin), and Tyr (Tiwaz; old High German, Zio; Anglo-Saxon Tio; from *tiwaz*, corresponding to Dieus, *deivos, divus,* which means, generically, " god "). Tiwaz has been seen as the *regnator omnium deus,*[8] the ancient Germanic sky god. Thor (Donar; Thunraz) is, like Indra and Jupiter, a god of tempest and combat. The distinction between Ouranos who " binds " his enemies and knows the future (he warns Kronos of the danger threatening him) and Zeus who fights " heroically " with his thunderbolts, or between the " magician " Varuṇa and the warrior Indra—these same differences occur, with some natural variations, in Germanic mythology. Thor is supremely the champion among the gods, the archetype of the German heroes; Odin, though he is also involved in innumerable battles, conquers without any effort thanks to his

[1] Nævius, fr. 15.
[2] Plautus, *Amphitr.*, 44 ff.
[3] Accius, *Clytemnestra,* fr. iii.
[4] *Mitra-Varuna*, Paris, 1940, p. 33; *Jupiter, Mars, Quirinus*, Paris, 1941, p. 81.
[5] Plutarch, *Romulus*, 18; Livy, i, 12.
[6] *Germania*, 39.
[7] Cf. Closs, " Die Religion des Semnonenstammes ", *passim.*
[8] See, for instance, Hommel, " Die Hauptgottheiten der Germanen bei Tacitus ", *AFRW*, vol. xxxvii.

" magic " (ubiquity, power of assuming different forms, ability to paralyse his adversary with fear, " binding " him). As Dumézil has shown,[1] the primitive Indo-Aryan double picture of " the magic sovereign " and " the hero sovereign ", the possessor of spiritual power and of physical power, is preserved here.[2]

Thus, in the case of Odin (Woden) and Thor (Donar), we are faced with sky gods, complete with the advantages that go with these two sorts of sovereignty, and modified by different influences and side developments. Odin (Woden), in particular, is a difficult case, and cannot be reduced to any simple definition. He developed along various different lines, taking in the attributes of agricultural deities and divinities of fertility, and also becoming a chthonian, master of the souls of dead heroes. The analogies between the Wodenist religion and the shamanism of the nomads of north and north-west Asia have recently become clearer and clearer.[3] Woden is " the great shaman " who stays hanging from the tree of the world for nine nights,[4] and discovers the runes, thus getting his magic powers (this is undoubtedly a reference to some initiation rite). His very name shows that he is master of *wut, furor religiosus* (*Wodan, id est furor*, says Adam of Bremen). Drunken joy, prophetic excitation, the magic teaching in the Scaldic schools— all these have their counterparts in shamanist techniques; this does not necessarily mean that Odin-Woden is a foreign god taken by the Germans (as some scholars have often tried to prove), but simply that later " specialization " invested him

[1] *Mythes et lieux des Germains*, Paris, 1939, p. 19 ff.

[2] We find the same double idea in Babylonian mythology. Ea, the divinity of water and of wisdom, does not struggle " heroically " with the primordial monsters, Apsu and Mummu, but " binds " them by magic incantations so as to kill them afterwards (*Enuma Elish*, i, 60–74). Marduk, having been invested by the assembly of the gods with the prerogatives of absolute sovereignty (which up till then had belonged to the sky god Anu, iv, 4 and 7), and having received from them the sceptre, throne and *palu* (iv, 29) sets out to conquer the sea monster Tiamat. We see a true " heroic " struggle. Marduk's chief weapon is always " the net ", " the gift of his father Anu " (iv, 49; in i, 83 Marduk is the son of Ea, but whatever his paternity was, it is of the essence of magical sovereignty). Marduk " binds " Tiamat (iv, 95), " chains him up ", and kills him (iv, 104). In the same way, he chains up all the gods and demons who helped Tiamat, and casts them into prisons and caves (iv, 111–14, 117, 120). Marduk gains his sovereignty by his heroic fighting, but also keeps the prerogatives of magic sovereignty.

[3] Cf. Closs, p. 665, and n. 62.

[4] *Havamal*, str. 139–41.

with different sorts of powers, thus making him like the more exotic gods.

The Celts believed in Taranis, who was certainly a sky god of storm (from the Celtic root *taran*, to thunder, cf. the Irish *torann*, " thunder "). The Baltic Perkunas (*perkunas*, lightning), and the proto-Slavic Perun (cf. the Polish *piorun*, thunder), were also supreme sky gods, manifesting themselves chiefly in storm. Their names have been connected with the Vedic divinity Parjanya and the Germanic Fjorgyn, mother of Thor, and recently with Phorkys, the father of the Pleiades.[1] And in both their names (*perkus*, *quercus*) and their cults, these sky divinities display a close relationship with the oak, and with various birds supposed to herald the weather (birds that herald a storm, or spring).[2] But, at least as they appear in history, they show a marked " specialization "; they are primarily divinities of storm; they govern the seasons, and bring rain, which makes them divinities of fertility. The oak of Dodona was consecrated to Zeus, but near it were the sacred doves, symbols of the great Earth Mother, which suggests that of old there was a hierogamy of the sky god of storm with the Great Goddess of fecundity, a phenomenon which we shall find elsewhere on a large scale.

26. STORM GODS

The " specialization " of sky gods into gods of hurricane and of rain, and also the stress on their fertility powers, is largely explained by the passive nature of sky divinities and their tendency to give place to other hierophanies that are more concrete, more clearly personal, more directly involved in the daily life of man. This fate results largely from the transcendence of the sky and man's ever-increasing " thirst for the concrete ". The " evolution " process of the sky gods is fairly complex. To make description of it easier, I should like to distinguish two lines of development: first, the god of the sky, master of the world, absolute sovereign (despot), guardian of the law; and second, god of the sky, creator, supremely male, spouse of the great Earth Goddess, giver of rain. I need not say that nowhere do we meet either of these two types alone, that

[1] Krappe, " Les Péléiades ", *RAR*, 1932, vol. xxxvi.
[2] Cf. Harrison, *Themis*, Cambridge, 1927, pp. 94 ff.

the lines of development are never parallel, but constantly cut across each other, that the sovereign is often the giver of rain, that the " fecundator " is often a despot. But what can unhesitatingly be said is that the process of specialization tends to mark out fairly clearly the spheres in which these two types of god exercise their power.

As a typical example of the first class—sovereigns and guardians of the law—take T'ien, Varuna, Ahura Mazda. The second class—that of the " fecundators "—is morphologically richer. But note, in all the figures grouped under this heading, the following constantly-recurring themes: marriage with the Earth Goddess; thunder, storm and rain; ritual and mythical connection with bulls. Among the gods of this second class— " fecundators " and also " storm gods "—one may place Zeus, Min and the Hittite god, but also Parjanya, Indra, Rudra, Hadad, Ba'al, Jupiter Dolichenus, Thor; in fact all that are known as storm gods. Each of the above-mentioned divinities naturally has his own individual " history ", making him more or less clearly different from the others in the list; applying the terms of chemistry to mythology one might say that varying components go to make up their " compositions ". But this we shall consider more closely when we come to study the " forms " of the various gods, not just their " power ". In this present section what we are primarily concerned with is the elements they have in common, the values they share. The most important of these are: the power of originating life (and hence their connection with bulls—the earth being very often pictured as a cow), thunder and rain; the epiphanies, in fact, of force and of violence, the necessary sources of those energies on which the life in the universe depends. Divinities of the atmosphere are quite certainly specializations of sky divinities, but however extreme the " specialization " may have been, it never manages to destroy their celestial character. We are thus driven to set the so-called storm gods beside the sky gods properly so called; and in both we shall find the same powers and the same attributes.

Take, for instance, the case of Parjanya, the Indian god of hurricanes. His celestial nature is clear: Parjanya is the son of Dyaus[1] and is sometimes confused with him; as, for instance,

[1] *RV*, vii, 102, 1.

when he is thought to be the spouse of Pṛthvī, goddess of the earth.[1] Parjanya rules over the waters and over all living creatures,[2] sends down the rains,[3] guarantees the fecundity of men, animals and plants[4] and the whole Universe trembles when he unleashes his storms.[5] Parjanya is more concrete and more dynamic than Dyaus, and is more successful in maintaining his place in the Indian pantheon. But that rank is no longer supreme. Parjanya no longer " knows " all, like Dyaus, nor is he sovereign like Varuṇa. His specialization has limited the bounds of his domain; and, more important still, even within those bounds he is not invulnerable. Another hierophany of storm and fertilizing energy could easily replace him if new rituals and new mythological creations were to demand it.

That is precisely what happened in Vedic times. Parjanya gave way to Indra, the most popular of all the Vedic gods (no fewer than two hundred and fifty hymns are addressed to him in the *Ṛg Veda* alone, as against ten to Varuṇa, and thirty-five to Mitra, Varuna and Āditya together). Indra is supremely the " hero ", the brave warrior of indomitable energy, the conqueror of the monster Vṛtra (who steals all the waters), insatiable consumer of *soma*. Whatever interpretations are advanced, we cannot miss seeing Indra's cosmic importance and his function as demiurge. Indra covers the sky,[6] is greater than all the earth,[7] wears heaven as his crown,[8] and the amount of *soma* he swallows is terrifying—he absorbed three lakes once in one draught.[9] Drunk with *soma* he kills Vṛtra, unleashes tornadoes, and makes the whole world tremble. Everything Indra does seems to overflow from his strength and bravado. He is a living personification of the exuberance of life, of cosmic and biological energy; he makes the sap in things circulate and the blood, puts the life into seeds, gives free play to rivers and seas, and bursts open the clouds. A thunderbolt (*vajra*) is the

[1] *AV*, xii, 1, 12, 42.
[2] *RV*, vii, 101, 2.
[3] v, 83; vii, 101, 102.
[4] v, 83, 1; vi, 52, 16; vii, 101, 1, 2.
[5] v, 83, 2.
[6] *RV*, i, 61, 8, 9.
[7] i, 102, 8; iii, 32, 11.
[8] i, 173, 6.
[9] vi, 17, 11.

weapon he uses to kill Vṛtra, and the Maruts, who are lesser
tornado-divinities under Indra's leadership, also have this
divine weapon. "Born of the laughter of lightning",[1] the
Maruts are constantly invoked not to hurl their "projectiles"[2]
against men and cattle, and not to kill them.[3]

Storms are the supreme unleashings of creative force;
Indra pours down the rain and governs moisture of every kind,
so that he is both god of fertility[4] and the archetype of the
forces that originate life.[5] He is ūrvavapati, "master of the
fields" and śiraspati, "master of the plough", he is "the bull
of the world",[6] he makes fields, animals and women fruitful;[7]
he is invoked at weddings that the bride may bear ten sons,[8]
and innumerable invocations refer to his inexhaustible power of
generating life.[9] All Indra's attributes and powers are inter-
related, and the spheres he governs correspondingly so.
Whether we see him sending thunderbolts to strike Vṛtra,
or setting the waters free, or sending the storm that goes
before rain, or absorbing fabulous amounts of soma, whether
we see him fertilizing the fields or see his fantastic sexual
powers, we are always faced with some manifestation of the
life force. His slightest gesture, even of display or boasting,
springs from his superabundance. The myth of Indra is a
perfect expression of the fundamental oneness of all abundant
manifestations of life. The dynamic force of fruitfulness is
the same at every level of things, and often the very words
themselves show that the things that produce fertility are
connected with each other, or come from the same root;
etymologically, varṣa, rain, is very close to vṛṣa, male. Indra
keeps the cosmic forces constantly in motion to circulate bio-
spermatic energy through the whole universe. He has an
inexhaustible reservoir of vitality, and it is upon this reservoir

[1] i, 23, 12.
[2] RV, vii, 56, 9.
[3] v, 55, 9; vii, 56, 17, etc.
[4] Cf. Hopkins, "Indra as God of Fertility", JAOS, vol. xxxvi.
[5] RV, vi, 46, 3, where he is called sahasramuṣka, "with a thousand testicles".
[6] AV, xii, 1, 6.
[7] Cf. Meyer, Trilogie, vol. iii, pp. 154 ff.
[8] Hiranyakeśin-Grhyasūtras, i, 6, 20, 2.
[9] Cf. Meyer, vol. iii, pp. 164 ff.

that the hopes of mankind are based.[1] But Indra is not a creator; he promotes life and diffuses it victoriously all over the universe, but he does not *make* it. The creative function with which every sky divinity is endowed is " specialized ", in Indra's case, into a generative and vitalizing mission.

27. FECUNDATORS

Indra is constantly compared to a bull.[2] His Iranian counterpart, Vrthraghna, appeared to Zarathustra as a bull, a stallion, a ram, a he-goat and a boar,[3] " so many symbols of the male and combative spirit, of the elementary forces of the blood."[4] Indra, too, is sometimes called a ram (*meṣa*).[5] These same animal epiphanies are also to be found in Rudra, a pre-Aryan divinity, absorbed into Indra. Rudra was the father of the Maruts and one hymn[6] recalls how " the bull Rudra created them in the bright breast of Prsni ". As a bull, the generating divinity of the sky united himself to a cow goddess of cosmic proportions. Prṣṇi was one of her names, Sabardugha another; but she remains always a cow procreating all things. The *Ṛg Veda*[7] speaks " of a cow Visvarupa who gives life to all "; in the *Atharva Veda*,[8] the cow unites herself with all the gods in turn and procreates on all cosmic levels; " the gods have life of the cow and men also, the cow becomes this universe vast as the empire of the Sun."[9] Āditi, mother of the Supreme Beings the Ādityas, is also represented as a cow.[10]

This bull-generation " specialization " of the gods of atmos-

---

[1] This very condensed presentation of the hierophany of Indra, at least as we have it in myth, does not exhaust Indra's function in Indian religion. Every divine figure is always involved in innumerable rites which I cannot go into in detail here. (It is important, for instance, to recall that Indra and his escort of Maruts are the archetypes of Indo-Aryan " societies of men ", cf. Stig Wikander, *Der arische Männerbund*, Lund, 1938, pp. 75 ff.). This is true of all the divinities discussed here.

[2] Cf. the texts grouped together by Oldenburg in his *Religion des Veda*, (Berlin, 1894), 2nd ed., p. 74; Hillebrandt, *Vedische Mythologie*, Breslau, 1929, vol. ii, p. 148.

[3] *Yast*, xiv, 7–25.

[4] Benveniste-Renou, *Vrtra et Vrthragna*, p. 33.

[5] Cf. *RV*, i, 51, 1.

[6] *RV*, ii, 34, 2.

[7] iii, 38, 8.

[8] x, 10.

[9] *AV*, x, 10, 34.

[10] Oldenberg, p. 205.

phere and fertility is not limited to India; we find it also in a
fairly wide area of Africa, Europe and Asia. But note at once
that such a " specialization " also betrays outside influences,
sometimes racial, sometimes religious. Indra, for instance,
shows traces of influences that are not Aryan (Rudra), but,
what is even more interesting to us at the moment, his personality has been altered and developed by elements which do not
belong to him as god of rain, storm and cosmic fertility. His
connection with bulls, for instance, and with *soma*, confer
upon him certain lunar prerogatives.[1] The moon governs
the seas and the rains, and all fertility is its gift (§§ 49 ff.);
the bull's horns came very early to be associated with the
crescent moon. I shall return to these complex developments
later. But always bear in mind that generative " specialization " forces the sky gods to take into their personality
every hierophany directly connected with the fertility of the
universe. When stress is laid on his meteorological (storm,
lightning, rain) and generative functions, a sky god must
necessarily not merely become the partner of the great earth-
moon mother, but also absorb her attributes; in Indra's case
these were *soma*, the bull and perhaps also some aspects of the
Maruts (in as much as they personify the wandering souls
of the dead).

The bull and the thunderbolt were very early on (by 2400 B.C.)
symbols connected with gods of the sky and weather.[2] In
archaic cultures, the bellowing of the bull was likened to
thunder and hurricanes (cf. the " bull-roarer " of the Australians); and both were epiphanies of fecundating forces.
That is why we keep coming upon them in the iconography,
rites and myths relating to all the weather-gods of the whole
Afro-Eurasian area. In pre-Aryan India the proto-historic
cults of Mohenjodaro and Baluchistan included the bull.
The " bulls' games " still preserved in the Deccan and Southern
India[3] existed in India before Vedic times in the third millennium B.C. (as witness a seal of Chauhudaro, round 2500 B.C.).
The pre-Dravidians, the Dravidians and the Indo-Aryans all

[1] Cf. Koppers, "Pferdeopfer und Pferdekult der Indogermanen", *WBKL*,
1935, pp. 338 ff.
[2] Cf. Malten, "Der Stier in Kult und mythischen Bild", *JDAI*, 1928, vol.
lxiii, pp. 110 ff.
[3] Autran, *Préhistoire du Christianisme*, Paris, 1941, vol. i, pp. 100 ff.

venerated the bull, either as an epiphany of the god of weather
and generation, or as one of his attributes. The temples of
Śiva are full of the images of bulls, for Siva's vehicle (*vahana*)
is the bull Nandin. The Kanarese *ko* which means ox, also
signifies sky, lightning, ray of light, water, horn, mountain.[1]
The complex religious whole made up of sky-lightning-fecundity
is here preserved as completely as it could be. The Tamil
ko(n) means divinity, but the plural *Kon-ar* means cowherds.[2]
There is possibly some connection between these Dravidian
words and the Sanskrit *gou* (Indo-European *gu-ou*) and the
Sumerian *gu(d)* which mean both " bull " and " powerful or
brave ".[3] We might also note the common origin of the
Semitic and the Greek and Latin words for bull (cf. the
Assyrian *shuru*, the Hebrew *shor*, the Phoenician *thor*, etc.,
and the Greek *tauros*, and Latin *taurus*) which confirms the
unity of this religious pattern.

In Iran, sacrifices of bulls were frequent, and Zarathustra
opposed them unwearyingly.[4] At Ur in the third millennium,
the god of the atmosphere was represented as a bull[5] and in
ancient Assyria, as in Asia Minor, the " god by whom men
swear " (originally, that is, a sky god) was in the form of a bull.[6]
The supremacy attained by such storm gods as Teshub, Hadad
and Ba'al in the religions of the Near East are very significant
in this connection. We might well dwell on these divinities
at greater length. We do not know the name of the supreme
god of the Hittites, spouse of the goddess Arinna; it was once
wrongly thought that he was called Zashhapunah.[7] His
name was written by means of two ideograms of Babylonian
origin, U and I M. The reading of this ideogram in the Luvian
language was Dattas, and the Hurrites called him Teshub.
He was a god of sky and hurricane, winds and lightning.
(In Akkadian, the ideogram I M had the sense of *zunnu*,

[1] Autran, p. 99.
[2] Autran, p. 96.
[3] On the term *gu-ou*, cf. Nehring, " Studien zur indogermanischen Kultur
und Urheimat ", *WBKL*, vol. iv, pp. 73 ff.
[4] *Yasna*, 32, 12, 14; 44, 20, etc.
[5] Malten, p. 103.
[6] Malten, p. 120.
[7] Furlani, *La Religione degli Hittiti*, Bologna, 1936, p. 35; *contra*, Dussaud,
" Les Religions des Hittites et des Hourrites, des Phéniciens et des Syriens ",
MA, vol. ii, p. 343.

" rain ", *sharu*, " wind ", *remanu* " thunder ").[1] His various
titles bear witness to his sky attributes and his position as
absolute sovereign: " king of the sky ", " lord of the country of
the Hatti ". The commonest epithet for him is " most powerful ", and he is symbolized by lightning, an axe or a club.[2]

Remember that in all near-eastern cultures " power " is
primarily symbolized by the bull; in Akkadian " breaking the
horn " is equivalent to " destroying the power ".[3] Arinna's
god was also represented in the form of a bull (images of him
have been found in all the temples) and the bull was his sacred
animal. In written texts, the two mythical bulls, Seris and
Hurris, are consecrated to him[4] or, according to some scholars,
are even his sons.[5] The only myth we know is that of his
battle with the serpent Illuyankas[6] in which we once more meet
the same theme of the battle between the god of storm and
fertility and a reptilian monster (like Indra and Vṛtra, or Zeus
and Typhon; the prototype is Marduk and Tiamat). Note
again the multitude of local epiphanies of this god; in the
account of Suppiluliumas twenty-one Us are mentioned,[7]
proving that they are native to all the areas inhabited by
Hittites. U was a popular god throughout Asia Minor and
Western Asia, though invoked under many different names.

The Sumero-Babylonians knew him by the names of Enlil
and Bel. Though third in their triad of cosmic gods, he was
the most important of the whole pantheon; he was the son of
Anu, the supreme sky god. Here again, you see, the well-
known phenomenon of the passing from a celestial *deus
otiosus* to an active and fecundating god. In Sumerian, his
name means " lord of the violent wind " (*lil*, " powerful
wind, hurricane "). Thus he is also called *lugal amaru*,
" divinity of the wind and hurricane ", and *umu*, " storm ",
En-ug-ug-ga, that is " master of storms ".[8] Similarly, Enlil
governs the waters, and it was he who produced the universal

[1] Cf. Jean, *La Regligion sumérienne*, Paris, 1931, p. 101.
[2] Furlani, p. 36.
[3] Cf. Autran, p. 74.
[4] Götze, *Kleinasien*, Münich, 1933, p. 133.
[5] Malten, p 107.
[6] Furlani, pp. 87 ff.; Dussaud, pp. 345–6.
[7] Furlani, p. 37.
[8] Furlani, *Religione babilonese-assira*, Bologna, 1928–9, vol. i, p. 118.

deluge. He is called " the powerful one ", *alim*, god of the horn, master of the universe, king of heaven and earth, Father Bel, the great warrior, etc.[1] His wife is Ningalla, " the great cow ", *umum rabetum*, " the great mother ", generally invoked as Beltu or Belit, " Mistress ".[2] His celestial origin and meteorological function are also shown by the name of his temple at Nippur, " the House of the Mountain ".[3] The " mountain " continues as a symbol of the sky divinity even when the latter has been " specialized " into a god of fecundity and sovereignty.

At Tel-Khafaje, in the oldest sanctuary known to us, the image of a bull is found next to that of the goddess mother.[4] The god El, who took first place in the early Phoenician pantheon, was called " bull " (*shor*) and also *El* (" merciful bull ").[5] But this god was supplanted at a very early date, by Ba'al, " Master, Lord ", whom Dussaud sees with good reason as the same as the god Hadad.[6] That Ba'al and Hadad are synonymous is also confirmed by the El-Amarna tablets.[7] Hadad makes his voice heard in thunder, hurls down lightning, and dispenses rain. The proto-Phoenicians compared Hadad to a bull: texts only lately deciphered describe how " the strength of Ba'al [that is to say, Hadad] struck Mot with his horns like wild bulls. . . ."[8] And in the myth " The Hunting of Ba'al ", Ba'al's death is compared to the death of a bull: " so fell Ba'al . . . like a bull ".[9] It is not surprising that Ba'al-Hadad has a consort Asherat (Anat, Ashtart), and that his son, Aleion, is a divinity of water, fertility and vegetation.[10] Bulls were sacrificed to Ba'al-Hadad (cf. the famous scene between Elias and the prophets of Ba'al on Mount Carmel). The

---

[1] Furlani, vol. i, pp. 118 ff.

[2] Furlani, p. 120.

[3] Furlani, p. 121.

[4] Autran, vol. i, p. 67.

[5] Dussaud, *Les Découvertes de Ras Shamra et l'ancien testament*, Paris, 1941, 2nd ed., p. 95.

[6] " La Mythologie phénicienne d'après les tablettes de Ras Shamra ", *RHR*, 1931, vol. civ, p. 362 ff.; " Le Vrai Nom de Ba'al ", *RHR*, 1936 *passim; Découvertes*, pp. 98 ff.

[7] " Mythologie phénicienne ", p. 362.

[8] Dussaud, " Le Sanctuaire et les dieux phéniciens de Ras Shamra ", *RHR*, 1932, vol. cv, p. 258.

[9] Dussaud, " Vrai nom de Ba'al ", p. 19.

[10] Dussaud, " Mythologie ", pp. 370 ff.; *Découvertes*, pp. 115 ff.

Assyrian Bel, successor of Anu and Enlil, is described as "divine bull"; and sometimes he is called Gu, "the ox" or "the great ram" (Dara-Gal).[1]

This interdependence between the "generative" and "celestial" symbols in all these types of storm god is noteworthy. Often Hadad, represented as a bull, bears the symbol of lightning.[2] But the lightning is sometimes in the shape of ritual horns.[3] The god Min, prototype of the Egyptian god Ammon, was similarly described as "the bull of his mother", and the "great bull" (*Ka wr*). Lightning was one of his attributes and his functions of raining and giving life are clear from one title describing him—"He who tears open the rain-bearing cloud". Min was not a god of local origin; the Egyptians knew that he had come with his consort, the cow Hathor, from the land of Pwnt, that is, from the Indian Ocean.[4] To conclude this very rapid summary of an extraordinarily rich subject (cf. the Bibliography), note that it was as a bull that Zeus carried off Europa (epiphany of the Great Mother), had his liaison with Antiope and attempted to violate her sister Demeter. And in Crete we can read a very strange epitaph: "Here lies the great Ox who was called Zeus."

28. THE SPOUSE OF THE GREAT MOTHER

As we can see, this structure made up of the rainy sky, bull and Great Goddess was one of the elements that united all the proto-historic religions of Europe, Africa and Asia. Undoubtedly the greatest stress is laid here on those functions of the sky god in bull form which bear on birth and plant life. What is primarily venerated in Min, Ba'al, Hadad, Teshub and other bull-gods of lightning who are husbands of Great Goddesses is not their celestial character but their potentialities as fecundators. That they are sacred is due to their sacred marriage with the great Earth Mother. Their celestial nature is considered of value for its life-bringing functions. The sky is primarily the place where thunder "bellows", where the clouds gather, and where the fertility of the fields is determined;

[1] Autran, *Préhistoire*, vol. i, pp. 69 ff.
[2] Ward, *The Seal Cylinders of Western Asia*, Washington, 1910, p. 399.
[3] Autran, vol. i, p. 89.
[4] Cf. Autran, *La Flotte a l'enseigne du poisson*, Paris, 1939, pp. 40 ff.

the place, in fact, which ensures the continuance of life on earth. The transcendence of the sky is seen mainly as expressed in the weather, and its " power " is simply an unlimited reservoir of seeds. This is sometimes shown in the very language used. The Sumerian *me* means " man, male ", and at the same time, " sky ". The gods of the weather (thunder, storm, rain) and of generation (the bull) lose their celestial autonomy, their absolute sovereignty. Each is accompanied, and often dominated, by a Great Goddess upon whom the fecundity of the universe ultimately depends. They are no longer the creators who made the cosmos, like the primordial sky gods, but simply fecundators and procreators at the biological level. Hierogamy with the goddess becomes their essential function. That is why we constantly come upon them in all fertility cults, and particularly those of the earth; but they never play the leading part in them; that is always played either by the Great Mother, or by a " son ", the god of vegetation who periodically dies and rises again.

In the end the " specialization " of sky gods may change their whole form radically; by abandoning their transcendence, by becoming " accessible ", and so indispensable to human life, by changing from *dei otiosi* into *dei pluviosi*, generative gods in the form of bulls, they are constantly taking to themselves functions, attributes and honours foreign to them, and for which they had no concern in their superb celestial transcendence.[1] Like every divine " form ", in their tendency to become the centre of every religious manifestation and to govern every region of the cosmos, the storm gods and the life-giving gods absorb into their personality and into their worship (particularly by their marriages with the Mother Goddess) elements which did not belong to their original celestial make-up.

Then, too, meteorological happenings are not always and necessarily explained by a sky divinity; the lightning-storm-

[1] We also observe the reverse happening: a local god that has become, owing to its " historical " circumstances, a supreme god, takes to itself the attributes of sky divinity. Assur, the divine protector of the town of the same name, borrowed the attributes of the supreme Creator and Sovereign and thus became one with the sky gods (cf. Knut Tallquist, *Der assyrische Gott*, Helsinki, 1932, pp. 40 ff.). *Enuma Elish*, which was read in Babylon on the fourth day of the New Year before Marduk, was read in Assyria before the statue of Assur (Labat, *Le Poème de la Création*, Paris, 1935, p. 59).

rain combination were sometimes looked on—by the Eskimos, for instance, by the Bushmen and in Peru—as a hierophany of the moon.[1] The bull's horns were long ago compared to a crescent and likened to the moon. Menghin[2] has established a connection between the crescent moon and the Aurignacian feminine figurines (holding a horn in one hand); idols in the form of an ox, often connected with the cult of the Great Mother (the moon) are frequent in the Neolithic Age.[3] Hentze[4] carried out a study of this lunar-life-giving pattern over a wide cultural area. Lunar divinities of the Mediterranean and of the East were represented under the form of a bull and invested with a bull's attributes. Thus, for instance, the Babylonian moon god, Sin, was called " the powerful calf of Enlil ", while Nannar, the moon god of Ur, was described as " powerful young bull of the sky, most wonderful son of Enlil ", or " the powerful one, the young bull with strong horns ", etc. In Egypt, the divinity of the moon was " the bull of the stars ".[5] We shall see later how coherent is this relationship between the earth-moon cults and the cults of fecundity. The rain— the storm god's " sowing "—fits in with the hierophany of the waters, which are the most important sphere the moon dominates. Everything connected with fecundity belongs, more or less directly, to the immense orbit of Moon-Waters-Woman-Earth. Sky divinities, by becoming " specialized " into virile and generative divinities, became firmly bound up with these prehistoric patterns, and have remained there, either assimilating them into their own personalities, or becoming part of them.

29. YAHWEH

The only sky gods of rain and fertility who managed to preserve their autonomy, despite unions with innumerable Great Goddesses, are those who developed along the lines of sovereignty; who held on to their sceptres, as well as their thunders and fecundating powers, and thus remained the guarantors of the order of the universe, guardians of the norms, and personifications of Law. Zeus and Jupiter are two such

[1] Koppers, " Pferdeopfer ", p. 376.
[2] *Weltgeschichte der Steinzeit*, Vienna, 1931, p. 148.
[3] Menghin, p. 448.
[4] *Mythes et symboles lunaires*, Antwerp, 1932, p. 95 ff.
[5] Koppers, p. 387.

gods. Naturally, these two ruling figures had personalities closely fashioned according to the peculiar leaning of the Greek and Roman mind towards the notions of norm and law. But rationalizations of this sort are only possible because based upon a religious and mythical intuition of the rhythms of nature, with their harmony and agelessness. T'ien, too, with his tendency to be revealed as a hierophany of Law and cosmic rhythm, is a good example of the sovereignty of the sky. We shall grasp these aspects better when we come to study the religious patterns of the sovereign and of sovereignty.

The " evolution " of the supreme God of the Hebrews is to be found on a plane that is in some ways parallel. Yahweh's personality and religious history are far too complex to be summed up in a few lines. Let me say, however, that his celestial and atmospheric hierophanies very early became the centre of those religious experiences which made later revelations possible. Yahweh displayed his power by means of storms; thunder is his voice and lightning is called Yahweh's " fire ", or his " arrows ".[1] The Lord of Israel declares his presence: " . . . thunders began to be heard and lightning to flash, and a very thick cloud to cover the mount "[2] while he was transmitting the Law to Moses. " And all Mount Sinai was on a smoke: because the Lord was come down upon it in fire ".[3] Deborah recalled with holy dread how at the Lord's footstep " the earth trembled and the heavens dropped water."[4] Yahweh warns Elias of his approach by " a great and strong wind . . . overthrowing the mountains, and breaking the rocks in pieces: the Lord is not in the wind. And after the wind an earthquake: the Lord is not in the earthquake. And after the earthquake a fire: the Lord is not in the fire. And after the fire a whistling of a gentle air."[5] The fire of the Lord descends on the holocausts of Elias[6] when the prophet prays that he will show himself and confound the priests of Ba'al. The burning bush in the story of Moses, and the pillar of fire and cloud which leads the Israelites through the desert are epiphanies

[1] Cf. Ps. xvii, etc.
[2] Exod. xix, 16.
[3] xix, 18.
[4] Judges v, 4.
[5] 3 Kings xix, 11–12.
[6] 3 Kings xviii, 38.

of Yahweh. And Yahweh's covenant with the descendants of Noe after his escape from the Flood is expressed by a rainbow: " I will set my bow in the clouds, and it shall be the sign of a covenant between me, and between the earth ".[1]

These hierophanies of sky and weather, unlike those of other storm gods, manifest above all the " power " of Yahweh. " God is high in his strength: and none is like him among the law-givers."[2] " In his hands he hideth the light, and commandeth it to come again. He showeth his friend concerning it. . . . At this my heart trembleth and is moved out of its place. Hear ye attentively the terror of his voice, and the sound that cometh out of his mouth. He beholdeth under all the heavens: and his light is upon the ends of the earth. After it a noise shall roar: he shall thunder with the voice of his majesty . . ."[3] The Lord is the true and only Master of the cosmos. He can make all things, annihilate all things. His " power " is absolute, which is why his freedom knows no bounds. Uncontested sovereign, he measures his mercy or his anger as he will: and this absolute liberty the Lord enjoys is the most effective revelation of his absolute transcendence and autonomy; for by nothing can the Lord be " bound "—nothing constrains him, not even good actions or obedience to his laws.

This notion of God's " power " as the only absolute reality is the jumping-off point for all later mystical thought and speculation on the freedom of man, and his possibility of achieving salvation by obedience to the Law and rigorous moral conduct. No one is " innocent " before God. Yahweh made a " covenant " with his people, but his sovereignty meant that it was quite possible for him to annul it at any moment. That he did not was due not to the " covenant " itself—for nothing can " bind " God—but to his infinite goodness. Throughout the religious history of Israel, Yahweh shows himself a sky god and storm god, creator and omnipotent, absolute sovereign and " Lord of Hosts ", support of the kings of David's line, author of all the norms and laws that make it possible for life on earth to go on. The " Law ", in every form, finds its basis and justification in a revelation from Yahweh. But unlike

[1] Gen. ix, 13.
[2] Job xxxvi, 22.
[3] Job xxxvi, 32–xxxvii, 4.

other supreme gods, who cannot contravene their own laws
(Zeus could not save Sarpedon from death),[1] Yahweh maintains
his absolute freedom.

30. THE SUPPLANTING OF SKY GODS BY FECUNDATORS

The substitution of gods of storm and gods of procreation
for the sky gods occurred also in worship. Marduk replaced
Anu in the feast of the New Year (§ 153). As for the great
Vedic sacrifice, the Aśvamedha, it was in the end offered to
Prajāpati (sometimes to Indra as well), having previously been
offered to Varuṇa, and as Varuṇa had taken the place of Dyaus,
it is most likely that this sacrifice of a horse was originally
performed in honour of the ancient Indo-Aryan sky god.
Into modern times the Uralo-Altaic races sacrificed horses to
supreme gods of the sky (§ 33). The essential and primitive
element of the Aśvamedha is its connection with the creation
of the world. The horse is identified with the cosmos and the
sacrificing of it symbolizes (that is, *reproduces*) the act of
creation. The meaning of this rite will be made clearer in
another chapter (§ 153 ff.). All I need stress here is the fact
that the Aśvamedha must be seen as fitting in with a creation
pattern on the one hand, and, on the other, its importance as
an initiation ceremony. That the Aśvamedha *is* at the same
time a ritual of initiation is shown clearly enough by the
following verses from the *Ṛg Veda*: " We have become immortal, we have seen the light, we have found the gods."[2]
Whoever knows the mystery of that initiation has triumphed
over the second death (*punarmṛtyu*) and fears death no longer.
The initiation is in fact a conquest of immortality and a change
over from the human to the divine state. This bringing together
of the conquest of immortality with a repetition of the act of
creation is significant; the offerer gets beyond the merely
human state and becomes immortal by a creation ritual. We
shall find the same connection between initiation and cosmogony in the mysteries of Mithra.

Like Prajāpati—to whom the sacrifice came later to be
offered—the sacrificed horse symbolized the universe. For the
Iranians, all cereals and plants grew from the body of the

---

[1] *Iliad*, xvi, 477 ff.
[2] viii, 48, 3.

primeval bull killed by Ahriman; in the Germanic tradition, the universe was taken from the body of the giant Ymir.[1] There is no need here to consider the implications of these creation myths, nor their parallels in the far east (Pan'ku, for instance) or Mesopotamia (the cosmos created by Marduk from the body of the monster Tiamat). All that interests us here is the *dramatic* nature of the act of creation as we have it in such myths: the Cosmos is no more created *ex nihilo* by the supreme divinity, but comes into existence by means of the sacrifice (or self-sacrifice) of a god (Prajāpati), a primeval monster (Tiamat, Ymir), of a super-man (Puruṣa), or a primeval animal (the bull Ekadath of the Iranians). The source of all these myths is to be found in a real or allegorical human sacrifice (Puruṣa means " man "); this is a pattern that has been found by Gahs to exist throughout a vast number of different races, and it is always connected with initiation ceremonies of secret societies.[2] The dramatic nature of the creative sacrifice of a primeval being shows that such stories of creation are not " primitive ", but represent stages in a long and complicated mythico-religious process that was highly developed even in prehistory.

The Aśvamedha is an excellent example to show the complexity of the rituals honouring sky gods. Substitutions, fusions and symbioses occur as often in the history of worship as in the history of the gods themselves. In the example I have taken, we can discover yet another substitution: the Indian sacrifice of a horse replaced the more ancient sacrifice of a bull (a bull was sacrificed in Iran, and the creation myth speaks of a primordial bull; Indra, in fact, was first pictured surrounded by bulls, though later by stallions; " Prajāpati is, indeed, the great bull ").[3] In Vedic writings they saw Aśvins, whose very name shows their connection with horses, riding, not horses, but humped cattle.[4]

The Aśvins, like the Dioscuri (*Dios kuroi*, cf. Lettish *dewa deli*, Lithuanian *diewo sunelei*), are the sons of the sky god.

---

[1] Güntert, *Arische Weltkönig*, pp. 315 ff.; Christensen, *Le Premier Homme et le premier roi dans l'histoire légendaire des Iraniens*, Uppsala, 1918, vol. i, pp. 11 ff; Koppers, " Pferdeopfer ", pp. 320 ff.

[2] Cf. Koppers, pp. 314 ff.

[3] *Śatapatha-Brāhmaṇa*, iv, 4, 1, 14; cf. vi, 5, 2, 5, 17, etc.

[4] Cf. R. Otto, *Gottheit d. Arier*, pp. 76 ff.

The myth about them owes much both to the hierophanies of the sky (dawn, Venus, the phases of the moon) and to the worship of the Gemini; and the belief (see the Bibliography) that the birth of twins presupposes the union of a mortal with a god, and particularly with a sky god, is extremely widespread. The Aśvins were always represented at the side of a feminine divinity, either Uṣā, goddess of Dawn, or Sūrya; the Dioscuri also accompanied a female figure, their mother or their sister: Castor and Pollux accompanied Helen, Amphion and Zethos their mother Antiope, Heracles and Iphikles their mother Alcmene, Dardanos and Iasion, Harmonia, and so on. Note that:

(a) The Aśvins, the Dioscuri, or whatever other name these mythical twins go by, are the sons of the sky god (most usually as a result of his union with a human woman);

(b) they are always with either their mother or their sister;

(c) their activity on earth is always beneficent. The Aśvins, like the Dioscuri, are healers, saving men from danger, protecting sailors, and so on. In a sense they are the representatives of the sacred power of the sky on earth, though they are undoubtedly more complex in form than that, and could not be adequately described merely as dispensers of that power. But whatever patterns of myth and of ritual the Dioscuri may claim, their beneficent activity is clear.

The Dioscuri did not achieve a leading role in religious life everywhere. Where the " god's sons " failed, the god's son succeeded. Dionysos was the son of Zeus, and his appearance in the religious history of Greece was a spiritual revolution. Osiris, in the same way, was the son of the sky (a goddess) and earth (a god); the Phoenician Aleion was the son of Ba'al, and so on. In every case these divinities had a close connection with vegetation, with suffering, death and resurrection, and with initiation. All of them are dynamic, able to feel suffering, redemptive. Not only the Aegean and Eastern mystery religions, but also the main streams of popular piety took shape around these gods, in name gods of vegetation, but primarily dramatic gods, taking on the destiny of man himself, like him experiencing passions, suffering and death. Never had god been brought so close to man. The Dioscuri helped and protected mankind; the saviour-gods even shared mankind's sufferings, died and rose from the dead to redeem them. That same " thirst for the concrete " which was forever thrusting the sky gods—with their remoteness, their impassibility, their indifference to the daily struggle—into the background, is shown in the importance given to the " son " of the sky god—to Dionysos, Osiris, Aleion and the rest. The " son " often invokes his heavenly father; but it is not his paternity that explains the all-important part he plays in the history of religion, but his " humanity ", the fact that he definitely shares the lot of mankind, even though he passes beyond it in his periodic resurrection.

31. SKY SYMBOLISM

We have looked at a series of sky divinities, or divinities closely connected with the hierophany of the sky. In every case we have observed the same phenomenon of the withdrawal of the sky gods in face of more dynamic, concrete and familiar theophanies. However, it would be quite wrong to limit the hierophanies of the sky to divine or semi-divine figures issuing from them. The sacred nature of the sky appears in innumerable rites and myths which are not, in appearance at least, directly connected with any sky god. The sacred as manifested by the sky lives on in men's religious experience, after the actual sky god has faded into the background, in the symbolism of " height ", " ascension ", " centre ", and so on. Then, too, we often find in such symbolism that while a fertilizing divinity has been substituted for the sky divinity, the celestial nature of the symbolism remains.

Mountains are the nearest thing to the sky, and are thence endowed with a twofold holiness: on one hand they share in the spatial symbolism of transcendence—they are " high ", " vertical ", " supreme ", and so on—and on the other, they are the especial domain of all hierophanies of atmosphere, and therefore, the dwelling of the gods. Every mythology has its sacred mountain, some more or less famous variation on the Greek Olympus. All sky gods have certain high places set apart for their worship. The symbolic and religious significance of mountains is endless. Mountains are often looked on as the place where sky and earth meet, a " central point " therefore, the point through which the *Axis Mundi* goes, a region impregnated with the sacred, a spot where one can pass from one cosmic zone to another. So, in Mesopotamian belief, " the Mountain of the Lands " unites earth and heaven,[1] and in Indian mythology Mount Meru rises up in the centre of the world; above it the Pole Star sends forth its light.[2] The Uralo-Altaic peoples also have a central mountain, Sumbur, Sumur or Semeru, above which hangs the Pole Star.[3] According to Iranian belief, the sacred mountain Haraberazaiti (Harburz) is at the centre of the earth and is fastened to the sky.[4] In the Edda, Himingbjorg is, as its name suggests, a " celestial mountain "; that is the point where the rainbow (Bifrost) touches the dome of heaven. Such beliefs are also to be found among the Finns, the Japanese and other peoples.

The mountain, because it is the meeting place of heaven and earth, is situated at the centre of the world, and is of course the highest point of the earth. That is why so many sacred places—" holy places ", temples, palaces, holy towns—are likened to " mountains " and are themselves made " centres ", become in some magic way part of the summit of the cosmic hill (cf. § 145). Mounts Tabor and Gerizim in Palestine were also " centres " and Palestine, the Holy Land, held therefore to be the highest place on earth, and to have been unaffected by the Flood. " The Land of Israel was not submerged by the deluge," says one rabbinic text.[5] To Christians, Golgotha is the centre of the world, for it is the peak of the cosmic mountain and the spot where Adam was created and buried. According to the tradition of Islam, the highest spot on earth is the Ka'aba for " the Pole Star proves that . . . it lies against the centre of heaven."[6]

The very names of some sacred temples and towers bear witness to this assimilation to the cosmic mountain: " the hill house ", " the house of the hill of all lands ", " the

---

[1] Jeremias, *Handbuch der altorientalischen Geisteskultur*, Berlin, 1929, p. 130.

[2] Kirfel, *Die Kosmographie der Inder*, Bonn-Leipzig, 1920, p. 15.

[3] These are Buriat beliefs: Holmberg-Harva, *Der Baum des Lebens*, Helsinki, 1923, p. 41.

[4] Texts quoted in Christensen, *Le Premier Homme*, vol. ii, p. 42.

[5] Quoted by Wensinck, *The Ideas of the Western Semites concerning the Navel of the Earth*, Amsterdam, 1916, p. 15; for other texts, Burrows, " Some Cosmological Patterns in Babylonian Religion ", in S. H. Hooke, *The Labyrinth*, London, 1934, p. 54.

[6] Text from Kisa'i, quoted by Wensinck, op. cit., p. 15.

mountain of storms ", " the union of earth and heaven " and so on.[1] The Ṣumerian term for *ziqqurat* is *u-nir* (hill), which Jastrow interprets as meaning " visible from afar ".[2] The *ziqqurat* was actually a " cosmic hill ", that is, a symbolic image of the cosmos; its seven levels represented the seven heavens of the planets (as at Borsippa), or were the colours of the world (as at Ur). The temple of Borobudur was itself an image of the cosmos and was built in the shape of a mountain. An extension of the sacredness of the temple (hill, centre of the world), to the whole town, made certain cities in the East " centres " themselves, peaks of the cosmic mountain, points of junction between the cosmic regions. Thus, Larsa was called, among other things, " the home of the junction between heaven and earth ", and Babylon, " the home of the foundation of the sky and the earth ", " the union of heaven and earth ", " the home of the luminous hill ", etc.[3] In China, the capital of the perfect sovereign stood at the exact centre of the universe,[4] that is, at the summit of the cosmic mountain.

We shall come back in a later chapter to this cosmological symbolism of the centre in which mountains play such an important part (§ 143). What we can note for the moment is the consecrating power of " height ". High places are impregnated with sacred forces. Everything nearer to the sky shares, with varying intensity, in its transcendence. " Height ", " what is higher " becomes transcendent, super-human. Every ascent is a breakthrough, as far as the different levels of existence are concerned, a passing to what is beyond, an escape from profane space and human status. I need hardly add that the sacred value of " height " is explained by the sacred value of the upper regions of air, and therefore event-ually by the sacredness of the sky itself. The mountain, the temple, the city, and so on are consecrate because they are given the attributes of the " centre "; originally, that is, they were assimilated into the highest point of the universe, and the point where heaven and earth meet. Consequently, the

---

[1] Dombart, *Der Sakralturm: I Teil: Ziqqurat*, Munich, 1920, p. 34.

[2] " Sumerian and Akkadian Views of Beginnings ", *JAOS*, 1917, vol. xxxvi, p. 289.

[3] Dombart, p. 35.

[4] Granet, *La Pensée chinoise*, Paris, 1934, p. 324.

consecration conferred by rituals of ascension and the climbing of hills or of ladders owes its power to the fact that it is placing the believer in a higher celestial sphere. The richness and variety of ascension symbolism may at first look chaotic but, seen together, all such rites and symbols are explained by the sacred value of " height ", that is, of the celestial. The transcending of the human condition by entering a sacred place (a temple or an altar), by some ritual consecration, or by dying, is expressed concretely as a " passage ", a " rising ", an " ascension ".

32. ASCENSION MYTHS

Death means transcending the human state and " passing to what is beyond ". In those religions which place the other world in the sky or in some higher sphere, the souls of the dead trudge up mountain paths, or clamber up a tree, or even up a rope.[1] The usual Assyrian expression for dying is " grappling oneself to the mountain ". And in Egyptian, *myny*, " grasp " or " grapple " is a euphemism for " die ".[2] The sun sinks between the mountains and the path of the dead to the other world always goes that way. Yama, the first to die in the mythical tradition of India, went by " the high passes " to show " the way to many men ".[3] Popular belief among the Uralo-Altaics is that the road taken by the dead goes up the hills; Bolot, a Kara-Kirghiz hero, like Kesar, the legendary king of the Mongols, enters the world beyond by going through a tunnel to the top of the hills—rather like an initiation trial. The shaman's journey to hell is made by climbing several very high mountains.[4] The Egyptians preserved in their funeral texts the expression *asket pet* (*asket* means " step ") which shows that the ladder offered to Ra for him to climb from earth to heaven is a real ladder.[5] " The ladder is in place for me to see the gods ", says the Book of the Dead.[6] " The

[1] For this latter see Van Gennep, *Mythes et légendes d'Australie*, Paris, 1906, nos. 17 and 66, and their notes.

[2] Zimmern, " Zum babylonischen Neujahrsfest ", *Berichte über d. Verhandl. d. Kgl. Sächs. Gesell. d. Wiss.*, Leipzig, 1918, vol. lxx, no. 5; vol. ii, p. 5, n. 2.

[3] *RV*, x, 14, 1.

[4] Eliade, *Le Chamanisme et les techniques archaïques de l'extase*, Paris, 1951, pp. 184 ff.

[5] W. Budge, *From Fetish to God in Ancient Egypt*, Oxford, 1934, p. 346.

[6] Weill, *Le Champ des roseaux et le champ des offrandes dans la religion funéraire et la religion générale*, Paris, 1936, p. 52.

gods are making him a ladder so that he can use it to go up to heaven."[1] In a great many tombs of the Old and Middle Kingdoms amulets have been found bearing a picture of a ladder (*maqet*) or a staircase.[2]

The same path by which the souls of the dead go to the other world is also taken by those who, because of some exceptional condition or because they have carried out some efficacious rite, manage to enter heaven even while they are alive. This idea of "ascension" into heaven by means either of a rope, a tree, or a ladder, is fairly widespread in all five continents. I will mention only a few examples.[3] The Dieri tribe of Australia have a myth of a tree growing, by the power of magic, as high as heaven.[4] The Numgahburran talk of two miraculous pines that grow till their tops touch the sky because a taboo has been violated.[5] The Mara tell of a similar tree which their ancestors used to climb till they got to heaven, and climb down again.[6] The Maori hero, Tawhaki's wife, who was a fairy from the sky, stayed with him only until their first child was born; after which she climbed up to the roof and disappeared. Tawhaki went up to heaven by clambering up a vine, and succeeded in getting back to earth afterwards.[7] In other variations of the story the hero reaches the sky by climbing a cocoa-tree, a rope, a spider's web, riding on a kite, and so on. In the Hawaiian islands, they say he climbed up the rainbow; at Tahiti, that he climbed a high mountain and met his wife on the way.[8] One fairly widespread myth in Oceania tells how the hero reached the sky by a "chain of arrows"; that is, by shooting one arrow into the sky, the second into the first, and so on till a chain of arrows stretched from heaven to earth.[9] Ascension by rope is to be found in Oceania,[10] in Africa,[11] in

[1] Weill, p. 28.
[2] Budge, *The Mummy*, Cambridge, 1925, pp. 324, 326.
[3] For further study, cf. Eliade, pp. 404 ff.
[4] Van Gennep, no. 32.
[5] Van Gennep, no. 44.
[6] Van Gennep, no. 49.
[7] Grey, *Polynesian Mythology and Ancient Traditional History of the New Zealanders*, Auckland, 1929, pp. 42 ff.
[8] Chadwick, *The Growth of Literature*, Cambridge, 1930, vol. iii, p. 273.
[9] Pettazzoni, " The Chain of Arrows.", *FRE*, vol. xxxv, pp. 151 ff.
[10] Dixon, *Oceanic Mythology*, Boston, 1916, pp. 156 ff.
[11] Werner, *African Mythology*, Boston, 1916, p. 135.

South America,[1] and North America.[2] In almost the same
places there exists the myth of ascension by a spider's web.
Climbing a ladder into the sky was known in ancient Egypt,[3]
Africa,[4] Oceania[5] and North America. And the ascent might
also be made by means of a tree,[6] a plant, or a mountain.[7]

33. ASCENSION RITES

For all these myths and beliefs there are corresponding
concrete rites of " rising " and " ascension ". The deter-
mining and consecrating of a place of sacrifice constituted a
sort of sublimation of the profane space: " In truth the
officiating priest makes himself a ladder and a bridge for
reaching the celestial world," states the *Taittirīya Samhitā*.[8]
In another passage, the same book shows the celebrant climbing
up a staircase; having got to the top of the stake of sacrifice,
he raises his hands and cries: " I have reached heaven, the
gods; I have become immortal ! " The ritual climbing up
to heaven is a *dūrohaṇa*, a " difficult climb ". A great many
similar expressions can be found in Vedic writings.[9] Kosingas,
priest-king of some of the Thracian peoples (the Kebrenioi
and Sykaiboai), threatens to leave his subjects and go to the
goddess Hera by climbing a wooden ladder.[10] Ascension to
heaven by means of a ceremonial climbing of a ladder was
probably part of the Orphic initiation.[11] We certainly find it in
Mithraic initiation. In the mysteries of Mithra the ceremonial
ladder (*climax*) had seven rungs, each made of a different metal.
According to Celsus (Origen, *Contra Celsum*) the first rung
was lead, and corresponded to the " heaven " of Saturn, the
second tin (Venus), the third bronze (Jupiter), the fourth iron
(Mercury), the fifth " the alloy of money " (Mars), the sixth

[1] Alexander, *Latin-American Mythology*, Boston, 1925, p. 271.
[2] Stith Thompson, *Motif Index of Folk Literature*, Helsinki, 1934, vol. iii, p. 7.
[3] Muller, *Egyptian Mythology*, Boston, 1918, p. 176.
[4] Werner, p. 136.
[5] Chadwick, p. 481.
[6] Sea Dyaks, Chadwick, p. 486; Egypt, Muller, p. 176; Africa, Werner, pp.
136 ff., etc.
[7] Cf. Stith Thompson, vol. iii, pp. 8–9.
[8] vi, 6, 4, 2.
[9] Cf. Coomaraswamy, *Svayamatrnna*, *passim*.
[10] Polyæmus, *Stratagematon*, vii, 22.
[11] Cf. Cook, *Zeus*, vol. ii, pp. 2, 124 ff.

silver (the moon) and the seventh gold (the sun). The eighth rung, Celsus tells us, represents the sphere of the fixed stars. By climbing this ceremonial ladder, the initiate was in fact going through the " seven heavens " and thus attaining the empyrean.

Even to-day among the Uralo-Altaic peoples the shamans carry out exactly the same ritual in their journey to heaven, and in their initiation ceremonies. The " ascension " is achieved either within the framework of an ordinary sacrifice— when the shaman goes with the offering (the soul of the sacrificed horse) to Bai Ulgen, the Supreme God—or on the occasion of the magic cure of invalids who consult them. The sacrifice of a horse, which is the chief religious ceremony of the Turco-Tatar races, takes place once a year and lasts two to three nights. The first evening a new yurt is set up containing a birch tree whose branches have been removed with nine steps cut into it (*tapty*). A white horse is chosen for the sacrifices; a fire is lit in the tent, the shaman passes his drum through the smoke, while calling on the spirits one after another, after which he goes out, and straddling the body of a goose made of rag and stuffed with straw, he waves his arms as if flying, and sings:

> Above the white heavens,
> Beyond the white clouds,
> Above the blue heavens,
> Beyond the blue clouds,
> Fly up to heaven, bird !

The aim of this rite is to seize hold of the soul of the sacrificed horse (*pura*), which is supposed to have fled as the shaman approached. Having seized the soul and brought it back, the shaman sets the " goose " free and sacrifices only the horse. The second part of the ceremony takes place the following evening, when the shaman takes the soul of the horse to Bai Ulgen. Having passed his drum through the smoke and put on his ritual vestments, having invoked Merkyut, bird of the sky, to " come singing " and " sit on his right shoulder ", the shaman begins his ascent. Lightly climbing up the notches of the ceremonial tree, the shaman goes one by one through all the nine heavens, and describes to his audience in great detail all that he sees and all that is happening in each. At the

sixth heaven he venerates the moon, in the seventh the sun.
At last, in the ninth, he is prostrate before Bai Ulgen, and offers
him the soul of the sacrificed horse. This episode is the climax
of the shaman's ecstatic ascension. He finds out whether the
sacrifice is accepted by Bai Ulgen and is given predictions
about the weather; the shaman then falls to the ground and
after a moment's silence wakes up as if from a deep sleep.[1]

The notches or steps made in the birch symbolize the spheres
of the planets. During the ceremony the shaman begs the
assistance of the various divinities whose specific colours
show their nature as planetary divinities.[2] As in the Mithraic
initiation ritual, and as with the walls of the city of Ecbatana,
which are all different colours[3] to symbolize the heavens of
the planets, the moon is in the sixth heaven and the sun in the
seventh. The number nine is a substitution for the older
number of seven grooves; for, to the Uralo-Altaics, the "pillar
of the world" has seven notches[4] and the mythical tree with
seven branches symbolizes the celestial regions.[5] The ascent
of the ceremonial birch tree is equivalent to the ascent of the
mythical tree that stands in the middle of the world. The hole
in the top of the tent is identified with the opening opposite
the Pole Star through which one may pass from one cosmic
level to the other.[6] The ceremonial is thus effected in a
"centre" (§ 143).

The same ascent takes place in the shamanic initiations.
Among the Buriats, nine trees are placed next to each other,
and the neophyte climbs to the top of the ninth and then goes
along the tops of all the others.[7] A birch is also placed in a
tent, and sticks out of the opening at the top; the neophyte
climbs with a sword in his hand till he is outside the tent, thus
effecting the journey to the last heaven. There is a rope
attaching the birch in the tent to the nine other birches and
on this rope hang scraps of different coloured cotton, represent-

[1] Radlov, *Aus Sibiren*, Leipzig, 1884, vol. ii, 19–51; Holmberg-Harva, *Rel. Vorst.*, p. 553 ff. ; Eliade, *Le Chamanisme*, pp. 176 ff.

[2] Holmberg-Harva, *Baum des Lebens*, p. 136.

[3] Herodotus, i, 98.

[4] Holmberg-Harva, pp. 25 ff.

[5] Holmberg-Harva, p. 137 and fig. 46.

[6] Holmberg-Harva, pp. 30 ff.

[7] Eliade, *Chamanisme*, pp. 116 ff.

ing the heavenly spheres. The rope is called the "bridge", and symbolizes the shaman's journey to the home of the gods. The shaman performs a similar ascent to heal the sick when they come to ask his help.[1] The mythical journeys into heaven performed by the Turco-Mongolian heroes bear a striking resemblance to the shamanist rites.[2] According to Yakut belief, there used once to be shamans who actually rose into the sky; spectators could see them gliding across the clouds with the sacrificed horse.[3] At the time of Genghis Khan, a Mongol shaman of repute would ascend to heaven on his charger.[4] The Ostyak shaman sang that he rose into the skies on a rope and pushed aside any stars that barred his way.[5] In the Uighur poem *Kudatku Bilik*, a hero dreamed that he was climbing a fifty-runged ladder, at the top of which a woman gave him water to drink; thus revived, he was able to get to heaven.[6]

34. ASCENSION SYMBOLISM

Indeed Jacob dreamt of a ladder reaching to heaven, and "the angels also of God ascending and descending by it."[7] The stone on which Jacob lay sleeping was a *bethel* and was placed "in the middle of the world", for it is there that the union of all the cosmic regions takes place (§ 81). In Islamic tradition, Mahomet saw a ladder rising from the temple of Jerusalem (the "centre" *par excellence*) into heaven, with angels on the right and on the left; the souls of the just went up this ladder to God.[8] Dante, too, in the heaven of Saturn, saw a golden ladder rising dizzily to the furthest sphere of heaven for the souls of the blessed to ascend.[9] The symbolism of steps, ladders and ascents has been preserved in Christian mysticism. Saint John of the Cross pictures the steps of mystical perfection as an ascent of Mount Carmel, and himself

---

[1] Holmberg-Harva, *Rel. Vorst*, pp. 546 ff.

[2] Eliade, *Chamanisme*, pp. 291 ff.

[3] Czaplicka, *Aboriginal Siberia*, Oxford, 1914, p. 238.

[4] Kopruluzade, *Influence du chamanisme turco-mongol sur les ordres mystiques musulmans*, Istanbul, 1929, p. 17.

[5] Chadwick, *Growth*, vol. iii, p. 204.

[6] Chadwick, p. 206.

[7] Gen. xxviii, 12.

[8] Asin Palacio, *Escatologia musulmana*, Madrid, 1942, p. 70.

[9] *Paradiso*, xxi–xxii.

illustrates it by a mountain with weary, winding paths up its side.

All mystical visions and ecstasies include a rising of some sort to heaven. We gather from Porphyry that Plotinus had this sort of heavenly ecstasy four times during the period when they lived together.[1] St. Paul too was " caught up even to the third heaven ".[2] The doctrine of the ascension of souls to the seven heavens—whether during initiation or after death— had tremendous vogue during the last centuries of the pre-Christian era. That it came from the East is certain;[3] but Orphism had as much to do with its spread in the Graeco-Roman world as Pythagorism. These traditions will be more usefully examined in a later chapter. But it is important to glance at them here because their final justification is to be found in the sacred character of the sky and upper regions. In whatever religious context you find them, whatever *sort* of value is placed upon them—shamanist rite or initiation rite, mystical ecstasy or oniric vision, eschatological myth or heroic legend—ascents, the climbing of mountains or stairs, flights into the air, and so on, all these things always signify a transcending of the human and a penetration into higher cosmic levels. Levitation in itself means a consecration or divinization. The ascetics of Rudra " walk on the way of the wind, for the gods have entered into them ".[4] Exponents of *yoga* and Indian alchemists fly in the air, and cover vast distances in a few moments.[5] To be able to fly, to have wings, becomes a symbolic formula for transcending human status; the ability to rise into the air indicates access to the ultimate realities. Obviously there is still a radical distinction, even in the phenomenology of ascents, between religious experience and the technique of the magician; a saint is " rapt " to heaven; Yogis, ascetics, magicians, " fly " by their own efforts. But in either case, it is their *ascent* that sets them apart from the mass of ordinary and uninitiated souls: they can enter the heavens which are impregnated with holiness, and become like gods. Their contact with the starry spaces makes them divine.

[1] *Vita Plot.*, 23.
[2] 2 Cor. xii, 2.
[3] Cf. Bousset, " Die Himmelreise der Seele ", *AFRP*, iv, pp. 155 ff.
[4] *RV*, x, 156, 2–3.
[5] Eliade, *Le Yoga: Immortalité et liberté*, Paris, 1954, p. 397.

35. CONCLUSIONS

Let me recapitulate briefly:

(a) The sky, of its very nature, as a starry vault and atmospheric region has a wealth of mythological and religious significance. " Height ", " being on high ", infinite space— all these are hierophanies of what is transcendent, what is supremely sacred. Atmospheric and meteorological " life " appears to be an unending myth. And the Supreme Beings of primitive races, as well as the Great Gods of the earliest civilizations of history, all display a connection—sometimes more, sometimes less, organic—with the sky, the air, and meteorological happenings.

(b) But these Supreme Beings cannot be explained simply as sky hierophanies. They are more than that; they have a " form " which indicates that they have a proper and exclusive mode of being which cannot, therefore, be explained simply in terms of events in the sky, or human experience. For these Supreme Beings are creators, good, eternal (" old "); they are founders of the established order and guardians of the laws— attributes which can be explained only partially by the hierophanies of the sky. This is the problem of the " form " of Supreme Beings, and I shall take it up in another chapter.

(c) Bearing in mind this unsolved problem—which is of some importance—we can discern in the " history " of Supreme Beings and sky gods one phenomenon which is extremely significant in the religious history of mankind: these divine figures tend to disappear from the cult. Nowhere do they play a leading part, but have become remote and been replaced by other religious forces: by ancestor-worship, worship of the spirits and gods of nature, spirits of fertility, Great Goddesses and so forth. It is noteworthy that such substituion almost invariably means a more concrete, more dynamic, more fertile divinity or religious force (such as the sun, the Great Mother, the male god, etc.). The conqueror always represents fecundity, or dispenses it; in other words, ultimately represents or gives *life*. (Even fear of the dead and of demons is simply fear that *life* may be threatened by those hostile powers which must therefore be exorcized and neutralized.) The profound meaning of this substitution will appear when we come to look at the religious significance of life and vital functions.

(*d*) Sometimes—as a result, no doubt, of the appearance of agriculture and religious forms connected with it—the sky god regains the field as a god of weather and storms. But such " specialization ", though giving him a great many attributes, limits his omnipotence. The storm god is dynamic and " strong ", he is the bull, he is the fecundator, the myths about him grow richer, and his cults become startling—but he is no longer the creator of the universe or of man, he is no longer omniscient; sometimes he is merely the spouse of the Great Goddess. It was against this storm god, the great male, orgiastic, rich in dramatic epiphanies, whose cults were lavish and bloody (with sacrifices and orgies) that the Semitic world produced its religious revolution, in form monotheistic, prophetic and messianic. It was in this struggle between Ba'al and Yahweh or Allah that " heavenly " values were brought anew into the field of man's life, as against " earthly " (money, fecundity, power); criteria of quality (the interiorization of faith, prayer, and love) as against those of quantity (the physical act of sacrificing, the all-importance of ritual gestures, etc.). But because " history " made it inevitable that these epiphanies of the elementary forces of life should be outgrown, that does not mean necessarily that they were without religious value. As I shall show, these primitive epiphanies were originally so many ways of sanctifying physical life; they became dead things only as they lost their original function by ceasing to be sacred and becoming simply vital, economic and social " phenomena ".

(*e*) In many cases the sun god replaced the sky god. The sun then became the giver of fecundity on earth and protector of life (see *infra*, § 36 ff.).

(*f*) Occasionally the ubiquity, the wisdom and the passivity of the sky god were seen afresh in a metaphysical sense, and the god became the epiphany of the order of nature and the moral law (as with the Maori Iho); the divine " person " gave place to the " idea "; religious experience (already meagre in the case of almost all the sky gods) gave place to theoretic understanding, or philosophy.

(*g*) A few sky gods preserved their position in people's religious life, or even strengthened it, by being seen as sovereign gods as well. These are those who were best able to maintain their supremacy in the pantheon (Jupiter, Zeus, T'ien) and those who were the subject of monotheist revolutions (Yahweh, Ahura Mazda).

(*h*) But even when religious life was no longer dominated by sky gods, the starry regions, sky symbolism, ascension myths and rites, all continued to hold an important place in the scheme of sacred things.

What is " on high ", " raised up ", is still a revelation of the transcendent in any religious setting. Divine " forms " may change; indeed the very fact that they are revealed as " forms " to man's mind, means that they *have* a history and follow a definite course; but the sacred meaning of the sky remains a living idea everywhere and in all circumstances. Worship grew away from it, and myths put other things in its place, but the sky retained its importance in symbolism. And this sky symbolism was the foundation of a number of rites (of ascension, of climbing upwards, of initiation, of coronation, etc.), myths (the Cosmic Tree, the Cosmic Mountain, the chain of arrows and so on) and legends like the magic flight. The symbolism of the " centre ", which plays such an important part in all the great religions of history, is made up of sky elements (sometimes quite clearly so, sometimes less clearly)— the Centre and Axis of the World, the point of communication between the three cosmic regions; it is only at a " centre " that a break-through can occur, a passing from one cosmic zone to another.

To sum up very briefly, one may say that " history " has effectively pushed into the background the divine " forms " of a celestial nature (as with Supreme Beings) or corrupted them (as storm gods or fecundators), but that " history "— which is simply man's ever-fresh experimentation and inter- pretation of the sacred—has not been able to do away with the direct and abiding revelation that the sky is something sacred; it is a revelation neither personal, nor temporal, and it is quite outside history. The symbolism of the sky has held its position in every religious framework, simply because its mode of being is outside time: in fact, this symbolism gives meaning and support to all religious " forms ", and yet never loses anything itself by so doing (§ 166 ff.).

RECENT DISCUSSION AND BIBLIOGRAPHY

The problem of the sky gods of less civilized races has been stated mainly in connection with Supreme Beings and " primitive monotheism ". Consequently, most of the works mentioned here look at these beings in general as divine " forms ", and only consider their celestial characteristics as a subsidiary question (apart, of course, from the works of Pettazzoni and Frazer, whose purpose is, precisely, an exhaustive illustration of those celestial qualities).

General Studies on primitive Supreme Beings: PETTAZZONI, R., " Allwissende höchste Wesen bei primitivsten Völkern ", *AFRW*, 1930, vol. xxix, pp. 108–29, 209–43 ; CLEMEN, C., " Der sogenannte Monotheismus der Primitiven ", *AFRW*, 1929, vol. xxviii, pp. 290–333; PETTAZZONI, R., *Saggi di Storia delle Religioni e di Mitologia*, Rome, 1946, pp. xii ff., 1 ff.; *L'onniscienza di Dio*, Turin, 1955.

On Baiame: HOWITT, A. W., *The Native Tribes of South-East Australia*, London, 1904, pp. 362 ff., 466 ff.; PETTAZZONI, R., *Dio*, vol. i (*L'Essere Celeste nelle Credenze dei Popoli Primitivi*), Rome, 1922, p. 2 ff.; SCHMIDT, W., *Der Ursprung der Gottesidee*, vol. i, 2nd ed., Münster, 1926, pp. 416–78; ibid., vol. iii, Münster, 1931, pp. 828–990, and the accompanying documentation.

On Daramulum: HOWITT, A. W., *Native Tribes*, pp. 494 ff., 528 ff.; PETTAZZONI, R., *Dio*, vol. i, pp. 6 ff.; SCHMIDT, W., *Ursprung*, vol. i, p. 410 ff.; vol. iii, pp. 718–827.

On Bunjil: MATTHEWS, R. H., *Ethnological Notes on the Aboriginal Tribes of New South Wales and Victoria*, Sydney, 1905, pp. 84–134, 162–71; VAN GENNEP, A., *Mythes et légendes d'Australie*, Paris, 1906, pp. 178 ff.; PETTAZZONI, R., *Dio*, vol. i, p. 16 ff.; SCHMIDT, W., *Ursprung*, vol. i, pp. 337–80; vol. iii, 650–717 (an effort to distinguish between the history of Bunjil and his transformations in myth).

On Munganngana: HOWITT, *Native Tribes*, pp. 616 ff.; SCHMIDT, *Ursprung*, vol. i, pp. 380–97; vol. iii, pp. 591–649. (Schmidt thinks that Munganngana was less affected by naturist mythology than any of the other Australian Supreme Beings.)

On the controversies about the Aranda and Loritja tribes: SCHMIDT, W., " Die Stellung der Aranda unter den australischen Stämmen ", *ZFE*, 1908, pp. 866–901; SCHMIDT, W., *Ursprung*, vol. i, pp. 434–49; cf. NIEUWENHUIS, A. W., " Der Geschlechtstotemismus an sich und als Basis der Heiratsklassen und des Gruppentotemismus in Australien ", *IAFE*, 1928, vol. xxix, pp. 1–52; *contra*: SCHMIDT, W., *Ursprung*, vol. iii, pp. 574–86, and VATTER, E., " Der Australische Totemismus ", *Mitteilungen aus dem Museum f. Völkerkunde in Hamburg*, 1925, vol. x, particularly pp. 28 ff., and 150; STREHLOW, C., and VON LEONHARDI, M., *Mythen, Sagen und Märchen des Aranda-Stammes in Zentral-Australien*, Frankfurt a. M., 1907; SPENCER, Baldwin, *The Arunta*, London, 1927, 2 vols. For the Lang-Hartland controversy about Andrew Lang's book, see *The Making of Religion*, London, 1898; HARTLAND, E. S., " The High Gods of Australia ", *FRE*, 1908, vol. ix, pp. 290–329; LANG, Andrew, " Australian Gods ", *FRE*, vol. x, pp. 1–46; HARTLAND, E. S., " High Gods: A Rejoinder ", *FRE*, pp. 46–57; Lang's answer, *FRE*, pp. 489–95. There is a long critical analysis by Schmidt, *APS*, 1908, iii, pp. 1081–107.

On Puluga: MAN, E. H., *On the Aboriginal Inhabitants of the Andaman Islands*, London, 1883; BROWN, A. R., *The Andaman Islanders*, Cambridge, 1922; a long controversy on the existence of a Supreme Being among the Andaman Islanders took place between W. Schmidt and A. R. Brown in the review *Man*, 1910, vol. xx, pp. 2 ff., 33 ff., 66ff., 84 ff.; cf. SCHMIDT, W., *Stellung der Pygmäenvölker*, Stuttgart, 1910, pp. 193–219, 241–67; id., " Die religiösen Verhältnisse der Andamanesen-Pygmäen ", *APS*, 1921–2, vols. xvi–xvii, pp. 978–1005; id., *Ursprung der Gottesidee*, vol. i, 2nd ed., pp. 160–3; for a general study cf. PETTAZZONI, R., *Dio*, vol. i, pp. 92–101; SCHMIDT, W., *Ursprung*, vol. iii, pp. 50–145, where the author attempts to distinguish Puluga's original characteristics from outside influences (naturism, animism, magic, matriarchy, lunar mythology; indeed Brown could find no trace of a supreme being among the islanders of the northern and central Andamans, but only a religion, matriarchal in form, worshipping Bilika; whereas in the south, Man's findings on Puluga are confirmed).

On the Semang Pygmies, the Sakai and the Yakem: SCHEBESTA, P., " Religiöse Anschauungen der Semang über die Orang hidop, die Unsterblichen ", *AFRW*, 1926, vol. xxiv, pp. 209–33; id., *Among the Forest Dwarfs of Malaya*, London, 1929; id., *Orang-Utan, Bei den Urwaldmenschen Malayas und Sumatras*, Leipzig, 1928; id., *Les Pygmées*, French ed., Paris, 1940, pp. 93 ff.; EVANS Ivor H. N., *Studies in Religion, Folk-lore and Custom in British North Borneo and the Malay Peninsula*, Cambridge, 1923; id., *Papers on the Ethnology and Archæology of the Malay Peninsula*, Cambridge, 1927; general study, PETTAZZONI, R., *Dio*, vol. i, pp. 101–18; SCHMIDT, W., *Ursprung*, vol. iii, pp. 152–279.

On the Negritos of the Philippines: VANOVERBERGH, Morice, " Negritos of Northern Luzon ", *APS*, 1925, vol. xx, pp. 148–99, 399–433; on religious life, pp. 434 ff.; SCHEBESTA, P., *Les Pygmées*, pp. 145 ff.; cf. also SKEAT, W. W., and BLAGDEN, O., *Pagan Races of the Malay Peninsula*, London, 1906.

On the sky gods of Africa: general study, PETTAZZONI, R., *Dio*, vol. i, pp. 186–259; FRAZER, J., *The Worship of Nature*, London, 1926, pp. 89–315; SCHMIDT, W., *Ursprung*, vol. iv (*Der Religionen der Urvölker Afrikas*), Münster, 1933; cf. also vol. i, pp. 167 ff.; vol. vi, 1935, *passim*; vol. vii, 1940, pp. 3–605, 791–826; vol. viii, 1949, pp. 569–717; vol. xii, 1955, pp. 761–899; vol. vii (*Die afrikänischen Hirten völker*), 1940; LE ROY, Mgr. A., *La Religion des Primitifs*, 7th ed., Paris, 1925 (translation of 1st ed., *The Religion of the Primitives*, London, 1923); SMITH, Edwin W., *African Ideas of God*, London, 1950; cf. also PETTAZZONI, R., *Miti e Leggende*, vol. i (*Africa, Australia*), Turin, 1948, pp. 3–401.

SPIETH, J., *Die Religion der Eweer*, Göttingen and Leipzig, 1911; HOLLIS, A. C., *The Masai*, Oxford, 1905, pp. 364 ff.; SMITH, E. W. and DALE, A. M., *The Ila-speaking Peoples of Northern Rhodesia*, London, 1920, vol. ii, pp. 198 ff.; TAUXIER, L., *La Religion Bambara*, Paris, 1927, pp. 173 ff.

On Nzambe (and *contra* Pettazzoni's statement, p. 210, that he is indifferent to human affairs), see also VAN WING, J., " L'Etre suprême des Bakongo ", *RSR*, vol. x, pp. 170–81.

On the African Pygmies: TRILLES, H., *Les Pygmées de la forêt equatoriale*, Paris, 1932; id., *L'Ame du Pygmée d'Afrique*, Paris, 1945; IMMEN-

ROTH, W., *Kultur u. Umwelt der Kleinwuchsigen in Afrika*, Leipzig, 1933, particularly pp. 153 ff.; SCHEBESTA, P., *Les Pygmées*, pp. 13 ff.

WANGER, W., in " The Zulu Notion of God ", *APS*, 1925, pp. 574 ff., suggests that the name of Unkulunkulu can be traced to a Sumerian proto-type, AN-gal-gal (the Zulu *un* being the same as the Sumerian *an*, *anu*, " heaven ", " God in heaven "). WIDENGREN, George (*Hochgottglaube im Alten Iran*, Uppsala-Leipzig, 1938, pp. 5–93), gives a wealth of material about African sky gods and compares them with the sky gods of Iran, pp. 394–5.

On the religions of Indonesia and Melanesia : PETTAZZONI, R., *Dio*, vol. i, pp. 109–85; CODRINGTON, R. H., *The Melanesians*, Oxford, 1891, pp. 116 ff.; LANG, Andrew, *The Making of Religion*, 3rd ed., 1909, pp. 200 ff.; DIXON, Roland B., *Oceanic Mythology*, Boston, 1916, *passim*; SCHARER, H., *Der Gottesidee der Ngadju Dajak in Süd-Borneo,* Leiden, 1946, pp. 15 ff., 175 ff.

On Tangaroa : cf. CRAIGHILL HANDY, E. S., *Polynesian Religion*, Honolulu, 1927, pp. 144 ff., and *passim*; WILLIAMSON, R. W., *Religious and Cosmic Beliefs of Central Polynesia*, Cambridge, 1933.

On Yelafaz : WALLESER, Sixtus, " Religiöse Anschauungen und Ge-bräuche der Bewohner von Jap, Deutsche Südsee ", *APS*, 1913, vol. viii, pp. 617, 629, etc., particularly pp. 613 ff.

On the worship and myths of Io : see HANDY, E. S. C., *Polynesian Religion*, pp. 36 ff.; id., " The Hawaiian Cult of Io ", *JPS*, 1941, vol. l, no. 3.

On the mythical pair, Heaven and Earth, see NUMAZAWA, F. Kiichi, *Die Weltanfänge in der japanischen Mythologie*, I ucerne, 1946; see also the bibliographies following Chapter VII.

On the sky gods of North America : PETTAZZONI, R., *Dio*, vol. i, pp. 260–73; DANGEL, R., " Tirawa, der höchste Gott der Pawnee ", *AFRW*, 1929, pp. 113–44; SCHMIDT, W., *Ursprung*, vol. ii, pp. 21–326 (the tribes of Central California), pp. 328–90 (the Indians of the North-West), pp. 391–672 (the Algonquins); vol. v, 1937, pp. 1–773, vol. vi, *passim*. General study by the same author : *High Gods in North America*, Oxford, 1933.

On the Supreme Divinities of South America : PETTAZZONI, R., *Dio*, vol. i, pp. 324–48 (*contra*: KOPPERS, W., *Unter Feuerland-Indianern*, Stuttgart, 1924, pp. 139–57); SCHMIDT, W., *Ursprung*, vol. ii, pp. 873–1033 (on the Indians of Tierra del Fuego, with particular reference to the researches of Gusinde and Koppers), vi, *passim*; GUSINDE, M., *Die Feuerland-Indianer*, vol. i, (*Die Selk'nam*), Mödling bei Wien, 1931, vol. ii (*Die Yamana*), Mödling bei Wien, 1937; KOPPERS, W., " Sur l'origine de l'idée de Dieu. A propos de la croyance en Dieu chez les Indiens de la Terre de Feu ", *NV*, Fribourg, 1943, pp. 260–91; id., " Die Erst-besiedlung Amerikas im Lichte der Feuerland-Forschungen ", *Bull. d. Schweizerischen Gesellschaft f. Anthropologie u. Ethnologie*, 1944–5, vol. xxi, pp. 1–15.

Vols. ii, v and vi of *Ursprung der Gottesidee* have a good bibliography, and an enormous analytical collection of religious material relating to the primitive beliefs of both Americas. Cf. *Ursprung*, vol. v, pp. 522 ff., 716 ff.; vol. vi, 1935, pp. 520 ff. But see also COOPER, J. M., " The

Northern Algonquin Supreme Being ", *Primitive Man*, 1933, vol. vi, pp. 41–112, and PETTAZZONI, R., *Miti e Leggende*, vol. iii (*America Setten-trionale*), Turin, 1953, particularly pp. 337 ff.

On the religions of the Arctic civilizations: general study, SCHMIDT, W., *Ursprung*, vol. iii, pp. 331–64; vol. vi, pp. 70–5, 274–81, 444–54; vol. vii, pp. 609–701: GAHS, A., " Kopf-, Schädel- und Langknochen-opfer bei Rentiervölkern ", *W. Schmidt-Festschrift*, Vienna, 1928, pp. 231–68.

On the Samoyeds: CASTREN, A., *Reisen im Norden in den Jahren 1838–1844*, Leipzig, 1953, pp. 229–33; LEHTISALO, T., " Entwurf einer Mythologie der Jurak-Samoyeden ", *Mémoires de la Soc. Finno-Ougrienne*, 1924, vol. liii; DONNER, K., *Bei den Samojeden in Sibirien*, Stuttgart, 1926; for exposition, general study and supplementary documentation, see SCHMIDT, W., *Urpsrung*, vol. iii, pp. 340–84.

The Koryaks: JOCHELSON, W., *The Koryak*, Leiden-New York, 1905–8, 2 vols.; Vol. VI of the Jesup North Pacific Expedition; CZAPLICKA, A., *Aboriginal Siberia. A Study in Social Anthropology*, Oxford, 1914, particularly pp. 261–9, 294–6; SCHMIDT, W., *Ursprung*, vol. iii, pp. 387–426.

The Ainu: BATCHELOR, J., *The Ainu and their Folk-lore*, London, 1901; LOWENTHAL, J., " Zum Ainu-Problem ", *MAGW*, 1930, vol. lx, pp. 13–19; STERNBERG, L., " The Ainu Problem ", *APS*, 1929, vol. xxiv, pp. 755–801 ; SCHMIDT, W., *Ursprung*, vol. iii, pp. 427–92; cf. also OHM, Thomas, " Die Himmelsverehrung der Koreaner ", *APS*, 1920–1, vols. xxxv–xxxvi, pp. 830–40.

The Eskimos: BOAS, F., *The Central Esquimo*, 6th Annual Report of the Bureau of American Ethnology, 1884–5, Washington, 1888, pp. 409–670; RASMUSSEN, Knud, *Intellectual Culture of the Iglulik Eskimos*, Copenhagen, 1930; id., *Intellectual Culture of the Caribou Eskimos*, Copenhagen, 1931; BIRKET-SMITH, F., " Über der Herkunft der Eskimo und ihre Stellung in der zirkumpolaren Kulturentwicklung ", *APS*, 1930, vol. xxv, pp. 1–23; THALBITZER, W., " Die kultischen Gottheiten der Eskimos ", *AFRW*, 1928, vol. xxvi, pp. 364–430; SCHMIDT, W., *Ursprung*, vol. iii, pp. 493–526.

The Ugrians and Turco-Mongols: KARJALAINEN, K. F., *Die Religion der Jugra-Völker*, vols. i–iii, Porvoo-Helsinki, 1921, 1922, 1927 (*FFC*, nos. 41, 44, 63); HOLMBERG-HARVA, Uno, *Die Religion der Tcheremissen*, Porvoo, 1926 (*FFC*, no. 61); id., *Siberian Mythology* (*The Mythology of all Races*, vol. iv, Boston, 1927); id., *Die religiösen Vorstellungen der altaischen Völker*, Helsinki, 1939 (*FFC*, no. 125); SCHMIDT, W., " Das Himmelsopfer bei den innerasiatischen Pferdezüchter Völkern ", *ES*, 1942, vol. vii, pp. 127–48; id., *Ursprung*, vol. ix, 1949, pp. 3–67 (Proto-Turks), 71–454 (Altai Tatars), 457–794 (Abakhan Tatars), vol. x, 1952, pp. 1–138 (Mongols), 139–470 (Buriats), 503–674 (Tunguses), 675–758 (Yukaghirs); vol. xi, 1954, pp. 1–398, 565–707 (Yakuts), 399–467 (Kara-gasses and Soyots), 469–567, 683–712 (Yenissei). Schmidt has given a synthesis of the religions of the pastoral peoples of Central Asia in vol. xi, pp. 565–704, and vol. xii, pp. 1–613. HAECKEL, Joseph, " Idolkult und Dual-system bei den Uiguren. Zum Problem des eurasiatischen Totemismus ", *AFV*, Vienna, 1947, vol. i, pp. 95–163.

On Ulgen: RADLOFF, W., *Proben der Völksliteratur der türkischen Stämme*, St. Petersburg, 1866, vol. i, pp. 147 ff.; ELIADE, M., *Le Cha-manisme*, pp. 175 ff.; SCHMIDT, W., *Ursprung*, vol. ix, pp. 172–215.

On the lunar elements in Ulgen (and his double, Erlik), cf. KOPPERS, W., " Pferdeopfer und Pferdekult der Indogermanen ", *WBKL*, Salzburg-Leipzig, 1936, vol. iv, pp. 279–412, pp. 396 ff.; HAECKEL, J., op. cit., pp. 142 ff.

On the cult of Tenre among the nomads of Kan-su: cf. MATHIAS, P., " Uiguren und ihre neuentdeckten Nachkommen ", *APS*, 1940–1, vols. xxxv-xxxvi, pp. 78–99, particularly pp. 89 ff. (Tenre is known as *Xan Tenre*, " the emperor of heaven ", or simply *tenre*, " heaven ". He is the creator of the universe, of life, of man, p. 89. Sacrifices, are offered to him, p. 90.)

On the Supreme Being of the sky among the Mo-so Lolos and the Tai: cf. Luigi Vannicelli, *La Religione dei Lolo*, Milan, 1944.

PALLISEN, N., " Die alte Religion des mongolischen volkes während der Herrschaft der Tschingisiden ", *Micro-Bibliotheca Anthropos*, Freiburg, 1953, vol. vii.

DONNER, Kai, " Über soghdisch nom ' Gesetz ' und samojedisch nom ' Himmel, Gott ' ", *SO*, Helsinki, 1925, vol. i, pp. 1–6. But see also SCHMIDT, W., *Ursprung*, vol. iii, pp. 505 ff.; ELIADE, M., *Le Chamanisme*, pp. 206 ff.

The Chinese sky god: DE GROOT, J. J. M., *The Religion of the Chinese*, New York, 1910, pp. 102 ff.; GRANET, Marcel, *La Religion des Chinois*, Paris, 1922, pp. 49 ff. According to E. Chavannes, Chang-ti, the " Supreme Lord " and T'ien, the " Sky " meant at first two distinct divine beings (rather like Ouranos and Zeus); cf. " Le Dieu du sol dans l'ancienne religion chinoise ", *RHR*, 1901, vol. xliii, pp. 125–246. On Chang-ti, cf. also SÖDERBLOM, N., *Das Werden des Gottesglaubens*, Leipzig, 1916, pp. 224 ff., which gives an excellent presentation of the non-naturist traits of the ancient Chinese god. See EBERHARD, W., *APS*, 1942–5, vols. xxxvii-xl, 977, for recent works on the subject; PETTAZZONI, *L'onniscienza di Dio*, Turin, 1955, pp. 400 ff.

On the prehistoric relations between the Proto-Turks and the Near East: EBERT, Max, *Reallexikon der Vorgeschichte*, vol. xiii, pp. 60 ff.; HERMES, G., " Das gezähmte Pferd im alten Orient ", *APS*, 1936, vol. xxxi, pp. 364–94; AMSCHLER, W., " Die ältesten Funde des Hauspferdes ", *WBKL*, vol. iv, pp. 498–516; HERZFELD, E., " Völker und Kultur-zusammenhänge im Alten Orient ", *DF*, Berlin, 1928, vol. v, pp. 33–67, particularly pp. 39 ff.; KOPPERS, W., " Urtürkentum und Urindogermanentum im Lichte der völkerkundlichen Universalsgechichte ", *Belleten*, den ayri basim, Istanbul, 1941, no. 20, pp. 481–525, pp. 488 ff. But cf. also A. M. Tallgren, " The Copper Idols from Galich and their Relatives ", *SO*, 1925, vol. i, pp. 312–41.

On the relations between the Proto-Turks and Indo-Europeans: this is discussed in the two full studies by KOPPERS, " Die Indogermanenfrage im Lichte der historischen Völkerkunde ", *APS*, 1935, vol. xxx, pp. 1–31, particularly pp. 10 ff.; and " Urtürkentum ", *passim*. Along the same lines, SCHRADER, O., *Reallexikon der indogermanischen Altertumskunde*, 2nd ed., Berlin-Leipzig, 1917-29, vol. ii, p. 24. Cf. also, NEHRING, Alfons, " Studien zur indogermanischen Kultur und Urheimat ", *WBKL*, vol. iv, pp. 9–229, particularly pp. 13 ff., 93 ff.; against his view, HAUER, J. W., " Zum gegenwärtigen Stand der Indogermanenfrage ", *AFRW*, 1939, vol. xxxvi, pp. 1–63, particularly pp. 14 ff. See also SCHMIDT, W., *Rassen und Völker in Vorgeschichte des Abendlandes*, vol. ii, Lucerne, 1946, pp. 171 ff., 192 ff., 208 ff.

The Indo-Europeans (protohistory, linguistics, cultures): HIRT, H., *Die Indogermanen*, Strasbourg, 1905–7, vols. i–ii; SCHRADER, O., *Reallexikon*; CHILDE, C. Gordon, *The Aryans*, London, 1926; *Germanen u. Indogermanen. Festschrift für Hermann Hirt*, Heidelberg, 1932–4, vols. i–ii; KOPPERS, W., " Indogermanenfrage "; NEHRING, A., " Studien zur indogermanischen Kultur und Urheimat "; HAUER, J. W., " Zum Gegenwärtigen Stand "; DUMEZIL, G., " Le nom des ' Arya ' ", *RHR*, 1941, no. 363, pp. 36–59.

On the divinity of the sky among the Indo-Aryans (Dieus, etc.): VON SCHRÖDER, L., *Arische Religion; I; Einleitung. Der Altarische Himmelsgott*, Leipzig, 1914; KRETSCHMER, P., *Einleitung in die Geschichte der griechischen Sprache*, Gottingen, 1896, pp. 77 ff.; FEIST, S., *Kultur, Ausbreitung und Herkunft der Indogermanen*, Berlin, 1913, pp. 319 ff.; WILKE, Georg, " Die Religion der Indogermanen in archäologischer Betrachtung", *MB*, Leipzig, 1923, no. 31, pp. 107 ff.; KOPPERS, W., " Die Religion der Indogermanen in ihren kulturhistorischen Beziehungen ", *APS*, 1921, vol. xxiv, pp. 1073–89; id., " Indogermanenfrage ", pp. 11 ff., 16 ff.; HOPKINS, S. Sturtevant, *Indo-European Deiwos and Related Words*, Philadelphia, 1932; NEHRING, A., " Studien ", pp. 195 ff.; KRETSCHMER, P., " Dyaus, Zeus, Diespiter und die Abstrakta im indogermanischen ", *GLA*, 1924, vol. xiii, pp. 101–14.

On Vedic India: for the texts, translations and an immense critical bibliography, see RENOU, L., *Bibliographie védique*, Paris, 1931, particularly pp. 170 ff. It is always useful to read the three volumes A. BERGAIGNE has devoted to *La Religion védique d'après les hymnes du Rig Veda*, Paris, 1878–83. There are exhaustive studies of the myths and beliefs in HILLEBRANDT, A., *Vedische Mythologie*, 2nd ed., Breslau, 1927–9, vols. i–ii, and KEITH, A. B., *The Religion and Philosophy of the Veda and Upanishads*, Harvard Oriental Series, nos. 21–2, Cambridge, Mass., 1925, 2 vols.

On the Aryan gods of the Mitani: cf. the present position of the question and an interpretative essay along the lines of a functional division into three, in DUMEZIL, G., *Naissance d'archanges*, Paris, 1945, pp. 15 ff.

On Varuṇa: GUNTERT, H., *Der arische Weltkönig und Heiland*, Halle, 1923, pp. 97 ff.; DUMEZIL, G., *Ouranos-Varuna*, Paris, 1934; id., *Mitra-Varuna*, Paris, 1940; Cf. GEIGER, B., *Die Amesa Spentas*, Vienna, 1916; LEVI, Sylvain, *La Doctrine du sacrifice dans les Brahmanas*, Paris, 1898; HOPKINS, E. W., *Epic Mythology*, Strasbourg, 1920. Kretschmer believes erroneously that Varuṇa came from the Hittite Arunash and was coloured with Asian and Babylonian ideas; cf. " Varuṇa und die Urgeschichte der Inder ", *WZKM*, vol. xxxiii, pp. 1 ff. On Varuṇa as " binder ", cf. ELIADE, M., " Les Dieux lieurs et le symbolisme des nœuds ", *RHR*, 1947–8, vol. cxxxiv, pp. 5–36; cf. *Images et Symboles*, Paris, 1952, ch. iii.

The Indo-European myth of a sky of stone uniting itself to the earth, which H. REICHELT has pieced together in " Der steinerne Himmel ", *IGF*, 1913, vol. xxxii, pp. 23–57, is not supported by the texts: cf. BENVENISTE and RENOU, *Vrtra and Vrthragna*, Paris, 1935, p. 191, n. 3.

On Iran: for texts, general study, criticism and bibliography, see PETTAZZONI, *La Religione di Zarathustra*, Bologna, 1920; GRAY, Louis H.,

The Foundations of the Iranian Religions, Bombay, Cama Oriental Institute, 1929; BENVENISTE, E., *The Persian Religion According to the Chief.Greek Texts*, Paris, 1929; BENVENISTE and RENOU, *Vrtra and Vrthragna*; NYBERG, H. S., " Questions de cosmogonie et de cosmologie mazdéennes ", *JA*, April–June 1929, pp. 193–310; July-Sept. 1931, pp. 1–124; Oct-Dec. 1931, pp. 193–244; id., *Die Religionen des alten Iran*, trans. Schaeder, Leipzig, 1938; WIDENGREN, Georg, *Hochgottglaube im Alten Iran*, Uppsala, 1938; DUMEZIL, G., *Naissance d'archanges*.

On Varuṇa and Ahura-Mazda: OLDENBERG, " Varuṇa und die Adityas ", *ZDMG*, 1896, vol. l, pp. 43 ff.; MEILLET, A., *La Religion indo-européenne*, reprinted in *Linguistique historique et linguistique générale*, Paris, 1921, pp. 323 ff.; Ahura-Mithra: DUMEZIL, G., *Mitra-Varuna*, pp. 59 ff.; *Naissance d'archanges*, pp. 30 ff.; HERTEL, J., *Die Sonne und Mitra im Awesta*, Leipzig, 1927; Cf. PAUL, Otto, " Zur Geschichte der iranischen Religionen ", *AFRW*, 1940, vol. xxxv, pp. 215–34, which disagrees with Nyberg; and similarly, WUST, W., ib., pp. 234–49. See also HEIMANN, Betty, *Varuna-Rta-Karma*, in *Festgabe H. Jacobi*, pp. 210–14.

On the Greek material there is one book which is as good as an entire library: COOK, A. B., *Zeus. A Study in Ancient Religion*, Cambridge, 1914–40, 5 vols. Cf. for a general picture, NILSSON, Martin P., *Geschichte der griechischen Religion*, vol. i, Munich, 1941; On Zeus as father of the gods, cf. CALHOUN, G., " Zeus the Father in Homer ", *TAAP*, 1935, vol. lxvi; NILSSON, M. P., " Vater Zeus ", *AFRW*, 1938, vol. xxxv, pp. 156 ff. On the myth of Ouranos: DUMEZIL, G., *Ouranos-Varuna*; STAUDACHER, W., *Die Trennung von Himmel u. Erde. Ein vorgriechischer Schöpfungmythus bei Hesiod und den Orphikern*, Tübingen, 1942.

On Rome, cf. DUMEZIL, *Jupiter, Mars, Quirinus*, Paris, 1941 and *Naissance de Rome*, Paris, 1944, ch. i; KOCH, Carl, *Der römische Juppiter*, Frankfurt a. M., 1937.

A general study of the ancient Germanic religions with a large critical bibliography has been given us by DE VRIES, Jan, *Altgermanische Religionsgeschichte*, vols. i–ii, Berlin and Leipzig, 1935, 1937. There are admirable analyses of the myths of sovereignty and the warrior myths in DUMEZIL's little book, *Mythes et dieux des Germains*, Paris, 1939. See also TONNELAT, Ernst, in " Les Religions des Celtes, des Germains et des anciens Slaves ", *MA*, Paris, 1948, vol. iii, pp. 323 ff. You will find a penetrating critique of the various modern trends in interpreting Germanic religions and a constructive attempt to integrate the study of those religions in the " culture-historical " method of the Viennese school in the two studies by CLOSS, Alois, " Neue Problemstellungen in der germanischen Religionsgeschichte ", *APS*, 1934, vol. xxix, pp. 477–96, and " Die Religion des Semnonenstammes ", *WBKL*, vol. iv, pp. 448–673; id., " Die Religion der Germanen in ethnologischen Sicht " in *Christus und die Religionen der Erde*, Vienna, 1951, vol. ii, pp. 267–365. Cf. also Hillebrecht HOMMEL, " Die Hauptgottheiten der Germanen bei Tacitus ", *AFRW*, vol. xxxvii, pp. 144 ff.; MUCH, R., *Die Germania des Tacitus*, Heidelberg, 1937; PETTAZZONI, R., " Regnator Omnium Deus ", *SMSR*, 1943–6, vols. xix–xx, pp. 142–56; HOFLER, Otto, *Germanische Sakralkönigtum*, vol. i, Tübingen, Münster, Cologne, 1952.

On Taranis, cf. CLEMEN, Carl, " Die Religion der Kelten ", *AFRW*, 1941, vol. xxxvii, p. 122; LAMBRECHTS, P., *Contributions à l'étude des divinités celtiques*, Bruges, 1942, pp. 54 ff.

On Perun : MANSIKKA, V. J., *Die Religion der Ostslavem*, vol. i, Helsinki, 1922 (*FFC*, no. 43, pp. 30–4, 54–7, 60–5, 379 ff.); BRÜCKNER, A., *Mitologia slava*, Bologna, 1923, pp. 58 ff. (He derives Perkun-Perun from the word for an oak tree); NIEDERLE, L., *Manuel de l'antiquité slave*, Paris, 1926, vol. ii, pp. 138 ff.; UNBEGAUN, B. O., " Les Religions des Celtes, des Germains, et des anciens Slaves ", *MA*, 1948, pp. 405–7.

Cf. also KRAPPE, A. H., " Les Péléiades ", *RAR*, 1932, vol. xxxvi, pp. 77 ff.; HARRISON, Jane, *Themis*, 2nd ed., Cambridge, 1927, pp. 94 ff.

On Indra, see also HOPKINS, J. Washburn, " Indra as God of Fertility ", *JAOS*, vol. xxxvi, pp. 242–68; CHARPENTIER, Jarl, " Indra. Ein Versuch die Aufklärung ", *MO*, Uppsala, 1931, vol. xxv, pp. 1–28; BENVENISTE and RENOU, *Vrtra et Vrthragua*, Paris, 1935, pp. 184 ff. Kretschmer (*Kleinasiatische Forschungen*, 1929, vol. i, pp. 297 ff.) thought he had discovered in the Hittite *innara* the original of the Indo-Iranian Indra, but Sommer has shown that this was in fact a Hittite goddess, Inara (with one " n "; cf. BENVENISTE and RENOU, p. 186). PRZYLUSKI, J. (" Inara and Indra ", *RHA*, vol. xxxvi, pp. 142–6) thinks that " the Vedic Indra and the Hittite Innara might both belong to a series of bisexual divinities, which were much the same as the Great Goddesses; the hermaphroditic Venus, *Fortuna barbata*, Zervan, Kala " (p. 146). But this is too superficial a view; it is not certain that the Great Goddess " was replaced by a Great God in the pantheons of the Semitic and Indo-European races " (p. 142); divine androgyny is not always a secondary phenomenon (cf. p. 160); ritual hermaphroditism cannot be explained in terms of hybrid cults, half way between worshipping a Great Goddess and a Great God.

Cf. also MACHEK, V., " Name und Herkunst des Gottes Indra ". *AOI*, 1941, vol. xii, nos. 3–4; DUMEZIL, G., *Tarpeia*, 1947, pp. 117 ff. There are copious references about Indra as god of fertility in MEYER, J. J., *Trilogie altindischer Mächte und Feste der Vegetation*, Zürich-Leipzig, 1937, 3 vols., particularly vol. iii, pp. 164 ff.

On sky gods in Mesopotamian religions, cf. the general works— MEISSNER, B., *Babylonien und Assyrien*, vols. i–ii, Heidelberg,1920–5; DHORME, E., *Choix de textes religieux assyro-babyloniens*, Paris, 1907; id., *La Religion assyro-babylonienne*, Paris, 1940; ibid., " Les religions de Babylonie et d'Assyrie ", *MA*, vol. ii, Paris, 1945 (this is the best study yet produced); FURLANI, Giuseppe, *La Religione Babilonese-Assira*, 2 vols., Bologna, 1928–9, which gives an exhaustive bibliography; JEAN, Charles, *La Religion sumérienne d'après les documents sumériens antérieurs à la dynastie d'Isin*, Paris, 1931; FURLANI, G., *La Religione degli Hittiti*, Bologna, 1936; DUSSAUD, René, " Les Religions des Hittites et des Hourrites, des Phéniciens et des Syriens ", *MA*, vol. ii, pp. 333–414.

Cf. also WARD, W. H. ,*The Seal Cylinders of Western Asia*, Washington, 1910; GOTZE, A., *Kleinasien*, in the series *Kulturgeschichte des Alten Orients*, vol. iii, 1, Munich, 1933.

On the similar elements to be found among the pre-Semites and pre-Indo-Europeans of Asia Minor and the Aegean, and the pre-Aryan peoples of the Indus, the following works by B. HROZNY are thought-provoking though not always convincing: *Die älteste Völkerwanderung u. die proto-indische Zivilisation*, Prague, 1939; *Die älteste Geschichte Vorderasiens*,

Prague, 1940, and the studies published in *AOI*, 1941 and onwards; also *Histoire de l'Asie Ancienne, de l'Inde, et de la Crète*, Paris, 1946.

On storm gods in the near East and their relations with the bull, the Great Mother and so forth, cf. MALTEN, L., " Der Stier in Kult und mythischen Bild ", *JDAI*, 1928, vol. lxiii, pp. 90–139; OTTO, E., *Beiträge zur Geschichte des Stierkultus in Aegypten*, Leipzig, 1938; AUTRAN, C., *La Préhistoire du Christianisme*, vol. i, Paris, 1941, pp. 39 ff.; NAMITOK, A., " Zeus Osogoa ", *RHR*, 1941, no. 364, pp. 97–109, particularly p. 102, n. 4, and 103, n. 6 (concerning the recent discoveries of the images of bulls in India, etc.); DHORME, E., *Les Religions de Babylonie*, pp. 96 ff.; SCHLOBIES, H., *Der akkadische Wettergott in Mesopotamien*, Leipzig, 1925; FURLANI, G., " La Frusta di Adad ", *Rendiconti d. Accad. dei Lincei, Classa di Scienze Morali*, 1932, pp. 574–86; TALLQUIST, K., *Akkadische Götterepitheta*, Helsinki, 1938, pp. 246 ff.; DUSSAUD, René, " La Mythologie phénicienne d'après les tablettes de Ras Shamra ", *RHR*, 1931, vol. civ, pp. 353–408; id., " Le Sanctuaire et les dieux phéniciens de Ras Shamra ", *RHR*, 1932, vol. cv, pp. 245–302; id., " Le Vrai Nom de Ba'al ", *RHR*, 1936, vol. cxiii, pp. 5–20; id., *Les Découvertes de Ras Shamra et l'Ancien Testament*, 2nd ed., Paris, 1941; id., " Peut-on identifier l'Apollon de Hierapolis ? ", *RHR*, 1942–3, no. 368, pp. 128–49, particularly pp. 138 ff.; NIELSON, Ditlef, *Ras Shamra Mythologie und biblische Theologie*, Leipzig, 1936; NAMITOK, A., " Le Nom du dieu de l'orage chez les Hittites et les Kassites ", *RHR*, July–Aug., 1939, pp. 21 ff.; ENGNELL, Ivan, *Studies in Divine Kingship in the Ancient Near East*, Uppsala, 1943, p. 213. The iconography of Hadad and Teshub: GRESSMANN, H., *Altorientalische Bilder zum Alten Testament*, 2nd ed., Berlin-Leipzig, 1926-7, nos. 317, 326, 330, 335, 339, 350, 345; CONTENAU, G., *Manuel d'archéologie orientale*, Paris, 1927– , vol. i, p. 206, fig. 129; vol. ii, p. 942; DEMIRCIOGLU, H., *Der Gott auf dem Stier. Geschichte eines religiösen Bildtypus*, Berlin, 1936.

On Jupiter Dolichenus, COOK, A. B., *Zeus*, vol. i, 1914, pp. 605–63; CUMONT, F., *Etudes Syriennes*, Paris, 1917, pp. 173–202; KAN, A. H., *Juppiter Dolichenus*, Lede, 1943.

On Egypt: cf. RUSCH, A., *Die Entwicklung der Himmelsgott in Nut zu einer Todesgottheit*, Leipzig, 1922; WAINWRIGHT, G. A., *The Sky-Religion in Egypt*, Cambridge, 1938; AUTRAN, C., *La Flotte à l'enseigne du poisson*, Paris, 1938; JUNKER, H., *Die Götterlehre vom Memphis*, Berlin, 1940, pp. 25 ff. on the sky god Our (*wr*).

On Thunder as the Supreme Being among North American tribes, SCHMIDT, *Ursprung*, vol. ii, pp. 55, 63, 71, 228 ff.; the thunder-bird in North American mythology, id., pp. 635 ff.; in African mythology, FRAZER, *The Worship of Nature*, p. 155; cf. HARRIS, Rendel, *Boanerges*, Cambridge, 1913, pp. 13 ff.; STITH THOMPSON, *Motif-Index of Folk-literature*, Helsinki, vol. i, 1932, pp. 80 ff.; TALLQUIST, Knut, " Himmels-gegenden und Winde. Eine semasiologische Studie ", *SO*, Helsinki, 1933, vol. ii.

F. Kern attempts to analyse the mythological process whereby the sky god of shepherd peoples becomes a god of storm in " Die Welt, worin die Griechen traten ", *APS*, 1929, vol. xxiv, pp. 167–219, particularly pp. 179 ff. Schmidt traces the same process (which he calls the hypostasis of a god of the universe into a god of the atmosphere) among the various groups of Eskimos (*Ursprung*, vol. iii, p. 505).

On the sovereignty of Yahweh, there is a rich bibliography in GRABAR'S "Le Thème religieux des fresques de la synagogue de Doura ", *RHR*, 1941, no. 363, p. 27, n. 1. On Yahweh's atmospheric epiphanies cf. SOMMER, A. Dupont, "Nubes tenebrosa et illuminans noctem ", *RHR*, 1942-3, no. 365, pp. 5-31; on the "glory" of Yahweh, cf. pp. 18 ff. and n. 1.

For material and bibliography on the myth of creation among the Iranians and the Germans: CHRISTENSEN, A., *Le Premier homme et le premier roi dans l'histoire légendaire des Iraniens*, Uppsala, 1918, 1931, 2 vols.; GÜNTERT, H., "Der arische Weltkönig und Heiland ", and SCHRÖDER, F. R., "Germanische Schöpfungsmythen ", *GRM*, 1931, vol. xix, pp. 1-26, and 81-99; BORTZLER, F., "Ymir. Ein Beitrag zu den Eddischen Weltschöpfungsvorstellungen ", *AFRW*, 1936, vol. xxxiii, nos. 3-4; KOPPERS, W., "Das magische Weltschöpfungsmysterium bei den Indogermanen ", *Van Ginneken-Festschrift*, Paris, 1937, pp. 149-55.

Of the wealth of bibliography on the *Aśvamedha*, the sacrificing of horses, and the Indo-European divinities that are either equine in form or ride horses, I will mention only: DUMONT, P., *L'Açvamedha*, Paris, 1927; NEGELEIN, J. von, *Das Pferd im arischen Altertum*, Königsberg i. Pr., 1903; MALTEN, L., "Das Pferd im Totenglauben ", *JKDAI*, Berlin, 1914, vol. xxix, pp. 179-256; HINDRINGER, R., *Weiheross und Rossweihe*, Munich, 1932; KOPPERS, W., "Pferdeopfer und Pferdekult der Indogermanen ", *WBKL*, 1935, pp. 279-411; BLEICHSTEINER, R., "Rossweihe u. Pferderennen im Totenkult der Kaukasischen Völker ", *WBKL*, 1935, pp. 413-95; against Koppers' thesis, cf. HAUER, *AFRW*, 1939, vol. xxxvi, pp. 23 ff.; WIESNER, L., "Fahren und Reiten in Alteuropa und im Alten Orient ", *AOR*, 1939, xxxviii, nos. 3-4; id., "Fahrende und Reisende Götter ", *AFRW*, 1941, vol. xxxvii, pp. 36-46; cf. SCHMIDT, W., *Rassen und Völker*, Lucerne, 1946-9, vol. ii, pp. 102 ff.

Cf. also the works already mentioned by HERMES, G., "Das gezähmte Pferd im neolitischen u. Frühbronzezeitlichen Europa ", *APS*, 1935, vol. xxx, pp. 805-23; 1936, vol. xxxi, pp. 115-29; id., "Das gezähmte Pferd im alten Orient ", *APS*, 1936, vol. xxxi, pp. 364-94; FLOR, F., "Das Pferd und seine kulturgeschichtliche Bedeutung ", *Wiener kulturhistorische Studien*, 1930, vol. i. For the cult of horses in Asia Minor, see ROSTOVTZEFF, *Syria*, vol. xii, pp. 48 ff. And for China and Japan, ERKES, E., "Das Pferd im alten China ", *TP*, 1940-1, vol. xxxvi; VAN GULIK, R. H., *Hayagriva. The Mantrayanic Aspects of the Horse Cult in China and Japan*, Leiden, 1935, particularly pp. 41 ff.

On the Aśvins, the Dioscuri, the Gemini, etc.: GÜNTERT, H., *Der arische Weltkönig*, pp. 253 ff.; HARRIS, Rendel, *The Cult of the Heavenly Twins*, Cambridge, 1906; EITREM, S., *Die göttlichen Zwillinge bei den Griechen*, Christiania, 1902; COOK, A. B., *Zeus*, vol. ii, pp. 1003 ff.; CHAPOUTHIER, F., *Les Dioscures au service d'une déesse*, Paris, 1935; KEITH, A. B., *Indian Mythology*, Boston, 1917, pp. 30 ff.; KRAPPE, A. H., *Mythologie universelle*, pp. 53-100; id., "La légende des Harlungen " in *Etudes de mythologie et de folklore germaniques*, Paris, 1928, pp. 137-74; STERNBERG, "Der antike Zwillingskult im lichte der Ethnologie ", *ZFE*, 1929, vol. lxi, pp. 152-200; id., "Der Zwillingskult in China u. die indischen Einflüsse ", *Baessler Archiv*, 1929, vol. xiii, pp. 31-46; NEGELEIN,

J. von, " Die aberglaubische Bedeutung der Zwillingsgeburt ", *AFRW*, 1906, vol. v, pp. 271–3; VAN GENNEP, A., *Tabou et totemisme à Madagascar*, Paris, 1911, p. 176.

On the sacred meaning and symbolism of the mountain, the " centre ", etc.: AUTRAN, C., *La Flotte à l'enseigne du poisson*, pp. 31 ff.; DUSSAUD, R., *Découvertes de Ras Shamra*, p. 100; JEREMIAS, A., *Handbuch der altorientalischen Geisteskultur*, 2nd ed., Berlin, 1929, pp. 130 ff.; ELIADE, M., *Cosmologie si alchimie babiloniana*, Bucharest, 1937, pp. 26 ff.; id., *Le Chamanisme et les techniques archaïques de l'extase*, Paris, 1951, pp. 235 ff.; id., *Images et Symboles*, Paris, 1952, ch. i; KIRFEL, W., *Die Kosmographie der Inder*, Bonn-Leipzig, 1920; HOLMBERG-HARVA, Uno, " Der Baum des Lebens ", *Annales Academicæ Scientiarum Fennicæ*, Helsinki, 1923, pp. 33 ff.; BURROWS, E., " Some Cosmological Patterns in Babylonian Religion ", in HOOKE, S. H., *The Labyrinth*, London, 1935, pp. 43 ff.; DOMBART, T., *Der Sakralturm: I: Ziqqurat*, Munich; id., *Der babylonische Turm*, Leipzig, 1930; JASTROW, M., " Sumerian and Akkadian Views of Beginnings ", *JAOS*, 1917, vol. xxxvi, pp. 274–99; VAN BUREN, E. Douglas, " Mountain Gods ", *ORA*, Rome, 1943, vol. xii, nos. 1–2.

On ascension symbolism (steps, stairs, etc.):

Egypt: BUDGE, Wallis, *From Fetish to God in Ancient Egypt*, Oxford, 1934, p. 346; id., *The Mummy*, 2nd ed., Cambridge, 1925, pp. 324, 327; WEILL, R., *Le Champ des roseaux et le champ des offrandes dans la religion funéraire et la religion générale*, Paris, 1936; MULLER, W. Max, *Egyptian Mythology*, Boston, 1918, p. 176; ELIADE, M., *Le Chamanisme*, pp. 415 ff.

India: COOMARASWAMY, A., " Svayamātr̥ṇṇā-Janua Coeli ", *CZ*, 1939, vol. ii, pp. 1–51; ELIADE, M., " Durohana and the Waking Dream ", *Art and Thought, A Volume in Honour of the late Dr. Ananda K. Coomaraswamy*, London, 1947, pp. 209 ff.

Polynesia: GREY, Sir George, *Polynesian Mythology and Ancient Traditional History of the New Zealanders* (a reissue), Auckland, 1929, pp. 42 ff.; CHADWICK, H. M. and N. K., *The Growth of Literature*, Cambridge, 1930, vol. iii, pp. 273 ff.; PETTAZZONI, R., " The Chain of Arrows; the Diffusion of a Mythical Motive ", *FRE*, vol. xxxv, pp. 151 ff.; id., *Saggi di Storia delle Religioni e di Mitologia*, Rome, 1946, pp. 63 ff.

Oceania: DIXON, Roland, *Oceanic Mythology*, Boston, 1916, pp. 139, 293 ff.; CHADWICK, op. cit., vol. iii, p. 481.

Africa: WERNER, Alice, *African Mythology*, Boston, 1925, pp. 135 ff.

America: ALEXANDER, H. B., *Latin-American Mythology*, Boston, 1920, pp. 271, 308; STITH THOMPSON, *Tales of the North American Indians*, Cambridge, Mass., 1929, pp. 283, 332 ff.

On the ascension motif, cf. STITH THOMPSON, *Motif-Index of Folk Literature*, Helsinki, 1934, vol. iii, pp. 7–10; ELIADE, M., *Le Chamanisme*, pp. 423 ff.

On the sacrificing of horses among the Turco-Mongols, the ascension symbolism of the Altaics, etc.: see RADLOV, W., *Aus Sibirien: Lose Blätter aus dem Tagebuch eines reisenden Linguisten*, vols. i–ii, Leipzig,

1884, pp. 19 ff.; CZAPLICKA, M. A., *Aboriginal Siberia*, Oxford, 1914; HOLMBERG-HARVA, Uno, " Der Baum des Lebens ", *Annales Academiæ Scientarum Fennicæ*, Helsinki, 1923; id., *Die Religion der Tcheremissen*, Porvoo, 1926, pp. 108 ff.; id., *Die religiösen Vorstellungen der altaischen Völker*, Helsinki, 1938; KOPRULUZADE, Mehmed Fuad, *Influence du chamanisme turco-mongol sur les ordres mystiques musulmans*, Istanbul, 1929; CHADWICK, Nora K., " Shamanism among the Tartars of Central Asia ", *JRAI*, 1936, vol. lxvi, pp. 75 ff.; SCHMIDT, W., *Ursprung*, vol. ix, pp. 278 ff.; vol. x, pp. 231 ff., 321 ff.; ELIADE, M., *Le Chamanisme*, pp. 175 ff.

III

THE SUN AND SUN-WORSHIP

36. HIEROPHANIES OF THE SUN AND "RATIONALIZATION"

IT was once thought, when the study of the history of religion was in its brave infancy, that sun-worship was common to all mankind. The first studies in comparative mythology disclosed traces of it pretty well everywhere. However, in 1870, Bastian, who was an ethnologist of some importance, realized that sun-worship is in fact to be found in very few parts of the world. And a half-century later, Sir James Frazer, reviewing the problem in connection with his painstaking researches into the worship of nature, noted[1] the lack of any coherence among the various solar elements to be found in Africa, Australia, Melanesia, Polynesia and Micronesia. The same lack of coherence is almost universal in the Americas. It is really only in Egypt, Asia and in primitive Europe that what we call sun-worship ever attained sufficient popularity to become at any time, as in Egypt for instance, really dominant.

If you consider that, on the other side of the Atlantic, the solar religion was developed only in Peru and Mexico, only, that is, among the two "civilized" peoples of America, the only two who attained any level of real political organization, then you cannot help discerning a certain connection between the predominance of sun religions and what I may call "historic" destinies. It could be said that where "history is on the march", thanks to kings, heroes, or empires, the sun is supreme. A great many other hypotheses, some frankly whimsical, have been put forward to explain this parallelism between sun worship and the spread of civilization in history. Some authors have even spoken of "Children of the Sun" spreading both the cult of the sun and the basic principles of civilization, during the course of endless migrations. I shall continue to leave the whole question of "history" on one side, and say here only that, compared with celestial figures, evidence of which we find almost everywhere, divine figures of the sun are rare.

[1] *The Worship of Nature*, London, 1926, p. 441.

I will return to those figures in a moment. But we must first forestall an error of perspective which might easily become an error of method. On the one hand, we must bear in mind that solar divine figures (gods, heroes and so on) do not exhaust the hierophanies of the sun any more than any other figures exhaust the hierophanies of which they are a part. And, on the other hand, we must realize that unlike other nature hierophanies, such as the moon or water, the sacred meaning expressed in the sun is not always clear to the modern Western mind. Or, more precisely, what *is* clear, and therefore easily grasped, in any sun hierophany is most often only what remains after a long process of rationalization has worn it away and it is brought to us, without our realizing it, by way of language, custom and culture. The sun has now become simply one of the commonplaces of what is in a vague sense religious experience, solar symbolism being reduced to little more than a series of gestures and phrases of no very vital significance.

It is not part of my scheme to try to explain the alterations that have affected the actual make-up of the sun hierophany in the experience of modern man. I do not therefore undertake to analyse how far the important astronomical and biological function that the last few centuries have discovered in the sun has not only altered modern man's attitude towards it and the relationship he can have with it by his own direct experience, but has also changed the nature of solar symbolism itself. One point will illustrate this: the orientation of intellectual activity from Aristotle onwards has done much to blunt our receptiveness towards the *totality* of sun hierophanies. What has happened in the case of the moon proves that this new intellectual orientation does not necessarily make the experience of the hierophany in itself impossible. No one, indeed, would maintain that a modern was *ipso facto* closed to the hierophanies of the moon. On the contrary, we can see as clearly as primitives how the symbols, myths and rites connected with the moon fit together. Perhaps the fact that the mentalities of the " primitive " and the " modern " respond so similarly to the sort of sacredness expressed by the moon can be explained by the survival even in the most totally rationalist outlook of what has been called " the nocturnal domain of the mind ".

The moon would be appealing to a layer of man's consciousness that the most corrosive rationalism cannot touch.

It is true that the " diurnal domain of the mind " is dominated by solar symbolism; that is, largely by a symbolism which, though perhaps not always artificially constructed, is often the result of a chain of reasoning. This does not mean that every rational element whatever in the hierophanies of the sun must automatically be a later and artificial development. As we saw earlier, reason is present in the most primitive hierophanies, and religious experience is not *a priori* incompatible with the intelligible. What is later and quite artificial is the *exclusive* primacy of reason. For religious life, which we may summarily define as the experience of kratophanies, hierophanies and theophanies, affects the whole of man's life, and it would be quite unreal to try to divide the mind into separate compartments. The primitive hierophanies of the sun give us an excellent example of this. As we shall see, they show a certain *apprehension of reality as a whole* as well as a coherent and intelligible structure of the *sacred*. But this intelligibility could never be reduced to a series of clear " rational truths " or to any experience not including hierophanies. Let me give an example: the connection between the sun and darkness or the dead, or the peculiarly Indian binomial, " sun-serpent ", however much they may be based on a total grasp of life and reality, will never be clear in any perspective that is purely rational.

37. THE " SOLARIZATION " OF SUPREME BEINGS

I pointed out in the last chapter (§ 17) the tendency for Supreme Beings of the sky to withdraw from the foreground of religious life and give place to magico-religious forces, or to divine figures that are more active, more useful, and generally more directly connected with " Life " Indeed, the passivity we noted in the Supreme Beings is, in the last analysis, simply their apparent indifference to the ever more complicated vicissitudes of human life. For motives of protection (against adverse powers, spells and so on), and positive help (for he wants to be assured of continued existence by means of fertility magic, and so forth), man feels more drawn to other religious " forms " and becomes progressively more dependent on them:

ancestors, civilizing heroes, Great Goddesses, magico-religious forces (such as *mana*), cosmic centres of fertility (the Moon, Waters, Vegetation and so on). And we have thus observed the phenomenon—general throughout the Indo-Mediterranean area—of the replacing of the supreme sky figure by an atmospheric and fecundating god, the spouse, or sometimes simply the acolyte and inferior, of the Great Mother of earth, moon, and plant-life, and sometimes the Father of a god of vegetation.

This passage from " creator " to " fecundator ", this slipping of the omnipotence, transcendence and impassiveness of the sky into the dynamism, intensity and drama of the new atmospheric, fertilizing, vegetation figures, is not without significance. It makes quite clear that one of the main factors in the lowering of people's conceptions of God, most obvious in agricultural societies, is the more and more all-embracing importance of vital values and of " Life " in the outlook of economic man. And, looking only at the Indo-Mediterranean area, it is interesting to realize that the supreme gods of Mesopotamia often combined the prerogatives of fertility with those of the sun. Marduk is one example of this[1] and the best known. But it is a trait found among other gods of the same type—others, that is, in the process of taking over the supremacy. It may even be said that these gods of vegetation display solar attributes as well, in so far as there are plant elements in the mystique and myth of divine sovereignty.[2]

This conjunction of sun and vegetation elements is clearly to be explained by the Sovereign's having the added role of storing and dispensing " Life ", both on the cosmic and on the social level. When, therefore, sky divinities gradually turn into sun divinities, it is the same sort of process which results, in other situations, in their transformation into gods of atmosphere and fecundation. The Hittites, for instance, had a sky god who tended very strongly, from the earliest historic times, to become a sun god[3] and had connections with cosmic and biological sovereignty—thus possessing elements of

[1] See H. Frankfort, " Gods and Myths on Sargonid Seals ", *Irak*, 1934, vol. i, p. 6.

[2] Cf. Engnell, *Studies in Divine Kingship in the Middle East*, Uppsala, 1943, pp. 21 ff., 54 ff.

[3] Cf. Götze, *Kleinasien*, Leipzig, 1933, p. 136.

vegetation which fitted him into the pattern of God-King-Tree of Life.[1]

In any case, this happened oftener and earlier than one might think from the evidence of the Ancient East which, we must remember, was dominated by the mystique of sovereignty. Even the oldest phases of primitive cultures display both a beginning of the transfer of the sky god's attributes to the sun god and an amalgamation of the Supreme Being with the sun god. The rainbow, looked on in so many places (§ 14) as a sky epiphany, is associated with the sun and becomes, for instance among the Fuegians, the " sun's brother ".[2] More often you will find a filiation established between the Supreme God of the sky and the sun. Among the Semang Pygmies, the Fuegians and the Bushmen, the sun is the " eye " of the Supreme God.[3] Vedic India and various other places witnessed something similar happening; see further on. Among the Wiradjuri and Kamilaroi of South-West Australia, the sun is looked on as Grogoragally in person, son of the Creator, a divine figure well-disposed towards mankind;[4] but under the influence, no doubt, of matriarchy, the moon is the second son of the Supreme Being.[5] The Samoyeds see the sun and moon as the eyes of Num (that is, the sky): the sun is the good eye, the moon the evil eye.[6] The Yuraks of the tundra round Obdursk celebrate a great winter feast at the first appearance of the sun, but they offer sacrifice to Num at it, which shows that the solemnity was originally connected with the sky. The Yuraks of the forests consider the sun, the moon, and " the thunderbolt bird " as symbols of Num; the tree on which they hang the heads of animals as an offering is called " tree of the sun ", though originally this sacrifice was in honour of Num.[7] With the Chukchi, the sun has taken the place of the supreme divinity; the major sacrifices are offered to good spirits, notably to the

---

[1] Cf. Engnell, p. 61.

[2] Schmidt, *Ursprung*, vol. ii, p. 938.

[3] Schmidt, vol. iii, p. 1087.

[4] Schmidt, vol. iii, p. 841.

[5] Schmidt, vol. iii, p. 844.

[6] Lehtisalo, *Entwurf einer Mythologie der Jurak-Samoyeden*, Helsinki, 1927, pp. 16 ff.

[7] Gahs, " Kopf- Schädel- und Langknochenopfer ", *Festschrift W. Schmidt* Mödling, 1928, p. 240.

light of the sun. According to Gahs, the introduction of sun worship into the whole of northern Asia was the work of these same Chukchi and of the Yukagirs.

38. AFRICA, INDONESIA

The turning of the Supreme Being of the sky into a sun god[1] is a phenomenon fairly common in Africa. A whole series of African tribes give the Supreme Being the name of " Sun "[2] Sometimes, as with the Munsh, the sun is taken for the son of the Supreme Being Awondo, and the moon for his daughter.[3] The Barotse, however, make the sun the " dwelling " of the god of the sky, Niambe, and the moon his wife.[4] Elsewhere we find the sky god assimilated to the sun by a kind of coalescence : among the Louyi, for instance, for whom Niambe *is* the sun,[5] or the Kavirondo, for whom the sun takes the place of the Supreme Being in worship.[6] The Kaffa still call their Supreme Being Abo which means both " Father " and " Sun ", and see him embodied in the sun. But according to one of the latest authorities on this tribe, F. H. Bieber,[7] this " solarization " is simply a later development, and Abo was, to start with, a god of light or of the sky.

It is interesting to note that the fact that he has become a sun god still does not keep for the African Supreme God any active importance in religious life. Among various Bantu tribes of East Africa and particularly, the Wajaggas of Kilimanjaro, the Supreme Being is Ruwa (which means " sun "); he dwells, indeed, in the sun, but he still preserves certain celestial traits including the passivity so characteristic of sky gods; and Ruwa is no more honoured than they are; it is

---

[1] " Solarization " often acts directly upon the structure of the Supreme Being as such, rather than as a sky god. But as we have not yet come to divine "forms", I would rather stress here the process of solarizing sky figures. This, of course, does not in any way imply that such figures alone represent the earliest personal divine forms known to history, nor that it does not sometimes happen that the Supreme Being becomes a sun god direct, without becoming *en route* a Supreme Being of the sky.

[2] Frazer, *Worship*, p. 315, n. 1 and 2.

[3] Frazer, p. 124.

[4] Frazer, p. 170.

[5] Frazer, p. 173.

[6] Frazer, p. 279.

[7] *Kaffa*, Münster, 1923, vol. ii, pp. 387 ff.

only in the last resort that they offer sacrifice to him or pray to him.[1]

You will find the same substitution in Indonesia. Puempalaburu, the sun god of the Toradja, gradually replaces I'lai, the sky god, and carries on his work of creating the universe.[2] The sun god, then, advances to the position of demiurge, just as in America, among the Tlingit, for instance, we see the demiurge, in the form of a crow, becoming identified with the sun, and receiving from the Supreme God of the sky whose servant or whose son he is, the mission to continue and complete the work of creation begun by him.[3] There we have the dynamic and organizing element that the sun divinity assumes which corresponds on a different plane to the fertility element in the gods of atmosphere (§ 26). But the sun god is no more *creative* than they are; like them he is subordinate to the creator, and holds the latter's mandate to complete the work of creation. However, the *solar demiurge* has secured what the majority of the *sun gods* who have been substituted for or amalgamated with the Supreme Being have not attained: a living importance in religious life and in myth. One has only to remember the major place held by the crow in North American mythology and by the eagle—a substitute for the sun, or symbol of it—in Arctic and Northern Asiatic mythology.

39. SOLARIZATION AMONG THE MUNDA

The best example of the Supreme Being turning into a sun god comes from the Kolarian tribes of India. The Mundas of Bengal put the sun, Sing-Bonga, first in their pantheon. He is a gentle god and does not interfere in men's affairs, yet he is not totally absent from the cult. He is offered sacrifices of white he-goats, or white cocks, and in August when the rice harvest is gathered, he is offered the first-fruits.[4] He is married to the moon, and seen as the author of creation, although his creation myth brings in as subordinate demiurges, the tortoise, the crab and the leech, who are each in turn ordered by Sing-Bonga to bring soil from the ocean bed.[5]

[1] Pettazzoni, *Dio*, pp. 223 ff.
[2] Pettazzoni, pp. 130 ff.
[3] Pettazzoni, p, 266.
[4] Dalton, *Descriptive Ethnology of Bengal*, Calcutta, 1872, p 198.
[5] Dalton, p. 185.

The Khond tribes of the province of Orissa adore as their supreme creator-god Bura Pennu (" god of light ") or Bela Pennu (" god of the sun "); the process of solarization is greatly assisted by the benevolent and in many ways passive nature of this divinity: Bela Pennu does not figure in the cult.[1] The Birhors of Chota Nagpur offer white he-goats or hens to their supreme divinity, the god of the sun, particularly when they are in great need or to ensure a good harvest. As one might guess, the Supreme Being who becomes connected with the sun owes his living place in the cult to the part he plays in the mechanics of " vital production ". The prayers that accompany libations and sacrifices offered to him make this fairly clear. When a child is born, its father offers a libation of water, faces east, and says, as he does it, the following words : " O Sing-Bonga, I am making this libation of water to thee. May milk flow from the mother's breast like this water ! "[2] And to ensure a good rice harvest, the head of the family makes the following promise to sacrifice a white hen : " I make this vow to thee, O Sing-Bonga. May grains grow in abundance, and I shall sacrifice this white fowl to thee at the time of the threshing." He then lets the white hen go and immolates a black one. That the sacrifice takes place on the day of the full moon in the month of Baishak (April–May), leaves us in no doubt as to its meaning : the black hen is offered to the divinity of earth and fields who has supreme jurisdiction over the fertility of the soil.[3] This is a typical example of what happens to the Supreme Being when he has become linked with the sun : the sun is made Supreme Being in place of the omnipotent, creating figure of the sky ; the presence of the sun god in the cult is due chiefly to his fecundating powers ; yet, even then, he is not looked on as infallibly efficacious, for the faithful are prudent enough to draw as well upon the forces of moon, earth and fields which have control over all fecundity.

The sun is also the Supreme Being of another Munda tribe, the Oraon, who call him Dharmesh. Their main religious preoccupation is undoubtedly that of appeasing the spirits, *bhut*.[4] However—as with the sky gods—when the help of all

[1] Dalton, p. 296.
[2] Chandra Roy, *The Birhors*, Ranchi, 1925, pp. 225 ff.
[3] Roy, pp. 373 ff.
[4] Dalton, p. 256.

other magico-religious forces proves to be illusory, the Oraon come back to Dharmesh: " Now we have tried everything, but we have still you to help us ! " And they sacrifice a white cock to him, exclaiming: " God, thou art our creator, have mercy on us ! "[1] Recent research has brought to light the existence of a genuine Supreme Being native to the Munda tribes, and also shows the relatively late date at which he was ousted by the sun and moon divinities. According to Bodding, the amalgamation of the Santali Supreme God, Thakkur, with the sun (this supreme being is also called Chanda, " sun ") was an equally late development. Rahmann has set out to study this solarization and lunarization of Supreme Beings among the Gond and the Munda tribes. And Koppers, in a notable comparative study (" Bhagwan, the Supreme Deity of the Bhils "), sets out to prove not only the authenticity of the Supreme Beings found among pre-Dravidian and pre-Aryan tribes, but also the possibility of influences on the Indo-European invaders.[2]

40. SOLAR CULTS

In Indonesia and the peninsula of Malacca, sun-worship is very sporadic. I have given a few examples of Indonesian Supreme Beings' becoming " solarized " (§ 38). Timor and the islands near it are the only exceptions. There the sun god still holds an important position although religious life, as in the rest of Indonesia, is dominated by the worship of the dead and of the spirits of nature. On Timor, the " Lord Sun ", Usi-Neno, is husband of " Lady Earth ", Usi-Afu, and the whole world is the result of their union. Nonetheless, the earth goddess still receives the greater part of their sacrifices; the sun receives only one great yearly sacrifice, at the time of the harvest.[3] On Wetter Island, north of Timor, the Supreme

---

[1] Frazer, *Worship*, p. 631.

[2] Such influence, unlikely as it may seem, cannot be *a priori* excluded. It has been often thought that certain aspects of Indian religious life—earth and burial rites, serpent-worship, symbols of the genital organs and so on—might be explained by the influence of aboriginal, non-Aryan inhabitants. And in the same way it has been thought possible for primitives to have a similar influence on the civilized. However, in recent times, a number of ethnologists deny that the most primitive tribes native to India, particularly the Munda, have ever had orgiastic cults, or that the Indo-Europeans could in any sense have derived them from them.

[3] Frazer, pp. 656 ff.

Being, solarized though he be, still retains traces of an original celestial nature; he is called the " great lord ", or the " old man on high " (cf. § 12 ff.). He dwells in the vault of heaven, but also in the sun, and embodies the principle of masculinity, while the earth is feminine. The ideas the natives have of him are fairly vague, and they offer sacrifice to him only in case of illness,[1] which certainly seems to indicate the sort of withdrawal from the forefront of religious experience made by the Supreme Beings of the sky.

East of Timor, in the Leti, Sarmata, Baber and Timor Laut archipelagoes, the sun is looked upon as the most important divinity and bears the name Upulero, the " Lord Sun ". Here again, it is simply because the sun god has become a fecundator that he has remained a living force. Indeed, his cult still indicates some features of his original loftiness and purity: Upulero has no images and is adored under the form of a lamp made with cocoa leaves. Yet the entire ritual centres on an entreaty for fecundity in the universe. Once a year, at the beginning of the rainy season, there is a great feast in honour of Upulero: it lasts an entire month, and its object is to ensure rain, the fertility of the fields and the wealth of the community. These tribes believe that at that moment the sun comes down into a fig tree to make his wife, the Earth Mother, fruitful. To make his coming easier a ladder of seven or ten rungs is erected on the fig tree (I mentioned earlier the sky symbolism of seven-runged ladders, cf. § 31). Then before this same fig tree, sacrifices of pigs and dogs are offered, and finally there breaks out, amidst singing and dancing, a collective orgy such as always goes with the mystique of agriculture (§ 138). The prayers that accompany it show the function of fecundator and depositary of food supplies attributed to the sun: " O Lord or Grandfather Sun, come down ! The fig-tree has put forth shoots; the former shoots have turned to leaves and have fallen off. The pig's flesh is ready, cut in slices. The canoes of the village are full to overflowing of offerings. Lord or Grandfather Sun, thou art invited to the feast. Cut and eat . . . O drink indeed ! . . . O come indeed, Lord or Grandfather Sun ! We expect that thou wilt give into our hands much ivory, much gold. Let the goats cast

[1] Frazer, p. 660.

two or three young apiece. Let the number of the nobles increase, let the number of the people increase or multiply. Replace the dead goats and pigs by living ones. Replace the rice and betel that are used up. Make the empty rice-basket full, make the empty sago-tub full . . . etc."[1]

41. DESCENT FROM THE SUN

Upulero can also produce children.[2] On Timor, moreover, certain chiefs are called " children of the sun "[3] and claim to be directly descended from the sun god. We should keep in mind this myth of the sun's creating man, and of the direct relationships between the sun god and certain classes of men. This is not a privilege of the sun god alone: as I shall point out in later chapters, because of the dialectic of hierophanies every sphere of nature—water, earth, plant-life—can claim some function relative to mən's creation; each of these spheres man recognizes as *absolute reality* and, at the same time, as a primordial source from which he gets being and life.

But in the case of the sun, this genealogy indicates something more: it expresses the changes that follow upon the solarization of the Supreme Being, or the turning of the sun into a " fecundator " and a " limited creator ", monopolized by certain societies of men or even certain families such as the families of chiefs or kings. Thus, in the Arunta tribe in Australia, the sun (which is female) holds a more important place than the moon (which is male) in the sense that it " is regarded as having a definite relationship to each individual member of the various [social] divisions ".[4] The Loritja[5] and the tribes of the south-east[6] also believe in such relationships. What the Australians see as " a definite relationship with each individual member " (for man *as such* is a creature of the supreme sky being himself, see § 12 ff.), becomes elsewhere crystallized into a direct relationship with the father or ancestor of the tribe—among, for instance, the Blackfoot Indians, and the

[1] Frazer, pp. 661–2.

[2] Frazer, p. 662.

[3] Frazer, p. 658.

[4] Spencer, *The Arunta*, London, 1927, vol. ii, p. 496.

[5] Strehlow and Von Leonhardi, *Mythen, Sagen und Märchen des Aranda-stammes in Zentral-Autralien*, Frankfurt a. M., 1907, vol. i, p. 16.

[6] Howitt, *Native Tribes of South-East Australia*, London, 1904, p. 427.

Arapahos.[1] The Korkus of India declare that they are descended from the union of the Sun and the Moon.[2] We find the same sort of relationships in more developed societies, but always limited to the king and noble families. However, in Australia, man's relations with the sun can be strengthened on another level, for man can attain identification with the sun through the ceremonial of initiation. The candidate smears his head with red, tears out his hair and beard, undergoes a symbolic death, and revives the next day as the sun is rising; this initiation drama identifies him with the sun-hero Grogoragally, the son of the creator.[3]

42. THE SUN AS HIEROPHANT AND PSYCHOPOMP

This Australian ceremonial brings in an important new element which explains the part played by the sun in a great many other cultures and historical contexts. Various Australian tribes show us the sun related to each individual member of the community. In the Wiradjuri and Kamilaroi tribes, which are at a lower stage of development than the Arunta and Loritja, these relationships are of a different order: they have the object of uniting the initiate with the sun hero, son of the Supreme Being of the sky. Initiation thus makes man, in a sense, son of the Supreme Being; more precisely, he becomes so anew as a result of his ritual death from which he rises identified with the sun. Now, these details prove that in the religion of tribes as primitive as the Wiradjuri and Kamilaroi the Supreme Being is superior to the sun and puts him in charge of saving man by means of initiations, but they prove something else too. They also indicate that the sun may still assume an important function in the sphere of burial beliefs, in all that concerns man's state after death. In addition, Grogoragally presents the souls of the dead individually to the Supreme Being;[4] he can present them because they are already initiated, that is, because they have already undergone death and resurrection, and have each become a " sun ". The sun in this

---

[1] Cf. Scmidt, *Ursprung*, vol. ii, pp. 662, 729, etc

[2] Frazer, p. 616.

[3] Schmidt, vol. iii, pp. 1056-7.

[4] Schmidt, loc. cit.

way becomes the prototype of the " dead man rising again every morning ". A whole series of beliefs connected with initiation and sovereignty—to which I shall be referring again soon—grow out of this raising of the sun into a god (hero) who does not die (as does the moon), but who passes through the empire of death every night and returns the next day eternal and unchanging.

Sunset is not recognized as a " death " of the sun (unlike the moon's three days in hiding) but as a descent into the lower regions, into the kingdom of the dead. Unlike the moon, the sun has the privilege of passing through hell without undergoing the condition of death. Nonetheless, its pre-destined journey through the lower regions still confers on it the prerogatives relating to death and burial. Thus even when it no longer holds a front place in the pantheon or in the religious experience of a given civilization, as the Supreme Being who has become a sun god or a fecundator, the sun still manifests a certain ambivalence which makes it capable of undergoing yet further developments.

This ambivalence might be expressed rather like this : though immortal, the sun descends nightly to the kingdom of the dead; it can, therefore, take men with it and, by setting, put them to death; but it can also, on the other hand, guide souls through the lower regions and bring them back next day with its light. That is its twofold function—as psychopomp to " murder " and as hierophant to initiate. It explains the belief, so widely held in New Zealand and the New Hebrides, that merely to glance at the setting sun may induce death.[1] The sun draws things, it " sucks in " the souls of the living with as much ease as it guides the souls of the dead to whom it acts as psychopomp through the western " gate of the sun ". The natives of the Torres Straits believe there is a mythical island called Kibu (" the gate of the sun ") somewhere in the west. The wind blows the souls of the dead there.[2] In the Hervey Islands, the natives think that the dead gather in bands and twice a year, at the time of the solstice, they try to follow the sun

---

[1] Williamson, *Religious and Cosmic Beliefs in Central Polynesia*, Cambridge, 1933, vol. i, p. 118; vol. ii, pp. 218 ff.

[2] Frazer, *The Belief in Immortality and the Worship of the Dead*, London, 1933, vol. i, p. 175.

when it sets, so as to get to the lower regions.[1] In other Polynesian islands, the westernmost tip of land is called " the souls' jumping-off place ".[2]

You will also find fairly widespread in Oceania the beliefs by which the dead sink with the sun into the sea, are carried in " boats of the sun ", or according to which the kingdom of the dead is where the sun sets.[3] Clearly, the fate of all the souls who plunge into the setting sun is not the same; not all gain what we may call " salvation ". That is the point at which the redemptive power of initiation enters, and the part played by the various secret societies in choosing the elect and separating them from the amorphous mass of common men (the separation expressed in the mystique of sovereignty and the " children of the sun "). Thus, in the Hervey Islands only those who die in battle are carried to heaven by the sun; everyone else who dies is devoured by the gods of the underworld, Akaranga and Kiru.[4]

The dichotomy between the hero or initiate and death by natural causes has some importance in the history of religion and I shall be returning to it in another chapter. Still looking for a moment at Oceania, it has long been observed[5] that traces of sun-worship run parallel with those of ancestor-worship: the two find common expression in the setting up of megalithic monuments. But Rivers has also found in Polynesia and in Micronesia very close connections between the distribution of megalithic monuments and secret societies.[6] And megalithic monuments are always linked to the worship of the sun. In the Society Islands, for instance, the megaliths (*marae*) face the rising sun, as does the Fijiian *nanga*, while in the Banks Islands, there is a custom of anointing a megalith with red clay to make the sun shine anew. Ancestor-worship (worship of the dead), secret societies with their initiations which guarantee a happy lot after death, and finally, sun-worship: these three elements, which seem to spring from quite

[1] Frazer, *Belief*, vol. ii, p. 239.

[2] Frazer, *Belief*, vol. ii, p. 241.

[3] Frobenius, *Die Weltanschauung der Naturvölker*, Weimar, 1898, pp. 135 ff., 165 ff.

[4] Frazer, *Belief*, vol. ii, p. 242.

[5] Rivers, *The History of Melanesian Society*, Cambridge, 1914, vol. ii, p. 549.

[6] Vol. i, p. 289; vol. ii, p. 248, pp. 429–30, 456–7.

different lines of thought, are none the less closely linked in fact;
they were virtually present together even in the most primitive
sun hierophanies, in Australia for instance.

Keep in mind that notion of " choice ", of " selection ",
bound up with the initiation and burial rituals practised in the
name of the sun.   Remember too that in different parts of the
world chieftains were supposed to be descendants of the sun;
Polynesian chiefs,[1] the heads of the Natchez and Inca tribes[2]
and the Hittite kings (called " my sun "), the Babylonian kings
(cf. the stone tablet of Nabu-apla-iddin) and the Indian king[3]
all had the title and character of " suns ", " children of the
sun ", " grandchildren of the sun ", or even mystically embodied
the sun as in the case of the Indian king.   Among the Masai
shepherds in Africa,[4] as in Polynesia,[5] only chieftains could be
identified with the sun after death.   In fact, there must be a
choice or selection carried out either in the ritual initiation of
a secret society, or by the initiation conferred by sovereignty.
The Egyptian sun religion is a perfect example of this, and it is
worth stopping to consider at some length.

43. EGYPTIAN SUN CULTS

The religion of Egypt was, more than any other, dominated
by sun-worship.   At an early date the sun-god had absorbed
various divinities such as Atum, Horus and the scarab god
Khopri.[6]   From the fifth dynasty onwards, the phenomenon
became general: a great many divinities were merged with the
sun producing the " solarized " figures Khnemu, Min-Ra,
Amon-Ra, etc.[7]   I do not think there is any need for us to
decide here between the rival hypotheses of Kees and Sethe
on the question of the historical sources of sun doctrine.
What is agreed is that this doctrine reached its zenith under
the fifth dynasty and that its success gave support both to the
notion of sovereignty and the work of the priests at Hieropolis.
But, as a good deal of recent research seems to prove, other

[1] Perry, *The Children of the Sun*, London, 1927, pp. 138 ff.
[2] Hocart, *Kingship*, London, 1927, pp. 12 ff.
[3] Laws of Manu, vii, 3; v, 96.
[4] A. Haberlandt, in Buschan's *Völkerkunde*, Stuttgart, 1907, vol. i, p. 567.
[5] Williamson, vol. ii, pp. 302 ff., 322 ff.
[6] Vandier, " La Religion égyptienne ", *MA*, Paris, 1944, vol. i, pp. 21, 55.
[7] Vandier, p. 149.

divine figures had earlier on been supreme, figures more ancient and more popular too—popular in this sense, that they never belonged exclusively to any privileged group.

It has long been recognized that Shu, god of atmosphere and therefore originally a sky figure, was later identified with the sun. But Wainwright thinks Amon too was a very early sky god, and H. Junker thinks Ur (wr), whose name means " the Great One ", was an ancient celestial Supreme Being; we do sometimes find Ur taking as his wife the goddess Nut, " the Great One " (wrt), as in the myth of the cosmic pair, Heaven and Earth (cf. § 84). The total absence of any reference to Ur on public (and therefore royal) monuments is due to his being a god of the people. Junker even tries to piece together Ur's history. It is, briefly, the story of his loss of the supreme place because of being constantly fitted into local theologies: he becomes an auxiliary of Ra's (we see him healing the sun's eyes, which were for a time blind), later merges with Atum and finally with Ra himself. I have not the knowledge to enable me to enter into the discussion provoked by Junker's studies. But I was persuaded to mention it because such Egyptologists as Capart and Kees appear to agree with him in the main. From the point of view of the history of religion, the career of Amon or that of Wr can be easily understood: I have already shown how Supreme Beings of a heavenly nature tend, if they do not fade into complete oblivion, either to change into gods of fecundation and weather, or else to become sun gods.

There have been, we said, two major factors in the establishment of Ra as supreme: the theology of Hieropolis and the mystique of sovereignty in which the sovereign was identified with the sun. A valuable support of this is the rivalry that lasted for some time between Ra as solar and (imperial) funeral god, and Osiris. The sun set in the Field of Offerings or Field of Rest to rise next day at the opposite side of the heavens in the Field of Reeds. These solar spheres which had been ruled over by Ra in pre-dynastic times gained in addition during the third and fourth dynasties a funeral signification. It was from the Field of Reeds that the Pharaoh's soul set off to meet the sun in heaven, to be guided by it to the Field of Offerings. At first, this ascent was no easy matter. In spite of his divine character, the Pharaoh had to fight the guardian of the " Field ", the Bull of Offerings, for the right to take up his abode in heaven. The Pyramid texts[1] refer to this heroic testing—of an initiatory character—which the Pharaoh had to undergo.

As time went on, however, the writings stopped mentioning any duel with the Bull of Offerings and the departed was said to climb to heaven[2] by a ladder or even sail across the starry seas till at last, guided by a goddess and in the guise of a glittering bull, he reached the Field of Offerings. It is the start of the degeneration of a heroic initiation myth (which may have also included a rite), into a political and social privilege. It is not as a " hero " that the Pharaoh has sovereign powers or attains the immortality of the sun; as supreme ruler he automatically receives immortality and need not attempt to prove himself a hero at all. This legal establishment of the Pharaoh's privileged state after death is as it were balanced by the victorious ascent of Osiris as a non-aristocratic god of death. I cannot set out here to discuss the conflict between Ra and Osiris, but it is clear enough even from the Pyramid texts. " Thou openest thy place in heaven among the stars of heaven, for thou art a star. . . . Thou watchest over Osiris, thou hast control of the dead, thou holdest thyself remote from them, thou art not of them," writes, we may guess, an apologist of imperial privilege and the solar tradition.[3]

The new god, though popular in form (accessible, that is, to other social classes), is no less powerful for that, and Pharaoh judges it wise to ask the sun's help against falling under Osiris' axe: " Ra Atum deliver thee not to Osiris who judges not thy heart and has no power over thy heart . . . Osiris, thou shalt not take possession of him, thy son [Horus] shall not have possession of him . . ."[4] The west, where the dead go, becomes the sphere of Osiris, while the east remains the sun. And in the Pyramid texts, Osiris' worshippers praise the west and disparage the east: " Osiris (N) does not walk in the eastern places, but walks in the western places, along the road of

---

[1] For instance, *Pyramid Texts*, pp. 293, 913, 914, 1432 ff.; Weill, *Le Champ des roseaux et le champ des offrandes*, Paris, 1936, pp. 16 ff.

[2] Cf., for instance, the Book of the Dead.

[3] *Pyr.*, p. 251; Weill, p. 116.

[4] *Pyr.*, pp. 145–6; Weill, p. 116.

Ra's followers ";[1] this is the exact opposite of what is commanded in the solar burial doctrine. Indeed, the test is simply a wild " osirianization " of an ancient formula with the terms reversed: " Walk not on the paths of the West, where those who set out do not go forward; but let (N) walk on the paths of the East, by the paths of Ra's followers."[2]

In time those texts increased. The sun resisted and won the field. Osiris, who had been obliged to claim the two heavenly fields simply because they had always been *the* spheres of death, in the end withdrew from them. But the retreat was not a defeat. Osiris had only attempted to gain possession of the sky because solar theology made it a scene necessary to the immortality of the Pharaohs. His eschatological message, though basically different from the heroic conquest of immortality—which degenerated later into the automatic acquisition of immortality by royal personages—had forced Osiris to lead the souls he wanted to save from annihilation along a heavenly, solar path. In any case, Osiris was merely completing the " humanist " revolution which had already altered eschatological thought in Egypt. In fact, we have actually seen how the idea that immortality was something heroic, requiring initiation, offered to a handful of privileged persons who could win it by a struggle, turned into an idea that immortality was given to all privileged persons. Osiris developed this profound change in the notion of immortality further in the direction of " democracy ": anyone could attain immortality by emerging victorious from the *trial*. The theology of Osiris took up and developed the notion of trial as a *sine qua non* of after life; but for the heroic, initiatory type of trial (the struggle with the Bull), it substituted trials of an ethical and religious nature (good works and so on). The archaic theory of heroic immortality gave way to a new conception, humbler and more human.

44. SOLAR CULTS IN THE CLASSICAL EAST AND THE MEDITERRANEAN

I should not have dealt in such detail with the conflict between Ra and Osiris except for the fact that it helps enormously towards understanding the nature of the secret societies

[1] *Pyr.*, p. 1531; Weill, p. 121.
[2] *Pyr.*, p. 2175; Weill, p. 121.

connected with the sun and death that I mentioned earlier. In Egypt, the sun was to remain to the last the psychopomp of a privileged class (the family of the Sovereign), yet sun-worship still played a leading role in the whole of Egyptian religion, at least the religion expressed in the monuments and writings. In Indonesia and Melanesia, the situation is different: there the sun was at one time psychopomp of *all* the initiates of secret societies; but its role, though still important, is not the only one. In those secret societies, the " ancestors "—led by the sun on the road of the west—play an equally important part. In Egyptian terms, it is a coming-together of Ra and Osiris. This coming-together does not damage the prestige of the sun, for do not forget that the sun's connection with the other world, with the spheres of darkness and of death, is clear in the most primitive solar hierophanies and is rarely lost to view.

The god Shamash provides us with a good example of how this works; Shamash holds a lower rank in the Mesopotamian pantheon than Sin, the Moon god, and is held to be Sin's son; he has never had an important part in mythology.[1] Nonetheless, the solar hierophanies of Babylon still retain traces of their former connection with the world beyond. Shamash is called the " sun of Etimme ", that is, of the *manes*; we are told of him that he " makes the dead live ".[2] He is the god of justice and the " lord of judgement " (*bel-dini*). From earliest times his temple was called the " house of the judge of the land ".[3] On the other hand, Shamash is the god of oracles, the patron of prophets and soothsayers,[4] a function that is always connected with the world of the dead and the domains of earth and burial.

In Greece and in Italy, the sun never occupied anything more than a secondary position. In Rome, sun-worship was introduced under the Empire through oriental ideas, and it developed in a rather exterior and artificial manner through the worship of the Emperors. Greek mythology and religion, however, preserved traces of certain " underworld " hiero-

[1] Meissner, *Babylonien und Assyrien*, Heidelberg, 1920–5, vol. ii, p. 21.

[2] Dhorme, " Les Religions de Babylonie et d'Assyrie ", p. 87.

[3] Dhorme, p. 64.

[4] Haldar, *Associations of Cult Prophets among the Semites*, Uppsala, 1945, pp. 1 ff.

phanies of the sun. The myth of Helios reveals relations with both the earth and the underworld. A whole collection of epithets—which Pestalozza[1] sees as the remnant of a Mediterranean religious heritage—bring out its organic connection with the plant world. Helios is *pythios* and *paian*—two attributes which he shares with Leto, one of the Great Goddesses of the Mediterranean—*chthonios* and *plouton*; Helios is also *titan*, an epiphany of generative energy. We are not specially concerned at the moment to know how far the sun's connection with the world of chthonian and sexual magic belongs to the Mediterranean substratum (in Crete, for instance, Helios takes the form of a bull, and becomes the spouse of the Great Mother, just as do most of the atmosphere gods) and how far it represents a later compromise effected by the events of history, between the matriarchal regime of the Mediterranean peoples and the patriarchy of the Indo-Europeans who came down from the north. For us it is something quite different that matters: the sun, which, looked at superficially from the point of view of reason alone, might be thought to be supremely an " intelligible " hierophany of the sky, and of light, was being worshipped as a source of the " dark " energies.

For Helios is not only *pythios*, *chthonios*, *titan*, and so on; over and above all this, he is in communication with the chosen world of darkness: sorcery and hell. He is the father of the sorceress Circe, and the grandfather of Medea, both illustrious specialists in nightplant philtres; and it was from him that Medea received her famous chariot drawn by winged serpents.[2] Horses are immolated to him on Mount Taygetus.[3] At Rhodes, during the feast in his honour, Halieia (from *halios*, the Doric form of *helios*), a chariot drawn by four horses is offered to him and then cast into the sea.[4] And horses and serpents both belong mainly to chthonian and funereal symbolism. And, lastly, the entry into Hades is called the " gate of the sun ", and " Hades " as pronounced during the Homeric age—" A-ides "—also brings to mind the notion of

---

[1] *Pagine di religione mediterranea*, Milan-Messina, 1945, vol. ii, pp. 22 ff.
[2] Euripides, *Medea*, 1321; Apollodorus, *Biblioth.*, i, 9, 25.
[3] Pausanias, iii, 20, 4.
[4] Festus, s. v. *October equus*.

what is " invisible " and what " renders invisible ".[1] The swing between light and darkness, solar and earthly, can therefore be taken as two alternating phases of one and the same reality. The hierophanies of the sun display, indeed, dimensions that the sun merely as such would lose in any purely rational or profane perspective. But those dimensions hold a definite place in any primitive system of myth and metaphysic.

45. INDIA: THE AMBIVALENCE OF THE SUN

We find such a system in India. Sūrya figures among the second rank of Vedic gods. The Ṛg Veda does indeed devote ten hymns to him, but he never attains any very high position. He is the son of Dyaus[2] but he is also known as the eye of heaven or the eye of Mitra and Varuṇa.[3] He sees a long way, he is " the spy " over all the world. According to the Puruṣa Sūkta,[4] the sun was born of the eye of the cosmic giant Puruṣa, and, at death, when man's body and soul become once more part of that cosmic giant, his eye will go back into the sun. So far, Sūrya's hierophanies reveal only his luminous aspect. But we also read in the Ṛg Veda that the sun's chariot is drawn by a horse, Etaśa,[5] or by seven horses,[6] and he is himself a stallion[7] or a bird,[8] or even a vulture or a bull;[9] and whenever a thing displays the essence or attributes of a horse it always has some chthonian or funereal significance. That significance is quite clear in the other Vedic variant on the sun god, Sāvitrī, who is often identified with Sūrya: he is a psychopomp and conducts souls to the place of the just. In some texts he bestows immortality on gods and men;[10] it is he who makes Tvaṣṭṛ immortal.[11] Whether as a psychopomp or a hierophant (conferring immortality) his mission is certainly an echo of the

[1] Kerenyi, " Vater Helios ", EJ, Zürich, 1943, p. 91.
[2] RV, x, 37, 2.
[3] i, 115, 1; x, 37, 1.
[4] RV, x, 90.
[5] vii, 63, 2.
[6] iii, 45, 6; i, 50.
[7] vii, 77, 3.
    i, 191, 9.
[9] v, 47, 3.
[10] iv, 54, 2, etc.
[11] i, 110, 3.

prerogatives that attached to the sun god in primitive societies.[1]

But in the *Ṛg Veda* itself, and particularly in the speculations of the Brahmaṇas, the sun is seen also in its dark aspects. The *Ṛg Veda*[2] describes one aspect as " shining " and the other as " black " (that is, invisible). Sāvitrī brings night as well as day[3] and is himself a god of night;[4] one hymn even describes his night journey. But this alternating of modalities also has an ontological significance. Sāvitrī is *prasavita niveśanah*,[5] " he who makes things come in and go out " ("making all creatures come in and go out ").[6] Bergaigne quite rightly stressed the cosmic import of this " reintegration ":[7] for Sāvitrī is *jagato niveśāni*, " making the world return "[8]— which really formulates a system of cosmology. Night and day (*naktośasā*, a dual feminine word) are sisters, just as the gods and the " demons " (*asura*) are brothers: *dvayāḥ prājāpatyāḥ, devās cāsurāśca*, " the children of Prajapati are of two sorts, gods and asuras ".[9] The sun fits into this divine bi-unity, and also displays in some myths, an ophidian (that is, " dark " or indistinct) aspect which would normally be the complete opposite of its immediate meaning. There are still traces of the serpentine myth of the sun to be found in the *Ṛg Veda*: originally " without feet ", Varuṇa gave him feet to walk with (*apade pada prati dhātave*).[10] He is the priest *asura* of all the *devas*.[11]

The sun's ambivalence is shown also in its behaviour towards men. It is, on the one hand, man's true progenitor : " When the [human] father thus emits him as seed into the womb, it is

---

[1] I am not of course speaking of " historical " connection, but of typological symmetry. Underlying the history, development, diffusion and changes of any hierophany is its basic structure. There is so little evidence that it is hard—and for our purpose scarcely necessary—to discover exactly how far the structure of any hierophany was first seen fully by all the members of a given society. All we need to do is specify what a hierophany *could mean* or could not mean.

[2] i, 115, 5.

[3] ii, 38, 4 ; v, 82, 8, etc.

[4] ii, 38, 1–6, etc.

[5] iv, 53, 6.

[6] vii, 45, 1, etc.

[7] *La Religion védique d'après les hymnes du Rig Veda*, Paris, 1878–83, vol. iii, pp. 56 ff.

[8] i, 35, 1.

[9] *Brhadāraṇyaka-Upaniṣad*, i, 3, 1.

[10] i, 24, 8.

[11] viii, 101, 12.

really the sun that emits him as seed into the womb ";[1] Coomaraswamy[2] quotes in this connection Aristotle[3]—" Man and the sun generate man "—and Dante:[4] ". . . the sun, who is the father of all mortal life ". On the other hand, the sun is sometimes identified with death, for he devours his children as well as generating them.[5] Coomaraswamy devoted several brilliant studies (cf. the Bibliography) to the mythical and metaphysical expressions of divine bi-unity as it is formulated in Vedic and post-Vedic writings. In my book *Mitul Rein-tegrarii* (*The Myth of Reintegration*) I traced the opposites that are found together in primitive rites, myths and metaphysics. We shall have to return to these problems later on. For the moment, note the primitive ambivalence of the sun hiero-phanies developed in the framework of extremely elaborate systems of symbolism, theology and metaphysics.

It would, however, be wrong to look on these developments as simply the stereotyped and artificial workings of a mere verbal machinery. The laborious hermeneutics were merely the statement in accurate terms of all the meanings the sun hierophanies *could have*. That those meanings cannot be reduced to a single brief formula (that is, to rational and non-contradictory terms), is shown by the fact that the sun can be realized in different and even contradictory ways within the compass of a single religion. Take Buddha, for instance. As *cakravartin*, or universal sovereign, Buddha was very early identified with the sun. So much so indeed, that E. Senart wrote a startling book in which he attempted to reduce the life story of Śākyamuni to a series of solar allegories. He undoubtedly overstated his point, but it is true none the less that the solar element dominates both the legend and the mystical apotheosis of Buddha.[6]

However, within the framework of Buddhism, as indeed that of all Indian mystical religions, the sun does not always have the supreme position. India's mystical physiology, particularly

---

[1] *Jaiminiya Upaniṣad Brāhmaṇa*, iii, 10, 4.

[2] In " The Sun-Kiss ", *JAOS*, vol. lx, p. 50.

[3] *Physics*, ii, 2.

[4] *Paradiso*, 22, 116.

[5] *Pañcaviṁśa Brāhmaṇa*, xxi, 2, 1.

[6] Cf. a recent work on this subject, " Buddha and the Sun God ", by B. Rowland (*CZ*, 1938, vol. i).

Yoga and Tantra, attributes to the sun a definite " physiological " and cosmic sphere as against that of the moon. And the aim common to all these Indian mystical techniques is not to achieve *supremacy* over one of these spheres, but to *unify* them, to effect, in other words, the reintegration of the two opposing principles. It is just one of the many variants on the myth and metaphysic of reintegration; in this case the balance of opposites is expressed in the cosmological formula sun-moon. Of course, all these mystical techniques are possible only to a tiny minority as compared with the mass of the Indian people, but this does not necessarily mean that they represent an " evolution " as regards the religion of that mass, for even " primitives " know that same sun-moon formula of reintegration.[1] Consequently, the hierophanies of the sun, like every other hierophany, can be seen as significant on totally different levels without its basic structure undergoing any apparent " contradiction ".

The final result of giving absolute supremacy to solar hierophanies as developed in one sense only, can be seen in the excesses of those ascetic Indian sects whose members go on staring at the sun till they become totally blind. This is a case of the " dryness " and " sterility " of a purely solar order of things, which carries its limited logic to extremes. The counterpart of it is a species of " decay from damp ", the turning of men into " seeds ", which occurs in those sects which give the same sort of total acceptance to the nocturnal, lunar or earthly order of things (cf. § 134 ff.). It is the almost automatic fate of those who accept only one aspect of the sun hierophanies to be driven to a state of " blindness " and " dryness ", while those who fix themselves exclusively upon the " nocturnal sphere of the mind " are led into a state of permanent orgy and dissolution—a return to a sort of larval state (as in our day the telluric sect of the " Innocents ").

46. SUN HEROES, THE DEAD AND THE ELECT

A great many primitive hierophanies of the sun were preserved in popular traditions, and fitted in more or less with other religious systems. There are flaming wheels which are

[1] See my study " Cosmical Homology and Yoga ", *JISOA*, June-Dec., 1937, pp. 199–203.

sent down from heights at the time of each solstice, especially the summer one; medieval processions, in which wheels were borne on chariots or boats, whose prototypes can be found in prehistoric times; the custom of fastening men to wheels, the ritual prohibiting the use of a spinning wheel on certain evenings of the year (round about the time of the winter solstice), and other phenomena still to be found among European peasant communities (Fortuna, the " wheel of fortune ", the " wheel of the year ", etc.), all of which are solar in their original form. There can be no question here of going into the problem of their historical origins. Remember, however, that from the Bronze Age onwards there was in Northern Europe a myth about the sun's stallion (cf. the sun-chariot of Trundholm), and as R. Forrer has shown in his study on *Les Chars cultuels préhistoriques*, the ritual chariots of prehistory, which were made to reproduce the movement of the heavenly bodies, can be looked on as the prototype of ordinary chariots later.[1]

But studies like Oskar Almgren's on the protohistoric cave-drawings of northern Europe, or O. Höfler's on the Germanic secret societies of antiquity and of the Middle Ages have brought out the complex character of " sun worship " in northern regions. This complexity cannot be explained as the effect of hybrid mixtures and syntheses, for primitive societies evince it as much as any. Indeed it indicates rather how primitive the cult is. Almgren and Höfler have pointed out the symbiosis of sun elements with funereal (as with the " Wild Hunt ") and those that relate to the earth and farming (the fertilization of fields by the wheel of the sun and so on). And some time back Mannhardt, Gaidoz and Frazer showed how the " year " and the wheel of fortune fit together and centre on the sun both in the agricultural magic and the religion of ancient European beliefs, and in modern folk lore.

The same religious pattern of sun-fertility-hero (or represent-

[1] Just as the ritual boat on which corpses were placed was the prototype for all boats. The point is an important one; it helps us to a better understanding of how human skills began. What is called man's conquest of nature was not so much the direct result of scientific discoveries as the fruit of man's various " situations " in the universe, situations determined by the dialectic of the hierophanies. Metallurgy, agriculture, the calendar and many other things began as a result of man's realizing one of his situations in the universe. I shall say more about this later.

ative of the dead) appears again more or less intact in other civilizations. In Japan, for instance, as part of the ritual drama of the " visitor " (a drama which includes elements of the cult connected with earth and agriculture) a group of young men with daubed faces, called the " Sun Devils ", go from farm to farm to ensure the fertility of the earth for the coming year, and they do this as representing their solar ancestors.[1] In European ceremonials, the bowling of blazing wheels at the time of the solstices also probably performs the magic function of restoring the sun's powers. Indeed, throughout the north, the gradual shortening of the days as the winter solstice approaches inspires fear that the sun may die away completely. In other places this state of alarm is expressed in apocalyptic visions: the falling or the darkening of the sun becomes one of the signs of the coming end of the world, of the conclusion, that is, of one cosmic cycle (generally to be followed by a new creation and a new human race). Indeed, the Mexicans ensured the immortality of the sun by constantly sacrificing prisoners to it so that their blood would renew its failing energies. But in this religion there always remains a dark fear that there will periodically be a collapse of the whole universe. However much blood is offered to it, the sun will one day fall; the apocalypse is part of the necessary rhythm of the universe.

Another important mythical pattern is that of solar heroes, particularly common among nomad shepherds, among the peoples, in fact, from whom the nations destined to " make history " have generally sprung. We find these sun heroes among African shepherds (the Hottentots, the Herreros, and the Masai for instance);[2] among the Turco-Mongols (for instance the hero Gesser Khan), the Jews (notably Samson) and above all, in all the Indo-European nations. Enough has been written to fill whole libraries on the myths and legends of the sun heroes, and traces of them can be found even in traditional lullabies. This mania of scholars for seeing the sun everywhere is not wholly baseless. There is no doubt that at one time or another the " sun hero " was in favour in all the races we have talked of. But we must be careful not

---

[1] That is, the " dead "; Slawik, " Kultische Geheimbünde der Japaner und Germanen ", WBKL, Salzburg-Leipzig, 1936, vol. iv, p. 730.

[2] Graebner, Das Weltbild der Primitiven, Munich, 1924, p. 65.

to reduce the sun hero to being simply a physical manifestation of the sun; neither his structure nor his place in myth is confined to merely the phenomena of the sun (dawn, rays, light, twilight, and so on). A sun hero will always present in addition a " dark side ", a connection with the world of the dead, with initiation, fertility and the rest. The myth of sun heroes is equally full of elements connected with the cult of sovereignty or of a demiurge. The hero " saves " the world, renews it, opens a new era which sometimes even amounts to a new organization of the universe; in other words, he still preserves the qualities of the demiurge of the Supreme Being. A career like that of Mithra who was at first a sky god, later became a sun god and later still a saviour (as the *Sol Invictus*), can to some extent be explained by this demiurgic function of ordering the world (all grains and plants grew up from the bull slain by Mithra).

There are further reasons against reducing sun heroes to solar phenomena in the way " naturalist " mythology does. Every religious " form " is basically " imperialist "—it constantly adopts the substance, attributes and honours of other—often very different—religious forms. Every form that gains the ascendancy tends to seek to be *all*, to extend its power over the whole of religious experience. We may therefore be quite certain that whenever a religious form that began by being solar (whether god, hero, ceremony, myth, or anything else) became supreme, it must have included elements from without, assimilated and integrated into it by its very nature of imperialist expansion.

I do not propose to conclude this brief study of the nature of sun hierophanies with any general summing-up. If I did I should only be stating the major themes I have stressed in the chapter: the solarization of Supreme Beings, the sun's connection with sovereignty, initiation and the élite, its ambivalence, its relations with the dead, with fertility, and so on. But it *is* worth underlining the close connection between solar theology and the élite—whether of kings, initiates, heroes or philosophers. Unlike other nature hierophanies, sun hierophanies tend to become the privilege of a closed circle, of a minority of the elect. The result is the hastening of the process of rationalization. In the Graeco-Roman world the sun, having become the "fire of intelligence", ended by becoming a "cosmic principle"; from a *hierophany* it turned into an *idea* by a process rather similar to that undergone by various of the sky gods (Iho, Brahman, etc.). Even Heraclitus says that "the sun is new each day". To Plato it was the image of the good as expressed in visible things;[1] to the Orphics it was the intellect of the world. Rationalization and syncretism advanced together. Macrobius[2] relates all theology to sun-worship, and sees in the sun Apollo, Liber-Dionysos, Mars, Mercury, Aesculapius, Hercules, Serapis, Osiris, Horus, Adonis, Nemesis, Pan, Saturn, Adad, and even Jupiter. The Emperor Julian, in his treatise *On the Sun King*, and Proclus in his *Hymn to the Sun*, offer their own syncretist and rationalist interpretations.

These last honours paid to the sun in the twilight of antiquity are not entirely devoid of significance; they are like palimpsests in which traces of the old writing can still be seen under the new—they still reveal traces of the true, primitive hierophanies: the dependence of the sun on God which recalls the very early myth of the solarized demiurge, its connections with fecundity and plant life and so on. But generally speaking, we find there only the palest shadow of what the sun hierophanies once meant, and constant rationalization makes it paler still. The philosophers, last among the "elect", thus at last completed the secularization of what was one of the mightiest of all the cosmic hierophanies.

---

[1] *Rep.*, 508 b, c.
[2] *Saturnalia*, i, chs. xvii–xxiii.

BIBLIOGRAPHY

On sun cults in general :
BOLL, F., *Die Sonne im Glauben und in der Weltanschauung der alten Völker*, Stuttgart, 1922; KRAPPE, A. G., *La Genèse des mythes*, Paris, 1938, pp. 81 ff.; FRAZER, Sir James, *The Worship of Nature*, London, 1926, vol. i, pp. 441 ff.; DECHELETTE, J., " Le Culte du soleil aux temps préhistoriques ", *RAR*, 1909, pp. 305 ff.; *Manuel d'archéologie préhistorique, celtique et gallo-romaine*, Paris, 1908– , vol. ii, pp. 413 ff.

On sun myths:
EHRENREICH, P., " Die Sonne im Mythos ", *Mythologische Bibliothek*, Leipzig, 1915-6, vol. viii, 1; OHLMARKS, Ake, *Heimdalls Horn und Odins Auge*, Lund, 1937, vol. i, pp. 32 ff., 257 ff., and *passim*.

On the " solarization " of the Supreme Being:
PETTAZZONI, R., *Dio*, Rome, 1922, vol. i, p. 367.

On the coexistence of solar and plant elements in Mesopotamian gods and religions:
Cf. FRANKFORT, H., " Gods and Myths on Sargonid Seals ", *Irak*, 1934, vol. i, pp. 2–29; ENGNELL, Ivan, *Studies in Divine Kingship in the Ancient Near East*, Uppsala, 1943; GÖTZE, A., *Kleinasien*, Leipzig, 1933; on Shamash, there is material and a bibliography in FURLANI, G., *La Religione babilonese-assira*, Bologna, 1928-9, vol. i, pp. 162-9; vol. ii, pp. 179-83, etc.; DHORME, E., *Les Religions de Babylonie et d'Assyrie*; also *MA*, Paris, 1945, vol. ii, pp. 60-7, 86-9; on Shamash and the art of divining; HALDAR, A., *Associations of Cult Prophets among the Ancient Semites*, Uppsala, 1945, pp. 1 ff.

On the solar elements in Arctic and northern Asiatic religions:
LEHTISALO, *Entwurf einer Mythologie der Jurak-Samoyeden*, Helsinki, 1927; GAHS, A., " Kopf-, Schädel- und Langknochenopfer bei Rentier-volkern ", *Festschrift W. Schmidt*, Mödling, 1928, pp. 231-68.

On solar religions among the Munda tribes:
Cf. DALTON, E. T., *Descriptive Ethnology of Bengal*, Calcutta, 1872; FRAZER, Sir J., *Worship of Nature*, pp. 614 ff.; BODDING, P. O., *Santali Folk Tales*, Oslo, 1925-7, vols. i–ii; RAHMANN, R., " Gottheiten der Primitivstämme im nordöstlichen Vorderindien ", *APS*, 1936, vol. xxxi, pp. 37–96; KOPPERS, W., " Bhagwan, The Supreme Deity of the Bhils ", *APS*, 1940-1, vols. xxxv-vi, pp.. 265-325.

On sun religions in Oceania:
RIVERS, W. H. R., " Sun-cult and Megaliths in Oceania ", *AA*, 1915, new series, xvii, pp. 431 ff.; id., *The History of Melanesian Society*, vols. i–ii, Cambridge, 1914; FRAZER, Sir J., *The Belief in Immortality and the Worship of the Dead*, vols. i–iii, London, 1913-24; WILLIAMSON, R. W., *Religious and Cosmic Beliefs in Central Polynesia*, vols. i–ii, Cambridge, 1933.

On the " Children of the Sun ":
PERRY, W. J., *The Children of the Sun*, 2nd ed., London, 1927; HOCART, A. M., *Kingship*, London, 1927.

On the sun religion in Egypt:
VANDIER, J., " La Religion égyptienne ", *MA*, Paris, 1944, vol. i, pp. 36 ff.; WAINWRIGHT, G. A., *The Sky-Religion in Egypt*, Cambridge, 1928; JUNKER, H., *Die Götterlehre von Memphis*, Berlin, 1940; id., " Der sehende und blinde Gott ", *Sitz. d. b. Akad. d. Wissensch.*, Munich,

1942; GARNOT, J. Sainte-Fare, *RHR*, July-Dec. 1944, vol. cxxviii, pp. 116-8; id., *RHR*, Jan.-June 1945, vol. cxxix, pp. 128 ff.; on the conflict between Ra and Osiris, WEILL, R., *Le Champ des roseaux et le champ des offrandes dans la religion funéraire et la religion générale*, Paris, 1936.

On the Sun-God among the Indo-Aryans:
See VON SCHRÖDER, L., *Arische Religion*, Leipzig, 1916, vol. ii, pp. 3-461; among the Mediterraneans and Greeks, COOK, A. B., *Zeus. A Study in Ancient Religion*, Cambridge, 1914, vol. i, pp. 197 ff.; PESTA-LOZZA, Uberto, *Pagine di religione mediterranea*, Milan-Messina, 1945, vol. ii, pp. 9 ff.; KERENYI, Karl, " Vater Helios ", *EJ*, Zürich, 1943, vol. x, 1944, pp. 81-124; KRAPPE, A. H., " Apollon ", *SMSR*, 1943-6, vols. xix-xx, pp. 115-32; traces of sun worship in Iran: WIDENGREN, G., *Hochgottglaube im alten Iran*, Uppsala, 1938, pp. 183 ff.; on primitive Italian sun religions, cf. KOCH, C., *Gestirnverehrung im alten Italien*, 1933, pp. 50 ff.; ALTHEIM, F., and TRAUTMANN, E., " Neue Felsbilder der Val Camonica. Die Sonne in Kult und Mythos ", *WS*, 1938, vol. xix, pp. 12-45.

On sun gods in Vedic India:
BERGAIGNE, A., *La Religion védique d'après les hymnes du Rig Veda*, Paris, 1878-83, 3 vols., vol. ii, pp. 160 ff., 379 ff.; vol. iii, pp. 38 ff., etc.

On the solar elements in the legend of Buddha:
Cf. ROWLAND, B., " Buddha and the Sun God ", *CZ*, 1938, vol. i, pp. 69-84; on the metaphysical implications of the sun myths: cf. COOMARASWAMY, A., " The Darker Side of the Dawn ", *Smithsonian Miscellaneous Collection*, Washington, 1935, vol. civ, no. 1; id., " The Sun Kiss ", *JAOS*, vol. lx, pp. 46-7, etc.

On sun worship in the Roman Empire:
SCHMIDT, Paul, " Sol Invictus. Betrachtungen zu spätrömischer Religion und Politik ", *EJ*, Zürich, 1944, vol. x, pp. 169-252.

On the wheel as a symbol of the sun among the Celts:
GAIDOZ, " Le Dieu gaulois du soleil ", *RAR*, 1884-5; LAMBRECHTS, Pierre, *Contributions à l'étude des divinités celtiques*, Bruges, 1942,. pp. 71 ff.

On solar cults and symbols in northern European prehistory and European folklore:
ALMGREN, O., *Nordische Felszeichnung als religiöse Urkunden*, Frank-furt a. M., 1934, *passim*, but particularly pp. 343 ff.; HÖFLER, O., *Kultische Geheimbünde der Germanen*, Frankfurt a. M., 1934, pp. 112 ff.; FORRER, R., " Les Chars cultuels préhistoriques et leurs survivances aux époques historiques ", *PHE*, 1932, vol. i, pp. 19-123; MANNHARDT, W., *Wald-und Feld-Kulte*, 2nd ed., Berlin, 1904-5, vol. i, pp. 591 ff.; FRAZER, J., *Baldur the Beautiful*, vol. i, pp. 106-327; DUMEZIL, G., *Loki*, Paris, 1948, pp. 225 ff.

On the connection between the earth and the sun among the Japanese:
SLAWIK, A., " Kultische Geheimbünde der Japaner und Germanen ", *WBKL*, Salzburg-Leipzig, 1936, vol. iv, pp. 675-764.

On the significance of solar symbolism in Christian theology: RAHNER, Hugo, " Das christliche Mysterium von Sonne und Mond ", *EJ*, Zürich, 1944, vol. x, pp. 305-404; DEONNA, W., " Les Crucifix de la Vallée de Saas (Valais); Sol et Luna. Histoire d'un thème iconographique ", *RHR*, 1946, vol. cxxxii, pp. 5-47; 1947-8, vol. cxxxiii, pp. 49-102.

IV

THE MOON AND ITS MYSTIQUE

47. THE MOON AND TIME

THE sun is always the same, always itself, never in any sense " becoming ". The moon, on the other hand, is a body which waxes, wanes and disappears, a body whose existence is subject to the universal law of becoming, of birth and death. The moon, like man, has a career involving tragedy, for its failing, like man's, ends in death. For three nights the starry sky is without a moon. But this " death " is followed by a rebirth: the " new moon ". The moon's going out, in " death ", is never final. One Babylonian hymn to Sin sees the moon as " a fruit growing from itself ".[1] It is reborn of its own substance, in pursuance of its own destined career.

This perpetual return to its beginnings, and this ever-recurring cycle make the moon *the* heavenly body above all others concerned with the rhythms of life. It is not surprising, then, that it governs all those spheres of nature that fall under the law of recurring cycles: waters, rain, plant life, fertility. The phases of the moon showed man time in the concrete sense—as distinct from astronomical time which certainly only came to be realized later. Even in the Ice Age the meaning of the moon's phases and their magic powers were clearly known. We find the symbolism of spirals, snakes and lightning —all of them growing out of the notion of the moon as the measure of rhythmic change and fertility—in the Siberian cultures of the Ice Age.[2] Time was quite certainly measured everywhere by the phases of the moon. Even to-day there are nomad tribes living off what they can hunt and grow who use only the lunar calendar. The oldest Indo-Aryan root connected with the heavenly bodies is the one that means " moon ":[3] it is the root *me*, which in Sanskrit becomes *māmi*, " I measure ".

[1] Furlani, *La Religione babilonese-assira*, Bologna, 1929, vol. i, p. 155.
[2] e.g., at Irkutsk; cf. Hentze, *Mythes et symboles lunaires*, Antwerp, 1932, pp. 84 ff., figs. 59, 60.
[3] Cf. Schrader, *Sprachvergleichung und Urgeschichte* (Jena, 1883), 2nd ed., pp. 443 ff.; W. Schultz, " Zeitrechnung und Weltordnung ", *MB*, Leipzig, 1924, no. 35, pp. 12 ff.

The moon becomes the universal measuring gauge. All the words relating to the moon in the Indo-European languages come from that root: *mās* (Sanskrit), *mah* (Avestic), *mah* (Old Prussian), *menu* (Lithuanian), *mena* (Gothic), *mene* (Greek), *mensis* (Latin). The Germans used to measure time by nights.[1] Traces of this ancient way of reckoning are also preserved in popular European traditions; certain feasts are celebrated at night as, for instance, Christmas night, Easter, Pentecost, Saint John's Day and so on.[2]

Time as governed and measured by the phases of the moon might be called " living " time. It is bound up with the reality of life and nature, rain and the tides, the time of sowing, the menstrual cycle. A whole series of phenomena belonging to totally different " cosmic levels " are ordered according to the rhythms of the moon or are under their influence. The " primitive mind ", once having grasped the " powers " of the moon, then establishes connections of response and even interchange between the moon and those phenomena. Thus, for instance, from the earliest times, certainly since the Neolithic Age, with the discovery of agriculture, the same symbolism has linked together the moon, the sea waters, rain, the fertility of women and of animals, plant life, man's destiny after death and the ceremonies of initiation. The mental syntheses made possible by the realization of the moon's rhythms connect and unify very varied realities; their structural symmetries and the analogies in their workings could never have been seen had not " primitive " man intuitively perceived the moon's law of periodic change, as he did very early on.

The moon measures, but it also unifies. Its " forces " or rhythms are what one may call the " lowest common denominator " of an endless number of phenomena and symbols. The whole universe is seen as a pattern, subject to certain laws. The world is no longer an infinite space filled with the activity of a lot of disconnected autonomous creatures: within that space itself things can be seen to correspond and fit together. All this, of course, is not the result of a reasoned analysis of reality, but of an ever clearer intuition of it in its totality. Though there may be a series of ritual or mythical side-

[1] Tacitus, *Germania*, ii.
[2] Kuhn, quoted in Hentze, p. 248.

commentaries on the moon which are separate from the rest, with their own somewhat specialized function (as, for instance, certain mythical lunar beings with only one foot or one hand, by whose magic power one can cause rain to fall), there can be no symbol, ritual or myth of the moon that does not imply all the lunar values known at a given time. There can be no part without the whole. The spiral, for instance, which was taken to be a symbol of the moon as early as the Ice Age, relates to the phases of the moon, but also includes erotic elements springing from the vulva-shell analogy, water elements (the moon=shell), and some to do with fertility (the double volute, horns and so on). By wearing a pearl as an amulet a woman is united to the powers of water (shell), the moon (the shell a symbol of the moon; created by the rays of the moon, etc.), eroticism, birth and embryology. A medicinal plant contains in itself the threefold effectiveness of the moon, the waters and vegetation, even when only one of these powers is explicitly present in the mind of the user. Each of these powers or " effectivenesses " in its turn works on a number of different levels. Vegetation, for instance, implies notions of death and rebirth, of light and darkness (as zones of the universe), of fecundity and abundance, and so on. There is no such thing as a symbol, emblem or power with only one kind of meaning. Everything hangs together, everything is connected, and makes up a cosmic whole.

48. THE COHERENCE OF ALL LUNAR EPIPHANIES

Such a whole could certainly never be grasped by any mind accustomed to proceeding analytically. And even by intuition modern man cannot get hold of all the wealth of meaning and harmony that such a cosmic *reality* (or, in fact, sacred reality) involves in the primitive mind. To the primitive, a lunar symbol (an amulet or iconographic sign) does not merely contain in itself all the lunar forces at work on every level of the cosmos —but actually, by the power of the ritual involved, places the wearer himself at the centre of those forces, increasing his vitality, making him more *real*, and guaranteeing him a happier state after death. It is important to keep stressing this fact that every religious act (that is, every act with a meaning) performed by primitive man has a character of *totality*, for there is always a danger of our looking upon the functions, powers and attributes of the moon as we discuss them in this chapter in an *analytic* and *cumulative* manner. We tend to divide what is and must remain a whole. Where we use the words " because ", and " therefore ", the mind of the primitive man would phrase it perhaps as " in the same way " (for instance, I say: because the moon governs the waters, plants are subject to it, but it would be more correct to say: plants and the waters are subject to it *in the same way* . . .).

The " powers " of the moon are to be discovered not by means of a succession of analytical exercises, but by intuition; *it reveals itself* more and more fully. The analogies formed in the primitive mind are as it were orchestrated there by means of symbols; for instance, the moon appears and disappears; the snail shows and withdraws its horns; the bear appears and disappears with the seasons; thus, the snail becomes the scene of a lunar theophany, as in the ancient religion of Mexico in which the moon god, Tecciztecatl, is shown enclosed in a snail's shell;[1] it also becomes an amulet, and so on. The bear becomes the ancestor of the human race, for man, whose life is similar to that of the moon, must have been created out of the very substance or by the magic power of that orb of living reality.

The symbols which get their meaning from the moon *are* at the same time the moon. The spiral is both a lunar hierophany—expressing the light-darkness cycle—and a sign by which man can absorb the moon's powers into himself. Lightning, too, is a kratophany of the moon, for its brightness recalls that of the moon, and it heralds rain, which is governed by the moon. All these symbols, hierophanies, myths, rituals, amulets and the rest, which I call lunar to give them one convenient name, form a whole in the mind of the primitive; they are bound together by harmonies, analogies, and elements held in common, like one great cosmic " net ", a vast web in which every piece fits and nothing is isolated from the rest. If you want to express the multiplicity of lunar hierophanies in a single formula, you may say that they reveal life repeating itself rhythmically. All the values of the moon, whether

[1] Cf. Wilke, " Die Religion der Indogermanen in archäologischer Betracht-ung ", *MB*, Leipzig, 1923, no. 31, p. 149, fig. 163.

cosmological, magic or religious, are explained by its modality of *being*: by the fact that it is " living ", and inexhaustible in its own regeneration. In the primitive mind, the intuition of the cosmic destiny of the moon was equivalent to the first step, the foundation of an anthropology. Man saw himself reflected in the " life " of the moon; not simply because his own life came to an end, like that of all organisms, but because his own thirst for regeneration, his hopes of a " rebirth ", gained confirmation from the fact of there being always a new moon.

It does not matter to us a great deal whether, in the innumerable beliefs centring upon the moon, we are dealing with adoration of the moon itself, of a divinity inhabiting it, or of a mythical personification of it. Nowhere in the history of religions do we find an adoration of any natural object in itself. A sacred thing, whatever its form and substance, is sacred because it reveals or shares in ultimate *reality*. Every religious object is always an " incarnation " of something: of the *sacred* (§ 3 ff.). It incarnates it by the quality of its being (as for instance, the sky, the sun, the moon or the earth), or by its form (that is, symbolically: as with the spiral-snail), or by a hierophany (a *certain* place, a *certain* stone, etc. becomes sacred; a certain object is " sanctified " or " consecrated " by a ritual, or by contact with another sacred object or person, and so on).

Consequently, the moon is no more adored in *itself* than any other object, but in what it reveals of the sacred, that is, in the power centred in it, in the inexhaustible life and reality that it manifests. The sacred reality of the moon was recognized either immediately, in the lunar hierophany itself, or in the forms created by that hierophany over the course of thousands of years—that is in the representations to which it had given birth: personifications, symbols or myths. The differences between these various forms are not the concern of this chapter. After all, what we are seeking here is mainly to explain the hierophany of the moon and all that it involves. There is no need even to confine ourselves to evidence that is obviously " sacred ", lunar gods, for example, and the rituals and myths consecrated to them. To the primitive mind, I repeat, everything that had a meaning, everything connected with *absolute reality*, had sacred value. We can observe the religious character of the moon with as much precision in the symbolism of the pearl or of the lightning as we can by studying a lunar divinity like the Babylonian Sin or the goddess Hecate.

49. THE MOON AND THE WATERS

Both because they are subject to rhythms (rain and tides), and because they sponsor the growth of living things, waters are subject to the moon. " The moon is in the waters "[1] and " rain comes from the moon "[2]; those are two *leitmotiven* in Indian thought. *Apām napāt*, " the son of water ", was in primitive times the name of a spirit of vegetation, but was later applied also to the moon and to the nectar of the moon, *soma*. Ardvisura Anahita, the Iranian goddess of water, was a lunar being; Sin, the Babylonian moon god, also governed the waters. One hymn brings out how fruitful his theophany is: " When thou floatest like a boat on the waters . . . the pure river Euphrates is filled with water to the full . . ."[3] One text of the " Langdon Epic " speaks of the place " whence the waters flow from their source, from the moon's reservoir ".[4]

All the moon divinities preserve more or less obvious water attributes or functions. To certain American Indian tribes, the moon, or the moon god, is at the same time the god of water. (This is true in Mexico, and among the Iroquois, to name two instances.) One tribe in central Brazil call the moon-god's daughter " Mother of the Waters ".[5] Hieronymo de Chaves said (in 1576), speaking of ancient Mexican beliefs concerning the moon, " the moon makes all things grow and multiply . . ." and " all moisture is governed by it ".[6] The link between the moon and the tides which both the Greeks and the Celts observed, was also known to the Maoris of New Zealand[7] and the Eskimos (whose moon divinities govern the tides).[8]

---

[1] *RV*, i, 105, 1.
[2] *Aitareya Brāhmaṇa*, viii, 28, 15.
[3] *Cuneiform Texts*, 15–17; 16 d.
[4] Quoted by Albright, " Some Cruces of the Langdon Epic ", *JAOS*, 1919 vol. xxxix, p. 68.
[5] Briffault, *The Mothers*, London, 1927, vol. ii, pp. 632 ff.
[6] Seler, *Gesammelte Abhandlungen*, Berlin, 1902, vol. iv, p. 129.
[7] Krappe, *La Genèse des mythes*, Paris, 1938, p. 110.
[8] W. Schmidt, *Ursprung*, vol. iii, 496.

From the earliest times it was recognized that rainfall followed the phases of the moon. A whole series of mythical characters, belonging to cultures as varied as the Bushman, Mexican, Australian, Samoyed and Chinese,[1] were marked by their power to cause rain and by having only one foot or only one hand. Hentze establishes quite fully that they are lunar in essence. And, too, there are numerous moon symbols in all images of them, and all their various rites and myths have a definite lunar character. While the waters and the rain are governed by the moon, and normally follow a fixed order—that is, they follow the phases of the moon—all disasters connected with them, on the other hand, display the moon's other aspect, as the periodic destroyer of outworn " forms " and, we may say, of effecting regeneration on the cosmic scale.

Flood corresponds to the three days of darkness, or " death ", of the moon. It is a cataclysm, but never a final one, for it takes place under the seal of the moon and the waters, which are pre-eminently the sign of growth and regeneration. A flood destroys simply because the " forms " are old and worn out, but it is always followed by a new humanity and a new history (§ 72). The vast majority of deluge myths tell how a single individual survived, and how the new race was descended from him. This survivor—man or woman—occasionally marries a lunar animal, which thus becomes ancestor to the race. So, for instance, one Dyak legend tells how a woman was the only survivor of a flood which followed upon the slaying of an immense boa constrictor, a " lunar animal ", and gave birth to a new humanity by mating with a dog (or, in some variants, with a stick for firing, found next to a dog).[2]

Of the numerous variants on the Deluge myth we will look at one—an Australian version (that of the Kurnai tribe). One day all the waters were swallowed by an immense frog, Dak. In vain the parched animals tried to make her laugh. Not until the eel (or serpent) began to roll about and twist itself round did Dak burst out laughing, and the waters thus rushed out and produced the flood.[3] The frog is a lunar animal, for a great

---

[1] Hentze, pp. 152 ff.

[2] Hentze, p. 24.

[3] Van Gennep, *Mythes et légendes d'Australie*, Paris, 1906, pp. 84–5.

many legends speak of a frog to be seen in the moon,[1] and it is always present in the innumerable rites for inducing rain.[2] Father Schmidt explains the Australian myth by the fact that the new moon halts the flow of the waters (Dak swallowing them).[3] And Winthuis,[4] who disagrees with Schmidt's interpretation, discerns an erotic meaning in this frog myth; but that would not, of course, disprove its lunar nature, nor the anthropogonic function of the deluge (which "creates" a new, regenerated, humanity).

Again in Australia we find another variant on the watery disaster produced by the moon. The moon asked man one day for some oppossum skins to wear at night as it was cold, and man refused; to avenge itself, the moon caused torrents of rain to fall and flood the whole area.[5] The Mexicans also believed that the moon caused the disaster, but under the guise of a young and beautiful woman.[6] However, there is one thing to note with all these catastrophes induced by the moon (most of them provoked by some insult paid to it, or by ignorance of some ritual prohibition—that is, by a "sin" indicating that man is backsliding spiritually, abandoning law and order, putting the rhythms of nature out of joint): and that is the myth of regeneration, and the appearance of a "new man". This myth fits in perfectly, as we shall see, with the redemptive functions of the moon and the waters.

50. THE MOON AND VEGETATION

That there was a connection between the moon, rain and plant life was realized before the discovery of agriculture. The plant world comes from the same source of universal fertility, and is subject to the same recurring cycles governed by the moon's movements. One Iranian text says that plants grow by its warmth.[7] Some tribes in Brazil call it "mother of grasses"[8] and in a great many places (Polynesia, Moluccas,

---

[1] Briffault, *The Mothers*, London, 1927, vol. ii, pp. 634–5.
[2] Briffault, ibid. ; Krappe, p. 321, n. 2.
[3] *Ursprung*, vol. ii, pp. 394–5.
[4] *Das Zweigeschlechterwesen*, Leipzig, 1928, pp. 179–81.
[5] Van Gennep, p. 46.
[6] Briffault, vol. ii, p. 573.
[7] *Yast*, vii, 4.
[8] Briffault, vol. ii, p. 629.

Melanesia, China, Sweden, etc.) it is thought that grass grows on the moon.[1] French peasants, even to-day, sow at the time of the new moon; but they prune their trees and pick their vegetables when the moon is on the wane,[2] presumably in order not to go against the rhythm of nature by damaging a living organism when nature's forces are on the upward swing.

The organic connection between the moon and vegetation is so strong that a very large number of fertility gods are also divinities of the moon; for instance the Egyptian Hathor, Ishtar the Iranian Anaitis, and so on. In almost all the gods of vegetation and fecundity there persist lunar attributes or powers—even when their divine " form " has become completely autonomous. Sin is also the creator of the grasses; Dionysos is both moon-god and god of vegetation; Osiris possesses all these attributes—moon, water, plant life and agriculture. We can discern the moon-water-vegetation pattern particularly clearly in the religious nature of certain beverages of divine origin, such as the Indian *soma*, and the Iranian *haoma*; these were even personified into divinities—autonomous, though less important than the major gods of the Indo-Iranian pantheon. And in this divine liquor which confers immortality on all who drink it, we can recognize the sacredness that centres round the moon, water and vegetation. It is supremely the " divine substance ", for it transmutes life into absolute reality—or immortality. *Amṛta*, ambrosia, *soma*, *haoma* and the rest all have a celestial prototype drunk only by gods and heroes, but there is a similar power in earthly drinks too—in the *soma* the Indians drank in Vedic times, in the wine of the Dionysiac orgies. Furthermore, these earthly drinks owe their potency to their corresponding celestial prototype. Sacred inebriation makes it possible to share—though fleetingly and imperfectly—in the divine mode of being; it achieves, in fact, the paradox of at once possessing the fulness of existence, and becoming; of being at once dynamic and static. The metaphysical role of the moon is to *live* and yet remain *immortal*, to undergo death, but as a rest and regeneration, never as a conclusion. This is the destiny

[1] Briffault, vol. ii, pp. 628–30.
[2] Krappe, p. 100.

which man is trying to conquer for himself in all the rites, symbols and myths—rites, symbols and myths in which, as we have seen, the sacred values of the moon exist together with those of water and of vegetation, whether the latter derive their sacredness from the moon, or constitute autonomous hierophanies. In either case we are faced with an *ultimate reality*, a source of power and of life from which all living forms spring, either of its substance, or as a result of its blessing.

The connections seen between the different cosmic levels that the moon governs—rain, plant life, animal and human fecundity, the souls of the dead—enter into even as primitive a religion as that of the Pygmies of Africa. Their feast of the new moon takes place a little before the rainy season. The moon, which they call Pe, is held to be the " principle of generation, and the mother óf fecundity ".[1] The feast of the new moon is reserved exclusively for the women, just as the feast of the sun is celebrated exclusively by the men.[2] Because the moon is both " mother and the refuge of ghosts " the women honour it by smearing themselves with clay and vegetable juices, thus becoming white like ghosts and moonlight. The ritual consists in preparing an alcoholic liquid from fermented bananas, which the women drink when they are wearied by their dancing, and of dances and prayers addressed to the moon. The men do not dance, nor even accompany the ritual on their tom-toms. The moon, " mother of living things ", is asked to keep away the souls of the dead and to bring fertility, to give the tribe a lot of children, and fish, game and fruit.[3]

51. THE MOON AND FERTILITY

The fertility of animals, as well as that of plants, is subject to the moon. The relationship between the moon and fecundity occasionally becomes somewhat complicated owing to the appearance of new religious " forms "—like the Earth-Mother, and the various agricultural divinities. However, there is one aspect of the moon that remains permanently evident, however many religious syntheses have gone towards making up these new " forms "; and that is the prerogative of fertility, of

[1] Trilles, *Les Pygmées de la forêt équatoriale*, Paris, 1933, p. 112.
[2] Trilles, p. 113.
[3] Trilles, p. 115 f.

recurring creation, of inexhaustible life. The horns of oxen, for instance, which are used to characterize the great divinities of fecundity, are an emblem of the divine *Magna Mater*. Wherever they are to be found in Neolithic cultures, either in iconography, or as part of idols in the form of oxen, they denote the presence of the Great Goddess of fertility.[1] And a horn is always the image of the new moon: " Clearly the ox's horn became a symbol of the moon because it brings to mind a crescent; therefore both horns together represent two crescents, or the complete career of the moon."[2] And also in the iconography of the prehistoric Chinese cultures of Kansu and Yang-kao you will often find symbols of the moon and symbols of fertility together—stylized horns are framed by a pattern of lightning-flashes (signifying the rain and the moon) and lozenges (which are a symbol of femininity).[3]

Certain animals become symbols or even " presences " of the moon because their shape or their behaviour is reminiscent of the moon's. So with the snail which goes in and out of its shell; the bear, which disappears in midwinter and reappears in the spring; the frog because it swells up, submerges itself, and later returns to the surface of the water; the dog, because it can be seen in the moon, or because it is supposed in some myths to be the ancestor of the race; the snake, because it appears and disappears, and because it has as many coils as the moon has days (this legend is also preserved in Greek tradition);[4] or because it is " the husband of all women ", or because it sloughs its skin (that is to say, is periodically reborn, is " immortal "), and so on. The symbolism of the snake is somewhat confusing, but all the symbols are directed to the same central idea: it is immortal because it is continually reborn, and therefore it is a moon " force ", and as such can bestow fecundity, knowledge (that is, prophecy) and even immortality. There are innumerable myths telling the disastrous story of how the serpent stole the immortality given to man by his god.[5] But they are all later variants on a primitive

[1] O. Menghin, *Weltgeschichte der Steinzeit*, Vienna, 1931, pp. 148, 448.
[2] Hentze, p. 96.
[3] Cf. Hentze, figs. 74–82.
[4] Aristotle, *Hist. Animal.*, ii, 12; Pliny, *Hist. Nat.*, xi, 82.
[5] Frazer, *Folklore in the Old Testament*, London, 1918, vol. i, pp. 66 ff.

myth in which the serpent (or a sea monster) guarded the sacred spring and the spring of immortality (the Tree of Life, the Fountain of Youth, the Golden Apples).

I can only mention here a few of the myths and symbols connected with the serpent, and only those which indicate its character of a lunar animal. In the first place, its connection with women and with fecundity: the moon is the source of all fertility, and also governs the menstrual cycle. It is personified as " the master of women ". A great many peoples used to think—and some think it to this day—that the moon, in the form of a man, or a serpent, copulates with their women. That is why, among the Eskimos for instance, unmarried girls will not look at the moon for fear of becoming pregnant.[1] The Australians believe that the moon comes down to earth in the form of a sort of Don Juan, makes women pregnant and then deserts them.[2] This myth is still current in India.[3]

Since the serpent is an epiphany of the moon, it fulfills the same function. Even to-day it is said in the Abruzzi that the serpent copulates with all women.[4] The Greeks and Romans also believed it. Alexander the Great's mother, Olympia, played with snakes.[5] The famous Aratus of Sicyon was said to be a son of Aesculapius because, according to Pausanias,[6] his mother had conceived him of a serpent. Suetonius[7] and Dio Cassius[8] tell how the mother of Augustus conceived from the embrace of a serpent in Apollo's temple. A similar legend was current about the elder Scipio. In Germany, France, Portugal and elsewhere, women used to be afraid that a snake would slip into their mouths when they were asleep, and they would become pregnant, particularly during menstruation.[9] In India, when women wanted to have children, they adored a cobra. All over the East it was believed that woman's first sexual contact was with a snake, at puberty or during men-

---

[1] Briffault, vol. ii, p. 585.

[2] Van Gennep, pp. 101–2.

[3] Krappe, p. 106.

[4] Finamore, *Tradizioni popolari abruzzesi*, Palermo, 1894, p. 237.

[5] Plutarch, *Vita. Alex.*, ii.

[6] ii, 10, 3.

[7] *Divus Augustus*, 94.

[8] 55, 1.

[9] Briffault, vol. ii, p. 664.

struation.[1]   The Komati tribe in the Mysore province of
India use snakes made of stone in a rite to bring about the
fertility of the women.[2]   Claudius Aelianus[3] declares that the
Hebrews believed that snakes mated with unmarried girls;
and we also find this belief in Japan.[4]   A Persian tradition says
that after the first woman had been seduced by the serpent,
she immediately began to menstruate.[5]   And it was said by the
rabbis that menstruation was the result of Eve's relations with
the serpent in the Garden of Eden.[6]   In Abyssinia it was
thought that girls were in danger of being raped by snakes
until they were married.   One Algerian story tells how a snake
escaped when no one was looking and raped all the unmarried
girls in a house.   Similar traditions are to be found among the
Mandi Hottentots of East Africa, in Sierra Leone and elsewhere.[7]

Certainly the menstrual cycle helps to explain the spread of
the belief that the moon is the first mate of all women.   The
Papoos thought menstruation was a proof that women and
girls were connected with the moon, but in their iconography
(sculptures on wood) they pictured reptiles emerging from
their genital organs,[8] which confirms that snakes and the
moon are identified.   Among the Chiriguanoes, various
fumigations and purifications are performed after a woman's
first menstrual period, and after that the women of the house
drive away every snake they come upon, as responsible for
this evil.[9]   A great many tribes look upon the snake as the
cause of the menstrual cycle.   Its phallic character, which
Crawley was one of the first ethnologists to demonstrate,[10] far
from excluding its connection with the moon, only confirms it.

[1] Briffault, vol. ii, p. 665.

[2] Frazer, *Adonis, Attis, Osiris*, London, 1936, pp. 81 ff.

[3] *Nat. Animal.*, vi, 17.

[4] Briffault, vol. ii, p. 665.

[5] Dähnhart, *Natursagen*, Leipzig, 1907, vol. i, pp. 211, 261.

[6] Eisenmenger, *Entdecktes Judentum*, vol. i, pp. 832 ff.; Briffault, vol. ii,
p. 666.

[7] Briffault, ibid.

[8] Ploss and Bartels, *Woman*, London, 1935, i, figs. 263, 267.

[9] Briffault, vol. ii, p. 668.

[10] *The Mystic Rose*, ed. Besterman, London, 1927, vol. i, pp. 23 ff.; vol. ii,
pp. 17, 133.

A great deal of the iconographical documentation which remains—both of the Neolithic civilizations of Asia (such as the idol of the Panchan culture, at Kansu,[1] and the sculptured gold of Ngan-Yang)[2] and of the Amerindian civilizations (such as the bronze discs of Calchaqui)[3]—show the double imagery of the snake decorated with lozenges (symbolizing the vulva).[4] The two together undoubtedly have an erotic meaning, but the coexistence of the snake (phallus) and lozenges also expresses an idea of dualism and reintegration which is a supremely lunar notion, for we find that same motif in the lunar imagery of " rain ", of " light and darkness ", and the rest.[5]

52. THE MOON, WOMAN, AND SNAKES

The moon then can also be personified as reptile and masculine, but such personifications (which often break away from the original pattern and follow a path of their own in myth and legend), are still fundamentally based on the notion of the moon as source of living reality, and basis of all fertility and periodic regeneration. Snakes are thought of as producing children; in Guatemala, for instance,[6] in the Urabunna tribe of central Australia (who believe themselves to be descended from two snakes which travelled about the world and left *maiaurli*, or " the souls of children " wherever they stopped), among the Togos in Africa (a giant snake dwells in a pool near the town of Klewe, and receiving children from the hands of the supreme god Namu, brings them into the town before their birth). In India, from Buddhist times (cf. the Jātakas), snakes were held to be the givers of all fertility (water, treasures; cf. 71). Some of the Nagpur paintings[7] depict the mating of women with cobras. A mass of beliefs in present day India evince the beneficent and fertilizing power of snakes: they

[1] Hentze, *Objets rituels, croyances et dieux de la Chine antique et de l'Amérique*, Antwerp, 1938, figs. 4–7.

[2] Hentze, fig. 8.

[3] Hentze, *Mythes*, fig. 136.

[4] Cf. Hentze, *Mythes*, pp. 140 ff.; *Objets rituels*, pp. 27 ff.

[5] Hentze, *Objets*, pp. 29 ff.

[6] Miller, *The Child in Primitive Society*, London, 1928, p. 16.

[7] Rivett-Carnac, *Rough Notes on the Snake-symbol in India*, Calcutta, 1879.

prevent women from being sterile and ensure that they will have a large number of children.[1]

There are a great many different woman-snake relationships, but none of them can be fully explained by any purely erotic symbolism. The snake has a variety of meanings, and I think we must hold its " regeneration " to be one of the most important. The snake is an animal that " changes ". Gressman[2] tried to see in Eve a primitive Phoenician goddess of the underworld, personified by a snake.[3] The Mediterranean deities are represented with snakes in their hands (the Arcadian Artemis, Hecate, Persephone and so on), or with snakes for hair (the Gorgon, Erinyes and others). And there are some central European superstitions to the effect that if, when a woman is under the moon's influence (that is, when she is menstruating), you pull out some of her hair and bury it, the hairs will turn into snakes.[4]

One Breton legend says that the hair of a witch turns into snakes.[5] This cannot therefore happen to ordinary women, except when under the influence of the moon, when sharing in the magic power of " change ". There is a great deal of ethnological evidence to show that witchcraft is a thing bestowed by the moon (either directly, or through the intermediary of snakes). To the Chinese, for instance, snakes are at the bottom of all magic power, while the Hebrew and Arabic words for magic come from words that mean " snakes ".[6] Because snakes are " lunar "—that is, eternal—and live underground, embodying (among many other things) the souls of the dead, they know all secrets, are the source of all wisdom, and can foresee the future.[7] Anyone, therefore, who eats a snake becomes conversant with the language of animals, and particularly of birds (a symbol which can also have a metaphysical meaning: access to the transcendent reality); this is a belief held by a

---

[1] Dubois, *Hindu Manners*, Oxford, 1899, p. 648; W. Crooke, *Popular Religion and Folklore of Northern India*, London, 1894, vol. ii, p. 133; Vogel, *Indian Serpent-Lore*, London, 1926, p. 19.

[2] " Mythische Reste in der Paradieserzählung ", *AFRW*, x, 345–67.

[3] Particularly pp. 359 ff.

[4] Ploss and Bartels, i, §103, ff.

[5] Briffault, vol. ii, p. 662.

[6] Noldeke, " Die Schlange nach arabischem Volksglauben ", *ZVS*, i, p. 413; Briffault, vol. ii, p. 663.

[7] Briffault, pp. 663–4.

tremendous number of races,[1] and it was accepted even by the learned of antiquity.[2]

The same central symbolism of fertility and regeneration governed by the moon, and bestowed by the moon itself or by forms the same in substance (*magna mater, terra mater*) explains the presence of snakes in the imagery and rites of the Great Goddesses of universal fertility. As an attribute of the Great Goddess, the snake keeps its lunar character (of periodic regeneration) in addition to a telluric one. At one stage the moon was identified with the earth and itself considered the origin of all living forms (§ 86). Some races even believe that the earth and the moon are formed of the same substance.[3] The Great Goddesses share as much in the sacred nature of the moon as in that of the earth. And because these goddesses are also funeral goddesses (the dead disappear into the ground or into the moon to be reborn and reappear under new forms), the snake becomes very specially the animal of death and burial, embodying the souls of the dead, the ancestor of the tribe, etc. And this symbolism of regeneration also explains the presence of snakes in initiation ceremonies.

53. LUNAR SYMBOLISM

What emerges fairly clearly from all this varied symbolism of snakes is their lunar character—that is, their powers of fertility, of regeneration, of immortality through metamorphosis. We could, of course, look at a series of their attributes or functions and conclude that all these various relationships and significations have developed one from another by some method of logical analysis. You can reduce any religious system to nothing by methodically breaking it down to its component parts and studying them. In reality, all the meanings in a symbol are present together, even when it may look as if only some of them are effective. The intuition of the moon as the measure of rhythms, as the source of energy, of life, and of rebirth, has woven a sort of web between the various

[1] Cf. Penzer, *Ocean of Story*, London, 1923, vol. ii, p. 108; Frazer, *Spirits of the Corn and of the Wild*, London, 1936, vol. i, p. 146; Stith Thompson, *Motif-Index of Folk-Literature*, Helsinki, 1934, vol. i, p. 315.

[2] Philostratos, *Vita Apol. Tyan.*, i, 20; cf. L. Thorndike, *A History of Magic and Experimental Science*, New York, 1923, vol. i, p. 261.

[3] Briffault, vol. iii, pp. 60 ff.; Krappe, *Genèse*, pp. 101 ff.

levels of the universe, producing parallels, similarities and unities among vastly differing kinds of phenomena. It is not always easy to find the centre of such a " web "; secondary centres will sometimes stand out, looking like the most important, or perhaps the oldest starting point. Thus the erotic symbolism of snakes has in its turn " woven " a system of meanings and associations which in some cases at least push its lunar connections into the background. What in fact we are faced with is a series of threads running parallel to or across each other, all fitting together, some connected directly with the " centre " on which they all depend, others developing within their own systems.

Thus the whole pattern is moon-rain-fertility-woman-serpent-death-periodic-regeneration, but we may be dealing with one of the patterns within a pattern such as Serpent-Woman-Fertility, or Serpent-Rain-Fertility, or perhaps Woman-Serpent-Magic, and so on. A lot of mythology has grown up around these secondary " centres ", and if one does not realize this, it may overshadow the original pattern, though that pattern is, in fact, fully implicated in even the tiniest fragments. So, for instance, in the snake-water (or rain) binomial, the fact that both these are subject to the moon is not always obvious. Innumerable legends and myths show snakes or dragons governing the clouds, dwelling in pools and keeping the world supplied with water. The link between snakes and springs and streams has been kept to this day in the popular beliefs of Europe.[1] In American Indian iconography, the serpent-water connection is very often found; for instance, the Mexican rain-god, Tlaloc, is represented by an emblem of two snakes twisted together;[2] in the same Borgia Codex[3] a snake wounded by an arrow means rainfall;[4] the Dresden Codex shows water in a vessel shaped like a reptile;[5] the Codex-Tro-Cortesianus[6] shows water flowing from a vase in the shape of a snake,[7] and there are many more examples.

[1] Cf., for instance, Sébillot, *Le Folklore de France*, Paris, 1905, vol. ii, pp. 206, 309 ff.
[2] Seler, *Codex Borgia*, Berlin, 1904, vol. i, p. 109, fig. 299.
[3] p. 9.
[4] Wiener, *Mayan and Mexican Origins*, Cambridge, 1926, pl. xiv, fig. 35.
[5] Wiener, fig. 112c.
[6] Wiener, p. 63.
[7] Wiener, fig. 123.

Hentze's researches[1] have quite conclusively proved that this symbolism is based on the fact that the moon supplies the rains. Sometimes the Moon-Snake-Rain pattern has even been kept in the ritual: in India, for instance, the annual ceremony of venerating the snake (*sarpabali*), as it is given in the *Gṛhyasūtras*, lasts for four months; it starts at the full moon in Śravaṇa (the first month of the rainy season) and finishes at the full moon in Mārgaśīrṣa (the first month of winter).[2] The *sarpabali* thus includes all three elements of the original pattern. Yet it is not quite right to think of them as three separate elements: it is a *triple repetition*, a " concentration " of the moon, for the rain and the snakes are not merely things that follow the rhythms of the moon, but are in fact of the same substance. Like every sacred thing, and every symbol, these waters and snakes achieve that paradox of being at once *themselves* and *something other*—in this case the moon.

54. THE MOON AND DEATH

As E. Seler, the student of Americana, wrote long ago, the moon is the first of the dead. For three nights the sky is dark; but as the moon is reborn on the fourth night, so shall the dead achieve a new sort of existence. Death, as we shall see later, is not an extinction, but a change—and generally a provisional one—of one's level of existence. Death belongs to another kind of " life ". And because what happens to the moon, and to the earth (for as people discovered the agricultural cycle they came to see the Earth as related to the Moon) proves that there is a " life in death " and gives the idea meaning, the dead either go to the moon or return to the underworld to be regenerated and to absorb the forces needed to start a new existence. That is why so many lunar divinities are in addition chthonian and funereal divinities (Min, Persephone, probably Hermes, and so on).[3] And why, too, so many beliefs see the moon as the land of the dead. Sometimes the privilege of repose on the moon after death is reserved to political or religious leaders; that is what the Guaycurus believe, and the Polynesians of Tokelau and others.[4] This is

[1] *Objets*, pp. 32 ff.
[2] Cf. Vogel, *Serpent Lore*, p. 11.
[3] Krappe, p. 116.
[4] Tylor, *Primitive Culture*, London, 1929, vol. ii, p. 70; Krappe, p. 117.

one of those aristocratic, or heroic systems, which concede immortality only to the privileged rulers or the initiated (" magicians "), which we also find elsewhere.

This journey to the moon after death was also preserved in highly developed cultures (India, Greece, Iran), but something else was added. To the Indians, it is the " path of the *manes* " (*pitṛyāna*), and souls reposed in the moon while awaiting reincarnation, whereas the sun road or " path of the gods " (*devayāna*) was taken by the initiated, or those set free from the illusions of ignorance.[1]   In Iranian tradition, the souls of the dead, having passed the Cinvat bridge, went towards the stars, and if they had been good they went to the moon and then into the sun, and the most virtuous of all entered the *garotman*, the infinite light of Ahura Mazda.[2] The same belief was kept in Manicheeism[3] and existed in the East as well. Pythagorism gave astral theology a further impulse by popularizing the idea of the empyrean : the Elysian Fields, where heroes and Caesars went after death, were in the moon.[4]   The " Isles of the Blessed ", and all the mythical geography of death, were set in the sky utilizing the moon, the sun, the Milky Way. Here, of course, we have clearly got formulæ and cults impregnated with astronomical speculation and eschatological gnosis. But even in such late developments as that it is not hard to identify the traditional key ideas : the moon as land of the dead, the moon as receiver and regenerator of souls.

The lunar sphere was only one stage in an ascension including several others (the sun, the Milky Way, the " outer sphere "). The soul rested in the moon, but as in the Upaniṣad tradition, only to await reincarnation, and a return to the round of life. That is why the moon has the chief place in forming organisms, but also in breaking them apart : " Omnia animantium corpora et concepta procreat et generata dissolvit."[5]   Its task is to " reabsorb " forms and recreate them. Only what is beyond the moon is beyond becoming : " Supra lunam sunt aeterna

---

[1] Cf. *Bṛhadāraṇyaka-Upaniṣad*, vi, 2, 16 ; *Chāndogya Upaniṣad*, v, 10, 1 ; etc.

[2] *Dadistan-i-Dinik*, 34 : West, *Pahlavi Texts* (in the series *Sacred Books of the East*), vol. ii, p. 76.

[3] Cf. the texts in F. Cumont's *Recherches sur le symbolisme funéraire des Romains*, Paris, 1942, p. 179, n. 3.

[4] Cumont, p. 184, n. 4.

[5] Firmicus Maternus, *De Errore*, iv, i, 1.

omnia."[1]   To Plutarch,[2] who believed man to be made up of three parts, body (*soma*), soul (*psyche*), and mind (*nous*), this meant that the souls of the just were purified in the moon while their bodies were given back to the earth and their minds to the sun.

To the duality of soul and mind correspond the two different itineraries after death to the moon and sun, rather like the Upaniṣad tradition of the " path of souls " and the " path of the gods ".   The path of souls is a lunar one because the " soul " has not the light of reason, or in other words, because man has not come to know the ultimate metaphysical reality: Brahman.   Plutarch wrote that man had two deaths: the first took place on earth, in the domain of Demeter, when the body became cut off from the psyche and the *nous* and returned to dust (which is why the Athenians called the dead *demetreioi*); the second takes place in the moon, in the domain of Persephone, when the psyche separates from the *nous* and returns into the moon's substance.   The soul, or psyche, remains in the moon, though holding on to dreams and memories of life for some time.[3]   The righteous are soon reabsorbed;   the souls which have been ambitious, self-willed, or too fond of their own bodies are constantly drawn towards earth and it is a long time before they can be reabsorbed.   The *nous* is drawn towards the sun, which receives it, to whose substance it corresponds.   The process of birth is the exact reverse:[4] the moon receives sun from the *nous*, and, coming to fruition there, it gives birth to a new soul.   The earth furnishes the body. Note the symbolism of the moon rendered fertile by the sun, and its relation to the regeneration of the *nous* and psyche, the first integration of the human personality.

Cumont[5] thinks that the dividing of the mind into *nous* and psyche comes from the East and is Semitic in nature, and he reminds us that the Jews believed in a " vegetative soul " (*nephesh*), which continued to dwell on earth for some time and a " spiritual soul " (*ruah*) which departed from the body

---

[1] Cicero, *De Republ.*, vi, 17, 17.

[2] *De Facie in Orbe Lunæ*, pp. 942 ff.; I am using the edition and commentary of P. Raingeard, Paris, 1935, pp. 43ff., 143 ff.

[3] pp. 994, ff.

[4] pp. 945, c, ff.

[5] *Symbolisme funéraire*, pp. 200 ff.

immediately after death.   He finds a confirmation of his theory
in eastern theology as it became popularized under the Roman
Empire, which describes the influences exercised by the layers
of atmosphere, the sun and the moon on a soul coming down
from the empyrean to the earth.[1]   It may be objected to this
hypothesis that this duality in the soul and its destiny after
death is to be found, in embryo at least, in the oldest Hellenic
traditions.   Plato held both the duality of the soul (*Phaedo*) and
its separation later into three.[2]   With regard to the astral
eschatology, the successive journeys of *nous* and psyche and
its elements from moon to sun and back cannot be found in
the *Timaeus*, and probably comes from some Semitic influence.[3]
But what we are specially concerned with at the moment is
the conception of the moon as the dwelling-place of the souls
of the dead, which we find expressed iconographically in the
carvings of the Assyrians and Babylonians, the Phoenicians,
the Hittites and the Anatolians, and which was later used in
funeral monuments all over the Roman Empire.[4]   Everywhere
in Europe the half-moon is to be found as a funeral symbol.[5]
This does not mean that it came in with the Roman and Eastern
religions fashionable under the Empire; for in Gaul for
instance,[6] the moon was a local symbol in use long before any
contact with the Romans.   The " fashion " merely brought
primitive notions up to date by formulating in new language
a tradition older than history.

55. THE MOON AND INITIATION

Death, however, is not final—for the moon's death is not.
" As the moon dieth and cometh to life again, so we also,
having to die, will again rise," declare the Juan Capistrano
Indians of California in ceremonies performed when the moon
is new.[7]   A mass of myths describe a " message " given to
men by the moon through the intermediary of an animal

[1] " Oracles Chaldéens ", in op. cit., p. 201.
[2] *Republ.*, iv, 434 e–441 c; x, 611 b–612 a; *Timæus*, 69 c–72 d.
[3] See also Guy Soury, *La démonologie de Plutarque*, Paris, 1942, p. 185.
[4] Cf. Cumont, pp. 203 ff.
[5] Cumont, pp. 213 ff.
[6] Cumont, p. 217.
[7] Frazer, *The Belief in Immortality and the Worship of the Dead*, London
1913, vol. i, p. 68.

(hare, dog, lizard or another) in which it promises that " as I die and rise to life again, so you shall also die and rise to life again ". From either ignorance or ill-will, the " messenger " conveys the exact opposite, and declares that man, unlike the moon, will never live again once he is dead. This myth is extremely common in Africa,[1] but it is also to be found in Fiji, Australia, among the Ainus and elsewhere.[2] It justifies the concrete fact that man dies, as well as the existence of initiation ceremonies. Even within the framework of Christian apologetics, the phases of the moon provide a good exemplar for our belief in resurrection. " Luna per omnes menses nascitur, crescit, perficitur, minuitur, consumitur, innovatur," wrote Saint Augustine. " Quod in luna per menses, hoc in resurrectione semel in toto tempore."[3] It is therefore quite easy to understand the role of the moon in initiations, which consist precisely in undergoing a ritual death followed by a " rebirth ", by which the initiate takes on his true personality as a " new man ".

In Australian initiations, the " dead man " (that is, the neophyte), rises from a tomb as the moon rises from darkness.[4] Among the Koryaks of north-eastern Siberia, the Gilyaks, Tlingits, Tongas and Haidas, a bear—a " lunar animal " because it appears and disappears with the seasons—is present in the initiation ceremonies, just as it played an essential part in the ceremonies of Paleolithic times.[5] The Pomo Indians of Northern California have their candidates initiated by the Grizzly Bear, which " kills " them and " makes a hole " in their backs with its claws. They are undressed, then dressed in new clothes, and they then spend four days in the forest while ritual secrets are revealed to them.[6] Even when no lunar animals appear in the rites and no direct reference is made to the disappearance and reappearance of the moon, we are driven to connect all the various initiation ceremonies with the lunar myth throughout the area of southern Asia and the

[1] Cf. Frazer, *Belief*, vol. i, pp. 65 ff.; *Folklore in the Old Testament*, London, 1918, vol. i, pp. 52–65; H. Abrahamsson, *The Origin of Death*, Uppsala, 1951.
[2] Frazer, *Belief*, pp. 66 ff.
[3] *Sermo CCCLXI, De Resurr.; PL*, xxxix, col. 1605; cf. Cumont, p. 211, n. 6.
[4] Schmidt, *Ursprung*, vol. iii, pp. 757 ff.
[5] Cf. the discussion in Hentze, *Mythes*, pp. 16 ff.
[6] Schmidt, vol. ii, p. 235.

Pacific, as Gahs has shown in a yet unpublished monograph.[1]

In certain of the shaman initiation ceremonies, the candidate is " broken in pieces "[2] just as the moon is divided into parts (innumerable myths represent the story of the moon being broken or pulverized by God, by the sun and so on).[3] We find the same archetypal model in the osirian initiations. According to the tradition recorded by Plutarch,[4] Osiris ruled for twenty-eight years and was killed on the seventeenth of the month, when the moon was on the wane. The coffin in which Isis had hidden him was discovered by Set when he was hunting by moonlight; Set divided Osiris' body into fourteen and scattered the pieces throughout Egypt.[5] The ritual emblem of the dead god is in the shape of the new moon. There is clearly an analogy between death and initiation. " That is why," Plutarch tells us, " there is such a close analogy between the Greek words for dying and initiating."[6] If mystical initiation is achieved through a ritual death, then death can be looked upon as an initiation. Plutarch calls the souls that attain to the upper part of the moon " victorious ", and they wear the same crown on their heads as the initiate and the triumphant.[7]

56. THE SYMBOLISM OF LUNAR " BECOMING "

" Becoming " is the lunar order of things. Whether it is taken as the playing-out of a drama (the birth, fulness and disappearance of the moon), or given the sense of a " division " or " enumeration ", or intuitively seen as the " hempen rope " of which the threads of fate are woven, depends, of course, on the myth-making and theorizing powers of individual tribes, and their level of culture. But the formulæ used to express that " becoming " are heterogeneous on the surface only. The moon " divides ", " spins ", and " measures "; or feeds, makes fruitful, and blesses; or receives the souls of the dead,

---

[1] An abridgement of which is given in Koppers' " Pferdeopfer und Pferde-kult ", pp. 314–17.

[2] Eliade, *Le Chamanisme et les techniques archaiques de l'extase*, Paris, 1951, pp. 47 ff.

[3] Cf. Krappe, pp. 111 ff.

[4] *De Iside.*

[5] *De Iside*, 18.

[6] *De Facie*, p. 943 b.

[7] *De Facie*, p. 943 d.

initiates and purifies—because it is living, and therefore in a perpetual state of rhythmic becoming. This rhythm always enters into lunar rituals. Sometimes the ceremonial will re-enact the phases of the moon as a whole, as does for instance the Indian *pūjā* introduced by Tantrism. The goddess Tripurasundari must, says one Tantric text,[1] be considered as actually being *in* the moon. One Tantric writer, Bhaskara Rājā, states definitely that the goddess' *pūja* must begin on the first day of the new moon, and last for the whole fifteen days of moonlight; this calls for sixteen Brahmans, each representing one aspect of the goddess (that is, one phase of the moon, one *tithi*). Tucci[2] notes quite rightly that the presence of the Brahmans can only be a recent innovation, and that in the primitive *pūjā*, other figures represented the " becoming " of the moon goddess. And, indeed, in *Rudra-yamālā*, a treatise of undoubted authority, we find the description of the traditional ceremony, *kumarī-pūjā*, or " the adoration of a maiden ". And that *pūjā* always started at the new moon and lasted fifteen nights. But instead of the sixteen Brahmans, there must be sixteen *kumarī* to represent the sixteen *tithi* of the moon. The adoration is *vṛddhibhedana*, that is, in order of age, and the sixteen maidens must be aged from one to sixteen. Each evening the *pūjā* represents the corresponding *tithi* of the moon.[3] Tantric ceremonial in general gives tremendous importance to woman and to female divinities;[4] in this case the parallel between the lunar form and the feminine is complete.

That the moon " measures " and " divides " is shown by primitive classifications as well as etymologies. In India, again, the *Bṛhadāraṇyaka Upaniṣad*[5] says that " Prajāpati is the year. It has sixteen parts; the nights are fifteen of them, the sixteenth is fixed. It is by night that it grows and decreases " and so on. The *Chāndogya Upaniṣad*[6] tells us that man is made up of sixteen parts and grows at the same time as food does. Traces

---

[1] *Lalitasahasranāma*, v, 255.
[2] " Tracce di culto lunare in India ", *RSO*, 1929–30, vol. xii, p. 424.
[3] Tucci, p. 425.
[4] Cf. Eliade, *Le Yoga: Immortalité et liberté*, Paris, 1957, pp. 256 ff.
[5] i, 5, 14.
[6] vi, 7, 1 ff.

of the octaval system abound in India: eight *mālā*, eight *mūrti*, etc.; sixteen *kāla*, sixteen *śakti*, sixteen *mātrikā*, etc.; thirty-two sorts of *dikṣa*, etc.; sixty-four *yoginī*, sixty-four *upacāra*, etc. In Vedic and Brahman literature the number four prevails. *Vāc* (the "logos") is made up of four parts,[1] *puruṣa* ("man", the "macanthrope") also.

The phases of the moon give rise to the most complex relationships in later speculative thought. Stuchen devoted a whole book to a study of the relations between the letters of the alphabet and the phases of the moon as conceived by the Arabs.[2] Hommel[3] has shown that ten or eleven Hebrew characters indicate phases of the moon (for instance, *aleph*, which means "bull", is the symbol of the moon in its first week and also the name of the sign of the zodiac where the moon's mansions begin, and so on). Among the Babylonians, too, there is a relationship between graphic signs and the phases of the moon,[4] and among the Greeks[5] and Scandinavians (the twenty-four runes are divided into three sorts or *aettir*, each containing eight runes).[6] One of the clearest and most complete assimilations of the alphabet (as a collection of sounds, that is, not as written) with the phases of the moon is to be found in a scholium of Dionysius Thrax, in which the vowels correspond to the full moon, the hard consonants to the half moon (the quarters), and the soft consonants to the new moon.[7]

57. COSMO-BIOLOGY AND MYSTICAL PHYSIOLOGY

These assimilations do not simply serve a function of classification. They are obtained by an attempt to integrate man and the universe fully into the same divine rhythm. Their meaning is primarily magic and redemptive; by taking to himself the powers that lie hidden in "letters" and "sounds", man places himself in various central points of cosmic energy and thus effects complete harmony between himself and all that is. "Letters" and "sounds" do the work of images,

---

[1] *RV*, i, 164, 45.

[2] *Der Ursprung des Alphabets und die Mondstationen*, Leipzig, 1913.

[3] *Grundriss der Geographie und Geschichte des alten Orient*, Munich, 1904, vol. i, p. 99.

[4] Winkler, *Die babylonische Geisteskultur*, 2nd ed., 1919, p. 117.

[5] Schultz, "Zeitrechnung und Weltordnung", *MB*, Leipzig, 1924.

[6] Schultz, *passim;* cf. Arntz, *Handbuch der Runenkunde*, Halle, 1935, pp. 232 ff.

[7] Dornseif, *Das Alphabet in Mystik und Magie*, Leipzig, 1925, p. 34.

making it possible, by contemplation or by magic, to pass from one cosmic level to another. To give only one example: in India, when a man is going to make a divine image, he must first meditate, and his meditation will include, among others, the following exercise (in which the moon, mystical physiology, the written symbol and the sound value together form a pattern of consummate subtlety): " Conceiving in his own heart the moon's orb as developed from the primal sound [*prathama-svara-parinatam*, i.e., evolved from the letter ' A '], let him visualize therein a beautiful blue lotus, within its filaments the moon's unspotted orb, and thereon the yellow seed-syllable *Tam* . . ."[1]

Clearly, man's integration into the cosmos can only take place if he can bring himself into harmony with the two astral rhythms, " unifying " the sun and moon in his living body. The " unification " of the two centres of sacred and natural energy aims—in this technique of mystical physiology—at reintegrating them in the primal undifferentiated unity, as it was when not yet broken up by the act that created the universe; and this " unification " realizes a transcendence of the cosmos. In one Tantric text,[2] an exercise in mystical physiology seeks to change " vowels and consonants into bracelets, the sun and moon into rings ".[3] The Tantric and Haṭhayoga schools developed to a very high degree these complex analogies between the sun, the moon and various " mystical " centres or arteries, divinities, blood and *semen virile*, etc.[4] The point of these analogies is first of all to unite man with the rhythms and energies of the cosmos, and then to unify the rhythms, fuse the centres and finally effect that leap into the transcendent which is made possible when all " forms " disappear and the primal unity is re-established. A technique like this is of course the polished product of a long mystical tradition, but we find the rudimentary groundwork of it as often among primitive peoples[5] as in the syncretist periods of the Mediter-

[1] *Kimcit-Vistara-Tārā-Sādhana*, no. 98 of *Sādhanamālā;* cf. Eliade, "Cosmical Homology and Yoga ", p. 199.

[2] Carya 11, *Kṛṣṇapada.*

[3] Eliade, p. 200.

[4] Cf. *Le Yoga: Immortalité et liberté*, pp. 257 ff. ; " Cosmical Homology ", p. 201.

[5] Cf. " Cosmical Homology ", p. 194, n. 2.

ranean religions (the moon influences the left eye and the sun the right:[1] the moon and the sun in funeral monuments as a symbol of eternity;[2] and so on).

By its mode of being, the moon " binds " together a whole mass of realities and destinies. The rhythms of the moon weave together harmonies, symmetries, analogies and participations which make up an endless " fabric ", a " net " of invisible threads, which " binds " together at once mankind, rain, vegetation, fertility, health, animals, death, regeneration, after-life, and more. That is why the moon is seen in so many traditions personified by a divinity, or acting through a lunar animal, " weaving " the cosmic veil, or the destinies of men. It was lunar goddesses who either invented the profession of weaving (like the Egyptian divinity Neith), or were famous for their ability to weave (Athene punished Arachne, for daring to rival her, by turning her into a spider),[3] or wove a garment of cosmic proportions (like Proserpine and Harmonia),[4] and so on. It was believed in medieval Europe that Holda was patroness of weavers, and we see beyond this figure to the chthonian and lunar nature of the divinities of fertility and death.[5]

We are obviously dealing here with extremely complex forms in which myths, ceremonials and symbols from different religious structures are crystallized, and they have not always come directly from the intuition of the moon as the measure of cosmic rhythms and the support of life and death. On the other hand, we find in them the syntheses of the moon and Mother Earth with all that they imply (the ambivalence of good and evil, death, fertility, destiny). Similarly, you cannot always limit every mythological intuition of a cosmic " net " to the moon. In Indian thought, for instance, the universe was " woven " by the air[6] just as breath (prāṇa) " wove " human

[1] Cumont, L'Egypte des astrologues, Brussels, 1937, p. 173.

[2] Cumont, Symbolisme funéraire, pp. 94, 208.

[3] Ovid, Metamorphoses, vi, 1 ff.

[4] Cf. Nonnus, Dionysiaca, xli, 294 ff.; Claudian, De Raptu Proserpinæ, i, 246 ff.; Krappe, Etudes de mythologie et de folklore germaniques, Paris, 1928, p. 74.

[5] Cf. Krappe, " La déesse Holda ", in Etudes, pp. 101 ff.; Liungman, " Traditionswanderungen: Euphrat-Rhein ", Helsinki, 1938, FFC, no. 119, pp. 656 ff.

[6] Brhadāraṅyaka-Up., iii, 7, 2.

life. Corresponding to the five winds that divide the Cosmos and yet preserve its unity, there are five breaths (*prāṇas*) " weaving " human life into a whole (the identity of breath and wind can be found as early as in Vedic writings).[1] What we have got in these traditions is the primitive conception of the living whole—whether cosmic or microcosmic—in which the different parts are held together by a breathing force (wind or breath) that " weaves " them together.

58. THE MOON AND FATE

The moon, however, simply because she is mistress of all living things and sure guide of the dead, has " woven " all destinies. Not for nothing is she envisaged in myth as an immense spider—an image you will find used by a great many peoples.[2] For to weave is not merely to predestine (anthropologically), and to join together differing realities (cosmologically) but also to *create*, to make something of one's own substance as the spider does in spinning its web. And the moon is the inexhaustible creator of all living forms. But, like everything woven, the lives thus created are fixed in a pattern: they have a destiny. The Moirai, who spin fates, are lunar divinities. Homer[3] calls them " the spinners ", and one of them is even called Clotho, which means " spinner ". They probably began by being goddesses of birth, but the later development of thought raised them to the position of personifications of fate. Yet their lunar nature was never totally lost to view. Porphyry said the Moirai were dependent on the forces of the moon, and an Orphic text looks on them as forming part (*ta mere*) of the moon.[4] In the old Germanic languages, one of the words for fate (Old High German *wurt*, Old Norse, *urdhr*, Anglo-Saxon *wyrd*) comes from an Indo-European verb *uert*, " turn ", whence we get the Old High German words *wirt*, *wirtel*, " spindle ", " distaff ", and the Dutch *worwelen*, " turn ".[5]

Needless to say, in those cultures in which Great Goddesses

---

[1] Cf. *AV*, xi, 4, 15.
[2] Cf. Briffault, vol. ii, pp. 624 ff.
[3] *Odyssey*, vi, 197.
[4] Krappe, *Genèse*, p. 122.
[5] Cf. Krappe, p. 103.

have absorbed the powers of the moon, the earth and vegetation, the spindle and distaff with which they spin the fates of men become two more of their many attributes. Such is the case of the goddess with the spindle found at Troy, dating from the period between 2000 and 1500 B.C.[1] This iconographic figure is common in the East: we find a distaff in the hand of Ishtar, of the Hittite Great Goddess, of the Syrian goddess Atargatis, of a primitive Cypriot divinity, of the goddess of Ephesus.[2] Destiny, the thread of life, is a long or short period of *time*. The Great Goddesses consequently become mistresses of time, of the destinies they create according to their will. In Sanskrit Time is *kāla*, and the word is very close to the name of the Great Goddess, *Kālī*. (In fact, a connection has been suggested between the two words.)[3] *Kāla* also means black, darkened, stained. Time is black because it is irrational, hard, merciless. Those who live under the dominion of time are subject to every kind of suffering, and to be set free consists primarily in the abolition of time, in an escape from the law of change.[4] Indian tradition has it that mankind is at present in the *Kālī-yuga*, that is, " the dark era ", the period of total confusion and utter spiritual decadence, the final stage in the completion of a cosmic cycle.

59. LUNAR METAPHYSICS

We must try to get a general picture of all these lunar hierophanies. What do they reveal? How far do they fit together and complement each other, how far do they make up a " theory "—that is, express a succession of " truths " which, taken together, could constitute a system? The hierophanies of the moon that we have noted may be grouped round the following themes: (*a*) fertility (waters, vegetation, women; mythological " ancestor "); (*b*) periodic regeneration (the symbolism of the serpent and all the lunar animals; " the new man " who has survived a watery catastrophe caused by the moon; the death and resurrection of initiations; etc.);

---

[1] Eliade, *Mitul reintegrarii*, Bucharest, 1942, p. 33.
[2] Cf. Picard, *Ephèse et Claros*, Paris, 1922, p. 497.
[3] Cf. J. Przyluski, " From the Great Goddess to Kala ", *IHQ*, 1938, pp. 67 ff.
[4] Cf. Eliade, " La Concezione della libertà nel pensiero indiano ", *ASA*, 1938, pp. 345–54.

(c) time and destiny (the moon " measures ", or " weaves " destinies, " binds " together diverse cosmic levels and heterogeneous realities); (d) change, marked by the opposition of light and darkness (full moon—new moon; the " world above " and the " underworld "; brothers who are enemies, good and evil), or by the balance between being and non-being, the virtual and the actual (the symbolism of hidden things: dusky night, darkness, death, seeds and larvæ). In all these themes the dominant idea is one of *rhythm* carried out by a succession of contraries, of " becoming " through the succession of opposing modalities (being and non-being; forms and hidden essences; life and death; etc.). It is a becoming, I need hardly add, that cannot take place without drama or *pathos*; the sub-lunar world is not only the world of change but also the world of suffering and of " history ". Nothing that happens in this world under the moon can be " eternal ", for its law is the law of becoming, and no change is final; every change is merely part of a cyclic pattern.

The phases of the moon give us, if not the historical origin, at least the mythological and symbolic illustration of all dualisms. " The underworld, the world of darkness, is typified by the waning moon (horns=crescents, the sign of the double volute=two crescents facing the opposite way, placed one on top of the other and fastened together=lunar change, a decrepit and bony old man). The higher world, the world of life and of growing light, is typified by a tiger (the monster of darkness and of the new moon) letting humanity, represented by a child, escape its jaws (the child being the ancestor of the tribe, likened to the new moon, the ' Light that returns ')."[1] These images come from the cultural area of primitive China, but light and darkness symbols were complementary there; the owl, a symbol of darkness, is to be found beside the pheasant, symbol of light.[2] The cicada, too, is at once related to the demon of darkness and to the demon of light.[3] At every cosmic level a " dark " period is followed by a " light ", pure, regenerate period. The symbolism of emerging from the " darkness " can be found in initiation rituals as well as

---

[1] Hentze, *Objets Rituels*, p. 55.

[2] Hentze, *Frühchinesische Bronzen*, Antwerp, 1938, p. 59.

[3] Hentze, pp. 66–7.

in the mythology of death, and the life of plants (buried seed, the "darkness" from which the "new plant" (*neophyte*) arises), and in the whole conception of "historical" cycles. The "dark age", *Kāli-yuga*, is to be followed, after a complete break-up of the cosmos, (*mahāpralaya*), by a new, regenerate era. The same idea is to be found in all the traditions that tell of cosmic historic cycles, and though it does not seem to have first entered the human mind with the discovery of the moon's phases, it is undoubtedly illustrated perfectly by their rhythm.

It is in this sense that we can talk of the positive value of periods of shadow, times of large-scale decadence and disintegration; they gain a suprahistorical significance, though in fact it is just at such times that "history" is most fully accomplished, for then the balance of things is precarious, human conditions infinitely varied, new developments are encouraged by the disintegration of the laws and of all the old framework. Such dark periods are a sort of darkness, of universal night. And as such, just as death represents a positive value in itself, so do they; it is the same symbolism as that of larvæ in the dark, of hibernation, of seeds bursting apart in the earth so that a new form can appear.

It might be said that the moon shows man his true human condition; that in a sense man looks at himself, and finds himself anew in the life of the moon. That is why the symbolism and mythology of the moon have an element of *pathos* and at the same time of consolation, for the moon governs both death and fertility, both drama and initiation. Though the modality of the moon is supremely one of change, of rhythm, it is equally one of periodic returning; and this pattern of existence is disturbing and consoling at the same time— for though the manifestations of life are so frail that they can suddenly disappear altogether, they are restored in the "eternal returning" regulated by the moon. Such is the law of the whole sublunary universe. But that law, which is at once harsh and merciful, can be abolished, and in some cases one may "transcend" this periodic becoming and achieve a mode of existence that is absolute. We saw (§ 57) how, in certain Tantric techniques, an attempt is made to "unify" the moon and the sun, to get beyond the opposition between things, to be reintegrated in the primeval unity. This myth of reintegration is to be found almost everywhere in the history of religion in an infinity of variations—and fundamentally it is an expression of the thirst to abolish dualisms, endless returnings and fragmentary existences. It existed at the most primitive stages, which indicates that man, from the time when he first realized his position in the universe, desired passionately and tried to achieve concretely (i.e., by religion and by magic together) a passing beyond his human status (" reflected " so exactly by the moon's). We shall be dealing with myths of this nature elsewhere, but I note them here, for they mark man's first attempt to get beyond his " lunar mode of being ".

BIBLIOGRAPHY

On lunar cults and myths in general:
SCHMIDT, W., *Semaine d'ethnologie religieuse*, 1914, vol. ii, pp. 294 ff., 341 ff.; KRAPPE, A. H., *La Genèse des mythes*, Paris, 1938, pp. 100 ff.; id., *Etudes de mythologie et de folklore germaniques*, Paris, 1928, pp. 74 ff.; DÄHNHARDT, O., *Natursagen*, Leipzig, 1907, vol. i; PREUSS, K. T., " Das Problem der Mondmythologie im Lichte der lokalen Spezialforschung ", *AFRW*, 1925, vol. xxiii, pp. 1–14; ROSCHER, W., *Uber Selene und Verwandles*, Leipzig, 1890; MUCH, Rudolf, " Mondmythologie und Wissenschaft ", *AFRW*, 1942, vol. xxxvii, pp. 231–61 (against the theories of H. LESSMANN, G. HUSSING, and W. SCHULTZ); TALLQUIST, Knut, " Månen i myt och dikt, foktro och Kult ", *SO*, Helsinki, 1947, vol. xii.

See also NIELSEN, D., *Die altarabische Mondreligion*, 1904; DUMEZIL, G., " Tityos ", *RHR*, 1935, vol. iii, 66–89; JACKSON, J. W., " The Aztec Moon-Cult and its Relation to the Chank-Cult of India ", *Manchester Memoirs*, Manchester, 1916, vol. lx, no. 5; HENTZE, C., *Mythes et symboles lunaires*, Antwerp, 1932; id., *Objets rituels, croyances et dieux de la Chine antique et de l'Amérique*, Antwerp, 1936; id., *Frühchinesische Bronzen*, Antwerp, 1938; but see KARLGREN, B., " Legends and Cults in Ancient China ", *BMAS*, Stockholm, 1946, no. 18, pp. 346 ff.

On the relations of the moon, serpents, sexuality, death and initiation: BRIFFAULT, R., *The Mothers*, London, 1927, vols. i–iii; FRAZER, Sir J., *The Belief in Immortality and the Worship of the Dead*, London, 1913, vol. i, pp. 60 ff.; id., *Folklore in the Old Testament*, vol. i, pp. 52 ff.; HENTZE, *Mythes et symboles*, *passim*; CAPELLE, P., *De Luna, Stellis, Lacteo Orbe Animarum Sedibus*, Halle, 1917; CUMONT, F., *Recherches sur le symbolisme funéraire des Romains*, Paris, 1942, pp. 182 ff., and *passim*.

On the mythical ancestor originating in the moon: KOPPERS, W., " Der Hund in der Mythologie der zirkumpazifischen Völker ", *WBKL*, 1930, vol. i, pp. 359 ff.; cf. also SCHEBESTA, P., *Les Pygmées*, p. 79.

On the relations of moon, waters and vegetation: SAINTYVES, P., *L'Astrologie populaire, etudiée spécialement dans les doctrines et les traditions relatives à l'influence de la lune*, Paris, 1937, pp. 230 ff. and *passim*; ELIADE, M., " Notes sur le symbolisme aquatique ", *CZ*, 1939, vol. ii, pp. 139–52: reprinted in *Images et symboles*, Paris, 1952, pp. 164–98; BIDEZ, J., and CUMONT, F., *Les Mages hellenisés*, Brussels, 1938, vol. ii, pp. 189, 227, 302 ff.; LIUNGMAN, W., *Traditionswanderungen: Euphrat-Rhein*, Helsinki, 1937–8, vol. ii, pp. 656 ff.

On the part played by the phases of the moon in reckoning time: SCHULTZ, Wolfgang, " Zeitrechnung und Weltordnung in ihren ubereinstimmenden Grundzugen bei den Indern, Iraniern, Keltern, Germanen, Litauern, Slawen ", *MB*, Leipzig, 1924, no. 35, pp. 12 ff., and *passim* (but see Much's criticisms in " Mondmythologie "); DORNSIEFF, Franz, *Das Alphabet in Mystik und Magie*, 2nd ed., Leipzig, 1925, pp. 82 ff.; HIRSCHBERG, Walter, " Der ' Mondkalender ' in der Mutterrechtskultur ", *APS*, 1931, vol. xxvi, pp. 461 ff.

On the traces of lunar cults at Ras-Shamra, cf. GASTER, Theodor, " A Canaanite Ritual Drama ", *JAOS*, vol. lxvi, pp. 49–76, particularly p. 60; on lunar cults among the Chaldean and Aramaic peoples, see DHORME,

E., *La Religion des Hébreux nomades*, 1937, pp. 87 ff.; ibid., *Les Religions de Babylonie et d'Assyrie*, *MA*, 1945, vol. ii, pp. 59 ff., 85 ff.

On the traces of lunar cults among the early Indian civilizations, cf. MACKAY, E. J. H., "Chanhu-Daro Excavations 1935–6", *APS*, 1943, vol. xx, on the number 16.

On the lunar elements in Varuṇa: OLDENBERG, H., *Die Religion des Veda*, pp. 178 ff. ; LOMMEL, H., *Les Anciens Aryans*, pp. 83 ff.; but see also WALK, L., *APS*, 1933, p. 235, and ELIADE, M., "Le 'Dieu Lieur' et le symbolisme des nœuds", *RHR*, 1948: reprinted in *Images et symboles*, pp. 120–56.

On the lunar elements in Tantrism: TUCCI, G., "Tracce di culto lunare in India", *RSO*, 1929–30, vol. xii, pp. 419–27; ELIADE, M., Cosmical Homology and Yoga", *JISOA*, June-December, 1937, pp. 199–203; cf. also, DASGUPTA, S., *Obscure Religious Cults as Background of Bengali Literature*, Calcutta, 1946, pp. 269 ff.

On the lunar elements in Iranian religions: WIDENGREN, G., *Hochgottglaube im Alten Iran*, Uppsala-Leipzig, 1938, pp. 164 ff.

On the lunar nature of cosmic and historic cycles: see ELIADE, M., *The Myth of the Eternal Return*, London, 1955, pp. 95 ff.

On lunar symbolism in Christian iconography: see RAHNER, Hugo, "Das christliche Mysterium von Sonne und Mond", *EJ*, Zürich, 1944, vol. x, pp. 305–404; DEONNA, W., "Les Crucifix de la vallée de Saas (Valais): Sol et luna", *RHR*, 1946, vol. cxxxii, pp. 5–37; 1947–8, vol. cxxxiii, pp. 49–102.

V

THE WATERS AND WATER SYMBOLISM

60. WATER AND THE SEEDS OF THINGS

To state the case in brief, water symbolizes the whole of potentiality; it is *fons et origo*, the source of all possible existence. " Water, thou art the source of all things and of all existence ! " says one Indian text,[1] summing up the long Vedic tradition. Waters are the foundations of the whole world;[2] they are the essence of plant life,[3] the elixir of immortality[4] like the *amṛta*;[5] they ensure long life and creative energy, they are the principle of all healing, and so on.[6] " May the waters bring us well-being ! " the Vedic priest used to pray.[7] " The waters are indeed healers; the waters drive away and cure all illnesses ! "[8]

Principle of what is formless and potential, basis of every cosmic manifestation, container of all seeds, water symbolizes the primal substance from which all forms come and to which they will return either by their own regression or in a cataclysm. It existed at the beginning and returns at the end of every cosmic or historic cycle; it will always exist, though never alone, for water is always germinative, containing the potentiality of all forms in their unbroken unity. In cosmogony, in myth, ritual and iconography, water fills the same function in whatever type of cultural pattern we find it ; it *precedes* all forms and *upholds* all creation. Immersion in water symbolizes a return to the pre-formal, a total regeneration, a new birth, for immersion means a dissolution of forms, a reintegration into the formlessness of pre-existence; and emerging from the water is a repetition of the act of creation in which form was first expressed. Every contact with water

---

[1] *Bhaviṣyottarapurāṇa*, 31, 14.
[2] *Śatapatha-Brāhmaṇa*, vi, 8, 2, 2; xii, 5, 2, 14.
[3] *Śat.-Br.*, iii, 6, 1, 7.
[4] *Śat.-Br.*, iv, 4, 3, 15, etc.
[5] *Śat.-Br.*, i, 9, 3, 7; xi, 5, 4, 5.
[6] *RV*, i, 23, 19 ff.; x, 19, 1 ff.; etc.
[7] *AV*, ii, 3, 6.
[8] *AV*, vi, 91, 3.

implies regeneration : first, because dissolution is succeeded by a " new birth ", and then because immersion fertilizes, increases the potential of life and of creation. In initiation rituals, water confers a " new birth ", in magic rituals it heals, and in funeral rites it assures rebirth after death. Because it incorporates in itself all potentiality, water becomes a symbol of life (" living water "). Rich in seeds, it fertilizes earth, animals and women. It contains in itself all possibilities, it is supremely fluid, it sustains the development of all things, and is therefore either compared or even directly assimilated with the moon. Its rhythms are fitted to the same pattern as the moon's; they govern the periodic appearance and disappearance of all forms, they give a cyclic form to the development of things everywhere.

Then, too, since prehistoric times, water, moon and woman were seen as forming the orbit of fertility both for man and for the universe. Water used to be represented, on Neolithic vases (of what is called the Walterniernburg-Bernburg civilization) by the sign $\vee\wedge\wedge\vee$ which is also the oldest Egyptian hieroglyph for flowing water.[1] Even in Paleolithic times, the spiral was a symbol of water and lunar fertility; when inscribed on a feminine idol, it united all these centres of life and fertility.[2] In the mythology of the American Indians, the hieroglyphic for water—a vase full of water into which a drop from a cloud is falling—is always associated with moon images.[3] The spiral, the snail (a lunar emblem), woman, water, fish, all belong essentially to the same symbolism of fertility, which applies to every level of nature.

In any analysis, there is always a danger of breaking apart or reducing to separate elements what was a single unity, a cosmos, in the minds that produced it. The same symbol may indicate or evoke a whole series of realities, which only profane experience would see as separate and autonomous. The many different symbolic values given to a single emblem or word in primitive languages continually show us that, to the mind that conceived it, the world appeared as an organic

---

[1] Kuhn, Epilogue to Hentze, *Mythes et symboles lunaires*, p. 244.

[2] Kuhn, p. 248.

[3] Cf. the reproductions of Sahagun, Codex Nuttal, etc., in Leo Wiener's volume, *Mayan and Mexican Origins*, Cambridge, 1926, pp. 49 ff., 84 ff.

whole. In Sumerian, *a* means " water ", but also " sperm, conception, generation ". In Mesopotamian carvings, for instance, the symbolic fish and water are emblems of fertility. Even to-day, among primitive peoples—not always in ordinary experience, but regularly in mythology—water is identified with semen. On Wakuta Island, there is a myth which describes a girl losing her virginity because she allowed rain to touch her body; and the most important myth on the Trobriand Islands tells how Bolutukwa, the mother of the hero Tudava, lost her virginity when a few drops of water fell from a stalactite.[1] The Pima Indians of New Mexico have a similar myth; a very beautiful woman (Mother Earth) was made pregnant by a drop of water that fell from a cloud.[2]

61. WATER COSMOGONIES

Though separate in time and space, these things none the less make up a cosmological whole. At every level of existence, water is a source of life and growth. Indian mythology has a great many variations of the theme of the primeval waters on which Nārāyaṇa floated, with the cosmic tree rising from his navel. In Puranic tradition, the tree is replaced by the lotus from whose centre Brahma (*abjaja*, " born of the lotus ") was born.[3] One by one other gods appear—Varuṇa, Prajāpati, Puruṣa or Brahman (Svayaṁbhū), Nārāyāṇa or Viṣṇu; they represent the different variants of the same cosmogonic myth—but the waters remain in them all. Later on, aquatic cosmogony became a common motif in iconography and the decorative arts: the plant or the tree rising from the mouth or the navel of a Yakṣa (a personification of fecund life), from the throat of a sea monster (*makara*), of a snail or of a " flowing vase "— but never directly from any symbol representing the earth.[4] For, as we have seen, water precedes and upholds all creation, all that is firmly established, every cosmic manifestation.

The waters on which Nārāyaṇa floated, carefree and happy, symbolize the state of rest and formlessness, the cosmic night.

---

[1] B. Malinowski, *The Sexual Life of Savages in North-Western Melanesia*, London, 1935, p. 155.

[2] Russell, " The Pima Indians ", *Annual Report of the Bureau of Ethnology*, xxvi, 1903–4 (Washington, 1908), p. 239.

[3] Cf. references in Coomaraswamy, *Yakṣas*, Washington, 1928, vol. ii, p. 24.

[4] Coomaraswamy, p. 13.

Even Nārāyaṇa is asleep. And from his navel, that is, from a
" centre " (cf. § 145), the first cosmic form comes to life: the
lotus, the tree, a symbol of the life-giving but unawakened
sap, of life which has not yet attained consciousness. All
creation is born of a single source and is supported by it. In
other versions, Viṣṇu, in his third reincarnation (as a giant
boar), goes down to the depths of the primeval waters, and
draws the earth up from the abyss.[1] This myth, Oceanian in
structure and form, is also preserved in European folklore
(cf. the Bibliography).

The Babylonian creation story also tells of a watery chaos, a
primordial ocean, *apsu* and *tiamat*; the first personified the
ocean of fresh water on which the earth was later to float,
and *tiamat* was the salty and bitter sea inhabited by monsters.
Enuma Elish, the creation poem, begins thus:

> When the heavens on high were not yet named,
> And the earth beneath was not yet called a name,
> And the primordial Apsu, who gave them birth
> And Mummu, and Tiamat, the mother of them all,
> Mingled all their waters into one . . .[2]

The tradition of the primeval waters, whence all the worlds
were born, can be found in a great many different versions in
ancient and " primitive " creation beliefs. I refer my readers
to the *Natursagen* of Dähnhardt,[3] and, for further bibliographical suggestions, to the *Motif-Index of Folk Literature*
by Stith Thompson.[4]

62. WATER AS UNIVERSAL MOTHER

Since water is the source of all things, in which all potentialities are contained, and in which all seeds thrive, it is easy to
see why there are myths and legends which make it the origin
of the human race, or of some section of it. On the south
coast of Java there is a *segara anakkan*, a " children's sea ".
The Karaja Indians in Brazil recall a mythological time when
" they still lived in the water ". Juan de Torquemada, describ-

---

[1] *Taittirīya Brāhmaṇa*, i, 1, 3, 5; *Śatapatha-Br.*, xiv, i, 2, 11; cf. *Rāmāyaṇa*,
Ayodhya-Khaṇḍa, CX, 4; *Mahābhārata*, Vana-Prāṇa, cxlii, 28–62, cclxxii,
49–55; *Bhagavata Purāṇa*, iii, 13; etc.
[2] i, 1–5.
[3] i, 1–89.
[4] Vol. i, pp. 121 ff.

ing the baptismal washing of newborn babies in Mexico, recorded some of the formulæ in which children were consecrated to the goddess Chalchihuitlycue Chalchiuhtlatonac, who was looked on as their real mother.

Before immersing a child in the water, they said: "Take this water, for the goddess [of the waters] Chalchihuitlycue Chalchiuhtlatonac is thy mother. May this bath cleanse thee of the sins and blemishes thou hast from thy parents. . . ." Then, touching the mouth, breast and head of the child with water, they added: "Receive, child, thy mother, Chalchihuitlycue, the goddess of the waters."[1] The ancient Karelians, the Mordvinians, the Estonians, the Cheremisses and other Finno-Ugrian peoples believed in a Water-Mother to whom women prayed for children.[2] Sterile Tatar women used to kneel and pray by a pool.[3] The creative forces of water are at their height in mud, *limus*. Illegitimate children were likened to the plants that grew in pools, and were pushed down into the mud at the edge of the pool, that inexhaustible source of life; they were thus ritually reintegrated into the impure life whence they came, like the coarse grass and the rushes that grow in swamps. Tacitus said of the Germans: "Ignavos et imbelles et corpore infames caeno ac palude, iniecta insuper crate mergunt."[4] Water nourishes life, rain fertilizes as does the *semen virile*. In the erotic symbolism of the creation, the sky embraces and fertilizes the earth with rain. The same symbolism is found universally. Germany is full of *Kinderbrunnen, Kinderteichen, Bubenquellen*.[5] In Oxfordshire, Child's Well is a fountain thought to make sterile women fertile.[6] Many beliefs of this sort have become entangled with the notion of "Mother Earth" and with the erotic symbolism of fountains. But, underlying these beliefs, and indeed all myths about human descent from the earth, vegetation, and stones, we find the same fundamental idea: Life, that is, *reality*, is somewhere concentrated in one cosmic substance

---

[1] Nyberg, *Kind und Erde*, Helsinki, 1931, pp. 113 ff.

[2] Holmberg-Harva, *Die Wassergottheiten der finnisch-ugrischen Völker*. Helsinki, 1913, pp. 120, 126, 138, etc.

[3] Nyberg, p. 59.

[4] *Germania*, 12.

[5] Dieterich, *Mutter Erde*, 3rd ed., Berlin, 1925, pp. 19, 126.

[6] McKenzie, *Infancy of Medicine*, London, 1927, p. 240.

from which all living forms proceed, either by direct descent or by symbolic participation. Water animals, particularly fish (which also serve as erotic symbols) and sea monsters, become emblems of the sacred because they stand for *absolute reality*, concentrated in water.

63. THE " WATER OF LIFE "

Symbol of creation, harbour of all seeds, water becomes the supreme magic and medicinal substance; it heals, it restores youth, it ensures eternal life. The prototype of all water is the " living water " which came to be seen as existing somewhere in the sky—just as there is a heavenly *soma*, a white *haoma* in the heavens, and so on. Living water, the fountains of youth, the Water of Life, and the rest, are all mythological formulæ for the same metaphysical and religious reality: life, strength and eternity are contained in water. This water is not, of course, accessible to everybody in every way. It is guarded by monsters. It is to be found in places which are hard to get to, and belongs to some sort of demons or divinities. To reach the source of " living water " and get possession of it involves a series of consecrations and " testings ", just as does the search for the " Tree of Life " (§ 108, 145). The " ageless river " (*vijara-nadī*) runs beside the miraculous tree spoken of in the *Kauśitaki Upaniṣad*.[1] And, in the Apocalypse,[2] the two symbols are also side by side: " And he showed me a river of water of life, clear as crystal, proceeding from the throne of God and of the Lamb . . . and on both sides of the river, was the tree of life."[3]

" Living Water " restores youth and bestows eternal life; and, by a gradual process which will become clearer in the course of this book, *all* water comes to be considered powerful for fertility or healing. Even in modern times, sick children have been dipped three times in the well of Saint Mandron, in Cornwall.[4] In France there are a considerable number of healing rivers[5] and fountains.[6] There are also certain rivers

[1] 1, 3.
[2] xxii, 1–2.
[3] Cf. Ezech. xlvii.
[4] McKenzie, pp. 238 ff.
[5] Sébillot, *Le Folklore de France*, Paris, 1905, vol. ii, pp. 327–87.
[6] Sébillot, pp. 256–91.

with a beneficent influence on love.[1]   And yet other waters are
esteemed in popular medicine.[2]   In India illnesses are cast
into the water.[3]   The Finno-Ugrians think that some illnesses
are the result of profaning or polluting flowing water.[4]   And
to conclude this brief glance at the wonderful powers of water,
I would remind you of the " new water " used in most spells
and popular medicaments.   " New water ", that is, the water
in a new vase, not profaned by everyday use, contains all the
values for creating and fostering life of the primeval Water.
It heals, because in a sense it remakes creation.   We shall be
seeing later how magic acts are a repetition of the creation of
the world, for they are projected into the mythological time
when the worlds were made, and they merely repeat the things
that were done then, *ab origine*.   With the use of " new "
water in popular medicine, what is being sought is the magic
regeneration of the patient by contact with primordial substance; the water absorbs his disease because of its power of
taking to itself and dissolving all forms.

64. THE SYMBOLISM OF IMMERSION

Purification by water has the same effects: in water everything is " dissolved ", every " form " is broken up, everything
that has happened ceases to exist; nothing that was before
remains after immersion in water, not an outline, not a " sign ",
not an " event ".   Immersion is the equivalent, at the human
level, of death, and at the cosmic level, of the cataclysm (the
Flood) which periodically dissolves the world into the primeval
ocean.   Breaking up all forms, doing away with all the past,
water possesses this power of purifying, of regenerating, of
giving new birth; for what is immersed in it " dies ", and,
rising again from the water, is like a child without any sin or
any past, able to receive a new revelation and begin a new and
real life.   As Ezechiel wrote:[5]   " I will pour upon you clean
water and you shall be cleansed."   And the prophet Zacharias[6]

[1] Sébillot, pp. 230 ff.
[2] Sébillot, pp. 460–6.
[3] Rönnow, *Trita Aptya, ϑine vedische Gottheit*, Uppsala, 1927, pp. 36–7.
[4] Manninen, *Die dämonistischen Krankheiten in finnischen Volksaberglauben*,
Helsinki, 1922, pp. 81 ff.
[5] xxxvi. 25.
[6] xiii. 1.

saw in spirit how " in that day there shall be a fountain open
to the house of David and to the inhabitants of Jerusalem:
for the washing of the sinner and of the unclean woman ".

Water purifies and regenerates because it nullifies the past,
and restores—even if only for a moment—the integrity of the
dawn of things. The Iranian water divinity, Ardvisura Anahita,
is called " the holy one who multiplies flocks . . . goods . . .
riches . . . land . . . who purifies the seed of all men . . . the
womb of all women . . . who gives them milk when they need
it . . .", etc.[1] Ablution purifies man from crime,[2] from the
unlucky presence of the dead,[3] from madness (the fountain of
Clitor, of Arcadia),[4] destroying sins as well as stopping the
process of mental or physical decay. It was done before all
the major religious acts, to prepare man for his entry into the
economy of the sacred. There were ablutions before going
into temples[5] and before sacrifices.[6]

The same ritual of regeneration by water explains why in
antiquity statues of divinities were immersed. The ceremony
of the sacred bath was generally performed in the cult of the
Great Goddesses of fertility and agriculture. The goddess's
flagging powers were thus strengthened, ensuring a good harvest
(immersion as a magic rite was supposed to produce rain) and
a rich increase in goods. The " bath " of the Phrygian mother,
Cybele, took place on the 27th of March (*Hilaria*). The
statue was immersed either in a river (at Pessinus, Cybele was
bathed in the Gallos), or a pool (as at Ancyra, Magnesia and
elsewhere).[7] Aphrodite was bathed at Paphos[8] and Pausanias
describes the *loutrophoroi* of the goddess at Sicyon.[9] In the
third century A.D., Callimachus[10] extols the bath of the goddess
Athene. This ritual is very common in the cults of Cretan and

---

[1] *Yasna*, 65.

[2] *Æneid*, ii, 717–20.

[3] Euripides, *Alcestis*, 96–104.

[4] Vitruvius, *De Architect.*, 8; Saintyves, *Corpus du folklore des eaux en France et dans les colonies françaises*, Paris, 1934, p. 115.

[5] Justin, *Apolog. I*, 57, 1.

[6] *Æneid*, iv, 634–40; Macrobius, *Sat.*, iii, 1, etc.

[7] Cf. Graillot, *Le Culte de Cybèle*, Athens, 1912, pp. 288, 251, n.4, etc.

[8] *Odyssey*, viii, 363–6.

[9] ii, 10, 4.

[10] *Hymn.*, v, 1–17, 43–54.

Phoenician goddesses,[1] and among certain Germanic tribes.[2]
Dipping a crucifix or a statue of Our Lady in water to end a
drought and produce rain was a thing done by Catholics
from the thirteenth century onwards, and went on, despite
ecclesiastical opposition, into the nineteenth and even the
twentieth centuries.[3]

65. BAPTISM

This immemorial and œcumenical symbolism of immersion
in water as an instrument of purification and regeneration was
adopted by Christianity and given still richer religious meaning.
St. John's baptism was directed not to healing the infirmities
of the flesh, but the redemption of the soul, the forgiveness of
sin. John the Baptist preached " the baptism of penance for
the remission of sins ",[4] but he added: " I indeed baptize
you with water; but there shall come one mightier than I . . .
he shall baptize you with the Holy Ghost and with fire."[5]
In Christianity, Baptism becomes the chief instrument of
spiritual regeneration, for immersion in the water of Baptism
is equivalent to being buried with Christ. " Know you not,"
wrote St. Paul,[6] " that all we who are baptized in Christ Jesus
are baptized in his death?" Man dies symbolically with
immersion, and is reborn, purified, renewed; just as Christ
rose from the tomb. " For we are buried together with him by
baptism into death; that, as Christ is risen from the dead by
the glory of the Father, so we also may walk in newness of life.
For if we have been planted together in the likeness of his
death, we shall be also in the likeness of his resurrection."[7]
Of the tremendous number of patristic texts interpreting the
symbolism of Baptism, I shall record only two here: the first
is concerned with the redemptive significance of the water,
the second with the baptismal symbolism of death and rebirth.
Tertullian[8] gives a long dissertation on the extraordinary

[1] Picard, *Ephèse et Claros*, Paris, 1922, p. 318.
[2] Hertha; cf. Tacitus, *Germania*, 40.
[3] Cf. Saintyves, pp. 212 ff., 215 ff.
[4] Luke iii. 3.
[5] Luke iii. 16.
[6] Rom. vi. 3.
[7] Rom. vi. 4 ff.
[8] *De Bapt.*, iii–v.

powers of water, an element in the creation of the world which
was sanctified from the first by God's presence. For water
was the first " seat of the divine Spirit, who gave it preference
over all the other elements. . . . The water was the first to be
commanded to bring forth living creatures. . . . Water was the
first to produce what has life, so as to prevent our being
astonished when one day it came to give birth to life in baptism.
In forming man himself, God used water to complete his work.
It is true that the earth gave the substance, but earth would
have been of no use for this work had it not been moist and
sodden. . . . Why should not that which produces life from the
earth also give the life of heaven ? . . . Therefore all natural
water, because of the ancient privilege with which it was
honoured from the first, gains the power of sanctifying in the
sacrament, as long as God is invoked to that effect. As soon
as the words are said the Holy Ghost, coming down from
heaven, rests upon the waters which he sanctifies with his
fruitfulness; the waters thus sanctified are in turn filled with
the power of sanctifying. . . . What used of old to heal the
body now heals the soul; what gave health in time gains
salvation in eternity. . . ."

The Old Man dies by being immersed in water, and gives
birth to a new, regenerate being. This symbolism is perfectly
expressed by John Chrysostom[1] who, speaking of the many
different meanings symbolized in Baptism, writes: " It represents death and burial, life and resurrection. . . . When we
plunge our head into water as into a tomb, the old man is
immersed, wholly buried; when we come out of the water,
the new man appears at that moment." All that one may call
the " prehistory " of Baptism sought the same object—death
and resurrection, though at different religious levels from that
of Christianity. There can be no question here of " influences "
or of " borrowings ", for such symbols are archetypal and
universal; they show man's position in the universe, while
at the same time evaluating his position in regard to his god
(to absolute *reality*), and to history. The symbolism of water
is the product of an intuition of the cosmos as a unity, and of
man as a specific mode of being in the cosmos.

[1] *Homil. in Joh.*, xxv, 2; Saintyves, p. 149.

66. THE THIRST OF THE DEAD

The funereal use of water is explained by the same elements that give it its function in the creation of the universe, in magic and in medicine; water " appeases the thirst of the dead man ", it dissolves him, it links him together with the seeds of things; water " kills the dead ", finally destroying their human status[1] that hell may reduce them to a sort of larval state, thus leaving their capacity for suffering unimpaired. In none of the various conceptions of death, do the dead die completely: they are given an elementary form of existence; it is a regression, rather than a total extinction. While waiting to return into the cosmic round (transmigration), or to be finally delivered, the souls of the dead *suffer* and that suffering is generally expressed as a *thirst*.

Dives, in the fires of hell, asks Abraham: " Have mercy on me and send Lazarus, that he may dip the tip of his finger in water to cool my tongue: for I am tormented in this flame."[2] An inscription found on an Orphic tablet (at Eleutherne) reads: " I burn, and am consumed with thirst . . ." During the ceremony of the Hydrophoria, water was poured into crevasses (*chasmata*) for the dead, and at the time of the Anthesteria, just before the spring rains, the Greeks believed that the dead were thirsty.[3] The thought that the souls of the dead suffered from thirst was particularly frightening to those peoples to whom heat and drought were a constant menace (in Mesopotamia, Anatolia, Syria, Palestine, Egypt), and it was chiefly among them that libations were made for the dead, and the happiness of the after-life was represented as a cool

---

[1] This notion was also held in philosophical speculation. " For souls, death is to become water," said Heraclitus (fr. 68). That is why " the dry soul is the wisest and the best " (fr. 74). The fear that moisture would " dissolve " the souls separated from their bodies, make them grow again and send them out once again into the round of the lower forms of life, was common in Greek soteriology. One Orphic fragment (Clement, *Strom.*, vi, 2, 17, 1; Kern, p. 226) says that " for the soul, water is death ", and Porphyry (*De Antro Nympharum*, 10–11) explains the leaning of the souls of the dead towards moisture by their desire for reincarnation. Later on the germinative function of water was depreciated, because the happiest lot after death came to be considered to be not reintegration into the cosmic round, but escaping from the world of organic forms into the empyrean, into the heavens. That is why such importance came to be given to the solar path of " dryness ".

[2] Luke xvi. 24.

[3] See references in Gernet, *Génie grec*, Paris, 1932, p. 262; Schuhl, *La formation de la pensée grecque*, Paris, 1934, pp. 119, n. 2, 210, n. 2.

place.[1] The sufferings of the after-life were expressed in terms as concrete as those describing every other human experience and primitive theory; the "thirst of the dead", and the "flames" of the Asian hells were replaced in the Nordic mind by terms expressing a cooler temperature (cold, frost, frozen swamps, etc.).[2]

But thirst and cold both express suffering, drama, agitation. The dead cannot always remain in the same state, a state that is merely a tragic defacement of their human one. Libations are intended to "satisfy" them, that is, to abolish their sufferings, and regenerate them by total "dissolution" in water. In Egypt, the dead are sometimes identified with Osiris, and thus may hope for an "agricultural destiny", their bodies germinating like seeds. On a burial stele now in the British Museum, the dead man addresses a prayer to Ra "that his body may grow as a seed".[3] But libations are not always to be taken in an "agricultural" sense; their object is not always "the germination of the dead man", his transformation into a "seed" and a *neophutos* (neophyte="new plant") but, primarily, his "appeasement", that is, the extinction of what remains of his human condition, his complete immersion in the "waters", so that he may achieve a new birth. The "agricultural destiny" that funeral libations sometimes include, is only one consequence of that final abolition of the human condition; it is a new mode of manifestation, rendered possible by the power water has not only to dissolve but also to germinate life.

67. MIRACULOUS AND ORACULAR SPRINGS

There are a great number of cults and rites connected with various springs, streams and rivers throughout history to correspond to these many different values given to water. All these cults are primarily based on the sacredness of water as such, as an element in the creation of the universe, but also on the local epiphany, on the manifestation of a sacred presence in some particular watercourse or spring. Such local epiphanies are independent of the religious structure superimposed

---

[1] Cf. Parrot, Le " Refrigerium " dans l'au-delà, Paris, 1937, passim; Eliade. CZ, 1938,i, pp. 203ff.

[2] Cf. Eliade, Insula lui Euthanasius, p. 95; CZ, i, p. 205.

[3] Parrot, p. 103, n. 3; CZ, i, p. 206, with further references.

on them. Water flows, it is " living ", it moves: it inspires, it heals, it prophesies. By their very nature, spring and river display power, life, perpetual renewal; they *are* and they are *alive*. Thus they have a certain autonomy, and their worship persists in spite of other epiphanies and other religious revolutions. Each continues always to reveal the sacred force that is peculiarly its own, and at the same time shares in the prerogatives of water as such.

The cult of water—and particularly of springs held to be curative, hot springs, salt springs and so on—displays a striking continuity. No religious revolution has ever put a stop to it; fed by popular devotion, the cult of water came to be tolerated even by Christianity, after the fruitless persecuting of it in the Middle Ages. (The reaction began in the fourth century with St. Cyril of Jerusalem.[1] Ecclesiastical prohibitions were made over and over again from the Second Council of Arles—443 or 452—until the Council of Trèves in 1227. In addition, a considerable number of polemics, pastoral letters and other documents mark out for us the struggle made by the Church against the cult of water.[2]) In some cases the cult seems to have lasted from the Neolithic age until the present day. In the hot spring of Grisy (in the commune of Saint-Symphorien-de-Marmagne) for instance, Neolithic and Roman " ex-votos " can be found.[3] Similar traces of Neolithic worship (silexes broken to show they were ex-votos) were found in the spring now called Saint-Sauveur (Compiègne Forest)[4]. Rooted in prehistory, the cult was passed down to the Gauls, and later the Roman Gauls, whence it was taken up and assimilated by Christianity. At Saint Moritz, until quite lately, there still stood ancient remains dating from the worship of the Bronze Age.[5] In the commune of Bertinoro (Province of Forli) religious remains from the Bronze Age are to be found near a modern well of chloro-saline water.[6] In England springs near some of the prehistoric barrows and megalithic monu-

---

[1] *Catech.*, xix, 8.

[2] Cf. Saintyves, *Corpus*, pp. 163 ff.

[3] Vaillat, *Le Culte des sources dans la Gaule antique*, pp. 97–8.

[4] Vaillat, p. 99.

[5] Pettazzoni, *La religione primitiva in Sardegna*, Piacenza, 1912, p. 102.

[6] Pettazzoni, pp. 102–3.

ments are held by the local inhabitants to be miraculous or beneficent.[1] And finally I think I should recall the ritual that took place at the lake of Saint Andéol (in the Aubrac Mountains) described by Saint Gregory of Tours (A.D. 544–95). The men came in their carts and feasted for three days by the lakeside, bringing as offerings linen, fragments of clothing, woollen thread, cheese, cakes and so on. On the fourth day there was a ritual storm with rain (clearly it was a primitive rite to induce rain). A priest, Parthenius, having in vain tried to convince the peasants to give up this pagan ceremonial, built a church to which the men eventually brought the offerings intended for the lake. However, the custom of throwing cakes and worn-out things into the lake remained alive till the nineteenth century; pilgrims continued to throw shirts and trousers into the lake, though they did not really know what their object was in doing so.[2]

We find an excellent example of continuity, in spite of the many changes in the religious framework surrounding the cult of water, in Pettazzoni's monograph on primitive religion in Sardinia. The early Sardinians worshipped springs, offering sacrifice to them and building sanctuaries beside them dedicated to Sarder Pater.[3] Beside the temples and the water, there took place ordeals, a religious phenomenon characteristic of the whole Atlanto-Mediterranean area.[4] Traces of these ordeals by water can still be seen in Sardinian beliefs and folklore. We also find the cult of water in Sicilian prehistory.[5] At Lilybaeum (Marsala) the Greek Sybil was superimposed on a primitive local cult centring around a cave flooded with water; the early Sicilians went there for ordeals or for prophetic retreats; during the time of the Greek colonization the Sybil held sway and prophesied, and in Christian times it became the scene of a devotion to Saint John the Baptist, to whom, in the sixteenth century, a church was built in the old cave

---

[1] Pettazzoni.

[2] Cf. Saintyves, pp. 189–95.

[3] Pettazzoni, pp. 29 ff., 58.

[4] In Lusitania, they still adored a local god, Tongoenabiagus, in Roman times; he seems to have been the god " of the water course by which one swears oaths " (Vasconcellos, *Religiões de Lusitania*, Lisbon, 1905, vol. ii, pp. 239 ff.).

[5] Pettazzoni, pp. 101 ff.

which is even to-day the object of pilgrimage for its miraculous waters.[1]

Oracles were often situated near water. Near the temple of Amphirais, at Oropos, those who were cured by the oracle threw a coin into the water.[2] The *pythia* prepared by drinking water from the Kassotis fountain. At Colophon, the prophet drank the water from a sacred spring which was in the grotto.[3] At Claros, the priest went down into the cave, drank some water from a mysterious fountain (*hausta fontis arcani aqua*) and replied in verse to any question he was asked (*super rebus quas quis mente concepit*).[4] That prophetic power emanates from water is a primitive intuition which we find in a great part of the world. The ocean, for instance, was called by the Babylonians " the home of wisdom ". Oannes, the mythical Babylonian character half man, half fish, rose from the Persian Gulf and revealed to man culture, writing and astrology.[5]

68. WATER EPIPHANIES AND DIVINITIES

The cult of water—rivers, springs and lakes—existed in Greece before the Indo-European invasions. Traces of this primitive cult were preserved up till the decline of Hellenism. Pausanias[6] could still examine and describe the ceremony that took place at the Hagno spring, on the side of Mount Lykaios, in Arcadia; the priest of the god Lykaios came there when there was a severe drought; he sacrificed a branch of oak and let it drop into the spring. The rite was an ancient one and part of the whole pattern of " rain magic ". Indeed, declares Pausanias, after the ceremony, a light breath like a cloud rose from the water, and it soon began to rain. We find there no religious personification; the power is in the spring itself, and that power, set in motion by the proper rite, governs the rain.

Homer speaks of the cult of rivers. The Trojans offered sacrifices of animals to the Scamander and threw living horses

---

[1] Pettazzoni, p. 101.

[2] Pausanias, i, 34, 4.

[3] Iamblichus, *De Myst.*, iii, 11.

[4] Tacitus, *Annals*, ii, 54; on the subject of the Oracle of Claros, cf. Picard, *Ephèse et Claros*, pp. 112 ff.

[5] Texts quoted in Jeremias, *Handbuch der altorientalischen Geisteskultur*, Berlin, 1929, pp. 39–40.

[6] viii, 38, 3–4.

into its waters; Peleus sacrificed fifty sheep into the springs of Spercheios. The Scamander had its priests; an enclosure and an altar were consecrated at Spercheios. Horses and oxen were sacrificed to Poseidon and the divinities of the sea.[1] Other Indo-European peoples also offered sacrifice to rivers; for instance the Cimbri (who sacrificed to the Rhône), the Franks, Germans, Slavs and others.[2] Hesiod[3] mentions the sacrifices celebrated when crossing a river. (This rite has numerous parallels in ethnology; the Masai, in West Africa, throw in a handful of grass whenever they cross a river; the Baganda, of central Africa, bring some coffee beans as an offering when they cross water, and so on.)[4] The Hellenic river gods were sometimes in the likeness of men; for instance, the Scamander fought against Achilles.[5] But for the most part they were represented as bulls.[6] The most famous river god of all was the Achelous. Homer even held him to be a great god, the divinity of all rivers, seas and springs. We have read of Achelous' struggles with Heracles; his cult was carried on in Athens, Oropos, Megara, and a great many other cities. Various interpretations have been given of its name, but it seems likely that the etymology is simply " water ".[7]

It would not assist our purpose to quote all the water mythology of the Greeks. It is vast and not at all clearly defined. Innumerable mythological figures appear in endless succession, all with the same theme—that water divinities are born of water. Some of those figures attained importance in myth or legend, as for instance Thetis, the sea nymph, or Proteus, Glaucos, Nereus, Triton—all Neptunian divinities still displaying in their appearance their connection with water, having the bodies of sea monsters, or the tails of fishes, or something of the sort. They live and govern in the depths of the sea. Like the element from which they are only imperfectly and never finally detached, these divinities are odd and

[1] Cf. references and bibliography in Nilsson, *Geschichte der griechischen Religion*, Munich, 1941, vol. i, p. 220, n. 3.

[2] Cf. Saintyves, p. 160.

[3] *Works and Days*, 737 ff.

[4] Cf. Frazer, *Folklore in the Old Testament*, vol. ii, pp. 417 ff.

[5] *Iliad*, xxi, 124 ff.

[6] References in Nilsson, p. 221, n. 10.

[7] Nillsson, vol. i, p. 222.

capricious; they do good and evil with equal carelessness, and, like the sea, they generally do evil. More than any other gods they live outside time and history. Closely bound up with the origin of the world, they only participate occasionally in what passes there. Their life is perhaps less divine than that of the other gods, but it is more regular and more closely connected with the element they represent.

69. NYMPHS

What Greek could boast that he knew the names of *all* the nymphs? They were the divinities of all flowing waters, of all springs and of all fountains. They needed hardly to be created by the Hellenic imagination; rather they were there, in the water, from the beginning of the world; all the Greeks had to give them was their human form and their name. They were created by the living, flowing water, by its magic, by the power emanating from it, by its babbling. The Greeks detached them as far as possible from the element to which they belonged. Once detached, personified, and invested with all the powers of water, they became subjects of legend, they were brought into epics, were petitioned to work wonders. They were usually the mothers of the local heroes.[1] As minor divinities of certain places, they were well known to men and they were the object of worship and received sacrifices. The most famous are the sisters of Thetis, the Nereids, or, as Hesiod still called them,[2] the Oceanides, the perfect Neptunian nymphs. Most of the others are divinities of springs. But they also dwell in caves where there is water. The " nymphs' cave " became a common-place in Hellenist literature, and the most " literary ", that is profane, formula, the furthest from the primitive religious sense, from the pattern of water-cosmic-cave-happiness-Fertility-Wisdom. The nymphs, once personified, entered into men's lives. They were divinities of birth (water=fertility) and *kourotrophoi*; they brought children up, and taught them to become heroes.[3] Nearly all the Greek heroes were brought up either by nymphs or by centaurs—that is, by superhuman beings who shared in nature's powers and could direct them.

[1] Nilsson, vol. i, pp. 227 ff.
[2] *Theog.*, 364.
[3] Cf. for instance, Euripides, *Helen.*, 624 ff.

Heroic initiations were never a thing of the family; nor were they generally " civic ", for they took place not in the city but in the forests, and woodlands.

That is why we find, alongside the veneration for nymphs (as for other spirits of nature), a fear of them. Nymphs often stole children; or, on other occasions, they would kill them out of jealousy. We find written on the tomb of one five-year-old girl: " I was lovable because I was good, and it was not death that bore me off but the Naiads."[1] Nymphs were also dangerous in another way; anyone who saw them in the heat of midday became mentally deranged. The middle of the day was the moment when the nymphs manifested themselves. Whoever saw them became seized with a nympholeptic mania; like Tiresias, who saw Pallas and Chariclo, or Actaeon, who came upon Artemis with her nymphs. That is why it was advisable, at midday, not to go near fountains or springs, or the shadow of certain trees. Later superstition had it that a prophetic madness would seize anyone who saw a form emerging from the water: *speciem quamdam e fonte, id est effigiem Nymphæ* (Festus). The prophetic quality of water remains in all these beliefs, though with inevitable adulterations and mythological embroideries. What persists above all is the ambivalent feeling of fear and attraction to water which at once destroys (for the " fascination " of the nymphs brings madness, the destruction of the personality) and germinates, which at once kills and assists birth.

70 POSEIDON, ÆGIR, ETC.

But above Achelous, Thetis and all the other minor water divinities is Poseidon. The sea, when it is angry, loses its feminine qualities of undulating seductiveness and lazy pleasure —and its mythological personification acquires a markedly masculine outline. When the universe was divided among the sons of Kronos, Poseidon was given power over the ocean. Homer knew him as the god of the seas; his palace was at the bottom of the Ocean, and his symbol was the trident (originally the teeth of the sea monsters). If Persson is right in reading the Mycenian inscription of Asima as *Poseidafonos*, then the god's name can be traced right back to the Mycenian

[1] *CIG*, 6291.

period.[1] Poseidon was also the god of earthquakes, which the Greeks held to be due to erosion by water. The furious waves breaking wildly on the shore were reminiscent of seismic tremors. Like the ocean itself, Poseidon was untamed, unhappy, faithless. The picture of him in myth has no moral qualities; he was too near the Neptunian origin to know any law apart from his own mode of existence. Poseidon reveals a certain cosmic condition: waters pre-existed creation, and rhythmically swallow it up once more; thus, the perfect autonomy of the sea, indifferent to gods, men and history, rocking itself in its own flowing, unconscious both of the seeds it bears and of the " forms " it possesses potentially, and which, indeed, it dissolves periodically.

In Scandinavian mythology, Ægir (*eagor*, " the sea ") personifies the limitless ocean. His wife is the perfidious Ran (*ræna*, " to plunder ") who takes her net over the whole sea, drawing whatever she meets down to her dwelling beneath it. Drowned men go to Ran, men thrown into the sea are sacrificed to her. Ægir and Ran have nine daughters, each representing one aspect of the ocean, one moment of the epiphany of the sea: Kolga (the untamed sea), Bylgja (the swell), Hrafn (the despoiler), Drafn (the waves seizing and dragging things along with them) and so on. At the bottom of the ocean there stands the magnificent palace of Ægir, where all the gods sometimes gather. There, for instance, took place the famous banquet round the vast cauldron which Thor stole from the giant Ymir (another spirit of the ocean)—a miraculous cauldron in which the drink used to make and stir itself; there Loki came to disturb the good will the gods bore each other (cf. *Lokasenna*) by calumniating them all together with their goddess-wives (he was finally punished by being bound to a rock at the bottom of the sea).

The miraculous cauldron of Ymir finds parallels in other Indo-Aryan mythologies.[2] It was used for making ambrosia, the drink of the gods. What particularly interests us here is the telling detail that most of the magic and mythological cauldrons were found at the bottom of the sea or of lakes.[3]

---

[1] Nilsson, vol. i, p. 416.
[2] Cf. Dumézil's *Le Festin d'immortalité*.
[3] A. C. Brown, quoted by Krappe, *La Genèse des Mythes*, Paris, 1938, p. 209.

The traditional city of the magic cauldron in Ireland, Murias, gets its name from *muir*, the sea. There is magic power in water; cauldrons, kettles, chalices, are all receptacles of this magic force which is often symbolized by some divine liquor such as ambrosia or " living water "; they confer immortality or eternal youth, or they change whoever owns them into a hero or a god, etc.

71. WATER ANIMALS AND EMBLEMS

Dragons, snakes, shell-fish, dolphins, fish and so on are the emblems of water; hidden in the depths of the ocean, they are infused with the sacred power of the abyss; lying quietly in lakes or swimming across rivers, they bring rain, moisture, and floods, thus governing the fertility of the world. Dragons dwell in the clouds and in lakes; they have charge of thunder-bolts; they pour down water from the skies, making both fields and women fruitful. We shall be reverting later to the many-sided symbolism of dragons, snakes, shells and such; in the present paragraph I shall merely glance at it, limiting myself to the Chinese and South-East Asian cultures. Dragons and snakes,[1] according to Tchouang Tseu, symbolize rhythmic life,[2] for the dragon stands for the spirit of water, whose har-monious fluctuations feed life and make all civilization possible. The dragon Ying gathers all the waters together and orders the rain, for he is himself the principle of moisture.[3] " When a drought grows acute, they make an image of the dragon Ying and it starts to rain."[4]

In early Chinese writings you often find a linking of dragon, thunderbolt and fertility.[5] " The beast of the thunder has the body of a dragon and a human head."[6] A girl can become pregnant from a dragon's saliva.[7] Fu-hsi, one of the founders

[1] The Chinese have never made a very clear distinction between the snake and the mythical creature (cf. Granet, *Danses et Légendes de la Chine ancienne*, Paris, 1926, vol. ii, p. 554).

[2] Cf. Granet, *La Pensée chinoise*, p. 135.

[3] Granet, *Danses*, vol. i, p. 353–6, n.

[4] Granet, *Danses*, p. 361; cf. Frazer, *The Magic Art and the Evolution of Kings*, London, 1936, vol. i, p. 297, on the subject of Chinese rain rituals using effigies of dragons.

[5] Cf. Granet, *Danses*, vol. i, pp. 344–50; vol. ii, p. 555; Karlgren, " Some Fecundity Symbols in Ancient China ", BMAS, p. 37, etc.

[6] Granet, *Danses*, vol. ii, p. 510.

[7] Karlgren, p. 37.

of Chinese civilization, was born in a pool associated with dragons.[1] " The father [of Kao-Chu] was called T'ai-kong; his mother was called the venerable Liou. The venerable Liou was one day resting beside a large pool and she dreamt that she met with a god; at that moment there was thunder, lightning, and great darkness; T'ai-kong went to see what was happening and he saw a scaly dragon on top of his wife; as a result she became pregnant and gave birth to Kao-Chu."[2]

In China the dragon—an emblem of sky and water—was constantly associated with the Emperor, who represented the rhythms of the cosmos and conferred fecundity on the earth. When the rhythms were disturbed when the life of nature or of society became troubled, the Emperor knew what he must do to regenerate his creative power and re-establish order. A king of the Hsia dynasty, to guarantee the development of his kingdom, ate dragons.[3] Thus you always find dragons appearing as guardians of the rhythms of life whenever the power by which the Hsia dynasty ruled was growing weak, or undergoing a rebirth.[4] At death, or even sometimes while still alive, the Emperor returned to heaven; so, for instance, Huang-ti, the Yellow Sovereign, was taken up to heaven by a bearded dragon, with his wives and councillors, seventy people in all.[5]

In Chinese mythology, which is that of a people living away from the sea, the dragon, emblem of water, has always got more definite sky powers than he has elsewhere. The fertility of water becomes centred in the clouds, in the world above. But the pattern fecundity-water-kingship (or holiness) is more closely adhered to in the South-East Asian mythologies in which the ocean is seen as the foundation of all reality and the giver of all powers. J. Przyluski has analyzed a great many Australasian and Indonesian legends and folk tales which all present one special feature: the hero owes his extraordinary status (of " king " or " saint ") to the fact that he was born of a water animal. In Annam, the first mythological king holds

---

[1] Chavannes, *Les Mémoires historiques de Sse-Ma-Tsien*, Paris, 1897, vol. i, pp. 3 ff.

[2] Chavannes, vol. ii, p. 325.

[3] Granet, *Chinese Civilization*, London, 1930, pp. 181–2.

[4] Ibid.

[5] Chavannes, vol. iii, pt. ii, pp. 488–9.

the title of *long quan*, "the dragon king". In Indonesia, according to Tchao-Jou-Koua, the kings of San-fo-ts'i bore the title, *long tsin*, "spirit, sperm of *naga*".[1] Nagi was a female water spirit who filled the same role in Australasia as the dragon in China. In her sea form, or as a "princess smelling of fish", Nagi mated with a brahman and founded a dynasty (the Indonesian version, also found in Champa, Pegu, Siam, etc.). According to one Palaung legend, the *nagi* Thusandi loved the prince Thuriya, son of the Sun;[2] three sons were born of their union: one became Emperor of China, one King of the Palaung, the third king in Pagan. *Sedjarat Malayou* tells us that King Souran went down to the bottom of the sea in a glass case, and as those who dwelt there received him well, he married the king's daughter. Three sons were born of this marriage and the eldest became King of Palembang.

In southern India it is believed that one of the ancestors of the Pallava dynasty married a Nagi, and received from her the insignia of kingship. The *nagi* motif comes into Buddhist legends, and can even be found in northern India, in Uddyana and Kashmir. The kings of Chota-Nagpur were also descended from a *nāga* (spirit of a snake) called Pundarika: this latter, it is said, had evil-smelling breath, a detail reminiscent of the "princess smelling of fish". According to a tradition preserved in southern India, the sage Āgastya was born with Vasiṣṭha in a vase of water, from the union of the gods Mitra and Varuṇa with the *apsaras* Urvasi. That is why he was called Kumbhasambhava (born of Kumbhamata, the vase-goddess) and Pitābdhi (swallower of the ocean). Agastya married the daughter of the Ocean.[3] The *Devy-Upaniṣad* tells how the gods asked the Great Goddess (*devi*) who she was

---

[1] Cf. Przyluski, " La Princesse à l'odeur de poisson et la nāgi dans les traditions de l'Asie orientale ", *EA*, Paris, 1925, vol. ii, p. 276.

[2] Note the opposition between serpent (fish, sea monster, symbol of water, of darkness, of the unseen) and sun (" son of the sun ", or Brahman, etc.; symbol of the seen)—an opposition done away with by a mythical marriage which founded a dynasty, which, in other words, opened a new epoch in history. Whenever one tries to " formulate "divinity, one finds a fusion of opposite principles (cf. Eliade, *Mitul Reintegrarii*, p. 52). In the myths of Indonesia and South-East Asia to which I refer above, this *coincidentia oppositorum* signifies the end of a cycle by a return to the primeval unity, followed by the establishment of a " dynasty ", or new cycle of history.

[3] Oppert, *On the Original Inhabitants of Bhāratavarsa or India*, Westminster, 1893, pp. 24, 67–8.

and whence she came, and she answered, among other things:
". . . My birthplace is in the water inside the sea, who knows it
obtains the abode of Devi." At the beginning the goddess
was the origin of all things: " I produce at first the father of
the world."[1]

All these traditions show very clearly the sacred importance
and consecrating power of water. Both sovereignty and
sanctity are the gift of sea spirits; magico-religious power lies
at the bottom of the sea and is given to the heroes[2] by female
beings (nagi, the " princess smelling of fish ", etc.). Serpent
genies did not dwell only in the seas and oceans but also in
lakes, pools, wells and springs. The worship of serpents and
serpent genies in India and elsewhere, in whatever setting we
find it, always preserves its magico-religious bond with water.[3]
Serpents and serpent genies are always found close to water,
or in charge of it; there are genies guarding the springs of life,
of immortality, of holiness, as well as all the emblems connected
with life, fecundity, heroism, immortality and " treasure ".

72. DELUGE SYMBOLISM

Almost all the traditions of deluges are bound up with the
idea of humanity returning to the water whence it had come,
and the establishment of a new era and a new humanity.
They display a conception of the universe and its history as
something " cyclic ": one era is abolished by disaster and a
new one opens, ruled by " new men ". This conception of
cycles is also shown by the convergence of the lunar myths
with themes of floods and deluges; for the moon is by far the
most important symbol of rhythmic development, of death
and resurrection. Just as the phases of the moon govern
initiation ceremonies—in which the neophyte " dies " to waken
to a new life—so too they are intimately connected with the

[1] The text can be found in Oppert, pp. 425–6; cf. my Le Yoga: Immortalité
et Liberté, pp. 346 ff.

[2] Are we justified in explaining the birth of the Greek heroes from nymphs
and naiads—water divinities too—by this same formula? Achilles was the son
of Thetis, a sea nymph. And note that local heroes were often descended from
naiads—Iphition, Sotnios and others. A local hero was often left behind by an
earlier, primitive, cult, a pre-Indo-European cult; he was " the master of the
place ".

[3] Cf. for instance, Vogel, " Serpent Worship in Ancient and Modern India, "
AOA, 1924, vol. ii, passim.

floods that annihilate the old humanity and set the stage for the appearance of the new. In the mythologies of the area round the Pacific, tribes are generally supposed to have sprung from some mythical moon animal which had escaped a watery disaster.[1] The tribes were descended either from a shipwrecked man whose life was saved, or the lunar animal which caused the flood to happen.

There is no need in this chapter to stress the rhythmic nature of this re-engulfing of all things by water and their periodic emergence—a rhythm which is at the root of all the geographical myths and apocalypses (Atlantis and so on). What I must point out is how widespread and how coherent these Neptunian mythological themes are. Water is in existence before every creation, and periodically water absorbs it all again to dissolve it in itself, purify it, enrich it with new possibilities and regenerate it. Men disappear periodically in a deluge or flood because of their " sins " (in most of the myths of the Pacific area the catastrophe was caused by some ritual misdemeanour). They never perish utterly, but reappear in a new form, return to the same destined path, and await the repetition of the same catastrophe which will again dissolve them in water.

I am not sure that one can call it a pessimistic conception of life. It is rather a resigned view, imposed simply by seeing the pattern made by water, the moon and change. The deluge myth, with all that it implies, shows what human life may be worth to a " mind " other than a human mind; from the " point of view " of water, human life is something fragile that must periodically be engulfed, because it is the fate of all forms to be dissolved in order to reappear. If " forms " are not regenerated by being periodically dissolved in water, they will crumble, exhaust their powers of creativity and finally die away. Mankind would eventually be completely deformed by " wickedness " and " sin "; emptied of its seeds of life and creative powers, humanity would waste away, weakened and sterile. Instead of permitting this slow regression into sub-human forms, the flood effects an instantaneous dissolution in water, in which sins are purified and from which a new, regenerate humanity will be born.

[1] Hentze, *Mythes et Symboles*, pp. 14, 24, etc.

73. SUMMING-UP

Thus all the metaphysical and religious possibilities of water fit together perfectly to make a whole. To the creation of the universe from water there correspond—at the anthropological level—the beliefs according to which men were born of water. To the deluge or disappearance of continents into the water (of which Atlantis is the perfect example)—a cosmic phenomenon which must of necessity be repeated periodically—there correspond at the human level, the " second death " of the soul (burial libations, " moisture " and *leimon* in hell, etc.) and the ritual, initiatory death of baptism. But, whether at the cosmic or the anthropological level, immersion in water does not mean final extinction, but simply a temporary reintegration into the formless, which will be followed by a new creation, a new life or a new man, depending on whether the reintegration in question is cosmic, biological, or redemptive. In form, the " deluge " is comparable to " baptism "; the burial libation, or the frenzy of nympholepsy, to the ritual washing of the new-born, or the ritual bathings of springtime which assure health and fertility. In whatever religious framework it appears, the function of water is shown to be the same; it disintegrates, abolishes forms, " washes away sins "—at once purifying and giving new life. Its work is to precede creation and take it again to itself; it can never get beyond its own mode of existence—can never express itself *in forms*. Water can never pass beyond the condition of the potential, of seeds and hidden powers. Everything that has form is manifested above the waters, is separate from them. On the other hand, as soon as it has separated itself from water, every " form " loses its potentiality, falls under the law of time and of life; it is limited, enters history, shares in the universal law of change, decays, and would cease to be itself altogether were it not regenerated by being periodically immersed in the waters again, did it not again go through the " flood " followed by the " creation of the universe ". Ritual lustrations and purifications with water are performed with the purpose of bringing into the present for a fleeting instant " that time ", that *illud tempus*, when the creation took place; they are a symbolic re-enactment of the birth of the world or of the " new man ". Any use of water with a religious intention brings together the two basic points in the rhythm of the universe: reintegration in water—and creation.

BIBLIOGRAPHY

Water Cosmogonies: WENSINCK, A. J., *The Ocean in the Literature of the Western Semites*, Amsterdam, 1919, particularly pp. 1–15, 40–56; DÄHNHARDT, Oscar, *Natursagen*, Leipzig, 1909, vol. i, pp. 1–89; THOMPSON, Stith, *Motif-Index of Folk Literature*, Helsinki, 1932, vol. i, pp. 121 ff.; COOMARASWAMY, Ananda K., *Yaksas*, Washington, 1928–31, vols. i–ii, HENTZE, Carl, *Mythes et Symboles Lunaires*, Antwerp, 1932; KRAPPE, A. H., *La Genèse des Mythes*, Paris, 1938, pp. 197 ff.

On the magic and religious significance of water: NINCK, M., " Die Bedeutung des Wassers im Kult und Leben der Alten ", *PS*, 1921, suppl. vol. xiv; SCHEFTELOWITZ, J., " Die Sündentilgung durch Wasser ", *AFRW*, 1914, pp. 353–412; on ritual purifications by water, PETTAZZONI, R., *La Confessione dei peccati*, Bologna, 1929, vol. i, pp. 2–3 (the Ewe and Bashilange), p. 18 (Sulka); HARTTE, K., *Zum semitischen Wasserkultus*, Halle, 1912; SMITH, Robertson, *Lectures on the Religion of the Semites*, 3rd ed., London, 1927, pp. 166 ff., 557 ff. (sacred waters); LAGRANGE, P., *Etudes sur les religions sémitiques*, Paris, 1905, pp. 158, 169; HOPKINS, E. W.; " The Fountain of Youth ", *JAOS*, 1905, vol. xxvi, pp. 1–67; BARNETT, L. D., " Yama, Gandharva and Glaucus ", *BSOAS*, 1926–8, vol. iv, pp. 703–16; RÖNNOW, K., *Trita Aptya, eine vedische Gottheit*, Uppsala, 1927, pp. 6 ff. (water demons), 14 ff. (Varuṇa, god of water), 36 ff. (illnesses driven out of people into water by magic), 64 ff. (the " water of life ") and so on; BOUCHE-LECLERCQ, A., *Histoire de la divination dans l'antiquité*, Paris, 1879–82, vol. ii, pp. 261–6 (oracles controlled by water divinities), 363–9 (the oracle of Poseidon); GLOTZ, G., *L'Ordalie dans la Grèce primitive*, Paris, 1904, pp. 11–69 (ordeals by sea), 69–79 (by springs, rivers and wells); FRAZER, J., *Folklore in the Old Testament*, London, 1918, vol. iii, pp. 304–6 (ordeals among the Israelites); SAINTYVES, P., *Les Vierges-mères et les naissances miraculeuses*, Paris, 1908, pp. 39–53 (water theogonies and water cults), 87–109 (miraculous births by means of sacred water); NYBERG, B., *Kind und Erde*, Helsinki, 1931, pp. 55 ff. (the birth of children, or of mythological ancestors from water); PESTALOZZA, U., *Pagine di religione mediterranea*, Milan, 1945, vol. ii, pp. 253 ff. (ritual union beside rivers); LAOUST, E., *Mots et choses berbères. Notes de linguistique et d'ethnographie*, Paris, 1920, pp. 202–53 (rain rites); BENOIT, F., " Le Rite de l'eau dans la fête du solstice d'été en Provence et en Afrique ", *RAN*, vol. lxv, nos. 1–3; BRUNOT, Louis, *La Mer dans les traditions et les industries indigènes à Rabat et Salé*, Paris, 1920, pp. 3–25 (sea demonology; the sea in medicine and magic); JOLEAUD, L., " Gravures rupestres et rites de l'eau en Afrique du nord " *JSA*, 1933, vol. iii, pp. 197–222; GOLDZIEHER, J., " Wasser als Dämonen-abwehrendes Mittel ", *AFRW*, 1910, vol. xiii, no. 1; WESENDONCK, O. von, *Das Weltbild der Iranien*, 1933, pp. 102 ff. (on the Iranian cult of water); ELIADE, M., " Notes sur le symbolisme aquatique ", *CZ*, 1939, vol. ii, pp. 131–52; BACHELARD, Gaston, *L'Eau et les rêves*, Paris, 1942.

On the symbolism of Baptism: LUNDBERG, P., *La Typologie baptismale dans l'ancienne Eglise*, Uppsala-Leipzig, 1942; DANIELOU, Jean, *Bible et Liturgie*, Paris, 1951, pp. 29–173; BEIRNAERT, Louis, S.J., " La Dimension mystique du sacrementalisme chrétien ", *EJ*, 1950, vol. xviii, pp. 255–86; ELIADE, M., *Images et symboles*, Paris, 1952, pp. 199 ff.

On the water symbolism of the spiral: SIRET, L., *Origine et signification du décor spirale*, Report of the 15th International Congress of Anthropology, Portugal, 1930, published in Paris, 1931, pp. 465–82.

On the worship of springs, streams, rivers; on Neptunian divinities: PETTAZZONI, R., *La Religione primitiva in Sardegna*, Piacenza, 1912, *passim*; DECHELETTE, J., *Manuel d'archéologie préhistorique, celtique et gallo-romaine*, Paris, 1908–14, vol. ii, a, pp. 166 ff. (votive axes found near springs and fountains), 444–53 (the cult of hot springs); JULLIAN, C., *Histoire de la Gaule*, 5th ed., Paris, 1924–6, vol. ii, pp. 129–37 (local divinities), vol. viii, pp. 313–31 (the continuity of water cults); TOUTAIN, J., *Les Cultes paiens dans l'empire romain*, Paris, 1907–20, vol. i, pp. 372–84 (water divinities; official cults); vol. iii, pp. 193–467 (native cults in Roman Gaul); VAILLAT, Claudius, *Le Culte des sources dans la Gaule antique*, Paris, 1934; there is a good bibliography of Gallic and Gallo-Roman cults in SAINTYVES, *Corpus du folklore des eaux en France et dans les colonies françaises*, Paris, 1934, pp. 24–35; VASCONCELLOS, Leite de, *Religiões da Lusitania*, Lisbon, 1905, vol. ii, pp. 198 ff. (river gods in early Celto-Lusitanian history); Lisbon, 1913, vol. iii, pp. 248 ff. (in Roman times); JEREMIAS, Alfred, *Handbuch der altorientalischen Geisteskultur*, 2nd ed., Berlin, 1929, pp. 39–40; REINACH, S., *Cultes, mythes et religions*, Paris, 1923, vol. v, pp. 250–4 (horses, nymphs, springs); TOUTAIN, J., " Le Culte des eaux (sources, fleuves, lacs) dans la Grèce antique " (in the volume *Nouvelles études de mythologie et d'histoire des religions antiques*, Paris, 1935, pp. 268–94; GRIMM, J., *Teutonic Mythology*, English ed., London, 1888, pp. 583–601; HOLMBERG-HARVA, Uno, *Die Wassergottheiten der finnisch-ugrischen Völker*, Helsinki, 1913; NIPPGEN, J., " Les Divinités des eaux chez les peuples finno-ougriens, Ostiaques et Vogoules ", *RETP*, 1925, pp. 207–16.

On the funeral use of water: PARROT, A., *Le " Refrigerium " dans l'au-delà*, Paris, 1937; ELIADE, M., " Locum Refrigerii . . . ", *Z*, 1938, vol. i, pp. 203–6.

On the cult of water in Christianity: there is a good bibliography in SAINTYVES, *Corpus du folklore des eaux*, pp. 20–1; texts, ibid., pp. 139–96; cf. SAINTYVES, " De l'immersion des idoles antiques aux baignades des statues saintes dans le christianisme ", *RHR*, cviii, 1933, pp. 135–83; reprinted in *Corpus*, pp. 197 ff.

Water folklore: HOPE, C., *The Legendary Lore of the Holy Wells of England, including Rivers, Lakes, Fountains and Springs*, London, 1893; GREGOR, W., " Guardian Spirits of Wells and Lochs ", *FRE*, 1892, vol. iii, pp. 67–73; BERENGER-FERAUD, L. J. B., *Superstitions et survivances étudiées au point de vue de leur origine et de leurs transformations*, Paris, 1895, 5 vols.; vol. i, pp. 207–304 (mythical dragons and snakes beside springs, lakes and so on); vol. ii, pp. 1–58 (the " powers " and spirits of water); vol. iii, pp. 167–214 (ritual rain gestures); vol. iv, pp. 291–360 (miraculous powers in fountains); SEBILLOT, Paul, *Le Folklore de France*, Paris, 1905, vol. ii, pp. 175–303; LAWSON, J. C., *Modern Greek Folklore and Ancient Greek Religion*, Cambridge, 1910, pp. 130–73 (the continued presence of nymphs in contemporary Greek folklore); RHYS, J., *Celtic Folk-Lore*, Oxford, 1901, pp. 354–400 (the folklore of wells); WEINHOLD, K., *Die Verehrung der Quellen in Deutschland*, Berlin, 1898; MANNINEN, Ilmari, *Die dämonistischen Krankheiten im finnischen Volks-aberglauben*, Helsinki, 1922, pp. 81–106; MCKENZIE, Daniel, *Infancy of*

Medicine, London, 1927, pp. 238 ff.; MASSANI, R. P., " Le Folklore des puits dans l'Inde et spécialement à Bombay ", *RHR*, 1931, vol. civ, pp. 221-71 ; cf. also the bibliography following the chapter on Vegetation (the " Fountain of Youth " and the " Tree of Life ").

Dragons in China and in Eastern Asia; the descent of sovereigns from the *nagi*: GRANET, Marcel, *Danses et légendes de la Chine ancienne*, Paris, 1926, 2 vols.; id., *Chinese Civilization*, London, 1930; id., *La Pensée chinoise*, Paris, 1934; KARLGREN, B., " Some Fecundity Symbols in Ancient China ", *BMAS*, Stockholm, 1930, no. 2, pp. 1-54; CHAVANNES (Ed.), *Les Mémoires historiques de Sse-Ma-Tsien*, Paris, 1897, vol. i; Paris, 1897, vol. ii; Paris, 1899, vol. iii, p. 2; GIESSELER, G., " Le Mythe du dragon en Chine ", *RAR*, 1917, 5th series, vol. vi, pp. 104-70; HOPKINS, L. C., " The Dragon Terrestrial and the Dragon Celestial. A Study of the Lung and Ch'en ", *JRAS*, 1931, pp. 791-806; 1932, pp. 91-7; PRZYLUSKI, J., " La Princesse à l'odeur de poisson et la Nāgī dans les traditions de l'Asie orientale ", *EA*, Paris, 1925, vol. ii, pp. 265-84; id., " Le Prologue-cadre des mille et une nuits et le thème de svayamvara ", *JA*, 1924, pp. 101-37; OPPERT, G., *On the Original Inhabitants of Bhārata-varsa or India*, Westminster, 1893; MATSUMOTO, Nobushiro, *Essai sur la mythologie japonaise*, Paris, 1928, pp. 46, 53 ff.; id., *Le Japonais et les langues Austre-Asiatiques*, Paris, 1928, pp. 35 ff.; ELIADE, M., *Le Yoga: Immortalité et Liberté*, Paris, 1957, pp. 346 ff.; princes born of *nāga* princesses, in Siam, India and Africa, cf. DANGEL, *SMSR*, 1938, vol. xiv, p. 180; KNOCHE, Walter, " Kindfisch-Märchen in Ozeanien ", *MAGW*, 1939, vol. lxix, pp. 24-33; RÖNNOW, K., " Kirāta ", *MO*, 1936, vol. iii (published 1944), pp. 90-169, 137, n. 1, points out that the frequent occurrence of the motif of the royal families of Northern India having sprung from serpents destroys the hypothesis of an Australasian influence; see too AUTRAN, C., *L'Epopée hindoue*, Paris, 1946, pp. 66-169; material and a bibliography on snake worship in India can be found in VOGEL, J. P., " Serpent-worship in Ancient and Modern India ", *AOA*, 1924, vol. ii, pp. 279-312; id., *Indian Serpent Lore, or, the Nāgas in Hindu Legend and Art*, London, 1926, pp. 35 ff.

On the flowing vase (a fertility symbol well known in the classical East): cf. VAN BUREN, E. D., *The Flowing Vase and the God with Streams*, Berlin, 1933; COMBAZ, G., *L'Inde et l'orient classique*, Paris, 1937, no. 174 ff.; id., " L'Evolution du stupa en Asie ", *Mélanges chinois et Bouddhiques*, Brussels, 1936, vol. iv, pp. 93 ff.

VI

SACRED STONES: EPIPHANIES, SIGNS AND FORMS

74. STONES AS MANIFESTING POWER

THE hardness, ruggedness, and permanence of matter was in itself a hierophany in the religious consciousness of the primitive. And nothing was more direct and autonomous in the completeness of its strength, nothing more noble or more awe-inspiring, than a majestic rock, or a boldly-standing block of granite. Above all, stone *is*. It always remains itself, and exists of itself; and, more important still, it *strikes*. Before he even takes it up to strike, man finds in it an obstacle —if not to his body, at least to his gaze—and ascertains its hardness, its roughness, its power. Rock shows him something that transcends the precariousness of his humanity: an absolute mode of being. Its strength, its motionlessness, its size and its strange outlines are none of them human; they indicate the presence of something that fascinates, terrifies, attracts and threatens, all at once. In its grandeur, its hardness, its shape and its colour, man is faced with a reality and a force that belong to some world other than the profane world of which he is himself a part.

We can hardly say that men have always adored stones simply as stones. The devotion of the primitive was in every case fastened on something beyond itself which the stone incorporated and expressed. A rock or a pebble would be the object of reverent devotion because it represented or imitated *something*, because it came from somewhere. Its sacred value is always due to that something or that somewhere, never to its own actual existence. Men have always adored stones simply in as much as they represent something *other* than themselves. They adored stones, or they used them as instruments of spiritual action, as centres of energy designed to defend them or their dead. And we may say from the start that most of the stones connected with worship were used as *instruments*; they helped towards getting something, towards ensuring possession of it. Their role was generally more magical than religious. Invested with certain sacred powers as a result of their origin or their shape, they were not *adored*, but *made use of*.

Imbelloni, in his researches over the whole Oceano-American area in which the word *toki* is used (an area extending from eastern Melanesia to the interior of both Americas) discovered all of the following meanings possible to it: (*a*) weapon of combat, of stone; axe; and by extension, any stone imple-ment; (*b*) emblem of dignity, symbol of power; (*c*) person having or exercising power, whether by heredity or by investiture; (*d*) ritual object.[1] The eneolithic " burial guards " were placed beside burial vaults to ensure their inviolability.[2] Menhirs seem to have played a similar role: that of the Mas d'Azais was set up vertically over a burial vault.[3] Stone was a protection against animals and robbers, and, above all, against " death " for, as stone was incorruptible, the soul of the dead man must continue to exist as itself (the phallic symbolism that these prehistoric burial stones later came to have made this meaning still clearer, for the phallus sym-bolized existence, power, continuance).

75. BURIAL MEGALITHS

Among the Gonds, one of the Dravidian tribes which pene-trated furthest into Central India, there is a custom whereby the son or the heir of a dead man must place beside the tomb four days after the burial a vast stone, sometimes nine or ten feet high. The transport of this stone (often brought from some distance away) is a matter of considerable effort and expense; that is why, in most cases, the building of the monu-ment is postponed for a long time and sometimes never achieved at all.[4] The English anthropologist Hutton thinks that these megalithic funeral monuments—common among the un-civilized tribes of India—were intended to " fasten down " the dead man's soul and provide a temporary dwelling for it near the living so as (while enabling it to influence the fertility

[1] " Les noms des haches lithiques ", *Festschrift W. Schmidt*, Vienna, 1928, p. 333.
[2] Octobon, " Statues-menhirs, stèles gravées, dalles sculptées ", *RAN*, 1931, p. 562.
[3] Octobon, p. 562.
[4] W. H. Schoobert, " The Aboriginal Tribes of the Central Provinces ", in the *Census of India*, 1931, vol. i (iii, b), p. 85; W. V. Grigson, *The Maria Gonds of Bastar*, London, 1938, pp. 274 ff.

of their fields by the powers its spiritual nature gave it) to prevent it from roaming about or becoming dangerous. This interpretation was confirmed by Koppers' recent researches on the most primitive tribes of central India, the Bhils, the Korku, the Mundas and the Gonds. The main points of Koppers' findings[1] on the history of the stone burial monuments of central India are these:

(a) That all such monuments are connected with the cult of the dead and are aimed at setting the dead man's soul at peace; (b) that in form they are comparable to the prehistoric European megaliths and menhirs; (c) that they are not placed on top of tombs or even beside them, but at some distance; (d) that, however, when there is a violent death involved as, for instance, that caused by lightning, snake or tiger, the monument is set up on the actual spot where the disaster took place.[2]

This last point reveals the original meaning of stone burial monuments, for a violent death lets loose a soul that is troubled and hostile, and full of resentment. When life is broken off suddenly, it is to be expected that the soul of the dead man will be inclined to carry on what remained to him of normal life near the community from which it has been cut off. The Gonds, for instance, heap up stones on any spot where someone has been killed by lightning, or by a snake, or by a tiger;[3] everyone who passes by adds a stone to the heap for the repose of the dead man's soul (this custom remains to this day in some parts of Europe, for instance in France, cf. § 76). Further, in some places (among the Dravidian Gonds) the consecration of burial monuments is accompanied by erotic rites like those we always find connected with the commemoration of the dead among agricultural peoples. The Bhils only

---

[1] These findings are fairly important, for the custom of setting up burial monuments does not seem to have been native to the Bhils, the most primitive people of Central India (p. 156), but to have come from the influence of megalithic peoples like the Dravidians and the Mundas (cf. Koppers, " Monuments to the Dead of the Bhils and Other Primitive Tribes in Central India ", *Annali Lateranensi*, 1942, vol. vi, p. 196). Since neither the Aryans, nor the founders of the prehistoric civilization of the Indus (third millennium B.C.) were megalithic peoples, the problem of the origin of the megalithic tradition in India remains unsettled. It may be due to Southern Asian or Australasian influence, or it may have to be explained by historical and (possibly indirect) genetic connections with the megalithic culture of European prehistory.

[2] Koppers, pp. 134, 151, 189, 197, 188.

[3] Koppers, p. 188.

set up these monuments for those who died by violence, or for chieftains, sorcerers and warriors, that peace might come to the souls of the "strong"—the souls, in other words, of all those who stood for force when they were alive or, as it were, " caught " it by their violent death.

The burial stone thus became the means of protecting life against death. The soul " dwelt " in the stone as, in other cultures, it dwelt in the tomb—looked on, similarly, as a " dead man's house ". The funeral megalith protected the living against possible harmful action by the dead; for death, as a state of indetermination, made possible certain influences, both good and bad. " Imprisoned " in a stone, the soul would be forced only to act beneficently: i.e., assisting fertilization. That is why, in so many cultures, stones thought to be inhabited by " ancestors " are instruments for fertilizing fields and women. The Neolithic tribes of the Sudan had " rain stones " which they thought of as ancestors who could produce rain.[1] In the Pacific Islands (New Caledonia, Malekula, Achin, and so on), certain rocks represent or even embody gods, ancestors or culture heroes;[2] J. Layard tells us that the central object on every altar in those areas of the Pacific is a monolith with a smaller cromlech, representing ancestors.[3]

Maurice Leenhardt writes[4] that " stones are the petrified spirits of ancestors ". That is an admirable way of putting it, but it is not, of course, to be taken literally. Stone is no " petrified spirit ", but a concrete representation, a provisional or symbolic " habitat " of that spirit. Elsewhere in his book Leenhardt himself admits[5] " that whether spirit, god, totem or clan, all these various conceptions have a single concrete representation, which is stone ". The Khasis of Assam believe that the Great Mother of the clan is represented by the cromlechs (*maw-kynthei*, " female stones ") and that the Great Father is present in the menhirs (*maw-shynrang*, " male

[1] Seligmann (C. G. and B. Z.), *Pagan Tribes of the Nilotic Sudan*, London, 1932, p. 24.

[2] Williamson, *The Social and Political Systems of Central Polynesia*, Cambridge, 1924, vol. ii, pp. 242–3, etc.

[3] Layard, " The Journey of the Dead ", in *Essays Presented to S. Seligman*, London, 1934, pp. 116 ff., etc.

[4] *Notes d'ethnologie néocalédonienne*, Paris, 1930, p. 183.

[5] p. 241.

stones ").[1] In other cultures, menhirs can even embody the supreme (sky) divinity. And as we saw earlier (cf. § 16), in a great many African tribes, the worship of the Supreme Being of the sky involves menhirs (sacrifices are brought to them) and other sacred stones.

76. FERTILIZING STONES

The cult is not, then, directed towards the stone as a material thing, but rather to the spirit that animates it, or the symbol that makes it sacred. Stones, rocks, monoliths, cromlechs, menhirs, etc. *become* sacred because they bear the mark of some spiritual force. While we are still looking at the cultures concerned with " ancestors ", with the dead being " fastened " to the stone so as to be used as an instrument for protecting and enriching life, consider a few more examples. In India, it is to the megaliths that young couples pray to have children.[2] The sterile women of Salem (in southern India) believe that the ancestors who can make them fruitful dwell in the cromlechs, and therefore they rub themselves against these stones after placing offerings for them (flowers, sandalwood, cooked rice).[3] The tribes of central Australia have similar notions. Spencer and Gillen instance the case of a huge rock known as Erathipa which has an opening in one side from which the souls of the children imprisoned in it watch for a woman to pass by so that they may be reborn in her. When women who do not want children go near the rock, they pretend to be old, and walk as if leaning on a stick, crying: "Don't come to me, I am an old woman ! "[4] The childless women of the Maidu tribe of northern California touch a rock shaped like a pregnant woman.[5] On the island of Kai (south-west of New Guinea) a woman who wants to have a child smears a stone with grease. The same custom is found in Madagascar.[6] It is interesting to note that these same " fertilizing stones " are also rubbed with oil by merchants who want their business to thrive. In India there is a belief that certain stones were born and reproduce

[1] Cf. Pettazzoni, *Dio*, p. 10.
[2] Hutton, *Census of India*, 1931, vol. i, p. 88.
[3] Cf. J. Boulnois, *Le Caducée et la symbolique dravidienne indo-méditerranéenne*, Paris, 1939, p. 12.
[4] *The Native Tribes of Central Australia*, London, 1899, p. 337.
[5] Hartland, *Primitive Paternity*, London, 1909, vol. i, p. 124 ff.
[6] Frazer, *Folklore in the Old Testament*, vol. ii, p. 75.

of themselves (*svayambhū*—" autogenesis "); for this reason
they are sought out and venerated by sterile women, who bring
them offerings.[1] In some parts of Europe and elsewhere,
young couples walk upon a stone to make their union fruitful.[2]
The Samoyeds prayed before a stone of curious shape known
as *pyl-paja* (" the woman-stone ") and made offerings of gold
to it.[3]

The idea implicit in all these rites is that certain stones have
the power to make sterile women fruitful, either because of the
spirits of the ancestors that dwell in them, or because of their
shape (the pregnant woman, " woman stone "), or because
of their origin (*svayambhū*, " autogenesis "). But the " theory "
that first produced these religious practices or by which they
are to be explained, may not always have been preserved in the
minds of those who still carry them out. In some cases, perhaps,
the original theory has been replaced or changed by a different
one; in others the original may have been totally forgotten,
following a successful religious revolution. We may note a
few instances of the latter. Faint traces of devotion to megaliths,
rocks or cromlechs, the remains of practices of " fertilizing "
by means of contact with stone, can be found even to-day
among the popular beliefs of Europe. This devotion is, as I
have said, fairly vague; in the district of Moutiers in Savoy,
the country people feel " religious fear and pious respect " for
the " Pierra Chevetta " (Owl Stone) about which they know
nothing save that it protects the village, and, as long as it
remains, neither fire nor flood can harm them.[4] In the district
of Sumène (*département* of Le Gard), the peasants fear cromlechs and keep away from them.[5] The women of the district
of South Annecy say an Our Father and a Hail Mary every
time they pass a certain pile of stones known as " the dead
man ". But this fear may be due to the belief that someone
is buried there.[6] In that same district women will kneel and

---

[1] Wilke, " Die Religion der Indogermanen in archäologsichen Betrachtung,"
MB, Leipzig, 1921, p. 99 ff.

[2] Cf. Frazer, vol. ii, pp. 403–5; Nyberg, *Kind und Erde*, Helsinki, 1931, pp.
66 ff., 239.

[3] Nyberg, p. 66.

[4] Van Gennep, in P. Saintyves, *Corpus*, vol. ii, p. 376.

[5] Hugues, in Saintyves, p. 390.

[6] Cf. Van Gennep, in Saintyves, p. 317.

cross themselves when they come to a pile of stone supposed
to cover the body of a pilgrim either murdered, or buried in a
landslide, and they always throw a little stone on to the pile.[1]
A similar custom can be found in Africa. The Hottentots
throw stones on to the tomb of the demiurge Heitsi Eibib,
and the Bantu tribes of the south perform the same ritual for
their demiurge Unkulunkulu.[2] From these few examples it
can be seen that religious fear of megaliths is only sporadic in
France, and generally determined by reasons other than belief
in the magic powers of stone (for instance, violent death).
The primitive conception of the fertility of consecrated stones,
cromlechs and menhirs was quite different. But almost everywhere some fraction of the practices resulting from it persist
even to-day.

77. " SLIDING "

The custom known as " sliding " was very widespread.
Young women wanting to have children slid along a consecrated
stone.[3] Another even more widespread ritual custom is
" friction ": friction is practised for health reasons as well,
but it is chiefly used by sterile women. At Decines (Rhône),
even quite recently, they used to sit on a monolith in the fields
near the place known as Pierrefrite. At Saint-Renan (Finisterre)
any woman who wanted to have a child slept for three nights
running on a huge rock, "the Stone Mare".[4] And young
brides used also to come there the first few nights after their
weddings, and rub their bellies against this stone.[5] This practice
can be found in a lot of places.[6] In some places, for instance
in the village of Moedan, in the district of Pont-Aven, women
who rubbed their stomachs against stone were sure of having
male children.[7] Even as late as 1923, countrywomen who came

[1] Saintyves, p. 332.

[2] Cf. Pettazzoni, pp. 198, 200.

[3] For examples see Saintyves, vol. ii, pp. 347, etc.; Sébillot, *Le Folklore de
France*, vol. i, pp. 335 ff.; Lang, *Myth, Ritual and Religion*, London, 1887, vol. i,
pp.96 ff.; Sartori in the *Handwörterbuch de sdeutsch en Aberglaubens, s.v.* "gleiten",
Leite de Vasconcellos, *Opusculos*, Lisbon, 1938, vol. vii, pp. 653 ff.

[4] Sébillot, pp. 339-40.

[5] Saintyves, vol. iii, p. 346.

[6] Cf. the index of the three volumes of the *Corpus, s.v.* " friction ", etc.

[7] Saintyves, vol. iii, p. 375.

to London used to clasp the pillars of Saint Paul's Cathedral to make them have children.[1]

Sébillot describes a custom which must belong in the same ritual pattern: "Around 1880, not far from Carnac, people who had been married for several years and not had children, came, when the moon was full, to a menhir; they removed their clothes and the woman began to run round the stone, trying to escape from her husband's pursuit; their relations kept watch all round to avoid profanation of the rite.[2] Such observances were probably more common in the past. Kings and clerics in the Middle Ages were constantly forbidding the cult of stones, and in particular the practice of seminal emission in front of stones."[3] But this last is rather more complicated, and cannot be explained—as can the practices of " sliding " and " friction "—simply in terms of the belief that cromlechs and menhirs possessed the power of directly "fertilizing". For one thing, mention is made of the season for sexual intercourse (" during the full moon ") which points to a trace of moon worship; and then, the practice both of marital intercourse and seminal emission before a stone results from a somewhat evolved conception of the sexualization of the mineral kingdom, of birth originating from stone and so forth, which corresponds to certain rites for the fecundation of stone.[4]

Most of the customs—as I said earlier—still preserve the belief that merely to touch the sacred rock or stone is all that is needed to make a sterile woman fertile. In Carnac, again, women used to come and sit on the cromlech of Cruez-Moquem with their dresses tucked up; a cross was set upon the stone precisely in order to put an end to this practice.[5] A great many other stones are known as " love stones ", or " marriage stones ", and are thought to have erotic powers.[6] In Athens,

[1] Mackenzie, *Infancy of Medicine*, London, 1927, p. 219, quoting newspaper reports.

[2] Sébillot, vol. iv, pp. 61–2; *Traditions et Superstitions de la Haute-Bretagne*, Paris, 1882, vol. i, p. 150.

[3] See Le Pontois, *Le Finisterre préhistorique*, Paris, 1929, p. 268.

[4] Eisler, " Kuba-Kybele ", *PS*, 1909, pp. 118–51; 161–209; cf. C. Hentze, *Mythes et symboles*, pp. 34 ff.

[5] Saintyves, vol. iii, p. 431.

[6] Cf. the index to *Corpus*, vol. i, *s.v.* " pierre d'amour ", " pierre de marriage ", etc.

pregnant women used to go up to the hill of the Nymphs and slide down the rock invoking Apollo, to ensure a successful confinement.[1]   There you have an excellent example of a rite's change of meaning, the stone of fertility becoming the stone of delivery.   Similar beliefs can be found attaching to stones in Portugal—merely by touching them a woman can be assured of a safe delivery.[2]

A great many megaliths help children to walk or ensure their good health.[3]   In the district of Amance, there is a stone with a hole in it; women kneel to it and pray for the health of their children, and throw money into the hole.[4]   Parents bring their children as soon as they are born to the " hole stone " of Fouvent-le-Haut and put them through the hole.   " It was a kind of baptism of stone, intended to preserve the child from all spells and bring him happiness."[5]   Even to-day, the sterile women of Paphos go through the hole in a certain stone.[6] We find the same custom in parts of England.[7]   Elsewhere, the women simply put their right hand into the opening because, they say, that is the hand that supports the child's weight.[8] At Christmas, and on St. John's day (that is, at the two solstices), candles were placed beside certain stones with holes in them, and oil was sprinkled on them which was later taken up and used as a medicine.[9]

The Church fought all these customs for a very long time.[10] That they survived not only ecclesiastical pressure, but even a century of anti-religious and anti-supersititious rationalism, shows how firmly established they were.   Almost all the other ceremonies to do with sacred stones (of devotion, fear, divining, and so on) have disappeared.   All that remains is the one essential: faith in their power of fertilizing.   Nowadays this faith has no reasoned theory behind it, but is supported by new legends or explained according to Christian interpretations

[1] See Hartland, *Primitive Paternity*, vol. i, p. 130.
[2] See Leite de Vasconcellos, *De Terra em terra*, Lisbon, 1927, vol. ii, p. 205; *Opusculos*, vol. vii, p. 652.
[3] Saintyves, vol. iii, pp. 36, 213, etc.; 98, 220, 330.
[4] See Saintyves, vol. ii, p. 401.
[5] Perrault Dabot, quoted in Saintyves, vol. ii, p. 403.
[6] Frazer, *Adonis, Attis, Osiris*, London, 1936, vol. i, p. 36.
[7] Frazer, *Balder the Beautiful*, London, 1936, vol. ii, p. 187.
[8] Saintyves, vol. ii, p. 403.
[9] Saintyves, vol. ii, p. 403.
[10] Cf. Saintyves, vol. i, *s.v.* " condamnations ", etc.

(on this rock a saint rested; a cross stands on that menhir; and so on). Yet one can still detect a certain theoretic formula somewhere between the two: stones, rocks, menhirs are places where fairies come and it is to them that offerings are brought (oil, flowers and such). No real worship is given to these beings but there is always something to ask them for.

The religious revolution effected by the conversion of Europe to Christianity did, in the end, destroy the whole primitive system which enshrined the ceremonial of fertility-giving stones. The honour paid by country people as late as the Middle Ages to everything connected with prehistoric times (with what is called the " Stone Age "), to their burial monuments, whether magic or religious, and to their stone weapons (" thunder-stones "), was not merely the result of a direct survival of the religious ideas held by their forefathers, but also of the fear, piety or superstitious admiration they felt for the men themselves; they were judged by the remains of their stone civilization. Country people—as we shall see—thought their primitive weapons were " thunder-stones " fallen from the sky; and menhirs, meteorites, and cromlechs were taken for traces of giants, fairies and heroes.

78. STONES WITH HOLES : " THUNDER-STONES "

I said just now that in the case of " fertilizing " stones and the worship of stones, the traditional " theory " behind the practice had been replaced (or at least affected) by a new theory. We find a striking example of this in the custom found even to-day in Europe, of putting newborn babies through the hole in a stone.[1] This rite quite clearly relates to a " rebirth ", conceived either as a birth from the divine womb through a stone symbolizing it, or as a rebirth through a solar symbol. The earliest peoples in Indian history thought stones with holes in them were emblems of the *yoni*, and the ritual action of going through that hole implied a regeneration by means of the feminine cosmic principle.[2] The religious " mill-stones " (*alv-kvarnar*) of pre-historic Scandinavia may have fulfilled a similar function; Almgren attributes to them a symbolic

[1] Cf. Rydh, " Symbolism in Mortuary Ceramics ", *BMAS*, 1929, p. 110.

[2] Cf. Marshall, *Mohenjo-Daro and the Indus Civilisation*, London, 1931, vol. i, p. 62.

meaning closely akin to that of the *yoni*.[1] But these ring-stones in India have a certain solar symbolism in addition. They are united to the " gate of the world ", *loka-dvāra*, through which the soul, too, may " pass beyond " (escape = *atimucyate*). The hole in the stone is called " the gate of deliverance " (*mukti-dvāra*) and can in no way be connected with any rebirth through the *yoni* (or womb of things), but only with being set free from the cosmos and from the karmic cycle, a deliverance bound up with the symbolism of the sun.[2] This is, in fact, a symbolism showing a different meaning in the primitive rite of passing through the ring-stone. In India, again, we find another example of a new theory taking the place of an old : the stone *śālagrāma* is sacred even now, because it is taken as symbol of Viṣṇu, and is married to the *tulasī* plant, symbol of the goddess Lakṣmī. Yet in fact the religious coupling of stone and plant was a primitive symbol of the " holy place ", of the primitive altar, and was so over the whole Indo-Mediterranean area (cf. § 97).

In a great many places, meteorites are looked upon as emblems or signs of fertility. The Buriats are convinced that certain stones " fallen from heaven " help to bring rain ; and in time of drought they offer sacrifice to them. Similarly, rather smaller stones are found in a great many villages, and offerings are made to them in the spring to ensure a good harvest.[3] Clearly, then, if the stone has a religious significance, it is because of its origin : it comes from a supremely sacred and fertile place. It fell from heaven with the rain-bringing thunder. All the beliefs relating to the fertility of " rain stones " are founded upon their meteoric origin, or the analogies felt to exist between them and some force, form or being governing rain. At Kota Gadang (Sumatra), for instance, there is a stone which is shaped vaguely like a cat. And as a black cat is introduced into certain of the rain-making rites, it seems likely that this stone is endowed with similar powers.[4] A close analysis of innumerable " rain stones " has always brought to light the

[1] Cf. *Nordische Felszeichnungen als religiöse Urkunden*, Frankfurt a. M., 1934, p. 246.

[2] Cf. Coomaraswamy, *The Darker Side of the Dawn*, Washington, 1935, p. 17, n. 22.

[3] Holmberg-Harva, *Die religiösen Vorstellungen der altaischen Völkern*, p. 153.

[4] Cf. Frazer, *The Magic Art and the Evolution of Kings*, London, 1936, vol. i, p. 308.

existence of a " theory " to explain their power of governing the clouds; it is something to do either with their shape, which has some " sympathy " with the clouds or with lightning, or with their celestial origin (they must have fallen from heaven), or with their belonging to " ancestors "; or perhaps they were found in water, or their shapes recall snakes, frogs, fishes or some other water emblem. The power of these stones never originates in themselves; they share in a principle, or embody a symbol, they express a cosmic " sympathy " or betray a heavenly origin. These stones are the *signs* of a spiritual reality beyond themselves, or the instruments of a sacred power of which they are merely containers.

79. METEORITES AND BETHELS

Meteorites offer us a suggestive example of the different sorts of symbolic value attaching to stones. The Ka'aba of Mecca and the black stone of Pessinus, a non-pictorial image of Cybele, the Great Mother of the Phrygians, brought to Rome during the last of the Punic wars, are the best known of all meteorites.[1] Their sacred character was due primarily to their heavenly origin. But they were at the same time images of the Great Mother, the earth goddess *par excellence*. Their sky origin can hardly have been forgotten, for popular belief attributed it to all prehistoric stone implements, which were called " thunder-stones ". Meteorites probably became images of the Great Goddess because they were seen as pursued by lightning, a symbol of the sky god. But, on the other hand, the Ka'aba was looked upon as the " centre of the world ". In other words, it was not merely the central point of the earth; directly above it, in the centre of the heavens, was the " gate of heaven ". Clearly, the Ka'aba, in falling from the sky, made a hole in it, and it was through this hole that a communication could be effected between earth and heaven. Through it passed the *Axis Mundi*.

Thus, meteorites are sacred, either because they have fallen from the sky, or because they betray the presence of the Great Goddess, or because they represent the " Centre of the World ". Whichever they are, they are *symbols* or *emblems*.

[1] Cf. the bibliography in my study, " Metallurgy, Magic and Alchemy ", Paris, 1938, *CZ*, vol. i, p. 3.

That they are sacred implies at once a cosmological theory and a clearly defined conception of the dialectic of hierophanies. " The Arabs adore stones," wrote Clement of Alexandria.[1] Like his monotheistic predecessors of the Old Testament, the Christian apologist, by the purity and intensity of his own religious experience (based on the revelation of Christ), was led to deny the old religious forms any spiritual value. Given the tendency in the spiritual make-up of Semites to confuse God with the material object representing him or displaying his power,[2] it is very likely that in Clement's time the greater number of the Arabs " adored " stones. Recent research, however, shows that the pre-Islamic Arabs venerated certain stones called by the Greeks and Romans *baytili*, a word taken from the Semitic and meaning " house of God ".[3] And such sacred stones were not venerated in the Semitic world only, but by all the peoples of North Africa even before their contacts with the Carthaginians.[4] But bethels were never adored simply as *stones*; they were adored in as much as they manifested a divine presence. They represented God's *house*, they were his sign, his emblem, and the repository of his power, or the unchanging witness of a religious act performed in his name. A few examples from the Semitic world will serve to make their meaning and function clearer.

On his way to Mesopotamia, Jacob went to Haran. " And when he was come to a certain place, and would rest in it after sunset, he took of the stones that lay there, and putting them under his head, slept in the same place. And he saw in his sleep a ladder standing upon the earth, and the top thereof touching heaven; the angels also of God ascending and descending by it; and the Lord, leaning upon the ladder, saying to him: I am the Lord God of Abraham thy father, and the God of Isaac. The land, wherein thou sleepest, I will give to thee and to thy seed. . . . And when Jacob awaked out of sleep he said: Indeed the Lord is in this place, and I knew it not. And trembling he said: How terrible is this place !

---

[1] *Protreptica*, iv, 46.

[2] Vincent, *La Religion des Judéo-Araméens d'Eléphantine*, Paris, 1937, p. 591.

[3] See Lammens, " Le Culte des bétyles et les processions religieuses dans l'Arabie préislamique ", *Bulletin de l'institut d'archéologie orientale*, Cairo, vol. xvii.

[4] Cf. Bel, *La Religion musulmane en Berberie*, Paris, 1938, vol. i, p. 80.

This is no other but the house of God and the gate of heaven. And Jacob, arising in the morning, took the stone, which he had laid under his head, and set it up for a title, pouring oil upon the top of it. And he called the name of the city, Bethel . . ."[1]

80. STONE EPIPHANIES AND SYMBOLISMS

Zimmern has shown that *Beth-el*, " house of God ", is both a name for God, and one of the words for a sacred stone or bethel.[2] Jacob went to sleep on a stone, at the place where heaven and earth opened on to each other; it was a " centre " like the " gate of heaven ". But the God who appeared to Jacob in his dream—was he indeed the God of Abraham, as the Bible text stresses, or was he a local divinity, the god of Bethel, as Dussaud thought in 1921 ?[3] The texts of Ras Shamra, which are invaluable evidence of the religious life of the Semites before Moses, show that *El* and *Bethel* are interchangeable names for the same divinity.[4] In other words, it *was* the God of his ancestors whom Jacob saw in his dream, and not a local divinity. But the bethel which he set up to consecrate the place was later venerated by the local population as a particular divinity, Bethel. The monotheist elite, faithful to Moses' message, struggled long against this " god ", and it is that struggle to which Jeremias is referring. " We may take it as read that, in the famous story of Jacob's vision, the God of Bethel has not yet become the god Bethel. But this identification and confusion may have occurred quite soon among the ordinary people."[5] Where, traditionally, Jacob saw the angels' ladder and the house of God, Palestinian peasants saw the god Bethel.[6]

But we must remember that, whatever god the local population may have seen in Bethel, no *stone* ever represented more than a *sign*, a dwelling, a theophany. The divinity was *manifest* by means of the stone, or—in other rituals—*witnessed* and

[1] Gen. xxviii. 11–13, 16–19.

[2] Cf. Dussaud, *Les Origines cananéennes du sacrifice israélite*, 2nd ed., Paris, 1941, p. 232.

[3] Dussaud, pp. 234 ff.; cf. Jer. xlviii. 13: " And Moab shall be ashamed of Chamos, as the house of Israel was ashamed of Bethel ".

[4] Cf. Dussaud, *Les Découvertes de Ras Shamra*, 2nd ed., Paris, 1941 pp. 97. 111.

[5] Vincent, p. 591.

[6] Cf. Eliade, *Insula lui Euthanasius*, p. 117.

sanctified a covenant made near it. This witness consisted,
in the minds of simple folk, in the divinity's being embodied
in the stone; and, to the elite, in the stone's being transfigured
by the divine presence. After completing the covenant between
Yahweh and his people, Josue " took a great stone, and set
it under the oak that was in the sanctuary of the Lord. And
he said to all the people: Behold, this stone shall be a testimony
unto you . . . lest perhaps hereafter you will deny it, and lie to
the Lord ".[1] God was also there as " witness " in the stones
set up by Laban when he made a league of friendship with
Jacob.[2] Such witness-stones were probably adored by the
Caananites as manifestations of the deity.

The elite who held to the monotheism of Moses struggled
against the frequent confusion between the *sign* of God's
presence, and the *incarnation* of the deity in a given object.
" You shall not make to yourselves any idol or graven thing
[masseba]: neither shall you erect pillars [maskit], nor set up
a remarkable stone in your land to adore it."[3] And in Numbers,[4]
God commands Moses to destroy the stones of worship that
he is going to find in Canaan: ". . . beat down their pillars,
and break in pieces their statues, and waste all their high places."
It is not a battle between faith and idolatry, but between two
theophanies, two moments of religious experience: on one
hand the primitive conception, identifying the divinity with
matter and adoring it in whatever form or place it appeared;
and on the other, a conception growing out of the experience
of an elite, that recognized the presence of God only in consecrated places (the Ark, the Temple and so on) and in certain
Mosaic rites aimed at strengthening that presence in the
believer's own mind. As usual, the religious reform took over
the old forms and objects of worship, altering their meaning
and their religious significance. The Ark of the Covenant in
which, traditionally, the Tables of the Law were kept, may well
have also contained at the beginning certain religious stones
made sacred by the presence of God. The reformers would
accept things of this sort and fit them into a different religious

[1] Josue xxiv. 26–7.
[2] Gen. xxxi. 44 ff.
[3] Levit. xxvi. 1.
[4] xxxiii. 52.

system, give them a quite different meaning.[1] Indeed, every reform is really directed against a defacement of the original experience; the confusion between *sign* and *divinity* had become very great among the simple people, and it was to avoid just such confusions that the Mosaic elite either abolished the signs (figured stones, carved images and the rest), or completely changed their meaning (as with the Ark of the Covenant). The confusion was not slow to reappear in another form, and dictated further reforms or, in other words, further restatements of the original meaning.

81. SACRED STONE, *Omphalos*, " CENTRE OF THE WORLD "

The stone upon which Jacob slept was not only the " House of God "; it was also the place where, by means of the angels' ladder, communication took place between heaven and earth. The bethel was, therefore, a centre of the world, like the Ka'aba of Mecca or Mount Sinai, like all the temples, palaces and " centres " consecrated by ritual (§143 ff.). Its being a " ladder " uniting heaven and earth derived from a theophany which took place at that spot; God, manifesting himself to Jacob on the bethel, was also indicating the place where he could come to earth, the point at which the transcendent might enter the immanent. As we shall see later, ladders of this kind are not necessarily placed in a definite, concrete geographical spot; the " centre of the world " can be consecrated by ritual in innumerable points of the globe without the authenticity of one invalidating the rest.

For the moment I will simply note a few beliefs about the *omphalos* (" navel ") of which Pausanias says:[2] " What the inhabitants of Delphi call *omphalos* is of white stone, and thought to be at the centre of the earth; and Pindar, in one of his odes, confirms this notion ". Much has been written on the subject (cf. the Bibliography). Rohde and J. H. Harrison think that the *omphalos* originally represented the stone placed on the tomb; Varro[3] mentions a tradition that the *omphalos* was the tomb of the sacred serpent of Delphi, Python: *quem*

---

[1] Cf. for instance, A. Bertholet, " Ueber kultische Motivverschiebungen ", *Sitz. Preuss. Akad. Wiss., Phil. Hist. Klasse*, 1938, vol. xviii.

[2] x, 16, 2.

[3] *De Lingua Latina*, vii, 17.

Pythonis aiunt tumulum. Roscher, who devotes three mono-graphs to this question, declares that the *omphalos* was from the first believed to be the " centre of the earth ". Nilsson[1] is not satisfied with either interpretation, and believes the conception of the burial stone and of the " centre of the world " both came after, and took the place of, a more " primitive " belief.

But, actually, both interpretations are " primitive ", and they are not mutually exclusive. A tomb, seen as a point of contact between the world of the dead, of the living, and of the gods, can also be a " centre ", an " *omphalos* of the earth ". To the Romans, for instance, the *mundus* represented the communi-cating point of the three spheres; " when the *mundus* is open, open too is the gate of the unhappy gods of the under-world ", writes Varro.[2] The *mundus* is not, of course, a tomb, but the symbolism of it will give us a clearer understanding of the similar function fulfilled by the *omphalos:* that it first originated with burial does not contradict the fact of its being a " centre ". The place where communication could be made between the world of the dead and that of the gods of the underworld was consecrated as a connecting link between the different levels of the universe, and such a place could only be situated in a " centre " (the manifold symbolic significance of the *omphalos* will be studied in its proper place when we come to analyse the theory and ritual function of the consecration of " centres ", §145).

When Apollo superseded the ancient earth religion of Delphi, he took over the *omphalos* and its privileges. Pursued by the Furies, Orestes was purified by Apollo beside the *omphalos*, the supremely sacred spot, in the " centre " where the three cosmic zones are linked, in the " navel " which guarantees by its symbolism a new birth and a reintegrated conscience. The manifold significance of the " centre stone " is even better preserved in Celtic traditions. Lia Fail, " the stone of Fail " (the name is doubtful; Fail might mean Ireland), starts singing when anyone worthy of being king sits on it; in ordeals, if the accused is innocent, he becomes white when he gets on to it; when a woman who is doomed to remain sterile comes near, the stone exudes blood; when if the woman will become a mother,

[1] *Geschichte*, vol. i, p. 189.
[2] Quoted by Macrobius, *Saturn.*, i, 16, 18.

it exudes milk.[1] Lia Fail is a theophany of the soil divinity, the
only divinity to recognise his master (the High King of Ireland),
the only one who controls the economy of fertility, and guarantees ordeals. There are also, of course, later phallic variants of
these Celtic *omphaloi* (cf. the bibliography); fertility, above all,
is an attribute of the " centre ", and emblems of it are often
sexual. That the Celts saw the religious (and implicitly the
political) significance of the centre is evidenced by such words as
medinemetum, mediolanum[2] which exist even today in French
place names.[3] Bearing in mind what we learn from Lia Fail
and some of the traditions preserved in France, we have good
reason to identify these " centres " with omphalic stones. In
the village of Amancy (district of La Roche), for instance, there
can be found—proof positive of the " centre "— a " Middle-
of-the-World Stone ".[4] The Pierra Chevetta in the Moutiers
district has never been covered by floods,[5] which seems to be a
faint echo of the " centre " that the deluge could never engulf
(§143).

82. SIGNS AND FORMS

The *omphalos*, in every tradition, is a stone consecrated by a
superhuman presence, or by symbolism of some kind. Like
bethels and *masseba*, or prehistoric megaliths, the *omphalos*
bears *witness* of something, and it is from that witness that it gets
its value, or its position in the cult. Whether they *protect* the
dead (like, for instance, neolithic megaliths), or become the
temporary dwellings of the souls of the dead (as among many
" primitives "), or witness a covenant made between man and
God, or man and man (as among the Semites), or owe their
sacred character to their shape or their heavenly origin (as with
meteorites etc.)—whether, in fact, they represent theophanies,
or points where the different zones of the universe touch, or
images of the " centre "—stones always draw their religious
significance from the presence of God transfiguring them, from
extra-human powers (the souls of the dead) embodied in them,

[1] Cf. Dumézil, *Jupiter, Mars, Quirinus*, Paris, 1941, pp. 228–9.
[2] Cf. Cæsar, *De Bello Gallico*, vi, 13: " media regio ".
[3] Saintyves, vol. ii, p. 328, with the bibliography.
[4] Saintyves, vol. ii, p. 327,
[5] Saintyves, vol. ii, p. 376.

or from the symbolism (erotic, cosmological, religious, or political) which gives them their setting. Religious stones are always *signs*, always represent something beyond themselves. From the simple elementary hierophany represented by boulders and rocks—which *strike* men's minds by their solidity, steadfastness and majesty—to the symbolism of *omphaloi* and meteorites, religious stones invariably *signify* something greater than man.

Obviously these " significations " will change, will be replaced by others, will sometimes become debased or sometimes strengthened. We cannot hope to analyse them in a few pages. Suffice it to say that there are some forms of stone worship which show traces of a regression to infantilism, and others which, either as a result of new religious experiences, or because they are fitted into different systems of cosmology, change so totally as to be almost unrecognizable. *History* modifies, transforms, debases, or, when a really strong religious personality comes on the scene, transfigures all theophanies. We shall be seeing later the meaning of the changes effected by history in the sphere of religious morphology. For the moment, we will merely note one example of the " transfiguration " of stone: the case of some Greek gods.

" If one goes far back in time," wrote Pausanias,[1] " one sees the Greeks paying honour not to statues, but to unwrought stones [*argoi lithoi*]". The figure of Hermes had a long and complex prehistory: the stones set along the sides of roads to " protect " and keep them were called *hermai*; only much later did an ithyphallic column with a man's head, a *hermes*, come to be taken as an image of the god. Thus Hermes, before becoming the " person " we know in post-Homeric religion and literature, was at first simply a theophany of stone.[2] These *hermai* indicated a presence, embodied a power, and at once protected and made fertile. That Hermes came to have the form of a man was due to the action of the Greek imagination, and the tendency people had from very early on more and more to personalize their divinities and sacred forces. We are witnessing an evolution here, but an evolution quite without any " purification " or " enrichment " of the divinity, an

[1] vii, 22, 4.
[2] Cf. Raingeard, *Hermès psychagogue*, Paris, 1935, pp. 348 ff.

evolution which merely alters the *formula* in which man first expressed his religious experience and his conception of the divinity. As time went on, the Greeks represented their experiences and concepts in different ways. Their minds, bold, elastic and fertile, gained wider horizons, and the old theophanies, losing their effectiveness in this new setting, also lost their meaning. The *hermai* only manifested a divine presence to minds that could receive the revelation of the sacred directly, from every kind of creative act, from every " form " and every " sign ". And so Hermes ceased to be one with the stone; his appearance became human, his theophany became myth.

The theophany of Athene displays the same development of a *sign* into a *person;* whatever its origin, the *palladium* certainly expressed from prehistoric times the direct power of the goddess.[1] Apollo Agyieus was at first no more than a stone pillar.[2] There was a small pyramid-shaped stone in the Gymnasium of Megara called Apollo Karinos; at Malea, Apollo Lithesios stood beside a stone, and the adjective Lithesios has recently been thought to come from *lithos*[3]—an etymology which Nilsson[4] regards as neither better nor worse than its predecessors. Certain it is that no other Greek god, not even Hermes, was surrounded by as many " stones " as Apollo. But Apollo did not rise out of stone any more than Hermes " was " stone; the *hermai* were simply a reminder of the loneliness of the roads, the fearsomeness of the night, and stood for the protection of traveller, house and field. And it was only because Apollo took possession of the old worshipping places that he also annexed their characteristic signs, stones, *omphaloi,* and altars, most of which were originally dedicated to the Great Goddess. This does not mean that a basically stone theophany of Apollo did not hold the field in the period before the god achieved his classic form: undressed stone indicated the divine presence far more effectively to the primitive religious mind than did any statue of Praxiteles to the sculptor's own contemporaries.

[1] Cf. Denyse de Lasseur, *Les Déesses armées,* Paris, 1919, pp. 139 ff.

[2] De Visser, *Die nichtmenschengestaltigen Götter der Griechen,* Leiden, 1903, pp. 65 ff.

[3] Solders, in *AFRW,* 1935, pp. 142 ff.

[4] *Geschichte,* vol. i, p. 189.

BIBLIOGRAPHY

On prehistoric funeral stones and megaliths: VON HEINE-GELDERN, " Die Megalithen Sudostasiens und ihre Bedeutung für die Klärung d. Megalithenfrage in Europa und Polynesien ", *APS*, 1928, vol. xxiii, pp. 276–315; the author tries to explain the origin and the functions of megaliths according to beliefs still obtaining among the people of south-eastern Asia: the " fixing " of the souls of the dead in stone; PERRY, W. J., *Megalithic Culture of Indonesia*, Manchester, 1918; RIESENFELD, A., *The Megalithic Culture of Melanesia*, Leiden, 1950; CLEMEN, Carl, *Urgeschichtliche Religion*, Bonn, 1932, vol. i, pp. 95 ff. (gives the state of the question, bibliography and a critical study); PETTAZZONI, R., *La Religione primitiva in Sardegna*, Piacenza, 1912, pp. 185 ff. (megaliths and cromlechs in Mediterranean and Atlantic Africa); KOPPERS, W., " Monuments to the Dead of the Bhils and Other Primitive Tribes in Central India. A Contribution to the Study of the Megalith Problem ", *Annali Lateranensi*, 1942, vol. vi, pp. 117–206; METZGER, Emile, *Les Sépultures chez les Prégérmains et les Germains des âges de la pierre et de bronze*, Paris, 1933 (this gives a good bibliography and brief indications of the distribution of megaliths). G. WILKE, KOSINNA, and BOSCH GIMPERA consider that the origins of megalithic architecture must be placed in the Iberian peninsula; from there it must have spread all over Europe; cf. OBERMAIER, Hugo, and GARCIO Y BELLIDO, Antonio, *El Hombre prehistorico y los origenes de la humanidad*, 2nd ed., Madrid, 1941, pp. 171 ff.; a good collection of photographs can be found in MONTEZ, Paulino, *Historia da arquitectura primitiva em Portugal. Monumentos dolmenicos*, Lisbon, 1942; list, description and bibliography in OCTOBON, " Statues-menhirs, stèles gravées, dalles sculptées ", *RAN*, 1931, pp. 291–579. P. Laviosa Zambotti supports the notion of the Egyptian origin of megalithic architecture; see *Origini e diffusione della civiltà*, Milan, 1947, pp. 238 ff.

The religious conceptions of the prehistoric and proto-historic peoples of the megalithic cultures (*Megalithkultur*) of Europe have lately been studied exhaustively by Dominik Josef Wölfel, in " Die Religionen des vordindogermanischen Europas ", *Christus und die Religionen der Erde*, Vienna, 1951, vol. i, pp. 170–297.

Cf. IMBELLONI, J., " La Première Chaîne isoglossémantique océano-américaine. Les noms des haches lithiques ", *Festschrift W. Schmidt*, Vienna, 1928, pp. 324–35.

On the part played by prehistoric stones (megaliths, cromlechs, menhirs, " thunderstones ", and so on) in popular beliefs, cf. SAINTYVES, P., *Corpus du folklore préhistorique en France et dans les colonies françaises*, Paris, 1934, vols. i–ii, 1936, vol. iii (a tremendous bit of research, embodying almost all the documentation available at the time of publication, and giving full regional bibliographies); REINACH, Salomon, " Les Monuments de pierre brute dans le langage et les croyances populaires ", *Cultes, Mythes, Religions*, 1908, vol. iii, pp. 366 ff.

On sacred stones among " primitives ", cf. the works of FRAZER, LÉVY-BRUHL, NYBERG, HARTLAND, KOPPERS, as referred to in the text, and also DAHMEN, F., " The Paliyans, a Hill-Tribe of the Palmi Hills (South India) ", *APS*, 1908, vol. iii, pp. 19–31, particularly p. 28 : " Mayandi, the god of the Paliyans and Puliyans, is usually represented by a stone, preferably one to which Nature has given some curious shape . . . "; LEENHARDT, M., *Notes d'ethnologie néocalédonienne*, Paris, 1930, pp. 243–5.

On stone as protector, fetish and amulet, KARSTEN, Rafael, *The Civilization of South American Indians*, London, 1926, pp. 362 ff.; NYBERG, B., *Kind und Erde*, Helsinki, 1931, pp. 65 ff., 141 ff.

On the myth of stone giants, cf. LEHMANN-NITSCHE, Robert, " Ein Mythenthema aus Feuerland und Nord-Amerika, Der Steinriese ", *APS*, 1938, vol. xxxiii, pp. 267–73.

On the myth of " petra genitrix " (a theme also to be found in Asia Minor and in the Far East) cf. LOWIS, A. von, " Nord-kaukasische Steingeburtssagen ", *AFRW*, 1910, vol. xiii, pp. 509–24; SEMPER, Max, *Rassen und Religionen im alten Vorderasien*, Heidelberg, 1930, pp. 179–86; DUMEZIL, G., *Légendes sur les Nartes*, Paris, 1930, pp. 75–7; SCHMIDT, *Grundlinien einer Vergleichung der Religionen und Mythologien der austronesischen Völker*, Vienna, 1910, pp. 408 ff.; PERRY, W. J., *The Children of the Sun*, 2nd ed., London, 1926, pp. 255 ff.; WILLIAMSON, R. W., *The Social and Political Systems of Central Polynesia*, Cambridge, 1924, vol. i, pp. 48, 57, 382; vol. ii, p. 304; JACKSON KNIGHT, W. F., *Cumæan Gates*, Oxford, 1936, pp. 9 ff.; LAYARD, John, *Stone Men of Malekula*, London, 1942, *passim*. On the relationship between stones and fertility (rain) among certain tribes of South America, HENTZE, C., *Mythes et symboles lunaires*, Antwerp, 1932, pp. 32–3, 35, etc.

On fertilization by stones with holes in them, in addition to the works mentioned in the text: SELIGMANN, S., *Der böse Blick*, Berlin, 1910, vol. ii, p. 27; DECHELETTE, J., *Manuel d'archéologie préhistorique, celtique et gallo-romaine*, Paris, 1906, vol. i, pp. 520 ff.; also Wagenvoort's article in *SMSR*, vol. xiv, p. 55.

On " conception and pregnancy stones " in popular Italian belief, cf. BELLUCCI, G., *Il Feticismo primitivo*, Perugia, 1907, pp. 36, 92 ff.; id., *Gli Amuletti*, Perugia, 1908, p. 19.

On " rain stones ": FRAZER, Sir J., *The Magic Art and the Evolution of Kings*, London, 1936, vol. i, pp. 304–7; id., *Folklore in the Old Testament*, London, 1918, vol. ii, pp. 58 ff.; EISLER, R., " Kuba-Kybele ", *PS*, 1909, vol. lxviii, p. 42, n. 222; WAGENVOORT, *SMSR*, vol. xiv, p. 53, n.; WAINWRIGHT, G. A., *The Sky-Religion in Egypt*, Cambridge, 1938, p. 76; KUNZ, G. F., *The Magic of Jewels and Charms*, Philadelphia-London, 1915, pp. 5 ff., 34; PERRY, W. J., *Children of the Sun*, p. 392.

On the myth of water gushing from the rock: cf. SAINTYVES, P., *Essais de folklore biblique*, Paris, 1932, pp. 139 ff.

On the " witness stones " in New Caledonia: LEENHARDT, M., *Notes d'ethnologie néocalédonienne*, pp. 30–1; among the ancient Antimerina VAN GENNEP, *Tabou et totémisme à Madagascar*, Paris, 1904, p. 186.

On the origins of stoning, see PETTAZZONI, R., " La grave mora ", *SMSR*, 1925, vol. i, p. 1 ff.

On meteorites, cf. ELIADE, M., " Metallurgy, Magic and Alchemy ", Paris, 1938, *CZ*, vol. i, p. 3.

On the manifold symbolic and religious significance of stone, BERTHOLET, Alfred, " Über kultische Motivverschiebungen ", *Sitz. Preuss. Akademie Wiss., Phil. Hist. Klasse*, 1938, vol. xviii, pp. 164–84, particularly 164–9.

On religious stones in India: OPPERT, G., " Der Sälagrāma Stein ", *ZFE*, 1902, vol. xxxiv, pp. 131–7; KIRFEL, W., " Vom Steinkult in Indien ", *Studien zur Geschichte u. Kultur des nahen u. fernen Osten, Paul Kahle zum 60 Geburtstag*, Leiden, 1935, pp. 163–72; in Japan: DEGUCHI, Y., " On the Traces of Stone Worship in Japan ", *Journal of the Anthropological Society of Tokyo*, Oct., 1908, vol. xxiv, no. 271 ; in Peru: MINNAERT, P., " Le Culte des pierres au Pérou ", *Bulletin de la société des américanistes de Belgique*, August, 1930.

On bethels, *masseba* and religious stones among the Semites: BEER, G., *Steinverehrung bei den Israeliten*, 1921; ROBERTSON SMITH, W., *The Religion of the Semites*, 3rd ed., London, 1927, pp. 200 ff., 568 ff.; LAGRANGE, P., *Etudes sur les religions sémitiques*, 2nd ed., Paris, 1905, pp. 194 ff.; LAMMENS, P., " Le Culte des bétyles et les processions religieuses dans l'Arabie préislamique ", *Bulletin de l'institut d'archéologie orientale*, Cairo, vol. xvii; DHORME, E., *La Religion des hébreux nomades*, Brussels, 1937, pp. 159–68; DUSSAUD, R., *Les Origines cananéennes du sacrifice israélite*, 2nd ed., Paris, 1941, pp. 222 ff.

On the god Bethel and the divinity of Bethel: cf. EISSFELDT, O., " Der Gott Bethel ", *AFRW*, 1930, vol. xxviii, pp. 1 ff.; VINCENT, A., *La Religion des Judéo-Araméens d'Eléphantine*, Paris, 1937, pp. 562 ff.

On sacred stones in Greece: HASBLUCK, F. W., " Stone Cults and Venerated Stones in the Græco-Turkish Area ", *Annual of the British School at Athens*, vol. xxi; DE VISSER, *Die nichtmenschengestaltigen Götter der Griechen*, Leiden, 1903, pp. 55 ff.; MAAS, E., " Heilige Steine ", *Rhein. Museum*, 1929, vol. lxxviii, pp. 1 ff.; RAINGEARD, P., *Hermès psychagogue*, Paris, 1935, pp. 344 ff.; NILSSON, Martin P., *Geschichte der griechischen Religion*, Munich, 1941, vol. i, p. 187 (with copious bibliographical references); on the Phrygian cults, PICARD, C., *Ephèse et Claros*, Paris, 1922, p. 474.

On the religious stones of the Celts and Germans: D'ARBOIS DE JUBAINVILLE, " Le Culte des menhirs dans le monde celtique ", *RC*, vol. xxvii, pp. 313 ff.; DE VRIES, Jan, *Altgermanische Religionsgeschichte*, Berlin, 1937, vol. ii, p. 100.

On the *omphalos*: ROHDE, E., *Psyche*, London, 1925, pp. 97 ff.; HARRISON, Jane, *Themis*, 2nd ed., Cambridge, 1927, pp. 396 ff.; ROSCHER, " Omphalos ", *Abh. Kön. Sachs. Gesell. Wiss. Phil.-Hist. Klasse*, 1913, vol. xxix, p. 9; id., " Neue Omphalosstudien ", id., 1915, vol. xxxi, p. 1; id., " Der Omphalosgedanke bei verschiedenen Völkern", *Sitz.-Berichte König. Sachs. Gesell. Wiss.*, Leipzig, 1918, vol. lxxx, p. 2; MERINGER, R., " Omphalos, Nabel, Nebel ", *WS*, 1913, vol. v, pp. 43–91; id., " Zum Roschers Omphalos ", *WS*, 1914, vol. vi; DEONNA, W., *REG*, 1915, pp. 444–5; 1917, p. 358, n. 10, etc.; PICARD, C., *Ephèse et Claros*, pp. 110, n. 5, 551, n. 7; ROBERT, R., *Thymèlé*, Paris, 1931, pp. 278–83. On Perdrizet's hypothesis (that the Delphic *omphalos* may have been an importation from Crete), and those of Homolle (that it may have had Egyptian influences), see PICARD, op. cit., p. 464, n. 4; cf. too STEINDORFF, G., " The So-Called Omphalos of Napate ", *JEA*, 1938, vol. xxiv, pp. 147–56. Suggestions and bibliography on the *omphalos* among the Celts, DUMEZIL, G., *Jupiter, Mars, Quirinus*, Paris, 1941, p. 229, n. 2–3.

See also the Bibliography for Chapter X.

VII

THE EARTH, WOMAN AND FERTILITY

83. THE EARTH MOTHER

" . . . Earth [Gaia], herself, first of all gave birth to a being
equal to herself, who could overspread her completely, the
starry heaven [Ouranos], who was to present the blessed gods
a secure throne forever ".[1]   This primeval pair gave birth to
the innumerable family of gods, Cyclops and other mythical
creatures (Cottos, Briareus, Gyges, " children filled with pride ",
each with a hundred arms and fifty heads).   The marriage
between heaven and earth was the first hierogamy; the gods
soon married too, and men, in their turn, were to imitate them
with the same sacred solemnity with which they imitated everything done at the dawn of time.

Gaia or Ge was fairly widely worshipped in Greece, but in
time other earth divinities took her place.   The etymology
suggests that in her the earth element was present in its most
immediate form (cf. Sanskrit *go*, " earth, place "; Zend *gava*,
Gothic, *gawi*, *gauja*, " province ").   Homer scarcely mentions
her; a chthonian divinity—and one belonging pre-eminently to
the pre-Hellenic substratum—would be unlikely to find a place
in his Olympus.   But one of the Homeric hymns is addressed to
her: " It is the earth I sing, securely enthroned, the mother of
all things, venerable ancestress feeding upon her soil all that
exists . . . To thee it belongs to give life to mortals, and to take
it from them . . . Happy the man favoured with thy good will !
For him the soil of life is rich with harvest; in his fields, the
flocks thrive, and his house is full of wealth."[2]

Aeschylus also glorifies her, for it is the earth that " gives
birth to all beings, feeds them, and receives back from them the
fertile seed."[3]   We shall see in a moment how genuine and
ancient is this formula of Aeschylus'.   And there is another
very old hymn which, Pausanias tells us, the Pleiades of Dodona
sang: " Zeus was, is and shall be, O Great Zeus; it is through

---

[1] Hesiod, *Theogony*, v, 126 ff.
[2] *To Earth*, 1 ff.
[3] *Choephori*, v, 127–8.

thy help that the Earth gives us her fruit. We call her our mother with good reason ".[1]

A great many beliefs, myths and rituals have come down to us which deal with the earth, with its divinities, with the Great Mother. As the foundation, in a sense, of the universe, the earth is endowed with manifold religious significance. It was adored because of its permanence, because all things came from it and all things returned to it. If one studied the history of a single religion, one might manage to state fairly exactly the function and development of its beliefs about the chthonian epiphanies. But if one is simply dealing with a study of religious forms, the thing becomes impossible; here, as in all our other chapters, we are looking at acts, beliefs and theories belonging to cycles of civilization differing in age, differing in nature. Let us, however, attempt to see the main threads in the pattern whose elements are listed in the indexes of works on the subject under such headings as Earth, Mother Earth, Earth Divinities, Earth Spirits, etc.

84. THE PRIMEVAL PAIR: SKY AND EARTH

The divine couple, Heaven and Earth, presented by Hesiod, are one of the *leitmotiven* of universal mythology. In many mythologies in which the sky plays the part of supreme divinity, the earth is represented as his companion, and as we saw earlier (§12 ff.), the sky has a place almost everywhere in primitive religious life. Let us recall some examples of this. The Maoris call the sky Rangi and the Earth Papa; at the beginning, like Ouranos and Gaia, they were joined in a close embrace. The children born of this infinite union—Tumata-nenga, Tane-mahuta and others—who longed for the light and groped around in the darkness, decided to separate from their parents. And so, one day, they cut the cords binding heaven to earth and pushed their father higher and higher until Rangi was thrust up into the air and light appeared in the world.[2]

---

[1] x, 12, 10.

[2] You remember that, in the myth Hesiod tells, too, Kronos castrates his father, but for a different reason: because Ouranos was giving birth unknowingly to monsters, which he then hid in Gaia's body. Lang thought the Greek myth could be explained in terms of the Maori. But while the latter is simply a creation myth, explaining the distance between sky and earth, the other can only be explained if one records the Indo-European religious notion of sovereignty, as G. Dumézil has shown in *Ouranos-Varuṇa* (Paris, 1934).

The creation motif of a primeval pair, Heaven and Earth, occurs in all the civilizations of Oceania, from Indonesia to Micronesia.[1] You find it in Borneo, among the Minehassa, in the northern Celebes (where Luminuut, the goddess of earth, is the chief divinity);[2] among the Toradja of the central Celebes (I-lai and I-ndora), in innumerable other Indonesian islands, and so on. In some places one also meets the motif of the sky and earth separated by force; at Tahiti, for instance, it is believed that this was effected by a plant which raised the sky up by growing.[3] This motif is quite widespread in other areas of civilization too.[4] We find the primeval couple, heaven and earth, in Africa; for instance, the Nzambi and Nzambi-Mpungu of the Bawili tribe, in the Gabon,[5] Olorun and Oduna (" the black ") among the Yoruba,[6] the divine couple of the Ewe, and of the Akwapim,[7] and so on. Among the Kumana, an agricultural tribe of southern Africa, the marriage between sky and earth takes on the same sense of cosmic fertility as it has in the hymns of the Pleiades of Dodona: " The Earth is our mother, the Sky is our father. The Sky fertilizes the Earth with rain, the Earth produces grains and grass."[8] And as we shall see, this formula covers a large part of the beliefs concerning agriculture. The divine couple also figure in the mythologies of the Americas. In southern California, the Sky is called Tukmit and the Earth Tamaiovit;[9] among the Navahos we find Yadilqil Hastqin (sky man) and his wife Nihosdzan Esdza (earth woman)[10]; among the Pawnees, in north America,[11] with the Sioux, the Hurons (one of the main tribes of Iroquois),[12] the Hopi, the Zuñi, in the West Indies, and elsewhere we find the same cosmic duality. In the mythologies of the East, it

---

[1] Staudacher, *Die Trennung von Himmel u. Erde*, Tübingen, 1942,; Numazawa, *Die Weltanfänge in der japanischen Mythologie*, Lucerne, 1946, pp. 138 ff., 305 ff.

[2] Cf. Pettazzoni, p. 130.

[3] Krappe, *Genèse*, p. 79.

[4] Cf. Krappe, pp. 78–9; Numazawa, pp. 317 ff.

[5] Pettazzoni, pp. 210, 212.

[6] Pettazzoni, p. 246.

[7] Pettazzoni, p. 241.

[8] Krappe, p. 78.

[9] Pettazzoni, p. 279.

[10] Pettazzoni, p. 282.

[11] Pettazzoni, p. 284.

[12] Pettazzoni, pp. 291, 315.

plays an equally important part in the creation of the universe. The " queen of the lands " (the goddess Arinna) and her husband U or Im, the god of storm, are the Hittite version;[1] the goddess of earth and the god of sky are the Chinese; Izanagi and Izanami the Japanese;[2] and so on. Among the Germanic peoples, Frigga, the wife of Tyr, and later of Othin, is in essence a goddess of earth. And it is merely a chance of grammar that the Egyptians had a goddess, Nut, to represent the sky (the word for sky was feminine), and a god, Geb, for the earth.

85. THE STRUCTURE OF CHTHONIAN HIEROPHANIES

It would be easy to multiply examples, but nothing would be gained by it. The mere listing of cosmological couples would indicate neither the essential structure of chthonian divinities nor their religious significance. In the myth of creation, the earth, though primeval, plays a passive part. Before there were myths to tell any stories about the earth, the mere *existence* of the soil was seen as significant in the religious sphere. The earth, to the primitive religious consciousness, was something immediately experienced and accepted; its size, its solidity, its variety of landscape and of vegetation, formed a live and active cosmic unity. The first realization of the religious significance of the earth was " indistinct "; in other words, it did not localize sacredness in the earth as such, but jumbled together as a whole all the hierophanies in nature as it lay around—earth, stones, trees, water, shadows, everything. The primary intuition of the earth as a religious " form " might be formularized thus: " The cosmos—repository of a wealth of sacred forces." We saw the notion of seeds, latencies and rebirth in the various meanings—religious, magical or mythological—given to water, but the primal intuition of the Earth shows it as the *foundation* of every expression of existence. All that *is* on earth, is united with everything else, and all make up one great whole.

The cosmic structure of these elemental intuitions makes it almost impossible for us to discern the element of earth as such. Men lived in their surroundings as a whole, and it is very hard

[1] Furlani, *La Religione degli Hittiti,* Bologna, 1936, pp. 18, 35.
[2] Numazawa, pp. 93 ff.

to distinguish, in such intuitions, what belongs properly to the earth from what is merely *manifested* through the earth: mountains, forests, water, vegetation. Only one thing can be said with certainty of these primary intuitions (whose religious nature I have already indicated clearly enough): that is, that they appear as *forms*, that they reveal realities, that they must, of necessity, obtrude themselves, that they strike the mind. The earth, with all that it supports and contains, has been seen from the first as an inexhaustible fount of existences, and of existences that reveal themselves directly to man.

What makes it quite certain that the hierophany of the earth was cosmic in form before being truly chthonian (which it became only with the appearance of agriculture), is the history of the beliefs as to the origin of children. Before the physiological causes of conception were known, men thought that maternity resulted from the direct insertion of the child into a woman's womb. We are in no way concerned here with the question of whether what entered the woman's womb was thought to be already a fœtus—which up till then had lived its life in caves, crevices, wells, trees and such—or whether they thought it merely a seed, or even the " soul of an ancestor ", or what they thought it was. What we are concerned with is the idea that children were not conceived by their father, but at some more or less advanced stage of development, they were placed in their mother's womb as a result of a contact between her and some object or animal in the country round about.

Although this problem belongs more to ethnology than to the history of religion properly so called, it may here help us to clarify the matter in hand. Man has no part in creation. The father was father to his children only in the legal sense, not the biological. Men were related to each other through their mothers only, and that relationship was precarious enough. But they were related to their natural surroundings far more closely than any modern, profane mind can conceive. They were literally, and in no mere allegorical sense, " the people of the land ". Either they were brought by water animals (fish, frogs, crocodiles, swans or some such), or they grew among rocks, in chasms or in caves, before being thrust by magic into their mother's womb; or before birth, they began life in water, in crystals, in stones, in trees; or they live—in an obscure,

pre-human form as " souls " of " child-ancestors "—in one of
the nearby cosmic zones.   Thus, to mention only a few examples,
the Armenians thought the earth was the " maternal womb,
whence men came forth ".[1]   The Peruvians believed that they
were descended from mountains and stones.[2]   Other peoples
placed the origins of children in caves, crevices, springs and so
on.   Even to-day there are people in Europe who believe
children " come " from pools, springs, rivers, trees and so on.[3]
What is significant about these superstitions is the cosmic
form the " earth " takes; it can be identified with the whole
surrounding area, with the microcosm, not merely with the
earth as such.   " The earth " here, means all that surrounds
man, the whole " place "—with its mountains, its waters and
its vegetation.

The human father merely *legitimizes* such children by a
ritual which has all the marks of adoption.   They belong, first
of all, to the " place ", to the surrounding microcosm.   The
mother has only received them; she has " welcomed " them,
and at the most, perfected their human form.   It is easy to
understand, from this, that the feeling of solidarity with the
surrounding microcosm, with the " place ", was a prevailing
one with man at this stage of his mental development—or,
rather, for man where he envisaged human life in this fashion.
We might say in a sense that *man was not yet born*, that he did
not yet realize that he belonged wholly to the biological species
he represented.   It might be better to consider that at this
stage his life was in a pre-natal phase: man still continued to
share, directly, in a life that was not his own, in a " cosmico-
maternal " life.   He had, we might say, a " phylogenetic "
experience of being, which he only partly understood; he felt
himself to have emerged from two or three " wombs " at the
same time.

It is not hard to realize that a background of this sort involved man in a certain number of specific attitudes regarding
both the cosmos and his fellow-men.   The precariousness of
human paternity was balanced by the solidarity existing between
man and various protective forces or substances in nature.

[1] Dieterich, *Mutter Erde*, Berlin, 1925, p. 14.
[2] Nyberg, *Kind und Erde*, Helsinki, 1931, p. 62.
[3] Dieterich, pp. 19 ff.

But, on the other hand, this solidarity with "place" could hardly inspire man to feel himself a creator in the biological order. The father, legitimizing his children, who had either come to him from some source in nature or were "the souls of ancestors", did not really have any children at all, but simply new members for his family, fresh tools for his work or his protection. The bond between him and his offspring was not really procreative. His biological life ended with himself and could never be passed on through other beings—though the Indo-Europeans came later to offer an interpretation of the feeling men have of family continuity, which was basically that the body is passed on directly (the parents creating the body, or "substance" of the child) while the soul descends indirectly from ancestors (the souls of ancestors were incarnate in the new-born).[1]

The earth, then, was, in the earliest of religious experiences or mythical intuitions, "the whole place" in which man found himself. A large number of the words for earth have etymologies which manifest impressions of space—"place", "wide", "province" (cf. *pṛthivī*, "the wide"), or primary impressions of sense, "firm", "what stays", "black", and so on. Any religious evaluation of the earth simply as such can only have occurred later on—in the pastoral cycle and, above all, in the agricultural cycle, to talk in terms of ethnology. Up till then, what one would call the "divinities of the earth" were really "divinities of the place"—in the sense of the cosmic surroundings.

86. CHTHONIAN MATERNITY

One of the first theophanies of the earth as such, and particularly of the earth as soil, was its "motherhood", its inexhaustible power of fruitfulness. Before becoming a mother goddess, or divinity of fertility, the earth presented itself to men as a Mother, *Tellus Mater*. The later growth of agricultural cults, forming a gradually clearer and clearer notion of a Great Goddess of vegetation and harvesting, finally destroyed all trace of the Earth-Mother. In Greece, the place of Gaia was taken by Demeter. However, certain ancient ethnological documents reveal relics of the old worship

[1] Cf. Eckhardt, *Irdische Unsterblichkeit*, Weimar, 1937, *passim*.

of the Earth-Mother. Smohalla, an Indian prophet of the Umatilla tribe, forbade his followers to dig the earth, for, he said, it is a sin to wound or cut, tear or scratch our common mother by the labours of farming. And he defended his anti-agricultural attitude by saying: " You ask me to plough the ground ? Shall I take a knife and tear my mother's bosom ? Then when I die she will not take me to her bosom to rest. You ask me to dig for stone ? Shall I dig under her skin for her bones ? Then when I die I cannot enter her body to be born again. You ask me to cut grass and make hay and sell it, and be rich like white men ! But how dare I cut off my mother's hair ? "[1]

Such a mystical devotion to the Earth-Mother is not an isolated instance. The members of a primitive Dravidian tribe of central India, the Baiga, carried on a nomadic agriculture, sowing only in the ashes left when part of the jungle had burnt away. And they went to such trouble because they thought it a sin to tear their mother's bosom with a plough.[2] In the same way some Altaic and Finno-Ugrian peoples thought it a terrible sin to pluck the grass, because it hurt the earth as much as it would hurt a man to pluck out his hair or his beard. The Votyaks, whose custom was to place their offerings in a ditch, were careful never to do it in the autumn, as that was the time when the Earth was asleep. The Cheremisses often thought the earth was ill, and at such times would avoid sitting on it. And there are many other indications that beliefs about Mother Earth persisted, even though sporadically, among both agricultural and non-agricultural peoples.[3] Earth religion, even if it is not, as some scholars believe, the oldest of man's religions, is one that dies hard. Once established in an agricultural framework, thousands of years may go by without its altering. In some cases there is no break in the continuity from prehistoric times to the present. The " dead man's cake ", for instance, (coliva in Rumanian) was known by the same name in ancient Greece, which had it as a heritage from prehistoric, pre-Hellenic times. Further examples of

---

[1] James Mooney, " The Ghost-Dance Religion and the Sioux Outbreak of 1890 ", *Annual Report of the Bureau of American Ethnology*, Washington, 1896, xiv, p. 721.

[2] Frazer, *Adonis, Attis, Osiris*, vol. i, p. 89.

[3] Cf. Nyberg, pp. 63 ff.

continuity within the enduring framework of agricultural earth religions will be mentioned later on.

In 1905 A. Dieterich published a book, *Mutter Erde, ein Versuch über Volksreligion*,[1] which soon became a classic work. Emil Goldmann[2] and others after him, and—more recently—Nilsson,[3] have put forward every sort of objection to Dieterich's theory, but it has never been totally disproved. Dieterich opens his study by recalling three customs practised in antiquity—the laying of newborn children upon the ground, the burial of children (by contrast with the cremating of adults), the placing of the sick and dying as near the earth as possible—from which he reconstructs the outline of the primitive earth-goddess, the " Earth-Mother-of-all-things " (*pammetor Ge*) mentioned by Aeschylus,[4] the Gaia of Hesiod's hymn. An impressive amount of material was gathered round these three primitive customs, and controversies took place which we need not go into here. But we may see what the things themselves teach us, and in what religious setting they are to be seen.

87. MAN'S DESCENT FROM THE EARTH

Saint Augustine,[5] following Varro, mentions the name of a Latin goddess, Levana, who raised children from out of the earth: *levat de terra*. Dieterich notes, in connection with this fact, the custom, still current in the Abbruzzi, of placing babies upon the earth as soon as they are washed and swaddled.[6] The same ritual took place among the Scandinavians, the Germans, the Parsees, the Japanese, and other races. The child was picked up by its father (*de terra tollere*), who thus expressed his recognition of it.[7] Dieterich interprets this rite as a way of dedicating the child to the earth, *Tellus Mater*, which is its true mother. Goldmann objects that the placing of a baby (or an ill or dying person) on the ground does not necessarily imply any descent from the earth, nor even any consecration to the Earth-Mother, but is simply intended to

[1] Leipzig-Berlin, 3rd ed., 1925, enlarged and completed by E. Fehrle.
[2] " Cartam levare ", *MIOG*, 1914, vol. xxv, pp. 1 ff.
[3] *Geschichte*, pp. 427 ff.
[4] *Prometheus*, 88.
[5] *De Civ. Dei*, iv, 11.
[6] *Mutter Erde*, p. 7.
[7] Nyberg, p. 31.

make a contact with the magic powers in the soil. Others[1] are of the opinion that this rite is meant to procure the child a soul, which comes to it from *Tellus Mater*.

We are obviously faced with two different interpretations, but they contradict each other only on the surface; both follow from the same primordial conception: that of the earth as the source at once of force, of " souls ", of fecundity—the fecundity of the Earth-Mother. Lying on the ground (*humi positio*) is a custom found frequently and among a great many peoples; among the Gurions of the Caucasus, and in some parts of China, women lie on the ground as soon as the pains of childbirth begin, so that they will be on the ground when their child is born;[2] the Maori women in New Zealand have their children beside a stream, in the bushes; in a lot of African tribes, it is usual for women to give birth in forests, sitting on the ground;[3] we find the same ritual in Australia, in Northern India, among the Indians of North America, Paraguay and Brazil.[4] Samter notes (p. 6) that this custom had been abandoned by the Greeks and Romans by historical times, but it certainly existed at one time; some statues of the goddesses of birth (Eilithyia, Damia, Auxeia) represent them kneeling in the exact position of a woman having a child straight on the ground.[5] In the Middle Ages in Germany, among the Japanese, in certain Jewish communities, in the Caucasus,[6] in Hungary, Rumanía, Scandinavia, Iceland, and elsewhere, the same ritual can be found. The expression " to sit on the ground " in Egyptian, was used in demotic writings to mean " giving birth ".[7]

The basic meaning of this extremely widespread ritual was undoubtedly the maternity of the earth. As we have seen, it was believed in a number of places that children came from wells, water, rocks, trees and so on; it goes without saying

---

[1] For instance Rose, in *Primitive Culture in Italy*, London, 1926, p. 133.

[2] Samter, *Geburt, Hochzeit und Tod*, Berlin, 1911, pp. 5 ff.

[3] Nyberg, p. 131, gives sources.

[4] Ploss and Bartels, *Woman: An Historical, Gynæcological and Anthropological Compendium*, London, 1935, vol. ii, §§ 278–80.

[5] See also Marconi, *Riflessi mediterranei nella più antica religione laziale*, Milan, 1939, pp. 254 ff.

[6] Nyberg, p. 133.

[7] Nyberg, p. 134.

that in others, children were thought to have " come from the earth ".[1] A bastard was known as *terrae filius*. When the Mordvinians want to adopt a child, they place it in a ditch in the garden where the protecting goddess, the Earth-Mother, is supposed to dwell.[2] This means that a child, to be adopted, must be born anew; and this is managed, not by the adopting mother imitating the act of giving birth on her knees (as e.g., with the Romans), but by placing the child on the bosom of its true mother, the earth.

It was natural that this notion of descent from the earth should, later, be replaced by a kindlier notion; a realization that the earth was the protectress of children, the source of all strength, and that it was to it (that is, to the maternal spirit dwelling in it) that newborn babies must be consecrated. That is why we so often find " earth cradles ": tiny babies were put to sleep or rest in ditches, in direct contact with the earth, or with the bed of ashes, straw, and leaves their mothers made for them there. The earth cradle is common both in primitive societies (the Australians and various Turco-Altaic peoples) and in higher civilizations (the Inca empire, for instance).[3] Unwanted children were never killed, but left on the ground by the Greeks and others. The Earth-Mother must take care of them; she must decide whether they were to live or die.[4]

A child " exposed ", abandoned to the will of the elements —water, wind, earth—is always a sort of defiance thrown in the face of fate. Entrusted to earth or water, the child will henceforward bear the social status of an orphan, and is in danger of dying, but he also has a chance to attain to some condition other than the human. Protected by nature, the abandoned child generally becomes a hero, king or saint. The legend giving his biography is simply repeating the myths about gods abandoned at birth. Remember that Zeus, Poseidon, Dionysos, Attis and innumerable other gods also shared the fate of Perseus, Ion, Atalanta, Amphion and Zéthos, of Oedipus, Romulus and Remus and the rest. Moses too was

[1] Cf. Dieterich, pp. 14 ff.; the myth of the man made of earth among the Australians, etc.; Nyberg, p. 62.

[2] Nyberg, p. 137.

[3] Cf. Nyberg, p. 160.

[4] Cf. Delcourt, *Stérilités mystérieuses et naissances maléfiques dans l'antiquité classique*, Paris, 1938, p. 64.

abandoned to the water, like the Maori hero Massi who was thrown into the sea, like the hero of the *Kalevala*, Vainamoinen, who " floated above dark waves ". The tragedy of the abandoned child is made up for by the mythological grandeur of the " orphan ", the primeval child, with his utter and invulnerable loneliness in the universe, his uniqueness. The appearance of such a child coincides with a moment in the dawn of things: the creation of the cosmos, the creation of a new world, of a new epoch of history (*Jam redit et virgo* . . .), a " new life "— at no matter what level of reality.[1] A child abandoned to the Earth-Mother, saved and brought up by her, no longer has any part in the common destiny of mankind, for he re-enacts the cosmological instant of " beginning ", and grows not in the midst of a family, but in the midst of the elements. That is why heroes and saints come from among abandoned children: merely by protecting the child, and preserving it from death, the Earth-Mother (or the Water-Mother) is dedicating it to a tremendous destiny which a common mortal could never attain.

88. REGENERATION

Another ritual following on from this belief in the Earth-Mother, is the burial of children's bodies. Grown men are burnt, but children are buried, so that they may return to the bosom of Mother Earth and be reborn again later on: *Terra clauditur infans.*[2] The Laws of Manu ordain that children under two must be buried, and forbid their cremation. The Hurons bury dead children under the road, so that they may be born again by creeping into the wombs of women who pass along it.[3] The Andaman Islanders bury children under the hearth, actually in their huts.[4] Note in this connection, too, burial " in the position of an embryo ", which is a practice found among a lot of peoples, to which I shall return when discussing the mythology of death.[5] The corpse is arranged in

[1] Cf. Eliade, *Commentarii la legenda Mesterului Manole*, Bucharest, 1943, p. 54.

[2] Juvenal, xv, 140.

[3] Dieterich, p. 22.

[4] Schebesta, *Les Pygmées*, p. 142.

[5] Van der Leeuw, " Das sogenannte Höckerbegräbnis und der ägyptische Tjkuw ", *SMSR*, 1938, vol. xiv.

the position of the embryo, so that the Earth-Mother may return it into the world. There are places where children are buried alive as offerings to the Earth Goddess; thus, in Greenland, the child was buried if the father was seriously ill; in Sweden, two children were buried alive during a plague; the Mayans offered similar sacrifices when there was a bad drought.[1]

Just as the child is laid on the ground at birth so that its true mother may legitimize it and assure it her divine protection, so children and grown men, when they are ill, are laid upon the ground—if not actually buried. This rite is the same as rebirth. Symbolic burial—partial or total—has the same magico-religious significance as immersion in water, baptism (§ 64). The sick man is reborn of it: he is born again. This does not merely mean taking hold of the forces of earth, but total regeneration. The practice is equally effective in getting rid of a serious sin, or curing a sickness of the mind (the latter being as great a danger to society as crime or physical illness). The sinner is placed in a barrel or a ditch cut into the earth, and when he emerges, " he is born a second time from his mother's womb ".[2] That is why the Scandinavians believe that a witch can be saved from eternal damnation if she is buried alive, and seed is immediately sown on top of her, and its crop gathered.[3] There is a similar belief concerning children who are dangerously ill; if one could bury them, and sow seed above them and give it long enough to grow, the children might get better. This belief is not hard to understand: the man (or witch, or child) is in this way given a chance to be reborn along with the plant.

Another rite, related to this, is that of placing the sick child for a moment in a crevice in the ground, or a hole in a rock, or the hollow of a tree.[4] This is part of a rather more complex belief: on the one hand, the purpose is to transfer the child's sickness into something else (tree, rock, ground); on the other, the actual birth is re-enacted (by emerging from the opening). Indeed, it is even possible that elements of the sun cult contribute to this rite—at least in some places (e.g., India;

[1] Nyberg, pp. 181 ff.
[2] Frazer, *Folklore in the Old Testament*, vol. ii, p. 33.
[3] Dieterich, pp. 28 ff.; Nyberg, p. 150.
[4] Nyberg, pp. 144 ff.

cf. § 78). But the basic idea is that of healing by a new birth—and, as we have seen, in most of their beliefs, agricultural peoples make a very close connection between this new birth and the contact with the Earth-Mother. That is the only explanation of one whole series of beliefs and customs relating to purification and the use of the earth as a means of healing. The earth is indeed imbued with power, as Goldmann says, but that power derives from its ability to bear fruit and its motherhood.

As we have seen, children are buried, even by people whose normal custom is to cremate their dead; this is in the hope that the womb of the earth will give them new life. The Maori word *whenna* means both " earth " and " placenta ".[1] And even the burial of grown men who die—or of their ashes, among those who practise cremation—is carried out for the same purpose. " Crawl to the earth, thy mother ", says the *Ṛg Veda*.[2] " Thou, who art earth, I place thee in the earth ", says the *Atharva Veda*.[3] " The earth is a mother; I am the son of the Earth, my father is Parjanya . . . Born of thee, mortals return into thee . . ."[4] When ashes and cremated bones are being buried, seeds are added to them, and the whole thing is sprinkled over a newly ploughed field, with the words: " May Sāvitrī sprinkle thy flesh in the bosom of our mother the Earth."[5] But such Hindu beliefs are not always as simple as may appear from these texts. The notion of a return into the Earth-Mother was completed by a later idea: that of man's reintegration into the whole Cosmos, a *restitutio ab integro* of mental powers and bodily organs into the original anthropo-cosmos (" Thy breath goes away to the winds, thy ear [that is, ' thy hearing '], to the points of the compass, thy bones return to the Earth ").[6]

The belief that the dead dwell underground till they return again to the light of day, to a new existence, shows why the kingdom of the dead is identified with the place from which

---

[1] Dieterich, p. 13, n. 13.
[2] x, 18, 10.
[3] xviii, 4, 48.
[4] *AV*, xii, 1, 11; 14.
[5] *Śatapatha Brah.*, xiii, 8, 2.
[6] *Aitareya Brāhmaṇa*, ii, 6, 13; etc.

children come; the Mexicans, for instance, believe that they come from a place called Chicomoztoc, the place of seven caves.[1] Whether because the dead were thought to know the future, or because the earth, because of its periodic reabsorbing of all living creatures, was thought to have oracular powers, certain ancient Greek oracles were situated beside crevices or earthern grottos. We know that there were earth oracles of this sort at Olympia and at Delphi, and Pausanias[2] mentions an oracle at Aigai, in Achaea, where the priestesses of Gaia foretold the future at the edge of a crevice in the earth. And it is hardly necessary to remind you of the tremendous number of " incubations " that took place as a result of sleeping on the ground.[3]

89. Homo-Humus

From all the beliefs we have so far looked at, the earth emerges as a mother, that is, as giving birth to living forms which it draws out of its own substance. The earth is " living " first of all because it is fertile. Everything that comes from the earth is endowed with life, and everything that goes back into the earth is given new life. The connection between *homo* and *humus* must not be understood simply to mean that man is earth because he is mortal but also that the fact that man can live is due to his being born of—and returning to—the *Terra Mater*. Not long ago, Solmsen[4] explained *mater* from *materies*; and although this is not in fact the true etymology (the original meaning of " matter " was, apparently, something like " heart of wood "), yet it has a place in a mythico-religious outlook: " matter " does the work of a mother, for it unceasingly gives birth. What we call life and death are merely two different moments in the career of the Earth-Mother as a whole: life is merely being detached from the earth's womb, death is a returning " home ". The wish so many people feel to be buried in their own country is simply a profane form of this mystical love of one's own earth, of this need to return to one's own home. The burial inscriptions of the Roman Empire demonstrate the joy of being buried in the soil of one's homeland: *Hic natus*

[1] Preuss, *AFRW*, vii, 234.
[2] vii, 25, 13.
[3] Deubner, *De Incubatione*, Leipzig, 1900, *passim*.
[4] Cf. Dieterich, p. 77.

hic situs est;[1] *Hic situs est patriæ*;[2] *Hic quo natus fuerat optans erat illo reverti*,[3] etc. And others witness the sorrow of not having this consolation: *Altera contexit tellus dedit altera nasci*,[4] and so on.[5] And, then, too, traitors were refused burial, because, Philostratus explains, they were not worthy " of being sanctified by the earth ".[6]

Water is a bearer of seeds; earth bears seeds too, but in the earth they all bring forth fruit quickly. Latencies and seeds may spend several cycles in water before they become manifest; but it can be said of the earth that it never rests; its work is to give birth unceasingly, to give form and life to whatever comes back to it lifeless and sterile. The waters are there at the beginning and end of every cosmic cycle; the earth is there at the beginning and end of every individual life. Everything emerges into being above the surface of the waters, and is once again reduced to its primeval formlessness as a result of a historical disaster (like the flood) or a cosmic one (*mahāpralaya*). Every expression of life is the result of the fertility of the earth; every form is born of it, living, and returns to it the moment its share of life is exhausted; returns to it to be reborn; but before being reborn, to rest, to be purified, to be regenerated. Water *precedes* every creation, every form; earth *produces* living forms. While the mythological destiny of water is to open and close cosmic cycles, the destiny of the earth is to stand at the beginning and end of every biological form and of every form sharing in the history of *place* (" men of the place "). Time—which, so to speak, sleeps as far as water is concerned— is alive and active in the earth's engendering. Living forms come and go with lightning speed. But the going is never definitive; the death of living forms is a hidden and provisional mode of existence; the living form as such, as a species, will never disappear till the end of the term allowed to earth by the waters.

---

[1] *CIL*, v, 5595.

[2] viii, 2885.

[3] v, 1703.

[4] xiii, 6429.

[5] For further examples see Brelich, *Aspetti della morte nelle inscrizioni sepolcrali dell'Impero Romano*, Budapest, 1937, pp. 36, 37.

[6] Quoted by Harrison *Prolegomena to the Study of Greek Religion*, London, 1907, p. 599.

90. COSMOLOGICAL SOLIDARITY

From the first moment when a form emerged from water, every direct organic bond between them was broken; between form and the pre-formal there is a gulf. But there is no such break between the earth and the forms engendered by it; these forms remain bound to their source, from which they are in any case separated only for a time, and to which they will return to rest, to be strengthened, and one day to reappear. That is why there is a magic, sympathetic bond between the earth and the organic forms it has engendered. Together they form a whole. The invisible threads binding the plants, animals and men in a given place to the soil from which they spring, which gave them birth and nourishes them, are woven together by that life which beats in the Mother as in her creatures. The solidarity between earth on one hand, and the vegetable, animal and human forms on the other, is due to the *life* which is the same in them all. Their unity is biological. And if any one of the modes of this life be polluted or deadened by a sin against life, all the other modes are tainted too because of their organic solidarity.

Any crime is a sacrilege and may bring serious consequences at every level of life, for the mere shedding of blood " poisons " the earth. And the disaster is manifested in the fact that fields, animals and men are all smitten with sterility. In the prologue to *Oedipus Rex*,[1] the priest laments the miseries that have fallen upon Thebes: " The city is dying, in the fruits of the earth, in the herds of oxen in the fields, in the birth pangs of the women, which end all with no births." A wise king, whose reign is based on justice, assures, on the contrary, the fertility of earth, animals and women. Ulysses declares to Penelope[2] that it is because he is renowned as a good king that the earth bears its harvest, that the trees are heavy with fruit, that the sheep have lambs as they should, and that the seas are alive with fish. Hesiod states this peasant notion of anthropocosmic harmony and fertility in this way: " Those who deal fairly and never depart from justice, whether to stranger or to citizen, see their town flourish, and the people within their walls thrive. The peace in which young men thrive is spread over their land, and

[1] 25 ff.
[2] *Odyssey*, xix, 109 ff.

wide-watching Zeus will not give them painful wars. Just law is never visited by famine or disaster. . . . The earth offers them abundant life; upon their mountains the oak bears acorns at its summit, and bees in its midst; their fleecy flocks are heavy with wool; their women give them sons like their fathers; they thrive in endless prosperity; and they never cross the sea, for the fertile soil gives them its harvest."[1] And an Iranian version of it runs like this: " Under the rule of the courageous Yama, there was neither cold nor heat, old age nor death, nor any envy created by demons. Fathers and sons alike had the air of young men of fifteen, as long as Yama reigned, the man of fine flocks, the son of Vivahvant."[2]

91. SOIL AND WOMAN

One of the salient features in all agricultural societies is the solidarity they see between the fertility of the land and that of their women. For a very long time the Greeks and Romans identified the soil with the womb, and agricultural labour with the act of generation. We find this same identification else-where, in a great many civilizations, and it gave rise to a large number of beliefs and rites. Aeschylus, for instance, says that Oedipus " dared to sow seed in the sacred furrow where he was himself formed, and plant there a bloody branch ".[3] In Sophocles there are abundant allusions: to " paternal furrows ",[4] to the " other furrows one may plough ",[5] to the " husbandman, master of a distant field, which he only visits once at seed-time " (Deianira, speaking of Heracles).[6] Dieterich, who gives numerous other references in addition to these classical texts,[7] also notes how often the *arat-amat* motif appears in the Latin poets.[8] But, as we might have expected, the comparison of woman with the ploughed furrow, of the act of generation to agricultural labour, is a widespread and very primitive intuition. And we must distinguish the several

[1] *Works and Days*, 225–37.
[2] *Yasna*, 9, 3–5. On the Indian traditions, see Meyer, *Sexual Life in Ancient India*, London, 1930, vol. i, pp. 286–7.
[3] *Seven Against Thebes*, 750 ff.
[4] *Œdipus Rex*, 1210.
[5] *Antigone*, 569.
[6] *Trachiniæ*, 30 ff.
[7] p. 47, n. 1 and 2; cf. V. Pisani, " La Donna e la terra ", *APS*, 1942, vol. xxxvii–xl, pp. 248 ff.
[8] pp. 78, 79.

elements which go to make up this mythico-religious whole: the identification of women with ploughland; the identification of the phallus with the plough; the identification of the labour of farming with the act of generation.

Let me say at once that the Earth-Mother and her human representative, woman, though they play a dominant part in this ritual pattern, do not play it alone. There is room not only for the earth or woman, but also for the man and the god. Fertility is preceded by a hierogamy. An old Anglo-Saxon charm used when the land was barren gives a perfect picture of the trust farming societies placed in that hierogamy: " Hail, Earth, Mother of men, be fertile in the god's embrace, be filled with fruit for man's use."[1] At Eleusis, the priest pronounced the ancient agricultural formula " Make it to rain !—Mayest thou bear fruit ! ", looking first to the sky, then to the earth. It is probable that this sacred marriage between heaven and earth was the primeval model both of the fertility of the land and of human marriage. A text from the *Atharva Veda*,[2] for instance, compares the bride and bridegroom to earth and heaven.

92. WOMAN AND AGRICULTURE

No one doubts that agriculture was discovered by women. Man was almost always in pursuit of game, or pasturing his flocks. Woman, on the other hand, with her keen, though circumscribed, powers of observation, was in a position to watch the natural phenomena of seeds falling and growing, and to try and reproduce those phenomena artificially. And then too, because she was linked up with the other centres of cosmic fertility—Earth and the Moon—woman also became endowed with the prerogative of being able to influence and distribute fertility. That is the reason for the dominant role played by women when agriculture was in its infancy—particularly when this skill was still the province of women—and which in some civilizations she still plays.[3] Thus, in Uganda, a barren woman is thought to be a danger to the

[1] Quoted in Krappe, *Etudes de mythologie et de folklore germaniques*, Paris, 1928, p. 62.

[2] xiv, 2, 71.

[3] See U. Pestalozza, " L'Aratro e la donna nel mondo religioso mediterraneo ", *Rendiconti, Reale Instituto Lombardo di Scienze e Lettere, cl. di Lettere*, 1942-3, vol. lxxvi, no. 2, pp. 324 ff.

garden, and her husband can seek a divorce simply on economic grounds.[1] We find the same belief in the danger to farming of female sterility in the Bhantu tribe, in the Indies.[2] In Nicobar it is thought that the harvest will be richer if the seed is sown by a pregnant woman.[3] In southern Italy, it is thought that everything undertaken by a pregnant woman will be a success, and that everything she sows will grow as the fœtus grows.[4] In Borneo ". . . the women play the principal part in the rites and actual operations of the *padi* culture; the men only being called in to clear the ground and to assist in some of the later stages. The women select and keep the seed grain, and they are the repositories of most of the lore connected with it. It seems to be felt that they have a natural affinity to the fruitful grain, which they speak of as becoming pregnant. Women sometimes sleep out in the *padi* fields while the crop is growing, probably for the purpose of increasing their own fertility, or that of the *padi*; but they are very reticent on this matter."[5]

The Orinoco Indians left the task of sowing maize and planting roots to their women; for " as women knew how to conceive seed and bear children, so the seeds and roots planted by them bore fruit far more abundantly than if they had been planted by male hands ".[6] At Nias, a palm tree planted by a woman has more sap than one planted by a man.[7] The same beliefs are to be found in Africa, among the Ewe. In South America, among the Jibaros, for instance, it is believed " that women exercise a special, mysterious influence on the growth of cultivated plants ".[8] This solidarity of woman with fertile furrows was preserved even after farming became a masculine skill, and the plough took the place of the primitive spade. This solidarity accounts for a great many rites and beliefs which we shall examine when we come to look at the various rituals of agriculture (§ 126).

[1] Briffault, *The Mothers*, London, 1927, vol. iii, p. 55.
[2] Lévy-Bruhl, *L'Expérience mystique et les symboles chez les primitifs*, Paris, 1938, p. 254.
[3] Temple, in Hastings' *Encyclopædia of Religion and Ethics*, vol. ix, p. 362.
[4] Finamore, *Tradizioni populari abruzzesi*, p. 59.
[5] Hose and MacDougall, *Pagan Tribes of Borneo*, i, iii, quoted by Lévy-Bruhl, *L'Expérience mystique*, p. 254.
[6] Frazer, *Spirits of the Corn and of the Wild*, vol. i, p. 124; see the whole chapter, " The Role of Woman in Agriculture "
[7] Lévy-Bruhl, p. 254.
[8] Karsten, quoted by Lévy-Bruhl, p. 255.

93. WOMAN AND FURROW

The identification of woman with the ploughed earth can be found in a great many civilizations and was preserved in European folklore. " I am the earth," declares the beloved in an Egyptian love song. The *Videvdāt* compares fallow land to a woman with no children, and in fairy tales, the barren queen bewails herself: " I am like a field on which nothing grows."[1] On the other hand, a twelfth-century hymn glorifies the Virgin Mary as *terra non arabilis quae fructum parturiit*. Ba'al was called " the spouse of the fields ".[2] And it was a common thing among all Semitic peoples to identify woman with the soil.[3] In Islamic writings, woman is called " field ", " vine with grapes ", etc. Thus the Koran:[4] " Your wives are to you as fields." The Hindus identified the furrow with the vulva (*yoni*), seeds with *semen virile*.[5] " This woman is come as a living soil: sow seed in her, ye men ! "[6] The Laws of Manu also teach that " woman may be looked upon as a field, and the male as the seed ".[7] Nārada makes this comment: " Woman is the field, and man the dispenser of the seed."[8] A Finnish proverb says that " maidens have their field in their own body ".[9]

Obviously, to identify woman with a furrow implies an identification of phallus with spade, of tilling with the act of generation. Such anthropo-telluric comparisons could only come in civilizations which understood both agriculture and the true causes of conception. In certain Australasian languages, the word *lak* means both phallus and spade. Przyluski has suggested that a similar Australasian term is at the root of the Sanskrit words *langūla* (tail, spade) and *lingam* (male generative organ).[10] The phallus-plough identification

---

[1] Van der Leeuw, *Religion in Essence and Manifestation*, London, 1938, p. 96.

[2] Robertson Smith, *Religion of the Semites*, London, 1923 ed., pp. 108, 536 ff.

[3] Robertson Smith, p. 537; cf. Dhorme, *La Religion des Hébreux nomades*, Brussels, 1937, p. 276.

[4] ii, 223.

[5] *Śatapatha-Brahmana*, vii, 2, 2, 5.

[6] *AV*, xiv, 2, 14.

[7] ix, 33.

[8] Cf. Pisani, " La Donna et la terra ", *APS*, 1942–5, vol. xxxvii–xl, *passim*.

[9] Nyberg, p. 232, n. 83.

[10] Cf. Bagchi, *Pre-Aryan and pre-Dravidian in India*, Calcutta, 1929, p. 11; Eliade, *Yoga*, p. 291; *Le Yoga: Immortalité et Liberté*, p. 410.

has even been represented pictorially.[1]   The origins of this
representation are much older: a drawing of a plough of the
Kassite period shows joined to it symbols of the generative
act.[2] Primitive intuitions of this sort take a long time to disappear not only from the spoken tongue, but even from the
vocabulary of serious writers.   Rabelais used the expression
" the member we call the husbandman of nature ".[3]

And finally, for examples of the identification of agricultural
labour with the act of generation, consider the myth of the
birth of Sītā, the heroine of *Rāmāyaṇa*.   Her father Janaka
(the name means " progenitor ") found her in his field while
he was ploughing, and called her Sītā, " furrow ".[4]   An
Assyrian text brings to us the prayer addressed to a god " whose
plough has fertilized the earth ".[5]

Even to-day, a lot of primitive peoples still use magic amulets
representing the generative organs to make the earth fruitful.[6]
The Australian aboriginals practise a most curious fecundation
ritual: armed with arrows which they carry in phallic fashion,
they dance round a ditch shaped like the female generative
organ; and conclude by planting sticks in the ground.[7]   It
must be remembered what a close connection there is between
woman and sexuality on one hand and tilling and the fertility
of the soil on the other.   Thus, there is one custom whereby
naked maidens must mark out the first furrows with the plough,[8]
a custom which calls to mind the archetypal union of the
goddess Demeter with Jason at the beginning of spring, in a
freshly sown furrow.[9]   All these ceremonies and legends will
yield up their meaning when we come to study the structure of
agricultural cults.

[1] Cf. the reproductions in Dieterich, pp. 107–8.
[2] Cf. Jeremias, *Handbuch der altorientalischen Geisteskultur*, Berlin, 1929,
p. 387, fig. 214.
[3] *Gargantua*, bk. ii, ch. 1.
[4] *Rāmāyaṇa*, ch. 66; cf. other references in Coomaraswamy, *The Rig Veda
as landnama bok*, pp. 15, 33.
[5] Quoted by Langdon, *Semitic Mythology*, Boston, 1931, p. 99.
[6] Dieterich, p. 94.
[7] See references in Dieterich, pp. 94 ff.; on the erotic meaning of the stick,
cf. Meyer, *Trilogie altindische Mächte und Feste der vegetation*, Zürich-Leipzig,
1937, vol. iii, pp. 194 ff.
[8] There is a wealth of material in Mannhardt, *Wald- und Feld-kulte*, Berlin,
1904–5, vol. i, pp. 553 ff.; Frazer, *The Magic Art*, vol. i, pp. 469ff.; 480 ff.
[9] *Odyssey*, v, 125.

94. SYNTHESIS

In all the mythological and ritual patterns we have examined, the earth is primarily honoured for its endless capacity to bear fruit. That is why, with time, the Earth-Mother imperceptibly turned into the Corn Mother. But the theophany of the soil never totally disappeared from the picture of " Mothers ", or earth divinities. To give but one example, we can perceive attributes that were originally those of the Earth-Mother in all the female figures of the Greek religion—Nemesis, the Furies, Themis. And Aeschylus[1] prays first to the Earth, then to Themis. It is true that Ge or Gaia was eventually replaced by Demeter, but the Hellenes never lost the consciousness of the bond between the goddess of cereals and the Earth-Mother. Euripides,[2] speaking of Demeter, says: " She is the Earth. . . . Call her what you will ! "

Agricultural divinities took the place of the primitive divinities of the soil, but this substitution did not involve the abolition of all the primeval rites. Underlying the " form " of the agricultural Great Goddesses, we can still detect the presence of the " mistress of the place ", the Earth-Mother, But the newer divinities are clearer in feature, more dynamic in their religious structure. Their history starts to involve emotion—they *live* the drama of birth, fertility and death. The turning of the Earth-Mother into the Great Goddess of agriculture is the turning of simple existence into living drama.

From the cosmic hierogamy of heaven and earth to the least of the practices that bear witness to the holiness of the soil, the same central intuition comes in as a constantly repeated *leitmotiv*: the earth produces living forms, it is a womb which never wearies of procreating. In every kind of phenomenon to which the epiphany of the soil has given rise—whether a " sacred presence ", a still formless divinity, a clearly-defined divine figure, or merely a " custom " that results from some confused memory of subterranean powers—everywhere we can discern the activity of motherhood, of an inexhaustible power of creation. This creation may be of a monstrous kind, as in Hesiod's myth of Gaia. But the monsters of the *Theogony* merely illustrate the endless creative resources of the

[1] *Eumenides*, 1.
[2] *Bacchæ*, 274.

Earth. In some cases the sex of this earth divinity, this universal procreatrix—does not even have to be defined. A great many earth divinities, and some divinities of fertility, are bisexual.[1] In such cases the divinity contains all the forces of creation— and this formula of polarity, of the coexistence of opposites, was to be taken up again in the loftiest of later speculation. All divinities tend to become *everything* to their believers, to take the place of all other religious figures, to rule over every sphere of the cosmos. And few divinities have ever had as much right or power to become *everything* as had the earth. But the ascent of the Earth-Mother to the position of the supreme, if not unique, divinity, was arrested both by her hierogamy with the sky and by the appearance of the divinities of agriculture. And traces of this tremendous story are preserved in the bisexuality of certain of the earth divinities. But the Earth-Mother never entirely lost her primitive prerogatives of being " mistress of the place ", source of all living forms, keeper of children, and womb where the dead were laid to rest, where they were reborn to return eventually to life, thanks to the holiness of Mother Earth.

[1] Cf. Nyberg, pp. 231, n. 69 and 72.

BIBLIOGRAPHY

The divine pair, Sky and Earth: PETTAZZONI, R., *Dio*, vol. i, pp. 130, 210, 241, etc.; KRAPPE, A. H., *La Genèse des mythes*, pp. 68 ff.; FISCHER, H. T., *Het Heilig Huwelik van Hemel en Aarde*, Utrecht, 1929; supplementary bibliographical suggestions in THOMPSON, Stith, *Motif-Index of Folk-Literature*, Helsinki, 1932, vol. i, p. 98; cf. also the bibliography following Chapter II. There is a great deal of ethnological research in STAUDACHER, W., *Die Trennung von Himmel und Erde*, Tübingen, 1942, and also in NUMAZAWA, F. Kiichi, *Die Weltanfänge in der japanischen Mythologie*, Lucerne, 1946; cf. ELIADE, M., "La Terre-Mère et les hiérogamies cosmiques", *EJ*, Zürich, 1954, vol. xxii.

On the Earth Mother: LANG, A., *Myth, Ritual and Religion*, London, 1887, pp. 299 ff.; DIETERICH, A., *Mutter Erde*, 3rd ed., Berlin, 1925, *passim;* LINDENAU, Max, "Ein vedischer Lobgesang auf die Mutter Erde als die grosse Allgottheit (*Ath. Ved.*, XII, 1)", *Festgabe Hermann Jacobi*, Bonn, 1926, pp. 248–58; MARCONI, Momolina, *Riflessi mediterranei nella più antica religione laziale*, Milan, 1939, *passim*; PESTALOZZA, U., *Pagine di religione mediterranea*, Milan, 1942, vol. i, *passim*; WEINSTOCK, S., "Tellus", *GLA*, 1933–4, vol. xxii, pp. 140–162; NOLDECKE, "Mutter-Erde bei den Semiten", *AFRW*, 1905, vol. viii, pp. 161 ff.; DHORME, E. P., "La Terre-Mère chez les Assyriens", *AFRW*, 1905, vol. viii, pp. 550 ff.; BRIEM, E., "Mutter Erde bei den Semiten", *AFRW*, 1926, vol. xxiv, pp. 179–95; NIELSEN, Dietlef, "Die altsemitische Mutter-göttin", *Zeitschr. der deutschen morgenländischen Gesel.*, 1938, pp. 504–31; HOLMBERG-HARVA, Uno, *Finno-Ugric Mythology*, Boston, 1927, pp. 239–459; WERNER, Alice, *African Mythology*, Boston, 1925, p. 125; STRUCK, B., "Nochmals 'Mutter Erde' in Afrika", *AFRW*, 1908, vol. xi, pp. 402 ff.; ALEXANDER, H. B., *North American Mythology*, Boston, 1916, pp. 91 ff.; FUCHS, Stefan, "The Cult of the Earth-Mother among the Nimar-Balahis", *IAFE*, vol. xl, pp. 1–8; for the Bhils' prayers to the Earth-Mother, see KOPPERS, W., "Bhagwan, The Supreme Deity of the Bhils", *APS*, 1940–1, vol. xxxv–xxxvi, pp. 265–325, particularly 272 and 273.

On the divinities and cults of the soil: THOMPSON, Stith, *Motif-Index*, vol. i, p. 83; NYBERG, B., *Kind und Erde*, Helsinki, 1931, pp. 230–1, n. 69; FRAZER, Sir J., *The Worship of Nature*, London, 1926, pp. 316–440; WALTER, E., "Die Erdgöttin der Tschuwaschen und Litauer", *AFRW*, 1899, vol. iii, pp. 358 ff.; WILKE, Georg, *Die Religion der Indogermanen in archäologischer Betrachtung*, Leipzig, 1923, pp. 97–107; VON WESEN-DONCK, "Aremati als arische Erd-Gottheit", *AFRW*, 1929, vol. xxxii, pp. 61–76; NESTLE, E., "Die 'jungfräuliche' Erde", *AFRW*, 1908, vol. xi, pp. 415 ff.

On the myth of Adam born of the Virgin Earth: VOLLMER, H., "Die Erde als jungfräuliche Mutter Adams", *ZNW*, 1911, vol. x, pp. 324 ff.; STARCK, W., "Eva-Maria", *ZNW*, 1934, vol. xxxiii, pp. 97–109; on the creation of man from the earth, there is a rich bibliography in BRIFFAULT, R., *The Mothers*, London, 1927, vol. iii, p. 57.

On the placing of children on the ground: DIETERICH, op. cit., pp. 7 ff.; SAMTER, E., *Geburt, Hochzeit und Tod*, Berlin, 1911, pp. 2 ff.; GOLD-MANN, E., "Cartam levare", *MIOG*, 1914, vol. xxxv, pp. 1 ff.; STRUCK,

B., " Niederlegen und Aufheben des Kindes von der Erde ", *AFRW*, 1907, vol. x, p. 158; supplementary suggestions and bibliography, NYBERG, B., op. cit., pp. 158 ff.; ROSE, H. J., *Primitive Culture in Italy*, London, 1926, p. 133; for a quantity of ethnographical research, see PLOSS and BARTELS, *Woman: An Historical, Gynæcological and Anthropological Compendium*, London, 1935, vol. ii, pp. 35 ff.; DELCOURT, Marie, *Stérilités mystérieuses et naissances maléfiques dans l'antiquité classique*, Paris, 1938, pp. 31 ff.; BRIFFAULT, *The Mothers*, vol. iii, p. 58; GRANET, Marcel, " Le Dépôt de l'enfant sur le sol. Rites anciens et ordalies mythiques ", *RAR*, 1922; reprinted in the volume *Etudes Sociologiques sur la Chine*, Paris, 1953, pp. 159–202.

On the identification of woman and field : in addition to the suggestions already given in the text, see DIETERICH, op. cit., pp. 46 ff.; FEHRLE, E., *Die kultische Keuschheit im Albertum*, Geissen, 1910, pp. 170 ff.; FARNELL, *The Cults of the Greek States*, Oxford, 1896–1909, vol. iii, pp. 106 ff.; LEVY-BRUHL, *Primitive Mentality*, London, 1923, pp. 315 ff.; ROBERTSON SMITH, *The Religion of the Semites*, 3rd ed., London, 1927, pp. 613 ff. (A propos Robertson Smith's remarks on Ba'al, " master of the earth ", cf. Lagrange, *Etudes sur les religions sémitiques*, 2nd ed., p. 97; DUSSAUD, R., *Origines cananéennes du sacrifice israélite*, Paris, 1941, p. 206; id., *Les Découvertes de Ras Shamra*, 2nd ed., Paris, 1941, p. 102; MEYER, J. J., *Trilogie altindischer Mächte und Feste der Vegetation*, Zürich-Leipzig, 1937, vol. i, p. 202; PESTALOZZA, U., " L'Aratro e la donna nel mondo religioso mediterraneo ", *Rendiconti, Reale Instituto Lombardo di Scienze e Lettere, Cl. di Lettere*, 1942–3, vol. lxxvi, no. 2, pp. 321–30; PISANI, Vittore, " La Donna e la terra ", *APS*, 1942–5, vol. xxxvii–xl, pp. 241–53 ; (a wealth of Indian and Græco-Latin material).

On ritual burials : DIETERICH, op. cit., pp. 28 ff.; NYBERG, B., op. cit., p. 150; FRAZER, Sir J., *Folklore in the Old Testament*, London, 1918, vol. ii, p. 33; BRELICH, A., *Aspetti della morte nelle inscrizioni sepolcrali dell'Impero Romano*, Budapest, 1937, pp. 9 ff.

On the rebirth of ancestors in newborn children : ECKHARDT, K. A., *Indische Unsterblichkeit*, Weimar, 1937; ASHLEY-MONTAGU, M. F., " Ignorance of Physiological Paternity in Secular Knowledge and Orthodox Belief among the Australian Aborigines ", *OA*, 1940–2, vol. xii, pp. 75–8.

On burial " in the shape of an embryo ", cf. VAN DER LEEUW, G., " Das sogenannte Hockerbegräbnis und der ägyptische Tjknw ", *SMSR*, 1938, vol. xiv, pp. 150–67.

On the " literary mythologies " of the earth, see BACHELARD, Gaston, *La Terre et les rêveries de la volonté*; id., *La Terre et les rêveries du repos*, Paris, 1948, 2 vols.

VIII

VEGETATION:
RITES AND SYMBOLS OF REGENERATION

95. A PRELIMINARY CLASSIFICATION

THE prophetess, the *Völva*, awoken from a deep sleep by
Odhin to reveal the beginning and end of the world to the
gods, declares:[1]

> I remember giants born at the dawn of time
> And those who first gave birth to me.
> I know nine worlds, nine spheres covered by the tree of the
> world,
> That tree set up in wisdom which grows down to the bosom of
> the earth.
> I know there is an ash tree they call Yggdrasil
> The top of the tree is bathed in watery white vapours,
> And drops of dew fall from it into the valley.
> It stands up green, forever, above the fountain of Urd.

The cosmos is pictured here as an immense tree. This ideogram of Scandinavian mythology has its counterpart in innumerable other traditions. Before noting each individually,
we might try to glance over the whole domain we are to study:
sacred trees, symbols, myths and rites of plant life. There is a
considerable amount of material; but it takes such a variety
of forms as to baffle any attempt at systematic classification.
Indeed, we meet sacred trees, and vegetation rites and symbols
in the history of every religion, in popular tradition the world
over, in primitive metaphysics and mysticism, to say nothing of
iconography and popular art. All this material comes from a
great variety of ages and cultures. Obviously the context of
Yggdrasil, for instance, or of the Tree of Life in Scripture, is
completely different from that of the " marriage of trees "
still practised to-day in India, or of the " May tree " borne
in ritual in the springtime in the villages of Europe. At the
level of popular piety, the ritual tree fulfills a role which the
tree symbolism that we can reconstruct from Near Eastern
documentation also implies, but that role is far from exhausting
all the depth and wealth of meaning the symbolism has. We

[1] *Völuspa*, st. 2 and 19.

can identify fairly clearly the starting points of certain fundamental notions (as, for instance, that of the cosmic tree or
vegetal rites of regeneration), and this to some extent helps us
to classify our material. But this question of the " history "
of the various motifs is only of secondary interest to our
particular study.

Before attempting to find out—if indeed it is possible to find
out—in what millennium, in what civilization and by what
means a given plant symbolism became widespread, before
even distinguishing the various ritual frameworks embodying
it, what matters to us at the moment is to find out the *religious
function* of trees, of plants, and of vegetal symbols in religious
life and the economy of the sacred, and then to see what that
function reveals and what it means; to see, in fact, to what
extent we are justified in seeking to find a coherent pattern
beneath the apparent polymorphousness of tree symbolism.
What we must find out is this: is there a close connection among
the significations—apparently so diverse—that " vegetation "
assumes, the meanings that give it its value in the various
contexts in which it is found—cosmology, myth, theology,
ritual, iconography, folklore ? Obviously the coherence we are
looking to find must be one which the very nature of the thing
imposes on our mind; a coherence displaying itself—wholly
or in part—from whatever level we look at it, whether it be that
of popular rite (such as the May procession at the beginning of
spring), or perhaps that of the ideogram of the " cosmic tree "
in Mesopotamian art or in Vedic writings.

We shall not know the answer to this question until we have
looked at a certain amount of evidence, and evidence of the
more important kind. But to avoid getting totally lost in the
labyrinth, I suggest a provisory classification of the vast amount
of material that faces us. Leaving aside all the religious values
and ceremonies of agriculture—which we shall be studying in a
separate chapter—we may distinguish in what we may call, for
want of a closer and more convenient formula, " vegetation
cults ", the following groupings:

(*a*) the pattern of stone-tree-altar, which constitutes an
effective microcosm in the most ancient stages of religious life
(Australia; China; Indochina and India; Phoenicia and the
Aegean);

(b) the tree as *image* of the cosmos (India; Mesopotamia; etc.);

(c) the tree as a cosmic theophany (Mesopotamia; India; the Aegean);

(d) the tree as *symbol of life*, of inexhaustible fertility, of absolute reality; as related to the Great Goddess or the symbolism of water (Yakṣa, for instance); as identified with the fount of immortality (" The Tree of Life "), etc.;

(e) the tree as *centre* of the world and *support* of the universe (among the Altaics, Scandinavians, etc.);

(f) *mystical bonds* between trees and men (trees giving birth to men; the tree as the repository of the souls of man's ancestors; the marriage of trees; the presence of trees in initiation ceremonies, etc.);

(g) the tree as symbol of the resurrection of vegetation, of spring and of the " rebirth " of the year (the " May " procession for instance, etc.).

This brief and obviously incomplete classification has at least the merit of drawing our attention from the start to those characteristics common to all the evidence. Without in any way anticipating the conclusions that will come from analysing that evidence, we may note at once that the tree represents—whether ritually and concretely, or in mythology and cosmology, or simply symbolically—the *living cosmos*, endlessly renewing itself. Since inexhaustible life is the equivalent of immortality, the tree-cosmos may therefore become, at a different level, the tree of " life undying ". And as this inexhaustible life was, in primitive ontology, an expression of the notion of *absolute reality*, the tree becomes for it a symbol of that reality (" the centre of the world "). Later on, when a new way of looking at metaphysical problems came to be added to the traditional ontology (in India, for example), the effort of the mind detaching itself from the rhythm of the cosmos and concentrating on its own autonomy, came to be designated as an effort to " cut the cosmic tree at its roots "—in other words, to get completely beyond all " appearances ", all representations, and beyond their source—the ever-flowing spring of universal life.

96. THE SACRED TREE

One wonders what mental synthesis, and from what special

characteristics of trees as such enabled primitive mankind to produce so vast and so coherent a symbolism. What we want is not so much to discern how a religious evaluation first came to be made, but to discover the oldest and therefore purest intuitions of it. It is certain that, to the primitive religious mind, the tree (or rather, certain specific trees) represented a *power*. And it must be added that that *power* was as much due to the tree as such as to any cosmological implications it had. To the primitive mind, nature and symbol were inseparable. A tree impressed itself on the religious consciousness by its substance and its shape, but this substance and this shape became significant just because they impressed themselves on the religious consciousness, because they were " singled out ", because, that is, they had " revealed " themselves. Neither the phenomenology nor the history of religion can by-pass the statement of this inseparable connection between nature and symbolism which the intuition of the sacred renders so valuable. It is not therefore correct to speak of a " tree cult ". No tree was ever adored for itself only, but always for what was revealed through it, for what it implied and signified. Magic and healing plants too, as we shall see later (§111 ff.), owe their efficacy to a mythological prototype. In studying the representations of the " sacred tree " in Mesopotamia and in Elam, Nell Parrot writes: " There is no cult of the tree itself; there is always some spiritual being hidden behind the representation ".[1] And another author, doing research in the same field, concludes that the sacred tree of Mesopotamia is more a symbol than a cult-object. " It is not the copy of a real tree embellished with any number of ornaments, but a completely artificial stylisation, and it seems to me to be, not so much a real object of worship, as a symbol with enormous power for good."[2] With only slight modifications, these conclusions are true elsewhere too.

Thus—and here we come back to the earliest intuitions of the sacred value of plants—it is in virtue of its *power,* in virtue of what it *expresses* (which is something beyond itself), that the tree becomes a religious object. But this power is in fact validated by an ontology: if the tree is charged with sacred

[1] *Les Représentations de l'arbre sacré sur les monuments de Mésopotamie et d'Elam*, Paris, 1937, p. 19.
[2] Danthine, *Le Palmier-dattier et les arbres sacrés dans l'iconographie de l'Asie occidentale ancienne*, Paris, 1937, pp. 163–4.

forces, it is because it is vertical, it grows, it loses its leaves and regains them and is thus regenerated (it " dies " and " rises " again) times without number, because it gives out latex, and so on. By simply being there (" power ") and by its natural laws of development (" regeneration "), the tree re-enacts what, to the primitive understanding, *is* the whole cosmos. The tree can, of course, become a *symbol* of the universe, and in that form we find it in more developed civilizations; but to a primitive religious mind, the tree *is* the universe, and it *is* so because it reproduces it and as it were sums it up as well as " symbolizing " it. This first notion of the " symbol ", by which symbols owe their validity to the fact that the reality they symbolize is embodied in them, will be defined more clearly when we come to approach the problem of the function and workings of symbols (§166 ff.).

All I want to point out here is the fact that the *Whole* exists within each *significant fragment*, not because the " law of participation " (as understood by Lévy-Bruhl) is valid, but because every significant fragment *reproduces* the Whole. A tree becomes sacred, while continuing to be a tree, because of the *power* it expresses; and if it becomes a *cosmic tree*, it is because what it *expresses* is a perfect reproduction of what the cosmos expresses. The sacred tree need not lose its concrete natural qualities to become symbolic (the date palm is so to the Mesopotamians, the oak to the Scandinavians, the *aśvattha* and the *nyagrodha* to the Hindus, etc.). Quite a number of mental stages must be gone through before the symbol becomes detached from concrete forms, before it becomes an abstract essence (cf. the quotation from Hélène Danthine above).

97. THE TREE AS MICROCOSM

The most primitive of the " sacred places " we know of constituted a microcosm, as Przyluski noted so rightly:[1] a landscape of stones, water, and trees. The Australian totem centre was very often situated in a sacred group of trees and stones. The triptych of tree, altar and stone to be found in the primitive " sacred places " of eastern Asia and India was brought to light by P. Mus,[2] though he saw it as developing

---

[1] *La Participation*, Paris, 1940, p. 41.
[2] *Bulletin de la soc. française de philosophie*, May-June, 1937, p. 107.

step by step in time (the sacred place starting off with a forest, and later becoming simply the pattern of tree, altar and stone), instead of seeing, as Przyluski rightly did, that all the elements were simultaneously coexistent. Indeed, the coupling of tree and stone is to be found in other parts of the primitive world. In the pre-Indian civilization of Mohenjo-Daro the sacred place consisted of an enclosure set up round a tree. Such sacred places were to be found all over India at the time when Buddha was preaching. The Pāli writings often mention the stone or altar (*veyaddi, manco*) placed beside a sacred tree, which formed the framework for the popular worship of the fertility divinities (the Yaksas). This ancient habit of associating trees with stones was accepted and absorbed by Buddhism. The Buddhist *caitya* was sometimes simply a tree, without any altar; but at other times, it was the rudimentary construction erected beside the tree.[1] Neither Buddhism nor Hinduism could weaken the religious significance of the ancient sacred places. The great religious syntheses of post-Buddhist India were obliged to take these sacred places into account, and in the end actually absorbed them into themselves and so ratified them completely.

The same continuity can be observed in Greece and in the Semitic world. From Minoan times right up till the twilight of Hellenism, we always find the tree used for worship beside a rock.[2] Primitive Semitic sanctuaries often consisted of a tree and a bethel.[3] The tree or *asera* (barkless trunk used in place of a green tree) came later to remain alone beside the altar. The Canaanites and Hebrews had their places of sacrifice " on every high hill and under every green tree ".[4] The same prophet recalls the sins of the children of Juda, the altars and images of Astarte which they set up under " their green trees upon the high mountains ".[5] A post, vertical and substantial, added to the sacred power present in the tree. The inscription—only partly decipherable—upon the archaic Sumerian monument known as " the figure with feathers ", says: " Ennamaz placed

---

[1] Cf. numerous examples in Coomaraswamy, *Yakṣas*, Washington, 1928, vol. i, pp. 12 ff.

[2] Nilsson, *Geschichte*, vol. i, p. 260.

[3] Robertson Smith, *Lectures on the Religion of the Semites*, 3rd ed., London, 1927, p. 187, etc.

[4] Jer. ii. 20; cf. iii. 6.

[5] Jer. xvii. 1–3.

the bricks surely; the princely dwelling made, he placed a great tree nearby; by the tree, he set up a pillar."[1]

The " sacred place " is a microcosm, because it *reproduces* the natural landscape; because it is a reflection of the Whole. The altar and the temple (or funeral monument, or palace), which are later developments of the primitive " sacred place ", are also microcosms, because they are *centres of the world*, because they stand at the very heart of the Universe and constitute an *imago mundi* (§143). The idea of " centre ", of absolute reality—absolute because it is a repository of the sacred—is implied in even the most primitive conceptions of the " sacred place ", and, as we have already seen, such conceptions always include a sacred tree. Stone stood supremely for reality : indestructibility and lastingness; the tree, with its periodic regeneration, manifested the power of the sacred in the order of life. And when water came to complete this landscape, it signified latencies, seeds, and purification (§60). The " microcosmic landscape " gradually became reduced in time to but one of its constituents, to the most important : the tree or sacred pillar. The tree came to express the cosmos fully in itself, by embodying, in apparently static form, its " force ", its life and its quality of periodic regeneration.

98. THE DIVINITY DWELLING IN TREES

The actual changing-over of the " sacred place " as an image of the microcosm to a cosmic tree conceived also as the dwelling of the divinity, is preserved admirably in a Babylonian incantation that has been translated by a great many orientalists :

> In Eridu there grows a black *kiskanu*, it was made in a holy place;
> Its radiance is of shining lapis-lazuli, it stretches towards the *apsu*
> It is the walking place of Ea in rich Eridu,
> Its dwelling is a place of rest for Bau . . .[2]

The tree *kiskanu* displays all the characteristics of the cosmic tree : it is at Eridu, which is a " centre of the world "; in a sacred place, that is in the centre of reality (§140 ff.); with its shining it resembles lapis lazuli, which is *the* cosmic symbol above all others (the starry night);[3] it spreads towards the

[1] Parrot, p. 43.
[2] Dhorme's rendering.
[3] Cf. Eliade, *Cosmologia si alchimie babiloniana*, Bucharest, 1937, pp. 51 ff.

ocean which surrounds and supports the world (are we to understand that this tree spreads towards the ocean *with its branches*, or in other words that it is an " inverted tree " like some cosmic trees ?); it is the dwelling place of the god of fertility and of the civilizing sciences (arts, agriculture, the skills of writing, and so on); and it is the place where Ea's mother, Bau, rests, who is the goddess of plenty, of flocks and of agriculture.

Kiskanu may be looked upon as one of the prototypes of the Babylonian " sacred tree ", whose frequent appearance in the iconography of the ancient East is very significant. Its position in iconography proves conclusively that the " sacred tree " we find in those places means something more than merely a tree cult, that it has a very clear cosmological significance. There are almost always symbols with the tree, heraldic figures or emblems which make its cosmic significance clear and complete. For instance, the earliest instance we have of it, a fragment of vase discovered by the Gautier expedition to Moussian, represents a stylized tree, surrounded by lozenges.[1] In Mesopotamian iconography, the tree is usually surrounded by goats, stars, birds or snakes. Each of these emblems has a definite cosmological meaning. Stars beside a tree are a sure indication that the tree has a cosmological significance.[2] An archaic sketch from Susa[3] shows a serpent rising up vertically to taste a tree (Toscane allies this scene to the tree-serpent motif and interprets it as a Babylonian prototype of the Bible story we know so well).

Iconography offers other related scenes: a bird poised on a tree, surrounded by goats;[4] the tree, the solar disc, and men, all ritually disguised as fish,[5] or the tree, winged spirits and the solar disc.[6] I have merely mentioned a few of the most significant and most common groups and do not, of course, claim to have exhausted the wealth of evidence from Mesopotamia. But the cosmological significance which the tree

[1] Parrot, 22. The mystical meaning of the lozenge is already present in Magdalenian art; cf. Hentze, *Mythes et symboles lunaires*, p. 124.
[2] Cf. for instance, figs. 8–9 in Parrot, reproducing objects from Elam of the second millennium; and the entire series of Babylonian cylinders, figs. 21 ff., etc.
[3] Parrot, fig. 12.
[4] Parrot, figs. 35–6, etc.
[5] Parrot, figs. 110, 111.
[6] Parrot, figs. 100, 104, etc.

continually has in these patterns is clear.[1] None of the emblems attached to trees can be interpreted in a naturist sense for the simple reason that nature itself was something quite different in Mesopotamian thought from what it is in modern thought and experience. We need only remind ourselves that to the Mesopotamians, as to primitive man in general, no being, no action that *means* anything has any effectiveness except in so far as the being has a heavenly prototype, or the action reproduces a primeval cosmological one.

99. THE COSMIC TREE

Indian tradition, according to its earliest writings,[2] represents the cosmos in the form of a giant tree. This idea is defined fairly formally in the Upaniṣads: the Universe is an inverted tree, burying its roots in the sky and spreading its branches over the whole earth. (It is not impossible that this image was suggested by the downpouring of the sun's rays. Cf. *Ṛg Veda*:[3] " The branches grow towards what is low, the roots are on high, that its rays may descend upon us ! ") The *Kaṭha-Upaniṣad*[4] describes it like this: " This eternal Aśvattha, whose roots rise on high, and whose branches grow low, is the pure [*śukram*], is the Brahman, is what we call the Non-Death. All the worlds rest in it ! " The *aśvattha* tree here represents the clearest possible manifestation of Brahman in the Cosmos, represents, in other words, creation as a descending movement. Other texts from the Upaniṣads restate still more clearly this notion of the cosmos as a tree. " Its branches are the ether, the air, fire, water, earth ", etc.[5] The natural elements are the expression of this " Brahman whose name is Aśvattha ".[6]

In the *Bhagavad-Gītā*, the cosmic tree comes to express not only the universe, but also man's condition in the world: " It is said that there is an indestructible tree, its roots above, its branches below, its leaves the hymns of the Veda; whoever knows it knows the Veda also. Its branches increase in height

---

[1] Cf. also the material listed by A. J. Wensinck in his interesting study of trees and birds as cosmological symbols in Western Asia, which Parrot makes no use of.

[2] e.g., *AV*, ii, 7, 3; x, 7, 38; etc.

[3] i, 24, 7.

[4] vi, 1.

[5] *Maitri Up.*, vi .7.

[6] Ibid.

and depth, growing on the *guṇas*; its buds are the objects of sense; its roots spread out from below, bound to actions in the world of men. In this world one cannot perceive the shape, nor the end, nor the beginning, nor the expanse of it. With the strong weapon of renunciation, one must first cut down this *aśvattha* with its powerful roots, and then seek the place from which one never returns . . . "[1] The whole universe, as well as the experience of man who lives in it and is not detached from it, are here symbolized by the cosmic tree. By everything in himself which corresponds with the cosmos or shares in its life, man merges into the same single and immense manifestation of Brahman. " To cut the tree at its roots " means to withdraw man from the cosmos, to cut him off from the things of sense and the fruits of his actions. We find the same motif of detachment from the life of the cosmos, of withdrawal into oneself and recollection as man's only way of transcending himself and becoming free, in a text from the *Mahābhārata*. " Sprung from the Unmanifested,[2] arising from it as only support, its trunk is *bodhi*, its inward cavities the channels of the sense, the great elements its branches, the objects of the senses its leaves, its fair flowers good and evil [*dharmādharmav*], pleasure and pain the consequent fruits. This eternal Brahma-tree [*brahmavṛkṣa*] is the source of life [*abjīva*] for all beings . . . Having cut asunder and broken the tree with the weapon of *gnosis* [*jananeña*], and thenceforth taking pleasure in the Spirit, none returneth thither again."[3]

100. THE INVERTED TREE

This is not the place for a philosophical exegesis on the texts quoted above. All we need here is to grasp this identification of the cosmos with the inverted tree. This mythological and metaphysical ideogram is not the only one of its kind. Masudi mentions[4] a Sabean tradition which has it that Plato declared man to be a plant turned upside down, whose roots stretch

[1] xv, 1–3.

[2] *Avyakta* or the *asat* of *AV*, x, 7, 21.

[3] *Aśvamedha Parva*, 47, 12–15, quoted by Coomaraswamy, " The Inverted Tree ", *The Quarterly Journal of the Mythic Society*, Bangalore, 1938, vol. xxix, no. 2, p. 20, from the version used by Śaṅkara in his commentary on the *Bhagavad Gītā*, xv, 1.

[4] *Morug-el-Dscheb*, 64, 6.

to heaven and whose branches to earth.[1] The same tradition
occurs in Hebraic esoteric teaching: " Now the Tree of Life
extends from above downward, and it is the Sun which illumin-
ates all."[2] The same thing occurs in the Islamic tradition of the
" Tree of Happiness ", whose roots are sunk in the furthest
heaven and whose branches spread over the earth.[3] Dante
represents the celestial spheres all together as the garland of a
tree whose roots are directed upwards:

> In questa quinta soglia
> Dell' albero che vive della cima,
> e fruta sempre, e mai non perde foglia.[4]

The " fifth lodgment " is the sphere of the planet Jupiter.
The " tree whose life is from its top " is a tree turned upside
down. Another Florentine poet, very much influenced by
Dante, Federigo Frezzi, describes " the most beautiful plant of
Paradise, the happy plant which preserves its life and renews
it " and " whose roots are above, in heaven, whose branches
grow towards earth ":

> Su dentro al cielo avea la sua radice
> e giù inverso terra i rami spande.[5]

Holmberg-Harva finds the same tradition in Finnish and
Icelandic folklore (op. cit., p. 55). The Lapps used to sacrifice
an ox every year to the god of vegetation, and on this occasion
a tree was placed near the altar with its roots in the air and its
branches on the ground.[6] In the Wiradjuri and Kamilaroi
tribes of Australia, the witch doctors had a magic tree which
they planted upside down. Having daubed the roots with
human blood, they burned it.[7] And in connection with this

---

[1] Quoted by Holmberg-Harva, " Der Baum des Lebens ", *AASF*, Helsinki,
1922–3, series B, vol. xvi, p. 54.

[2] *Zohar*, Beha' Alotheka, with reference to Ps .xix. 6; quoted by Coomaraswamy, p. 21.

[3] Cf. Wensinck, " Tree and Bird as Cosmological Symbols in Western Asia ",
Verhandelingen der Koninklijke Akademie van Wettenschappen, Amsterdam, 1921,
vol. xxii, p. 33; Asin Palacio, *La Escatologia musulmana en la Divina Comedia*,
2nd ed., Madrid, 1942, p. 235.

[4] " On this fifth lodgment of the tree, whose life is from its top, whose fruit
is ever fair, and leaf unwithering ". (*Paradiso*, xviii, 28 ff., Cary's translation.)

[5] *Il Quadriregio*, bk. iv, ch. ii, quoted by A. Graf, *Miti, leggende, e superstizioni
del medio Evo*,Turin, 1925, p. 157.

[6] Ibid; cf. Kagarow, " Der Umgekehrte Schamanenbaum ", *AFRW*, 1929, p.
183.

[7] Schmidt, *Ursprung*, vol. iii, pp. 1030 ff.

custom, Schmidt notes the initiation ceremonies used in another Australian tribe, the Yuin;[1] a young man, acting as if dead, is buried, and a bush is placed on top of him. When the neophytes, candidates for initiation, come near him, the young man shakes the bush, and then rises and comes out of the tomb. The bush, Schmidt tells us, represents the celestial Tree of the Stars.[2]

101. YGGDRASIL

The cosmic tree, together with either birds,[3] horses or tigers,[4] is also to be found in primitive China; there, as elsewhere, it is sometimes confounded with the Tree of Life. What this confusion means will become clearer in the pages that follow. We find this combination of cosmic tree and mythical lunar animal in an example of Mayan iconography which shows a jaguar attached to the Tree of Life.[5] Among the Arctic peoples, and those around the Pacific, the Cosmic Tree—with its branches spreading to the third or even the seventh heaven— plays a central role, both in mythology and in ritual. It is often related to the mythological ancestor, men thinking themselves descended from an ancestor born of a tree.[6] Further on I shall be dwelling at length on these myths of man's descent from a cosmologico-vegetal symbol.

Yggdrasil is a Cosmic Tree *par excellence*. Its roots go to the very heart of the earth, where hell and the kingdom of the giants are to be found.[7] Near it is the miraculous fountain of Mimir (" meditation ", " memory "), where Odhin left one eye as a pledge, and where he constantly returns to refresh and enrich his wisdom.[8] The fountain of Urd is also to be found near Yggdrasil; there the gods hold daily council and deliver justice. The Norns water the giant tree with the water of this fountain to revive its youth and vigour. Heidrun, the goat, an eagle, a stag and a squirrel dwell in the branches of Yggdrasil; the viper Nidhoggr is at its roots, and constantly

---

[1] Schmidt, pp. 757 ff.; 806.
[2] Cf. also Hentze, *Mythes et Symboles*, pp. 182 ff.
[3] Hentze, pl. vi.
[4] Hentze, pl. vii, viii, fig. 148.
[5] This scene figures in the Codex Borbonicus, fig. 149 (Hentze).
[6] Eliade, *Chamanisme*, Paris, 1951, pp. 244 ff.
[7] *Völuspa*, 19; *Grimnismal*, 31.
[8] *Völuspa*, 28, 39.

tries to destroy it. Every day the eagle gives battle to the viper (a cosmological motif often found in other civilizations as well).[1] When the universe trembles to its foundations in the cataclysm predicted by the *Völuspa*, and which will put an end to the world to inaugurate a new, paradisal, era, Yggdrasil will be severely shaken, but not brought down.[2] This apocalyptic conflagration, announced by the prophetess, will not result in the complete disintegration of the cosmos.

Kaarle Krohn attempted to explain the myth of Yggdrasil by the Tree of Life in the Old Testament, and Sophus Bugge by the story of the Cross of Christ. But neither is a satisfactory hypothesis. Odhin tethers his horse to Yggdrasil, and it is hard to think that this very central motif of Scandinavian mythology can be of such late date. Holmberg-Harva[3] notes quite rightly that the presence of the eagle upon Yggdrasil—a detail absent from the biblical tradition—brings this cosmological symbol rather closer to those of Northern Asia. The fight between the eagle and the snake, like the struggle between Garuḍa and the reptile—a very common motif in Indian mythology and iconography—is a cosmological symbol of the struggle between light and darkness, of the opposition of the two principles, that of the sun and that of the underworld. It is hard to say whether or no any Judaeo-Christian elements have come into the notion of the Yggdrasil, for from what Holmberg-Harva has discovered of the affinities between this cosmic tree of Scandinavian myth and those of Northern Asia, it cannot strictly be shown to have originated with them. In any case, Alfred Detering has shown, in a well-documented work, *Die Bedeutung der Eiche seit der Vorzeit*[4] that the embodiment of the Cosmic Tree and the Tree of Life in an oak tree by the Indo-Europeans may be traced right back to prehistoric times, and that it was anyhow the proto-Germanic peoples who developed this myth in the north of Europe. The amalgamation of the Cosmic Tree with the Tree of Life is also found among the Teutons. We have already noted the identification of a sacred or mythical tree with one definite botanical species (the *aśvattha* with the Indians; the date palm with the

---

[1] Cf. Eliade, *Mitul Reintegrarii*, Bucharest, 1942, pp. 41 ff.; 52.
[2] *Völuspa*, 45.
[3] " Der Baum des Lebens ", p. 67.
[4] Leipzig, 1939.

Mesopotamians and so on). In the case of Yggdrasil, the presence of the oak on prehistoric monuments, the unbroken succession of motifs representing the sacred tree as an oak, and the oak leaves used in decorative and religious art, make it abundantly clear that this conception is an autochthonous one.

102. PLANT EPIPHANIES

A divinity manifested in a tree is a motif that runs through all Near-Eastern plastic art; it can also be found in the whole Indo-Mesopotamo-Egypto-Aegean area.[1] Most often, the scene represents the epiphany of some divinity of fertility. The cosmos reveals itself to us as a manifestation of the creative powers of God. Thus, at Mohenjo-Daro (in the third millennium B.C.), we find a divine epiphany in a *ficus religiosa*;[2] the tree is stylized in a manner reminiscent of the Mesopotamian sacred tree. Even in Vedic texts, we find traces of a plant theophany. Besides the *aśvattha*, a symbol of the cosmos, and Brahman revealed in a tree (§99), one may also discern in those of the Vedic documents which express a " popular religious experience ", which, in other words, preserve the concrete, primitive formulæ, other expressions of the manifestation of God in vegetation. " O Herbs ! Oh, you who are mothers ! I hail you as goddesses ! " exclaims the *Yajur Veda*.[3] A long hymn from the *Ṛg Veda*[4] is devoted to plants, with particular reference to their healing and regenerating powers (a suggestion of the Herb of Life and of Immortality). The *Atharva Veda*[5] praises a plant, calling it: " Divinity born of the Earth Goddess ". This same theophany at the vegetal level explains the " lord of plants", Vanaspati, whose cult is mentioned in the *Ṛg Veda*.[6] Because of the cosmic prototype from which they derive their powers, herbs make childbirth easier, increase man's generative powers, and assure fertility and wealth. That is why it is even sometimes commanded to offer animal sacrifice

[1] Cf. also Pestalozza, *Pagine di religione mediterranea*, Milan, 1945, vol. ii, p. 260.
[2] Marshall, *Mohenjo-Daro and the Indus Civilization*, London, 1931, vol. i, pl. xii, fig. 18.
[3] iv, 2, 6.
[4] x, 97.
[5] iv, 136, 1.
[6] vii, 34, 23; x, 64, 8.

to plants.[1] The *Śatapatha Brahmaṇa*[2] formulates the pattern of the generative energy in the cosmos as made up of thunder, rain, and plants. Here the sacred is made manifest in the essential act of the renewal of vegetative life.

An excellent example of a theophany in a tree is the famous bas-relief of Assur,[3] which represents the god with the upper part of his body coming out of a tree. Beside him is "water pouring out" of an inexhaustible vase, which symbolises fertility. A goat, an attribute of divinity, is feeding off the leaves of the tree. In Egyptian iconography we find the motif of the Tree of Life out of which divine arms come laden with gifts, and pouring the water of life out of a vase.[4] Clearly, the theophany indicated by these examples and the motif of the "Tree of Life" have to some extent become blended together, and it is easy to see how this would occur: the divinity revealed in the cosmos in the form of a tree is at the same time a source of regeneration and "life without death", a source to which man turns, for it seems to him to give grounds for his hopes concerning his own immortality. Among the relationships within the pattern formed by tree, cosmos and divinity, there is symmetry, association, and fusion. The gods that we call gods of vegetation are often represented in the form of trees: Attis and the fir tree, Osiris and the cedar, etc. Artemis, of the Greeks, is sometimes present in a tree. Thus at Boiai in Laconia a myrtle was adored under the title of Artemis Soteira. Beside Orchomena in Arcadia, there was a wooden image of Artemis Kedreatis in a cedar tree.[5] Images of Artemis were sometimes ornamented with branches. We are familiar with the plant epiphany of Dionysos, sometimes called Dionysos Dendritis.[6] Remember too the oracular sacred oak tree of Zeus at Dodona, the laurel of Apollo at Delphi, the wild olive tree of Heracles at Olympia, to name only a few. However, there is evidence in only two places in Greece of any tree cult:

[1] Cf. for instance *Taittirīya Samhitā*, ii, 1, 5, 3.

[2] ix, 3, 3, 15.

[3] In the Berlin Museum; Parrot, fig. 69.

[4] Bergema, *De Boom des Levens in Schrijft en Historie*, Hilversum, 1938, figs. 91–3; Marconi, *Riflessi mediterranei nella più antica religione laziale*, Milan, 1939, figs. 41–2.

[5] Pausanias, iii, 22, 12.

[6] Harrison, *Prolegomena*, pp. 425 ff.

the tree at Cithaeron, which Pentheus is supposed to have
climbed to spy on the Maenads, and which the oracle had
ordered to be worshipped as a god,[1] and the plane tree of
Helen, in Sparta.

One very clear example of a plant theophany can be seen in
the cult of the (pre-Aryan) Indian goddess, Durgā. The texts
we quote are late ones, but their popular nature means that
they certainly go back a long way. In the *Devī-Mahātmya*[2]
the goddess declares: "Then, O Gods, I shall nourish
[literally, I will uphold] the whole universe with these plants
which support life and grow from my very body during the
rainy season. I shall then become glorious upon the earth like
Sakamhari ['bearer of herbs' or 'who feeds the herbs']
and in that same season, I shall destroy the great *asura* called
Durgama [the personification of drought]." In the rite of
Navapatrika (the nine leaves) Durgā is called "she who dwells
in the nine leaves".[3] And one could give many more examples
from India to illustrate this.[4] We shall be returning to this
point when we come to discuss other aspects of the religious
significance of trees.

103. VEGETATION AND GREAT GODDESSES

One of the most common and constant patterns is this Great-
Goddess-vegetation-heraldic-animals-priests. The scope of this
work allows me to note only a few of the considerable number
of examples which are to hand. The presence of the goddess
beside a plant symbol confirms one meaning that the tree
possesses in archaic iconography and mythology: that of
being an *inexhaustible source of cosmic fertility*. In the pre-
Aryan civilization of the Indus valley, of which we have learnt
such a lot from the excavations at Harrappa and Mohenjo-
Daro, the identification of the Great Goddess with vegetation
is represented either by association—nude goddesses of the
Yakṣinī type beside a *ficus religiosa*,[5] or by a plant emerging
from the goddess's genital organs.[6] Effigies of the *ficus*

[1] Pausanias, ii, 2, 7.
[2] Ch. xcii, vv. 43–4.
[3] Cf. Eliade, *Le Yoga*, p. 376.
[4] Cf. Meyer, *Trilogie altindische Mächte und Feste der Vegetation*, vol. iii,
passim.
[5] e.g., Marshall, vol. i, fig. 63–7.
[6] Marshall, vol. i, p. 52.

religiosa are fairly numerous,[1] as are those representing the Great Goddess naked[2]—an iconographic motif common to chalcolithic civilization all over Afro-Asia, including Egypt. The sacred tree is in an enclosure, and sometimes a naked goddess rises between two branches of a *ficus religiosa* growing in the centre of a circle. It is clearly indicated in iconography that this signifies a holy place and a " centre " (§ 142 ff.).

All over Africa[3] and in India[4] sap-filled trees symbolize divine motherhood, and are therefore venerated by women, as well as sought out by the spirits of the dead who want to return to life. The goddess-tree motif, whether or not it is completed by the presence of heraldic animals, was preserved in Indian iconography, whence, though not without gaining a certain admixture of water-cosmogony ideas, it passed into popular art, where we still find it to-day. The bonds linking the two symbols of water and of plants, are, in any case, easy to see. Water bears seeds, all seeds. Plants—rhizome, bush, lotus flower—express the *manifestation* of the cosmos, the appearance of *forms*. It is noteworthy that in India, cosmic images are represented as coming out of a lotus flower. A rhizome with flowers signifies creation actually taking place, " the fact of being firmly established above the waters ". That floral and water motifs are present together with plant and woman motifs is due to the central notion of inexhaustible creation, symbolized by the cosmic tree which is identified with the Great Goddess.

This conception is firmly rooted both in Vedic and Puranic creation beliefs (the divinity *manifests* him or herself, as well as the universe, as emerging from a lotus floating upon water), and in the Indo-Iranian conception of the miraculous plant, *soma*. As for this last, remember that *soma* is often pictured in the *Ṛg Veda* as a spring or stream,[5] but also as a paradisal *plant*, which the texts, and particularly the late Vedic and post-Vedic texts, place in a vase (a water symbol, cf. § 61). One finds the grounds for such multiformity if one remembers all that *soma* implies: it assures life, fertility, regeneration—

[1] For instance, pl. xii, figs. 16, 20, 21, 25, 26.
[2] Marshall, pl. i, figs. 48, 50.
[3] Frazer, *The Magic Art*, vol. ii, pp. 316 ff.
[4] Meyer, vol. iii, p. 195.
[5] Cf. Hillebrandt, *Vedische Mythologie*, Breslau, 1927, vol. i, pp. 319 ff.

in other words, exactly what water symbolism implies, and plant symbolism actually states. The theft of the *soma* in *Mahābhārata* I, indicates its double nature, both liquid and vegetal; though it is shown to be a miraculous drink, yet we are told that Garuda " tore it up " (*samutpatya*) as if it were a herb.[1] The symbolism of the Upaniṣads presents the same association, water-tree; " the ageless river " (*vijara-nadī*: that which regenerates) is found beside the tree that upholds all.[2] Both mystic springs are situate in heaven, just as it is in heaven that we find if not the actual substance, at least the prototype, of all the drinks that regenerate and bestow immortality—white *hom*, *soma*, the divine honey of the Finns, and the rest.

The same water-tree association can be found in Jewish and Christian traditions. Ezechiel[3] describes the miraculous waters issuing from under the temple, with fruit-bearing trees along their banks (the symbolic and metaphysical significance of the water whose source is under the temple, like that of the trees, cannot give us a moment's doubt: for the temple is " the centre of the world ", cf. § 142). The Apocalypse[4] takes up, making it even clearer, the cosmological and redemptive expression of water and tree together. " And [the angel] showed me a river of water of life, clear as crystal, proceeding from the throne of God and of the Lamb. In the midst of the street thereof, and on both sides of the river, was the tree of life, bearing twelve fruits, yielding its fruits every month: and the leaves of the tree were for the healing of the nations." The Biblical prototype of this is, of course, in Eden: " The tree of life also in the midst of paradise: and the tree of knowledge of good and evil. And a river went out of the place of pleasure to water paradise, which from thence is divided into four heads."[5] The temple, the place sacred above all others, is the equivalent of its heavenly prototype—the Garden of Paradise.

104. ICONOGRAPHIC SYMBOLISM

The association of water and plant symbols is explained

---

[1] xxxiii, 10.
[2] *Kauśitaki Up.*, i, 3.
[3] lxvii.
[4] xxii. 1–2.
[5] Gen. ii. 9–10.

extremely coherently in the creation belief which underlies
Indian decorative art. Coomaraswamy[1] gives us the following
formula for it: a rhizome of lotus with plenty of leaves and
flowers (*latā-kāma, māla-kāma*), often supporting or enclosing
flowers and animals (cf. *śakuna-yatthi*), emerging from the
mouth or navel of a Yakṣa or some other water symbol,
such as a full vase (*pūrṇa-ghata*), or the open throat of a
makara, or of an elephant with a fish tail. The "full vase"
is a symbol we find in other spheres, always connected with the
"plant of Life" or some emblem of fertility. Thus, after the
era of King Gudea, the "sacred tree" disappeared from the
Akkado-Sumerian scene, and was replaced by a "plant of
life", coming from a vase.[2] The "full vase" is always held
by a god or demi-god, never a man. Sometimes the "vase"
is left out and the water flows straight from the actual body of
the divinity.[3] There could hardly be a clearer way of expressing
the belief that life and regeneration flow directly from the divine
substance, or, more precisely, from the perfectly manifest
revelation of that substance, from the theophany.

To correspond in mythology to the decoration motif of
the rhizome emerging from a water emblem, there is the
Puranic conception of the birth of Brahma. The god is called
abjaja, "born of the lotus", which rises from the navel of
Viṣṇu.[4] Coomaraswamy[5] has shown the Vedic origins and
foundations of this idea. What the symbol of the "lotus
(or rhizome) emerging from water (or an emblem of water)"
expresses is the cosmic process itself. The water represents
the unmanifest, seeds, hidden powers; the floral symbol
represents manifestation, the creation of the universe. Varuna,
as god of water,[6] rain and fertility, was originally the root of
the Tree of Life, the source of all creation.[7]

105. GREAT GODDESS—TREE OF LIFE

The association between the Great Goddess and the Tree

[1] *Yakṣas*, vol. ii, pp. 2–3.
[2] Parrot, p. 59.
[3] Cf. Van Buren, *The Flowing Vase and the God with Streams*, Berlin, 1933,
figs. 6, 13, etc.
[4] *Agni Purāṇa*, ch. xlix.
[5] Vol. ii, p. 25.
[6] Cf. a wealth of reference in Meyer, vol. iii, p. 207.
[7] *RV*, i, 24, 7; cf. Coomaraswamy, vol. ii, 29.

of Life occurred also in Egypt. One relief depicts Hathor in a heavenly tree (undoubtedly the Tree of Immortality), giving food and drink to the soul of a dead man—in other words, assuring him continuity of life, survival.[1] This picture must be seen in relation to the series of representations of the goddess's hands filled with gifts, or her head and shoulders emerging from a tree, and giving the soul of the dead man something to drink. There is a parallel series of the goddess of destiny seated upon the lower boughs of an enormous tree symbolizing heaven, on all the branches of which are written the names of the Pharaohs and their destinies.[2] The same motif is to be found in popular Altaic beliefs (those of the Yakuts, etc.):[3] at the foot of the seven-branched tree of life is " the goddess of the ages ".

The same association is to be found in the myth and cult of Mesopotamia. Gilgamesh comes upon a miraculous tree in a garden, and near it the divinity Siduri (i.e., the " maiden ") described as *sabitu*, that is " the woman with wine ".[4] Autran indeed explains this as meaning that Gilgamesh meets her beside a vine: in the Near East, the vine was identified with the " herb of life " and the Sumerian sign for " life " was originally a vine leaf.[5] This wonderful plant was sacred to the Great Goddesses. The Mother Goddess was at first called " the mother vine ", or the " goddess vine ".[6] Albright has proved[7] that in primitive versions of the Gilgamesh legend, Siduri held a more important place. Gilgamesh asks immortality of her directly. Jensen identifies her with the nymph Calypso in the *Odyssey*.[8] Like Calypso, Siduri had the appearance of a young girl, wore a veil, carried bunches of grapes and dwelt in the place from whence the four springs came;[9] her island was placed at " the navel of the sea "[10] and the nymph could give

---

[1] Cf. the figure on p. 58 of Wallis Budge's *From Fetish to God in Ancient Egypt*, Oxford, 1934.

[2] F. Max Müller, *Egyptian Mythology*, Boston, 1918, p. 53.

[3] Holmberg-Harva, " Baum des Lebens ", p. 97.

[4] Autran, *Préhistoire du Christianisme*, vol. i, p. 143.

[5] Autran, p. 142.

[6] Langdon, *Tammuz and Ishtar*, Oxford, 1914, p. 43.

[7] In " The Babylonian Sage Ut-Napistim nuqu ", *JAOS*, 1918, vol. xxxviii.

[8] v, 68 ff.

[9] v, 70.

[10] *Omphalos thalasses*; *Odyssey*, i, 50.

heroes immortality, the heavenly ambrosia with which she tempted Ulysses also.[1]

Calypso was one of the innumerable theophanies of the Great Goddess, revealing herself at the " centre of the world ", beside the *omphalos*, the Tree of Life and the four springs. And the vine was the vegetal expression of immortality—just as wine remained the symbol of youth and everlasting life, in primitive traditions (cf. " eau de vie ", Gaelic *uschabheagh*, which means, literally, " water of life ", the Persian *maie-i-shebab*, " drink of youth ", the Sumerian *gestin*, " tree of life ").[2] The *Mishna*[3] declares that the Tree of the Knowledge of Good and Evil, in Genesis, was a vine. The Book of Enoch[4] places this vine or tree of the knowledge of good and evil between seven mountains, as, of course, also does the Epic of Gilgamesh.[5] The snake-goddess, Hannat, could taste of the fruit of the tree, just as Siduri and Calypso were allowed to. Grapes and wine went on symbolizing wisdom until quite late.[6] But the primitive conception of vine-cosmic-tree-tree-of-knowledge-and-redemption was preserved extraordinarily coherently in Mandeism. In that gnosis, wine (*gufna*) is the embodiment of light, wisdom and purity. The archetype of wine (*qadmaia*) is in the higher, heavenly world. The archetypal vine is water within, its leaves are made up of " spirits of light ", and its nodes are fragments of light. From it spring the streams of sacred water intended to satisfy men's thirst; the god of light and of wisdom, the redeemer (*Manda d'haiie*), is also identified with the vine of life (*gufna d'haiie*) and the vine is held to be a cosmic tree because it spreads over the heavens, and its grapes are the stars.[7]

The motif, vine and naked woman, also passed into the apocryphal Christian legends. For instance, in *Questions and Answers*,[8] a late compilation translated into Rumanian from

---

[1] v, 135 ff.

[2] Cf. Albright, " The Goddess of Life and Wisdom ", *JASS*, 1920, vol. xxxvi, p. 276.

[3] *Sanhedrin*, 70, a.

[4] xxiv. 2.

[5] Albright, p. 283.

[6] Cf. Prov. viii. 19.

[7] Albright, p. 266.

[8] *Intrebari si Raspunsuri*, cxxvii.

the Slavonic before the seventeenth century, we are told that Pilate found his wife naked in a vineyard, near a vine which had sprung up from out of the bloodstained clothes of Christ, and had miraculously borne fruit. (The legend is bound up with the motif of a creation of plants following the sacrifice of a divinity or violent death of a hero.)[1]

In the areas of Greece and the Aegean, the pattern of goddess-tree-mountain-heraldic-animals is similarly frequent. Remember the great ring of Mycenae,[2] which depicts a religious scene in which the goddess, a hand on her naked breast, sits under the Tree of Life near a series of cosmological emblems: double-headed stone axe, sun, moon, water (the four springs). The scene is very like a Semitic relief reproduced by Holmberg-Harva[3] depicting the goddess seated on a throne near the sacred tree and holding the divine child in her arms. A coin from Myra (Lycia) shows the theophany of the goddess in the midst of the tree.[4] From the Aegean, too, we may mention the gold ring of Mochlos, depicting the goddess in a boat with an altar and a tree,[5] and the famous scene of the dance before the sacred tree.[6]

All these associations we find in myth and iconography are not the result of mere chance, nor are they without religious and metaphysical significance. What do they mean, these associations of goddess and tree, or goddess and vine, with their surrounding cosmological emblems and heraldic animals ? They mean that here is a " centre of the world ", that here is the source of life, youth and immortality. The trees signify the universe in endless regeneration; but at the heart of the universe, there is always a tree—the tree of eternal life or of knowledge. The Great Goddess personifies the inexhaustible source of creation, the ultimate basis of all reality. She is simply the expression, in myth, of this primeval intuition that sacredness, life and immortality are situate in a " centre ".

[1] Cf. Eliade, " La Mandragore et les mythes de la ' naissance miraculeuse ' ", *CZ*, 1942, vol. iii, p. 25.

[2] Cf. Nilsson, *Geschichte*, vol. i, pl. 17, 1.

[3] Fig. 30.

[4] Cook, *Zeus*, Cambridge, 1925, vol. ii, 1, p. 681, fig. 620.

[5] Nilsson, pl. 13, 6.

[6] Nilsson, pl. 13, 5; cf. Persson, *The Religion of Greece in Prehistoric Times*, Berkeley and Los Angeles, 1942, pp. 36 ff.; and fig. 3.

106. THE TREE OF KNOWLEDGE

" In the midst " of Paradise stood the Tree of Life and the
Tree of the Knowledge of Good and Evil,[1] and God forbade
Adam to eat the fruit of the Tree of Knowledge: ". . . for
in what day soever thou shalt eat of it, thou shalt die the
death."[2] Yet God makes no mention of the Tree of Life.
Is this last simply the same as the Tree of Knowledge, or—
as some scholars believe[3]—was the Tree of Life "hidden"
only to become identifiable and therefore accessible at the
moment when Adam should snatch at the knowledge of good
and evil, or, in other words, of wisdom? I am inclined to this
second hypothesis. The Tree of Life can bestow immortality,
but it is not easy of attainment. It is " hidden "—like the herb
of immortality which Gilgamesh went to find at the bottom
of the sea; or it is guarded by monsters, like the golden apples
in the Garden of the Hesperides. That these two trees—of
life and of wisdom—should be together is not such a paradox
as it may at first seem. We find it in other primitive traditions
as well; at the eastern entry to heaven, the Babylonians placed
two trees: the Tree of Truth and the Tree of Life; and one
text from Ras Shamra tells us that Aleion gave Ltpn wisdom
and eternity together.[4]

The serpent induced Adam and Eve to eat of the Tree of
Knowledge, promising them that its fruit would bring them
not death but divinity. " No, you shall not die the death.
For God doth know that in what day soever you shall eat
thereof, your eyes shall be opened: and you shall be as gods,
knowing good and evil."[5] Was the serpent saying that man
was to become like God simply by knowing good and evil, or
because, becoming omniscient, he would be able to " see "
where the Tree of Life was, and thus achieve immortality?
If taken literally, the Bible text seems to say this: " And
[the Lord] said: Behold Adam is become as one of us, knowing
good and evil: now, therefore, lest perhaps he put forth his

[1] Gen. ii. 9.

[2] ii. 17.

[3] Cf. Paul Humbert, *Etudes sur le récit du paradis et a chute dans la Genèse*
Neuchatel, 1940, pp. 22 ff.

[4] Humbert, p. 22.

[5] Gen. iii. 4–5.

hand and take also of the tree of life and live for ever. And
the Lord God sent him out. . . ."[1]

For those who see the Genesis story as simply one of many
myths, constructed on the same general principle, certain
questions arise. Man could attain divinity only by eating of the
fruit of the second tree: the Tree of Immortality. Why, then,
did the serpent tempt Adam to eat of the Tree of Knowledge
which would only give him wisdom ? If the serpent prefigured
the spirit of evil, and therefore opposed man's attaining immortality, he must have " prevented " man from going to the
Tree of Life. The serpent was the obstacle in man's search for
the source of immortality, for the Tree of Life. This interpretation will be confirmed by other traditions we shall come
to later. But another explanation is offered by some of the
serpent's tempting: he wanted to gain immortality for himself
(as, in some myths, he succeeded in doing), and he needed to
discover the Tree of Life, hidden among all the other trees of
Paradise, so that he might be the first to eat of its fruit; that
is why he urged Adam to " know good and evil "; Adam, with
his knowledge, would have revealed to him where the Tree of
Life was.

107. THE GUARDIANS OF THE TREE OF LIFE

The pattern: primeval man (or hero) in search of immortality, Tree of Life, and serpent or monster guarding the
tree (or preventing man by its trickery from eating of it),
appears in other traditions as well. What these things (man,
tree and serpent) mean together is clear enough: immortality
is hard of attainment; it is contained in a Tree of Life (or
Fountain of Life), placed in some inaccessible spot (at the end
of the earth, at the bottom of the sea, in the land of darkness,
on top of a very high hill, or in a " centre "); a monster
(or serpent) guards the tree and the man who succeeds, after a
great many efforts, in approaching it, must fight the monster
and vanquish it, if he is to take hold of the fruits of immortality.

The combat with the monster seems, from all one can see,
to have had the quality of an initiation; man must " prove
himself ", become a " hero ", to have the right to possess
immortality. Anyone who cannot defeat the dragon or the

[1] Gen. iii. 22–3.

serpent can have no access to the Tree of Life, can never attain
immortality.   The hero's struggle with the monster is not
always a bodily one. Adam was defeated by the serpent
without any struggle in the heroic sense (as was the case with
Heracles, for instance); he was defeated by the serpent's
trick in persuading him to try and become like God, to violate
the divine order, and thus condemn himself to death. In the
Bible text, of course, the serpent is not presented as the " protector " of the Tree of Life, but from the results of its temptation,
we may well think of him as such.

The Babylonian hero, Gilgamesh, fared no better. He too
sought to attain immortality; what happens is that he is
struck with sadness by the death of his friend Enkidu and
laments : " Must I too lie down one day like him, and never
more awake ? "[1] He knows there is only one man in the world
who can help him—the sage Ut-Napishtim, who escaped the
deluge, and whom the gods have granted life immortal—and
to his dwelling, which stands somewhere at " the mouth of
the rivers ", Gilgamesh accordingly turns his steps. The way
is long, laborious, fraught with obstacles like every road to a
" centre ", to Paradise or to a source of immortality. Ut-
Napishtim lives on an island surrounded by the waters of death,
which the hero, in spite of everything, manages to cross. It is
fitting that Gilgamesh should stand powerless before some of
the trials to which Ut-Napishtim submits him; he does not,
for instance, succeed in watching for six days and nights running. His fate is determined beforehand; he will not attain
to eternal life, he cannot become like the gods, for he has none
of their qualities.

However, at the instance of his wife, Ut-Napishtim reveals
to Gilgamesh the existence of a " thorny " herb (that is a
herb hard of access) at the bottom of the sea, which, though it
will not confer immortality, will indefinitely prolong the youth
and life of whoever eats of it. Gilgamesh fastens stones to his
feet and goes down to search the bottom of the sea. Having
found the herb, he pulls a sprig from it, then unfastens the
stones, and rises again to the surface. On the road to Uruk,
he stops to drink at a spring; drawn by the scent of the plant,

[1] Tablet VIII; the passage is quoted by Virolleaud, " Le Voyage de Gilgamesh au Paradis ", *RHR*, 1930, vol. ci, p. 204.

a snake draws near and devours it, thus becoming immortal. Gilgamesh, like Adam, has lost immortality because of his own stupidity and a serpent's trick.   Just as he could not emerge victorious from the trials Ut-Napishtim set him, so he could neither keep what he had got with the help of so much kindness (for in the course of his journey he was helped by Sabitu, by Urnashabi—Ut-Napishtim's boatman—and by Ut-Napishtim himself and his wife). The monster, the serpent, was thus the adversary *par excellence* of man's immortality. When, much earlier than Gilgamesh, the legendary King Etana of Kish begged the sun and the god Anu to give him the " herb of life " so that his wife could provide him with an heir, he was taken up into the sky by an eagle which had, by the trick of a serpent, been cast into a ditch. The conflict between the serpent and the eagle is, as we have seen (§ 101), a leitmotif of Eurasian mythology.

108. MONSTERS AND GRYPHONS

Iranian tradition, also, has a tree of life and regeneration which grows on earth and has a prototype in heaven. Earthly *haoma*, or " yellow " *hom*—which, like the *soma* of Vedic writings, is thought of sometimes as a plant, and sometimes as a spring—grows among mountains;[1] Ahura Mazda planted it first on Mount Haraiti.[2] Its prototype is in heaven; and it is the heavenly *haoma* or *gaokerena* (white *hom*), which gives immortality to all who taste of it, and which is to be found among thousands of other medicinal herbs at the source of the waters of Ardvisura, on an island· in the lake Vourakasa.[3] This " white *hom* was made to abolish decrepitude. It is this which will effect the regeneration of the universe and the immortality which will follow from it. It is the king of plants ".[4] " Whoever eats of it becomes immortal ".[5] Ahriman counters this creation of Ahura Mazda's, by creating a lizard in the waters of Vourakasa to attack the miraculous tree Gaokerena.[6] Yima, the first man in Iranian mythological tradition, was

[1] *Yasna*, x, 3–4.
[2] *Yasna*, x, 10.
[3] *Videvdat*, xx, 4; *Bundahisn*, xxvii, 4.
[4] *Bundahisn*, i, 1, 5.
[5] *Bundahisn*, xxvii, 5.
[6] *Bund.*, xviii, 2; cf. the serpent Nidhoggr attacking the roots of Yggdrasil.

immortal,[1] but like Adam, he lost immortality through sin;
" He lied, and began to think of lying words contrary to the
truth."[2] It is as a result of Yima's sin that men are mortal
and unhappy.[3]

The serpent is present beside the Tree of Life in other
traditions, too, probably as a result of Iranian influences.
The Kalmuks tell how a dragon is in the ocean, near the tree
Zambu, waiting for some of the leaves to fall so that he can
devour them. The Buriats believe in the serpent Abyrga
beside the tree in a " lake of milk ". In some Central Asiatic
versions, Abyrga is coiled round the actual tree trunk.[4]

There are gryphons or monsters guarding all the roads to
salvation, mounting guard over the Tree of Life, or some other
symbol of the same thing. When Hercules went to steal the
golden apples from the garden of the Hesperides, he had either
to kill or put to sleep the dragon guarding them. Whether the
hero did this himself, or had it done for him by Atlas—while
for a moment Hercules supported the heavenly globe in his
place—is of secondary importance. What matters is that
Hercules was successful in these heroic " trials " and took the
golden apples. The golden fleece of Colchis was also guarded
by a dragon, which Jason had to kill to obtain it. There are
serpents " guarding " all the paths to immortality, that is,
every " centre ", every repository where the sacred is concentrated, every *real* substance. They are always pictured
round the bowl of Dionysos,[5] they watch over Apollo's gold
in far-off Scythia,[6] they guard the treasures hidden at the bottom
of the earth, or the diamonds and pearls at the bottom of the
sea—in fact, they guard every symbol embodying the sacred,
or able to bestow *power*, *life* or *omniscience*. In the Baptistery
at Parma, dragons mount guard over the Tree of Life. The
same motif can be seen in a bas-relief in the Museum of the
Cathedral of Ferrara.[7]

[1] *Yasna*, ix, 3–5.
[2] *Yast*, xix, 33–4.
[3] Cf. A. Christensen, *Le Premier Homme et le premier roi dans l'histoire légendaire des Iraniens*, Uppsala, 1931, vol. ii, pp. 13 ff.
[4] Homberg-Harva, *Finno-Ugric Mythology and Siberian Mythology*, Boston,
1927, pp. 356 ff.
[5] Carcopino, *La Basilique pythagoricienne*, p. 229.
[6] Herodotus, iii, 116.
[7] Hartlaub, *Arcana Artis*, p. 294.

109. THE TREE AND THE CROSS

The Tree of Life is the prototype of all miraculous plants that bring the dead to life, heal the sick, restore youth, and so on. Thus, on Mount Oshadi there are four wonderful herbs: " One of them, priceless herb, resurrects the dead, another pulls arrows out of wounds, a third closes sores . . ."[1] The herb *mṛtasamjīvanī*, which brings the dead to life, is undoubtedly the most precious. But there is also a " great herb ", *saṁdhani*, which has power to reunite the members of a dead body.[2] Chinese legends tell of a marvellous island from which crows bring a herb that can bring back to life warriors dead for three days. The same belief exists in Iran. The herb that brings the dead to life was also known to the Roman world,[3] and its powers were famous in all European legends.[4] When, according to the legend, King Solomon asked the Queen of Sheba to give him immortality, she spoke to him of a plant to be found growing amongst rocks. Solomon met a " white-haired man ", an old man walking with the herb in his hand, and he gave it to Solomon gladly, for as long as he kept it he could not die. For the herb gave immortality alone, not youth.[5]

The wood of the true cross was supposed to bring the dead to life, and Helena, mother of the Emperor Constantine, went to look for it.[6] The wood had this power because the cross was made out of the Tree of Life which stood in the Garden of Eden.[7] In Christian iconography the cross is often depicted as the Tree of Life (cf. the Bibliography). A tremendous number of legends about the wood of the cross and Seth's journey to Paradise were current right through the Middle Ages in all Christian countries. They sprang originally from the *Apocalypse of Moses*, the *Gospel of Nicodemus*, and the

[1] *Rāmāyaña*, Yuddha Khaṇḍa, 26, 6.

[2] *Mahābhārata*, i, 76, 33.

[3] Pliny, *Hist. Nat.*, 25, 5.

[4] For the Rumanians of Macedonia, cf. Candrea, *Iarba Fiarelor*, Bucharest, 1928, p. 20.

[5] Wünsche, " Die Sagen vom Lebensbaum und Lebenswasser. Altorientalischem Mythen ", *Ex Oriente Lux*, Leipzig, 1905, vol. i, nos. 2–3, p. 15 ff.

[6] Albiruni, *The Chronology of the Ancient Nations*, trans. Sachau, London, 1879, p. 292.

[7] Wünsche, p. 39.

Life of Adam and Eve. I will glance briefly at the most widely accepted version.[1] When Adam had lived for 932 years in the Hebron valley, he was struck down with a fatal illness and sent his son Seth to ask the angel who stood guard at the gate of Paradise for the oil of mercy. Seth follows the tracks of Adam and Eve's footsteps, where the grass has never grown and, coming to Paradise, he imparts Adam's wish to the archangel. The archangel advises him to look three times into Paradise. The first time Seth sees the water from which four rivers flow, and a dried-up tree above it. The second time, a serpent coils itself round the trunk. The third time he looks, he sees the tree rise up to heaven; at its top is a newborn child, and its roots spread down to the regions of the underworld (the Tree of Life stood at the centre of the universe and it passed as an axis through the three cosmic spheres). The angel tells Seth the meaning of what he has seen, and announces to him that a Redeemer is to come. At the same time he gives him three seeds from the fruit of the fatal tree of which his parents ate, and tells him to place them upon Adam's tongue; he says that Adam will die in three days. When Adam hears Seth's story he laughs for the first time since being banished from Paradise, for he realizes that mankind will be saved. When ne dies, the three seeds Seth has placed on his tongue rise up in the valley of Hebron, three trees growing with a single span till the time of Moses. And he, knowing their divine origin, transplants them to Mount Tabor or Horeb (the " centre of the world "). The trees remain there for a thousand years till the day David gets an order from God to take them to Jerusalem (which is also a " centre "). After a great many further episodes (the Queen of Sheba refusing to place her foot on their wood, etc.), the three trees become one tree, and the cross of the Redeemer is made of it. The blood of Christ, crucified at the centre of the Earth, on the very spot where Adam was created and buried, falls upon " the skull of Adam ", and thus, redeeming him from his sin, baptizes the father of mankind.[2]

A German medieval conundrum[3] speaks of a tree whose roots are in hell, and whose summit at the throne of God,

[1] Cf. Graf, *Miti, leggende e superstizioni*, pp. 59 ff.
[2] Cf. Eliade, *Cosmologie si alchimie babiloniana*, Burcharest, 1937, p. 53.
[3] Wünsche, op. cit., p. 13.

while its branches contain the whole world; and this tree is the cross. For Christians, indeed, the Cross is the support of the world: " Quapropter lignum crucis coeli sustinet machinam, terrae fundamenter corroborat, adfixos sibi homines ducit ad vitam ", wrote Firmicus Maternus.[1] In eastern legends, the cross is the bridge or the ladder along which men's souls rise to God;[2] standing as it does at the " centre of the world "; it is a thoroughfare between heaven, earth and hell. In some versions the wood of the cross has seven notches in it like the cosmic trees representing the seven heavens.[3]

110. REJUVENATION AND IMMORTALITY

As in the myth of the " Fountain of Life ", we find varying notions about miraculous herbs and fruits; some rejuvenate, others give long life, others even confer immortality. Each of these notions has developed and altered according to the ways of thought imposed by the genius of a given race, the mingling of cultures, and the varying notions of social classes. " The plant of immortality and youth ", for instance, was envisaged quite differently in India and in the Semitic world. The Semites thirsted for immortality, for immortal life; the Indians sought for the plant that would regenerate and rejuvenate them. That is why the medicinal and alchemical diets in India were merely to prolong life by hundreds of years, and to make those who undertook them sexually potent (*balavān strīṣṇu*). The myth of Śyāvana shows perfectly the profane ideal of the Indian: not *immortality* but *rejuvenation*. Śyāvana made an agreement with the Aśvins whereby they were to rejuvenate him and in return, he would give them *soma*, the divine ambrosia. The Aśvins took him to the " fountain of youth " of Sarasvatī, and when Śyāvana came back, he was godlike in his youth and splendour.[4]

An Indian who welcomed existence and loved life did not want to keep it indefinitely, but only to have a very long youth. Immortality was not the sort of thing to tempt sages or mystics —they longed for liberation, not a permanent continuation of

---

[1] *De Errore Profanarum Religionum*, 27, 1.
[2] Holmberg-Harva, " Baum des Lebens ", p. 133.
[3] Cf. Cartojan, *Cartile populare in literatura româneasca*, Bucharest, 1929, vol. i, p. 123.
[4] Cf. *Śatapatha-Br.*, iv, 1, 5; etc.

existence; they sought final detachment from the cosmos, and the acquisition of complete spiritual autonomy—not a mere continuation in time, even an endless one. We find the same with the Greeks; they did not long for immortality, but for youth and long life. In most of the legends relating to Alexander the Great, he is astonished that anyone should seek immortality.[1] The myth of regeneration and rejuvenation, as thought of by the Indians, was known to Europeans not only indirectly, as transmitted by the Semitic world, by Islam, but directly too, from the writings of those who had been to the East. The " Letter of Prester John " (1160–65) says that the Indus surrounded Paradise, and that three days' journey away was a spring which, if anyone swallowed three mouthfuls of its water, would make him like a young man of thirty for the rest of his days.[2] Del Rio and Peter Maffeius declare that the Indians of Bengal and the Ganges valley live to be three hundred or even three hundred and thirty years old.[3] Gervasius tells how Alexander the Great, in his search for the " water of life " in India, found some apples which the priests there took to extend their life to four hundred years.[4] In Scandinavian mythology, the apple is the fruit that regenerates and rejuvenates. The gods eat apples and stay young until the *ragna rok*, until the end of the present cycle of the universe.

These examples serve to show what a difference there is between the Indian ideal and the Semitic, but each of these mythological themes, in its turn, goes on altering even within the same racial group which formulated it. The spiritual levels of myth on the one hand, and of legend, superstition and custom on the other, are totally different. The peasant community and the cultured few will have utterly different ways of understanding and interpreting the myth of the herb of regeneration or immortality. And yet, in all the variants upon this same central theme—whatever differences may have arisen from ethnic genius, or social group, or simply from the vicissitudes which must occur when such a theme is transmitted —we can easily identify the essential unity. In this case, we

---

[1] Cf. Hopkins, " The Fountain of Youth ", *JAOS*, 1905, vol. xxvi, pp. 19, 20; and Wallis Budge, *Alexander the Great*, London, 1896, p. 93.
[2] Hopkins, p. 19.
[3] Hopkins, p. 24.
[4] Hopkins, p. 19

find, underlying every version of the miraculous herb, the original prototype: the Tree of Life; reality, sacred power and life centring in a marvellous Tree which stands in a " centre ", in an inaccessible world, and of which only the elect may eat.

111. THE ARCHETYPE OF SIMPLES

The magic and curative power of certain herbs is also derived from a heavenly prototype of the plant in question, or from the fact that it was first picked by a god. No plant is of value in itself; its value is in its relation to an archetype, or in the repeating of a set of actions or words which make the plant sacred by setting it apart from its profane surroundings. The words of two English incantations of the sixteenth century, which accompanied the picking of herbs with curative powers, make clear the origins of their healing efficacy: they grew for the first time (*ab origine*, that is) on the sacred hill of Calvary (at the centre of the earth).

> Haile be thou, holie herbe, growing on the ground
>   All in the mount Caluarie first wert thou found.
> Thou art good for manie a sore, and healest manie a wound;
>   In the name of sweet Jesus, I take thee from the ground.
>   (1584)
> Hallowed be thou, Vervein [verbena], as thou growest on the
>   ground,
> For in the Mount of Calvary, there thou wast first found.
> Thou healedst our Saviour Jesus Christ, and staunchest his
>   bleeding wound;
> In the name of [Father, Son, Holy Ghost] I take thee from the
>   ground.   (1608)[1]

The efficaciousness of these herbs is attributed to the fact that their prototype was discovered at a decisive cosmic moment (*in illo tempore*) upon Mount Calvary. Their sacredness comes from having healed the wounds of the Redeemer. The efficaciousness of the herb when it is picked is due solely to the fact that whoever picks it is repeating that primeval action of healing. That is why one ancient formula of in-cantation says: " We are going to pick herbs to lay them against the wounds of the Saviour."[2] The power of the herb can also

[1] Ohrt, " Herba, Gratia Plena ", *FFC*, Helsinki, 1929, no. 28, p. 17.
[2] Ohrt, p. 18.

be attributed to the fact that a divine being planted it. " Who planted thee ? " the herbalist asks the true-love plant. " It was Our Lady . . . for my healing."[1]   Sometimes the herb must be picked in the name of Jesus.[2]

These formulæ of Christian folk magic were the continuation of an ancient tradition.   In India, for instance, the herb *kapitthaka* (*Feronia elephantum*) cures sexual impotence, for *ab origine*, the Gandharvas used it to give Varuṇa back his virility.   Consequently the ritual picking of the herb is an effective repetition of the Gandharvas' action.   " Thee that the Gandharvas dug for Varuṇa, whose virility was dead, thee here we dig, a penis-erecting herb."[3]   Artemisia (*damana*) is picked with the following prayer: " Blessed be thou, Kāmadeva, who dost dazzle us all.   I pick thee with the good will of Viṣṇu ", etc.[4]

A long invocation in the Paris Papyrus[5] indicates the extraordinary status of picked herbs: " Thou wast sown by Cronos, picked by Hera, preserved by Ammon, begotten by Isis, nourished by rain-giving Zeus; thou hast grown thanks to the Sun and the dew.   Thou art the dew of all the gods, the heart of Hermes, the seed of the first gods, the eye of the sun, the light of the moon, the dignity of Osiris, the beauty and splendour of heaven, etc. . . . As thou raisedst up Osiris, arise thyself ! Rise as the Sun !   Thy grandeur is as high as its zenith; thy roots are as deep as the abyss, etc. . . . Thy branches are the bones of Minerva; thy flowers the eye of Horus; thy seeds the seed of Pan, etc. . . . ; I follow Hermes.   I pluck thee with good fortune, the Good Spirit, at the lucky hour, on the day that is right and suitable for all things."   The herb there addressed and picked has the significance of a cosmic tree. To obtain it is to obtain all the powers residing in it as a repository of force, life and sacred power.   This incantation is clearly the product of eclectic Graeco-Egyptian magic—its author was undoubtedly a learned man, but it is no less genuine for that; indeed, the majority of folk incantations are, as we know, the work of scholars debased by a long process of

---

[1] Cf. Delatte, *Herbarius*, Liège-Paris, 1938, p. 97, n. 3.
[2] Delatte, pp. 93 ff.
[3] *AV*, iv, 4, 1; Whitney and Lanman's translation.
[4] *Padma Purāṇa*, quoted by Meyer, *Trilogie*, vol. i, p. 48.
[5] Delatte, p. 100.

infantilization. The identification of a medicinal herb with a tree in which the god is manifest is perfectly legitimate in the nature of primitive spirituality; as we have already seen, to " primitives ", any object in the world around may acquire a sacred value if it can be linked with a prototype in the world of heaven.

To Christians, medicinal herbs owed their efficacy to the fact that they were first found on Calvary. To the ancients, herbs owed their curative properties to having been discovered *first* by the gods. One herbalistic treatise recommends the following opening to an invocation: " Betony, which wast first discovered by Aesculapius, or by Chiron the centaur . . ."[1] Or its efficaciousness might be due to the fact of having been planted by the divinity: " Basil, I beg thee by the supreme divinity who made thee to be born . . ."; " Castor-oil plant, in the name of the all-powerful God who made thee to be born . . ."; " You, powerful plants, you whom the Earth Mother has created and given to all the nations . . ."[2]

In popular Christian tradition, too, the herb owes its medicinal properties to the fact that God has given it quite exceptional powers. In France the following formula is pronounced: " Sacred herb, which hast neither been sowed, nor planted, show forth the power God has given thee ! "[3] Sometimes, the plant is divine; the *Cyranides*, a herbalistic text, for instance, calls bryony divine, queen of the gods, mother of plants, mistress of earth, heaven and water.[4] That is why gathering is a ritual, carried out in a state of ceremonial purity, accompanied by prayers and sacrifices to ward off certain dangers, and so on. It is no mere matter of simply picking a plant, a certain botanical species; it is re-enacting a primeval action (when the divinity picked it for the first time) and thus gaining possession of a substance impregnated with the sacred, a lesser version of the Tree of Life, the source of all healing.

112. THE TREE AS AXIS MUNDI

The myths and legends which relate to the Tree of Life there

[1] Delatte, p. 102.
[2] Ancient texts quoted by Delatte, pp. 102, 104.
[3] Delatte, p. 103.
[4] Delatte, p. 103.

often include the idea that it stands at the centre of the
universe, binding together earth, heaven and hell. This detail
of mythical topography has a special significance in the beliefs
of the Nordic and central Asiatic and, more particularly, the
Altai and Germanic peoples, but its origin is probably eastern
(Mesopotamian). The Altai peoples believed, for instance,
that " at the earth's navel grows the highest tree of all, a giant
fir whose branches rise up to the home of Bai-Ulgen "—that
is, to heaven.[1] Often this tree is found at the top of a mountain,
at the centre of the earth. The Abakhan Tatars talk of an iron
mountain on which there grows a seven-branched birch tree,
which apparently symbolizes the seven heavens (an ideogram
which would seem to be Babylonian in origin). In the hymns
of the Vasyugan Ostiak shamans, the cosmic tree, like the sky,
has seven levels; it passes through all the heavenly spheres
and buries its roots in the depths of the earth.[2]

When he goes up to heaven, in the course of his mystic
voyage, the shaman climbs up a tree with nine or seven notches
(§33). Generally, however, he makes his ascent up a ritual
pillar which also has seven notches, and which is, naturally,
also supposed to be at the centre of the earth.[3] The sacred
pole or tree is a symbol of the cosmic pillar which is at the
middle of the universe upholding the world. The Altai peoples
believe that the gods attach horses to this cosmic pillar and the
constellations moving around it. The Scandinavians have a
similar notion: Odhin tethers his horse to Yggdrasil (literally
" Odhin's horse "). The Saxons called this cosmic pillar
Irminsul—*universalis columna quasi sustinens omnia* (Rudolf of
Fulda). The Indians too have the notion of a cosmic axis,
represented by a pillar or Tree of Life, at the centre of the
universe.[4] In Chinese mythology the miraculous tree grows
at the centre of the universe, where the perfect capital
is to be found; it unites the Nine Springs with the Nine
Heavens. They call it " standing wood " (*Kien-Mou*), and
they say that at midday nothing upright standing near it can

[1] Holmberg-Harva, " Baum des Lebens ", 52.

[2] Eliade, *Le Chamanisme*, Paris, 1951, pp. 245 ff.

[3] Holmberg-Harva, *Finno-Ugric Mythology*, p. 338; " Der Baum des Lebens ",
pp. 26 ff.; Eliade, *Le Chamanisme*, pp. 120 ff.

[4] Coomaraswamy, *Elements of Buddhist Iconography*, Harvard, 1935, p. 83;
Mus, *Barabudur*, Hanoi-Paris, 1935, vol. i, pp. 117 ff.

cast any shadow.[1] This cosmic tree is similar to the Pillar, the support of the world, " axis of the universe " (*axis mundi*), of the Altaic and northern European cosmologies. In these myths the tree expresses absolute reality in its aspect of norm, of a fixed point, supporting the cosmos. It is the supreme prop of all things. And, consequently, communication with heaven can only be effected near it, or by means of it.

113. THE MYTH OF MAN'S DESCENT FROM A PLANT SPECIES

The same notions of life and of reality symbolized by plant life explain what I will call, for want of any more precise term, " the mystical relations between trees and men ". The most explicit of these mystical relations seems to be the descent of a given race from some plant species. A tree or bush is held to be the mythical ancestor of the tribe. Generally this ancestral tree is closely connected with the moon cult; the mythical ancestor, identified with the moon, is represented under the form of a certain plant. Thus certain Miao groups worship the bamboo as their ancestor. The same beliefs are to be found among the aboriginals of Formosa, the Tagalog of the Philippines, the Ya-Lang (Yunnan), and in Japan. For the Ainus, the Ghiliaks, and the Koreans, trees enter into the (lunar) cult of ancestors.[2] The Australian tribes round Melbourne believed that the first man was born of a mimosa.[3] One myth very widespread in Indo-China tells how mankind was wholly annihilated by the deluge, apart from one brother and sister, who had a miraculous escape in a pumpkin. Although they were loth to do so, the two married and the girl gave birth to a pumpkin; and from its seeds, sown upon hill and plain, arose the races of men.[4]

We find that same myth, with inevitable distortions (a distortion of the concept of " the ancestor ") even in India. Sumati, wife of King Sagara of Ayodhya, to whom sixty thousand sons had been promised, gave birth to a pumpkin from which sixty thousand children emerged.[5] One episode in the *Mahā-*

---

[1] Granet, *La Pensée chinoise*, p. 324.

[2] Hentze, *Mythes et symboles*, p. 158 ff.

[3] Van Gennep, *Mythes et légendes d'Australie*, p. 14.

[4] Matsumoto, *Essai sur la mythologie japonaise*, Paris, 1929, pp. 120 ff.

[5] *Rāmāyaṇa*, i, 38 ; *Mahābhārata*, iii, 106, etc.

bhārata[1] tells how " twins, Kṛpi and Kṛpa, were born to Gautama, son of Śaradvat, of a clump of reeds ".[2] There is further evidence of this notion of the mythical descent of various aboriginal Indian tribes from some plant or other. Udumbara, the Sanskrit name of the *Ficus glomerata*, means both the province of Punjab and its inhabitants.[3] One tribe in Madagascar are called Antaivandrika, which means literally, the people of (the tree) *vandrika*, and their neighbours, the Antaifasy, are descended from a banana tree: " From that banana tree there came out one day a fine little boy, who in a little while became very tall and strong . . . he had many children and grandchildren, and they were the ancestors of this tribe; they are still sometimes called the children of the banana tree."[4]

I could easily multiply examples. We might note the Iranian tradition of the origins of the first human pair; when the first man, Gayomard, succumbed to the blows of the evil spirit, his seed entered the earth and, forty years later, gave birth to a plant *rivas* which, in turn, was changed into Masyagh and Masyanagh.[5] But the Iranian brings in an additional element: the violent death of Gayomard. In two of my earlier works,[6] I studied this mythological motif of the origin of plants from the sacrifice (or violent death) of a primeval giant, and also the legendary theme of the appearance of plants from the blood or the body of a god or hero basely murdered. I shall be returning in another context to the conclusions I reached in these two works. However, what I want to look at at the moment is the solidarity between man and some kind of plant, a solidarity envisaged as a continuous circulation of life between the human and the plant. A human life which has been abruptly cut off is carried on in a plant; the latter, in its turn, if it is cut or burnt, gives birth to an animal or another plant which eventually finds a human form once more. We might sum up the theory implied in these legends thus: human life

[1] i, 63, v. 2456 ff.

[2] Cf. also Przyluski, " Les Empalés ", *Mélanges chinois et bouddhiques*, Brussels, 1936, vol. iv, p. 18.

[3] Przyluski, " Un Ancien Peuple du Penjab: les Udumbara ", *JA*, 1926, p. 36.

[4] Van Gennep, *Tabou et totémisme à Madagascar*, Paris, 1904, p. 300.

[5] Cf. the bibliography in *CZ*, vol. iii, p. 21.

[6] " Ierburile de sub Cruce " and " La Mandragore et les mythes de la naissance miraculeuse ", *CZ*, vol. iii.

must be completely lived out if it is to exhaust all its potentialities of creation and expression; if it is interrupted suddenly, by violent death, it will tend to extend itself in some other form: plant, fruit, flower. I will mention only a few examples of this: on battlefields where a number of heroes have been slain, roses or eglantines will grow;[1] violets grew up from the blood of Attis, and roses and anemones from that of Adonis when these two young gods were dying; from the body of Osiris there grew wheat and the *maat* plant and all kinds of herbs, and so on. The death of all these gods is in some way a re-enactment of the cosmogonic act when the worlds were created, which as we know, was the result of the sacrifice of a giant (Ymir is the type), or the self-sacrifice of a god.

But what chiefly interests us in the present chapter is the flowing of life between the two levels—vegetal and human. The fact that a race can be descended from a plant presupposes that the source of life is concentrated in that plant; and therefore that the human modality exists in it in a state of potentiality, in seed form. The Warramunga tribe of Northern Australia believe that " the spirits of children ", the size of a grain of sand, exist in certain trees, whence they sometimes come and enter the wombs of their mothers through the navel.[2] We are here seeing a process of rationalization of the primitive concept of the descent of the race from a tree; not only is the mythical ancestor born of a tree, but every newborn child comes directly and concretely from the substance of that tree. The source of reality and life seen in the tree has not put forth its creative power once and for all to give birth to the mythical ancestor—it continues its creation unceasingly with every individual man. That is a concrete and rationalist interpretation of the myth that the human race is descended from the very source of life expressed in plant species. But the theory underlying these rationalist variants remains the same: ultimate reality, with its powers to create, is concentrated (or expressed) in a tree.

The beliefs that the souls of ancestors are in some way attached to certain trees from which they pass as embryos into women's wombs form a compact group with a great many

---

[1] " Ierburile de sub Cruce ", p. 16.

[2] Spencer and Gillen, *Northern Tribes of Central Australia*, London, 1904, p. 331.

variations.[1]   In China it was thought that there was a tree to correspond to every woman; she would have as many children as it had flowers.   Sterile women would adopt a child to make flowers grow on their particular tree, so that they might become fertile.[2]   What is important in all these customs is this notion of the constant flowing of life between the plant level—as source of never-failing life—and the human;   men are all simply projections of the energy of the same vegetal womb, they are ephemeral forms constantly produced by the overabundance of plants.   Man is an ephemeral appearance of a new plant modality.   When he dies, or, rather, abandons his human condition, he returns—as " seed " or as " spirit "—to the tree.   In fact, these concrete formulæ merely express a change of level. Men again become one with the womb of all things, again acquire the status of seed, again become germs.   Death is a renewal of contact with the source of all life.   We find this same basic conception in all the beliefs connected with the Earth-Mother and the mystiques of agriculture.   Death is simply a change of modality, a passing to another level, a reintegration into the womb of all things.   If reality and life are expressed in terms of vegetation, the reintegration is merely a change of form: the dead man changes from the form of a man to the form of a tree.

114. TRANSFORMATION INTO PLANTS

The circulation of life between these two levels has been preserved in a good number of legends and folk stories which may be classed in two kinds: (a) the transformation of a murdered human being into a flower or tree; (b) miraculous fertilization by a fruit or a seed.   In earlier works I have gone into these two motifs in some detail; here I will only quote a few examples.   In a Santali tale published by Bodding,[3] seven brothers kill their sister, intending to eat her.   The youngest alone, who was also the most compassionate, could not bring himself to eat the body of his sister and buried the piece that fell to him in the earth.   Some time later a beautiful bamboo

---

[1] Cf. Frazer, *The Magic Art*, vol. ii, p. 50 ff.

[2] Hartland, *Primitive Paternity. The Myth of Supernatural Birth in Relation to the History of the Family*, London, 1909, vol. i, p. 148.

[3] *Santali Folk Tales*, Oslo, 1929, vo ii ,pp. 297 ff.

grew up on the spot. A man, passing by, saw it, and wanted to cut a piece of it to make a fiddle. But as soon as he struck it with his axe, he heard a voice calling: " Stop! Stop! do not cut so high! Cut lower! " So he struck the tree near its roots, only to hear the voice again, " Stop! do not cut so low! Cut higher! " At last, after hearing the voice twice more, the bamboo fell to his axe. The man made a fiddle of it, and it played gloriously " because that maiden was inside it ". One day the girl came out of the fiddle and became the wife of the musician—and her brothers were swallowed up by the earth.

This motif is very widespread in folklore. It can be summed up in this formula: a wonderful girl (a fairy) comes out of a fruit (pomegranate, lemon, orange) that is either miraculous in itself or has been won with great difficulty by a hero ; a slave or a very ugly woman kills her and takes her place, so becoming the hero's wife; a flower or a tree grows up from the body of the maid (or she is changed into a bird, or a fish which is killed by the ugly woman and thus gives birth to a tree); and finally the heroine reappears from the fruit (or bark, or a splinter of the wood) of the tree. Thus in an Indian tale from the Punjab, the murdered wife is turned into a lily; the false princess breaks it in bits, but from it there grows up a bunch of mint, and then a beautiful climbing plant. In the Deccan the story is of a jealous queen who drowns a girl in a pool. From it rises a sunflower, and from its ashes, when it is burnt, grows a mango.[1]

The story also crops up in Europe, though there it is mixed up with the secondary theme of the " substituted fiancée " and the " magic pin ". As in the Asiatic variant, the heroine undergoes several metamorphoses. In one Tuscan tale, the heroine turns into an " enormous eel " which, in turn, is killed and thrown into a bed of dog-roses. She then turns into an " extraordinarily large " dog-rose which is offered to the prince as a curiosity. A voice comes from the rose: " Gently! Do not strike me! " The prince cuts open the rose with a pen-knife and the beautiful maiden appears safe and sound. In the Greek version, the girl is turned into a little goldfish, then a lemon tree. Just as an old man seizes his axe to cut it down, he hears a voice: " Strike high! Strike low! Do not strike

[1] Cf. " Ierburile ", p. 15; " La Mandragore ", p. 34.

the middle for you will wound a maiden! "[1] That, of course, is very like the Santali story. In the Rumanian tale *The Three Golden Pomegranates*, the heroine is turned by a gypsy into a bird and ordered to be killed; from the bird's blood there grows a fine tall fir tree.[2]

115. RELATIONS BETWEEN MEN AND PLANTS

In all these stories the movement of life between man and plants is a dramatic one; the heroine, as one might say, disguises herself by taking the form of a tree when her life is cut short. It is a sort of provisional regression to the vegetal level. She carries on her life " hiding " under a new form. However, there are also folk stories which preserve the other primitive motif of this man-plant circuit—that of swallowing a seed or smelling a flower to acquire fertility. In Rumanian versions of the story of the Three Pomegranates, one of the parents is given an apple by a saint and, after eating it, gives birth to a child. (An old man who had eaten an apple given to him by a saint, found a girl-child being born from his thigh.)[3] One of the classic examples in folk literature is in the *Pentameron*,[4] in which a young virgin becomes pregnant after eating a rose leaf. Ovid[5] mentions the tradition that Mars was born of Juno without Jupiter having any part in it, because the goddess Flora had touched Juno with a flower. Penzer has assembled a number of these stories of conception by some heavenly fruit (cf. the Bibliography).

The man-plant circuit, preserved in dramatic form in folklore, is also expressed in a great many beliefs. At Mecklenburg, the placenta of every newborn child is buried at the foot of a young fruit tree; in Indonesia, a tree is planted on the spot where the placenta is buried.[6] Both these customs express the mystical solidarity between the growth of the tree and the growth of the man. Sometimes this solidarity exists between a tree and a whole tribe. Thus the Papus, for instance, believe

---

[1] E. Cosquin, *Les Contes Indiens et l'Occident*, Paris, 1922, pp. 84–5; " La Mandragore ", p. 34.

[2] Saineanu, *Basmele Românilor*, Bucharest, 1898, pp. 307 ff.

[3] Saineanu, pp. 308, 309.

[4] ii, 8.

[5] *Fasti*, v, 255.

[6] Van der Leeuw, *Religion in Essence and Manifestation*, London, 1938, p. 56.

that if anyone cuts down a certain tree they too will die.[1]
The Dolgan shamans plant a tree when they first feel their
vocation to magic; and after their death, the tree is torn up.
The Yurak shamans of the tundra north of Obolsk place two
sjadai (idols) in front of the tree to guard it, for if the tree were
to be destroyed, they too would perish.[2] In Europe, when a
royal heir is born, they still plant a lime tree. In the Bismarck
Archipelago, when a child is born, a coconut is planted; and
when the tree gives its first fruits, the child is held to be an
adult; the *mana* of a native chief will increase in proportion
as his tree is sturdy.[3] The mystical sharing of life between men
and trees forms a theme well known to folklore everywhere:
if the flowers of one kind of tree are fading or falling it is a
sign that a hero is threatened by danger or death. Other folk
beliefs of Europe also imply the myth that men are descended
from a tree; thus, around Nierstein in Hesse, there is a vast
lime tree " which provided children for the whole region ".[4]
In the Abruzzi it is said that new born children come from a
vine.[5]

116. THE TREE THAT REGENERATES

Trees are also the protectors of newborn children; they make
the birth easy, and then watch over the lives of tiny children
just as the earth does. The examples I quote will show very
clearly the parallels between earth and vegetation in their
religious significance. In any case, trees are simply another
expression of the inexhaustible life and reality which the earth
represents too. Underlying all the beliefs relating to earth or
plant ancestry, and the protection both earth and trees exercise
over the newly-born, we find an experience, and a " theory "
expressing it, of ultimate reality, the source of Life, the womb
of all forms. The earth, or the plant life growing upon it,
appears as *that which exists*, which exists as living, as endlessly
prolific, but in continual palingenesis. Merely touching or even

[1] Nyberg, *Kind und Erde*, p. 77.

[2] Holmberg-Harva, " Die religiösen Vorstellungen der altaischen Völker ",
Helsinki, 1939, *FFC*, no. 125, pp. 280–1; Emsheimer, " Schamanentrommel
und Schamanenbaum ", *ES*, 1946, no. 4, pp. 168 ff.

[3] Van der Leeuw, p. 56.

[4] Hartland, vol. i, p. 43.

[5] Hartland, p. 44.

approaching trees is beneficial, strengthening, fertilizing—and the same with the earth. Leto gave birth to Apollo and Artemis while kneeling in a meadow and touching a sacred palm tree with one hand. Queen Māha-Māyā gave birth to Buddha at the foot of a *śāla* tree while grasping one of its branches. Engelmann[1] and Nyberg[2] have assembled a wealth of ethnological evidence to show how common was the custom of women having their children near, or at the foot of, a tree. By merely being born near a source of life and healing, the child is sure of the best possible destiny. He will be free of illness, beyond the reach of evil spirits or accidents. His birth—like those taking place upon the ground—is, in a sense, a birth *in* his mother rather than of her; the real mother is Vegetation, and she will take care of him. And in this connection, we may note the custom which has existed from antiquity and is preserved even today among simple folk, of swaddling the child as soon as it is born and rubbing it with herbs, green branches or straw.[3] Direct contact with the embodiments of power and life can be nothing but favourable to the newborn child. Primitive cradles were made of green branches or ears of wheat. Dionysos, like all the children in ancient Greece, was placed as soon as he was born in a basket (*liknon*) in which the first fruits of the harvest were carried.[4] There is the same custom in present-day India[5] and elsewhere.[6] The rite is an ancient one; in Sumerian hymns we are told how Tammuz was placed at birth in a basket used for putting grain from the fields in.[7]

To place a sick child in the hollow of a tree implies a new birth, a regeneration.[8] In Africa and Sind, a sick child is cured by passing between two fruit trees joined together; the illness remains in the trees.[9] In Scandinavia, not children only, but sick adults too may be cured by going through the hollow of a

[1] *Die Geburt bei den Urvölkern*, Vienna, 1884, pp. 77 ff.

[2] *Kind und Erde*, pp. 207 ff.

[3] Nyberg, pp. 210 ff.

[4] Cf. Mannhardt, *Mythologische Forschungen*, Strasbourg, 1884. p, 369; Dieterich, *Mutter Erde*, pp. 101–4.

[5] Hastings, *Encycl. Rel. Ethics*, vol. ii, p. 682.

[6] Frazer, *Spirits of the Corn*, pp. 5–11.

[7] Jeremias, *Handbuch der altorientalischen Geisteskultur*, 2nd ed., Berlin ,1929, p. 345; *Allgemeine Religionsgeschichte*, Munich, 1918, p. 219.

[8] Mannhardt, *Wald- und Feldkulte*, Berlin, 1904, vol. i, pp. 32 ff.

[9] Nyberg, p. 216.

tree. Fertilizing plants, like curative herbs, owe their efficacy to this same principle: life and force are embodied in vegetation. The Hebrews called illegitimate children " children of herbs "; the Rumanians, "children of flowers ". We find the same terms elsewhere—among the natives of New Caledonia, for instance. Certain herbs have fertilizing powers; Lia had a son, Issachar, by Jacob, because of some mandrakes Ruben found in the fields.[1] All these miraculous and medicinal herbs are simply watered down and rationalized versions of their mythical prototypes: the herb which raises the dead, the herb of eternal youth, the herb that cures every sickness.

117. THE MARRIAGE OF TREES

Another ceremonial which shows the feeling of solidarity between men and plants is known as the " marriage of trees ". It is a custom common in India,[2] and occurs sporadically among certain groups of gypsies (those in Transylvania, for instance). The marriage of trees is generally performed when women have been married several years and still have no children. At an auspicious day and hour, husband and wife repair to a pool, and each plants a sapling there; the woman a young fig tree, the husband a mango tree. The planting is carried out in a proper ritual fashion, preceded by baths and so on. The woman attaches the stem of the *vepu*, or female tree, to the trunk of the *ārasu* or male tree, and then waters them from the pond; then both perform the *pradaksina* (ritual clockwise procession) three, twenty-seven, or a hundred and eight times. If one of the trees dries up it is a bad sign. That is why everything possible is done to make them grow normally; they are fenced round and so on. Their marriage is held to play a large part in the woman's fertility. After some time, these trees become the object of a cult, particularly when a *nāgakkal*, representing two cobras twined together, carved in stone, is placed near their twined trunks.[3]

This custom, practised on a large scale in India, presupposes that the wedding of two different plant species can have an influence on the woman's fertility. In other parts of India, the

[1] Gen. xxx. 14 ff.
[2] Cf. Frazer, *The Magic Art*, vol. ii, pp. 24 ff.
[3] Boulnois, *Le Caducée*, Paris, 1931, pp. 8 ff.

marriage of plants is performed at the same time as the marriage
of the human pair. In the Punjab, when a man marries for the
third time, they celebrate the marriage of a bamboo (*Acacia
arabica*) or an *Asclepia gigantesca*. In Nepal every girl from
among the *Newari* is married to a *bel* (a small tree) from her
youth; the spouse is then thrown into the water.[1] Weddings
between trees are effected for other purposes: the good luck
and wealth of the community for instance. A parallel custom
to this marrying of trees is the placing of a stick (*daṇḍa*) from
the *udumbara* tree between a young couple for the first few
nights after their wedding; the stick represents the Gandharvas
who, as we know, had the *jus primæ noctis*.[2] The sacred erotic
and fertilizing power of the Gandharvas, embodied in the wood,
was considered as consummating the marriage with the bride
before this was done by her husband.

118. THE MAY TREE

As we have seen, trees and plants in general always embody
inexhaustible life—which, in primitive ontology, corresponds
to absolute reality, to the " sacred " par excellence. The
cosmos is symbolized by a tree; the divinity is manifested in
the form of a tree; fertility, wealth, luck, health—or, on a
higher level, immortality, or eternal youth—are concentrated
in herbs or trees; mankind, or the tribe, is descended from a
plant species; human life takes refuge in plant forms if it is cut
short by some plot before its end is due; in short, all that *is*,
all that is *living* and *creative*, that is in a state of continual
regeneration, expresses itself in plant symbols. The cosmos
was pictured as a tree because, like one, it is periodically
regenerated. Spring is a resurrection of all life, and consequently of human life. In that cosmic act, all the forces of
creation return to their first vigour. Life is wholly reconstituted;
everything begins afresh; in short, the primeval act of the
creation of the cosmos is repeated, for every regeneration is a
new birth, a return to that mythical moment when for the first
time a form appeared that was to be constantly regenerated.

A great many rituals of vegetation imply the idea that the
whole of mankind is regenerated by an active participation in

[1] Nyberg, p. 201.
[2] Cf. Meyer, *Trilogie*, vol. iii, pp. 192 ff.

the resurrection of the plant world. European folk traditions have kept traces or fragments of ancient rites in which the coming of spring was hastened by adorning a tree and carrying it ceremonially in procession. Indeed, there still exists in Europe the custom of bringing a tree from the forest in spring, at the beginning of summer or on the feast of John the Baptist and setting it up in the middle of the village; or, in some places, everyone goes into the woods and cuts green branches to hang in the house and assure the prosperity of its master. This is known as bringing in the May.[1] In England, young people, or groups of little girls used to go from house to house on the first of May, wearing crowns of leaves and flowers, singing and asking for presents. In the Vosges, the ceremony takes place on the first Sunday of May. In Sweden, they bring a " Maypole " (*Maj stång*) into the house generally at the summer solstice; it is a fir tree with its branches stripped off, decorated with artificial flowers and toys and so on. Wherever this custom is found (from Scotland and Sweden to the Pyrenees and the Slav countries) the " Maypole " gives an occasion for general jollity ending with a dance round the pole. The chief part is usually played by young people or children. It is a feast of spring but, like all such manifestations, can turn into something of an orgy (§137).

Philip Stubbes, an English Puritan writer, in his *Anatomie of Abuses* (London, 1583), roundly condemns these survivals of paganism. For, he says, young persons of both sexes spend the night in the forests; Satan is their God; and when they bring the Maypole (" this stinkyng ydol rather ") into the village they dance a pagan dance round it. Only a third of the girls return home " undefiled ".[2] In spite of all the Church's resistance, May Day continued to be celebrated. Nor was it abolished even by the most far-reaching social changes; they only succeeded in altering the name. At Périgord and in many other places, the May Tree became a symbol of the French Revolution; it was called " the Tree of Liberty ", but the peasants danced the same ancient rounds about it as their ancestors.[3]

---

[1] Mannhardt, *Wald- und Feldkulte*, vol. i, pp. 312 ff.; Frazer, *The Magic Art*, vol. ii, pp. 59 ff.; id., *The Golden Bough*, abridged ed., London, 1924, pp. 120 ff.

[2] Quoted by Frazer in *The Magic Art*, vol. ii, p. 66; *The Golden Bough*, abridged ed., p. 123.

[3] A. Mathiez, *Les Origines des cultes révolutionnaires*, Paris, 1904, p. 32.

The first of May is nowadays celebrated as a feast of labour and of liberty; to the modern mind, this day still holds some vague memories of the myth of the regeneration and betterment of the community which is illustrated in all the traditionalist societies.

In many places when the Maypole is solemnly carried in, the previous year's tree is burnt.[1] The consumption of the wood by fire is probably another rite of the regeneration of the plant world and the beginning of the new year, for in India[2] and in classical antiquity[3] a tree was ceremonially burnt at the new year. This celebration, with the burning of the tree, was often in India the occasion of an orgy; the Bihars of the United Provinces (Agra and Oudh) for instance, set fire to the *sālmali* tree, and then gave themselves over to a collective orgy.[4] The ash of the tree is full of apotropaic and fertilizing qualities. It wards off sickness, the evil eye, and evil spirits.[5] In Europe the ashes remaining from the burnt Maypole, or firebrands from it, are scattered about the fields at Christmas or Carnival time to improve and multiply the crops.

All of this makes sense if we see it as a single ritual whole: the regeneration of plant life and the regeneration of " the year " (for remember that the New Year began in March with a great many peoples of the ancient East). The magic and fertilizing powers of the sacrificial wood are attributed also to the ash and charcoal;[6] they have " power " because they resemble a prototype (the ash of a tree burnt ceremonially at the beginning of the year, on St. John's day, etc.). Or trees or wood that are ceremonially burnt may become efficacious simply by their return to potency, by reverting to the state of " seed ", which results from burning; the " power " they represent or embody is unable to display itself formally any more and becomes concentrated into the ash or charcoal.

The coming of the May is often celebrated not only by a tree or Maypole but also by images in human form, ornamented

---

[1] Mannhardt, pp. 177 ff., pp. 186 ff.
[2] Meyer, vol. i, p. 101.
[3] Liungman, "Traditionswanderungen: Euphrat-Rhein", Helsinki, 1938, *FFC*, no. 119, vol. ii, p. 127.
[4] Crooke, " The Holi: A Vernal Festival of the Hindus ", *FRE*, vol. xxv, p. 59; other examples in Meyer, vol. i, p. 101, n. 2.
[5] In India, Crooke, p. 63; Meyer, pp. 107 ff.
[6] Cf. a wealth of documentation and references in Meyer, vol. i, pp. 157 ff.

with leaves and flowers, or even by an actual person embodying the power of vegetation or some mythical expression of it. Thus in northern Bavaria a tree called Walber is carried in procession to the centre of the village, and with it a young man, covered in straw, also called the " Walber ". The tree is stood in front of a tavern and the whole village dance round it; the young man called the Walber stands simply for the human counterpart of the powers of vegetation. The same sort of thing takes place among the Slavs of Carinthia who, on St. George's day, decorate a tree and cover a young man, who is known as "Green George", in green branches. After the songs and dances essential to every spring festival, an effigy of " Green George ", or even the young man himself, is thrown into the water. In Russia the tree has gone, and " the Green George " is only the young man dressed in green. In England, on May Day, " Jack-in-the-Green ", a chimney-sweep covered with leaves and ivy,[1] used to dance at the head of a whole group of sweeps. And when the dance was done, the sweeps made a collection among the audience.

All May ceremonies conclude with some sort of collection. The groups that go through villages with leaves and flowers, whether they are processsions, or carrying flower images or themselves represent plants, receive gifts at every house (and even the gifts have a traditional character: eggs, dried fruits, certain sorts of cake, etc.). If people refuse to give they are warned—either in verse or prose, according to the custom of the place—that they will not have good crops, that their orchard will not yield much fruit, that their wines will not do well, and so on. The group assume the right to punish the niggardly, because they are the messengers of vegetation. They do so both because avarice is dangerous to the community as a whole, and with a dramatic occurrence like the coming of spring, food, the substance of life, must circulate generously within the community in order that the cosmic circuit of life's substance may be kept in motion (trees, flocks, harvests); and because the group, by announcing the good news of spring, feel that they are performing a ceremonial action of interest to the whole community, and that such a performance should

---

[1] Frazer, *The Magic Art*, vol. ii, pp. 75 ff.; *The Golden Bough*, abridged ed., pp. 126–9.

be rewarded: the group *sees* spring before anyone else, *brings* it to the village, *shows* it to the others and *hastens* its coming with song, dance and ritual.

119. " KING " AND " QUEEN "

Indeed, in some places the coming of the May is an occasion for all sorts of competitions, choosing the sturdiest pair (to be " king " and " queen "), ritual wrestling, etc. All such tests, whatever their original meaning, came to be aimed at stimulating the energies of nature. The day usually starts with a race to the Maypole, or a competition among the young men and boys to see who can climb it the quickest. I will give a few examples only: in Saxony the ceremony took place on May 1, or Whitsunday, and consisted first in bringing young trees from the forest (*majum quærere*) to decorate the houses, then in setting up one tree, the May, solemnly in the centre of the village. Its branches were cut off, except perhaps a few of the topmost ones which were laden with gifts (sausages, eggs, cakes). Then young men competed, in some regions, to see who could most quickly climb to the top, in others, who could run quickest to where the Maypole stood. Sometimes there was a race on horseback.[1] The winner was borne shoulder-high and given honours. At one time he was presented with a red cloth by the prettiest girls.

In Silesia, the winner of the race on horseback was called " King of Pentecost " and his fiancée the " Queen of Pentecost ". The loser was made to play the part of a buffoon. He was obliged to eat thirty bread rolls and drink four litres of strong drink before the " king " arrived; the king, bearing a bunch of May and a crown, and with a cortège made up of all the village, was finally brought to the inn. There, if the buffoon had succeeded in eating and drinking all he should and was in a state to welcome the king with a speech and a glass of beer, his reckoning was paid by the king; otherwise, the buffoon had to pay his own reckoning. After Mass, the procession set forward again with the king and the buffoon at its head, wearing the crown of Pentecost, and stopped at every farm to ask for gifts in money or in kind " to buy soap and wash the beard of the fool ". Custom decreed that all the " knights " in the

[1] Frazer, *The Magic Art*, vol. ii, pp. 66 ff.

king's cortège might seize whatever eatables they found in the house, except those that were locked up. The cortège then went towards the house where the king's fiancée lived. She was called the " Queen of Pentecost ", and they gave her presents. The king had the right to put up the Maypole in front of the house of the farmer he worked for where it remained until the following year. Finally everyone returned to the fountain and the king and queen led the dancing.[1]

120. SEXUALITY AND VEGETATION

In some places (in France, England, and Bohemia, for instance), it was the custom to choose a May Queen. But most of the folk traditions of Europe retain the primeval pair under one name or another: king and queen, master and mistress, betrothed couple, lovers (as in Sicily and Sardinia). It is unquestionably a watered-down version of the old image of a young couple spurring on the creative forces of nature by mating ritually on ploughed land (cf. §135 ff.) to re-enact the cosmic hierogamy of Sky and Earth. This couple would always lead the procession carrying the Maypole from farm to farm collecting gifts. They were often looked upon thereafter as married. In other cultural patterns and frameworks the ceremonial pair lost their original meaning (of a sacred marriage), and became part of a whole ritual orgy. And in some cases it is hard to see exactly how far a given rite is expressing an erotic symbolism and how far simply a symbolism of earth and agriculture. Life is a single thing; the various levels of cosmic life fit together (moon-woman-earth; sky-rain-man; etc.) and even cut across each other at certain central points (all the cosmological attributes of the moon, night, water, earth, seeds, birth, regeneration, resurrection and so on are present, virtually at least, in woman, and can be actualized and increased by feminine rituals or hierogamies). We must therefore constantly direct our attention to this totality of units which in one sense gives rise to all the rituals and in another results from them. Vegetation cults, above all, must be interpreted in the light of the original bio-cosmological conception which gave rise to them. That they appear so various is often

[1] Drechsler, *Sitte, Brauch, und Volksglauben in Schlesien*, Breslau, 1901, vol.i, pp. 125–8; Frazer, *The Magic Art*, vol. ii, pp. 84 ff.

merely an illusion of modern vision; basically they flow from
one primitive ontological intuition (that the *real* is not only
what *is* indefinitely the same, but also what *becomes* in organic
but cyclic forms), and converge towards one object—that of
assuring the regeneration of the powers of nature by one means
or another.

Thus, in certain islands of the Amboina group, for instance,
when the clove plantations seem poor, the men go to them
during the night with nothing on, and try to fertilize the trees,
crying " Cloves ! " Among the Bagandas of central Africa,
any woman who gives birth to twins shows by that proof of her
fertility that she is a centre of life and can fertilize the banana
trees; if a banana leaf is placed between her legs and pushed
away by her husband during intercourse, it gains such extraordinary powers that the farmers from neighbouring villages
will try to get hold of it and are ready to pay a lot for it.[1]
In both cases, we have an application of human sexuality to
vegetative life; an application that is grotesque, over-concrete,
and limited to individual objects (certain trees, certain women)
—not projected by magic over the whole pattern, over life as a
whole.

These exceptional cases confirm the principle implied in the
sacred marriage, in the springtime union of young couples on
ploughed land, in the races and competitions used to stimulate
the forces of plant life during certain festivals of spring and
summer, in the May King and Queen, and so on. In all of
them we perceive the desire to spur on the circuit of bio-cosmic
energy, and particularly vegetative energy, on a vast scale. As
we have seen, it is not always a question of man's stimulating
vegetation with ceremonial and hierogamy; often it is human
fertility which is stimulated by plant life (as for instance with
the marriage of trees in India; fertility coming through fruits
and seeds, through the shadow of a tree and so on). It is the
same closed circuit of the substance of life springing up from
every cosmic level, but being concentrated and thrust into
certain centres (woman, vegetation, animals) according to
man's needs. This circulation of the substance of life and
sacred powers among the various bio-cosmic levels, a circulation

[1] Frazer, *The Magic Art*, vol. ii, pp. 101 ff.; *The Golden Bough*, abridged ed.
p. 137.

directed by man for his own immediate gain, was later to be used as the best way of attaining immortality or the " salvation " of the soul (cf. the Graeco-Oriental mysteries).

121. FIGURES REPRESENTING VEGETATION

What is essential to all vegetation festivals as they remain in the traditions of Europe is the ritual display of the tree and the blessing given to the starting year. All this will become clearer in the light of the examples I am going to give. The changes the calendar has undergone over the course of years may sometimes disguise this element of regeneration, of " beginning afresh " which we can trace in so many springtime customs. The reappearance of the plants opens a new cycle of time; plant life is reborn, " starts again " every spring. The origin common to both groups of ceremonies—the display of the Maypole and the beginning of a new " time "—can be clearly seen in quite a number of traditions. In some places, for instance, the custom is to " kill " the May King, who represents vegetation and stimulates its growth. In Saxony and Thuringia, groups of young boys go out to find the " wild man ", clothed in leaves and hiding in the forest; they take hold of him and fire blanks at him from their guns.[1] In Czechoslovakia on Shrove Tuesday, a group of young men disguise themselves and set out to pursue the " king " in a hunt through the town, catch him, try him and condemn him to death. The king, who has a long neck composed of a large number of hats on top of each other, is then decapitated. Around Pilsen (Czechoslovakia) the king appears dressed in grass and flowers, and after the trial can try to escape on horseback. If he is not caught he can remain king for another year; otherwise his head is cut off.[2]

Among European folk traditions, we find two other ceremonies which are closely connected with these spring festivals, and fulfil similar functions in the same ceremonial system of the rebirth of the year and its vegetation. The first is the " death and burial of the Carnival " and the second the " battle between

[1] Frazer, *The Golden Bough*, abridged ed., pp. 296 ff.; *The Dying God*, London, 1936, pp. 205 ff.

[2] Frazer has good reason to see in this a parallel to the ritual of the priest of Nemi; in just the same way, this priest in ancient Italy fought for his life and if he got away could continue to carry out his functions. The Czechoslovakian custom is also reminiscent of the *regifugium;* cf. Frazer, *The Golden Bough*, abridged ed., p. 229; *The Dying God*, p. 213.

winter and summer ", followed by the driving out of Winter
(or Death) and the bringing in of Spring. The date on which this
custom occurs varies; but generally Winter is driven out (and
Death murdered) on the fourth Sunday of Lent or (as with the
Czechs) a week later; in some German villages of Moravia, it
takes place on the Sunday after Easter. This difference, like the
difference we observe in the various May rituals (May 1,
Whitsun, the beginning of June, feast of St. John the Baptist,
etc.) is in itself an indication of how the ceremony changed
date in passing from one place to another, and in working its
way into different ritual systems. This is not the place to go
into the origins and meaning of the Carnival; what interests
us here is the concluding act of the festivals; an effigy of the
" Carnival " is, in a great many places, " condemned to death "
and executed (the method of the execution varies—sometimes
it is burnt, sometimes drowned, sometimes beheaded). The
" putting to death of the Carnival " is often accompanied by
general tussles; nuts are thrown at the grotesque creature itself,
or everyone pelts everyone else with flowers or vegetables. In
other places (around Tübingen, for instance) the figure of the
Carnival is condemned, decapitated and buried in a coffin in
the cemetery after a mock ceremony. This is called " Carnival's
funeral ".[1]

The other episode which is of the same sort is the driving
out or killing of " Death " in various forms. The most widespread custom in Europe is this: children make a guy from
straw and branches and carry it out of the village saying: " We
are carrying Death to the water ", or something of the sort;
they then throw it into a lake or well, or else burn it. In Austria,
all the audience fight round Death's funeral pyre to get hold of a
bit of the effigy.[2] There we see the fertilizing power of Death—
a power attaching to all the symbols of vegetation, and to the
ashes of the wood burnt during all the various festivals of the
regeneration of nature and the beginning of the New Year. As
soon as Death has been driven out or killed, Spring is brought
in. Among the Saxons of Transylvania, while the boys are
bearing the effigy of Death out of the village, the girls are

---

[1] Frazer, *The Golden Bough*, abridged ed., pp. 302 ff.; *The Dying God*, pp.
220 ff.

[2] Frazer, *The Golden Bough*, p. 314; *The Dying God*, pp. 230 ff.

preparing for the coming of Spring, personified by one of themselves.[1]

Elsewhere it is young men who bring the Summer in and this ceremony is another variant on the Maypole ceremony; boys go to the forest and cut down a young tree, remove its branches, decorate it, and then come back to the village and go from house to house singing that they are bringing Summer and asking for gifts.[2]   Liungman has shown[3] that this folk custom sprang from the original series of Carnival celebrations, that is, from the opening of the " New Year " (§153).   In Switzerland, Swabia and Ostmark we find, even in the present century, the effigy of Winter or " Grandmother " being driven out at Carnival time.[4]   An eighth-century religious writer notes that the Germanic tribes *in menso februario hibernum credi expellere*.   In some places witches were burnt at carnival time (as personifications of Winter; there are similar traditions in India),[5] or else the effigy of Winter was attached to a wheel or something of the sort.

As for the second part—the bringing in of Summer— Liungman declares that it, too, originated in the primitive Carnival.   This second part consists in displaying a creature, usually some bird (first in the ancient East;[6] and in classical antiquity since when it passed through the Balkans to central and northern Europe),[7] or else a leafy branch, or bunch of flowers—in short, something heralding spring as the Maypole does (cf. *eiresione* in Greece).[8]   The verses sung while Winter is driven out and Spring brought in are the same that were sung at the Carnival; the same threats are made to those who refuse gifts.[9]   For, like the Carnival and all the ceremonies derived from it, this festival ends with the collection of gifts.[10]

---

[1] Frazer, *The Golden Bough*, pp. 312, 313; *The Dying God*, pp. 207 ff.

[2] Frazer, *The Golden Bough*, p. 311.

[3] " Traditionswanderungen: Rhein-Jenissei ", Helsinki, 1941. *FFC*, no. 130, *passim*.

[4] Liungman, " Rhein-Jenissei ", p. 19.

[5] Meyer, vol. i, pp. 83 ff.

[6] Cf. Liungman, " Euphrat-Rhein ", I, pp. 352 ff.

[7] Liungman, II, pp. 1100 ff.

[8] Nilsson, *Geschichte*, I, 113 ff.

[9] Liungman, " Rhein-Jenissei ", pp. 44 ff.

[10] Liungman, p. 22.

122. RITUAL CONTESTS

There is one more custom which we should note here: the contest between Summer and Winter, an episode that is acted out partly by a contest between the representatives of the two seasons, and partly in a long dialogue in verse in which each character takes it in turns to declaim a stanza. As Liungman has shown,[1] this is far less widespread than the ceremony of driving out Winter and bringing in Spring, which suggests that it is of more recent origin. I will give only a few examples. In Sweden, at the May festival, there is a contest between two groups of knights. The group representing Winter are dressed in fur and throw snow and ice balls; the others wear branches and flowers. The Summer group finally win and the ceremony ends in general feasting. Along the Rhine, Winter appears dressed in straw and Summer in ivy. Naturally the fighting ends with Summer as victor, and the young man playing the part of Winter is flung to the ground and all his straw covering removed. The actors later take it in turns to go into houses with a magnificent crown of flowers, and demand gifts.[2]

The most common form the contest takes is going from house to house with each " season " taking it in turns to recite a stanza. Liungman has collected a considerable number of variants of this song praising in turn winter and summer. He considers[3] the literary form itself to be no older than the fifteenth century A.D., but the mythological prototype of the contest is undoubtedly very ancient. After noting innumerable medieval and ancient literary traditions (*Des Poppe Hofton*, a fifteenth-century manuscript, Hans Sachs' poem *Gesprech zwischen dem Sommer und Winter*, 1538, the Latin poem *Conflictus Veris et Hiemis* of the eighth or ninth century, Virgil's third Eclogue, Theocritus' fifth Idyll and so on),[4] Liungman sets forth, and rejects,[5] the various hypotheses put forward by the scholars (for instance the fight between Xanthos and Melanthos, the " light " and the " dark ", which Usener

---

[1] " Der Kampf zwischen Sommer und Winter ", Helsinki, 1941, *FFC*, no. 130, pp. 118 ff.

[2] Frazer, *The Golden Bough*, pp. 316, 317; *The Dying God*, pp. 246 ff.

[3] " Der Kampf ", p. 159.

[4] " Der Kampf ", pp. 124 ff.

[5] " Der Kampf ", pp. 146 ff.

considers the prototype of the motif we are considering) and himself states his conviction that the mythological prototype is the fight between Tiamat and Marduk, a struggle commemorated in Babylonian ritual at the beginning of each year.[1]

I agree with the Swedish scholar's conclusions about the mythological prototype (he speaks further of the struggle between vegetation and its adversary, drought; Osiris and Set in Egypt, Aleion and Mot for the Phoenicians, etc.) for, as I have shown a number of times in this work, every ritual is the repetition of a primal action which took place *in illo tempore*. But as to the historical spreading of this motif, I do not know how far the results of Liungman's research may be considered final. He himself points out[2] that the struggle between Summer and Winter is to be found among the Eskimos and the Yakuts, though he cannot say whether the custom came from the Mesopotamo-European tradition or from some other source. The struggle itself is a ritual for stimulating the forces of birth and of plant life. The contests and fights which take place in so many places in the spring or at harvest time undoubtedly spring from the primitive notion that blows, contests, rough games between the sexes and so on, all stir up and increase the energies of the whole universe. What we are primarily concerned with is the *model*, the *archetype* upon which these customs rest: all these things are done because they were done *in illo tempore* by divine beings, done to fit in with a ritual order then being established.

We find these ceremonial fights in a great many primitive religions, for instance in the most ancient strata of the cult of Osiris and the protohistoric religions of Scandinavia.[3] The same contests occur in Europe to-day, as part of this same series of spring celebrations; thus, on 29th June, feast of SS. Peter and Paul, the " burial of Kostroma " was celebrated in Russia—Kostroma being a mythical figure symbolizing the rhythmic life and death of vegetation. It was accompanied by contests and then lamentations.[4] The death and resurrection of Kostrubonko (another name for the same well known

---

[1] " Der Kampf ", p. 151.
[2] " Der Kampf ", p. 184.
[3] Cf. Almgren, *Nordische Felszeichnungen als religiöse Urkunden*, Frankfurt a. M., 1934.
[4] Frazer, *The Golden Bough*, p. 318; *The Dying God*, pp. 261 ff.

spring god of Slavonic origin, we are told by A. Bruckner)[1] were always celebrated in Russia by a chorus of girls singing:

> Dead, dead is our Kostrubonko
> Dead ! he who was dear to us is dead !

Then, suddenly one of them cried:

> Come back to life ! Our Kostrubonko has come back to life !
> He who was dear to us has come back to life ![2]

Although Bruckner is convinced that the rite and the name of the god are both genuinely proto-Slavonic in origin, the lamentation of the girls followed by their joy at Kostrubonko's resurrection recalls the traditional pattern of the drama of the eastern vegetation divinities.

123. COSMIC SYMBOLISM

We can pick out one charactertistic that all these folk ceremonies have in common: they celebrate a cosmic event (spring or summer) by using some symbol of vegetation. A tree, flower or animal is displayed; a tree is ceremonially decorated and carried in procession, or if not a tree, then a piece of wood, a man dressed in leaves, or some effigy; there are sometimes contests, fights, or scenes acted out relating to a death or a resurrection. For a moment, the life of the whole human group is concentrated into a tree or some effigy of vegetation, some symbol intended to represent and consecrate the thing that is happening to the universe: spring. It is as if the human group were incapable of expressing its joy and assisting in the arrival of spring on a larger scale (objectively speaking), on any scale embracing all nature. Man's joy, and his co-operation in effecting the final victory of vegetal life, are restricted to a microcosm: a branch, a tree, an effigy, a person in fancy dress. The presence of nature is indicated by a single object (or symbol). It is no pantheist adoration of nature or sense of being at one with it, but a feeling induced by the presence of the symbol (branch, tree or whatever it may be), and stimulated by the performing of the rite (processions, contests, fights, and the rest). This ceremonial is based on a comprehensive notion of the sacredness of all living force as

[1] *La Mitologia slava*, Bologna, 1923, p. 128.
[2] Frazer, *The Golden Bough*, pp. 318 ff.; *The Dying God*, pp. 261–2.

expressed at every level of life, growing, wearing itself out and being regularly regenerated. This " bio-cosmic sacredness " is personified in many different forms, changing, it would seem, to suit mood or circumstance. A spirit of vegetation appears from time to time in a mythical creation, lives, becomes widespread, and finally vanishes. What remains, what is basic and lasting, is the " power " of vegetation, which can be felt and manipulated equally well in a branch, an effigy or a mythological figure. But it would be wrong to see a more authentic religious significance in a ceremony built round a mythical person (such, for instance, as Kostrubonko) than in a ceremony in which there is only a *sign* (branch, or maypole, or some such). These are differences which, it must be realized, flow simply from differences in the mythological creativity of the various societies, or even from a chance of history. In neither case do they matter very much. In all of them we find the same basic idea and the same inclination to celebrate in a microcosm what is happening in the whole cosmos, to celebrate it symbolically.

What matters, I repeat, is not only the *expression* of the power of plant life, but the *time* when it is effected. It takes place not only in space but in time too. A new stage is beginning: in other words, repetition is being made of the initial mythical act of regeneration. That is why we find the ceremonies of vegetation celebrated—in all sorts of places and at all sorts of periods—between carnival time and the feast of St. John. It was not the actual appearance of spring which produced the vegetation rituals; it is not a question of what has been called a " naturist religion ", but of a ritual drama adapted to fit the different dates in question. Yet in every case the drama kept its original form: it is a *re-actualization* of the primeval act of regeneration. We have seen, too, that when the new Maypole arrives, the previous year's is burnt, that the effigies of Carnival, of Winter, of Death and Vegetation are also burnt and that their ashes are often in high demand for their powers of giving life and warding off evil. Liungman, however, notes[1] that some tree-trunks are also burnt at other times: for instance the Slavs of the southern Danube have the custom of burning a tree or branch which they call Badnjak

[1] " Euphrat-Rhein ", II, pp. 1027 ff.

at Christmas, the New Year or the Epiphany. The Badnjak burns for several days running in each house, and its ash is then spread over the fields to make them fertile; it thus enriches the family and increases its flocks. The Bulgars even used incense, myrrh and olive oil to honour the Badnjak; this custom, which dates very far back in the Balkans, is to be found over all of Europe, and must there be very ancient.

Of course there are places where trees are burnt at quite different times. In the Tyrol, it is the first Thursday in Lent when a log is carried in solemn procession; in Switzerland it is on Christmas Eve, at the New Year and at Carnival time. And then the ceremony of carrying and burning the " log of Christ " or the carnival tree (in the West) is performed by the same characters as bring in the Maypole; we find the King and Queen, the Moor, the Wild Man, the Buffoon and so on;[1] and the same actors and the same ritual tree reappear at weddings. Liungman thinks that all the customs involving the solemn bringing in and burning of a tree are derived from the ancient custom of burning trees on the first of May, the beginning of the new year. For one thing, in the Balkans and elsewhere, the custom was shifted to the time of Christmas and New Year; for another, in the West it became attached to Mardi Gras (the Carnival), then to the first of May, to Pentecost and St. John's day.[2] What it is interesting to note here is the cosmico-temporal significance which this custom of burning trees had (and always kept, though gradually less so). Burning was, and remained, a ritual of regeneration, or beginning-again, and at the same time it was the commemoration of an action performed *in illo tempore*. The magico-vegetal significance took second place in this ritual; its expressed object was to commemorate the opening of the year. We can therefore conclude that, in this particular ritual, the metaphysical notion came before the concrete experience of the coming of spring.

124. SUMMING-UP

One must not be confused by the almost unlimited abundance of plant hierophanies. Though many and varied they can be

[1] " Euphrat-Rhein ", p. 1036.
[2] " Euphrat-Rhein ", p. 1051.

reduced to coherence fairly simply. To take but two of the things we have looked at, it is obvious that the main difference between, for instance, the Cosmic Tree and the May procession is the difference between a cosmological *ideogram* and a *ritual*. The formulæ for carrying out a rite are not those for stating an ideogram, myth or legend. But all of them express the same idea: that vegetation is the manifestation of *living reality*, of the life that renews itself periodically. The myths about trees giving birth to men, the vegetation rituals of spring, the legends telling how simples originated, or how the heroes of the old tales were turned into plants, are all expressing, by means of symbol or drama, the same notional conviction: the plant world embodies (or signifies, or shares in) the *reality* of which *life* is made, which creates untiringly, which is ever reborn in an innumerable variety of forms, and is never worn out. Touching a tree to become pregnant or to protect a newborn child implies a definite and complete conception of the *reality* and *life* embodied in vegetation, and that same notion is implied in the ideogram of the Cosmic Tree or the myths of the Tree of Life; in each case, Life is manifested through a plant symbol. And so we are back at the idea of vegetation becoming a hierophany—that is, embodying and displaying the sacred—in so far as it *signifies* something *other than itself*. No tree or plant is ever sacred simply as a tree or plant; they become so because they *share* in a transcendent reality, they become so because they *signify* that transcendent reality. By being consecrated, the individual, "profane" plant species is transubstantiated; in the dialectic of the sacred a part (a tree, a plant) has the value of the whole (the cosmos, life) a profane thing becomes a hierophany. Yggdrasil was the symbol of the Universe, but to the Germans of old any oak tree could become sacred if it partook of this archetypal condition, if it "repeated" Yggdrasil. Similarly, to the Altai peoples *any* birch tree might be consecrated and so become the Tree of the World, and by mounting it ritually the shaman would in reality be climbing beyond the heavens.

What are classed together as "vegetation cults", therefore, are more complex than the name suggests. Through vegetation it is the whole of life, it is nature itself which is renewed in its manifold rhythms, which is "honoured", urged on, prayed to.

The forces of plant life are an epiphany of the life of the whole universe. Because man's lot is cast in with that nature and he thinks he can use that life for his own ends, he takes " signs " of vegetation and uses them (Maypoles, blossoming branches, the marriage of trees, and all the rest) or venerates them (" sacred trees " and so on). But there has never been any real vegetation cult, any religion solely built upon plants and trees. Even in the most " specialized " religions (the fertility cults, for instance), when plant life has been adored and used in the cult, other forces of nature have too. What are generally known as " vegetation cults " are really seasonal celebrations which cannot be accounted for merely in terms of a plant hierophany, but form part of far more complex dramas taking in the whole life of the universe. Indeed, it is sometimes hard to separate vegetation elements from the religious elements connected with the Earth-Mother, or Eros, or ancestor worship, or the sun, or the New Year, or any number of other things. Here I have set them apart so that we might get a clearer impression of the nature of plant hierophanies. But as with all primitive religious experience, all the various hierophanies (plants, the Earth-Mother, Eros and so on) in actual fact appear side by side and already form part of some sort of system. Using plant " symbols " and giving honour to plant " signs " *signifies* life in its every expression, the tireless and fruitful workings of nature. These references to life and to nature must not be taken to mean some sort of pantheist experience, some mystical way of getting in touch with cosmic life. For, as I noted earlier (§ 123), it is not the natural phenomenon of spring, the actual occurrence itself which inspires the rituals of springtime, but it is, on the contrary, the ritual which confers its significance upon the coming of spring; it is the symbolism and the ceremonial which show the full meaning of the renewal of nature and the start of a " new life "; in other words, the periodic recurrence of a new creation.

In this brief summary I have not mentioned the so-called " gods of vegetation " simply because the term lends itself to a good deal of confusion. Though there are plant epiphanies connected with some divinities, it would be hard to reduce them to a plant hierophany. The gods always reveal more than a mere plant hierophany would; their " form ", their career, and their nature go far beyond the simple revelation of living reality, of life renewed with the seasons. To understand properly what a " god of vegetation " is, one must first understand what a " god " is at all.

BIBLIOGRAPHY

Cf. also the bibliography for Chapter IX, especially the works of Mannhardt, Frazer, and J. J. Meyer.

On the sacred tree: PARROTT, Nell, *Les Représentations de l'arbre sacré sur les monuments de Mésopotamie et d'Elam*, Paris, 1937; DANTHINE, Hélène, *Le Palmier-dattier et les arbres sacrés dans l'iconographie de l'Asie occidentale ancienne*, Paris, 1937; WENSINCK, A. J., " Tree and Bird as Cosmological Symbols in Western Asia ", *Verhandelingen der Koninklijke Akademie van Wettenschappen*, Amsterdam, 1921, vol. xxii, pp. 1–56; COOMARASWAMY, A., *Yakṣas*, Washington, 1928–31, 2 vols.; NILSSON, M. P., *Geschichte der griechischen Religion*, Munich, 1941, vol. i, pp. 194 ff., 260 ff.; PRZYLUSKI, J., *La Participation*, Paris, 1940, pp. 41 ff.; HENTZE, C., *Mythes et symboles lunaires*, Antwerp, 1932, pp. 41 ff.; BERGEMA, H., *De Boom des Levens in Schrift en Historie*, Hilversum, 1938, pp. 337 ff.

On the inverted tree: COOMARASWAMY, A., " The Inverted Tree ", *The Quarterly Journal of the Mythic Society*, Bangalore, 1938, vol. xxix, no. 2, pp. 1–38; KAGAROW, E., " Der umgekehrte Schamanenbaum ", *AFRW*, 1929, p. 183; ritual inverted trees: HOLMBERG-HARVA, Uno, " Der Baum des Lebens ", *AASF*, Helsinki, 1922–3, series B, vol. xvi, pp. 17, 59, etc.; id., *Finno-Ugric and Siberian Mythology*, Boston, 1927 (in the series *The Mythology of All Races*), pp. 349 ff.; BERGEMA, op. cit., p. 275, n. 116; ELIADE, M., *Le Chamanisme*, Paris, 1951, pp. 244 ff.

On Yggdrasil and on the Cosmic Tree among the early Germans, cf. the references and bibliography in DE VRIES, Jan, *Altgermanische Religionsgeschichte*, Berlin-Leipzig, 1937, vol. ii, pp. 402 ff.; REUTER, *Germanische Himmelskunde*, Munich, 1934, pp. 229 ff.; BERGEMA, op. cit., p. 551.

On the Great-Goddess-Vegetation-Emblematic-Animal-Water pattern: MARSHALL, Sir John, *Mohenjo-Daro and the Indus Civilization*, London, 1931, vol. i, figs. 63–7, pp. 52 ff.; CONTENAU, G., *La Déesse nue babylonienne*, Paris, 1914, *passim*; id., *Le Déluge babylonien*, Paris, 1941, pp. 159 ff.; AUTRAN, C., *La Préhistoire du Christianisme*, Paris, 1941, vol. i, pp. 124 ff.; ALBRIGHT, W. F., " The Babylonian Sage Ut-Napistim Nuqu ", *JAOS*, 1918, vol. xxxviii, pp. 60–5; id., " The Goddess of Life and Wisdom," *JASS*, 1920, vol. xxxvi, pp. 258–94; id., " Some Cruces in the Langdon Epic ", *JAOS*, 1919, vol. xxxix, pp. 65–90; id., " The Mouth of the Rivers ", *JASS*, 1919, vol. xxxv, pp. 161–95; id., " Gilgamesh and Enkidu, Mesopotamian Genii of Fecundity ", *JAOS*, 1920, vol. lx, pp. 307–35; NILSSON, M. R., *Geschichte der griechischen Religion*, vol. i, pp. 260 ff.; HOLMBERG-HARVA, U., " Der Baum des Lebens ", pp. 83 ff.; HENTZE, C., *Frühchinesische Bronzen und Kultdarstellungen*, Antwerp, 1937, pp. 129 ff.; MARCONI, Momolina, *Riflessi mediterranei nella più antica religione laziale*, Milan, 1939; PERSSON, Axel W., *The Religion of Greece in Prehistoric Times*, Berkeley and Los Angeles, 1942; BERNADIN, S. A., *De mannelijke en de vrouwelijke godheid van de boomcultus in Minoische godsdienst*, Amsterdam, 1942; PESTALOZZA, U., *Pagine di religione mediterranea*, Milan, 1945, vol. ii.

On the Tree of Life and the Tree of the Knowledge of Good and Evil, see the discussion of the most recent interpretations in: SCHMIDT, Hans, *Die Erzählung von Paradies und Sündefall*, Tübingen, 1931; HUMBERT,

Paul, *Etudes sur le récit du paradis et de la chute dans la Genèse*, Neuchâtel, 1940; BERGEMA, op. cit., pp. 120 ff.

On the journey of Gilgamesh and the " plant of life ", CONTENAU, G., *L'Epopée de Gilgamesh* (translation with commentary), Paris, 1939; discussed in FURLANI, G., *La Religione babilonese-assira*, Bologna, 1921, vol. ii, pp. 50 ff. (p. 83, no. 69, bibliography; also DHORME, E., *Les Religions de Babylonie et d'Assyrie*, Paris, 1945, pp. 328 ff.; VIROLLEAUD, C., " Le Voyage de Gilgamesh au paradis ", *RHR*, 1930, vol. ci, pp. 202–15.

The Iranian texts have been collected and translated by BARNETT, L. D., " Yama, Gandharva and Glaucus ", *BSOAS*, 1926–8, vol. iv, pp. 703–16, particularly pp. 709 ff.; CHRISTENSEN, A., *Le Premier homme et le premier roi dans l'histoire légendaire des Iraniens*, Uppsala-Leiden, 1931, vol. ii, pp. 11 ff.

The eastern legends of the Tree of Life have been studied by August Wünsche, " Die Sagen vom Lebensbaum und Lebenswasser. Altorientalische Mythen ", *Ex Oriente. Lux*, Leipzig, 1905, vol. i, nos. 2–3; HOPKINS, E. W., " The Fountain of Youth ", *JAOS*, 1905, vol. xxvi, pp. 1–67; FRIENDLÄNDER, Israel, *Die Chadirlegende und der Alexanderroman*, Leipzig, 1913; HOLMBERG-HARVA, Uno, " Der Baum des Ledens," *passim*; BERGEMA, H., *De Boom des Levens*, pp. 238 ff.

On the divine origins of simples and magic plants: ELIADE, " Ierburile de sub Cruce ", first published in the *Revista Fundatülor Regale*, November, 1939, pp. 4 ff.; id., " La Mandragore et les mythes de la *naissance miraculeuse* ", *CZ*, 1942, vol. iii, pp. 1–48, particularly pp. 22 ff.; OHRT, F., " Herba, Gratia Plęna. Die Legenden der älteren Segensprüche über den göttlichen Ursprung der Heil- und Zauber-kraüter ", Helsinki, 1929, *FFC*, no. 82; DELATTE, A., *Herbarius. Recherches sur le cérémonial usité chez les anciens pour la cueillette des simples et des plantes magiques*, 2nd ed., Liège-Paris, 1938.

On the legends and iconography of the wood of the Cross: WÜNSCHE, A., " Lebensbaum ", pp. 33 ff.; GRAF, Arturo, *Miti, leggende e superstizioni del Medio Evo*, Turin, 1925, pp. 61 ff. (bibliography, p. 126, n. 6); CARTOJAN, N., *Cărtile populare în literatura românească*, Bucharest, 1929, vol. i, p. 123; BERGEMA, op. cit., pp. 503 ff.; WALK, L., " Lebensbaum-Kreuzesbaum: II; Kirchenkunst ", *OZK*, vol. ix, pp. 53–7; BALTRUSAITIS, J., " Quelques survivances des symboles solaires dan l'art du Moyen Age ", *GBA*, 6th series, vol. xvii, pp. 75–82; NAVA, A., " *Albero di Jesse* nella cattedrale d'Orvieto e la pittura bizantina ", *RIASA*, vol. v, pp. 363–76; HILDBURGH, W. L., " A Medieval Brass Pectoral Cross ", *AB*, 1932, vol. xiv, pp. 79–102; DETERING, A., *Die Bedeutung der Eiche seit der Vorzeit*, Leipzig, 1939, p. 126, fig. 51.

On the Tree of Life as axis of the Universe: HOLMBERG-HARVA, U., " Baum des Lebens," pp. 26 ff.; id., *Finno-Ugric Mythology*, p. 338; COOMARASWAMY, A., *Elements of Buddhist Iconography*, Harvard University Press, 1935, p. 82; MUS, P., *Barabudur*, Hanoi-Paris, 1935, vol. i, pp. 117 ff., 440 ff.; GRANET, M., *La Pensée chinoise*, Paris, 1935, p. 324; LECHER, G., " The Tree of Life in Indo-European and Islamic Cultures ", *AI*, 1937, vol. iv, pp. 369–416; BAUERREISS, Romuald, *Arbor Vitæ. Der* " *Lebensbaum* " *und seine Verwendung in Liturgie, Kunst und Brauchtum des Abendlandes*, Munich, 1938; ELIADE, M., *Le Chamanisme*, pp. 244

ff.; cf. the bibliography of Chapter II for reference to the trees of the Shamans, etc.).

On the Cosmic Tree: KRAPPE, A. H., *The Science of Folklore*, London, 1930, p. 233; HENTZE, C., *Mythes et symboles lunaires*, Antwerp, 1932, p. 155 ff.; WILKE, G., " Der Weltenbaum und die beiden Kosmischen Vögel in der vorgeschichtlichen Kunst ", *MB*, vol. xiv, 1922, pp. 73–99.

On the heavenly tree: 1 Enoch, 24–5: SAINEANU, L., *Basmele Românilor*, Bucharest, 1898, pp. 449–57; EMSHEIMER, E., " Schamanentrommel und Trommelbaum ", *ES*, 1946, no. 4, pp. 166–81; ELIADE, M., *Le Chamanisme*, pp. 51 ff., 160 ff.

On mythological descent from a plant species: BAUMANN, H., *Schöpfung und Urzeit des Menschen im Mythos afrikanischer Völker*, Berlin, 1936, pp. 224 ff.; VOLHARDT, E., *Kannibalismus*, Stuttgart, 1939, pp. 456 ff.; ENGELMANN, G. J., *Die Geburt bei den Urvölkern. Eine Darstellung der Entwicklung der heutigen Geburtskunde aus den natürlichen Gebrauchen aller Rassen*, Vienna, 1884, pp. 77 ff.; HARTLAND, E. S., *Primitive Paternity. The Myth of Supernatural Birth in Relation to the History of the Family*, London, 1909, vol. i, pp. 44 ff.; HENTZE, C., *Mythes et symboles lunaires*, pp. 155 ff.; KRAPPE, A. H., *La Genèse des mythes*, Paris, 1938, pp. 278 ff.; VAN GENNEP, A., *Mythes et légendes d'Australie*, Paris, 1906, pp. 14 ff.; MATSUMOTO, N., *Essai sur la mythologie japonaise*, Paris, 1929, pp. 120 ff.; PRZYLUSKI, J., " Un Ancien peuple du Penjab: les Udumbara ", *JA*, 1926, pp. 25–36; BAGCHI, P. C., *Pre-Aryan and Pre-Dravidian in India*, Calcutta, 1929, p. 154; PRZYLUSKI, J., " Les Empalés ", *Mélanges chinois et bouddhiques*, Brussels, 1936, vol. iv, pp. 1–51; ELIADE, M., " Ierburile de sub Cruce "; id., " La Mandragore et les mythes de la naissance miraculeuse ", *CZ*, 1940–2, vol. ii, pp. 3–48; the Iranian texts relating to the birth of Mashyagh and Mashyanagh from the *rivās* plant have been collected and translated by A. Christensen in *Le Premier homme et le premier roi dans l'histoire légendaire des Iraniens*, Uppsala, 1918, vol. i, pp. 21 ff., 73, etc.

On trees as healing and as protecting children: NYBERG, B., *Kind und Erde*, pp. 195 ff.

On the changing into a plant of a heroine killed by a trick: SAINEANU, L., *Basmele Românilor*, pp. 307 ff.; GOSQUIN, E., *Les Contes indiens et l'occident*, Paris, 1922, pp. 84 ff.; ELIADE, M., " Ierburile de Sub Cruce ", pp. 15 ff.; id., " La Mandragore ", pp. 34 ff.

On conception by fruit and flowers: there is a bilbiography in BOLTE and POLIVKA, *Ammerkungen zu den Kinder- und Haus-märchen der Brüder Grimm*, Leipzig, 1913–30, 4 vols., vol. ii, p. 125; vol. iv, p. 257; PENZER, N. M., *The Pentamerone of Giambattista Basile*, London, 1932, p. 158 ff.; THOMPSON, Stith, *Motif-Index of Folk-Literature*, Helsinki, 1935, vol. v, p. 302 ff.

On the marriage of trees : FRAZER, Sir J., *The Golden Bough*, abridged ed., London, 1922, pp. 114 ff.; SCHMIDT, Richard, *Liebe und Ehe in alten und modernen Indien*, Berlin, 1904, pp. 406 ff.; NYBERG, B., op cit., pp. 195 ff.; BOULNOIS, J., *Le Caducée et la symbolique dravidienne indo-méditerranéenne de l'arbre, de la pierre, du serpent et de la déesse-mère*, Paris, 1931, pp. 8 ff.; ABBOT, J., *The Keys of Power. A Study of Indian Ritual and Belief*, London, 1932, pp. 335 ff.

For the May ceremonies, the works of Mannhardt, Frazer, J. J. Meyer and Waldemar Liungman quoted in the text. Cf. too RUNEBERG, Arne, *Witches, Demons and Fertility Magic*, Helsinki, 1947.

On the feast of the Holi: CROOKE, W., " The Holi: A Vernal Festival of the Hindus ", *FRE*, vol. xxv, pp. 55–83; id., *Popular Religion and Folklore of Northern India*, London, 1894, pp. 342 ff. (2nd ed., vol. ii, pp. 197, 318); MEYER, J. J., *Trilogie, altindische Mächte und Feste der Vegetation*, Zürich-Leipzig, 1937, vol. i (*Kama*), pp. 16 ff., with a wealth of bibliography.

On the burial of the Carnival, the expulsion of Death, the combat between Summer and Winter: FRAZER, Sir J., *The Dying God, passim*; LIUNGMAN, W., " Traditionswanderungen: Euphrat-Rhein ", I–II, *FFC*, Helsinki, 1937–8, nos. 118–9, *passim*; id., " Traditionswanderungen: Rhein-Jenissei. Eine Untersuchung über das Winter- und Todaustragen und einige hierhergehörige Braüche ", I, *FFC*, Helsinki, 1941, no. 129; id., " Der Kampf zwischen Sommer und Winter ", *FFC*, Helsinki, 1941, no. 130; MEYER, J. J., *Trilogie*, vol. i, pp. 199 ff.

AGRICULTURE AND FERTILITY CULTS

125. AGRICULTURAL RITES

AGRICULTURE displays the mystery of the rebirth of plant
life in a more dramatic manner. In the rites and skills of
farming man is intervening actively; plant life and the sacred
forces of the plant world are no longer something outside him;
he takes part by using and fostering them. To the " primitive ",
agriculture, like all other basic activities, is no merely profane
skill. Because it deals with life, and its object is the marvellous
growth of that life dwelling in seed, furrow, rain and the spirits
of vegetation, it is therefore first and foremost a ritual. It
was so from the beginning and has always remained so in
farming communities, even in the most highly civilized areas
of Europe. The husbandman enters and becomes part of a
sphere of abundant holiness. His actions and labours have
solemn consequences because they are performed within a
cosmic cycle and because the year, the seasons, summer and
winter, seed-time and harvest-time build up their own essential
forms, each taking on its own autonomous significance.

We must first of all note the tremendous importance of time
and the rhythm of the seasons in the religious experience of
agricultural societies. The husbandman is not only dealing
with a sacred sphere as regards space—the fertile soil, the forces
at work in seed, bud and flower—but his work is part of and is
governed by a pattern of time, the round of the seasons.
Because farming communities are thus bound up with the
closed cycles of time, a great many ceremonies connected with
the driving out of " the old year " and the coming of the
" new year ", the driving out of " ills " and the regeneration of
" powers ", are always found interwoven with the rites of
agriculture. The rhythms of nature come to link them together
and increase their efficacy. A somewhat optimistic view of
existence gradually results from this long dealing with the soil
and its seasons; death is established as no more than a provisional change in the mode of being; winter is never final, for
it is followed by a complete regeneration of nature, by a

manifestation of new and boundless forms of life; nothing really dies—all is taken up again into primal matter and rests, waiting for another spring. Any vision of the world founded upon rhythm must have certain dramatic moments; to live out in ritual the rhythms of the universe means above all to live amid manifold and contradictory tensions.

Farm labour is a rite; partly because it is performed upon the body of the Earth-Mother and unleashes the sacred powers of vegetation, but partly also because it involves the farmer's being integrated into certain beneficent or harmful periods of time; because it is an activity involving certain dangers (such as the anger of the spirit who was master of the land before it was cleared); because it presupposes a series of ceremonies of varying form and origin intended to assist the growth of cereals and hallow the work of the farmer; and finally because it brings him into a sphere which is, in a sense, also under the jurisdiction of the dead. It would be impossible to list here even the more important groups of beliefs and rites linked with agriculture. The problem has been approached often, from Mannhardt and Frazer, to Rantasalo, J. J. Meyer and Walde-mar Liungman. I will be satisfied with giving the most significant rites and beliefs, dealing for preference with the areas that have been most methodically studied, such as the Finnish and Estonian to which Rantasalo has devoted five volumes: *Der Ackerbau im Volksaberglauben der Finnen und Esten mit entsprechenden Gebrauchen der Germanen verglichen.*[1]

126. WOMAN, SEXUALITY AND AGRICULTURE

I have already noted (§ 93) the solidarity which has always existed between woman and agriculture. It is not so long since the custom still prevailed in Eastern Prussia for a naked woman to go to the fields to sow peas.[2] Among the Finns, women used to bring the first seed to the fields in a cloth worn during menstruation, in the shoe of a prostitute, or the stocking of a bastard,[3] thus increasing the fertility of the grain through contact with things connected with persons characterized by a strong note of eroticism. The beetroot sown by a woman are

[1] 1919–25.
[2] Rantasalo, vol. ii, p. 7.
[3] Ibid., vol. ii, pp. 120 ff.

sweet, those sown by a man, bitter.[1] Among the Estonians,
flax seed is always brought out to the fields by young girls.
The Swedes allow flax to be sown only by women. Again,
with the Germans, it is women, and particularly married and
pregnant women, who sow the grain.[2] The mystical connection
between the fertility of the soil and the creative force of woman
is one of the basic intuitions of what one may call " the
agricultural mentality ".

Clearly, if women can have such influence upon the plant
world, ritual marriage and even collective orgy will, *a fortiori*,
have the most excellent effects upon the fertility of the crops.
We shall be looking later (§ 138) at a number of rites attesting
the decisive influence of erotic magic upon agriculture. For
the moment it is worth remembering that Finnish peasant
women used to sprinkle the furrows before they were sown with
a few drops of milk from their breasts.[3] The custom may be
interpreted in several ways: an offering to the dead, a magic
way of changing a sterile field into a fertile one, or simply
the influence of sympathy between a fruitful woman, a mother,
and the sowing. Similarly, we may note, as more than simply a
ritual of erotic magic, the role of ceremonial nakedness in the
work of agriculture. In Finland and Estonia, they used sometimes to sow at night, naked, saying softly: " Lord, I am naked !
Bless my flax ! "[4] The object is certainly to make the crop
thrive, but also to protect it against the evil eye or the depre-
dations of rabbits. (The sorcerer also goes naked when he is
driving off spells and other scourges from the crops.) In
Estonia the farmers guarantee a good harvest by doing their
ploughing and harrowing naked.[5] Hindu women, during a
drought, go out naked and pull a plough through the fields.[6]
And also in connection with this erotic farming magic, we may
note the fairly common custom of sprinkling the plough with
water before its first ploughing of the year. Here the water does
not only symbolize rain, but also has a seminal significance.
In Germany the ploughmen are often sprinkled with water, and

[1] Ibid., vol. ii, p. 124.
[2] Vol. ii, p. 125.
[3] Rantasalo, vol. iii, p. 6.
[4] Ibid., vol. ii, pp. 125 ff.
[5] Ibid., pp. 76–7.
[6] J. J. Meyer's bibliography, *Trilogie*, vol. i, p. 115, n. 1.

also in Finland and Estonia.[1] An Indian text makes it clear
that rain fills the same role here as does the semen in the
relations between man and woman.[2] And as agriculture became more developed, it tended to give man a more and more
important role. If woman was identified with the soil, man
felt himself to be one with the seeds which make it fertile.
In Indian ritual[3] grains of rice personified the sperm which
made women fruitful.

127. AGRICULTURAL OFFERINGS

These few examples, drawn from an extraordinarily rich
collection, make clear the ritual nature of the work of agriculture.
Woman, fertility, sexuality, and nudity are so many centres of
sacred power, so many starting-points for ceremonial drama.
But even apart from these " centres " which reveal primarily
the solidarity among all the various expressions of bio-cosmic
fertility, the work of agriculture is itself established as a ritual.
As for a sacrifice or any other religious ceremony, a man may
only begin to work in the fields in a state of ritual purity.
When sowing begins—and later, harvesting—the worker
must be washed, bathed, dressed in clean clothes, and so on.
The series of ritual actions performed at seed time and at
harvest time are similar. This is no mere coincidence: sowing
and reaping are the culminating points in the agricultural
drama. The actions with which they are begun are simply
sacrifices intended to make them a success. So the first seeds
are not sown, but thrown down beside the furrow as an offering
to various spirits (the dead, the winds, the " goddess of the
wheat ", etc.); similarly, at the harvest, the first ears are left
aside for the birds, or for the angels, the " Three Virgins ", the
" Mother of the Wheat ", and so on. And the sacrifices
which take place at seed time are repeated when the harvesting
and threshing begin.[4] The Finns and German sacrificed rams,
lambs, cats, dogs and other animals.[5]

You may wonder to whom and for what object these sacrifices

---

[1] Rantasalo, vol. iii, pp. 134 ff.
[2] *Śatapatha Brāhmāṇa*, vii, 4, 2, 22 ff.
[3] Cf. for instance, *Aitareya Brāhmaṇa*, i, 1.
[4] Cf. Rantasalo, vol. iii, pp. 39–61; v, p. 179, etc.
[5] Ibid., vol. iv, pp. 120 ff.

were offered. A great deal of ingenuity and patient research has gone towards trying to answer these questions. There is no doubt as to the ritual nature of these customs, and clearly their object is to ensure a good harvest. But the success of the harvest depends on innumerable forces, and it is only natural that we should find a certain confusion in the various ways in which they are personified and classified. It is natural, too, that the representation of these sacred forces, present by implication at least in the agricultural drama, should vary as between one cultural type and another and one people and another, even though it may have had a single origin; such representations have been, in their turn, absorbed into varying cultural and religious patterns, and interpreted in different, if not contradictory, ways even within the same nation (as for instance, in northern Europe, the changes the Germanic tribes underwent in their religious notions during the period of migration; or the influence of Christianity in Europe, of Islam in Africa and in Asia).

128. THE " POWER " OF THE HARVEST

What we can be fairly clear about is the basic outline of the drama. Thus we can perceive that the endless variety of agricultural rites and beliefs all involve the recognition of a *force manifested in the harvest*. This " force " may be conceived as impersonal, like the " power " of so many things and actions, again it may be represented in mythical forms, or concentrated in certain animals or certain human beings. The rituals, whether simple or elaborated into complicated dramas, are intended to establish favourable relations between man and these " powers ", and to ensure that the powers will continue to be regenerated from time to time. Sometimes the power embodied and acting in the harvest is approached in such a way that it is hard to be sure whether the rite is setting out to honour a mythical figure representing it, or simply to keep the power itself active. There is a widespread custom of leaving the last ears of corn standing in a field; they are left for " the spirit of the neighbour's house ", or for " those who dwell under the earth ", or for " Odhin's horses ", according to the Finns, Estonians and Swedes,[1] for the " gute Frau ", " arme Frau "

[1] Rantasalo, vol. v, pp. 73 ff.

or "Waldfräulein" in Germany,[1] or for the "Wife of the Corn" or the "Holzfrau".[2]

As Jan de Vries remarks,[3] we will find the meaning of this custom in an anxiety not to exhaust the essence, the vivifying "force" of the crop. Similarly, the last few fruits were never taken from any tree, a few tufts of wool were always left on the sheep, and, in Estonia and Finland, the chests the wheat is kept in are never completely emptied, and farmers, after drawing water, always pour a few drops back into the well so that it will not dry up. The ears that are not cut maintain the force of the plant and the field. This custom—which derives from the elemental idea of "power" consuming itself, but never totally, and then rebuilding its strength by its own magic forces—later came to be interpreted as an offering to the mythical personifications of the forces of vegetation, or to the various spirits related directly or otherwise to the plant world.

But commoner still and more dramatic is the ritual for cutting the first—or the last—sheaf in a field. The "force" of the whole of vegetation dwells in that sheaf, just as it is concentrated in the few ears that are not cut down. But this first or last sheaf, with its weight of sacred power, may be treated in quite opposite ways. In some places the men rush forward to be first to cut it, whereas in others this last sheaf is avoided by them all. Sometimes it is borne in procession to the farmhouse, elsewhere it is thrown down in a neighbour's field. There is no doubt that the last sheaf contains in itself a sacred force, whether to help or harm; men compete either to possess or be rid of it. This ambivalence in no way gainsays the nature of the sacred, but it is most likely that these contradictory ideas of the value of the last sheaf result from two parallel ritual scenarios concerned with the manipulation and distribution of the "power" embodied in vegetation. The Germans made one sheaf of the first and last ears and placed it on the table, for it brought good luck.[4] To the Finns and Estonians the first sheaf—borne ceremoniously to the farmhouse—brings a blessing on the whole house, protects it from

---

[1] Mannhardt, *Wald- und Feldkulte*, Berlin, 1904, vol. i, p. 78.
[2] Frazer, *Spirits of the Corn*, vol. i, pp. 131 ff.
[3] " Contributions to the Study of Othin ", Helsinki, 1931, *FFC*, no. 94, pp. 10 ff.
[4] Rantasalo, vol. v, p. 189.

illness, thunderbolt and other evils, and preserves the gathered corn from rats. Widespread, too, is the custom of keeping the first sheaf in the main bedroom of the farmhouse during meals and for one entire night (Germany, Estonia and Sweden).[1] In some places it is given to the cattle to protect and bless them.

In Estonia the first sheaf has prophetic powers; if they scatter the ears from it about in a certain way the girls will find out which of them will be the first married. On the other hand in Scotland, whoever cuts the last sheaf—known as " the maiden "—will be married before a year is out, and as a result the harvesters will resort to all sorts of strategems to get hold of it.[2] In a lot of countries the last handful of wheat cut is called " the bride ".[3] In some parts of Germany, the price of wheat during the coming year can be guessed from the first sheaf.[4] In Finland and Estonia, the harvesters hurry to get to the last row of wheat. The Finns call it " baby's cradle ", and believe that whichever woman binds it will become pregnant. There too, and in the Germanic lands, it is quite common to find the custom of making the last ears into an outsize sheaf to ensure a good harvest for the following year; that is why at seed time some grains from this sheaf are mixed in with the seed.[5]

129. MYTHICAL PERSONIFICATIONS

In all these beliefs and customs, the object is the " power " of the crop as such, as a " sacred force "—not as transfigured in any mythical personification. But there are a great many other ceremonies which imply more or less clearly, a " power " expressed in a person. The figures, names and importance of these personifications will vary: " Mother of the Wheat " in the Anglo-Germanic countries, or " Great Mother ", " Mother of the Wheat-Ear ", " Old Strumpet ",[6] " Old Woman " or " Old Man " with the Slavs and others,[7] " Mother

[1] Rantasalo, vol. v, p. 171.

[2] Frazer, *The Golden Bough*, p. 107; *Spirits of the Corn*, vol. i, p. 163.

[3] Frazer, *The Golden Bough*, p. 408; *Spirits of the Corn*, vol. i, p. 162.

[4] Rantasalo, vol. v, pp. 180 ff.

[5] Rantasalo, vol. v, pp. 63 ff.

[6] Mannhardt, *Mythologische Forschungen*, Strasbourg, 1884, pp. 319–22.

[7] Frazer, *The Golden Bough*, p. 401; *Spirits of the Corn*, vol. i, pp. 142 ff.

of the Harvest ", " the Old One " to the Arabs,[1] " the Old
Man " (*djedo*) or " the Beard " (the beard of the Saviour, of
Saint Elias or Saint Nicholas to the Bulgarians, Serbs and
Russians);[2] and many other names are given to the mythical
figure who is supposed to dwell in the last sheaf of wheat.

Among non-European peoples we find similar terminology
and ideas. Thus the Peruvians think that all plants used as
food are animated by a divine force which ensures their growth
and fertility; an effigy of " the Mother of the Maize " (*zara-
mama*), for instance, is made of stalks of maize put together
to look like a woman, and the natives believe that " as a mother,
she has the power to produce a lot of maize ".[3] They keep
this effigy until the next year's harvest, but when the year is
about half over, the " witch doctors " ask whether she has
the strength to last and if the *zara-mama* answers that she is
failing, she is burnt and they make a new " Mother of the
Maize " so that the maize seed shall not die out.[4] The Indo-
nesians have a "spirit of the rice", a power which makes their
rice grow and bear fruit; thus they treat the rice when it is in
flower as they would a pregnant woman, and take steps to
capture the " spirit " and imprison it in a basket, and carefully
keep it in the granary where the rice is kept.[5] If the crop is
withering, the Karens of Burma believe that the soul (*kelah*)
of the rice has departed from it and that the harvest is lost if
they cannot bring it back. They therefore address certain
words to the " soul ", to the force which seems to have stopped
acting in the plant: " O come, rice-*kelah*, come ! Come to the
field. Come to the rice. With seed of each gender, come.
Come from the river Kho, come from the river Kaw; from the
place where they meet, come. Come from the West, come
from the East. From the throat of the bird, from the maw of
the ape, from the throat of the elephant. Come from the
sources of rivers and their mouths. Come from the country
of the Shan and Burman. From the distant kingdoms, come.
From all granaries come. O rice-*kelah*, come to the rice."[6]

[1] Liungman, " Euphrat-Rhein ", I, p. 249.
[2] Liungman, " Euphrat-Rhein ", I, pp. 251 ff.
[3] Mannhardt, *Myth. Forsch.*, pp. 342 ff.; cf. Frazer, *Spirits*, vol. i, p. 172.
[4] J. de Acosta, quoted by Frazer, *Spirits*, vol. i, pp. 172 ff.
[5] Ibid., vol. i, pp. 180 ff.
[6] Frazer, *Spirits*, vol. i, pp. 189–90.

The Minangkabauers of Sumatra think that rice is guarded by a female spirit called Saning Sari, who is also called *indoea padi* (literally, " Mother of the Rice "). Certain stalks of rice, grown with special care and transplanted to the middle of the field, represent this *indoea padi* whose exemplary vigour works in a compulsive and beneficient way upon the entire crop.[1] The Tomoris of the Celebes also have a " Mother of the Rice " (*ineno pae*).[2] In the Malay peninsula, W. W. Skeat[3] was present at ceremonies connected with the " Mother of the Child Rice " which showed that for three days after the " soul of the Child Rice " was brought to the house, the farmer's wife was looked upon as a woman who was having a baby. On the islands of Java, Bali and Sombok, two handfuls of rice chosen from the plants ready for gathering are solemnly betrothed and married. The married pair are taken to the house and placed in the barn " to allow the rice to multiply ".[4] In these last examples there are two ideas intermingled: the force which makes the plant grow and the magic fertilizing power of marriage.

It might be said that the " force " at work in vegetation is most completely personified when the harvesters make the last ears into an effigy as near to the human form as they can, generally that of a woman; or else they take a real person and cover him with straw, and call him by the name of the mythical being he is supposed to represent; he will then always have a certain ceremonial part to play. Thus in Denmark, an effigy known as " the Old One " (*gammelmanden*) is decked in flowers and brought with every attention to the house. But in some cases, the last sheaf was twisted to resemble a human being, with a head, arms, and legs, and was thrown into a neighbour's field, not yet reaped.[5] Among the Germans, the " Old Woman " or the " Old Man " was thrown into a neighbour's field, or else brought into the house and kept until the next year's harvest. This mythical being was sometimes identified with whichever of the harvesters cut the last sheaf,

[1] Ibid., pp. 191–2.
[2] Ibid., p. 192.
[3] *Malay Magic*, London, 1900, pp. 225–49.
[4] *Spirits*, vol. i, pp. 199 ff.
[5] Rantasalo, vol. v, p. 52.

with a stranger who happened to walk along by the field, or with the farmer himself. In Sweden, for instance, the girl to cut down the last ears had to fasten them round her neck, take them to the house, and dance with them as her partner in the celebrations that took place at the end of the harvest.[1] In Denmark this girl would dance with a guy made of these last ears and weep because she was a " widow "—wed to a mythical being doomed to die.[2]

Sometimes the human representatives of the " power " embodied in the harvest are treated with great respect, sometimes the reverse. This ambivalence would seem to result from the two different functions fulfilled by whoever cuts the last sheaf; he is honoured as being identified with the " spirit " or " power " of agriculture; he is hated and threatened with death as being, on the contrary, looked upon as its destroyer. Thus, in various Germanic countries, whoever gives the final stroke of the flail is said to have " knocked down the Old Man " or " caught the Old Man ", and must carry the straw guy into the village amid general laughter and mockery, or in some cases must throw it, without being observed, into the field of a neighbour who has not yet finished his threshing.[3] In Germany, the last reaper or the girl who binds the last sheaf is fastened to the sheaf and led with great ceremony into the village and there given the best dishes at the feast.[4]

In Scotland, the last sheaf was called " the Old Woman " (*caileach*), and everyone tried to avoid being the one to cut it because, they believed, whoever did would be obliged to feed an imaginary old woman until the next harvest came round.[5] The Norwegians thought that *skurekail* (" the Reaper ") lived unseen in the fields throughout the year, eating the farmer's wheat. He was taken prisoner in the last sheaf which was made into a guy known as *skurekail*.[6] Some accounts say that the figure was thrown into the field of a neighbour who had not finished reaping, who would then have to feed it for the next year. Among the Slavs, on the other hand, whoever

---

[1] Rantasalo, vol. v, p. 57.
[2] De Vries, " Contributions to the Study of Othin ", pp. 17 ff.
[3] Frazer, *Spirits*, vol. i, pp. 133 ff.; *The Golden Bough*, p. 402.
[4] Mannhardt, *Myth. Forsch.*, pp. 20–5.
[5] Frazer, *Spirits*, vol. i, pp. 140 ff; *The Golden Bough*, p. 403.
[6] Rantasalo, vol. v, p. 51.

cut the " Baba " (the Old Woman) was thought to be lucky, and would have a child within the year.[1]   Round Cracow, whoever bound the last sheaf was called " Baba " or " Grand-mother ", and bundled up in straw, leaving only his head free; he was thus carried to the farmhouse in the last cart and the whole family sprinkled him with water.   For a whole year he kept the name Baba.[2]   In Carinthia, whoever bound the last sheaf was covered in straw and thrown into the water.   The Bulgars called the last the " Queen of the Wheat "; they dressed it in a woman's gown, paraded it through the village, and then threw it into the river to ensure enough rain for the next harvest; or sometimes they burnt it and sprinkled the ashes over their fields to make them more fertile.[3]

130. HUMAN SACRIFICE

The custom of sprinkling or even throwing into water who-ever represented vegetation is extremely widespread, and so is that of burning the straw figure and spreading the ashes upon the soil. All these actions have a definite ritual significance and are part of a scenario which was, in some places, preserved in its entirety, and which we must understand if we are to understand any agricultural ceremonies.   In Sweden, for instance, if a foreign woman comes into the neighbourhood, she is bound with straw and called the " Woman of the Wheat ". In the Vendée the farmer's wife assumes this role; she is carried, wrapped in straw, to the threshing-machine and placed under it; she is then removed from the grain and it alone is threshed, but the woman is bounced up and down on a blanket as if she were corn to be winnowed.[4]   In this case there is a complete identification between the " power " of the grain and its human representative; the farmer's wife undergoes, symbolically, all that is done to the wheat, which must submit to a series of rites to regenerate and pacify the " power " concentrated in its last sheaf.

In many other parts of Europe, any stranger who comes near a field during reaping, or near the place where the grain is

[1] Frazer, *Spirits*, vol. i, p. 145.
[2] Mannhardt, *Myth. Forsch.*, p. 330.
[3] Ibid., p. 332.
[4] Frazer, *Spirits*, vol. i, p. 149; *The Golden Bough*, p. 406.

threshed, is jestingly warned that he will be killed.[1] In other
places they bite the ends of his fingers, or touch their scythes
to his neck, and so on.[2] In some parts of Germany, the
stranger is tied up by the reapers and must pay a fine before
being set free. The game is accompanied by songs which make
their meaning quite clear; in Pomerania, for instance, the head
reaper declares:

> The men are ready,
> The scythes are bent,
> The corn is great and small,
> The gentleman must be mowed.

And in the district of Stettin:

> We'll stroke the gentleman
> With our naked sword,
> Wherewith we shear meadows and fields.[3]

Similar treatment greets the stranger who comes near the
threshing floor: he is captured, bound and threatened.

It seems probable that we see in this the remains of a ritual
scenario involving a real human sacrifice. This does not mean
that every farming community that now greets the roving
stranger with mock capture and threats once went in for
human sacrifice at harvest time. It is most likely that all these
agricultural ceremonies spread from a small number of places
of origin (Egypt, Syria, Mesopotamia) over the whole world,
and that a great many races only got hold of scraps of the
scenario as it was at first. Even in classical antiquity, human
sacrifice at harvest-time was no more than a faint memory from
times long past. One Greek legend, for instance, tells of a
bastard son of the Phrygian king Midas, Lityerses, famous
for his immense appetite and his preoccupation with reaping
his wheat. Any stranger who happened to pass by his field
was entertained by Lityerses, and then brought out to the field
and forced to reap alongside him. If he reaped less well,
Lityerses bound him up into a sheaf, cut off his head with the
scythe and threw his body down on the ground. But at last,
Heracles challenged Lityerses, won the reaping match, cut

---

[1] Mannhardt, *Myth. Forsch.*, pp. 38 ff.; Frazer, *Spirits*, vol. i, pp. 251 ff.;
The Golden Bough, pp. 429 ff.
[2] Liungman, " Euphrat-Rhein ", I, p. 260, n. 2.
[3] Mannhardt, *Myth. Forsch.*, pp. 39 ff.; Frazer, *Spirits*, vol. i, pp. 228–9.

his head off with the scythe and threw his body into the river
Meander, which suggests that that is what Lityerses may have
finally done with his victims.[1]   The Phrygians did, in fact,
probably offer human sacrifice during the harvest; and there
are indications that such sacrifice also took place in other
parts of the eastern Mediterranean.

131. HUMAN SACRIFICE AMONG THE AZTECS AND KHONDS

We possess evidence of human sacrifice being offered for the
harvest by certain peoples of Central and North America, in
some parts of Africa, a few Pacific islands, and by a number of
the Dravidian tribes of India.[2]   In order to get a clear grasp of
the nature of these human sacrifices, we will limit ourselves
here to a small number of examples, but those we will examine
in detail.

Sahagun has left us a detailed description of the maize rites
of the Aztecs of Mexico.   As soon as the plant began to
germinate, they went to the fields " to find the god of the maize "
—a shoot which they brought back to the house and offered
food, exactly as they would to a god.   In the evening, it was
brought to the temple of Chicome-coatl, goddess of sustenance,
where a group of young girls were gathered, each carrying a
bundle of seven ears of maize saved from the last crop,
wrapped in red paper and sprinkled with sap.   The name given
to the bundle, *chicomolotl* (the sevenfold ear), was also the
name of the goddess of the maize.   The girls were of three
different ages, very young, adolescent, and grown up—symbolizing, no doubt, the stages in the life of the maize—and their
arms and legs were covered in red feathers, red being the
colour of the maize divinities.   This ceremony, intended simply
to honour the goddess and obtain her magic blessing upon the
newly-germinated crop, did not involve any sacrifice.   But
three months later, when the crop was ripe, a girl respresenting
the goddess of the new maize, Xilonen, was beheaded; this
sacrifice opened the door to using the new maize profanely,
for food, which seems to suggest that it was in the nature of
an offering of the first-fruits.   Sixty days later, at the conclusion of the harvest, there was another sacrifice.   A woman

[1] Cf. Mannhardt, *Myth. Forsch.*, pp. 1 ff.;   Frazer, *Spirits*, vol. i, pp. 216 ff.
[2] Cf. Frazer, *Spirits*, vol. i, pp. 265, etc.;   *The Golden Bough*, pp. 431 ff.

representing the goddess Toci, " our Mother " (the goddess of the maize gathered for using), was beheaded and immediately afterwards skinned. One priest arrayed himself in the skin, while a piece taken from the thigh was carried to the Temple of Cinteotl, god of the maize, where another participant made himself a mask out of it. For several weeks, this person was looked upon as a woman in childbirth—for what this rite probably meant was that Toci, once dead, was reborn in her son, the dried maize, the grain that would provide the winter's food. A whole series of ceremonies followed upon these: the warriors marched by (for, like many eastern gods and goddesses of fertility, Toci was also the goddess of war and of death), dances were performed and, finally, the king, followed by all his people, threw everything that came to hand at the head of the person representing Toci and then withdrew. It seems as though Toci ended up as a scapegoat, and took upon herself, when she was driven out, all the sins of the community, for the person who played the part bore the skin to a fortress at the frontier and left it hanging there with its arms wide. And the mask of Cinteotl was taken there as well.[1] Other American tribes, like the Pawnees, used to sacrifice a girl, cut her body up and bury each piece in a field.[2] And that same custom of cutting up a body and placing the pieces in furrows occurs in certain African tribes also.[3]

But the best known example of human sacrifice in connection with agriculture is that practised until about the middle of the nineteenth century by the Khonds, a Dravidian tribe of Bengal. Sacrifices were offered to the earth goddess, Tari Pennu or Bera Pennu, and the victim, who was known as the Meriah, was either bought from his parents, or born of parents who had themselves been victims. The sacrifices took place upon certain stated feast days or when something exceptional happened, but the victims were always voluntary ones. The Meriahs lived happily for years, looked upon as consecrated beings; they married other " victims " and were given a piece of land as a dowry. Ten or twelve days before the

[1] Sahagun, *Historia General de las Cosas de Nueva Espana*, Fr. trans., Paris, 1880, pp. 94 ff.; A. Loisy, *Essai sur le sacrifice*, Paris, 1920, pp. 237, 238.

[2] Frazer, *Spirits*, vol. i, pp. 175 ff.

[3] Ibid., pp. 179 ff.

sacrifice, the victim's hair was cut off—a ceremony at which everyone assisted, for the Khonds considered this sacrifice as being offered for the good of all mankind. Then followed an indescribable orgy—and this is something we shall meet in a great many festivals relating to agriculture and natural fertility—and the Meriah was brought in procession from the village to the place of sacrifice which was usually a forest as yet untouched by the axe. There the Meriah was consecrated; he was anointed with melted butter and curcuma and decked with flowers, and seems to have been identified with the divinity, for the throng pressed round to touch him, and the homage offered him bordered on adoration. They danced to music around him, and calling upon the earth they cried: " O God, we offer thee this sacrifice; give us good crops, good weather and good health ! " They then addressed the victim: " We have purchased thee, not seized thee by force; now, according to our custom, we sacrifice thee and there is no sin to us ! " The orgies are suspended for the night, but taken up again in the morning and last till midday when all once more gather round the Meriah to watch the sacrifice. There are different ways of killing the Meriah: drugged with opium, he is bound and his bones are crushed, or he is strangled, or cut in pieces, or slowly burnt over a brazier, and so on. What matters is that all who are present, and thus every village that has sent its representative to the ceremony, should be given a morsel of the sacrificed body. The priest carefully shares out the pieces and they are at once sent to all the villages and there buried with great pomp in the fields. What is left, particularly the head and bones, is burned, and the ashes spread over the plough-lands with the same object—to ensure a good harvest. When the British authorities forbade human sacrifice, the Khonds used certain animals in place of the Meriahs (a he-goat or a buffalo).[1]

132. SACRIFICE AND REGENERATION

To find the meaning of these human sacrifices we must look into the primitive theory of the seasonal regeneration of the forces of the sacred. Clearly, any rite or drama aiming at the regeneration of a " force " is itself the repetition of a primal,

[1] Cf. Frazer, *Spirits*, vol. i, pp. 245 ff.; *The Golden Bough*, pp. 434 ff.

creative act, which took place *ab initio*. A regeneration sacrifice
is a ritual " repetition " of the Creation. The myth of creation
includes the ritual (that is, violent) death of a primeval giant,
from whose body the worlds were made, and plants grew.
The origin of plants and of cereals in particular is connected
with this sort of sacrifice; we have seen (§ 113 ff.) that herbs,
wheat, vines, and so on grew from the blood and the flesh of a
mythical creature ritually sacrificed " at the beginning ", *in
illo tempore*. The object in sacrificing a human victim for the
regeneration of the force expressed in the harvest is to repeat
the act of creation that first made grain to live. *The ritual
makes creation over again*; the force at work in plants is
reborn by suspending time and returning to the first moment of
the fulness of creation. The victim, cut to pieces, is identified
with the body of the primeval being of myth, which gave life
to the grain by being itself divided ritually.

This, we may say, is the pattern drama from which originated
every human or animal sacrifice intended to strengthen and
increase the harvest. Its most clear and immediate meaning
is simply that of regenerating the sacred force at work in the
crops. Fertility is, in itself, a fulfilment, and thus a full
functioning of all the possibilities hitherto only virtual.
" Primitive " man lived in constant terror of finding that the
forces around him which he found so useful were worn out.
For thousands of years men were tortured by the fear that the
sun would disappear forever at the winter solstice, that the
moon would not rise again, that plants would die forever, and
so on. The same anxiety seized him whatever the " power " he
saw manifested: this power is a precarious one, one day it
may wear out. It was particularly acute when faced with such
seasonal manifestations of " power " as vegetation, whose
rhythm includes moments of apparent extinction. And the
anxiety became sharper still when the disintegration of the
" force " appeared to be the result of some interference on the
part of man: the gathering of the first fruits, the harvest, and
so on. In this case sacrifices known as " the first-fruits "
were offered to reconcile man with the forces at work in them
and obtain permission for him to use them without danger.
These rites also mark the start of a new year, a new, " regenerated ", period of time. Among the Kaffirs of Natal, and the

Zulus, a dance takes place in the king's kraal after the celebrations of the New Year, during which all kinds of fruits
are cooked upon a new fire kindled by the witch doctors, in
new vessels used for no other purpose. Only after the king
has given everyone present some of this pudding of first-fruits
can any fruit be used for food.[1] Among the Creek Indians,
the ritual of offering the first-fruits coincides with that of
purification and the expulsion of evils and sins. All fires are
put out and the priests kindle a new fire by friction; all purify
themselves by fasting eight days, taking emetics and so on.
Only after the year has been thus " renewed " is permission
given to use the harvested grain.[2]

In these ceremonials of the first-fruits we can distinguish
several different elements: there is, first of all, the danger that
goes with the consuming of a new harvest, either of wearing
out the species of plant in question, or of calling down on
oneself the reprisals of the " force " dwelling in it; then
follows the necessity of warding off this danger by the ritual
consecration of the first fruits and by preliminary purification
(" the expulsion of sin ", as with the scapegoat) and regeneration of the community; and this takes place through a
" renewal of time ", that is by starting afresh with an unsullied
primeval time (every new year is a new creation of time, cf.
§ 153). We saw how with the Aztecs the driving out of the old
year and with it all evil and sin took place simultaneously with
the sacrifice to the goddess of maize. The dramatic ceremony
included military parades, mimed contests, and so on, such
as we also find in other agricultural ceremonies (for instance,
in the oldest rituals of Osiris).

133. END-OF-THE-HARVEST RITUALS

We will end this brief discussion of farming ceremonies by
noting a few of the customs that occur later, when the
harvest is brought into the barns. The Finns open the harvest
by sacrificing the first lamb born during the year. Its blood
is poured into the earth and its entrails are given as " wages
to the Bear ", " to the guardian of the fields ". The meat is

---

[1] Frazer, *Spirits*, vol. ii, pp. 66–8.

[2] Ibid., pp. 72–5; see Eliade, *The Myth of the Eternal Return*, London, 1955,
p. 5.

roasted and eaten in common in the fields; three pieces are left on the earth for the " spirit of the land ". The Finns also have the custom of preparing certain dishes at the beginning of the harvest—probably dating back to a ceremonial feast.[1] One Estonian account speaks of one part of the fields being known as the " pit of offerings " where the first-fruits of each year's harvest were placed.[2] We have seen that the harvest has preserved a ritual character even to-day; the three first sheaves are cut in silence; the Estonians, Germans and Swedes do not cut the first few ears.[3] This last is a very widespread custom and the ears left as offerings are destined in different beliefs either for " Odhin's horse ", " the cow of the Forest Woman ", " the mice ", " the Seven Daughters of the Storm " (Bavaria) or the " maiden of the woods ".[4]

There were various ceremonies for the time when the wheat was being carted into the barns; for instance, throwing a handful of grains over the left shoulder with the words: " Those are for the mice ". The fact that it was the left shoulder shows that the offering was connected with the dead. The Germans, on the other hand, had the custom of breaking the first pieces of hay brought into the barn, saying: " This is food for the dead." In Sweden, bread and wine were brought into the barn to win the goodwill of the spirit of the place.[5] During the threshing, a few ears were left aside for the spirit of the threshing-floor. The Finns said that the offering was made " to make the wheat grow equally high the next year."[6] Another Finnish tradition is that the sheaf that remains unthreshed belongs to the spirit of the earth (*mannhaltia*). Elsewhere it is thought that the spirit of the earth (*talonhaltia*) comes on Easter night to thresh the three sheaves left in the autumn. Some people call these untouched sheaves which are left as an offering " the sheaves of the spirits ". Among the Swedes, the last sheaf is not threshed but left in the field until the following year's harvest " to make the year fruitful ".[7]

---

[1] Rantasalo, vol. v, pp. 160 ff.
[2] Ibid., p. 166.
[3] Ibid., pp. 168 ff.
[4] Ibid., pp. 186 ff.
[5] Rantasalo, vol. v, pp. 191–7.
[6] Ibid., p. 201.
[7] Ibid., pp. 203–6.

Undoubtedly many of these offerings were to some extent connected with the dead. The relationship between the dead and the fertility of the fields is an important one, and we shall be returning to it. Note for the moment the complete symmetry between the offerings made at the *start* of the sowing, of the harvesting, and of the threshing or the bringing in. The cycle closes with the communal harvest festival in the autumn (in the north, at Michaelmas) which includes feasting, dancing, and the offering of sacrifice to various spirits.[1] This ceremony brings the farming year to a close. The agricultural elements that enter into the winter feasts are due to the fact that the fertility cults are linked with the cults of the dead. The dead who are to protect the grain sown in the earth also hold sway over the harvest gathered into the barns which is to feed the living during the winter.

The similarity between the rituals with which farming *begins* and *ends* deserves notice. Through it stress is laid on the fact that the ceremonial of agriculture is a closed cycle. The " year " becomes a sealed unity. Time loses the relative sameness it had in pre-agricultural societies. It is not simply divided by its seasons, but marked off into a series of complete unities: " the old year " is totally different from the " new year ". *The regeneration of the force that dwells in plant life has a power to regenerate human society through this renewing of time.* The " old year " is driven out with the sins of the community (§ 152). This idea of periodic regeneration extends to other spheres—that of sovereignty, for one. It is the same main idea that inspires and nourishes hope in the possibility of a spiritual regeneration through initiation. And lastly, in direct connection with these beliefs in periodic regeneration effected by the ceremonials of agriculture, we also find innumerable rituals of " orgy ", of a temporary return to the primeval chaos, of reintegration into that formless unity which existed before Creation.

134. SEEDS AND THE DEAD

Agriculture as a profane skill and as a cult touches the world of the dead on two quite different levels. The first is the solidarity with the earth; like seeds, the dead, too, are buried

[1] Ibid., p. 221.

and enter a dimension of the earth accessible to them alone. And then, too, agriculture is pre-eminently a handling of fertility, of life reproducing itself by growth; and the dead are specially drawn by this mystery of rebirth, of the cycle of creation, and of inexhaustible fertility. Like seeds buried in the womb of the earth, the dead wait for their return to life in their new form. That is why they draw close to the living, particularly at those times when the vital tension of the whole community is at its height, that is, during the fertility festival—when the generative powers of nature and of mankind are evoked, unleashed and stirred to frenzy by rites and orgies. The souls of the dead thirst for any sort of biological abundance, or organic excess, for any such overflowing of life compensates for the poverty of their own nature and projects them into a swirling flow of potentialities and of the seeds of life.

The communal feast represents just this concentration of vital energy; a feast, with all the excesses that go with it, is therefore equally indispensable to farming festivals and to the commemoration of the dead. At one time the banquets used to take place actually beside the tombs, so that the dead might regale themselves with the superabundance of life let loose so near them. In India, beans were pre-eminently the offering brought to the dead, because they were also held to be an aphrodisiac.[1] In China, the marriage bed was put in the darkest place in the house, where the seeds were kept and above the very spot where the dead were buried.[2] The connection between ancestors, crops and sexual life was so close that the cults relating to all three were often so mingled as to become one. Among Nordic peoples, Christmas (Yule) was both the feast of the dead and an honouring of fertility and life. At Christmas there were tremendous banquets, and often that was the time for weddings, and also for attending to the tombs.[3]

The dead return at such times to take part in the fertility rites of the living. In Sweden, women keep a piece of their wedding cake in the bundle of possessions with which their tombs are to be endowed. Similarly in both the Nordic countries

---

[1] Meyer, *Trilogie*, vol. i, p. 123.

[2] Granet, *La Religion des Chinois*, Paris, 1922, pp. 27 ff.

[3] H. Rydh, " Seasonal Fertility Rites and the Death Cult in Scandinavia and China ", *BMAS*, Stockholm, 1931, no. 3, pp. 69–98.

and China, women are buried in their bridal robes.[1] The "arch of honour" over the path of the newly married couple is identical with the one raised at the cemetery to receive the corpse. The Christmas tree (originally, in the north, a tree with only its topmost leaves left on, a " may ") was used both at weddings and at funerals.[2] I shall be coming later to the *post mortem* " marriages " which signify the desire to obtain for the dead the most vital condition possible and a fulness of generative power.

If the dead are trying to grasp at the kind of life and growth proper to the living, the living have an equal need of the dead to protect their seeds and their crops. The Earth-Mother, or Great Goddess of Fertility, governs the fate of seeds and that of the dead in the same way. But the dead are sometimes closer to man, and it is to them that the husbandman turns to bless and sustain his work. (Black is the colour both of earth and of the dead.) Hippocrates tells us that the spirits of the dead make seeds grow and germinate, and the author of the *Geoponica* says that the winds (or souls of the dead) give life to plants and everything else.[3] In Arabia, the last sheaf, known as " the Old Man ", is reaped by the owner of the field himself, laid in a tomb and buried with prayers that " the wheat may be reborn from death to life."[4] Among the Bambaras, when they have laid a body in the grave and are preparing to cover it, they beseech : " May the winds, as they blow from north or south, from east or west, be kind to us ! Give us rain ! Let us have an abundant harvest ! "[5] At seed time the Finns bury in the earth dead bones (taken from the cemetery and returned there after the harvest), or objects belonging to someone dead. If they have neither, they make do with some earth from the cemetery, or from a cross-roads over which the dead have passed.[6] The Germans used to scatter on their fields, together with the seed, some earth from a fresh tomb,

[1] Ibid., p. 92.

[2] Ibid., p. 82.

[3] Quoted by Harrison, *Prolegomena to the Study of Greek Religion*, Cambridge, 1922, p. 180.

[4] Liungman, " Euphrat-Rhein ", I, p. 249.

[5] T. R. Henry, " Le Culte des esprits chez les Bambara ", *AOS*, 1908, iii, pp. 702–17, 711.

[6] Rantasalo, vol. iii, pp. 8 ff.

or the straw upon which someone has died.[1] Snakes, supremely
the animals of death, protect the crops. In spring, as sowing
began, sacrifices were offered to the dead to ask them to protect
and care for the crops.[2]

135. AGRICULTURAL AND FUNERAL DIVINITIES

The connection of the dead with fertility and agriculture can
be seen even more clearly when we come to study the feasts or
divinities relating to either pattern of worship. A divinity of
plant and earth fertility generally becomes a divinity of death
too. Holika, originally represented in the form of a tree,
later became the divinity of the dead and the genie of plant
fertility.[3] A vast number of genies of vegetation and growth,
belonging by nature and origin to the earth, were assimilated,
to the point of becoming unrecognizable, with the amorphous
world of the dead.[4] In early Greece both the dead and the
grain were placed in earthen pots. Wax candles were offered
to the gods of the underworld as to those of fertility.[5] Feronia
was called *dea agrorum sive inferorum*.[6] Durgā, the great
goddess of fertility, worshipped in a great many local cults,
and in particular vegetation cults, became also the chief
divinity of the spirits of the dead.

With regard to the feasts, we may note simply that the ancient
Indian commemoration of the dead took place during the
reaping and was the main festival of the harvest as well.[7] We
have seen that the same thing occurred in the Nordic countries.
In antiquity, the worship of the Manes was celebrated along
with the rites of vegetation. The major feasts of agriculture
or fertility came to coincide with the feasts in honour of the
dead. At one time Michaelmas (September 29) was the feast
both of the dead and of the harvest all over north and central
Europe. And the funerary cult came to have more and more
influence upon fertility cults, absorbing their rites and turning
them into offerings or sacrifices to the souls of ancestors. The

[1] Ibid., p. 14.
[2] Ibid., p. 114.
[3] Meyer, *Trilogie*, vol. i, pp. 140, 152.
[4] Ibid., vol. ii, p. 104.
[5] F. Altheim, *Terra Mater*, Giessen, 1931, p. 137.
[6] Ibid., p. 107.
[7] Meyer, vol. ii, p. 104.

dead are " those who dwell under the earth ", and their good-will must be won. Grains thrown over the left shoulder, as offerings made " to the mouse ", are meant for them. Recon-ciled, fed, their goodwill sought after, they protect and increase the crops. The " Old Man " or " Old Woman ", whom peasants look upon as the personification of the " powers " and fertility of the soil, comes to have a sharper outline under the influence of beliefs concerning the dead; such figures take on the nature and characteristics of the " ancestors ", the spirits of the dead.

This phenomenon is particularly observable in the case of the Germanic peoples. Odin, god of death, leader of the " Wild Huntsmen " of the souls who can find no rest, took over a number of agricultural rites. At Yule, the feast specially devoted to the dead which the Germans held at the winter solstice, the last sheaf of the year's harvest is brought and formed into the image of a man or a woman, a cock, goat or some other animal.[1] It is significant that the animal forms used to express the " power " of vegetation are the same as those used to represent the souls of the dead. There comes a moment in the history of the two cults when one can no longer be clear whether a " spirit " manifesting itself in the form of a beast represents the souls of them that are no more, or is an animal embodiment of the earth-plant force. This symbiosis has given rise to innumerable difficulties, and controversies still rage between scholars as to, for instance, the agricultural or funereal nature of Odin, the origins of the Yule ceremonies, and so on. What we are in fact faced with is a number of ritual and mythological patterns in which death and rebirth are intermingled and become simply different moments in one preter-human reality. The areas over which fertility cults and cults of the dead impinge upon each other are so many and so important that it is hardly surprising that their symbiosis and fusion should be succeeded by a new religious synthesis based on a fuller understanding of the significance of man's existence in the universe.

We find this synthesis in its most complete form in the second millennium B.C. in the Aegean-Asiatic world, and it was that that made possible the development of the mystery religions.

[1] See De Vries, " Othin ", p. 21.

The mingling of the two cults began in northern Europe and in China in prehistoric times,[1] but it was probably only later that a full synthesis came to be expressed coherently. It is certain that the winter solstice was of far greater importance in northern Europe than in the Mediterranean south. Yule was the emotionally charged feast of this decisive moment in the universe, and at it the dead gathered round the living, for it was then that the " resurrection of the year ", the coming of spring, was prophesied. The souls of the dead are drawn by anything " beginning ", anything " coming to life ": a new year (which, like every beginning, is a symbolic re-enactment of the creation), a new outburst of life amid the torpor of winter (endless banquets, libations and orgies, marriage feasts), a new spring. The living come together to stimulate the energies of the declining sun by their own physical excesses; their hopes and fears centre upon vegetation, on what will happen to the next harvest. The two courses—of agriculture and of the after-life—cut across each other and merge together, coming at last to form a single mode of existence, larval, pregerminative.

136. SEXUAL LIFE AND THE FERTILITY OF THE FIELDS

The seeds themselves must be helped, or at least " accompanied " in the process of growing. This solidarity of all forms and actions of life was one of the most essential concepts of primitive man, and he turned it to magical advantage by following the principle that *whatever is done in common will have the most favourable results*. The fertility of women influences the fertility of the fields, but the rich growth of plants in turn assists women towards conceiving. The dead give their assistance to both, hoping at the same time that both sources of fertility will give them the energy and power to re-enter the flow of life. When the critical moment arrives and the barley starts to germinate, the Ewe negroes of West Africa take measures to ward off disaster by means of ritual orgies. A number of girls are offered as brides to the python god. The marriage is consummated in the temple by the priests, the god's representatives, and the girls, or wives, thus consecrated, carry on a sacred prostitution in the enclosure of the sanctuary for

[1] Cf. for instance, H. Rydh, " Symbolism in Mortuary Ceramics ", *BMAS*, Stockholm, 1929, no. 1, pp. 71–120.

some time. This sacred marriage is said to be performed to ensure the fertility of the soil and the animals.[1]

The part played by the priests shows this as a developed form of the ritual which started by being simply the mating of as many couples as possible in the fields as they grew green. That is what used to take place in China, where young men and girls used to mate on the ground in the springtime with the conviction that by their action they were assisting the regeneration of nature by helping forward every form of germination, summoning the rain, and laying the fields open to the workings of fertility.[2] In Hellenic tradition, too, we find traces of similar youthful matings taking place upon newly germinated furrows, with the union of Jason and Demeter as prototype. The Pipiles of central America sleep apart from their wives for four nights so as to be specially potent on the actual night before the sowing starts. A few couples had to be actually mating during the sowing. In some places, in Java, when the rice was blossoming, husband and wife mated in the field.[3] Even in recent times, in northern and central Europe, examples are to be found of marriages ritually consummated in the fields, and the close bond between vegetation and sexuality is demonstrated by the presence of the sacred tree (the " May ") at wedding celebrations.[4] In the Ukraine this custom used to exist: on St. George's day, after the priest has blessed the crops, young couples used to roll on the furrows. In Russia, it was the priest himself who was rolled on the ground by the women—not only to consecrate the crops, surely, but as part of some confused memory of the primeval hierogamy.[5] Elsewhere the sacred marriage has become merely a ceremonial dance by a couple decked with ears of wheat, or an allegorical marriage of the " fiancée of the wheat " with her " fiancé ". Such marriages are celebrated with great pomp; in Silesia, the young couple were driven in a decorated nuptial chariot accompanied by all the inhabitants from the field to the village.[6]

[1] Frazer, *Adonis*, vol. i, pp. 65 ff.
[2] Granet, *La Religion des Chinois*, p. 14.
[3] Frazer, *The Magic Art*, vol. ii, pp. 98 ff ; *The Golden Bough*, p. 136.
[4] Cf. references in Mannhardt, *Wald- und Feldkulte*, vol. i, pp. 480 ff.
[5] Frazer, *The Magic Art*, vol. ii, p. 103; *The Golden Bough*, p. 137.
[6] Frazer, *Spirits of the Corn*, vol. i, p. 163; *The Golden Bough*, p. 409.

Notice that the customs observed in Europe at harvest time are similar to those that take place in the spring, heralding the appearance of vegetation. In both, the " power " or " spirit " is directly represented by a tree or a sheaf of wheat, or by a human couple, and both ceremonies have a fertilizing influence on the crops, flocks and women:[1] and in each you see that same need felt by primitive man to do things " in common ", to " be together ". The couple personifying the power or genie of vegetation are in themselves a centre of energy, and able to increase the forces of the power they represent. The magic force of vegetation is increased by the very fact of being " represented ", personified, we might say, by a young couple with the richest possible erotic *capabilities*, if not actual *realizations*. This couple, the " bridegroom " and " bride ", are nothing more than an allegorical reflection of what once took place in very fact: they are repeating the primeval action of the sacred marriage.

137. THE RITUAL FUNCTION OF THE ORGY

Orgies usually correspond to some hierogamy. Unbounded sexual frenzy on earth corresponds to the union of the divine couple. As young couples re-enact that sacred marriage on the ploughed fields, all the forces of the community are supposed to increase to their highest point. When the Oraon people celebrate the marriage of the sun god with the Earth goddess in May, the priest has intercourse with his wife in public, after which an indescribable orgy takes place.[2] In some of the islands west of New Guinea and north of Australia (the Leti and Sarmata groups), similar orgies occur at the beginning of the rainy season.[3] Men cannot do better than imitate the example of the gods, particularly if the prosperity of the whole world and, above all, the course of animal and vegetable life, depends on their doing so. Their excesses fulfil a definite and useful role in the economy of the sacred. They break down the barriers between man, society, nature and the gods; they help force, life and the seeds of things to move from one level to another, from one zone of reality to the rest. What

---

[1] Frazer, *Spirits*, vol. i, p. 164; *The Golden Bough*, p. 410.
[2] Frazer, *Adonis*, vol. i, p. 46; *The Magic Art*, vol. ii, p. 148.
[3] Frazer, *The Golden Bough*, p. 136.

was emptied of substance is replenished; what was shattered into fragments becomes one again; what was in isolation merges into the great womb of all things. The orgy sets flowing the sacred energy of life. Moments of crisis or abundance in nature are especially the occasion for unleashing an orgy. In a lot of places, the women run naked over the fields during a drought, so as to stimulate the virility of the sky and provoke rain. In others, weddings and the birth of twins are celebrated with orgies—as, for instance, among the Baganda in Africa and the Fiji islanders.[1] The orgies practised in connection with the drama of vegetation, and particularly with the ceremonials of agriculture, are even simpler to explain. The earth must be reawakened, the sky aroused so that the great cosmic marriage—rain—will take place in the best possible conditions to make the grain ripen and bear fruit, the women to have children, the animals to multiply and the dead to fill their emptiness with the force of life.

The Kana of Brazil stimulate the powers of reproduction in earth, animals and men, by a phallic dance miming the act of generation; the dance is followed by a collective orgy.[2] Traces of phallic symbolism can also be discerned in the farming ceremonies of Europe; for instance the " Old Man " is sometimes represented in phallic form, and the last sheaf is called " the Strumpet "; or sometimes it is given a black head with red lips, which were originally the magic-symbolic colours of the female genital organs.[3] And we may also remember the excesses that took place during certain ancient feasts of vegetation, such as the Romans' Floralia (27th April), when young men paraded naked along the streets, or the Lupercalia, when young men used to touch women to make them fertile, or the Holi, the chief Indian vegetation feast, when anything might happen.

Till quite lately the Holi preserved all the marks of a collective orgy, let loose to excite and bring to boiling-point the forces of creation and reproduction throughout nature. All decency was forgotten, for the matter was far more serious than mere

[1] Cf. Meyer, Trilogie, vol. i, p. 69, n. 1.

[2] See Meyer, vol. i, pp. 71 ff.

[3] Mannhardt, Myth. Forsch., pp. 19, 339; also the Handwörterbuch d. deutschen Aberglaubens, vol. v, cols. 281, 284, 302.

respect for norms and customs; it was a question of ensuring that life should go on. Great groups of men and children wandered through the streets, singing, shouting, and sprinkling themselves with *holi* powder and water dyed red—red being pre-eminently the colour of life and generative energy. Whenever they met a woman or even saw one through the window curtains, tradition required them to hurl the most appalling obscenities and insults. The magic power of obscene insults was widely appreciated, and occurs even in highly developed cults (cf. the Thesmophoria of Athens, etc.). During the feasts of Bali, too, the Hindus were allowed tremendous sexual liberty—apart from incest, any union was permitted.[1] The Hos of north-eastern India practised tremendous orgies during harvest time, which they justified by the idea that vicious tendencies were aroused in both men and women and must be satisfied if the equilibrium of the community were to be established. The debauchery common during harvest festivals in central and southern Europe was condemned by a great many Councils, notably the Council of Auxerre in 590, and by numerous authors in the Middle Ages, but in some places it nevertheless survives to this day.[2]

138. ORGY AND REINTEGRATION

Orgies were not found only in the setting of agricultural ceremonies, although they always remained closely connected with rites of regeneration (like the " new year ") and fertility. The metaphysical significance and psychological function of the orgy will emerge more clearly from other chapters of this work. We may, however, note at once the complete analogy between, on the one hand, the phenomenon of agriculture and its mystique, and, on the other, the orgy as a way of expressing the life of the community as a whole. Like seeds that lose their shape in the great underground merging, disintegrating and becoming something different (germination), so men lose their individuality in the orgy, combining into a single living unity. They effect thus a total fusion of emotions in which neither " form " nor " law " is observed. They try once more to enter the primal, pre-formal, chaotic state—a state that

[1] The Puranic texts are in Meyer, vol. ii, pp. 108 ff.
[2] Cf. Meyer, vol. ii, p. 113.

corresponds in the cosmological order to the chaotic formlessness before the creation—using the power of imitative magic
to assist the merging of the seeds into the one womb of the
earth. Man returns to a biocosmic unity, even though that
unity involves a regression from the nature of *person* to that of
seed. In a sense, the orgy transports man to an agricultural
state. By abolishing norm, limit, and individuality, by opening
himself to the experiences of earth and night, man achieves
the state of the seeds decomposing in the earth, losing their
form to give birth to a new vegetation.

Among the other functions it fulfils in the spiritual and
psychological economy of a community, the orgy also makes
possible, and prepares the way for, " renewal ", the regeneration
of life. The awakening of an orgy may be compared with the
appearance of the green shoots in the field: a new life is
beginning, and the orgy has filled man with substance and with
energy for that life. And further, by bringing back the mythical
chaos that existed before the creation, the orgy makes it
possible for creation to be repeated. For a time man goes
back to the amorphous, nocturnal state of chaos that he may
be reborn, more vigorous than ever in his daylight self. Like
immersion in water (§ 64), the orgy destroys creation while at
the same time regenerating it; man hopes, by identifying
himself with formless, pre-cosmic existence, to return to himself restored and regenerated, in a word, " a new man ". We
can discern in the nature and function of the orgy this same wish
to repeat a primeval action: Creation bringing order into
chaos. In this pattern of everyday life broken up here and
there by orgies (Saturnalia, carnivals, etc.), we can see that
vision of life as a rhythm made up of activity and sleep, of
birth and death, and that notion of a cosmos made up of
cycles, that was born of chaos and returns to it through a
catastrope or *mahāpralaya*, a " great dissolution ". All
monstrous forms, of course, are degradations of this basic
idea of the rhythm of the universe, and the thirst for regeneration
and renewal. But such aberrant forms are not the starting
point from which we must set out to understand the origin
and function of the orgy, for every feast of its very nature
involves something of an orgy.

139. AGRICULTURAL MYSTICISM AND REDEMPTION

What I must stress is the redemptive nature of the mystique of agriculture even in its non-orgiastic forms. Plant life, which is reborn by means of apparent disappearance (the burying of seed in the earth) offers at once an example and a hope; the same thing may happen to the souls of the dead. True, this spectacle of rhythmic regeneration is not something that simply happens, presenting itself directly to man's contemplation; in primitive belief it was due in equal measure to human rites and actions. Regeneration was won through magical acts, through the Great Goddess, through the presence of woman, through the power of Eros and the working together of the whole of nature (with rain, warmth and all the rest). Furthermore, all this is possible only because it is a repetition of the primeval action—either by ritual marriage, the regeneration of time (the "new year"), or an orgy that makes present once again the archetypal chaos. Nothing is achieved without effort, a man's living can be earned only by working, that is, by acting in conformity with the norms of life, by repeating primeval actions. Thus, the hopes that men of farming communities have formed for themselves from their experience of plant life have been from the first directed towards *action*, towards *doing*. Man may hope for regeneration if he follows a certain course, if he acts according to certain patterns. The action, the rite, is indispensable. We shall have to remember this point when we come to study the mystery religions of antiquity, which not only preserved traces of agricultural ceremonies, but which could never have become initiatory religions at all had they not had behind them a long stream of agricultural mysticism going back to pre-history; if, that is, man had not for thousands of years observed the periodic regeneration of plant life and learnt from it the solidarity of man and seed, and the hope that regeneration might be achieved after death and by means of death.

We are used to thinking that the discovery of agriculture made a radical change in the course of human history by ensuring adequate nourishment and thus allowing of a tremendous increase in the population. But the discovery of agriculture had decisive results for a quite different reason. It was neither the increase of the population nor the overabundance of food that determined the course of history, but rather it was the *theory* that man evolved with that discovery. What he himself *saw* in the grain, what he himself *learnt* from dealing with it, what he *understood* from seeing how the seed lost its identity in the earth, it was all this that made up his decisive lesson. Agriculture taught man the fundamental oneness of organic life; and from that revelation sprang the simpler analogies between woman and field, between the sexual act and sowing, as well as the most advanced intellectual syntheses: life as rhythmic, death as a return, and so on. These syntheses were essential to man's development, and were possible only after the discovery of agriculture. One of the most important bases of hope in a redemption is to be found in the prehistoric mystique of agriculture: like seed hidden in the earth, the dead can hope to return to life in a new form. And yet the pessimistic, even sceptical, vision of life also finds its origin in the contemplation of the plant world: for man is like the flower of the field . . .

PRESENT IDEAS ON THE SUBJECT AND BIBLIOGRAPHY

The appearance of W. Mannhardt's *Wald- und Feldkulte*, Berlin, 1875–7; 2nd edition, 1904–5, 2 vols., marks an important date in the history of vegetation and agriculture cults. It is an absolute mine of information upon folklore and ethnography collected, classified and interpreted by the German scholar in the light of his hypothesis of the " demons of vegetation ". A volume of complementary studies, *Mythologische Forschungen*, Strasbourg, 1884, appeared shortly after his death. His contemporaries took some time to appreciate the importance of Mannhardt's hypotheses. As J. J. Meyer recalls (in the appendix to his *Trilogie*, vol. iii, p. 284), Franz Pfeiffer, the student of Germanic ethnology, spoke of the author of *Wald- und Feldkulte* as " a mere collector of references ", and the majority of scholars scarcely bothered to read him. Mannhardt's theory would probably never have become so widely accepted had Sir James Frazer's work not given it such solid backing. It was primarily due to Frazer's immense erudition and real literary talent that the category of " vegetation demons " managed to dominate all studies of ethnology and history of religion up till the first World War. Mannhardt's research won the field through the medium of *The Golden Bough*. The first edition of *The Golden Bough* came out in 1891 in two volumes; the second edition in three in 1900 and the third in twelve, between 1911 and 1918 (this last was re-edited a great many times). An abridged version without notes appeared in 1924. A complementary volume, *Aftermath*, was published in 1937. The volumes in the *Golden Bough* series dealing particularly with the rites and myths of vegetation and agriculture are *Adonis, Attis, Osiris* (2 vols.), and *Spirits of the Corn and of the Wild*. We may remember the verdict given by Goldenweiser (*Anthropology*, London, 1937, p. 531) upon *The Golden Bough*: " Negligible as theory, indispensable as a collection of material on primitive religion." Cf. also C. W. von SYDOW, " The Mannhardtian Theories About the Last Sheaf and the Fertility Demons from a Modern Critical Point of View ", *FRE*, 1937, vol. lxxv, pp. 291–309; Gudmund HATT, " The Corn Mother in America and in Indonesia ", *APS*, 1951, vol. lxxvi, pp. 853–914.

The problem of the sacred in vegetation and agricultural ritual went on being argued long after Frazer's works had appeared. I will give here the names of only a few of the more important publications: A. V. RANTASALO " Der Ackerbau im Volksaberglauben der Finnen und Esten mit entsprechenden Gebrauchen der Germanen verglichen ", 5 vols. (*FFC*, nos. 30, 31, 32, 55, 62; Sortavala-Helsinki, 1919–25)—a wealth of information, partially previously unpublished; Jan DE VRIES, " Contributions to the Study of Odhin, Especially in his Relation to Agricultural Practices in Modern Popular Lore ", (Helsinki, 1931, *FFC*, no. 94); J. J. MEYER, *Trilogie altindische Mächte und Feste der Vegetation*, Zürich-Leipzig, 1937, 3 vols., which makes use primarily of the Puranic writings and a series of ethnological parallels (cf. too W. RUBEN's review in *APS*, 1939, pp. 463 ff.); Waldemar LIUNGMAN, " Traditionswanderungen: Euphrat-Rhein ", I–II (Helsinki, 1937–8, *FFC*, nos. 118–9, 2 vols., particularly pp. 103 ff., and 1027 ff.) What is interesting in Liungman's work is not so much the material he uses (for the Swedish scholar depends almost solely on Frazer for this) but his evaluation of the Mannhardt and Frazer hypothesis (carrying on, in this regard, the criticisms of A. Lang,

Anitschkoff, A. Haberlandt, Von Sydow and others), and his attempt to discover the " history " of how the agricultural rites and myths of the ancient East spread to the Germanic north. I must add, however, that his " history " does not invariably seem to me to be convincing.

Mannhardt (*Wald- und Feldkulte*, 2nd ed., vol. i, pp. 1–155) bases his hypothesis that there is a " spirit of the tree " (*Baumseele*) upon the following facts: (1) the general tendency to compare the universe and man to a tree; (2) the custom of linking the fate of a man with the life of a tree; (3) the primitive belief that a tree was not only a dwelling for the " spirit of the forest " (*Waldgeist*), but is also inhabited by other genies, benign or hostile, some of whom (like the hamadryads) have a life bound up organically with the life of the tree; and (4) the custom of using trees to punish criminals upon. The individual " spirits " of the trees merge, thought Mannhardt, (op. cit., vol. i, p. 604) into a collective spirit of the forest.

But, as Liungman points out (vol. i, p. 336), such a collectivization or " totalization " of individual " spirits " cannot be deduced from the facts. Mannhardt argued along the rationalist, associationist lines of his day. By a series of artificial combinations he recreated in his own way the phenomenon he was proposing to explain: the " spirit of the tree " would give rise to a " spirit of the forest " which, in its turn, would merge with the " spirit of the wind " and produce a " general spirit of vegetation." Mannhardt (op. cit., vol. i, pp. 148 ff.) thought this new synthesis could be proved by the presence of certain forest genies in the cornfields—the " green ladies ", the " Holzfräulein " and others. But these associations of woodland genies with agricultural " spirits " are quite fortuitous, and in the final analysis they prove nothing. This arbitrary reconstruction of the Great Spirit of vegetation does not end with merging the spirits of farm and forest. Mannhardt deelares that the plant genie (or *Baumseele*) which, as the demon of vegetation, is embodied in a tree, is transformed into a personification of spring or summer, and is also called by those names (ibid., vol. i, p. 155). In point of fact, each of these mythical forms corresponds to an original institution, and they cannot be analytically deduced one from another. Each of them depends upon a specific ritual which is in turn based on a general religious theory. Liungman (op. cit., vol. i, p. 341) is quite right to replace this " demon of vegetation " with a " specialized " sacred *force* in vegetation; I would prefer to call it a plant hierophany. Liungman thinks that the sacrifice to the divinities of vegetation is derived from sacrifices offered with the object of regenerating a sacred force, and above all, from the " sacrifice of the son " (ibid., vol. i, p. 342). We may also note the criticism made by the Swedish scholar of Mannhardt and Frazer's hypothesis about the existence of a specifically Germanic " demon of vegetation "; for, he asks (p. 346), how then explain the fact that the rites and beliefs relating to this demon are commoner in the southern Germanic lands than in the northern ? Liungman believes the Germanic beliefs can be traced back to an oriental original which, in turn, was derived from southern influences felt at the time of the great migrations, but he does not succeed in making this thesis entirely satisfactory.

The Swedish scholar believes that the human sacrifices offered to benefit the harvest have their roots in Egypt, particularly in pre-Osirian rituals from among which he reconstructs the most ancient forms of this kind: in prehistoric times, a man was bound up in a sheaf of papyrus (a prototype of the *ded* pillar), and his head cut off; his body was dropped into water or cut into pieces, or perhaps the genital organ was thrown into a pool and the rest of the body buried in the fields. When the sacrifice took place there was also'a ritual battle between two forces. A later form of this ritual identified Osiris, "the Old Man", with the beheaded or mutilated man bound in the sheaf, and Set, the figure embodying drought, with whoever struck the blow or threw him in the water. Osiris' vengeance was effected by sacrificing an animal representing Set (goat, goose, or perhaps pig or hare). These ceremonies took place at the end of the harvest (mid-May). The rising of the Nile began on June 17; the myth was that Isis was then looking for Osiris. All the men gathered on the bank and wept the slain god. It may have been as part of the same thing that they held the ritual procession of lighted boats on the Nile. At the beginning of August Isis (the betrothed of the Nile), represented by a conical pillar with ears of wheat decorating its top, was symbolically fertilized by the dams of the Nile being broken. The goddess conceived Horus. Then Thoth put together the pieces of Osiris' body and the god was thus restored. The event was commemorated by the "gardens of Osiris". Ritual ploughing and sowing took place at the beginning of November, and the germination of the seeds showed that Osiris was reborn.

It was from these rites, as performed more or less fully on the Syrian coast, in Mesopotamia, Anatolia and Greece, that all the agricultural ceremonials and dramas of the whole world developed even to some extent in the ancient world, and more later, through the channels of Christianity and Islam (Liungman, "Euphrat-Rhein", I, pp. 103 ff.). The Germanic and Slavonic peoples must have borrowed the rituals of agriculture by contact with eastern Europe and the Balkans (see further O. GRUPPE, *Die griechischen Kulte*, Leipzig, 1887, §26, pp. 181 ff.; *Geschichte der klassischen Mythologie und Religionsgeschichte*, Leipzig, 1921, §77, p. 190).

Liungman's hypothesis gives new perspectives to the study of agricultural ceremonies and beliefs, but though it can be confirmed in the European and Afro-Asiatic spheres, it can hardly explain the American versions; cf. Gudmund HATT, "The Corn Mother in America and Indonesia", *APS*, 1951, xlvi, pp. 853–914; M. ELIADE, "La Terre-Mère et les hierogamies cosmiques", *EJ*, 1953. What, however, we can with certainty accept from the Swedish scholar's research is the oriental origin (Egypt, Syria, Mesopotamia) of the agricultural ceremonial conceived as a sacrifice of regeneration embodied in a dramatic pattern (see too A. MORET, "Rituels agraires de l'ancien Orient", *Mélanges Capart*, Brussels, 1935, pp. 311–42; A. M. BLACKMAN, "Osiris as the Maker of Corn", *SA*, 1938, I. On Indian material and the symbolism of the "death of the corn", see Ananda COOMARASWAMY, "Atmayajna: Self-Sacrifice", *HJAS*, 1942, vi, particularly pp. 362–3.

It remains to determine whether the almost universal custom of identifying an animal (male or female goat, pig, horse, cat, fox, cock, wolf, and so on) with the last sheaf, of making the last few ears into a likeness of that animal, which is itself an embodiment of the power of the harvest and of the "corn spirit"—whether these customs and rites (the symbolic slaying of the animal) can be traced back to the Egyptian or oriental archetype. Frazer, as we know, explains this identifying of the "spirit of the corn" with an animal by an association which the earliest husbandmen must have made between the animals that hid amongst the crops and fied as the last sheaf was cut (*Golden Bough*, pp. 447 ff.; *Spirits*, vol. i, pp. 270 ff.) and the magic power of vegetation. But the great scholar does not make it clear how horses, bulls, wolves and such could have hidden in the fields. And, similarly, the hypothesis he puts forward that the vegetation divinities of the ancient world were first conceived as animals (Dionysos as goat and bull, Attis and Adonis as pigs, etc.) is simply the arbitrary creation of a rationalist mind. Liungman, for his part, believed that these animals which came in time to personify the " power " or " spirit " of the harvest, were later forms which had in general lost their original sense as the Setian animals sacrificed to avenge the murder of Osiris by Set and to assist the harvest. The Swedish scholar gives this also as an explanation of why red animals, and particularly bulls, were sacrificed in Egypt : red hair was an attribute of Set and, therefore, any creature that had it was identified with him and sacrificed to avenge the death of Osiris (op. cit., vol. i, p. 263). The bull sacrificed in Greece (at the *Bouphonia*, etc.), the indications we have that a bull's shape and name were given to the last sheaf in Europe, the bull sacrificed and eaten in France at harvest time, the mutilation or sacrifice of goats during the harvest, etc., the sacrifice of the pig (Egypt; in Austria and Switzerland the last sheaf was called a " sow "), the ritual slaying of red-haired dogs, foxes and so on—all this, Liungman thinks, is the result of the direct or indirect handing down of the sacrifice of animals representing Set.

This hypothesis does not seem to me to be borne out by all the facts everywhere. The sacrifice of bulls and oxen, for instance, has its roots in Mediterranean pre-history, which the Osirian drama can have had no bearing upon. No one can doubt the cosmogonic meaning of these sacrifices, and the fact that they are performed in connection with agricultural ceremonies is because of the mystical symmetry which can always be found between every act of creation and the archetypal creation of the cosmos. The generative power of bull, goat, pig, gives an adequate explanation of what the sacrifice means in relation to the agricultural ritual; fertilizing energy, concentrated in these animals, is set free and distributed over the fields. The same pattern of thought explains the frequency with which orgies and erotic rituals accompany agricultural celebrations. Liungman's attempt to reconstruct the pre-Osirian ritual explains neither the divinity of Osiris nor the origin of the Osirian myth. The difference between the Egyptian ritual drama which took place at the harvest time and the drama of Osiris, is as great as the difference between adultery and *Madame Bovary* or *Anna Karenina*. The myth, like the novel, signifies primarily an autonomous act of creation by the mind.

For a different interpretation of the ceremonials of agriculture see A. Loisy, *Essai historique sur le sacrifice*, Paris, 1920, pp. 235 ff. E. A. Westermarck, *The Origin and Development of the Moral Ideas*, London, 1905, vol. i, pp. 441-51, explains the sacrifice of the Khonds by the " principle of substitution ", a convenient but rather summary formula which does not take in the full complexity of the matter. On the Meriah, see also L. de la Vallee-Poussin, *Indo-européens et Indo-iraniens* (new ed.), Paris, 1936, pp. 375-99; A. W. Macdonald, " A Propos de Prajapati ", *JA*, 1952, pp. 323-32.

On the influence of the dead upon agriculture see Frazer, *The Belief in Immortality*, vol. i, London, 1913, pp. 247 ff.; id., *The Fear of the Dead in Primitive Religion*, London, 1933-6, i, pp. 51 ff., 82 ff.

On the relationship between agricultural feasts and marriage, sexuality, etc., see also H. K. HAEBERLIN, " The Idea of Fertilization in the Culture of the Pueblo Indians ", *American Anthropological Association, Memoirs,* 1916, vol. iii, pp. 1 ff.; M. GRANET, *Festivals and Songs of Ancient China,* London, 1932, pp. 166 ff.; B. MALINOWSKI, *Coral Gardens and their Magic,* London, 1935, vol. i, pp. 110 ff., 119 (sexual purity and agricultural labour), pp. 219 ff. (prosperity magic). On the analogy between field and woman see GASTER, *AOA,* 1933, v, p. 119; id., " A Canaanite Ritual Drama ", *JAOS,* lxvi, 49-76, p. 63.

On the earth mysticism and " spiritual mechanics " obliging those who adhere solely to the nocturnal realm of the mind to " decompose underground " (as, for instance, with the modern sect of the " Innocents " in Russia and in Rumania), cf. my own book *Mitul Reintegraii,* Bucharest, 1942, pp. 24 ff.

On the obscene rituals connected with agriculture see MANNHARDT, *Myth. Forsch.,* pp. 142-3; *Wald- und Feldkulte,* vol. i, pp. 424-34; cf. also *RH,* lvi, p. 265; *RES,* iii, p. 86.

There is a wealth of material on the fertilization of fields by sacred chariots in E. HAHN, *Demeter und Baubo,* Lübeck, 1896, pp. 30 ff.

Cf. U. HAHN, " Die deutschen Opfergebrauche bei Ackerbau und Viehzucht ", (*Germanistische Abhandlungen,* by K. WEINHOLD, vol. iii); E. A. ARMSTRONG, " The Ritual of the Plough ", *FRE,* 1943, liv, no. 1; F. ALTHEIM, *Terra Mater,* Giessen, 1931; H. RYDH, " Seasonal Fertility Rites and the Death Cult in Scandinavia and China ", *BMAS,* 1931, no. 3, pp. 69-98.

On the origin and spread of agriculture in Europe, see P. LAVIOSA-ZAMBOTTI, *Le Più Antiche culture agricole europee,* Milan, 1943; id., *Origini e diffusione della civiltà,* Milan, 1947, pp. 175 ff. For the religious concepts of the earliest agricultural cultures see A. E. JENSEN, *Das religiöse Weltbild einer frühen Kultur,* Stuttgart, 1948. On matriarchy, the reader should consult W. SCHMIDT, *Das Mutterrecht,* Vienna, 1955.

Cf. also the bibliographies following Chapters VII and VIII.

X

SACRED PLACES:
TEMPLE, PALACE, " CENTRE OF THE WORLD "

140. HIEROPHANIES AND REPETITION

EVERY kratophany and hierophany whatsoever transforms the place where it occurs: hitherto profane, it is thenceforward a sacred area. Thus, for the Kanakas of New Caledonia " an innumerable number of rocks and stones with holes in them in the bush have some special meaning. One crevice is helpful if you want rain, another is the dwelling of a totem, one place is haunted by the vengeful spirit of a murdered man. In this way the whole landscape is alive and its smallest details all mean something; nature is rich with human history."[1] To put it more precisely, nature undergoes a transformation from the very fact of the kratophany or hierophany, and emerges from it charged with myth. Basing himself on the observations of A. R. Radcliffe-Brown and A. P. Elkin, Lévy-Bruhl very rightly stressed the hierophanic nature of sacred places: " To these natives, a sacred spot never presents itself to the mind in isolation. It is always part of a complexus of things which includes the plant or animal species which flourish there at various seasons, as well as the mythical heroes who lived, roamed or created something there and who are often embodied in the very soil, the ceremonies which take place there from time to time, and all the emotions aroused by the whole."[2]

According to Radcliffe-Brown, the cardinal point in this complexus is " the local totem centre ", and in most cases one can discern a direct bond—a " participation ", to use Lévy-Bruhl's word—between the totem centres and certain figures of myth who lived at the beginning of time and created totem centres then. It was in these places of hierophany that the primal revelations were made; it was there that man was taught how to nourish himself and how ensure a constant supply of food. And all the rituals connected with food celebrated within the limits of the sacred area, of the totem centre, are simply an

---

[1] Leenhardt, *Notes d'archéologie néocalédonienne*, Paris, 1930, pp. 23–4.
[2] *L'Expérience mystique et les symboles chez les primitifs*, Paris, 1938, p. 183.

imitation and reproduction of the things done *in illo tempore* by mythical beings. " Bandicoots, oppossum, fish and bees were pulled out of their holes in this way by the heroes of olden (*bugari*) times."[1]

In fact the idea of a sacred place involves the notion of repeating the primeval hierophany which consecrated the place by marking it out, by cutting it off from the profane space around it. In the next chapter I shall show how a similar idea of repetition underlies the idea of sacred time, and is the basis of innumerable ritual systems as well as, in general, of the hopes all religious men entertain in regard to personal salvation. A sacred place is what it is because of the permanent nature of the hierophany that first consecrated it. That is why one Bolivian tribe, when they feel the need to renew their energy and vitality, go back to the place supposed to have been the cradle of their ancestors.[2] The hierophany therefore does not merely sanctify a given segment of undifferentiated profane space; it goes so far as to ensure that sacredness will continue there. *There*, in *that* place, the hierophany repeats itself. In this way the place becomes an inexhaustible source of power and sacredness and enables man, simply by entering it, to have a share in the power, to hold communion with the sacredness. This elementary notion of the place's becoming, by means of a hierophany, a permanent " centre " of the sacred, governs and explains a whole collection of systems often complex and detailed. But however diverse and variously elaborated these sacred spaces may be, they all present one trait in common: there is always a clearly marked space which makes it possible (though under very varied forms) to communicate with the sacred.

The continuity of hierophanies is what explains the permanence of these consecrated spots. That the Australian aboriginals went on visiting their traditional secret places was not because of any pressure of economic circumstances, for, as Elkin points out, once they had entered the service of the white men, they depended on them for their food and their whole economy.[3] What they sought from these places was to remain in mystical

---

[1] A. P. Elkin, quoted by Lévy-Bruhl, p. 186.
[2] Lévy-Bruhl, pp. 188-9.
[3] Lévy-Bruhl, pp. 186-7.

union with the land and with the ancestors who founded the civilization of the tribe. The need the aboriginals felt to preserve their contact with those scenes of hierophany was essentially a religious one; it was nothing more than the need to remain in direct communion with a " centre " producing the sacred. And these centres were only with the greatest difficulty robbed of their importance—they were passed on like an heirloom from tribe to tribe, from religion to religion. The rocks, springs, caves and woods venerated from the earliest historic times are still, in different forms, held as sacred by Christian communities today. A superficial observer might well see this aspect of popular piety as a " superstition ", and see in it a proof that all community religious life is largely made up of things inherited from prehistoric times. But what the continuity of the sacred places in fact indicates is the autonomy of hierophanies; the sacred expresses itself according to the laws of its own dialectic and this expression comes to man *from without*. If the " choice " of his sacred places were left to man himself, then there could be no explanation for this continuity.

141. THE CONSECRATION OF SPACE

In actual fact, the place is never " chosen " by man; it is merely discovered by him;[1] in other words, the sacred place in some way or another reveals itself to him. The " revelation " is not necessarily effected by means of anything directly hierophanic in nature (*this* place, *this* spring, *this* tree); it is sometimes effected through the medium of a traditional technique originating out of and based upon a system of cosmology. One such process used to " discover " these sites was the *orientatio*.

Obviously, as we shall see in a moment, it was not only for sanctuaries that spaces must be consecrated. The building of a house also involves a transformation of profane space. But, in every case, the spot is always indicated by something *else*, whether that something be a dazzling hierophany, or the principles of cosmology underlying *orientatio* and geomancy, or perhaps, simplest, of all, by a " sign " expressing a hierophany, generally some animal. Sartori assembled a great deal of evidence[2] on the animal signs thought to ratify places chosen

[1] Van der Leeuw, *Religion in Essence and Manifestation*, pp. 393–4.
[2] " Uber das Bauopfer ", *ZFE*, 1898, vol. xxx, p. 4, note.

for human dwellings. The presence or absence of ants or mice may be a decisive sign of a hierophany. Sometimes a domestic animal, a bull for instance, is let loose; in a few days' time a search is made for it, and it is sacrificed on the spot where it is found, which is recognized as the place for building the town.

"All sanctuaries are consecrated by a theophany," wrote Robertson Smith.[1] But this does not mean that *only* sanctuaries are so consecrated. The remark can be extended to cover the dwellings of hermits or saints, and, in general, all human habitations. "According to the legend, the Moslem ascetic who founded El-Hemel at the end of the sixteenth century stopped beside a spring for the night, and stuck his stick in the earth. Next day he tried to pull it out to go on his way but found that it had taken root and was shooting buds. He saw in this an indication of the will of God and made his dwelling on the spot."[2] All the places where saints lived, prayed, or were buried are, in turn, sanctified, and are therefore cut off from the profane space around them by an enclosure or an embankment of stones.[3] We have already met (§ 75) these same piles of stones marking places where men died violent deaths (by lightning, snake-bite and so on); in that case the violent death possesses the value of a kratophany or hierophany.

The enclosure, wall, or circle of stones surrounding a sacred place—these are among the most ancient of known forms of man-made sanctuary. They existed as early as the early Indus civilization (at Mohenjo-Daro, for instance, cf. § 97) and the Ægean civilization.[4] The enclosure does not only imply and indeed signify the continued presence of a kratophany or hierophany within its bounds; it also serves the purpose of preserving profane man from the danger to which he would expose himself by entering it without due care. The sacred is always dangerous to anyone who comes into contact with it unprepared, without having gone through the "gestures of approach" that every

---

[1] *Lectures on the Religion of the Semites*, p. 436.

[2] René Basset, quoted by Saintyves, *Essais de folklore biblique*, Paris, 1923, p. 105.

[3] Examples of this in Morocco will be found in Westermarck, *Pagan Survivals in Mahometan Civilization*, London, 1933, p. 96.

[4] Cf. the reproductions of Minoan and Mycenian rings in Axel W. Persson's *The Religion of Greece in Prehistoric Times*, Berkeley (Cal.), 1942, nos. 6, 7, 15, 16, etc.

religious act demands. " Come not nigh higher," said the Lord
to Moses, " put off the shoes from thy feet : for the place where-
on thou standest is holy ground."[1] Hence the innumerable rites
and prescriptions (bare feet, and so on) relative to entering the
temple, of which we have plentiful evidence among the Semites
and other Mediterranean peoples.[2] The ritual importance
of the thresholds of temple and house[3] is also due to this
same separating function of limits, though it may have taken
on varying interpretations and values over the course of time.

The same is the case with city walls : long before they were
military erections, they were a magic defence, for they marked
out from the midst of a " chaotic " space, peopled with demons
and phantoms (see further on), an enclosure, a place that was
organized, made cosmic, in other words, provided with a
" centre ". That is why in times of crisis (like a siege or an
epidemic), the whole population would gather to go round the
city walls in procession and thus reinforce their magico-
religious quality of limits and ramparts. This procession round
the city, with all its apparatus of relics and candles, was sometimes purely magico-symbolic in form : the patron saint of
the town was offered a coiled waxen taper as long as the peri-
meter of the wall. All these defence measures were extremely
widespread in the Middle Ages,[4] but are to be found in other
times and in other places as well. In northern India, for
instance, in time of epidemic, a circle is described around the
village to stop the demons of the illness from entering its
enclosure.[5] The " magic circle ", in such favour in so many
magico-religious rituals, is intended to set up a partition
between the two areas of different kinds.

142. THE " CONSTRUCTION " OF THE SACRED SPACE

The supremely sacred places—altars and sanctuaries—were,
of course, constructed according to the traditional canons.
But, in the last analysis, this construction was based on a
primeval revelation which disclosed the archetype of the sacred

[1] Exod. iii. 5.
[2] Picard, *Ephèse et Claros*, Paris, 1922, p. 271, n. 3.
[3] See for instance, Frazer, *Folklore in the Old Testament*, vol. iii, pp. 1–18.
[4] Cf. Saintyves, *Essai de folklore biblique*, pp. 189 ff.
[5] W. Crooke, *Popular Religion and Folklore of Northern India*, London, 1894
vol. i, pp. 103–42.

space *in illo tempore*, an archetype which was then indefinitely copied and copied again with the erection of every new altar, temple or sanctuary. We find examples everywhere of this construction of a sacred place following an archetypal pattern. We will look at only a few—taken from the Near and Far East. Take, for instance, the Iranian *maga*. Nyberg, breaking away from the previous interpretations of this term (Geldner translated it by *Bund, Geheimbund*), relates it to the *maya* of the *Videvdat*[1] (which indicates an act of purification performed in a consecrated place with nine ditches), and sees in it the sacred place where all impurity was done away with and the union of heaven and earth made possible.[2] It was in this carefully marked space that the experience of the group Nyberg calls the " Gatha community " took place.[3]

The erection of the Vedic altar of sacrifice is more instructive still in this matter. The consecrating of the spot followed a twofold symbolism. On one hand, the building of the altar was conceived as a creation of the world.[4] The water with which the clay was mixed was the same as the primeval waters: the clay forming the altar's foundation, the earth; the side walls the surrounding atmosphere and so on.[5] On the other hand, the building of the altar was a symbolic integration of time, its "materialization in the very body of the altar". " The altar of fire is the year. . . . The nights are the stones surrounding it and there are 360 of them because there are 360 nights in the year; the days are the *yajuṣmati* bricks, for there are 360 of them; and there are 360 days in the year."[6] The altar thus becomes a microcosm existing in a mystical space and time quite distinct in nature from profane space and time. To speak of building an altar is, in the same breath, to speak of a repetition of the creation of the world. The profound significance of this repetition will appear in a little while (§ 151 ff.).

The same sense of a cosmogony is also apparent in the construction of the *mandala* as practised in the Tantric schools.

[1] 9, 1–33.
[2] *Yasna*, 53.
[3] *Die Religionen des Alten Iran*, Leipzig, 1938, pp. 147 ff.
[4] e.g. *Śatapatha-Brahmaṇa*, vi, 5, 1 ff.
[5] *Śat.-Br.*, i, 9, 2, 29, etc.
[6] *Śat.-Br.*, x, 5, 4, 10.

The word means " circle "; the Tibetan renderings of it are either " centre " or " what surrounds ". The thing itself is a series of circles which may or may not be concentric, inscribed in a square. Inside this diagram, outlined on the ground with a coloured thread or trails of coloured powder, images of the various Tantric divinities are placed. The *mandala* is both an *imago mundi* and a symbolic pantheon. The initiation consists in the neophyte's penetration into the various zones or stages of the *maṇḍala*. The rite may be looked on with equal justice as the equivalent of the *pradakṣiṇa*, the well-known ceremonial of going round a temple or sacred monument (*stūpa*), or as an initiation by way of ritual entry into a labyrinth. The assimilation of the temple with the *maṇḍala* is obvious in the case of Borobudur[1] and the Indo-Tibetan temples built under the influence of Tantric doctrine.[2] All these sacred constructions represent the whole universe in symbol: their various floors or terraces are identified with the " heavens " or levels of the cosmos. In one sense, every one of them reproduces the cosmic mountain, is, in other words, held to be built at the " centre of the world ". This symbolism of the centre, as I shall show, is as much involved in the building of towns as of houses: every consecrated place, in fact, is a " centre "; every place where hierophanies and theophanies can occur, and where there exists the possibility of breaking through from the level of earth to the level of heaven.

Any new human establishment of any sort is, in a sense, a reconstruction of the world (§ 151). If it is to *last*, if it is to be *real*, the new dwelling or town must be projected by means of the construction ritual into the " centre of the universe ". According to many traditions, the creation of the world was begun in a centre and for this reason the building of towns must also develop round a centre. Romulus dug a deep trench (*fossa*), filled it with fruit, covered it again with earth, and having set up an altar (*ara*) over it, traced a rampart round it with his plough (*designat moenia sulco*).[3] The trench was a *mundus*, and as Plutarch points out,[4] " they gave the name of world [mundus]

---

[1] P. Mus, *Barabudur*, Paris-Hanoi, 1935, vol. i, p. 320.
[2] Cf. G. Tucci, " Il Simbolismo architettonico dei Tempi di Tibet occidentale", *Indo-Tibetica*, Rome, 1949, vols. iii and iv.
[3] Ovid, *Fasti*, iv, 821–5.
[4] *Romulus*, 12.

to that trench as to the universe itself ". This *mundus* was the point of intersection for the three cosmic spheres.[1] It is likely that the primitive pattern for Rome was a square inscribed in a circle: the twin tradition of the circle and the square was so widespread as to suggest it.[2]

On the other hand, the chthonic significance of the circular monuments of the Greeks (*bothros*, *tholos*, *thymele*, etc.) so forcefully brought forward in F. Robert's recent research,[3] must not mislead us. It has not yet been shown whether this single interpretation is not, in fact, the result of an Aegean " specialization ", for sacred monuments of every kind, even funeral monuments (cf. the Indian *stūpa*), normally offer a far wider cosmological meaning—an intersection of all cosmic levels—which turns every such construction into a " centre ". Africa displays, in this matter, an example from which we can learn much, in which the chthonian element does not disguise the cosmogonic inspiration. It is the ceremonial for founding towns used by the Mande tribe, which Frobenius describes[4] and which Jeanmaire[5] and Kerenyi[6] compare with good reason to the ceremonial of the founding of Rome. This African ritual, while including chthonian and agricultural elements (the sacrifice of a bull and erection of an altar, phallic in form, over its generative organ), is based on a cosmogonic idea. The founding of a new town repeats the creation of the world; once the spot has been confirmed by ritual, a square or circular enclosure is put round it with four gates corresponding to the four points of the compass. As Usener had already shown,[7] towns are divided into four in imitation of the Cosmos; in other words, they are a copy of the Universe.

143. THE " CENTRE OF THE WORLD "

As I have devoted several earlier works to the symbolism of

---

[1] Macrobius, *Sat.*, i, 16, 18.

[2] Cf. A. H. Allcroft, *The Circle and the Cross*, London, 1927.

[3] *Thymélé*, Paris, 1939.

[4] *Monumenta Africana*, Frankfurt, 1929, vol. vi, pp. 119–24; *Histoire de la civilisation africaine*, p. 155.

[5] *Couroi et Courètes*, Paris, 1931, pp. 166 ff.

[6] C. G. Jung-K. Kerenyi, *Introduction to a Science of Mythology*, London, 1951, pp. 24 ff.

[7] *Götternamen*, pp. 190 ff.

the " centre " and its cosmological implications[1] I will give only
a few examples here. To take in all the facts in a single broad
view, one may say that the symbolism in question expresses
itself in three connected and complementary things:

1. The " sacred mountain " where heaven and earth meet,
stands at the centre of the world;

2. Every temple or palace, and by extension, every sacred
town and royal residence, is assimilated to a " sacred mountain"
and thus becomes a " centre ";

3. The temple or sacred city, in turn, as the place through
which the Axis Mundi passes, is held to be a point of junction
between heaven, earth and hell.

Thus, in Indian belief, Mount Meru stands in the middle
of the world, and the polar star shines above it. This idea is
shared by the Uralo-Altaics, Iranians and Germans;[2] it is
found even among such " primitives " as the Pygmies of
Malacca[3] and seems also to be part of the symbolism of prehistoric monuments.[4] In Mesopotamia, a central hill (the
" mountain of the lands ") joins the Sky to the Earth.[5] Tabor,
the name of the mountain in Palestine, may well have started
as *tabbur*, meaning " navel ", *omphalos*[6]; and Mount Gerizim
was known as " the navel of the earth " (*tabbur eres*).[7] It was
because Palestine was so high—near the summit of the cosmic
mountain in fact—that it was not covered by the Flood.[8] To
Christians, Golgotha was the centre of the world; it was both
the topmost point of the cosmic mountain and the spot where
Adam was created and buried. The Saviour's blood was therefore sprinkled over Adam's skull buried at the very foot of the
cross, and thus redeemed him.[9]

In the matter of temples and towns being assimilated to the

[1] *Cosmologie si alchimie babiloniana*, Bucharest, 1937; *Comentarii la legenda
Mesterului Manole*, Bucharest, 1943; *The Myth of the Eternal Return*, London,
1955, *passim*.
[2] Cf. *The Myth of the Eternal Return*, *passim*.
[3] Schebesta, *Les Pygmées*, Paris, 1940, p. 156.
[4] W. Gaerte, " Kosmische Vorstellungen im Bilde prähistorischer Zeit ",
APS, 1914, vol. ix, pp. 956–79.
[5] A. Jeremias, *Handbuch d. altorientalischen Geisteskultur*, Berlin, 1929, p. 130.
[6] E. Burrows, " Some Cosmological Patterns in Babylonian Religion ", in
The Labyrinth, ed. S. H. Hooke, London, 1935, p. 51.
[7] Judges, ix. 37.
[8] Wensinck, *The Ideas of the Western Semites concerning the Navel of the
Earth*, Amsterdam, 1916, p. 15.
[9] References to this in *Cosmologie si alchimie babiloniana*, Bucharest, 1937, p. 35.

cosmic mountain, the Mesopotamian terminology is clear: temples were called the " mountain house ", the " house of the mountain of all lands ", the "mountain of storms ", the " bond between sky and earth ", and so on.[1] A cylinder dating from the time of King Gudea says that " the [god's] bedroom which he [the king] built, was like to the cosmic mountain ".[2] Every eastern city stood at the centre of the world. Babylon was a *Bab-ilani*, a " door of the gods ", for it was there that the gods came down to earth. The Mesopotamian ziqqurat was, properly speaking, a cosmic mountain (cf. § 31). The temple of Borobudur is also an image of the cosmos and is built in the shape of a mountain.[3] When a pilgrim climbs it, he is coming close to the centre of the world, and on its highest terrace he breaks through into another sphere, transcending profane, heterogeneous space, and entering a " pure earth ".

Cities and sacred places have the same significance as the summits of the cosmic mountains. That is why Jerusalem and Sion were not covered by the Flood. And, in Islamic tradition, the highest point of the earth is the Ka'aba, because the polar star shows that it is opposite the centre of the sky.[4] In the capital of the perfect Chinese sovereign, the sundial must give no shadow at midday on the day of the summer solstice. There exists such a capital at the centre of the Universe, near the miraculous tree " Standing Wood " (*Kien-mou*), where the three cosmic spheres of heaven, earth and hell intersect.[5]

Indeed, by the very fact of being placed at the centre of the Cosmos, the temple or sacred city is always a meeting place for the three cosmic regions. *Dur-an-ki*, " bond between Heaven and Earth ", was the title of the sanctuaries of Nippur, Larsa and probably of Sippar too.[6] Babylon had a great many names, among them " house of the foundation of heaven and earth ", " bond between heaven and earth ".[7] But it was also in Babylon that the earth made connection with the underworld,

---

[1] Cf. Dombart, *Der Sakralturm: I: Zikkurat*, Munich, 1920, p. 34.

[2] Albright, " The Mouth of the Rivers ", *AJSL*, 1919, vol. xxxv, p. 173.

[3] Mus, vol. i, p. 356.

[4] Text from Kisa'i, quoted by Wensinck, p. 15.

[5] Cf. Granet, *La Pensée chinoise*, Paris, 1934, p. 324.

[6] Burrows, pp. 46 f.

[7] Jeremias, p. 113.

for the town was built upon *bab-apsi*, " gate of Apsu "[1]—
apsu signifying the waters of the chaos that preceded creation.
We find this same tradition with the Hebrews. The rock of
Jerusalem went down deep into the waters below the earth
(*tehom*). It is said in the Mishna that the Temple stands exactly
above *tehom* (the Hebrew equivalent of *apsu*). And as Babylon
had its " gate of *apsu* ", the rock of the Temple of Jerusalem
closed " the mouth of the *tehom* ".[2] We come upon similar
notions in the Roman world. " When the *mundus* is open it
is, so to speak, the gate of the gloomy gods of the underworld
which is open," says Varro.[3] The Italic temple, too, was the
sphere where the superior (divine), earthly, and subterranean
worlds met.

We have already pointed out (§ 81) that the *omphalos* was
looked upon as the " navel of the earth ", that is as the " centre
of the universe." Though the *omphalos* has certain meanings
connected with the earth and burial, that does not *a priori*
prevent its having any cosmological bearing. The symbolism
of the " centre " embraces a number of different ideas: the
point of intersection of the cosmic spheres (the channel joining
hell and earth; cf. the *bethel* of Jacob, § 79 f.); a place that is
hierophanic and therefore *real*, a supremely " creational "
place, because the source of all reality and consequently of
energy and life is to be found there. Indeed, cosmological
traditions even express the symbolism of the centre in terms
borrowed from embryology: " The Holy One created the
world like an embryo. As the embryo proceeds from the navel
onwards, so God began to create the world from its navel
onward, and from there it was spread out in different directions."[4] *Yoma* declares: " The world has been created
beginning with Sion."[5] And in the *Rg Veda* too,[6] the universe
is seen as spreading out from a single central point.[7]

Buddhist tradition offers the same idea: creation began from

[1] Burrows, p. 50.
[2] Texts quoted in Burrows, p. 55.
[3] Quoted by Macrobius, *Sat.*, i, 16, 18.
[4] Texts quoted by Wensinck, p. 19.
[5] Wensinck, p. 16.
[6] For instance, X, 149.
[7] Cf. Kirfel's commentary in *Die Kosmographie der Inder*, Bonn-Leipzig, 1920, p. 18.

a summit, from a point, that is, at once central and transcendent. " As soon as he was born, the Bodhisattva planted
his feet firmly on the ground and, turning to the north, took
seven strides, reached the pole and cried, ' It is I who am at the
top of the world. . . . [*aggo'ham asmi lokassa*], it is I who
am the firstborn of the world [*jetto'ham asmi lokassa*]' ! "[1]
Indeed, by gaining the summit of the Cosmos, Buddha *became
contemporaneous with the beginning of the world*. Buddha (by
the very fact of entering the " centre " from which the whole
universe grew) magically abolished time and creation and
placed himself in the timeless moment which was before the
world was created.[2] We will consider this in a moment; every
" construction ", and every contact with a " centre " involves
doing away with profane time, and entering the mythical *illud
tempus* of creation.

Since the creation of the world began in a given centre, the
creation of man could only take place on that same spot, *real*
and *living* in the highest degree. According to Mesopotamian
tradition, man was fashioned at the " navel of the earth " out
of U Z U (flesh), S A R (bond), K I (place, earth), where
Dur-an-ki, the " bond between heaven and earth " was too.[3]
Ormuzd creates the primeval bull, Evagdath, and the primeval
man, Gayomard, at the centre of the world.[4] Paradise, where
Adam was formed from the slime, was, of course, at the centre
of the cosmos. Paradise was the " navel of the earth ", and,
in one Syrian tradition, was set " on a mountain higher than
all the rest ".[5] According to the Syrian *Book of the Cave of
Treasures*, Adam was created at the centre of the earth on the
very spot where the Cross of Christ was later to be set up.[6]
The same traditions were preserved in Judisam.[7] The Jewish
Apocalypse and the *midrashim* go so far as to say that Adam
was made in Jerusalem;[8] and since he was buried on the very

---

[1] *Majjhimanikāya*, iii, 123.
[2] Mus, *La Notion du temps réversible;* Eliade, *Sapta padani kramati*.
[3] Texts in Burrows, p. 49.
[4] Texts in Christensen, *Le Premier Homme et le premier roi*, Uppsala, 1918,
vol. i, pp. 22 ff.
[5] Wensinck, p. 14.
[6] *The Book of the Cave of Treasures*, translated by Wallis Budge, London,
1927, p. 53.
[7] Cf. O. Dähnhardt, *Natursagen*, Leipzig, 1907, vol. i, p. 112.
[8] Texts in Burrows, p. 57.

spot where he had been created, at the centre of the world, on Golgotha, the Saviour's blood, as we have seen earlier, redeemed him directly.

144. COSMIC PATTERNS AND CONSTRUCTION RITES

The creation of the world is the exemplar for all constructions. Every new town, every new house that is built, imitates afresh, and in a sense repeats, the creation of the world. Indeed, every town, every dwelling stands at the " centre of the world ", so that its construction was only possible by means of abolishing profane space and time and establishing sacred space and time.[1] Just as the town is always an *imago mundi*, the house also is a microcosm. The threshold divides the two sorts of space; the home is equivalent to the centre of the world. The central pillar in the dwellings of the primitive peoples (*Urkulturen* of the Graebner-Schmidt school) of the Arctic and North America (Samoyeds, Ainus, Indians of northern and central California, Algonquins) is likened to the cosmic axis. When the dwelling is of a different shape (as, for instance with the shepherds and cattle-breeders of central Asia), and the house is replaced by the yurt, the mystical and religious function of the central pillar is assured by the opening in the roof through which the smoke escapes. When its inhabitants are offering sacrifice, they bring into the yurt a tree, the top of which goes through that opening.[2] The sacrificial tree with its seven branches symbolizes the seven spheres of heaven. Thus the house on the one hand corresponds to the universe, and on the other is looked upon as situate at the " centre " of the world, with the opening for smoke directly facing the polar star. Every dwelling, by the paradox of the consecration of space and by the rite of its construction, is transformed into a " centre ". Thus, all houses—like all temples, palaces and cities—stand in the selfsame place, the centre of the universe. It is, we must remember, a transcendent space, quite different in nature from profane space, and allows of the existence of a multiplicity and even an infinity of " centres ".

[1] Cf. Eliade, *Myth of the Eternal Return*, pp. 6 ff.
[2] References in Eliade, *Le Chamanisme et les techniques archaïques de l'extase*, Paris, 1951, pp. 117 ff. and *passim*.

In India, just before a house is built, the astrologer will decide which foundation stone must be laid upon the head of the serpent upholding the world. The master mason sticks a stake into the appointed spot, so as to " fasten down " the head of the earth-serpent firmly, and so avoid earthquakes.[1] Not only does the construction of the house take place in the centre of the world, but in a sense it also repeats the creation. We know, indeed, that in innumerable mythologies the worlds came from the cutting up of a primeval monster, often serpentine in form. Just as all dwellings are, by magic, placed at the " centre of the world ", so too their building takes place in the *same* moment of the dawn of the creation of the worlds (§ 152 ff.). Like sacred space, mythical time can be repeated *ad infinitum* with every new thing man makes.

145. THE SYMBOLISM OF THE " CENTRE "

There is a mass of myths and legends in which a Cosmic Tree symbolizes the universe (with seven branches corresponding to the seven heavens), a central tree or pillar upholds the world, a Tree of Life or a miraculous tree confers immortality upon all who eat its fruit, and so on (cf. § 97 ff.). Each one of these myths and legends gives its own version of the theory of the " centre ", in as much as the tree embodies absolute reality, the course of life and sacred power, and therefore stands at the centre of the world. Whether it is a Cosmic Tree, a Tree of Everlasting Life or a Tree of the Knowledge of Good and Evil, the road leading to it is a " hard path ", sown with obstacles : the tree is in inaccessible places, guarded by monsters (§ 108). Not everyone who tries reaches it, nor, once arrived, manages to win the duel he must fight with the monster mounting guard. It is the lot of heroes to defeat all these obstacles, and slay the monster which guards the approach to the tree or herb of immortality, the Golden Apples, the Golden Fleece, or whatever it may be. As we have had occasion to discover in earlier chapters, the thing that symbolizes absolute reality, sacred power and immortality, is hard of access. Symbols of this sort are situated in a " centre "; in other words they are always closely guarded and to get to them

[1] References in Eliade, *Comentarii*, pp. 72 ff.

is equivalent to an initiation, a "heroic" or "mystical" conquest of immortality.

Without being over-hasty in deciding the original meaning and function of labyrinths, there is no doubt that they included the notion of defending a "centre". Not everyone might try to enter a labyrinth or return unharmed from one; to enter it was equivalent to an initiation. The "centre" might be one of a variety of things. The labyrinth could be defending a city, a tomb or a sanctuary but, in every case, it was defending some magico-religious space that must be made safe from the uncalled, the uninitiated.[1] The military function of the labyrinth was simply a variant on its essential work of defending against "evil", hostile spirits and death. Militarily, a labyrinth prevented the enemy's getting in, or at least made it very difficult, while it admitted those who knew the plan of the defences. Religiously, it barred the way to the city for spirits from without, for the demons of the desert, for death. The "centre" here includes the whole of the city which is made, as we have seen, to reproduce the universe itself.

But often the object of the labyrinth was to defend a "centre" in the first and strictest sense of the word; it represented, in other words, access to the sacred, to immortality, to absolute reality, by means of initiation. The labyrinth rituals upon which initiation ceremonies are based (at Malekula, for instance) are intended for just this—to teach the neophyte, during his sojourn on earth, how to enter the domains of death without getting lost. The labyrinth, like any other trial of initiation, is a difficult trial in which not all are fitted to triumph. In a sense, the trials of Theseus in the labyrinth of Crete were of equal significance with the expedition to get the golden apples from the garden of the Hesperides, or to get the golden fleece of Colchis. Each of these trials is basically a victorious entry into a place hard of access, and well defended, where there is to be found a more or less obvious symbol of power, sacredness and immortality.

But this is far from meaning that this "hard journey" only occurs in those initiatory or heroic trials I have named. We find it in many other circumstances. There are, for instance, the complicated convolutions of certain temples, like that of

[1] Cf. W. F. Jackson Knight, *Cumæan Gates*, Oxford, 1936, *passim*.

Borobudur, pilgrimages to holy places (Mecca, Hardwar, Jerusalem, and so on), the sufferings of the ascetic who is ever seeking the path towards himself, towards the " centre " of his being. The way is arduous and fraught with peril because it is, in fact, a rite for passing from the profane to the sacred, from the passing and illusory to reality and eternity, from death to life, from man to god. To reach the " centre " is to achieve a consecration, an initiation. To the profane and illusory existence of yesterday, there succeeds a new existence, real, lasting and powerful.

At a closer examination, the dialectic of sacred places and, above all, of the " centre ", seems to be contradictory. One collection of myths, symbols and rituals agree in stressing the difficulty of entering a " centre " without coming to grief; and yet there is a whole further set of myths, symbols and rituals which make it clear that this centre is quite easy of access. Pilgrimage to the Holy Places is difficult, but any visit to any church is a pilgrimage. The Cosmic Tree, one might say, is inaccessible, yet it is perfectly legitimate to bring a tree representing the Cosmic Tree into every man's yurt. The journey to the " centre " is fraught with obstacles, and yet every city, every temple, every house *is* at the centre of the universe. The supreme rite of initiation is to enter a labyrinth and return from it, and yet every life, even the least eventful, can be taken as the journey through a labyrinth. The sufferings and trials undergone by Ulysses were fabulous, and yet any man's return home has the value of Ulysses' return to Ithaca.

146. " NOSTALGIA FOR PARADISE "

In short, all the symbolisms and equations we have looked at prove that, however different sacred space may be from profane, man cannot live except in this sort of sacred space. And when there is no hierophany to reveal it to him, he constructs it for himself according to the laws of cosmology and geomancy. Thus, although the " centre " is conceived as being " somewhere " where only the few who are initiated can hope to enter, yet every house is, none the less, thought of as being built at this same centre of the world. We may say that one group of traditions evinces man's desire to place himself at the " centre of the world " without any effort, while another stresses the difficulty, and therefore the merit, of attaining it. I do not at the moment want to determine the history of each of these traditions. The fact that the first—according to which it is easy to construct a centre in every man's house—can be found almost everywhere induces us, if not to decide at once that it is the more primitive, at least to see it as significant, as characteristic of mankind as a whole. It shows up very clearly a specific condition of man in the cosmos—what we may call " the nostalgia for Paradise ". I mean by this the desire to be always, effortlessly, at the heart of the world, of reality, of the sacred, and, briefly, to transcend, by natural means, the human condition and regain a divine state of affairs: what a Christian would call the state of man before the Fall.

Furthermore, the assimilation of the pillar of the house to the axis of the world among people of primitive cultures, as well as their belief, studied elsewhere,[1] that it is relatively easy to link heaven and earth, enables us to state with confidence that man's desire to place himself naturally and permanently in a sacred place, in the " centre of the world ", was easier to satisfy in the framework of the older societies than in the civilizations that have come since. Indeed, this result became harder and harder to achieve. The myths about " heroes " who alone are in a position to enter a " centre " became commoner as the civilizations producing them became more developed. The notions of merit, courage, strong personality, initiatory trials and so on, played an increasingly important part, and were fed and assisted by the ever more exclusive emphasis on magic, and on the idea of personal power.

But in either case, the nostalgia for paradise is expressed with equal force. Even where the tradition of a closely guarded " centre " is dominant, we find a great many " equivalents " of it situated at ever more accessible levels. We can even talk of " easy substitutes " for the centre, just as we saw (§ 111) that the Tree of Life and the Herb of Immortality found " easy substitutes " in magic, pharmacology and popular medicine in the sense that *any* magic or medicinal plant might take their place. In short, from whatever angle one looks at it, the dialectic of sacred space always reveals this nostalgia for paradise.

These facts are extremely interesting; they suggest and indeed

[1] *Le Chamanisme*, pp. 235 ff., 423 ff.

provide a most precious contribution to the setting up of a genuine philosophic anthropology. They have, first of all, the advantage of showing, in a humanity still " at the ethnological level ", as the usual expression has it, a spiritual attitude which only its limited means of expression (symbols, rites and " superstitions " exhaust it) distinguishes from the developed and coherent systems of theology and metaphysics. But that very poverty and crudeness of expression gives special weight to the spiritual attitude expressed. Its authenticity and the important part it plays in the lives of primitive and half-civilized peoples, prove at all events that the problems of metaphysics and theology are far from being a recent discovery of the human mind, or from representing an aberrant or passing phase in the spiritual history of mankind.

But this dialectic of paradoxes—that sacred space is accessible and inaccessible, unique and transcendent on the one hand, repeatable at will on the other—must also be looked at from another point of view. It brings us back directly to what I called the ambivalence of the sacred (§ 6 ff.). We saw that the sacred attracts and repels, is useful and dangerous, brings death as well as immortality. This ambivalence also enters into the formation of the complex and contradictory morphology of sacred space. Its negative qualities (inaccessible, dangerous, guarded by monsters and so on) can quite certainly be explained by the " terrible " aspect of the sacred (*tabu*, danger and the rest), and vice versa.

Lastly, a word must be said about the " easy substitutes for sacred space " and in particular for the " centre ". That they were invented by the series, and at lower and lower and more and more accessible levels (assimilations of every kind resulted in *anything's* being able to become a " centre ", a labyrinth, a symbol of immortality and so on) bears witness to a reproduction which we can almost call mechanical, of a single archetype in variants ever more " localized " and " crude ". This is not the place to go any more deeply into the make-up and function of these archetypes, which we have already met in earlier chapters of this book: *any* tree can become the Cosmic Tree, *any* water can be identified with the primeval waters, and so on. I have devoted a study to this particular subject[1] and we

[1] *The Myth of the Eternal Return.*

shall be returning to it later. Here we need only point out that
the " dynamics " and " physiology " of sacred spaces enable
us to affirm the existence of an archetypal sacred place which
can be " actualized " through hierophanies and through the
consecration of places everywhere. As I have said, there can
be a multiplicity of " centres ", because the nature of sacred
space admits the coexistence of an infinity of places in a single
centre. And the " dynamic ", the " actualization " of this
multiplicity is possible because it is the repetition of an archetype.
I have already shown that the archetype can be repeated at
any level man wishes, and under any form, however crude
(as with the sacred tree, sacred waters, etc.); what seems to me
significant is not the fact that the archetype is open to crude
imitations (repetitions), but the fact that man *tends*, even at
the lowest levels of his " immediate " religious experience, to
draw near to this archetype and make it present. If this does
reveal to us something about man's place in the cosmos it
is not the fact that the Tree of Life can be abased to fit any
magico-medical superstition, nor that the symbol of the centre
can be reduced to such an " easy substitute " as the home;
no; it is *the need that man constantly feels to " realize "
archetypes* even down to the lowest and most " impure "
levels of his immediate existence; it is this longing for transcendent forms—in this instance, for sacred space.

BIBLIOGRAPHY

On sacred space in general: VAN DER LEEUW, G., *Religion in Essence and Manifestation*, London, 1938, pp. 393 ff.; GUARDINI, R., *Von heiligen Zeichen*, pp. 71 ff.; BOGORAS, W., "Ideas of Space and Time in the Conception of Primitive Religion", *AA*, new series, April, 1917, pp. 205–66; NISSEN, H., *Orientation*, Berlin, 1906–7, *passim* (vols. i–iii of *Studien zur Geschichte der Religion*, Berlin, 1906–10); GRANET, N., *La Pensée chinoise*, pp. 91 ff.; CUILLANDRE, J., *La Droite et la gauche dans les poèmes homériques*, Paris, 1941; SOUSTELLE, J., *La Pensée cosmologique des anciens méxicains*, Paris, 1940, pp. 56 ff.; DEFFONTAINES, Pierre, *Géographie et religions*, Paris, 1948.

On construction rituals: SARTORI, Paul, "Über das Bauopfer", *ZFE*, 1898, vol. xxx, pp. 1–54; SEBILLOT, P., *Les Travaux publics et les mines dans les traditions et les superstitions de tous les pays*, Paris, 1894, pp. 85–120; id., *Le Folklore de France*, Paris, 1906, vol. iv, pp. 89–99; recent bibliography to be found in ELIADE, M., *Comentarii la legenda Mesterului Manole*, Bucharest, 1943, particularly pp. 37 ff.; COCCHIARA, "Il Ponte di arta e i sacrifici di costruzione", *Annali del Museo Pitrè*, Palermo, 1950, vol. i, pp. 38–81.

On the *circumambulatio:* SAINTYVES, P., "Le Tour de la ville et la chute de Jericho", in *Essais de folklore biblique*, Paris, 1923, pp. 177–204; PAX, W., *WS*, 1937, vol. viii, pp. 1–88; MUS, P., *Barabudur*, Paris-Hanoi, 1935, vol. i, pp. 68 ff., 94 ff., and *passim*.

On *mandalas:* DE VISSER, M. W., *Ancient Buddhism in Japan*, Paris, 1921, vol. i, pp. 159–75; ZIMMERN, H., *Kunstform und Yoga*, Berlin, 1926, pp. 94 ff.; TUCCI, G., "Il Simbolismo archittectonico dei tempi di Tibet occidentale", *Indo-Tibetica*, Rome, 1938, vols. iii–iv; id., *Teoria e pratica del mandala*, Rome, 1949; SUZUKI, E., "Mandara", *Eastern Buddhism*, vol. vii, May, 1936; ELIADE, M., *Techniques du Yoga*, Paris, 1948, pp. 185 ff.; id., *Le Yoga: Immortalité et liberté*, Paris, 1954, pp. 233 ff.

On the *mundus:* DEUBNER, L., "Mundus", *HE*, 1933, vol. lviii, pp. 276–87; HEDBUND, "Mundus", *EJ*, 1933, vol. xxxi, pp. 53–70; ALLCROFT A. H., *The Circle and the Cross*, London, 1927, *passim*; ROBERT, F., *Thymélé. Recherches sur la signification et la destination des monuments circulaires dans l'architecture religieuse de la Grèce*, Paris, 1939, pp. 181, 255 and *passim*.

On the "symbolism of the centre": ELIADE, M., *Cosmologie si Alchimie Babiloniana*, Bucharest, 1937, pp. 31 ff.; *Comentarii la legenda Mesterului Manole*, Bucharest, 1943, pp. 72 ff.; *The Myth of the Eternal Return*, London, 1955, pp. 12–16 ff.; *Images et Symboles*, Paris, 1952, pp. 33 ff.; GAERTE, W., "Kosmische Vorstellungen im Bilde prähistorischer Zeit: Erdberg, Himmelsberg, Erdnabel und Weltströme", *APS*, 1914, vol. ix, pp. 956–79; BURROWS, Eric, "Some Cosmological Patterns in Babylonian Religion", in *The Labyrinth*, ed. S. H. Hooke, London, 1935, pp. 45–70; WENSINCK, A. J., *The Ideas of the Western Semites concerning the Navel of the Earth*, Amsterdam, 1916; DOMBART, T., *Der Sakralturm; I; Zikkurat*, Munich, 1920; ALLBRIGHT, W. F., "The Mouth of the Rivers", *AJSL*, 1919, vol. xxxv, pp. 161–95.

On the *omphalos*, see the bibliography for Chapter VI.

On the Cosmic Tree see the bibliography for Chapter VIII.

On the labyrinth, see JACKSON KNIGHT, W. F., *Cumæan Gates: A Reference of the Sixth Æneid to the Initiation Pattern*, Oxford, 1936; KERENYI, Karl, " Labyrinth-Studien ", *Albæ Vigilæ*, Amsterdam-Leipzig, 1941, vol. xv.

On the labyrinth rituals at Malekula, see DEACON, Bernard A., *Malekula. A Vanishing People of the New Hebrides*, London, 1942, pp. 340 ff., 649 ff.

XI

SACRED TIME AND THE MYTH OF ETERNAL RENEWAL

147. THE HETEROGENEOUSNESS OF TIME

The problem we come to in this chapter is among the most difficult in all religious phenomenology. The difficulty is not simply that magico-religious time and profane time are different in nature; it is rather more the fact that the actual *experience of time as such* is not always the same for primitive peoples as for modern Western man. Sacred time does differ from profane; but, further, this latter reckoning itself differs in nature according to whether we are speaking of primitive or of modern society. It is not easy, at first, to determine whether this difference arises from the fact that the primitive's experience of profane time has not yet become completely detached from his ideas of mythico-religious time. But certainly this experience of time gives the primitive a kind of permanent " opening " on to religious time. To simplify the explanation and to some extent to anticipate the results of our study of it, we might say that the very nature of the primitive's experience of time makes it easy for him to change the profane into the sacred. But as this problem is primarily of interest to philosophic anthropology and sociology, we shall only consider it in so far as it brings us to a discussion of hierophanic time.

The problem we are dealing with is, in fact, this: in what is sacred time distinguishable from the " profane " duration that comes before and after it? The phrase " hierophanic time ", we see at once, covers a collection of widely varying things. It may mean the time during which a ritual takes place and therefore a *sacred time*, a time essentially different from the profane succession which preceded it. It might also mean mythical time, reattained by means of a ritual, or by the mere repetition of some action with a mythical archetype. And, finally, it might also indicate the rhythms of the cosmos (like the hierophanies of the moon) in that those rhythms are seen as revelations—that is, manifestations—of a fundamental sacred power behind the cosmos. Thus, an instant or a fragment of time might *at any moment* become hierophanic: it need only witness the occurrence of a kratophany, hierophany or theophany to become transfigured, consecrated, remembered because repeated, and therefore repeatable forever. All time of whatever kind " opens " on to sacred time—in other words, is capable of revealing what we may for convenience call the *absolute*, the supernatural, the superhuman, the superhistoric.

To the primitive mind, time is not homogeneous. Even apart from the possibility of its being " hierophanized ", time as such appears under different forms, varying in intensity and purpose. Lévy-Bruhl, following Hardeland, counted five distinct sorts of time believed by the Dyaks to vary, each by its special quality, the pattern of a single day—in this case a Sunday: (1) Sunrise, favourable for the beginning of any work. Children born at this moment are lucky; but one must never choose this time to set off for hunting, fishing or travelling. One would meet with no success; (2) About nine in the morning: an unlucky moment; nothing begun then will succeed, but if one sets out on the road one need not fear bandits; (3) Midday: a very lucky time; (4) Three in the afternoon: a time of battle, lucky for enemies, bandits, huntsmen and fishermen, unlucky for travellers; (5) About sunset: a shorter " lucky time ".[1]

Examples are not hard to find. Every religion has its lucky and unlucky days, its best moments even on the lucky ones, " concentrated " and " diluted " periods of time, " strong " and " weak " times, and so on. One point we must bear in mind from now on is the realization that time was seen as not being homogeneous even apart from all the valuations it came to receive in the framework of any given ritual system: certain periods are lucky and certain the reverse. In other words, time can be seen to have a new dimension that we may call hierophanic, as a result of which succession, by its very nature, takes on not only a particular cadence, but also varying " vocations ", contradictory " dynamisms ". Obviously this hierophanic dimension of time can be displayed, can be " caused ", by the rhythms of nature, as with the Dyaks' five sorts of time, or the crises of the solstice, the phases of the

[1] *Le Surnaturel et la nature dans la mentalité primitive*, Paris, 1931, pp. 18–19.

moon and the rest; it may equally well be " caused " by the actual religious life of human societies, under such forms as those winter festivals which centre around the dead season of agricultural life, and so on.

Various authors have lately pointed out the social origins of the rhythms of sacred time (for instance Mauss and Granet); but it cannot be denied that the rhythms of the cosmos also played a leading role in the " revelation " and ordering of these systems of reckoning. We have only to recall how very important were the religious values placed upon the course of the moon (§ 47 ff.) or the stages of plant life (§ 139) in the spiritual fate of primitive man. The ideas of rhythm and of repetition to which we shall have occasion to return during the course of this chapter, may be considered as having been " revealed " by the hierophanies of the moon quite independent of later exemplifications of rhythm and repetition in the framework of social life as such. It has been said[1] that the social " origin " of the reckoning of sacred time is borne out by the discrepancies between religious calendars and the rhythms of nature. In point of fact this divergence in no way disproves the link between man's systems of reckoning and the rhythms of nature; it simply proves on the one hand the inconsistency of primitive reckoning and chronometry, and on the other the non-" naturalist " character of primitive piety, whose feasts were not directed to any natural phenomenon in itself but to the religious aspect of that phenomenon.

Plant hierophanies (§ 123) brought home to us how very movable in the calendar the spring festival was. I have also shown that what characterized this spring festival was the metaphysical and religious significance of the *rebirth* of Nature and the *renewal* of life, rather than the " natural " phenomenon of spring as such. It was not because a calendar did not accord with astronomical time that sacred time was always arranged independently of the rhythms of nature. It was simply that those rhythms were only thought to be of value in so far as they were hierophanies, and this " hierophanization " of them set them free from astronomical time which served them rather as a sort of womb. A " sign " of spring might

---

[1] Hubert and Mauss, " La Représentation du temps dans la religion et la magie ", *Mélanges d'histoire des religions*, 1909, pp. 213 ff.

reveal *spring* before " nature's spring " made itself felt (§ 123);
the sign marked the *beginning* of a new era and nature's spring
would soon come to confirm it—not as a mere phenomenon
of nature but as a complete renewal and recommencement of
all cosmic life. Of course the notion of renewal included a
renewal of individuals and of society as well as of the cosmos.
This is not the first time in this book that I have pointed out
how, in the view of primitive spirituality, all things return to a
unity, all levels correspond.

148. THE UNITY AND CONTIGUITY OF HIEROPHANIC TIME

The heterogeneousness of time, its division into " sacred "
and " profane ", does not merely mean periodic " incisions "
made in the profane duration to allow of the insertion of sacred
time; it implies, further, that these insertions of sacred time
are linked together so that one might almost see them as
constituting another duration with its own continuity. The
Christian liturgy for a given Sunday is one with the liturgy
for the previous Sunday and the Sunday following. The
sacred time in which the mystery occurs of the tran-
substantiation of bread and wine into the Body and Blood of
Christ is different not only in quality from the profane succession
from which it is detached like a space enclosed between the
present and the future; not only is this sacred time linked
with that of the Masses preceding and following it, but it can
also be looked on as a continuation of all the Masses which
have taken place from the moment when the mystery of tran-
substantiation was first established until the present moment.
The profane succession, on the other hand, which flows between
two Masses, not being transformed into sacred time, cannot
have any connection with the hierophanic time of the rite:
it runs parallel, so to speak, to sacred time which is thus
revealed to us as a *continuum* which is interrupted by profane
intervals in appearance only.

What is true of time in Christian worship is equally true of
time in all religions, in magic, in myth and in legend. A ritual
does not merely repeat the ritual that came before it (itself
the repetition of an archetype), but is linked to it and continues
it, whether at fixed periods or otherwise. Magic herbs are
picked in those critical moments which mark a breaking-

through from profane to magico-religious time—as, for instance, midnight on the feast of St. John. For a few seconds —as with the " herb of iron " (the Rumanian *iarba fiarelor*), and with ferns—popular belief has it that the heavens open and magic herbs receive extraordinary powers so that anyone picking them at that moment will become invulnerable, invisible and so on.

These instants of hierophany are repeated every year. In the sense that they form a " succession "—sacred in nature, but a succession none the less—it may be said that they *are continuous*, and go to make up a single, unique " time " over the years and centuries. This does not prevent these instants of hierophany from recurring periodically; we might think of them as momentary openings onto the Great Time, openings which allow this same paradoxical second of magico-religious time to enter the profane succession of things. The notions of recurrence and repetition occupy an important place in both mythology and folklore. " In the legends of sunken churches, castles, towns and monasteries, the curse is never a final one: it is renewed from time to time; every year, every seven years or every nine years, on the date of the catastrophe, the town rises again, the bells ring, the lady of the castle comes out of hiding, the treasures are laid open, the guards sleep: but at the time fixed, the spell closes in again and everything disappears. These periodic recurrences are almost enough to prove that the dates themselves bring back the same happenings."[1]

149. PERIODIC RECURRENCE—THE ETERNAL PRESENT

In religion as in magic, the periodic recurrence of anything signifies primarily that a mythical time is *made present* and then used indefinitely. Every ritual has the character of happening *now*, at this very moment. The time of the event that the ritual commemorates or re-enacts is made *present*, " re-presented " so to speak, however far back it may have been in ordinary reckoning. Christ's passion, death and resurrection are not simply *remembered* during the services of Holy Week; they really happen *then* before the eyes of the faithful. And a convinced Christian must feel that he is *contemporary* with these

[1] Hubert and Mauss, p. 205.

transhistoric events, for, by being re-enacted, the time of the theophany becomes actual.

The same may be said of magic. We saw (§ 111) that people set off to hunt for simples with the words: " We will gather herbs to lay on the wounds of the Saviour." By her magic rite, the healer makes herself contemporary with Christ's passion; the herbs she picks owe their power to the fact that they *are* placed (or at least *can be* placed) on Christ's wounds, or grow at the foot of the cross. Her incantation takes place in the present. We are told how a healer met the Blessed Virgin or some other saint; told her of someone's illness, and was told by her what remedy to use, and so on. I will limit myself to one example, taken from Rumanian folklore (which has abundant material to choose from). " Nine brothers with nine different fathers met, all dressed the same, with nine well-ground hoes, and nine sharpened axes; they went half-way across the bridge of bronze; there they met Saint Mary; she was coming down a ladder of wax and began to ask them questions: ' Where are you going, you nine brothers with nine different fathers, all dressed the same ? ' ' We are going to the hill of Galilee to cut down the tree of Paradise.' ' Leave the tree of Paradise there. Go to Ion for his warts. Cut them off, chop them up and throw them to the bottom of the sea '."[1]

The scene is laid in that mythical time before the tree of Paradise had been cut down, and yet it takes place *now*, at this very moment while Ion suffers from pimples. The invocation does not simply invoke the Blessed Virgin's power, for all powers, even the divine, become weakened and lost if exercised in profane time; it establishes a different time, magico-religious time, a time when men *can* go and cut down the tree of Paradise, and Our Lady *comes down* in person on a heavenly ladder. And it is no merely allegorical establishment of it but a real one. Ion and his affliction are contemporary with the Virgin's meeting with the nine brothers. This contemporaneity with the great moments of myth is an indispensable condition for any form of magico-religious efficaciousness. Seen in this light, Søren Kierkegaard's effort to express the Christian status as " being contemporary with Jesus " is less revolutionary than

[1] Pavelescu, *Cercetari asupra magiei la Romanii din Muntii Apuseni*, Bucharest, 1945, p. 156.

it at first sounds; all Kierkegaard has done is to formulate in new words an attitude common and normal to primitive man.

Periodic recurrence, repetition, the eternal present: these three marks of magico-religious time taken together explain what I mean by saying that this time of kratophany and hierophany is not homogeneous with profane time. Like all the other essential activities of human life (hunting, fishing, gathering fruit, agriculture and the rest) which later became " profane " activities—though never totally so—rites too were revealed by the gods or by " ancestors ". Every time the rite, or any significant action (hunting, for instance) is repeated, the archetypal action of the god or ancestor is being repeated, that action which took place at the beginning of time, or, in other words, in a mythical time.

But this repetition also has the effect of establishing the mythical time of the gods and ancestors. Thus, in New Guinea, when a master mariner went to sea he personified the mythical hero Aori: " He wears the costume which Aori is supposed to have worn, with a blackened face and (in a way prematurely) the same kind of *love* in his hair which Aori plucked from Iviri's head. He dances on the platform and extends his arms like Aori's wings. . . . A man told me that when he went fish shooting (with bow and arrow) he pretended to be Kivavia himself."[1] He did not implore Kivavia's favour and help; he identified himself with the mythical hero. In other words, the fisherman lived in the mythical time of Kivavia just as the sailor identifying himself with Aori lived in the transhistoric time of that hero. Whether he *became* the hero himself, or merely a *contemporary* of the hero's, the Melanesian was living in a *mythical present* that could not possibly be confused with any profane kind of time. By repeating an archetypal action, he entered a sacred, an historical time, and this entry could only take place if profane time were done away with. We shall see further on how important it was for primitive man thus to do away with profane time.

150. THE RESTORATION OF MYTHICAL TIME

By every sort of ritual, and therefore by every sort of significant

---

[1] F. E. Williams, quoted by Lévy-Bruhl, *La Mythologie primitive*, Paris, 1935, pp. 163–4.

action (hunting, fishing, etc.) the primitive is placing himself in
" mythical time ". For " the mythical period, *dzugur*, must
not be thought of simply as past time, but as present and future,
and as a state as well as a period ".[1] That period is " creative "[2]
in the sense that it was then, *in illo tempore*, that the creation
and arranging of the Cosmos took place, as well as the revelation
of all the archetypal activities by gods, ancestors or culture
heroes. *In illo tempore*, in the mythical period, anything was
possible. The species were not yet fixed and all forms were
" fluid ". (There are memories of that fluidity even in the
most highly developed mythological traditions; in Greek
mythology, for instance, the time of Ouranos, or of Cronos,
cf. § 23.) On the other hand, this same fluidity of " forms "
will be, at the other end of time, one of the signs of the end of
the world, of the moment when " history " comes to an end
and the whole world begins to live in sacred time, in eternity.
" The wolf shall dwell with the lamb: and the leopard shall
lie down with the kid."[3] Then *nec magnos metuent armenta
leones*, " herds of cattle shall not fear great lions ".[4]

It would be impossible to overstress the tendency—observable
in every society, however highly developed—to bring back that
time, mythical time, the Great Time. For this bringing-back
is effected without exception by every rite and every significant
act. " A rite is the repetition of a fragment of the original
time." And " the original time is the model for all times.
What took place once upon a day is forever repeated. One
need only know the myth to understand what life is about ".[5]
As for the expression and significance of the myth, we will
consider exactly how far this formula of Van der Leeuw's is
true: " One need only know the myth to understand what
life is about." Let us note, for the moment, these two marks of
mythical time (or, it may be, sacred, magico-religious or hierophanic time); (1) its repeatability (in the sense that every
significant action reproduces it); and (2) the fact that, though
it is looked upon as transhistoric, beyond all succession,

---

[1] A. P. Elkin, quoted by Lévy-Bruhl, *Mythologie primitive*, p. 7.

[2] Lévy-Bruhl, p. 8.

[3] Isa. xi. 6.

[4] Virgil, Fourth Eclogue, 22.

[5] Van der Leeuw, *L'homme primitif et la religion*, Paris, 1940, pp. 120, 101.

and in a sense in eternity, this sacred time has, *in history*, a "beginning"—namely, that moment when the divinity created the world or set it in order, or that moment when the ancestor or civilizing hero made the revelation of any given activity, etc.

From the point of view of primitive spirituality, every beginning is *illud tempus*, and therefore an opening into the Great Time, into eternity. Marcel Mauss was right in saying that "the religious things that take place in time are legitimately and logically looked upon as taking place in eternity".[1] Indeed, every one of these "religious things" indefinitely repeats the archetype; in other words, repeats what took place at the "beginning", at the moment when a rite or religious gesture was, being revealed, at the same time expressed in history.

As I shall show at greater length later on, history, in the view of the primitive mind, coincides with myth: every *event* (every occurrence with any meaning), simply by being *effected in time*, represents a break in profane time and an irruption of the Great Time. As such, every event, simply by happening, by taking place in time, is a hierophany, a "revelation". The paradox of this event-being-also-hierophany, this historic-time-being-also-mythical-time is a paradox in appearance only; we have merely to try and place ourselves in the conditions of mind which produced it. For the primitive, at bottom, finds meaning and interest in human actions (in farm labour, for instance, or social customs, sexual life, or culture) in so far as they repeat actions revealed by his gods, culture heroes, or ancestors. Anything outside the framework of these meaningful actions, having no superhuman model, has neither name nor value. But all these archetypal actions were revealed then, *in illo tempore*, during a time outside recorded history, mythical time. By being revealed, they broke through profane time and brought mythical time into it. But, in the same act, they also created a "beginning", an "event" which entered the dreary and monotonous perspective of profane time (the time in which meaningless actions come and go) and thus produced "history", the series of "events with meanings" so different from the succession of automatic and meaningless acts. Thus, though

[1] " Représentation du Temps ", p. 227.

it may seem paradoxical, what we may call the " history " of primitive societies consists solely of the mythical events which took place *in illo tempore* and have been unceasingly repeated from that day to this. All that the modern thinks of as truly " historic ", that is, as unique and done once and for all, is held by the primitive to be quite devoid of importance as having no mythico-historic precedent.

151. NON-PERIODIC RECURRENCE

These observations contribute equally to our understanding of myth (§ 156 ff.) and to the explanation of that mythical, hierophanic, magico-religious time which is the subject of this chapter. We are now in a position to understand why sacred, religious time, is not always reproduced periodically; while a given feast (taking place of course in hierophanic time) will be repeated periodically, there are other actions which appear to be profane—but *only* appear to be—which, while they too were established in an *illud tempus*, can take place *at any time*. Man may set off at any time to hunt or to fish, and thus imitate a mythical hero, embodying him, re-establishing mythical time, leaving profane time, repeating the myth-history. To return to what I said a moment ago, *any* time may become a sacred time; at any moment succession may be changed to eternity. Naturally, as we shall see, the periodic recurrence of sacred time has an important place in the religious notions of all mankind; but it is extremely significant that the same contrivance of imitating an archetype and repeating an archetypal action can do away with profane time and transform it into sacred, quite apart from any periodic rites; it proves, on the one hand, that the tendency to " hierophanize " time is something essential, independent of any systems based on the framework of social life, independent of the normal means of abolishing profane time (like the " old year ") and establishing sacred (the " new year ") to which we shall be returning in a moment; and on the other hand, it reminds us of the " easy substitutes " we saw for establishing sacred space (§ 146). Just as a " centre of the world ", which is, by definition, in some inaccessible place, can nevertheless be constructed anywhere without any of the difficulties described by the myths and heroic legends, so too sacred time, generally established by communal feasts set by the calendar, may be attained at any time and by anyone, simply by repeating an archetypal, mythical gesture. It is important that we remember henceforth this tendency to go outside the frameworks of society in establishing sacred time: it is important in a way we shall very soon see.

152. THE REGENERATION OF TIME

Festivals take place in sacred time, or, in other words, as Marcel Mauss points out, in eternity. But there are some seasonal feasts—certainly the most important ones—which give us a glimpse of something more: the wish to destroy the profane time that is past and establish a " new time ". In other words, the seasonal feasts which close one cycle of time and open another set out to achieve a *complete regeneration of time*. As I have elsewhere[1] studied in some detail the ritual scenarios marking the end of the old year and beginning of the new, I will give here only a summary glance at this important question.

The morphology of seasonal ritual drama is a very rich one. The researches of Frazer, Wensinck, Dumézil and other authors cited in the bibliography, make it possible to formulate the substance of it in the following way. The end of the year and beginning of the new year are marked by a series of rites: (1) purgations, purifications, the confessing of sins, driving off of demons, expulsion of evil out of the village and so on; (2) the extinguishing and rekindling of all fires; (3) masked processions (with the masks representing the souls of the dead), the ceremonial reception of the dead, who are entertained (with banquets, etc.) and led back at the end of the feast to the borders of the territory, to the sea, or the river, or wherever it may be; (4) fights between two opposing teams; (5) an interlude of Carnival, Saturnalia, reversal of the normal order, " orgy ".

Needless to say, nowhere does the scenario for the end of the old year and beginning of the new include all these rites—and in any case this list does not exhaust them, for it omits the initiations and marriages by abduction which take place in some areas. All of them are none the less part of the same

[1] *In The Myth of the Eternal Return.*

ceremonial framework. Each—at its own level, with its own particular outlook—aims at abolishing the time that composed the cycle now being brought to a close. Thus the purgation, the purifications, the burning of effigies of the " old year ", the driving out of demons and witches, and generally of everything that represents the past year—all this is done to destroy the whole of the past, to *suppress* it. By extinguishing all fires, " darkness " is established, the " cosmic night " in which all " forms " lose their outlines and become confused. At the cosmological level, this " darkness " is identified with chaos, as the rekindling of the fires symbolizes creation, the re-establishing of forms and of limits. The masks which embody the ancestors, the souls of the dead paying ceremonial visit to the living (in Japan, Germany, and elsewhere) are also a sign that all barriers have been destroyed and all forms of life merged together. In this paradoxical interval between two " times " (between two Cosmoses) communication between the living and the dead becomes possible, between determinate forms and what is preformal, " larval ". In a sense it may be said that in the " darkness " and " chaos " established by the liquidation of the old year, all forms merge together and the coalescence of all things (" night "—" deluge "—" dissolution") makes possible an effortless, automatic *coincidentia oppositorum* at every level of existence.

This wish to abolish time can be seen even more clearly in the " orgy " which takes place, with varying degrees of violence, during the New Year ceremonies. An orgy is also a regression into the " dark ", a restoration of the primeval chaos, and as such precedes all creation, every manifestation of ordered form. The fusion of all forms into one single, vast, undifferentiated unity is an exact reproduction of the " total " mode of reality. I pointed out earlier (§ 138) the function and meaning of the orgy, at once sexual and agricultural; at the cosmological level, the " orgy " represents chaos or the ultimate disappearance of limits and, as time goes, the inauguration of the Great Time, of the " eternal moment ", of non-duration. The presence of the orgy among the ceremonials marking the periodic divisions of time shows the *will to abolish the past totally by abolishing all creation*. The " merging together of forms " is illustrated by overthrowing social conditions (during the Saturnalia, the slave was master, the master obeyed his slaves; in Mesopotamia the king was dethroned and humiliated); by combining opposites (matrons were treated as courtesans, and so on); and by the suspension of all norms. Licence is let loose, all commands are violated, all contraries are brought together, and all this is simply to effect the dissolution of the world—of which the community is a copy—and restore the primeval *illud tempus* which is obviously the mythical moment of the *beginning* (chaos) and the end (flood or *ekpyrosis*, apocalypse).

153. YEARLY REPETITION OF THE CREATION

That this is the meaning of the carnivalesque orgy at the end of the year is confirmed by the fact that the chaos is always followed by a new creation of the cosmos. All these seasonal celebrations go on to a more or less clear symbolic repetition of the creation. I will give only a few examples. During the new year ceremonial of the Babylonians, *akitu* (lasting for twelve days), they used to recite the creation poem, *Enuma Elish*, several times in the temple of Marduk; thus by oral magic and the rites that went with it, they brought into the present the struggle between Marduk and the sea-monster Tiamat, a struggle which took place *in illo tempore*, and which, through the god's final victory, put an end to the chaos. The Hittites had a similar custom: as part of the feast of the New Year, they recounted and re-enacted the archetypal duel between Teshub the god of the weather and the serpent Iluyankash.[1] The single combat between Marduk and Tiamat was acted out by a conflict between two groups of men,[2] and this ritual also occurs among the Hittites (at the time of the New Year),[3] and the Egyptians.[4] The turning of chaos into cosmos was reproduced: " May he continue to conquer Tiamat ", they cried, " and cut short his days ! " The struggle, Marduk's victory and the creation of the world thus became actually present.

[1] Cf. Gotze, *Kleinasien*, Leipzig, 1933, p. 130.
[2] Labat, *Le Caractère religieux de la royauté assyro-babylonienne*, Paris, 1939, p. 99.
[3] Gotze p. 130.
[4] Ivan Engnell, *Studies on Divine Kingship in the Ancient Near East*, Uppsala, 1943, p. 11.

At the time of the *akitu*, they also celebrated the *zakmuk*, the
" feast of lots ", so called because lots were then drawn for
every month of the year; in other words, they were *creating*
the next twelve months according to a notion shared by a
great many other traditions. A whole series of rituals was
connected with these: Marduk's descent into hell, the
humiliation of the king, the driving out of ills in the guise of a
scapegoat, and finally the marriage of the god with Sarpanitum
—a marriage which the king re-enacted with a temple handmaid
in the goddess' sanctuary[1] and which must have been the signal
for a short time of communal licence. We thus see a reversion
to chaos (in which Tiamat is supreme, and all forms become
confused) followed by a new creation (the victory of Marduk,
all fates determined, and a sacred marriage or " new birth ").
At the moment when the old world was dissolving into primeval
chaos, they thus also effected the abolition of the old time, of
what a modern would call the " history " of the cycle coming
to an end.

In the primitive mind, the old time consisted of the profane
succession of all the events without meaning, events, that is,
with no archetypal models; " history " is the remembrance
of those events, of what can only really be called " unmeanings "
or even sins (in as much as they are divergences from the
archetypal norms). As we saw, to primitives, true history
is not that, but myth; all that true history records are the
archetypal actions displayed by the gods, the ancestors or the
culture heroes, during the mythical time, *in illo tempore*. To
the primitive, all repetitions of archetypes take place outside
profane time; it follows then, that, on the one hand, such
actions cannot be " sins ", divergences from the norm, and
on the other, they have no connection with ordinary succession,
the " old time " that is periodically abolished. The driving
out of demons and spirits, the confessing of sins, the purifications
and, specially, the symbolic return of the primeval chaos—
all this indicates the abolition of profane time, of the old time
during which occurred all the meaningless events and all the
deviations.

Once a year, then, the old time, the past, the remembrance of
all events not archetypal in character (in short, " history "

[1] Labat, p. 247.

in our sense of the word), are abolished. The symbolic repetition of the creation which follows this symbolic annihilation of the old world regenerates *time in its entirety*. For it is no mere matter of a feast, bringing " the eternal moment " of sacred time into profane succession; it is further, as I have said, the total annihilation of all the profane time that made up the cycle now coming to an end. In the wish to *start a new life in the midst of a new creation*—an aspiration clearly present in all the ceremonies for beginning one year and ending another—there also enters the paradoxical desire to attain to an historic existence, to be able to live only in sacred time. What is meant is a regeneration of time in its totality, a transforming of succession into " eternity ".

This need for a complete regeneration of time (which can be effected by repeating the creation every year) has been preserved even in traditions which are anything but primitive. I mentioned the things done in the Babylonian new year festival. The creation elements are equally obvious in the corresponding Jewish ceremonial. " When the time of the year returneth ",[1] " in the end of the year ",[2] there took place the struggle of Yahweh with Rahab, the defeat of the sea monster (the counterpart of Tiamat) by Yahweh and the victory over the waters which was equivalent to a repetition of the creation of the worlds, and at the same time, the salvation of men (victory over death, a guarantee of food for the coming year and so on).[3]

Wensinck points out still more traces of the primitive idea of the annual re-creation of the Cosmos, which were preserved in Jewish and Christian traditions.[4] The world was created during the months of Tishri or Nisan, that is, during the rainy season, the ideal cosmogonic period. To Eastern Christians, the blessing of water at the Epiphany also has a cosmogonic significance. " He [God] has created the heavens anew, because sinners have worshipped all the heavenly bodies; has created the world anew which had been withered by Adam,

---

[1] Exod. xxxiv. 22.

[2] Exod. xxiii. 16.

[3] Cf. Johnson, " The Role of the King in the Jerusalem Cultus ", in *The Labyrinth*, ed. S. H. Hooke, London, 1938, pp. 97 ff.

[4] " The Semitic New Year and the Origin of Eschatology ", *AOA*, 1923, vol. i, p. 168.

a new creation arose from his spittle."[1] " Allah is he who effects the creation, hence he repeats it."[2] This eternal repeating of the creative act, which makes every New Year the inauguration of an era, enables the dead to return to life and upholds the faithful in their hope of a resurrection of the flesh. This tradition also remains among Semitic peoples[3] as well as Christians.[4] " The Almighty awakens the bodies [at Epiphany] together with the spirits."[5]

A Pahlavi text, translated by Darmesteter[6], says that " It is in the month of Fravartin, on the day of Xurdhath, that the Lord Orhmazd will cause the resurrection and the second body, and the world will be saved from powerlessness with demons, *drugs* . . . And there will be plenty in all things; no one will have any more desire for food; the world will be pure and man will be free from the opposition [of the evil spirit], and immortal forever." Kazwini says that on the day of Nawroz, God will raise the dead, " give them back their souls and give his orders to the sky to rain upon them, and that is why people have the custom of pouring water on that day ".[7] The close connection among the ideas of " creation by water " (aquatic cosmogony; periodic flood regenerating " historic " life; rain), of birth and of resurrection, are borne out by this phrase from the Talmud: " God hath three keys, of rain, of birth, of raising the dead."[8]

Nawroz, the Persian New Year, is at the same time the feast of Ahura Mazda (celebrated on " Orhmazd day " of the first month) and the day when the creation of the world and of man took place.[9] It is on the day of the Nawroz that " renovating

[1] St. Ephraim the Syrian, *Seventh Hymn on the Epiphany*, 16; Wensinck, " The Semitic New Year and the Origin of Eschatology ", *AOA*, 1923, vol. i, p. 169.

[2] *Qur'an*, xxix, 20 ff.

[3] Lehman and Pedersen, " Der Beweis für die Auferstehung im Koran ", *Der Islam*, v, pp. 54–61.

[4] Wensinck, p. 171.

[5] St. Ephraim the Syrian, *First Hymn on the Epiphany*, 1.

[6] *Zend-Avesta*, Paris, 1892-3, vol. ii, p. 640, n. 138.

[7] *Cosmography*, quoted by A. Christensen, *Le Premier homme et le premier roi*, Uppsala, 1918–34, vol. ii, p. 147.

[8] *Ta'anith*, ch. 1; Wensinck, p. 173.

[9] Cf. the texts assembled by J. Marquart, " The Nawroz, its History and Significance ", *Journal of the Cama Oriental Institute*, Bombay, 1937, no. xxxi, particularly 16 ff.

the creation " takes place.[1] According to the tradition handed
on by Dimashki,[2] the king proclaimed: "This is a new day
of a new month of a new year; all that time has worn out
must be renewed!" It is on that day, too, that the fate of
men is determined for the whole year.[3] On the night of the
Nawroz, innumerable fires and lights are to be seen,[4] and
libations and purifications by water are performed to ensure
plenty of rain in the coming year.[5]

At the time of the "Great Nawroz", too, everyone sowed
seven sorts of grain in a jar, and "drew from their growth
conclusions as to the year's harvest".[6] This is a custom similar
to that of "fixing lots" in the Babylonian new year, and exists
even to-day in the new year celebrations of the Mandeans and
the Yezidis. Again, it is because the New Year repeats the
creation that the twelve days between Christmas and Epiphany
are still looked on as foreshadowing the twelve months of the
year; peasants all over Europe judge the temperature and
rainfall to be expected during each of the months to come by the
"meteorological signs" of those twelve days.[7] The rainfall
for each month was also decided in this way during the Feast
of Tabernacles.[8] The Indians of Vedic times thought of the
Twelve Days of the middle of the winter as an image and
replica of the whole year,[9] and this same concentration of
the year into twelve days also appears in Chinese traditions.[10]

154. REPETITIONS OF THE CREATION ATTACHED TO PARTICULAR OCCASIONS

All these things we have been looking at have one trait in
common: they presuppose the notion that time is periodically
regenerated by symbolic repetition of the creation. But the

---

[1] Albiruni, *The Chronology of Ancient Nations*, trans. Sachau, London, 1879,
p. 199.

[2] Christensen, vol. ii, p. 149.

[3] Albiruni, p. 201; Kazwini, in Christensen, vol. ii, p. 148.

[4] Albiruni, p. 200.

[5] Albiruni, pp. 202-3.

[6] Albiruni, p. 202.

[7] Cf. Frazer, *The Scapegoat*, London, 1936, pp. 315 ff.; Dumézil, *Le Problème
des Centaures*, Paris, 1929, pp. 36 ff.

[8] Wensinck, p. 163.

[9] *RV*, iv, 33.

[10] Granet, *La Pensée chinoise*, p. 107.

repetition of the creation is not narrowly bound up with communal ceremonies for the New Year. In other words, " old ", " profane ", " historic " time can be abolished and mythical, " new " regenerated time established *by repeating the creation* even during the course of the year and quite apart from the communal rites mentioned just now. Thus, for the Icelanders, the taking possession of land (*landnama*) was equivalent to the transformation of chaos into cosmos[1] and, in Vedic India, taking possession of an area was confirmed by the erection of a fire altar, regarded in fact as a repetition of the creation. The fire altar, in effect, reproduced the universe, and setting it up corresponded to creating the world; and whenever anyone built an altar of this sort, he was repeating the archetypal act of creation and " building " time.[2]

The Fijians called the ceremony of inaugurating a new chieftain the " creation of the world ".[3] The same idea can be found, though not necessarily so explicitly, in more developed civilizations, where every enthronement is equivalent to a re-creation or regeneration of the world. The first decree the Chinese emperor promulgated on his accession to the throne was to determine a new calendar, and before establishing a new order of time, he abolished the old.[4] Assurbanipal saw himself as a regenerator of the cosmos, for, he said, " since the time the gods, in their friendliness, did set me on the throne of my fathers, Ramman has sent forth his rain . . . the harvest was plentiful, the corn was abundant . . . the cattle multiplied exceedingly ".[5]

The prophecy of the Fourth Eclogue, *magnes ab integro saeclorum nascitur ordo* . . . can in a sense be applied to every sovereign. For with every new sovereign, however insignificant he may be, a " new era " is begun. A new reign was looked upon as a regeneration of the nation's history, if not of the history of the world. We should be wrong to reduce these high-sounding formulæ to what they came to be only as

[1] Van der Leeuw, *L'Homme primitif et la religion*, p. 110.
[2] Cf. *Śatapatha-Brahmana*, vi, 5, i, ff.; " The fire-altar is the year " . . . ibid., x, 5, 4, 10; " Of five layers consists the fire-altar [each layer is a season], five seasons are a year, and the year is Agni [the altar] ", ibid., vi, 8, 1, 15.
[3] Hocart, *Kingship*, Oxford, 1927, pp. 189–90.
[4] Granet, *La Pensée chinoise*, p. 97.
[5] Quoted by Jeremias in Hastings, *Encyclopædia of Religion and Ethics*, vol. i, p. 187 b.

monarchies declined: mere boasting by the sovereign and flattery by his courtiers. The hope of a " new era " inaugurated by the new ruler was not only genuine and sincere, but also quite natural, if one looks at it with the vision of primitive man. In any case, there is not even any need of a new reign to open a new era; it is enough to have a wedding, the birth of a child, the building of a house or anything else of the sort. Man and the universe go on being regenerated, the past is destroyed, mistakes and sins are done away with, by any and every means, and nothing can stop it happening. However differently they may be expressed, all these means of regeneration are equally effective: they annihilate the time that is past, and abolish history by constantly going back to *illud tempus*.[1]

Thus, to go back to the Fijians, they repeat the creation of the world, not only when a new chieftain is crowned, but again every time the harvest is endangered.[2] Whenever the rhythms of nature are upset and life as a whole is threatened, the Fijians save themselves by returning *in principiuo*—they await, in other words, the re-establishing of the cosmos, not by a process of *repair*, but by *regeneration*. Similar ideas are behind the meaning of the " beginning ", the " new ", the " virginal ", and so on, in popular medicine and in magic (" new water ", the " new pitcher ", the symbolism of the child, of the virgin, of the " immaculate ", and so on). We saw (§ 149) how magic can make actual a mythical event which guarantees the power of the medicine and the cure of the patient. The symbolism of " the new ", the " not yet begun ", also guarantees the concurrence in time of the thing done now with the mythical, archetypal event. As with a threatened harvest, a cure is got not by any sort of patching up but by a *new beginning*, which involves the return to *illud tempus*. (It is not essential that a sorcerer carrying out these rites should realize the theory underlying them; it is enough for the rites in question to flow from the theory implicit in them; cf. § 3.)

Similar ideas, although of course disfigured by irrelevant additions and inevitable corruptions, can be seen in the techniques of mining and metallurgy.[3] On the other hand,

[1] See *Myth of the Eternal Return*, chs. ii–iii.
[2] Hocart, p. 190.
[3] Cf. Eliade, " Metallurgy, Magic and Alchemy ", *CZ*, Paris, 1938, vol. i, *passim*.

initiation ceremonies (such as the " death " of the old man
and " birth " of the new) are based on the hope that the past—
" history "—may be abolished and a new time established.
If the symbolism of water (§ 63 ff.) and the moon played so
important a part in the spiritual life of primitive men, it was
precisely because it made the continued abolition and re-
establishing of " forms ", periodic disappearance and reappearance, the eternal return (which was in fact a return to
the *beginnings*), clear and obvious. At every level—from
cosmology to soteriology—the notion of regeneration is bound
up with the conception of a new time, that is, with belief in
man's sometimes being able to attain to *an absolute beginning*.

155. TOTAL REGENERATION

This obsession with regeneration is also expressed in all the
myths and doctrines of cyclic time, which I studied in *The Myth
of the Eternal Return*. Belief in a time that is cyclic, in an
eternal returning, in the periodic destruction of the world and
mankind to be followed by a new world and a new, regenerated,
mankind—all these beliefs bear witness primarily to the desire
and hope for a periodic regeneration of the time gone by, of
history. Basically, the cycle in question is a Great Year, to
use a term very common in Graeco-Oriental terminology:
the Great Year opens with a creation and concludes with a
Chaos, that is, by a complete fusion of the elements. A cosmic
cycle includes a " creation ", an " existence " (or " history ",
wearing-out, degeneration), and a " return to chaos " (*ekpyrosis,
ragnarok, pralaya*, submergence of Atlantis, apocalypse).
Structurally, a Great Year is to the year what a year is to the
month and the day. But what is interesting to us at the moment
is chiefly the hope of *a total regeneration of time* that is evident
in all the myths and doctrines involving cosmic cycles; every
cycle is an *absolute* beginning because all the past, all " history ",
has been completely abolished by reverting in a single instant
to " chaos ".

We thus find in man at every level, the same longing to
destroy profane time and live in sacred time. Further, we see
the desire and hope of regenerating time as a whole, of being
able to live—" humanly ", " historically "—in eternity, by
transforming successive time into a single eternal moment.

This longing for eternity is a sort of parallel to the longing for paradise which we looked at in the last chapter (§ 146). To the wish to be always and naturally in a sacred place there corresponds the wish to live always in eternity by means of repeating archetypal actions. The repetition of archetypes shows the paradoxical wish to achieve an ideal form (the archetype) in the very framework of human existence, to be in time without reaping its disadvantages, without the inability to " put back the clock ". Let me point out that this desire is no " spiritual " attitude, which depreciates life on earth and all that goes with it in favour of a " spirituality " of detachment from the world. On the contrary, what may be called the " nostalgia for eternity " proves that man longs for a concrete paradise, and believes that such a paradise can be won *here*, on earth, and *now*, in the present moment. In this sense, it would seem that the ancient myths and rites connected with sacred time and space may be traceable back to so many nostalgic memories of an " earthly paradise ", and some sort of " realizable " eternity to which man still thinks he may have access.

BIBLIOGRAPHY

VAN DER LEEUW, G., *Religion in Essence and Manifestation*, London, 1938, pp. 384 ff.; id., *L'Homme primitif et la religion, passim*; DUMEZIL, G., " Temps et Mythes ", *Recherches philosophiques*, 1935-6, vol. v, pp. 235-51; REUTER, H., *Die Zeit: eine religionswissenschaftliche Untersuchung*, Bonn, 1941; COOMARASWAMY, Ananda K., *Time and Eternity*, Ascona, 1947.

HUBERT, H., and MAUSS, M., " La Représentation du temps dans la religion et la magie ", *Mélanges d'histoire des religions*, 1909, pp. 190-229; SAINTYVES, P., " Les Notions de temps et d'éternité dans la magie et la religion ", *RHR*, 1919, vol. lxxix, pp. 74-104; NILSSON, M. P., " Primitive Time Reckoning " (*Reg. Societas Humaniorum Letterarum Lundensis Acta*, Lund, 1920, vol. i); CAVAIGNAC, E., " Calendriers et fêtes religieuses " *RHR*, 1925, vol. ii, pp. 8 ff.

GRANET, M., *Danses et légendes de la Chine ancienne*, Paris, 1928, pp. 114 ff., 230 ff.; LEVY-BRUHL, *Primitives and the Supernatural*, London, 1936, *passim*; DANGEL, R., " Tagesanbruch und Weltenstehung ", *SMSR*, 1938, vol. xiv, pp. 65-81; LEHMANN, F. R., " Weltuntergang und Welterneuerung im Glauben schriftloser Völker ", *ZFE*, 1939, vol. lxxi, pp. 103-15; SOUSTELLE, J., *La Pensée cosmologique des anciens Mexicains*, Paris, 1940, pp. 79 ff.; LEENHARDT, Maurice, *Do Kamo. La Personne et le mythe dans le monde mélanésien*, Paris, 1947, pp. 96 ff.; VAN DER LEEUW, G., " Urzeit und Endzeit ", *EJ*, 1950, vol. xvii, pp. 11-51; PUECH, Henri-Charles, " La Gnose et le temps ", *EJ*, 1951, vol. xx, pp. 57-113; CORBIN, Henri, " Le Temps cyclique dans le Mazdéisme et dans l'Ismaélisme ", *EJ*, 1951, vol. xx, pp. 149-217; RINGGREN, Helmer, *Fatalism in Persian Epics*, Uppsala, 1952, pp. 9 ff.

JEREMIAS, Alfred, *Handbuch der altorientalischen Geisteskultur*, 2nd ed., Berlin, 1929, pp. 239 ff., 295 ff., 313 ff.; JOHNSON, A. J., " The Role of the King in the Jerusalem Cultus ", in *The Labyrinth*, ed. S. H. Hooke, London, 1938, pp. 73-111; CARCOPINO, J., *Virgile et le mystère de la IVe Eclogue*, revised and augmented edition, Paris, 1943.

CHRISTENSEN, A., *Le Premier Homme et le premier roi dans l'histoire légendaire des Iraniens*, Uppsala, 1918-24, 2 vols.; DUMEZIL, G., *Le Problème des Centaures*, Paris, 1929; LEHMANN and PEDERSEN, " Der Beweis für die Auferstehung im Koran ", (*Der Islam*, vol. v, pp. 54-61); WENSINCK, A. J., " The Semitic New Year and the Origin of Eschatology ", *AOA*, 1923, vol. i, pp. 158-99; MARQUART, J., " The Nawroz, its History and Significance ", *Journal of the Cama Oriental Institute*, Bombay, 1937, no. xxxi, pp. 1-51; SCHEFTELOWITZ, J., *Die Zeit als Schicksalsgottheit in der indischen und iranischen Religion*, Stuttgart, 1929; HERTEL, J., " Das indogermanische Neujahrsopfer im Veda ", Leipzig, 1938.

ELIADE, M., *The Myth of the Eternal Return*, London. 1955, chs. ii and iii; id., *Images et Symboles*, Paris, 1952, ch. ii.

On the *akitu*, *zakmuk* and the New Year in Babylon, see PALLIS, S. A., *The Babylonian Akitu Festival*, Copenhagen, 1926; ZIMMERN, H., " Zum babylonischen Neujahrsfest ", pts. i-ii, *Berichte über d. Verhandl. d. Kgl. Sachs. Gesell. d. Wiss.*, Leipzig, 1906-18, vol. xviii, 3; lxx, 5; FRAZER, Sir J. G., *The Scapegoat*, p. 355; LABAT, R., *Le Caractère religieux de la royauté assyro-babylonienne*, Paris, 1939, p. 95; PETTAZZONI, R., " Der babylonische Ritus des Akitu und das Gedicht der Weltschöpfung ", *EJ*, 1950, vol. xix, pp. 703-30.

XII

THE MORPHOLOGY AND FUNCTION OF MYTHS

156. CREATION MYTHS—EXEMPLAR MYTHS

ACCORDING to the Polynesian myth, in the beginning there existed only the primordial waters, plunged in cosmic darkness, From "within the breathing-space of immensity", Io, the supreme god, expressed the desire to emerge from his repose. Immediately, light appeared. Then he went on: "Ye waters of Tai-Kama, be ye separate. Heavens, be formed!" And thus, through Io's cosmogonic words, the world came into existence. Recalling these "ancient and original sayings . . . the ancient and original cosmological wisdom (*wananga*), which caused growth from the void . . .", a Polynesian of to-day, Hare Hongi, adds with eloquent awkwardness:

> And now, my friends, there are three very important applications of those original sayings, as used in our sacred rituals. The first occurs in the ritual for planting a child in the barren womb. The next occurs in the ritual for enlightening both mind and body. The third and last occurs in the ritual on the solemn subject of death, and of war, of baptism, of genealogical recitals and such like important subjects, as the priests most particularly concerned themselves in.
>
> The words by which Io fashioned the universe—that is to say, by which it was implanted and caused to produce a world of light—the same words are used in the ritual for implanting a child in a barren womb. The words by which Io caused light to shine in the darkness are used in the rituals for cheering a gloomy and despondent heart, the feeble aged, the decrepit; for shedding light into secret places and matters, for inspiration in song-composing and in many other affairs, affecting man to despair in times of adverse war. For all such ritual includes the words [used by Io] to overcome and dispel darkness. Thirdly, there is the preparatory ritual which treats of successive formations within the universe, and the genealogical history of man himself.

The cosmogonic myth thus serves the Polynesians as an archetypal model for all "creations", at whatever level they occur: biological, psychological, spiritual. The main function of myth is to determine the exemplar models of all ritual, and of all significant human acts. Innumerable ethnologists have shown that this is the case. " Among the Marind-anim " (of Dutch New Guinea), writes P. Wirz, " myth is, properly speaking, as much the basis of all the great feasts at which masked *Dema* actors appear as of the secret cults."[1] As we have seen (§ 150), even apart from actions that are strictly religious, myths are also the models for the other significant human actions, as, for instance, navigation and fishing.

What is interesting about the Polynesian creation myth is just this manifold application to circumstances which, in appearance at least, do not involve religious life at all; the act of procreation, " the cheering of a despondent heart, the feeble aged and the decrepit ", inspiring the composing of songs, going to war. The cosmogony thus provides a *model*, whenever there is a question of *doing something* ; often it is something " living ", something " animated " (in the biological, psychological or spiritual order), as with the cases given above, but it is also sometimes a question of making something apparently quite inanimate—a house, a boat, a State, etc.; remember the cosmogonic model for the building of houses, palaces and towns (§ 143 ff.).

These mythical models are not only to be found in "primitive" traditions: an Indian metaphysical treatise, the *Bṛhadāraṅyaka-Upaniṣad*, gives us the ritual for procreating a boy. It transforms the act of generation into a hierogamy. The human pair are identified with the cosmic pair: " I am the Sky," says the husband, " thou art the Earth " (*dyaur aham, pṛthivī tvam*).[2] Conception becomes a creative act of cosmic proportions, involving a whole series of gods : " May Viṣṇu prepare the womb; may Tvaṣṭṛ fashion the forms; may Prajāpati cause [the seed] to flow, may Dhātṛ place the seed within thee."[3] The hierogamy of sky and earth, or of sun and moon, is often thought of in quite literal terms : *ut maritus supra feminam in coitione iacet, sic cælum supra terram.*[4] It would be a mistake to see this notion of the hierogamy as occurring only with the " primitive mentality " : the same anthropomorphism is used

---

[1] Quoted by Lévy-Bruhl, *La Mythologie primitive, Le Monde mythique des Australiens et des Papous*, Paris, 1936, p. xvii.

[2] vi, 4, 20.

[3] vi, 4, 21.

[4] Hollis, *The Masai*, Oxford, 1905, p. 279; Krappe, *Mythologie Universelle*, Paris, 1930, p. 370, n. 1.

even in the most developed symbolism of alchemy, relating to the union between the sun and moon,[1] and in other cases of *coniunctio* between cosmological or spiritual principles.[2] In short, the hierogamy preserves its cosmological character independent of the varied contexts in which it may be found, and however anthropomorphic the formulæ in which it may be expressed.

Whether or not it includes a hierogamy, the creation myth, in addition to its important function as model and justification for all human activities, also constitutes the archetype of a whole complexus of myths and ritual systems. Every idea of renewal, of beginning again, of restoring what once was, at whatever level it appears, can be traced back to the notion of " birth " and that, in its turn, to the notion of " the creation of the cosmos ". We came across similar identifications in our study of the rituals and symbolism bound up with the rebirth of plant life (§ 118 ff.): each return of spring re-presents the cosmogony, every *sign* of the resurrection of vegetation is equivalent to a total manifestation of the universe, and that is why, as we saw (§ 123), the *sign*—a branch, a flower, or an animal—is carried in procession from house to house to be *shown* to everyone: it is a proof that " spring has come ", not necessarily nature's spring, the physical phenomenon, but the resurrection of life. The ritual dramas which took place either at the New Year (§ 152 f.) or at the coming of spring (the combat of spring and winter, the expulsion of death, the execution of winter or of death, and so on; cf. § 121 f.), are simply so many fragmentary and " specialized " versions of one and the same myth, which stems from the cosmogonic myth.

Every year the world is remade. It may happen, as in Mesopotamia, for instance, that the creation is re-enacted explicitly (by the recitation of the creation poem). But even when we are not told that the creation is being imitated traces of it are still clear to see (the putting out and relighting of fires, visits from the dead, contests between rival parties, initiations, marriages, orgies, and so on; cf. § 152). These New Year or Spring rituals are not, of course, always explicitly connected

[1] See, for instance, G. Carbonelli, *Sulle Fonti storiche della chimica e dell' alchimia in Italia*, Rome, 1925, p. 43, fig. 49; C .G. Jung, *Psychology and Alchemy*, London, 1953, p. 317, fig. 167.

[2] See Jung, p. 395, fig. 226, fig. 268, etc.

with a " myth "; and some are connected with secondary myths whose accent is not on the function of creation. But, taken together, all the sacred acts, all the " signs " effected at the New Year or at the beginning of spring—whether they be in essence symbolic or ritual, mythological or legendary—present a common framework; all express, more or less clearly, the drama of the creation. In this sense they all are part of the cosmogonic myth although, in more cases than one, there is no question of " myths " properly so called, but only of rituals or " signs ". Thus the " sign " heralding spring can be looked on as a cryptic or " concentrated " myth, for the very displaying of the sign is equivalent to proclaiming the creation. A true myth describes an archetypal event in words (in this case the creation of the world), while a " sign " (in this case a green branch or an animal) evokes the event simply by being shown. I shall shortly give some examples which will make clearer the relation between the myth properly so called and these other categories of magico-religious phenomena which we may call " cryptic " or " concentrated " myths.

157. THE COSMOGONIC EGG

A creation myth of the Society Islands tells of Ta'aroa, " ancestor of all the gods " and creator of the universe, sitting " in his shell in darkness from eternity. The shell was like an egg revolving in endless space."[1] This motif of the cosmogonic egg which we find in Polynesia[2] is also common to ancient India,[3] Indonesia,[4] Iran, Greece,[5] Phœnicia,[6] Latvia, Estonia, Finland,[7] the Pangwe of West Africa,[8] Central America and the west coast of South America (according to Frobenius' map[9]). The centre from which this myth originated is probably to be located in India or Indonesia. What are specially important to us are the ritual or mythological parallels of the

[1] Handy, *Polynesian Religion*, Honolulu, 1927, p. 12.
[2] Cf. Dixon, *Oceanic Mythology*, Boston, 1916, p. 20.
[3] *Śatapatha-Br.*, xi, 1, 6, 1 ff.; Laws of Manu, 1, 5 ff., etc.
[4] Numazawa, *Die Weltanfänge in der japanischen Mythologie*, Lucerne-Paris, 1946, p. 310; Krappe, p. 397.
[5] Harrison, *Prolegomena to the Study of Greek Religion*, pp. 627 ff.
[6] Numazawa, p. 309.
[7] Numazawa, p. 310; Krappe, p. 414.
[8] Krappe, p. 371, n. 1.
[9] Reproduced by W. Liungman in " Euphrat-Rhein ", I, p. 21, fig. 1.

cosmogonic egg; in Oceania, for instance, it is believed that man is born of an egg[1]; in other words, the creation of the cosmos here serves as a model for the creation of man, the creation of man copies and repeats that of the Cosmos.

Then, too, in a great many places the egg is connected with the symbols and emblems of the renovation of nature and vegetation; the new year trees, Maypoles, Saint John's trees and so on, are decorated with eggs or egg-shells.[2] We know that all these emblems of vegetation and the New Year in some way sum up the myth of periodic creation. The tree is itself a symbol of nature and her unwearying renewal, and when the egg is added to it, it confirms all these cosmogonic values. Hence the major role it plays in the East in all the new year dramas. In Persia, for instance, coloured eggs are the appropriate gifts for the New Year which, even to-day, is still called the Feast of Red Eggs.[3] And the red eggs given at Easter in the Balkan countries are probably also left over from a similar ritual pattern used to celebrate the coming of spring.

In all these cases, as in those we are coming to, the ritual power of the egg cannot be explained by any empirical or rationalist interpretation of the egg looked upon as a seed: it is founded on the symbol embodied in the egg, which bears not so much upon birth as upon a *rebirth* modelled on the creation of the world. Otherwise there could be no explanation for the important place eggs hold in the celebration of the New Year and the feasts of the dead. We have already seen the close connection between the cult of the dead and the start of the year; at the New Year, when the world is re-created, the dead feel themselves drawn towards the living and can hope, up to a point, to return to life. Whichever of these ritual and mythological patterns we turn to, the basic idea is not that of ordinary birth, but rather the *repeating of the archetypal birth* of the cosmos, the imitation of the cosmogony. During the Hindu vegetation feast, Holi, which is also a feast of the dead, the custom in some places is to light fires and cast into them two little statuettes, one of a man, the other of a woman,

---

[1] Indonesia, Dixon, p. 160, pp. 169 ff.; Melanesia, Dixon, p. 109; Polynesia, Micronesia, Dixon, p. 109, n. 17.

[2] Mannhardt, *Baumkultus*, pp. 244 ff.; pp. 263 ff.; etc.

[3] Lassy, *Muharram Mysteries*, Helsinki, 1916, pp. 219 ff.; Liungman, " Euphrat-Rhein ", I, p. 20.

representing Kāmadeva and Rati; with the first statuette an egg and a living hen are also thrown on to the fire.[1] When it takes this form, the feast symbolises the death and resurrection of Kāmadeva and Rati. The egg strengthens and assists the resurrection which, again, is not a birth, but a " return ", a " repetition ".

We find symbolism of this sort even in some prehistoric and proto-historic societies. Clay eggs have been found in a great many tombs in Russia and in Sweden[2]; with good reason Arne sees them as emblems of immortality. In the ritual of Osiris, various ingredients (diamond-dust, fig flour, aromatic spices and so on) are shaped into an egg—though we do not yet fully apprehend for what function.[3] The statues of Dionysos found in Bœotian tombs all have an egg in one hand[4] to symbolize a return to life. This explains the Orphic prohibition against eating eggs,[5] for the prime object of Orphism was to escape from the unending cycle of reincarnation—to abolish, in other words, the periodic return to life.

I will conclude with a few other instances of how the egg is used in ritual. There is, first, its role in the agricultural rituals still in use in modern times. To ensure that the grain would grow, Finnish peasants used to keep an egg in their pockets throughout the time of sowing, or place an egg in the ploughed earth.[6] The Estonians eat eggs during ploughing time " to have strength ", and the Swedes throw eggs down on ploughed fields. When the Germans are sowing flax they sometimes put eggs with it, or put an egg in the field, or eat eggs during the time of sowing.[7] The Germans still have the custom of burying blessed Easter eggs in their fields.[8] The Cheremisses and the Votyaks throw eggs up in the air before they start their sowing[9]; on other occasions they would bury an egg among the furrows

---

[1] Crooke, " The Holi: A Vernal Festival of the Hindus ", *FRE*, vol. 25, p. 75.
[2] T. J. Arne, *La Suède et l'Orient*, Uppsala, 1914, p. 216.
[3] Liungman, " Euphrat-Rhein ", I, pp. 141 ff.
[4] Nilsson, *Geschichte*, vol. i, p. 565.
[5] Rohde, *Psyche*, London, 1925, p. 357, n. 2; Harrison, p. 629.
[6] Rantasalo, " Der Ackerbau in Volksaberglauben der Finnen und Esten mit entsprechenden Gebräuchen der Germanen verglichen ", *FFC*, Helsinki, 1919–25, no. 32, pp. 55–6.
[7] Rantasalo, p. 57.
[8] Rantasalo, p. 58.
[9] Rantasalo, p. 58.

as an offering to the Earth Mother.[1] The egg is at once an
offering to the gods of the underworld and an offering used
frequently in the cult of the dead.[2] But whatever ritual pattern
it is linked with, the egg never loses its primary meaning: it
ensures the *repetition* of the act of creation which gave birth
in illo tempore to living forms. When they pick a simple, some
people put an egg on the spot to ensure that another herb will
grow there in its place.[3]

In each of these examples, the egg guarantees the possibility
of *repeating the primeval act,* the act of creation. In a sense,
therefore, we may speak of ritual variants on the creation myth.
For we must get used to dissociating the idea of " myth " from
" word " and " fable " (cf. the Homeric use of *mythos*: "word",
" discourse ") and connecting it with " sacred action ", " significant gesture " and " primeval event ". Not only is all that is
told about the various events that took place and characters
who lived *in illo tempore* mythical, but everything connected,
directly or indirectly, with those primeval events and characters
is mythical also. In as much as it is linked with the scenarios
for the New Year or the return of spring, the egg represents a
manifestation of creation and—in the framework not of
empirical and rational, but of hierophanic experience—a
summing up of the cosmogony.

From one point of view, every myth is " cosmogonic "
because every myth expresses the appearance of a new cosmic
" situation " or primeval event which becomes, simply by
being thus expressed, a paradigm for all time to come. But
it is wiser not to become bound by any formulæ, nor to reduce
all myths to a single prototype as did some of the really important scholars of a few generations ago—tracing all mythology back to epiphanies of the sun or moon. What I think
more useful than the classifying of myths and seeking for their
possible " origins ", is the study of their structure and the part
they play in the spiritual experience of primitive man.

158. WHAT MYTHS REVEAL

The myth, whatever its nature, is always a precedent and an

---

[1] Holmberg-Harva, *Die Religion der Tcheremissen*, Porvoo, 1926, p. 179.
[2] Martin Nilsson, " Das Ei im Totenkult der Alten ", *AFRW*, 1908, xi.
[3] Delatte, *Herbarius*, Liège-Paris, 1938, p. 120.

example, not only for man's actions (sacred or profane), but also as regards the condition in which his nature places him; a precedent, we may say, for the expressions of reality as a whole. " We must do what the gods did in the beginning "[1]; " Thus the gods acted, thus men act."[2] Statements of this kind give a perfect indication of primitive man's conduct, but they do not necessarily exhaust the content and function of myths; indeed one whole series of myths, recording what gods or mythical beings did *in illo tempore*, discloses a level of reality quite beyond any empirical or rational comprehension. There are, among others, the myths we may lump together as the myths of polarity (or bi-unity) and reintegration, which I have studied by themselves in another book.[3] There is a major group of mythological traditions about the " brotherhood " of gods and demons (for instance, the *devas* and *asuras*), the " friendship " or consanguinity between heroes and their opponents (as with Indra and Namuki), between legendary saints and she-devils (of the type of folklore's Saint Sisinius and his sister the she-devil Uerzelia), and so on. The myths giving a common " father " to figures embodying diametrically opposed principles still survive in the religious traditions which lay the stress on dualism, like the Iranian theology. Zervanism calls Ormuzd and Ahriman brothers, both sons of Zervan, and even the Avesta bears traces of the same idea.[4] This myth has in some cases also passed into popular traditions: there are a number of Rumanian beliefs and proverbs calling God and Satan brothers.[5]

There is another category of myths and legends illustrating not merely a brotherhood between opposing figures, but their paradoxical convertibility. The sun, prototype of the gods, is sometimes called " Serpent " (§ 45) and Agni, the god of fire, is at the same time a " priest Asura "[6]—essentially a demon; he is sometimes described[7] as " without feet or head, hiding

---

[1] *Śatapatha-Br.*, vii, 2, 1, 4.

[2] *Taittirīya-Br.*, 1, 5, 9, 4.

[3] *Mitul Reintegrarii*, Bucharest, 1942.

[4] For instance *Yasna*, 30, 3–6; see also Nyberg's commentary, " Questions de cosmogonie et de cosmologie mazdéennes ", *JA*, 1929, pp. 113 ff.

[5] Cf. Zane, *Proverbele Romanilor*, Bucharest, 1895–1901, vol. vi, p. 556.

[6] *RV*, vii, 30, 3.

[7] *RV*, iv, i, ii.

both his heads " just like a coiled snake. The *Aitareya Brāh-mana*[1] declares that Ahi-Budhnya is invisibly (*parokṣena*) what Agni is visibly (*pratyakṣa*); in other words, the serpent is simply a virtuality of fire, while darkness is light in its latent state. In the *Vājasaneyī Saṁhitā*,[2] Ahi-Budhnya is identified with the sun. *Soma*, the drink which bestows immortality, is supremely " divine ", " solar ", and yet we read in the *Ṛg Veda*[3] that *soma*, " like Agni, slips out of its old skin ", which seems to give it a serpentine quality. Varuṇa, sky god and archetype of the " Universal Sovereign " (§ 21), is also the god of the ocean, where serpents dwell, as the *Mahābhārata* explains; he is the " king of serpents " (*nāgarājā*) and the *Atharva Veda*[4] even goes so far as to call him " viper ".

In any logical perspective, all these reptilian attributes *ought not* to fit a sky divinity like Varuṇa. But myth reveals a region of ontology inaccessible to superficial logical experience. The myth of Varuṇa discloses the divine bi-unity, the apposition of contraries, all attributes whatever brought to their totality within the divine nature. Myth expresses in action and drama what metaphysics and theology define dialectically. Heraclitus saw that " God is day and night, winter and summer, war and peace, satiety and hunger: all opposites are in him."[5] We find a similar formulation of this idea in an Indian text which tells us that the goddess " is *śrī* [splendour] in the house of those who do good, but *alaksmi* [the opposite of Laksmī, goddess of good luck and prosperity] in the house of the wicked."[6] But this text is simply making clear in its own way the fact that the Indian Great Godesses (Kālī and the rest) like all other Great Goddesses, possess at once both the attributes of gentleness and of dread. They are at once divinities of fertility and destruction, of birth and of death (and often also of war). Kālī, for instance, is called " the gentle and benevolent ", although the mythology and iconography connected with her are terrifying (Kālī is covered in blood, wears a necklace of human skulls, holds a cup made out of a skull,

---

[1] ii, 36.
[2] v, 33.
[3] ix, 86, 44.
[4] xii, 3, 57.
[5] Fr. 64.
[6] *Markandeya Purāṇa*, 74, 4.

and so on), and her cult is the bloodiest anywhere in Asia. In India, every divinity has a " gentle form " and equally a " terrible form " (*krodha-mūrti*). In this, Śiva may be looked on as the archetype of a tremendous series of gods and goddesses for he rhythmically creates and destroys the entire universe.

159. *Coincidentia Oppositorum*—THE MYTHICAL PATTERN

All these myths present us with a twofold revelation: they express on the one hand the diametrical opposition of two divine figures sprung from one and the same principle and destined, in many versions, to be reconciled at some *illud tempus* of eschatology, and on the other, the *coincidentia oppositorum* in the very nature of the divinity, which shows itself, by turns or even simultaneously, benevolent and terrible, creative and destructive, solar and serpentine, and so on (in other words, actual and potential). In this sense it is true to say that myth reveals more profoundly than any rational experience ever could, the actual structure of the divinity, which transcends all attributes and reconciles all contraries. That this mythical experience is no mere deviation is proved by the fact that it enters into almost all the religious experience of mankind, even within as strict a tradition as the Judæo-Christian. Yahweh is both kind and wrathful; the God of the Christian mystics and theologians is terrible and gentle at once and it is this *coincidentia oppositorum* which is the starting point for the boldest speculations of such men as the pseudo-Dionysius, Meister Eckhardt, and Nicholas of Cusa.

The *coincidentia oppositorum* is one of the most primitive ways of expressing the paradox of divine reality. We shall be returning to this formula when we come to look at divine " forms ", to the peculiar structure revealed by every divine " personality ", given of course that the divine personality is not to be simply looked upon as a mere projection of human personality. However, although this conception, in which all contraries are reconciled (or rather, transcended), constitutes what is, in fact, the most basic definition of divinity, and shows how utterly different it is from humanity, the *coincidentia oppositorum* becomes nevertheless an archetypal model for certain types of religious men, or for certain of the forms religious experience takes. The *coincidentia oppositorum* or transcending of all attributes can be achieved by man in all sorts of ways. At the most elementary level of religious life there is the orgy: for it symbolizes a return to the amorphous and the indistinct, to a state in which all attributes disappear and contraries are merged. But exactly the same doctrine can also be discerned in the highest ideas of the eastern sage and ascetic, whose contemplative methods and techniques are aimed at transcending all attributes of every kind. The ascetic, the sage, the Indian or Chinese " mystic " tries to wipe out of his experience and consciousness every sort of " extreme ", to attain to a state of perfect indifference and neutrality, to become insensible to pleasure and pain, to become completely self-sufficient. This transcending of extremes through asceticism and contemplation also results in the " coinciding of opposites "; the consciousness of such a man knows no more conflict, and such pairs of opposites as pleasure and pain, desire and repulsion, cold and heat, the agreeable and the disagreeable are expunged from his awareness, while something is taking place within him which parallels the total realization of contraries within the divinity. As we saw earlier (§ 57),[1] the oriental mind cannot conceive perfection unless all opposites are present in their fulness. The neophyte begins by identifying all his experience with the rhythms governing the universe (sun and moon), but once this " cosmisation " has been achieved, he turns all his efforts towards *unifying* the sun and moon, towards taking into himself the *cosmos as a whole*; he remakes in himself and for himself the primeval unity which was before the world was made; a unity which signifies not the chaos that existed before any forms were created but the undifferentiated *being* in which all forms are merged.

160. THE MYTH OF DIVINE ANDROGYNY

Another example will illustrate more clearly still the efforts made by religious man to imitate the divine archetype revealed in myth. Since all attributes exist together in the divinity, then one must expect to see both sexes more or less clearly expressed together. Divine androgyny is simply a primitive formula for the divine bi-unity; mythological and religious thought, before expressing this concept of divine two-in-oneness in metaphysical

[1] Cf. Eliade, *Cosmical Homology and Yoga.*

terms (*esse* and *non esse*), or theological terms (the revealed and unrevealed), expressed it first in the biological terms of bisexuality. We have already noted on more than one occasion how archaic ontology was expressed in biological terms. But we must not make the mistake of taking the terminology superficially in the concrete, profane ("modern") sense of the words. The word "woman", in myth or ritual, is never just woman: it includes the cosmological principle woman embodies. And the divine androgyny which we find in so many myths and beliefs has its own theoretical, metaphysical significance. The real point of the formula is to express—in biological terms—the coexistence of contraries, of cosmological principles (male and female) within the heart of the divinity.

This is not the place to consider the problem which I discussed in my *Mitul Reintegrarii*. We must simply note that the divinities of cosmic fertility are, for the most part, either hermaphrodites or male one year and female the next (cf. for instance the Estonians' "spirit of the forest"). Most of the vegetation divinities (such as Attis, Adonis, Dionysos) are bisexual, and so are the Great Mothers (like Cybele). The primal god is androgynous in as primitive a religion as the Australian as well as in the most highly developed religions in India and elsewhere (sometimes even Dyaus; Puruṣa, the cosmic giant of the *Rg Veda*,[1] etc.). The most important couple in the Indian pantheon, Siva-Kālī, are sometimes represented as a single being (*ardhanariśvara*). And Tantric iconography swarms with pictures of the God Śiva closely entwined with Śakti, his own "power", depicted as a feminine divinity (Kālī). And then, too, all of Indian erotic mysticism is expressly aimed at perfecting man by identifying him with a "divine pair", that is, by way of androgyny.

Divine bisexuality is an element found in a great many religions[2] and—a point worth noting—even the most supremely masculine or feminine divinities are androgynous. Under whatever form the divinity manifests itself, he or she is ultimate reality, absolute power, and this reality, this power, will not let itself be limited by any attributes whatsoever (good, evil, male, female, or anything else). Several of the most ancient

[1] x, 90.
[2] Cf. Bertholet, *Das Geschlecht der Gottheit*, Tübingen, 1934.

Egyptian gods were bisexual.[1]   Among the Greeks, androgyny
was acknowledged even down to the last centuries of Antiquity.[2]
Almost all the major gods in Scandinavian mythology always
preserved traces of androgyny: Odhin, Loki, Tuisco, Nerthus,
and so on.[3]   The Iranian god of limitless time, Zervan, whom
the Greek historians rightly saw as Chronos, was also androgynous[4] and Zervan, as we noted earlier, gave birth to twin
sons, Ormuzd and Ahriman, the god of " good " and the god
of " evil ", the god of " light " and the god of " darkness ".
Even the Chinese had a hermaphrodite Supreme Divinity, who
was the god of darkness and of light[5]; the symbol is a consistent one, for light and darkness are simply successive aspects
of one and the same reality; seen apart the two might seem
separate and opposed, but in the sight of the wise man they
are not merely " twins " (like Ormuzd and Ahriman), but
form a single essence, now manifest, now unmanifest.

Divine couples (like Bel and Belit, and so on) are most
usually later fabrications or imperfect formulations of the
primeval androgyny that characterizes all divinities.   Thus,
with the Semites, the goddess Tanit was nicknamed " daughter
of Ba'al " and Astarte the " name of Ba'al ".[6]   There are
innumerable cases of the divinity's being given the title of
" father and mother "[7]; worlds, beings, men, all were born of
his own substance with no other agency involved.   Divine
androgyny would include as a logical consequence monogeny
or autogeny, and very many myths tell how the divinity drew
his existence from himself—a simple and dramatic way of
explaining that he is totally self-sufficient.   The same myth was
to appear again, though based this time on a complex metaphysic, in the neo-Platonic and gnostic speculations of late
Antiquity.

[1] Budge, *From Fetish to God in Ancient Egypt*, Oxford, 1934, pp. 7, 9.

[2] Cf. for instance Jung-Kerenyi, *Introduction to a Science of Mythology*, pp.
70 ff.

[3] Cf. e.g. De Vries, *Handbuch der germanischen Religionsgeschichte*, vol. ii,
p. 306; id., *The Problem of Loki, FFC*, no. 110, Helsinki, 1933, pp. 220 ff.

[4] Benveniste, *The Persian Religion According to the Chief Greek Texts*, Paris,
1929, pp. 113 ff.

[5] Cf. Hentze, *Frühchinesische Bronzen und Kultdarstellungen*, Antwerp, 1937,
p. 119.

[6] Bertholet, p. 21.

[7] Bertholet, p. 19.

161. THE MYTH OF HUMAN ANDROGYNY

Corresponding to this myth of divine androgyny—which reveals the paradox of divine existence more clearly than any of the other formulæ for the *coincidentia oppositorum*—there is a whole series of myths and rituals relating to human androgyny. The divine myth forms the paradigm for man's religious experience. A great many traditions hold that the " primeval man ", the ancestor, was a hermaphrodite (Tuisco is the type) and later mythical variants speak of " primeval pairs " (Yama—that is, " twin "—and his sister, Yami, or the Iranian pair Yima and Yimagh, or Mashyagh and Mashyanagh). Several rabbinical commentaries give us to understand that even Adam was sometimes thought of as androgynous. In this case, the " birth " of Eve would have been simply the division of the primeval hermaphrodite into two beings, male and female. " Adam and Eve were made back to back, attached at their shoulders; then God separated them with an axe, or cut them in two. Others have a different picture: the first man, Adam, was a man on his right side, a woman on his left; but God split him into two halves ".[1] The bisexuality of the first man is an even more living tradition in the societies we call primitive (for instance in Australia, and Oceania)[2] and was even preserved, and improved upon, in anthropology as advanced as that of Plato[3] and the gnostics.[4]

We have a further proof that the androgyny of the first man must be seen as one of the expressions of perfection and totalization in the fact that the first hermaphrodite was very often thought of as spherical (Australia; Plato): and it is well known that the sphere symbolized perfection and totality from the time of the most ancient cultures (as in China). The myth of a primordial hermaphrodite spherical in form thus links up with the myth of the cosmogonic egg. For instance, in Taoist tradition, " breathing "—which embodied, among other things, the two sexes—merged together and formed an egg, the Great One; from this heaven and earth were later detached. This

---

[1] *Bereshit rabbah*, I, 1, fol. 6, col. 2; etc.; for further texts, see A. Krappe, " The Birth of Eve ", *Occident and Orient, Gaster Anniversary Volume*, London, 1936, pp. 312–22.

[2] Cf. the works of Winthuis.

[3] *Symposium*.

[4] Cf. *Mitul Reintegrarii.*, pp. 83 ff.

cosmological schema was clearly the model for the Taoist techniques of mystical physiology.[1]

The myth of the hermaphrodite god and bisexual ancestor (or first man) is the paradigm for a whole series of ceremonies which are directed towards a *periodic returning* to this original condition which is thought to be the perfect expression of humanity. In addition to the circumcision and subincision which are performed on young aboriginals, male and female respectively, with the aim of transforming them into hermaphrodites,[2] I would also mention all the ceremonies of " exchanging costume " which are lesser versions of the same thing.[3] In India, Persia, and other parts of Asia, the ritual of " exchanging clothes " played a major part in agricultural feasts. In some regions of India, the men even wore false bosoms during the feast of the goddess of vegetation who was, herself, also, of course, androgynous.[4]

In short, from time to time man feels the need to return—if only for an instant—to the state of perfect humanity in which the sexes exist side by side as they coexist with all other qualities, and all other attributes, in the Divinity. The man dressed in woman's clothes is not trying to make himself a woman, as a first glance might suggest, but for a moment he is effecting the unity of the sexes, and thus facilitating his total understanding of the cosmos. The need man feels to cancel periodically his differentiated and determined condition so as to return to primeval " totalization " is the same need which spurs him to periodic orgies in which all forms dissolve, to end by recovering that " oneness " that was before the creation. Here again we come upon the need to destroy the past, to expunge " history " and to start a new life in a new Creation. The ritual of " exchanging costumes " is similar in essence to the ceremonial orgy; and, indeed, these disguises were very often the occasion for actual orgies to break loose. However, even the wildest

[1] Cf. H. Maspero, " Les Procédés de nourrir le principe vital dans la religion taoiste ancienne ", *JA*, April-June, 1937, p. 207, n. 1.

[2] See the studies of Winthuis, Roheim, etc.

[3] Cf. for the Greeks, Nilsson, *Griechische Feste*, pp. 370 ff.; at carnival time, Dumézil, *Le Problème des Centaures*, Paris, 1929, pp. 140, 180, etc.; in India, Meyer, *Trilogie*, vol. i, pp. 76, 86, etc.; during the spring festivals in Europe, ibid., vol. i, pp. 88 ff.; Crawley-Besterman, *The Mystic Rose*, new ed., London, 1927, vol. i, pp. 313 ff., etc.

[4] Meyer, vol. i, pp. 182 ff.

variants on these rituals never succeeded in abolishing their essential significance—of making their participants once more share in the paradisal condition of " primeval man ". And all these rituals have as their exemplar model the myth of divine androgyny.

If I wished to give more examples of the paradigmatic function of myths I should only have to go again through the larger part of the material given in the preceding chapters. As we have seen, it is not simply a question of a paradigm for ritual, but for other religious and metaphysical experience as well, for " wisdom ", the techniques of mystical physiology and so on. The most fundamental of the myths reveal archetypes which man labours to re-enact, often quite outside religious life properly so called. As a single example : androgyny may be attained not only by the surgical operations that accompany Australian initiation ceremonies, by ritual orgy, by " exchanging costumes " and the rest, but also by means of alchemy (cf. *rebis*, formula of the Philosophers' Stone, also called the " hermetic hermaphrodite "), through marriage (e.g. in the Kabbala), and even, in romantic German ideology, by sexual intercourse.[1] Indeed, we may even talk of the " androgynization " of man through love, for in love each sex attains, conquers the " characteristics " of the opposite sex (as with the grace, submission, and devotion achieved by a man when he is in love, and so on).

162. MYTHS OF RENEWAL, CONSTRUCTION, INITIATION AND SO ON

In no case can a myth be taken as merely the fantastic projection of a " natural " event. On the plane of magico-religious experience, as I have already pointed out, nature is never " natural ". What looks like a natural situation or process to the empirical and rational mind, is a kratophany or hierophany in magico-religious experience. And it is by these kratophanies or hierophanies alone that " nature " becomes something magico-religious, and, as such, of interest to religious phenomenology and the history of religions. The myths of the " gods of vegetation " constitute, in this regard, an excellent example of the transformation and significance of a " natural " cosmic event. It was not the periodic disappearing and re-

[1] See the references in my book, *Mitul Reintegrarii*, pp. 82 ff.

appearing of vegetation which produced the figures and myths of the vegetation gods (Tammuz, Attis, Osiris, and the rest); at least, it was not the mere empirical, rational, observation of the " natural " phenomenon. The appearing and disappearing of vegetation were always felt, in the perspective of magico-religious experience, to be a *sign* of the periodic creation of the Universe. The sufferings, death and resurrection of Tammuz, as they appear in myth and in the things they reveal, are as far removed from the " natural phenomenon " of winter and spring as *Madame Bovary* or *Anna Karenina* from an adultery. Myth is an autonomous act of creation by the mind: it is through that act of creation that revelation is brought about— not through the things or events it makes use of. In short, the drama of the death and resurrection of vegetation is revealed by the myth of Tammuz, rather than the other way about.

Indeed, the myth of Tammuz, and the myths of gods like him, disclose aspects of the nature of the cosmos which extend far beyond the sphere of plant life; it discloses on the one hand, the fundamental *unity* of life and death, and on the other, the hopes man draws, with good reason, from that fundamental unity, for his own life after death. From this point of view, we may look upon the myths of the sufferings, deaths and resurrections of the vegetation gods as paradigms of the state of mankind: they reveal " nature " better and more intimately than any empirical or rational experience and observation could, and it is to maintain and renew that revelation that the myth must be constantly celebrated and repeated; the appearing and disappearing of vegetation, in themselves, as " cosmic phenomena ", signify no more than they actually are: a periodic appearance and disappearance of plant life. Only myth can transform this *event* into a *mode of being*: on one hand, of course, because the death and resurrection of the vegetation gods become archetypes of all deaths and all resurrections, whatever form they take, and on whatever plane they occur, but also because they are better than any empirical or rational means of revealing human destiny.

In the same way, some of the cosmogonic myths, telling how the universe was made out of the body of a primeval giant, if not of the body and blood of the creator himself, became the model not only for the " rites for building " (involving, as we know, the sacrifice of a living being to accompany the setting up of a house, bridge or sanctuary) but also for all forms of " creation " in the broadest sense of the word. The myth revealed the nature of all " creations "—that they cannot be accomplished without an " animation ", without a direct giving of life by a creature already possessing that life; at the same time it revealed man's powerlessness to create apart from reproducing his own species—and even that, in many societies, is held to be the work of religious forces outside man (children are thought to come from trees, stones, water, " ancestors ", and so on).

A mass of myths and legends describe the " difficulties " demi-gods and heroes meet with in entering a " forbidden domain ", a transcendent place—heaven or hell. There is a bridge that cuts like a knife to cross, a quivering creeping plant to get through, two almost touching rocks to pass between, a door to be entered that is open only for an instant, a place surrounded by mountains, by water, by a circle of fire, guarded by monsters, or a door standing at the spot " where Sky and Earth " meet, or where " the ends of the Year " come together.[1] Some versions of this myth of trials, like the labours and adventures of Hercules, the expedition of the Argonauts and others, even had a tremendous literary career in antiquity, being constantly used and remodelled by poets and mythographers; they, in their turn, were imitated in the cycles of semi-historic legend, like the cycle of Alexander the Great, who also wandered through the land of darkness, sought the herb of life, fought with monsters, and so on. Many of these myths were, without doubt, the archetypes of initiation rites (as for instance, the duel with a three-headed monster, that classic " trial " in military initiations).[2] But these myths of the " search for the transcendent land " explain something else in addition to initiation dramas; they show the paradox of getting beyond opposition, which is a necessary part of any world (of any " condition "). Going through the " narrow door ", through the " eye of the needle ", between " rocks that

---

[1] *Jaiminīya Upaniṣad Brāhmaṇa*, i, 5, 5; i, 35, 7–9, etc.; for some of these mythological themes see Cook, *Zeus*, Cambridge, 1940, vol. iii, 2, Appendix P, " Floating Islands ", pp. 975–1016; Coomaraswamy, " Symplegades ", in *Homage to George Sarton*, New York, 1947, pp. 463–88.

[2] Studied by Dumézil in *Horace et les Curiaces*, Paris, 1942.

touch ", and all the rest, always involves a pair of opposites (like good and evil, night and day, high and low, etc.).[1] In this sense, it is true to say that the myths of " quest " and of " initiation trials " reveal, in artistic or dramatic form, the actual act by which the mind gets beyond a conditioned, piece-meal universe, swinging between opposites, to return to the fundamental oneness that existed before creation.

163. THE MAKE-UP OF A MYTH: VARUNA AND VṚTRA

Myth, like symbol, has its own particular " logic ", its own intrinsic consistency which enables it to be " true " on a variety of planes, however far removed they may be from the plane upon which the myth originally appeared. I remarked earlier in how many ways and from how many differing standpoints the creation myth is "true"—and therefore effective, "usable ". For another example, let us turn once again to the myth and structure of Varuṇa, sovereign sky god, all-powerful, and, upon occasions, one who " binds " by his " spiritual power ", by " magic ". But his cosmic aspect is more complex still: as we saw, he is not only a sky god, but also a moon and water god. There was a certain " nocturnal " keynote in Varuṇa—possibly from a very early date indeed—upon which Bergaigne, and, more recently, Coomaraswamy, have laid great stress. Bergaigne pointed out[2] that the commentator of *Taittirīya Saṁhitā*[3] speaks of Varuṇa as " he who envelops like darkness ". This " nocturnal " side of Varuṇa must not be interpreted only in the atmospheric sense of the " night sky ", but also in a wider sense more truly cosmological and even metaphysical: night, too, *is* potentiality, seed, non-manifestation, and it is because Varuna has this "nocturnal" element that he can become a god of water,[4] and can be assimilated with the demon Vṛtra.

This is not the place to go into the " Vṛtra-Varuna " problem, and we must be content with noting the fact that the two beings have more than one trait in common. Even leaving aside the probable etymological relationship between their two

[1] Cf. Coomaraswamy, p. 486.

[2] *La Religion védique d'après les hymnes du Rig-Veda*, Paris, 1878–83, vol. iii, p. 113.

[3] i, 8, 16, 1.

[4] Bergaigne, vol. iii, p. 128.

names,[1] we should note that both are connected with water, and primarily with " water held back " (" Great Varuṇa has hidden the sea ")[2] and that Vrtra, like Varuna, is sometimes called *māyin*, or magician.[3] From one point of view, these various identifications with Vṛtra, like all Varuṇa's other attributes and functions, fit together and help to explain each other. Night (the non-manifest), water (the potential, seeds), transcendence and impassivity (both marks of supreme gods and sky gods) are linked both mythologically and metaphysically with, on the one hand, every kind of being that " binds " and, on the other, the Vrtra who " holds back ", " stops " or " imprisons " the waters. At the cosmic level, Vṛtra, too, is a " binder ". Like all the great myths, the myth of Vṛtra has thus got many meanings, and no single interpretation exhausts it. We might even say that one of the main functions of myth is to determine, to authenticate the levels of reality which both a first impression and further thought indicate to be manifold and heterogeneous. Thus, in the myth of Vṛtra, besides other significations, we note that of returning to the non-manifest, of a " stopping ", of a " bond " preventing " forms "—the life of the Cosmos, in fact—from manifestation. Obviously we must not push the parallel between Vrtra and Varuna too far. But there can be no denying the structural connection between the " nocturnal ", " impassive ", " magician ", Varuna, " binding " the guilty from afar, and Vṛtra " imprisoning " the waters. Both are acting so as to stop life, and bring death, the one on an individual, the other, on a cosmic scale.

164. MYTH AS " EXEMPLAR HISTORY "

Every myth, whatever its nature, recounts an event that took place *in illo tempore*, and constitutes as a result, a precedent and pattern for all the actions and " situations " later to repeat that event. Every ritual, and every meaningful act that man performs, repeats a mythical archetype; and, as we saw (§ 150), this repetition involves the abolition of profane time and

---

[1] Bergaigne, vol. iii, p. 115, etc.; Coomaraswamy, *Spiritual Authority and Temporal Power*, New Haven, 1942, pp. 29 ff.

[2] *RV*, IX, 73, 3.

[3] For instance ii, 11, 10.

placing of man in a magico-religious time which has no connection with succession in the true sense, but forms the " eternal
now " of mythical time. In other words, along with other
magico-religious experiences, myth makes man once more
exist in a timeless period, which is in effect an *illud tempus*, a
time of dawn and of " paradise ", outside history. Anyone
who performs any rite transcends profane time and space;
similarly, anyone who " imitates " a mythological model or
even ritually assists at the retelling of a myth (taking part in it),
is taken out of profane " becoming ", and returns to the Great
Time.

We moderns would say that myth (and with it all other
religious experiences) abolishes " history " (§ 150). But note
that the majority of myths, simply because they record what
took place " in illo tempore ", themselves constitute an
exemplar history for the human society in which they have
been preserved, and for the world that society lives in. Even
the cosmogonic myth is history, for it recounts all that took place
ab origine; but we must, I need hardly say, remember that it
is not " history " in our sense of the word—things that took
place once and will never take place again—but exemplar
history which can be repeated (regularly or otherwise), and
whose meaning and value lie in that very repetition. The
history that took place at the beginning must be repeated
because the primeval epiphanies were prolific—they could not
be fully expressed in a single manifestation. And myths too
are prolific in their content, for it is paradigmatic, and therefore
presents a *meaning*, creates something, tells us something.

The function of myths as exemplar history is further apparent
from the need primitive man feels to show " proofs " of the
event recorded in the myth. Suppose that it is a well known
mythological theme: such and such a thing happened, men
became mortal, seals lost their toes, a mark appeared on the
moon, or something similar. To the primitive mind this theme
can be clearly " proved " by the fact that man *is* mortal,
seals *have* no toes, the moon has *got* marks on it. The myth
which tells how the island of Tonga was fished up from the
bottom of the sea is proved by the fact that you can still see
the line used to pull it up, and the rock where the hook caught.[1]

---

[1] Ehnmark, *Anthropomorphism and Miracle*, Uppsala-Leipzig, 1939, pp. 181–2.

This need to prove the truth of myth also helps us to grasp what history and " historical evidence " mean to the primitive mind. It shows what an importance primitive man attaches to things that have *really happened*, to the events which actually took place in his surroundings; it shows how his mind hungers for what is " real ", for what *is* in the fullest sense. But, at the same time, the archetypal function given to these events of *illud tempus* give us a glimpse of the interest primitive people take in realities that are significant, creative, paradigmatic. This interest survived even in the first historians of the ancient world, for to them the " past " had meaning only in so far as it was an example to be imitated, and consequently formed the *summa* of the learning of all mankind. This work of " exemplar history " which devolved upon myth must, if we are to understand it properly, be seen in relation to primitive man's tendency to effect a concrete realization of an ideal archetype, to live eternity " experientially " here and now—an aspiration which we studied in our analysis of sacred time (§ 155).

165. THE CORRUPTION OF MYTHS

A myth may degenerate into an epic legend, a ballad or a romance, or survive only in the attenuated form of " superstitions ", customs, nostalgias, and so on; for all this, it loses neither its essence nor its significance. Remember how the myth of the Cosmic Tree was preserved in legend and in the rites for gathering simples (§ 111). The " trials ", sufferings, and journeyings of the candidate for initiation survived in the tales of the sufferings and obstacles undergone by heroes of epic or drama before they gained their end (Ulysses, Aeneas, Parsifal, certain of Shakespeare's characters, Faust, and so on). All these " trials " and " sufferings " which make up the stories of epic, drama or romance can be clearly connected with the ritual sufferings and obstacles on the " way to the centre " (§ 146). No doubt the " way " is not on the same initiatory plane, but, typologically, the wanderings of Ulysses, or the search for the Holy Grail, are echoed in the great novels of the nineteenth century, to say nothing of paperback novels, the archaic origins of whose plots are not hard to trace. If to-day, detective stories recount the contest between a criminal and a detective (the good genie and wicked genie, the dragon and fairy prince of the old stories), whereas a few generations back, they preferred to show an orphan prince or innocent maiden at grips with a "villain", while the fashion of a hundred and fifty years ago was for "black" and turgid romances with "black monks", "Italians", "villains", "abducted maidens", "masked protectors" and so on, such variations of detail are due to the different colouring and turn of popular sentiment; the theme does not change.

Obviously, every further step down brings with it a blurring of the conflict and characters of the drama as well as a greater number of additions supplied by "local colour". But the patterns that have come down from the distant past never disappear; they do not lose the possibility of being brought back to life. They retain their point even for the "modern" consciousness. To take one of a thousand examples: Achilles and Søren Kierkegaard. Achilles, like many other heroes, did not marry, though a happy and fruitful life had been predicted for him had he done so; but in that case he would have given up becoming a *hero*, he would not have realized his unique success, would not have gained immortality. Kierkegaard passed through exactly the same existential drama with regard to Regina Olsen; he gave up marriage to remain himself, unique, that he might hope for the eternal by refusing the path of a happy life with the general run of men. He makes this clear in a fragment of his private Journal[1]: " I should be happier, in a finite sense, could I drive out this thorn I feel in my flesh; but in the infinite sense, I should be lost." In this way a mythical pattern can still be realized, and is in fact realized, on the plane of existential experience, and, certainly in this case, with no thought of or influence from the myth.

The archetype is still creative even though sunk to lower and lower levels. So, for instance, with the myth of the Fortunate Islands or that of the Earthly Paradise, which obsessed not only the imagination of the secular mind, but nautical science too right up to the great age of seafaring discoveries. Almost all navigators, even those bent on a definite economic purpose (like the Indian route), *also* hoped to discover the Islands of the Blessed or the Earthly Paradise. And we all know that there were many who thought they had actually found the Island of

[1] viii, A 56.

Paradise. From the Phoenicians to the Portuguese, all the memorable geographical discoveries were the result of this myth of the land of Eden. And these voyages, searches, and discoveries were the only ones to acquire a spiritual meaning, to create culture. If the memory of Alexander's journey to India never faded it was because, being classed with the great myths, it satisfied the longing for " mythical geography "— the only sort of geography man could never do without. The Genoese commercial ventures in Crimea and the Caspian Sea, and the Venetian in Syria and in Egypt, must have meant a very advanced degree of nautical skill, and yet the mercantile routes in question " have left no memory in the history of geographical discovery ".[1] On the other hand, expeditions to discover the mythical countries did not only create legends: they also brought an increase of geographical knowledge.

These islands and these new lands preserved their mythical character long after geography had become scientific. The " Isles of the Blessed " survived till Camoens, passed through the age of enlightenment and the romantic age, and have their place even in our own day. But the mythical island no longer means the garden of Eden: it is Camoens' Isle of Love, Daniel Defoe's island of the " good savage ", Eminescu's Island of Euthanasius, the " exotic " isle, a land of dreams with hidden beauties, or the island of liberty, or perfect rest—or ideal holidays, or cruises on luxury steamers, to which modern man aspires in the mirages offered to him by books, films or his own imagination. The *function* of the paradisal land of perfect freedom remains unchanged; it is just that man's view of it has undergone a great many displacements—from Paradise in the biblical sense to the exotic paradise of our contemporaries' dreams. A decline, no doubt, but a very prolific one. At all levels of human experience, however ordinary, archetypes still continue to give meaning to life and to create " cultural values ": the paradise of modern novels and the isle of Camoens are as significant culturally as any of the isles of medieval literature.

In other words man, whatever else he may be free of, is forever the prisoner of his own archetypal intuitions, formed at the moment when he first perceived his position in the

[1] Olschki, *Storia letteraria delle scoperte geografiche*, Florence, 1937, p. 195.

cosmos. The longing for Paradise can be traced even in the most banal actions of the modern man. Man's concept of the *absolute* can never be completely uprooted: it can only be debased. And primitive spirituality lives on in its own way not in action, not as a thing man can effectively accomplish, but as a *nostalgia* which creates things that become values in themselves: art, the sciences, social theory, and all the other things to which men will give the whole of themselves.

BIBLIOGRAPHY

General information: KRAPPE, A. H., *Mythologie universelle*, Paris, 1930; id., *La Genèse des mythes*, Paris, 1938; GRAY, L. H., and MOORE, G. F. (ed.), *The Mythology of All Races*, Boston, 1916–32, 13 vols., illus.; GUIRAND, F. (ed.), *Mythologie générale*, Paris, 1935; CINTI, J., *Dizionario mitologico*, Milan, 1935; PETTAZZONI, R., *Miti e Leggende: I: Africa e Australia*, Turin, 1947; *III: America Settentrionale*, 1953.

The "naturist" school of mythology: MULLER, Max, *Comparative Mythology*, Oxford, 1856 (reproduced in vol. ii of *Chips from a German Workshop*); id., *Contributions to the Study of Mythology*, London, 1896; COX, W., *An Introduction to the Science of Comparative Mythology*, London, 1881–3; KUHN, Adalbert, *Mythologische Studien*, Gutersloh, 1886, vol. i; DE GUBERNATIS, Angelo, *Zoological Mythology*, London, 1872; id., *La Mythologie des plantes ou des légendes du règne végétal*, Paris, 1878–82, 2 vols.

The "astral" school of mythology: STUCKEN, E., *Astralmythen der Hebræer, Babylonier und Ägypter*, Leipzig, 1896–1907; SIECKE, E., *Liebesgeschichte des Himmels*, Strasbourg, 1892; id., *Mythologische Briefe*, Berlin, 1901; LESMANN, *Aufgaben und Ziele der vergleichenden Mythenforschung (Mythologische Bibliothek, I)*, Leipzig, 1908; BOKLEN, E., *Adam und Qain im Lichte der vergleichenden Mythenforschung*, Leipzig, 1907; id., *Die Enstehung der Sprache im Lichte des Mythos*, Berlin, 1922; VON SPIESS, K., *Prähistorie und Mythos*, Wiener Neustadt, 1910; LANGER, F., *Intellektual-Mythologie, Betrachtungen über das Wesen des Mythus und der mythologischen Methode*, Leipzig-Berlin, 1917.

The mythological, anthropological and ethnographical school: LANG, Andrew, *Modern Mythology*, London, 1897; id., *Myth, Ritual and Religion*, London, 1901, 2 vols.; id., *Custom and Myth*, new ed., London, 1904; id., *The Making of Religion*, 3rd ed., London, 1909; STEINTHAL, H., "Allgemeine Einleitung in die Mythologie", *AFRW*, 1900, vol. iii, pp. 249–73, 297–323; EHRENREICH, Paul, "Die Mythen und Legenden der Südamerikanischen Urvölker und ihre Beziehungen zu denen Nordamerikas und der alten Welt", *ZFE*, 1905, suppl.; id., *Die allgemeine Mythologie und ihre ethnologischen Grundlagen (Mythologische Bibliothek, vol. iv, no. 1)*, Leipzig, 1910; JENSEN, A. E., *Das religiöse Weltbild einer frühen Kultur*, Stuttgart, 1948; id., *Mythos und Kult bei Naturvölkern*, Wiesbaden, 1951.

The creation myths: LUKAS, Franz, *Die Grundbegriffe in dem Kosmogonien der alten Völker*, Leipzig, 1893; id., "Das Ei als kosmogonische Vorstellung", *Zeit. f. Verein für Volkskunde*, 1894, vol. iv, pp. 227–43; GUNKEL, Hermann, *Schöpfung und Chaos in Urzeit und Endzeit. Eine religionsgeschichtliche Untersuchung über Gen. I und Ap. Joh. 12*, Gottingen, 1895; BAUMANN, H., *Schöpfung und Urzeit des Menschen im Mythus der afrikanischen Völker*, Berlin, 1936; NUMAZAWA, F. Kiichi, *Die Weltanfänge in der japanischen Mythologie*, Lucerne-Paris, 1946.

Monographs on various mythological systems: CUSHING, F. H., "Outlines of Zuñi Creation Myths", *Bulletin of the Bureau of Ethnology*, Washington, 1896, vol. xiii; BOAS, F., "Tsimshian Mythology", *Bulletin of the Bureau of Ethnology*, Washington, 1916, vol. xxxi; JENSEN, A. E., *Hainuwele*, Frankfurt am Main, 1939; MACDONELL, A. A., *Vedic Mythology*, Strasbourg, 1897; HOPKINS, E. W., *Epic Mythology*, Strasbourg, 1915; FRAZER, Sir J. G., *Myths of the Origin of Fire*, London, 1930; see also *The Mythology of All Races*.

On Greek mythology and the structure of Greek myths: GRUPPE, O., *Griechische Mythologie und Religionsgeschichte*, Munich, 1906, 2 vols.; id., *Geschichte der Klassischen Mythologie und Religionsgeschichte*, Leipzig, 1921; ROSE, H. J., *A Handbook of Greek Mythology, Including its Extension to Rome*, London, 1928; NILSSON, Martin P., *The Mycenian Origin of Greek Mythology*, Cambridge, 1932; DORNSIEFF, Franz, *Die archaische Mythenerzählung*, Berlin, 1933; SCHUHL, P. M., *Essai sur la formation de la pensée grecque*, Stuttgart, 1940; FEHR, Karl, *Die Mythen bei Pindar*, Zürich, 1936; FRUTIGER, P., *Les Mythes de Platon*, Paris, 1930; UNTERSTEINER, Mario, *La Fisiologia del mito*, Milan, 1946; ROSE, H. J., *Modern Methods in Classical Mythology*, St. Andrews, 1930.

JUNG, C. G., and KERENYI, K., *Introduction to a Science of Mythology*, London, 1951; KERENYI, K., " Mythologie und Gnosis ", *EJ*, 1940–1, Leipzig, 1942, pp. 157–229; id., *Die Geburt der Helena*, Zürich, 1945; id., *Prometheus. Das griechische Mythologem von der menschlichen Existenz*, Zürich, 1946.

Myths and Rituals: HOOKE, S. H. (ed.), *Myth and Ritual*, London, 1934; id., *The Labyrinth*, London, 1935, particularly HOOKE, S. H., " The Myth and the Ritual Pattern ", pp. 213–33; HOCART, A. N., *The Life-giving Myth*, London, 1952, pp. 263–81; KLUCKHOHN, C., " Myths and Rituals, a General Theory ", *Harvard Theological Review*, 1942, vol. xxxv, pp. 45–79.

Mythical thought: MALINOWSKI, B., *Myth in Primitive Psychology*, London, 1926; PREUSS, K. T., *Der religiöse Gehalt der Mythen*, Tübingen, 1933; VAN DER LEEUW, G., *Religion in Essence and Manifestation*, London, 1938, particularly pp. 413 ff.; id., *L'Homme primitif et la religion*, Paris, 1930, passim; LEVY-BRUHL, *La Mythologie primitive. Le monde mythique des Australiens et des Papous*, Paris, 1936; CAILLOIS, Roger, *Le Mythe et l'homme*, Paris, 1938; EHNMARK, Erland, *Anthropomorphism and Miracle*, Uppsala-Leipzig, 1939; LEENHARDT, Maurice, *Do Kamo. La Personne et le mythe dans le monde mélanésien*, Paris, 1947, particularly pp. 220 ff.

CASSIRER, E., *Die Begriffsform im mythischen Denken*, Leipzig, 1922 (*Studien der Bibliothek Wartburg*, vol. i); id., *Sprache und Mythos. Ein Beitrag zum Problem der Götternamen*, Leipzig, 1925 (id., vol. vi); COOMARASWAMY, Ananda K., " Angel and Titan. An Essay in Vedic Ontology ", *JAOS*, 1935, vol. lv, pp. 373–419; id., *The Darker Side of the Dawn* (*Smithsonian Miscellaneous Collections*, vol. xciv, no. 1), Washington, 1935; id., " Sir Gawain and the Green Knight: Indra and Namuci ", *Speculum*, 1944, vol. xix, pp. 2–23; id., " On the Loathly Bride ", id., 1945, vol. xx, pp. 391–404; id., " Symplegades ", *Homage to George Sarton*, New York, 1947, pp. 463–88; ELIADE, M., " Les Livres populaires dans la littérature roumaine ", *CZ*, 1939, vol. ii, published 1941, pp. 63–75; id., *Mitul Reintegrarii*, Bucharest, 1942; id., " Le Dieu lieur et le symbolisme des nœuds ", *RHR*, July-Dec., 1947, vol. cxxxiv; id., *The Myth of the Eternal Return*, London, 1955; id., *Images et Symboles. Essais sur le symbolisme magico-religieux*, Paris, 1952.

Methodological questions: STEINTHAL, H., " Allgemeine Einleitung in die Mythologie ", *AFRW*, 1900, vol. iii, pp. 249–73, 297–323; FARNELL, L. R., " The Value and the Methods of Mythologic Study ", *Proceedings of the British Academy*, 1919, vol. ix, pp. 37–51; NILSSON, M. P., "Moderne mythologische Forschung ", *Scientia*, 1932, vol. li; ROSE, J. H., " Myth-ology and Pseudo-Mythology ", *FRE*, 1935, vol. xlvi, pp. 9–36.

XIII

THE STRUCTURE OF SYMBOLS

166. SYMBOLIC STONES

IT is rare for a magico-religious phenomenon not to involve symbolism in some form or other. The material I have presented in the preceding chapters affords ample proof of this. This, of course, is not to deny the fact that every magico-religious object or event is either a kratophany, a hierophany or a theophany. But we are often faced with *mediate* kratophanies, hierophanies or theophanies, effected by sharing in or becoming part of a magico-religious system which is always a symbolic system or symbolism. Thus, to give but one example, we saw how certain stones become sacred because they embody the souls of the dead (" ancestors "), or because they manifest or represent a sacred force or divinity, or again because a solemn covenant or religious event took place nearby, and so on. But there are a great many other stones which acquire a magico-religious quality because of a mediate hierophany or kratophany, or in other words because of a symbolism which endows them with magic or religious significance.

The stone Jacob slept on when he saw in his dream the angels' ladder only became sacred because it was the scene of a hierophany. But other bethels or *omphaloi* are sacred because they stand at the " centre of the world " and consequently at the point of junction between the three cosmic zones. Clearly the " centre " is itself a sacred zone, and therefore anything embodying or representing it also becomes sacred and can, as a result, be considered a hierophany. But at the same time it is quite true to say that a bethel or *omphalos* is a " symbol " of the centre inasmuch as it bears within it a supra-spatial reality (the " centre ") and inserts it into profane space. In this case the " hierophanization " is effected by an obvious symbolism directly revealed by the actual " form " of the stone (the " form ", in this case, being of course that grasped by magico-religious rather than empirical or rational experience). But other magic stones, " precious " or healing, draw their significance from a symbolism not always so clear.

I will give a few examples which show the development of a more and more complex symbolism such as we could never find in any of the stone symbolisms we have looked at so far.

Jade is a precious stone which played a considerable part in the ancient symbolism of China.[1] In the social order it embodied sovereignty and power; in medicine it was a panacea and was taken internally to obtain the regeneration of the body[2]; it was also thought to be the food of the spirits, and the Taoists believed that it guaranteed immortality[3]; hence the importance of jade in alchemy, and the place it has always held in burial beliefs and practices. We read in the writings of the alchemist Ko-Hung: " If there is gold and jade in the nine apertues of the corpse, it will preserve the body from putrefaction."[4] And T'ao Hung-King (fifth century) gives us the following details: " When on opening an ancient grave the corpse looks alive, then there is inside or outside of the body a large quantity of gold and jade. According to the regulations of the Han dynasty, princes and lords were buried in clothes adorned with pearls and with boxes of jade, for the purpose of preserving the body from decay."[5] Recent archæological researches have borne out what these texts tell us about funeral jade.[6]

But jade only embodies all these powers because it embodies the cosmological principle *yang*, and is consequently endowed with a whole collection of solar, imperial and indestructible qualities. Like gold, because jade contains *yang* it becomes a centre filled with cosmic energy. That it can be used for so many things follows logically because *yang* itself has so many different values. And if we sought to delve into the prehistory of the cosmological formula *yang-yin*, we should come up against another cosmological formula and another symbolism which justified the using of jade.[7]

[1] See Laufer, *Jade. A Study of Chinese Archæology and Religion*, Chicago, 1912, *passim*.

[2] Laufer, p. 296.

[3] De Groot, *Religious Systems of China*, Leyden, 1892–1910, vol. i, pp. 271–3.

[4] Laufer, p. 299.

[5] Laufer, p. 299.

[6] Eliade, " Notes sur le symbolisme aquatique ", p. 141; republished in *Images et Symboles*, Paris, 1952, p. 179.

[7] Cf. Karlgren, *Some Fecundity Symbols in Ancient China*, Stockholm, 1936.

With the pearl, we can trace back its primitive symbolism even to prehistory. I devoted an earlier study to doing so.[1] Pearls and shells have been found in prehistoric tombs; they were used in magic and medicine; they were offered in ritual to river gods and others; they had a leading position in various Asiatic cults; women wore them for luck in love, and fertility. At one time pearls and shells had magico-religious significance everywhere; bit by bit their use became restricted to sorcery and medicine[2]; until nowadays the pearl has only an economic and æsthetic value in certain social classes. This lowering of the metaphysical significance from the " cosmological " to the " æsthetic " is in itself an interesting phenomenon to which we shall have occasion to return, but we must first seek the answer to another question: why should the pearl have any magical, medicinal or funeral meaning? This was because it was " born of the waters ", because it was " born of the moon ", because it represented the *yin* principle; because it was found in a shell, which symbolizes a femininity wholly creative. Everything works to transform the pearl into a " cosmological centre " bringing together the prerogatives of moon, woman, fertility, and birth. Pearls are filled with the germinative force of the water in which they were formed; " born of the moon "[3], they have a share in its magic powers and were worn by women for that reason; the sexual symbolism of shells communicates to them all the forces involved in it; and finally the similarity between the pearl and the fœtus endows it with generative and obstetrical properties (a *pang* mussel " being pregnant with the pearl is like the woman's having the fœtus in the womb ", says one Chinese text.[4] All the magic, medicinal, gynæcological and funereal properties of pearls spring from this triple symbolism of water, moon and woman.

In India the pearl becomes a panacea; it is effective against hæmorrhages, jaundice, madness, poisoning, eye troubles, consumption, and other things.[5] In European medicine it

---

[1] Ch. iv of *Images et Symboles*.
[2] Cf. *Images et Symboles*, p. 190 ff.
[3] *AV*, iv, 10.
[4] Quoted by Karlgren, p. 36.
[5] Cf. *Images et Symboles*, p. 192.

was mainly used for melancholia, epilepsy, and madness[1]; as you see, most of the illnesses concerned are "lunar" maladies (melancholia, epilepsy, hæmorrhage, etc.). Its antitoxic properties can have no other explanation; the moon was the cure for every kind of poisoning.[2] But the value put upon the pearl in the East came chiefly from its aphrodisiac, fertilizing and talismanic qualities. When it was placed in tombs as close to the dead as possible, it united them with the cosmological principle it itself contained: moon, water, woman. In other words, it regenerated the dead by placing them within a cosmic rhythm which is supremely cyclic, involving (in the pattern of the moon's phases) birth, life, death, rebirth. When a dead man is covered in pearls,[3] he enters upon a "lunar" career; he may hope to return to the cosmic circuit, for he is imbued with all the moon's powers of creating living forms.

167. THE DEGRADATION OF SYMBOLS

It is easy to see that what constitutes the manifold significance of the pearl is primarily the framework of symbolism surrounding it. Whether we interpret that symbolism so as to stress its sexual elements, or whether we choose to trace it back to a prehistoric ritual pattern, the one thing that remains certain, is its cosmological nature. In all primitive societies the emblems and functions of woman retain a cosmological value. We cannot say with any precision at what moment in prehistory the pearl acquired the different prerogatives I have listed. But we can be certain that it did not become a magic stone till the time when man became conscious of the cosmological pattern of Water, Moon, and Change, till he discovered the rhythms of nature governed by the moon. The "origins" of the symbolism of the pearl, then, were not empirical but theoretical. Only afterwards did that symbolism come to be interpreted and "lived" in varying ways, at last to degenerate into the superstition and economic-cum-æsthetic value that is all the pearl stands for to-day.

We may complete our record by looking at a few magico-

---

[1] *Images et Symboles.*

[2] *Harṣacarita*, quoted in *Images et Symboles*, p. 191.

[3] *Images et Symboles*, pp. 178 ff.

religious stones. First comes *lapis lazuli*, the blue stone held
in such high honour in Mesopotamia, which was sacred because
of its cosmological significance; it stood for the starry night
and the god of the moon, Sin. Certain stones which the
Babylonians held to be of great gynæcological value later
passed into Greek medicine. One of these, the " stone of
pregnancy " (*aban*e-ri-e*), was identified by Boson with the
lithos samios of Dioscorides; another, *aban*rami*, " the stone of
love ", of "fertility", seems to be the same as the *lithos
selenites* of Dioscorides. Stones of this kind drew their
efficacy for childbirth from their connection with the moon.
The obstetrical value of jasper, *aban*ashup*, was due to the fact
that by being broken it gave birth in its " womb " to several
other stones; the symbol in this case is obvious. The
gynæcological function of jasper was handed on by the Babylonians to the Graeco-Roman world where it persisted right
up till the Middle Ages. A similar symbolism explains the
favour the *aetites* or " eagle stone " enjoyed in the ancient
world; *utilis est, mulieribus praegnantibus*, declares Pliny[1];
when it was shaken an odd noise seemed to come from within
it as if it hid another stone in its " womb ". The power of these
gynæcological and obstetrical stones flowed directly either from
their connection with the lunar principle, or from some oddity
in their shape which must indicate some peculiar origin.
Their magic essence flowed from their " life ", for they " live ",
have a sex, are pregnant. Nor in this are they an exception.
All other stones and metals also " live " and have a sex[2];
it is only that their life is calmer, their sexuality more indistinct;
they " grow " in the womb of the earth, following their own
drowsy rhythm; very few " come to maturity " (the Indians
think the diamond to be *pakva* (ripe), whereas the crystal is
kaccha (unripe).[3]

The " snake-stone " offers a very good example of a symbol
displaced and changed. In many places, precious stones
were thought to be fallen from the heads of snakes or dragons.
Hence the idea that the diamond is poisonous and must not be

[1] *Nat. Hist.*, xxxvi; 21, 149–51.
[2] Cf. Eliade, " Metallurgy, Magic and Alchemy ", Paris, 1938, *CZ*, vol. i, *passim*.
[3] Cf. " Metallurgy ", p. 37.

allowed to touch anyone's lips because it was once in a snake's throat (a belief that started in India and came later to the Hellenistic and Arab world).[1]   The belief that precious stones come from snakes' spittle covered a very wide area, from China to England.[2]   In India it was thought that the *nāgas* carried certain magic, shining stones in their throats and heads.   When Pliny declared that *dracontia* or *dracontites* was a stone formed in the brains (*cerebra*) of dragons,[3] he was only giving a rationalization of beliefs that originated in the East.   The rationalizing process is marked even more clearly with Philostratus,[4] who says that the eye of some dragons is a stone of " blinding brilliance ", endowed with magic powers; he adds that sorcerers, when they have adored reptiles, cut off their heads and take out precious stones.

The origin and the theory underlying these legends and so many others are not far to seek: it is the ancient myth of "monsters" (snakes, dragons), watching over the "Tree of Life ", or some specially consecrated place, or some sacred substance, or some absolute value (immortality, eternal youth, the knowledge of good and evil, and so on).   Remember that all the symbols of this absolute reality are always guarded by monsters which only allow the elect to pass; the " Tree of Life", the tree with the golden apples or the golden fleece, " treasures " of every kind (pearls from the ocean bed, gold from the earth and so on) are protected by a dragon and anyone who wants to attain to one of these symbols of immortality must first give proof of his " heroism " or his " wisdom " by braving all dangers and finally killing the reptilian monster. From this ancient mythological theme, via many processes of rationalization and corruption, are derived all beliefs in treasure, magic stones and jewels.   The Tree of Life, or the tree with the golden apples, or the golden fleece, which symbolized a state of *absoluteness* (gold meant " glory ", immortality, etc.)—became a golden " treasure " hidden in the ground and guarded by dragons or serpents.

[1] See Laufer, *The Diamond.   A Study in Chinese and Hellenistic Folklore*, Chicago, 1915, p. 40–44.

[2] See my study, " Piatra Sarpelui ", *Mesterului Manole*, Bucharest, 1939.

[3] *Nat. Hist.*, xxxvi, 10.

[4] *Vita Apol. Tyan.*, iii, 7.

The metaphysical *emblems* guarded and defended by serpents turned into concrete *objects* which were to be found on the foreheads, eyes or throats of their guardians. What was originally valued as a *sign* of the absolute later took on—for different social strata or through a degeneration of its first meaning—its own magical, medicinal or æsthetic values. In India, for instance, diamonds were an emblem of absolute reality; the word for diamond, *vajra*, also meant lightning, the symbol of Indra, an emblem of the incorruptible. In this pattern of ideas—power, incorruptibility, lightning, cosmic expression of virility—the diamond was sacred in as much as, in the mineralogical order, it embodied these things. In a different framework of ideas—the " popular " picture of absolute reality guarded by a monster—the diamond was valued for its reptilian origin. It was the same origin (though by then it was sinking to lower and lower levels) which conferred upon diamonds their magic and medicinal properties: they were a protection against snakebite, like so many other " snake-stones " (carbuncle, borax, bezoar, and others). Certain of these " snake-stones " were in fact taken from the heads of snakes, where people sometimes found hard stony masses. But they were only found there because someone expected to find them there. Belief in the " snake-stone " is to be found over an immense area, and yet it was not until quite lately and only in a few places that hard and stony excrescences have actually been found on some snakes. In fact it is only in very rare cases that a " snake-stone " is actually a stone taken from the head of a snake; the enormous majority of magic and medicinal stones, whether or not they have any reptilian nickname, are connected with snakes in some way simply because of the original myth which can, as we have seen, be reduced to a metaphysical theme: " a monster guarding the emblems of immortality ". There is no doubt that a great many of these legends and superstitions are derived not from the primeval mythological formula itself but from the innumerable lateral or " corrupt " variants to which it gave birth.

168. INFANTILIZATION

I have purposely limited myself to these examples from but

one area so as to show, on the one hand, the manifold ramifications of the symbol, and, on the other, the processes of rationalization, degeneration and infantilization which any symbolism undergoes as it comes to be interpreted on lower and lower planes. As we have shown, it is often a question of variants " popular " in appearance but learned in origin—in the last case metaphysical (cosmological, etc.)—which can be easily recognized (as with the snake-stone) and bear all the marks of a process of infantilization. This process might also take place in a good many other ways. Two of the commonest are either for a "learned" symbolism to end up by being used in lower social strata so that its original meaning degenerates, or for the symbol to be taken in a childish way, over-concretely, and apart from the system it belongs to. I have given a few examples of the first category (" snake-stones ", pearls, and so on). Here is another equally illuminating one. A very old Rumanian peasant recipe prescribes: " When a man or an animal is constipated, write on a clean plate the words: Phison, Gehon, Tigris, Euphrates: and wash it with virgin water; let the sick man drink it and he will be cured; if it is an animal, pour it through its nose."[1] The names of the four biblical rivers which watered the garden of Paradise could, in the perspective of magical religion, purify every kind of " cosmos ", and for that reason also the microcosm of a human or animal body. In this case the infantilization is obvious in the simple, concrete way in which the symbolism of purification by the waters of paradise is interpreted: a man is to absorb the water which has touched the four written words . . .

For the second sort of infantilization of symbols (where there is not necessarily any " history ", and " descent " from a scholarly to a popular level), there are a great many examples in Lévy-Bruhl's excellent book, *L'Expérience mystique et les symboles chez les primitifs.*[2] Most of the evidence given by the French scholar shows the symbol as a substitute for the sacred object or as a means of establishing a relationship with it, and with this sort of substitution there must inevitably be a process of infantilization—and that not only among " primitives ", but even in the most developed societies. To give one example,

[1] Eliade, *Les Livres populaires*, p. 74.
[2] pp. 169–299.

take the following case quoted from Lévy-Bruhl: " In equatorial Africa, on the high Ogooue, the *ocibi* antelope, explained a Bamba chieftain, only grazes at night. During the day it sleeps or chews the cud without ever moving. This habit led the natives to make it their symbol of fixity. They are convinced that all those who have eaten its meat together when a new village is being established, will never leave it to live anywhere else."[1] In the minds of the natives, the symbol communicates itself concretely by participation, just as the four words written on the plate can, in the infantilized magic just quoted, " purify " a constipated subject. But this varying of interpretation does not exhaust the original symbol, nor the ability of " primitives " to attain to a coherent symbolism. This, I must repeat, is only one instance of an infantilism of which there are great numbers of examples in the religious experience of every civilized people. Primitives, too, are capable of a coherent symbolism, a symbolism built up on cosmological and theological principles, as much of the material given in earlier chapters proves (the " centre " symbolism found among Arctic, Hamitic and Finno-Ugrian races; the communication among the three cosmic zones for the Malacca Pygmies; the symbolism of the rainbow, the mountain, cosmic creeping plants, and so on, among the Australians, Oceanians and others). But we shall be returning later to this capacity of primitives and primitive races for evolving theory.

For the moment, let us simply note the fact of the coexistence in primitive as well as developed societies of a coherent symbolism alongside an infantilized one. We will lay aside the problem of what causes this infantilization and the question whether it may be simply the effect of the human condition as such. Here we need only realize clearly that, whether coherent or degenerate, the symbol always has an important part to play in all societies. Its function remains unchanged: it is to transform a thing or an action into *something other* than that thing or action appears to be in the eyes of profane experience. To go back, once again, to the examples already given— whether *omphalos*, or symbol of the " centre ", whether a precious stone like jade or pearl, or a magic stone like the " snake-stone "—every one of these stones is significant in

[1] pp. 257–8.

man's magico-religious experience in so far as it manifests some symbolism or other.

169. SYMBOLS AND HIEROPHANIES

Seen in this way, the symbol is carrying further the dialectic of the hierophany: everything not directly consecrated by a hierophany becomes sacred because of its participation in a symbol. Most of the primitive symbols discussed by Lévy-Bruhl are substitutes for or ways of entering into relationship with sacred objects of some sort or another. One need only glance through an exhaustive list such, for instance, as E. Douglas Van Buren's *Symbols of the Gods in Mesopotamian Art*, to realize that a whole series of symbolic signs or things owe their sacred significance and function to the fact that they fit into the " form " or epiphany of some divinity (ornaments, attire, signs of the gods; things carried by them, and so on). But these are not all the symbols there are: there are others which came before the historic " form " of the divinity—I mean such things as plant symbols, the moon, the sun, lightning, certain geometric designs (crosses, pentagons, rhombuses, swastikas and so on). A lot of these symbols were annexed by the divinities dominating the religious history of Meso-potamia: Sin, the moon god, took the sign of the crescent; Shamash the solar disc, and so on. Though there are others which remained to some extent independent of the gods (certain weapons, for instance, certain architectural symbols, various signs like the " three points ", and so on), many, indeed most, were adopted in turn by a great many different divinities, which suggests that they existed before the various pantheons of Mesopotamia. Then too, the handing on of symbols from one god to another is a phenomenon fairly common in the history of religion. Thus in India, for instance, *vajra*, both " lightning " and " diamond " (symbolizing universal sovereignty, incorruptibility, absolute reality, etc.), passed from Agni to Indra and later to Buddha. And there are many similar cases.

From these considerations it is clear that the majority of hierophanies are susceptible of becoming symbols. But the important part played by symbolism in the magico-religious experience of mankind is not due to this convertibility of hierophanies into symbols. It is not only because it continues a hierophany or takes its place that the symbol is important; it is primarily because it is able to carry on the process of hierophanization and particularly because, on occasions, it is *itself* a hierophany—it itself reveals a sacred or cosmological reality which no other manifestation is capable of revealing. Thus, to show how one hierophany is carried further by a symbol, all the amulets and " signs " in which the moon is present (the crescent, the half-moon, the full moon, etc.), draw their efficaciousness from the fact of that presence; in one way or another, they share in the sacred power of the moon. They are, one might say, lesser epiphanies of the moon. But it is certainly not this diminished and sometimes indistinct epiphany (like the crude reproduction of a crescent moon on little votive loaves)[1] which accounts for the importance of amulets and talismans; it is in the actual symbol itself that we must seek the reason. The process is quite clear in a great many of the ceramic ornaments and designs of early Chinese and Eurasiatic history which " symbolize " the phases of the moon by means of various contrasts of black and white (signifying light and darkness).[2] All these drawings and ornaments have a magico-religious function and significance.[3] But the lunar *epiphany* can scarcely be discerned in them and what gives them that significance is lunar *symbolism*.

Further, while a hierophany presupposes a break in religious experience (for there always exists, in one form or another, a *breach* between the sacred and the profane and a *passage* from one to the other—which breach and passage constitute the very essence of religious life), symbolism effects a permanent solidarity between man and the sacred (though this is somewhat indistinct in that man only becomes conscious of it from time to time). A talisman, or jade, or pearls, permanently project anyone wearing them into the sacred zone represented (that is, symbolized) by the ornament in question; and this permanence can only be effected by means of a magico-religious experience which presupposes a breach between profane and sacred. We

---

[1] Cf. for the Mesopotamians, Van Buren, " Symbols of the Gods in Mesopotamian Art ", *Analecta Orientalia*, Rome, 1945, vol. xxiii, p. 3.

[2] Cf. the works of Hentze.

[3] Cf. Hanna Rydh, " Symbolism in Mortuary Ceramics ", *BMAS*, Stockholm, 1929, vol. i, *passim*.

saw (§ 146) that the " easy substitutes " for the Cosmic Tree, the Axis of the Universe, the temple and so on, are always represented by a symbol of the centre (a central pillar, or hearth or something similar). Every dwelling is a " centre of the world " because, in one way or another, its symbolism is the same as that of the centre. But, as we have already had occasion to note, a " centre " is hard to get to, and the fact that it is put at the disposal of everyone is an indication of what I have called " the nostalgia for paradise ", the desire to be, permanently, without effort, and even to some extent unconsciously, in a supremely sacred zone. Similarly, we may say that symbolism is an indication of man's need to extend the hierophanization of the World *ad infinitum*, to keep finding duplicates, substitutes and ways of sharing in a given hierophany, and further, a tendency to identify that hierophany with the universe as a whole. We shall be returning at the end of this chapter to this major function of symbols.

170. THE COHERENCE OF SYMBOLS

Strictly speaking, the term " symbol " ought to be reserved for the symbols which either carry a hierophany further or themselves constitute a " revelation " which could not be expressed by any other magico-religious form (rite, myth, divine form, etc.). However, in the wider sense, *anything* can be a symbol or can play the part of a symbol, from the most rudimentary kratophany (which in some way " symbolizes " the magico-religious power embodied in a thing) to Christ himself who (prescinding from the question of the reality of his own claims) can at the least be held to be a "symbol " of the miracle of divinity incarnate in man.

In the present terminology of ethnology, the history of religion and philosophy, both senses of the word are allowed, and as we have already had occasion to point out, both senses are supported by the magico-religious experience of all of mankind. However, the authentic nature and function of symbols can best be grasped by a closer study of symbols as a prolongation of hierophanies and an autonomous form of revelation. We considered above the lunar symbolism in prehistoric and protohistoric art. Drawings of this kind certainly do carry the hierophany of the moon a stage further, but looked at as a whole they reveal more than any one of the other lunar epiphanies. They assist us to distinguish from among those epiphanies *the symbolism of the moon* which can " reveal " more than all the other lunar epiphanies put together, and at the same time can show simultaneously and panoramically what the other epiphanies only show successively and in part. The symbolism of the moon makes clear the actual structure of lunar hierophanies; the emblem of a lunar animal (*t'ao-t'ie*, the bear and so on) or a black and white drawing embodying the face of the " ancestor ", reveals equally all the prerogatives of the moon, and the fate of Man and the Universe in its rhythmic and constant pattern of change.[1]

Similarly the sacred power of water and the nature of water cosmologies and apocalypses can only be revealed as a whole by means of the water symbolism which is the only " system " capable of including all the individual revelations of innumerable hierophanies. Of course this water symbolism is nowhere concretely expressed, it has no central core, for it is made up of a pattern of interdependent symbols which fit together into a system: but it is none the less real for that. We have only to recall (§ 73) the consistency of the symbolism of immersion in water (Baptism, the Flood, submersion of Atlantis), of purification by water (Baptism, funeral libations), of the time before the creation (the waters, the " lotus ", or the " island ", and so on), to recognize that here is a well organized " system ". This system is obviously implied in every water hierophany on however small a scale, but is more explicitly revealed through a symbol (as for instance " the Flood " or " Baptism "), and is only fully revealed in water symbolism as displayed in *all* the hierophanies.

From a brief review of the preceding chapters it is clear that we are faced with, respectively, a sky symbolism, or a symbolism of earth, of vegetation, of sun, of space, of time, and so on. We have good cause to look upon these various symbolisms as autonomous " systems " in that they manifest more clearly, more fully, and with greater coherence what the hierophanies manifest in an individual, local and successive fashion. And I have tried, whenever the evidence in question allowed of it, to interpret a given hierophany in the light of its proper symbolism

[1] Cf. the studies of Hentze.

so as to discover its deepest significance. It is not, I need hardly say, a question of arbitrarily " deducing " any sort of symbolism from an elementary hierophany; nor is it a question of rationalizing a symbolism to make it more clear and consistent, as was done with the symbolism of the sun in the closing years of antiquity (§ 46). The primitive mind did genuinely have the experience of seeing each hierophany in the framework of the symbolism it implied, and did always really *see* that symbolic system in every fragment which went to make it up. And the fact that some ceased to see it, or came to attain only to an infantile symbolism, does not impair the validity of the structure of symbolism. For a symbolism does not depend upon being understood; it remains consistent in spite of every corruption and preserves its structure even when it has been long forgotten, as witness those prehistoric symbols whose meaning was lost for thousands of years to be " rediscovered " later.

It does not matter in the least whether or not the " primitives " of to-day realize that immersion in water is the equivalent both of a Deluge and of the submerging of a continent in the sea, and that both symbolize the disappearance of an " outworn form " in order that a " new form " may appear. Only one thing matters in the history of religion; and that is the fact that the immersion of a man or a continent, together with the cosmic and eschatological meaning of such immersions, are present in myth and ritual; the fact that all these myths and all these rituals fit together, or, in other words, make up a symbolic system which in a sense pre-existed them all. We are therefore, as we shall see in a moment, quite justified in speaking of a " logic of symbols ", of a logic borne out not only by magico-religious symbolism, but also in the symbolism expressed in the subconscious and transconscious activity of man.

One of the characteristics of the symbol is the many senses it reveals at once. A moon or water symbol holds good at every level of reality, and all the levels are displayed at once. The diptych of light and darkness, for instance, symbolizes at once the day and night of nature, the appearance and disappearance of any sort of form, death and resurrection, the creation and dissolution of the cosmos, the potential and the actual, and so on. This variety of meanings coming together in a single symbol is equally true at the fringe of religious life,

As I showed (§ 166), jade in China fulfilled or presented a magico-religious function, but that function was not the whole of the symbolism of jade: jade also had the values of a symbolic language in the sense that the number, colour and arrangement of bits of jade that a woman wore not only made that woman one with the universe or its seasons, but further indicted her " identity "—showing, for instance, whether she was a maiden, a married woman or a widow, to what family and what social class she belonged, from what part she came, whether her husband or fiancé were travelling, and much else besides. Similarly, too, in Java, the symbolism of the designs or colours of the *batik* declared the sex and social position of whoever wore it, the season and " occasion " on which it was worn, and so on[1]; the same systems are to be found all over Polynesia.[2]

From this point of view, symbolism appears to be a " language " understood by all the members of the community and meaningless to outsiders, but certainly a " language " expressing at once and equally clearly the social, " historic " and psychic condition of the symbol's wearer, and his relations with society and the cosmos (certain kinds of jade or *batik* were worn in the spring, some just before farming operations, some at the equinox or the solstice, and so on). In short, the symbolism of clothing made a human being one both with the cosmos and with the community to which he belonged, while making his fundamental identity clear to the eyes of every member of that community. Several ideas are expressed together here—becoming one with the cosmos, making clear one's position in regard to society—as so many functions with the same urge and the same object. They all converge towards a common aim: to abolish the limits of the " fragment " man is within society and the cosmos, and, by means of making clear his deepest identity and his social status, and making him one with the rhythms of nature—intergrating him into a larger unity: society, the universe.

171. THE FUNCTION OF SYMBOLS

This function of unification is certainly of considerable

---

[1] Mus, *Barabudur*, vol. i, p. 332.

[2] Sayce and March, " Polynesian Ornament and Mythography; or, a Symbolism of Origin and Descent ", *JRAI*, 1893, vol. xxii, *passim*.

importance, not only to man's magico-religious experience, but to his experience in general. Whatever its context, a symbol always reveals the basic oneness of several zones of the real. We have only to recall the tremendous " unifications " effected by the symbols of water or of the moon, whereby so many biological, anthropological and cosmic zones and levels are identified along various lines. Thus, firstly, symbolism carries further the dialectic of hierophanies by transforming things into *something other* than what they appear to profane experience to be: a stone becomes a symbol for the centre of the world, and so on; and then, by becoming symbols, signs of a trans-cendent reality, those things abolish their material limits, and instead of being isolated fragments become part of a whole system; or, better, despite their precarious and fragmentary nature, they embody in themselves the whole of the system in question.

At best, a thing that becomes a symbol tends to become one with the Whole, just as the hierophany tends to embody all of the sacred, to include *in itself* all the manifestations of sacred power. Every stone in a Vedic altar, by becoming Prajāpati, tends to become identified with the whole Universe, just as every local goddess tends to become the Great Goddess and finally to take to herself all the sacred powers possible. This " imperialism " among religious " forms " will be more clearly seen in the companion volume I shall devote to those " forms ". For the moment, let us note that this tendency to annexation can also be found in the dialectic of the symbol. This is not merely because every symbolism aims at integrating and unifying the greatest possible number of zones and areas of human and cosmic experience, but also because every symbol tends to identify with itself as many things, situations and modes of existence as it can. The symbolism of water or the moon will tend to take to itself whatever concerns life and death, that is all change and all " forms ". And a symbol like the pearl will tend to represent both these systems (moon and water) at once by embodying in itself almost all the manifestations of life, femininity, fertility and the rest. This " unification " is in no sense a confusion; the symbolism makes it possible to move from one level to another, and one mode of existence to another, bringing them all together, *but never merging them*.

We must realize that the tendency of each to become the Whole is really a tendency to fit the " whole " into a single system, to reduce the multiplicity of things to a single " situation " in such a way as also to make it as comprehensible as it can be made.

I have dealt elsewhere with the symbolism of bonds, knots and nets.[1] There I considered the cosmological significance of Vṛtra's " binding " of the waters and the cosmocratic significance of Varuṇa's " bonds "; the " binding " of one's enemies either magically or with actual ropes, the imprisoning of corpses, the myths in which the gods of the underworld catch in their nets men or the souls of the dead; the symbolism of the " bound " or " chained " man (India, Plato), of the untangling of the maze of thread and the solving of a problem of living. And I showed that we are always faced with the same symbolic pattern expressed more or less completely at the many levels of magico-religious life (cosmology, the myth of the Terrible Sovereign, aggressive or defensive magic, the mythology of the underworld, initiation dramas, etc.). In every case there is an archetype seeking expression at every level of magico-religious experience. But, more significant still, this symbolism of " binding " and " loosing " reveals man's specific situation in the universe, a situation that no other hierophany by itself would be capable of revealing; one might even say that it is only this symbolism of bonds that fully reveals to man his ultimate situation and enables him to express it to himself coherently. And, further, the articulations of this symbolic system make clear how identical are the situations of all who are " conditioned " (the " captive ", the " bewitched ", or simply man in the face of his own fate), and how inevitably they find their symbols.

172. THE LOGIC OF SYMBOLS

We have, therefore, every reason to speak of a " logic of symbols ", in the sense that symbols, of every kind, and at whatever level, are always consistent and systematic. This logic goes beyond the sphere of religious history to rank among the problems of philosophy. Indeed (and I have said this

[1] " Le ' Dièu lieur ' et le symbolisme des nœuds ", *Images et Symboles*, ch. iii.

elsewhere in studying the symbolism of " ascent ") the figments of what we call the subconscious (dreams, fantasies, imagination) the creative activities of psychopathic states and the rest, present a structure and a significance that harmonize perfectly both with the myths and rituals of ascension, and with the metaphysics of ascent.[1] There is not really any genuine break in continuity between the spontaneous figments of the sub-conscious (ascension dreams, for instance) and the theories worked out in the waking state (such as the metaphysic of spiritual ascent and elevation). This faces us with two problems : first, whether we can still talk exclusively of a subconscious—would it not be more correct to presuppose also the existence of a " trans-conscious " ?—and second, whether we are right in saying that the creations of the subconscious have a different structure from those of the conscious mind. But they are problems which can only be discussed in their true perspective, which is one of philosophy.

I should, however, like to stress one point—that a great many figments of the subconscious seem to have the characteristic of in a sense copying or imitating archetypes which seem not to proceed exclusively from the subconscious sphere. It often happens that a dream or a psychosis takes the same form as a spiritual act which is, in itself, completely intelligible, with no intrinsic contradiction, quite " logical ", and therefore spring-ing from conscious (or trans-conscious) activity. This obser-vation is such as to throw a certain amount of light on the problem of hierophanies in general and symbols in particular. Almost everywhere in the history of religion we have come across the phenomenon of an "easy" imitation of the archetype, which I have termed infantilism. But we saw how, similarly, infantilism tends to carry hierophanies on *ad infinitum*; that it tends, in other words, to put the sacred into every slightest thing, or ultimately, to put the Whole into every tiniest part. Such a tendency is not in itself aberrant, for the sacred does in fact tend to become one with profane reality, to transform and consecrate all creation. But infantilism almost always has a character of facility, of automatism and often even of arti-ficiality. We might therefore discern a parallel between the

[1] Cf. " Dūrohana and the ' Waking Dream ' ", *Art and Thought*, London, 1947, pp. 209–13.

tendency of the subconscious to imitate the forms of the conscious or trans-conscious mind in its creations and the tendency of infantilism to prolong hierophanies *ad infinitum*, to repeat them at every possible level and often in a quite mechanistic and crude fashion: both tendencies have in common the characteristic traits of facility and automatism. But there is something else: the desire to make all creation one and do away with multiplicity. This desire is also, in its own way, an imitation of the activity of reason since reason also tends to unify reality—a tendency which, carried to an extreme, would abolish Creation; however, the creations of the subconscious and the infantilization of hierophanies, are rather more a movement of *life* towards rest, towards a return to the original state of matter: inertia. On another plane and as part of another dialectical necessity, life—in tending towards rest, stability and Unity—is pursuing the same course as the mind in its urge towards unification and stability.

To be properly established, these statements would call for a whole series of comments that I cannot hope even to outline here. I have attempted to look at them briefly simply because they help us to understand, as a whole, the tendency to effect easy substitutes for hierophanies, and the extremely important part played by symbolism in magico-religious life. What we may call *symbolic thought* makes it possible for man to move freely from one level of reality to another. Indeed, " to move freely " is an understatement: symbols, as we have seen, identify, assimilate, and unify diverse levels and realities that are to all appearances incompatible. Further still: magico-religious experience makes it possible for man himself to be transformed into a symbol. And only in so far as man himself becomes a symbol, are all systems and all anthropo-cosmic experiences possible, and indeed in this case his own life is considerably enriched and enlarged. Man no longer feels himself to be an " air-tight " fragment, but a living cosmos open to all the other living cosmoses by which he is surrounded. The experiences of the world at large are no longer something outside him and therefore ultimately " foreign " and " objective "; they do not alienate him from himself but, on the contrary, lead him towards himself, and reveal to him his own existence and his own destiny. The cosmic myths and the whole world of ritual thus appear as existential experiences to primitive man: he does not lose himself, he does not forget his own existence when he fulfils a myth or takes part in a ritual; quite the reverse; he finds himself and comes to understand himself, because those myths and rituals express cosmic realities which ultimately he is aware of as realities in his own being. To primitive man, every level of reality is so completely open to him that the emotion he felt at merely *seeing* anything as magnificent as the starry sky would have been as strong as the most " intimist " personal experience felt by a modern. For, thanks chiefly to his symbols, the *real existence* of primitive man was not the broken and alienated existence lived by civilized man to-day.

BIBLIOGRAPHY

On the symbolism of magic stones, " thunderstones ", and precious stones: ANDREE, R., *Ethnographische Parallelen, Neue Folge*, Leipzig, 1889, pp. 30-41; KUNZ, G. F., *The Magic of Jewels and Charms*, Philadelphia-London, 1915, pp. 108 ff.; SKEAT, Walter W., " Snakestones and Stone Thunderbolts as a Subject for Systematic Investigation ", *FRE*, 1912, vol. xxxiii, pp. 45-80, particularly 60 ff.; BLINKENBERG, C., *The Thunderweapon in Religion and Folklore*, Cambridge, 1911; PERRY, W. J., *Children of the Sun*, 2nd ed., London, 1927, pp. 384 ff.; SAINTYVES, P., " Pierres magiques: bétyles, haches-amulettes et pierres de foudre ", *Corpus de folklore préhistorique*, Paris, 1934, vol. ii, pp. 7-276.

On the symbolism of jade: LAUFER, B., *Jade, A Study of Chinese Archæology and Religion*, Chicago, 1912; KARLGREN, B., " Some Fecundity Symbols in Ancient China ", *BMAS*, Stockholm, 1930, no. 2, pp. 1-54, especially 23 ff.; GIESLER, G., " Les Symboles de jade dans le taoisme ", *RHR*, 1932, vol. cv., pp. 158-81.

On the symbolism of the pearl: KUNZ, G. F., and STEVENSON, C., *The Book of the Pearl*, London, 1908; JACKSON, J.W., *Shells as Evidence of the Migration of Early Culture*, Manchester, 1917; ZYKAN, J., " Drache und Perle ", *Artibus Asiæ*, 1936, vol. vi, pp.1-2; ELIADE, M., " Notes sur le symbolisme aquatique ", *CZ*, 1939, vol. ii, pp. 131-52; reprinted in *Images et Symboles*, pp. 164-98.

On the symbolism of lapis lazuli: DARMSTÄDTER, E., " Der babylonisch-assyrisch Lasurstein ", *Studien zur Geschichte der Chemie, Festgabe Ed. von Lippmann*, Berlin, 1937, pp. 1-8; ELIADE, M., *Cosmologie si alchimie babiloniana*, Bucharest, 1936, pp. 51-8.

On the symbolism of the diamond: LAUFER, B., *The Diamond. A Study in Chinese and Hellenistic Folk-Lore*, Field Museum, Chicago, 1915; PENZER, N. M., *The Ocean of Story*, London, 1929, 4 vols., vol. ii, p. 299; THORNDIKE, L., *A History of Magic and Experimental Science*, New York, 1923– , vol. i, p. 496, vol. ii, pp. 262-3.

On gynæcological stones, *ætites*, etc.: BOSON, G., " I Metalli e le pietre nelle iscrizioni sumero-assiro-babylonesi ", *Rivista degli Studi orientali*, 1916, vol. ii, pp. 279-420, esp. 412-13; KUNZ, G. F., *The Magic of Jewels*, pp. 173-8; LAUFER, *The Diamond*, p. 9, n. 1; BIDEZ, J., and CUMONT, F., *Les Mages hellénisés*, Paris, 1938, vol. ii, p. 201.

On the symbolism of " snakestones ": SKEAT, W. W., " Snakestones and Stone Thunderbolts ", *passim*; KUNZ, *The Magic of Jewels*, pp. 201-40; HALLIDAY, W. R., " Of Snake-stones ", *Folklore Studies Ancient and Modern*, London, 1924, pp. 132-55; SELIGMANN, S., *Die magische Heil- und Schutzmittel*, Stuttgart, 1927, pp. 282 ff.; VOGEL, J. P., *Indian Serpent Lore*, London, 1926, pp. 25 ff., 218 ff.; SHEPHARD, O., *Lore of the Unicorn*, London, 1931, pp. 128, 131, 290-1, etc.; ELIADE, M., " Piatra Sarpelui ", *Mesterului Manole*, Bucharest, 1939, pp. 1-12.

On architectonic symbolism, see the bibliography for Chapter X; in addition, COMBAZ, G., " L'Évolution du stupa en Asie: les symbolismes du Stupa ", *Mélanges chinois et bouddhiques*, Brussels, 1936, vol. iv, pp. 1-125; MUS, P., *Barabudur, passim*; ANDRAE, Walter, *Die ionische Saüle, Bauform oder Symbol?*, Berlin, 1930.

On prehistoric and Eurasiatic symbolism: GÄRTE, W., " Die symbolische Verwendung des Schachbrettmusters im Altertum ", *MB*, 1914, vol. vi, pp. 349 ff.; WILKE, G., " Mystische Vorstellungen und symbolische Zeichen aus Indoeuropäischer Urzeit,", *MB*, 1914, vol. vi; RYDH, Hanna, " Symbolism in Mortuary Ceramics ", *BMAS*, Stockholm, 1929, vol. i, pp. 71-120; KARLGREN, B., " Some Fecundity Symbols in Ancient China ", *BMAS*, Stockholm, 1930, vol. ii, pp. 1–54; HENTZE, Carl, *Mythes et symboles lunaires*, Antwerp, 1932; WILLIAMS, C. A. S., *Outlines of Chinese Symbolism and Art Motives*, Shanghai, 1932; SALMONY, Alfred, " The Magic Ball and the Golden Fruit in Ancient Chinese Art ", *Art and Thought*, London, 1947, pp. 105–9 ; CAMMANN, Schuyler, " Cosmic Symbolism of the Dragon Robes of the Ch'ing Dynasty ", *Art and Thought*, pp. 125–9; SIMPSON, William, *The Buddhist Praying Wheel. A Collection of Material Bearing upon the Symbolism of the Wheel and Circular Movements in Custom and Religious Ritual*, London, 1896.

On Polynesian symbolism: SAYCE, A. H., and MARCH, H. C., " Polynesian Ornament and Mythography: or, a Symbolism of Origin and Descent ", *JRAI*, 1893, vol. xxii, pp. 314 ff.; GREINER, R. H., " Polynesian Decorative Designs ", *BMB*, Honolulu, 1922, no. 7.

On middle-eastern and Roman symbolism: DANZEL, T. W., *Symbole, Dämonen und heiligen Türme*, Hamburg, 1930; VAN BUREN, E. Douglas, " Symbols of the Gods in Mesopatamian Art ", *Analecta Orientalia*, Rome, 1945, vol. xxiii; CUMONT, Franz, *Recherches sur le symbolisme funéraire des Romains*, Paris, 1942; see also the bibliography for Chapter VIII.

On symbolism in general: THURNWALD, R., " Das Symbol im Lichte der Völkerkunde ", *Zeitschrift f. Æsthetik u. allgem. Kunstwiss*, vol. xxi, pp. 322–37; DEONNA, W., "Quelques réflexions sur le symbolisme ", *RHR*, 1924, vol. lxxxix, pp. 1–66; GUENON, René, *Le Symbolisme de la croix*, Paris, 1932; CAILLET, E., *Symbolisme et âmes primitives*, Paris, 1936; LEVY-BRUHL, L., *L'Expérience mystique et les symboles chez les primitifs*, Paris, 1938; COOMARASWAMY, Ananda, *Elements of Buddhist Iconography*, Harvard University Press, 1935; id., " The Inverted Tree ", *The Quarterly Journal of the Mythic Society*, Bangalore, 1938, vol. xxix, no. 2, pp. 1–39; id., " The Symbolism of the Dome ", *IHQ*, 1935, vol. xiv, no. 1, pp. 1–56; id., " The Iconography of Dürer's ' Knots ' and Leonardo's ' Concatenation '", *The Art Quarterly*, 1944, vol. vii, pp. 109–28; id., *Figures of Speech and Figures of Thought*, London, 1946; ELIADE, M., " Secret Languages ", (in the Rumanian, *Revista Fundatiilor Regale*, Bucharest, Jan.-March, 1938); id., " Durohaṇa and the Waking Dream ", *Art and Thought*, London, 1947, pp. 209–13; id., " Le Dieu lieur et le symbolisme des nœuds ", *RHR*, 1947–9; reprinted in *Images et Symboles*, pp. 120–63.

CONCLUSIONS

IF it is true, as I said at the beginning of this book (§ 1), that the simplest definition of the sacred remains " the opposite of the profane ", it is also clear from the succeeding chapters that the dialectic of hierophanies tends endlessly to reduce the spheres that are profane and eventually to abolish them. Some of the highest religious experiences identify the sacred with the whole universe. To many a mystic the integrated quality of the cosmos is itself a hierophany. " The whole universe, from Brahma down to a blade of grass is one form or another of Him ", exclaims the *Mahānirvāṇa Tantra*,[1] taking up an extremely old and well-known Indian saying. This " He ", *Ātman-Brahman*, is manifest everywhere: " Haṁsa, he is enthroned in the pure [Sky], resplendent [god] he is enthroned in the upper air, officiating he is enthroned upon the altar, host, he is enthroned in his dwelling. He is enthroned in man, in every oath, in the Law, in the firmament."[2] That this is more than a simple idea classed, rightly or wrongly, as pantheist, is shown by the words of Léon Bloy speaking of the ". . . mystery of Life, which is Christ: *Ego sum Vita*. Whether the Life is in men, animals or plants, it is always Life, and when the moment, the imperceptible instant called death comes, it is always Christ who withdraws, as much from a tree as from a human being."[3]

It is clear that this is not " pantheism " in our sense, but what we might call " panontism ". To Bloy, Christ, like the *Ātman-Brahman* of Indian tradition, is to be found in all that *is*, or rather in everything that *exists in an absolute manner*. And as I have shown so often, the *real* in archaic ontology is primarily identified with a " force ", a " life ", a fertility, an abundance, but also with all that is strange or singular—in other words with everything that exists most fully or displays an exceptional mode of existence. Sacredness is, above all, *real*. The more religious a man is the more real he is, and the more he gets away from the unreality of a meaningless change. Hence man's tendency to " consecrate " his whole life. Hiero-

---

[1] ii, 46.
[2] *Katha Upaniṣad*, v, 2.
[3] *Le Mendiant ingrat*, vol. ii, p. 196.

phanies consecrate the universe; rituals consecrate Life. This consecration can also be effected in an indirect way, by transforming life itself into a ritual. " Hunger, thirst, continence are in man [what is] a consecration [in sacrifice], *dikṣā*. Food and drink the pleasure he has corresponding to the [ceremonies called] *upasāda*; laughter, good cheer and love correspond to the canticles and recitations [*stuta-Sāstra*]. Mortification [*tapas*], almsgiving, honesty, the respect for life [*ahiṁsā*] and truth are in him gifts [given to the officiating priests]."[1] When I come, in the companion volume to this, to look at the development and functions of rites, I shall have occasion to show the mechanism by which physiological and psychological activities are transformed into ritual activities. The ideal of the religious man is, of course, that everything he does should be done ritually, should, in other words, be a *sacrifice*. In every primitive society or any society that lives by tradition, the work to which every man is called constitutes a sacrifice of this kind. On that account, every act is liable to become a religious act, just as every natural object is liable to become a hierophany. In other words, any moment may be inserted into the Great Time and thus project man into eternity. Human existence therefore takes place simultaneously upon two parallel planes: that of the temporal, of change and of illusion, and that of eternity, of substance and of reality.

On the other hand, we have also observed the existence of the contrary tendency—resistance to the sacred, a resistance which appears even at the very heart of religious experience. Man's ambivalent attitude towards the sacred, which at once attracts and repels him, is both beneficent and dangerous, can be explained not only by the ambivalent nature of the sacred in itself, but also by man's natural reactions to this transcendent reality which attracts and terrifies him with equal intensity. Resistance is most clearly expressed when man is faced with a *total demand* from the sacred, when he is called upon to make the supreme decision—either to give himself over completely and irrevocably to sacred things, or to continue in an uncertain attitude towards them.

This resistance to the sacred carries with it, in the perspective of existential metaphysics, a *flight from reality*. In that same

[1] *Chāndogya-Up.*, iii, 17, 1–4.

perspective the " general " corresponds to the profane, to the illusory, to the meaningless. The symbol of the " journey towards the centre " must be translated into the language of contemporary metaphysics as a journey towards the centre of one's own being and away from unreality. It can happen that this resistance to a total absorption of life by the sacred arises even within the bosom of the Churches; it is not unusual for the latter to have to defend man against the excesses of religious, and especially of mystical, experience, and against the risk of secular life's being totally abolished. These instances of resistance, which I shall analyse in my companion volume, indicate to some extent the growing awareness of the essential part played by " history ", the growing importance which the values of human life tend to attain, particularly in the more developed religions, chief among them that life's capacity to have its *being in history* and to *make* history. We saw the importance accorded to vital values even in the earliest phases of religion: remember how the dynamic, organizing, fertilizing divinities always came to the fore (§ 26 ff.). As time went on, the attraction of vital values continued to grow, largely in the form of an ever livelier interest in human values as such, and finally in history. Man's existence as a historic existence took on a significance if not directly religious, at least beyond the human. In the next volume I shall be examining how far " history " is capable of being seen as part of the sacred process and how far religious values have been created or developed by the historical process. But even now we can see that the " nostaliga for paradise " and the " easy substitutes " for the major religious experiences and symbols point to the direction in which we must look for a solution to this problem. For that " nostalgia " and those " easy substitutes " show historical man's deep-rooted repugnance to abandoning himself totally to sacred experience as clearly as they show his powerlessness to resign that experience wholly.

 I have not tried to study religious phenomena in their historical framework, but merely as hierophanies. That is why, in order to throw light on the nature of water hierophanies, I did not scruple to place Christian Baptism side by side with the myths and rites of Oceania, America or Græco-Oriental antiquity, ignoring the differences between them—or, in other words, history. In so far as our attention was turned directly upon the religious significance to the believer, our ignoring of historical perspective was completely justified. Of course, as I noted at the beginning (§ 1), there is no hierophany that is not, from the date of its first becoming manifest, " historic ". From the very fact of man's recognizing a revelation of the sacred that revelation, upon whatever plane it is effected, becomes historic. History comes in as soon as man, according as his needs inspire, experiences the sacred. The handling and passing on of hierophanies also accentuates their " historiciza- tion ". Yet their structure remains the same in spite of this and it is precisely this permanence of structure that makes it possible to know them. The gods of the sky may have under- gone innumerable transformations: but their celestial structure remains nonetheless the permanent element, the constant of their personality. Innumerable fusions and additions may arise in any divine figure of fertility, but its chthonian or agricultural structure will not be impaired by them. Indeed, we may go further: there *is* no religious form that does not try to get as close as possible to its true archetype, in other words, to rid itself of " historical " accretions and deposits. Every goddess tends to become a Great Goddess, taking to herself all the attributes and functions that belong to the archetypal Great Goddess. So much so that we can identify a double process in the history of things religious: on the one hand, the con- tinual brief appearance of hierophanies with the result that the manifestation of the sacred in the Universe becomes ever more fragmentary; on the other, the unification of those hierophanies because of their innate tendency to embody their archetypes as perfectly as they can and thus wholly fulfil their own nature.

It would be a mistake to see syncretism as merely a late religious phenomenon which could only have occurred as a result of a contact between several highly developed religions. What we call syncretism can be seen at every point in the course of religious life. Every farming spirit of the countryside, every tribal god, is the culmination of a long process of being assimil- ated and identified with other divine forms adjacent to it. But it must be pointed out that these assimilations and fusions are not due solely to historical circumstance (the mingling of two neighbouring tribes, the conquest of a given area and so on);

the process takes place as a result of the very nature of hierophanies; whether or not a hierophany comes into contact with another religious form, like or unlike itself, it will tend, in the religious consciousness of those who perceive it as such, to be expressed as totally, as fully as possible. This fact explains a phenomenon which we find everywhere from end to end of the history of religion: the ability of every religious form to rise, to be purified, to become nobler—for a tribal god, for instance, to become by means of a new epiphany, the god of a monotheistic religion, or for a minor goddess of the countryside to turn into the Mother of the Universe.

All these apparently contradictory movements of unification and of fragmentation, of identification and of separation, of attraction and of resistance or repulsion, all of them will become easier to grasp when, having looked at the various methods of approaching and handling the sacred (prayers, offerings, rites and the rest), we can enter upon the problem of the *history* of religious phenomena. This study I have left for my companion volume. Here, at the conclusion of this, I should like simply to declare that almost all the religious attitudes man has, he has had from the most primitive times. From one point of view there has been no break in continuity from the " primitives " to Christianity. The dialectic of the hierophany remains one, whether in an Australian *churinga* or in the Incarnation of the Logos. In both cases we are faced with a manifestation, vastly different obviously, of the sacred in a fragment of the universe; in both is implicit the problem of the " personality " or " impersonality " of the epiphany. We saw (§ 8), that in the case of the elementary hierophanies (like *mana*), there is not always any means of telling whether the revelation of the sacred is personal or impersonal in form ; generally it is both, for the " primitive " is far less preoccupied with the difference between personal and impersonal than with that between real (powerful, etc.) and unreal. And we shall discover this same polarity expressed in innumerable formulæ in the most highly developed religions and mysticisms.

That the major religious attitudes came into existence once and for all from the moment when man first became conscious of the position he stood in within the universe, does not mean that " history " has had no effect on religious experience in itself. Quite the reverse. Everything in man's life, even his physical life, has its echoes in his religious experience. Discovering the techniques of hunting, farming, metallurgy and so on did not merely alter man's material life; it went further, and affected man's spirituality, perhaps even more fruitfully. Thus agriculture opened the door to a whole series of revelations which could not have been produced in the pre-agricultural world. Needless to say, economic and social changes, and even historical events are not enough in themselves to account for religious phenomena as such, but the transformations the material world has undergone (agriculture, metallurgy and so on) have offered the mind new ways of embracing reality. And we can say that if history *has* had any influence upon religious experience, it is in this sense: that events have presented man with novel and different modes of being, of discovering his own nature, and of giving magic and religious significance to the universe. I will give just one example: one of the most fundamental elements in the religious revolution undertaken by Zarathustra was his opposition to the bloody sacrifice of animals.[1] It is evident that this attitude was produced by, among other things, the economic interests of a society turning from a pastoral to an agricultural way of life. But this historical event was given religious meaning and importance by Zarathustra: the abolishing of bloody sacrifices became, thanks to him, a means of spiritual discipline and ennoblement; the renunciation of this species of rite opened a new perspective of contemplation; in short, the historical event made possible a novel religious experience and the discovery of new spiritual values. It goes without saying that the evolution may easily take the opposite direction: that the noble religious experiences of primitive societies became harder and harder to attain as a result of the changes " history " introduced into those societies. In some cases it would be no exaggeration to speak of absolute spiritual catastrophes (such, for instance, as the swallowing up of the ancient societies in the economic framework of colonialist and semi-industrialist societies).

But though history may be capable either of assisting or of paralysing new religious experiences, it can never manage to

---

[1] Cf. the praise of the primeval Bull, *Yasna*, 29; the respect for cattle, *Yasna*, 12, 1, etc.

abolish the need for religious experience. Indeed, we may go further and say that the dialectic of hierophanies allows of the spontaneous and complete *rediscovery* of all religious values, whatever they may be and at whatever historical stage may be the society or individual who rediscovers them. The history of religion can thus, in the last analysis, be expressed in terms of the drama of the losing and refinding of those values, a loss and rediscovery which are never, nor can ever be, final.

NAME INDEX

466

SUBJECT INDEX

MIRCEA ELIADE was born in Bucharest in 1907 and received degrees from the universities of Bucharest and Calcutta. His teaching and research have taken him to England, Italy, Sweden, Portugal, Spain, Germany, France, Greece, and the United States, where he is presently Professor of the History of Religions at the University of Chicago. He is the author of numerous books and articles.

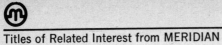

Titles of Related Interest from MERIDIAN

The Study of Religion from MERIDIAN

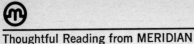

Thoughtful Reading from MERIDIAN

Philosophy Books from MERIDIAN

(0452)

☐ **JONATHAN EDWARDS: Basic Writings selected and edited by Ola Elizabeth Winslow.** These selections extend from Edwards' first essays as a youthful prodigy to the great sermons and treatises of his maturity; they offer both a fascinating record of spiritual evolution and a body of intellectual achievement of truly enduring import.
(004896—$4.95)

☐ **EXISTENTIALISM FROM DOSTOEVSKY TO SARTRE selected and introduced by Walter Kaufmann.** Revised and expanded. The basic writings of existentialism, many never before translated, including Kierkegaard, Nietzsche, Kafka, and Camus. (006686—$6.95)

☐ **EXISTENTIALISM, RELIGION, AND DEATH: THIRTEEN ESSAYS by Walter Kaufmann. With a special Introduction by the author.** With essays spanning twenty years, this book blends critical scholarship with the voice of personal experience and is an invaluable companion to *Existentialism from Dostoevsky to Sartre.* (006481—$6.95)

☐ **THE SOCIAL SOURCES OF DENOMINATIONALISM by Richard H. Niebuhr.** Professor Niebuhr traces the roles of social, economic, and political aspects of American democracy in the emergence of denominations. "One of the real classics of the sociology of religion." —Everett C. Hughes, *American Journal of Sociology.*
(006317—$9.95)

☐ **THE AGE OF BELIEF: The Medieval Philosophers edited by Anne Fremantle.** Basic writings of the most important philosophers from the 5th to 15th century, including St. Augustine, Boethius, Abelard, St. Bernard, St. Thomas Aquinas, Duns Scotus, William of Ockam and others. (007208—$3.95)

All prices higher in Canada.

Buy them at your local bookstore or use this convenient coupon for ordering.

NEW AMERICAN LIBRARY
P.O. Box 999, Bergenfield, New Jersey 07621

Please send me the MERIDIAN BOOKS I have checked above. I am enclosing $_____(please add $1.50 to this order to cover postage and handling). Send check or money order—no cash or C.O.D.'s. Prices and numbers are subject to change without notice.

Name_____

Address_____

City_____State_____Zip Code_____

Allow 4-6 weeks for delivery
This offer subject to withdrawal without notice.